D1242858

A DICTIONARY OF IRISH BIOGRAPHY
SECOND EDITION

THE EDITOR

Henry Boylan has had a distinguished career as a public servant and man of letters. A graduate of Trinity College, Dublin, he worked for Radio Éireann and in the 1950s became an executive director of Gaeltarra Éireann. He was for a time assistant secretary of the Department of Lands and chairman of a semi-state company which successfully harvested and processed seaweed on the west coast of Ireland. In addition to radio plays and adaptations, he has written four other books, including a highly acclaimed biography of Wolfe Tone in the Gill's Irish Lives series. Between the first edition and this revised and expanded edition, he has devoted almost ten years' work to *A Dictionary of Irish Biography*.

A Dictionary of
Irish
Biography

Second Edition

Henry Boylan

Gill and Macmillan

Published in Ireland by
Gill and Macmillan Ltd
Goldenbridge
Dublin 8
with associated companies in
Auckland, Delhi, Gaborone, Hamburg, Harare,
Hong Kong, Johannesburg, Kuala Lumpur, Lagos, London,
Manzini, Melbourne, Mexico City, Nairobi,
New York, Singapore, Tokyo
© Henry Boylan 1988
Print origination by Graphic Plan, Dublin
Printed in England by Camelot Press, Southampton

British Library Cataloguing in Publication Data
Boylan, Henry
    Dictionary of Irish biography.—2nd ed.
    1. Irish persons. Biographies, to 1988
    I. Title
    920'.0415

    ISBN 0-7171-1574-7 hardback
    ISBN 0-7171-1631-X paperback

FOR PATRICIA

All history becomes subjective, in other words there is properly no history; only biography.

Emerson

CONTENTS

NOTES

Irish versions of names are used only when the subjects are known better, or only, thus; otherwise the English version is used. Brian Merriman, for example, was known only by that name.

A short glossary of Irish words is appended hereunder to assist readers not familiar with Irish affairs.

Dáil (Éireann)	Lower house in Irish parliament.
Gaeltacht	Irish-speaking parts of Ireland, principally along western seaboard.
Oireachtas	National parliament; also, festival of Irish culture, held annually.
Seanad (Éireann)	Upper house in Irish parliament.
Sinn Féin	'Ourselves': political movement founded by Arthur Griffith.
Taoiseach	Prime minister.
Tánaiste	Deputy prime minister.
TD	Member of Dáil.

Since this book went to press in July 1988, it has not been possible to include persons who have died between that date and the date of publication.

ABBREVIATIONS

BD	Bachelor of Divinity
c.	circa
CB	Companion of the Order of the Bath
CBS	Christian Brothers' Schools
CID	Criminal Investigation Department
CIE	Companion of the Order of the Indian Empire
CMG	Companion of the Order of St Michael and St George
CSI	Companion of the Order of the Star of India
DD	Doctor of Divinity
DIAS	Dublin Institute for Advanced Studies
DMP	Dublin Metropolitan Police
DU	Dublin University
ESB	Electricity Supply Board
FRS	Fellow of the Royal Society
GAA	Gaelic Athletic Association
GOC	general officer commanding
GPO	General Post Office
IRA	Irish Republican Army
IRB	Irish Republican Brotherhood
KCB	Knight Commander of the Order of the Bath
MBE	Member of the Order of the British Empire
MC	Military Cross
MIAL	Member of the Irish Academy of Letters
MRIA	Member of the Royal Irish Academy
NS	National School
NUI	National University of Ireland
NUU	New University of Ulster
OBE	Officer of the Order of the British Empire
QC	Queen's Counsel
QUB	Queen's University, Belfast
RA	Royal Academy
RAF	Royal Air Force
RBAI	Royal Belfast Academical Institution
RCPI	Royal College of Physicians of Ireland
RCSI	Royal College of Surgeons in Ireland
RDS	Royal Dublin Society
RHA	Royal Hibernian Academy
RIA	Royal Irish Academy
RIAM	Royal Irish Academy of Music
RIC	Royal Irish Constabulary
RUI	Royal University of Ireland
SDLP	Social Democratic and Labour Party
TCD	Trinity College, Dublin
UCC	University College, Cork
UCD	University College, Dublin
UCG	University College, Galway
UK	United Kingdom
UN	United Nations

UNESCO	United Nations Educational, Scientific and Cultural Organisation
USA	United States of America
USSR	Union of Soviet Socialist Republics
VC	Victoria Cross

PREFACE

IT is one hundred years since M. H. Gill and Son published *A Compendium of Irish Biography*, compiled by Alfred John Webb (1834–1908). It held the field for fifty years, until 1928, when *A Concise Dictionary of Irish Biography*, by Dr John S. Crone (1858–1945) appeared under the imprint of the Talbot Press. The present work appears a further fifty years on, thus conforming to a pleasing rhythm of publication.

In 1913 Arthur Griffith contributed to the Dublin *Evening Telegraph* a series of short biographies of Irish men of letters and workers in the language revival movement. That year, in *Sinn Féin*, he appealed for help in compiling a Dictionary of Irish Biography. Evidently his political activities prevented him from proceeding with the undertaking. A revised and enlarged edition of Crone's *Dictionary* appeared in 1937 but the additional entries were few in number. The need for an up-to-date Dictionary of Irish Biography seemed clear.

The first decision concerning the present work was that no living person should be included. This rule is followed by the great *Dictionary of National Biography*. One need hardly seek for further justification, but there are good and obvious reasons for the rule. A man's best work may well be done in his last years or those years may be clouded by sudden overwhelming disaster. Until his life is ended, it is not possible to present the full picture.

There remained the problem of the formulation of a criterion governing the selection of entries. Should it be Irish birth, or education in Ireland or the extent of the subject's contribution to Irish life or history? The editors of *The Oxford Book of Irish Verse* considered that a poet might be Irish by birth, descent or adoption. Discussing this point in his essay 'Irishness' (*Writers and Politics*), Dr Conor Cruise O'Brien offers an alternative concept: 'Irishness is not primarily a question of birth or blood or language: it is the condition of being involved in the Irish situation, and usually of being mauled by it.' This is picturesque but unsafe as a guide in the context of general biography, for would it not admit a long list of English, from Robert Devereux, second Earl of Essex, to Augustine Birrell, chief secretary in Dublin in 1916, who fell from grace primarily through their involvement in the Irish situation, but who were English to the core? Birth in Ireland has been taken as the prime requirement but this is modified to admit those who, though born abroad, had an Irish parent, or were of Irish descent, lived and worked in Ireland or made a considerable contribution to Irish affairs. The chief example is Éamon de Valera, and clearly it would have been absurd to exclude him because of his American birth. It would have been equally absurd to have excluded Maria Edgeworth, born in Oxfordshire; James Connolly, born in Edinburgh; Countess Markievicz, born in London, or James Larkin, born in Liverpool.

Sir Alfred Chester Beatty was included, although he was born in New York and did not begin his connection with Ireland until his fifties, because he was the first to be made an honorary citizen of Ireland (the second was Dr Tiede Herrema) and because of the princely generosity of his bequests to Ireland. A Dictionary of Irish Biography would be lacking, in the opinion of the editor, if it omitted either Sir Alfred or the engaging Charles Bianconi, whose 'long cars' opened up the south of Ireland before the railway era.

It became clear in the early stages of the work that a further process of selection would be necessary, to contain the material within reasonable bounds. The selection inevitably became, to a degree, personal and subjective, but nevertheless certain guiding principles were kept steadily in view. After the chief events in a subject's life were ascertained, the vital questions were put: what had he or she left to posterity, by what will they be remembered? Did they affect the history of Ireland, influence events or play a part in some event which persists in a legend or song? 'Remember Orr', 'Armour of Ballymoney', 'Dolly's Brae', 'Hickey of Maynooth': these slogans and names awaken tribal memories that are not easily put to rest. Artists fared best under this examination, for, after all, by definition they create, they are 'makers'. But there are degrees of excellence between artists and a special problem arises in respect of Gaelic poets of the eighteenth century and earlier. Their poetry speaks for them but very little is known about many of them save that they were born, struggled and died. To take two examples, biographical material relating to Aindrías Mac Craith and Séamus Dall Mac Cuarta is scarce, although local tradition abounds. All of the best known, in the double sense that their poetry is familiar and that reasonably full accounts of their personal lives have survived, have been included and recent work by scholars in this field, regrettably meagre, has been drawn upon.

In the preface to the second edition of his *Irish-English Dictionary*, Father Pádraig Ó Duinnín wrote: 'Led by the lure and prompted by the pathos of unfinished or undeveloped undertakings, I have expended twenty years of severe labour...'. He was but one of a devoted band of scholars, men of modesty and charm, who became drawn to the study of Irish and whose names and work are remembered now only by students and professors. It is the editor's hope that publication of this Dictionary will help to save from oblivion and recall to the general reader the names and achievements of Osborn Bergin, R. I. Best, Father Edmund Hogan, Standish Hayes O'Grady and others, and re-awaken interest in their work.

The Flight of the Earls in 1607 marked the beginning of the exodus of Irishmen seeking on the Continent careers denied them at home. In the succeeding centuries many emigrants won distinction in the armies of France, Austria and Russia. Dr Richard Hayes has recorded the exploits of many of the Wild Geese, particularly those who went to France after the Treaty of Limerick of 1691, in his *Biographical Dictionary of Irishmen in France*. These soldiers of fortune included men like Count Peter de Lacy, who became field-marshal in the Russian army and Count Lavall Nugent, field-marshal in the Austrian army, who took the field against Napoleon III in the Battle of Solferino at the age of eighty-two. Here again, only those whose lives have been recorded in sufficient detail have been included.

Ireland has contributed many distinguished actors and actresses to the English stage and it is irritating to find that they are often annexed to England in English reference books. Even *The Oxford Companion to the Theatre* falls into this error, describing, for example, Dorothy Jordan and Peg Woffington as 'English actresses'.

Readers may be disappointed in finding that names familiar in legend and half-history are omitted. It must be remembered that fifth-century Ireland is a lost world, virtually closed to both historians and archaeologists, and so, *a fortiori*, are the centuries before that. There is, therefore, no entry for Queen Maeve, or other semi-mythological figures. Even for later personages, like Gráinne Mhaol, reliable biographical material is scanty. Irish saints form another group of whose recorded lives much is folklore and little is fact. Contemporary—or near contemporary—sources, yield valuable if meagre information concerning our major saints, Patrick, Columbanus, Colmcille and Brendan. For legends, attributed miracles and fabulous exploits, the reader must go elsewhere.

The editor has aimed at steering a middle course between the brevity of Crone's *Concise Dictionary* and the diffuseness of Webb's *Compendium*, at giving the important facts and events of the subject's career in chronological order and including, where possible, a sentence or quotation 'to give the flavour of the man'. 'The flavour of the man' influenced the choice of description, whether 'poet', 'politician', 'soldier' or 'explorer'; no occasion was found to use the quaintly old-fashioned word 'civilian', sometimes occurring in the *Dictionary of National Biography*. 'Politician' has been used freely to describe those whose lives were spent in the practice of politics; no reason was seen for regarding this as an unworthy calling. 'Patriot' was used sparingly and, it must be conceded, is a very personal choice; the editor is resigned to protests at the names chosen as deserving the appellation.

A large number of men of Irish birth distinguished themselves in the service of the British Empire, rising to the rank of general or admiral, becoming ambassadors, or being knighted for administrative services. Others reached equal eminence as ecclesiastics or 'divines', another old-fashioned word found frequently in the *DNB*. The careers of these men exhibit a monotonous sameness and few had any relevance to Ireland. In accordance with the general guiding principles set out above, only those who showed strong individuality are included. The question was put: is there a reason why the general reader might want to read about this person, or would he be of interest only to a descendant or a specialist in a narrow field? Time deals harshly with many reputations.

Some curious discoveries were made in the course of the research for this work. The most striking was the poor quality of many biographies, especially those written by devoted sons or daughters, recalling Carlyle's observation, 'A well-written Life is almost as rare as a well-spent one.' He also wrote, 'No great man lives in vain. The history of the world is but the biography of great men.'

The editor wishes to place on record his gratitude to the many people who helped and encouraged him in the preparation of this work. Miss Margaret Coffey, now returned to her native Melbourne, Australia, bore the brunt of the research involved. Mr Patrick Raftery made his extensive collection of books of Irish interest freely available. Professor Tomás de Bhaldraithe, the late Mr Austin Clarke, Mr Valentin Iremonger, the late Dr Vincent Barry, Professor Kevin B. Nowlan, the late Mr Dónal Foley and Mr Seán MacMathúna, all made helpful suggestions and indicated useful sources. Many other friends encouraged him, by their continuing interest, to persevere in an undertaking which has occupied him for seven years, and which might well have overwhelmed him without their support. The staffs of Trinity College Library, the National Library, the Royal Irish Academy, and of the cuttings library of the *Irish Times* were at all times patient and helpful. The editor records his gratitude to his wife, who read the manuscript at different stages and helped him in many ways.

It only remains to say that it is hoped that the work will be of interest to the common reader and bring to him the stories of many gifted Irish men and women, which it were a pity he should never hear. Errors and omissions are the fault of the editor alone. It is also his hope that any such may be repaired in future editions.

Henry Boylan,
July 1978

PREFACE TO THE SECOND EDITION

The editor again records his gratitude to the many people whose interest and practical help encouraged him in this undertaking. To the names mentioned in the Preface to the first edition must be added those of Diarmuid Breathnach, Deaglán de Bréadún, Liam de Paor, Professor L. M. Cullen, Tony Farmar, Proinsias Mac Aonghusa, Mr Justice Niall St J. McCarthy, Dr Seán Mac Réamoinn, Tony O'Riordan and C.E.F. Trench. As with the first edition, Fergal Tobin of Gill and Macmillan gave invaluable guidance and advice throughout.

Henry Boylan,
July 1988

A

ABERNETHY, JOHN (1680–1740), dissenting clergyman. Born Co. Derry, 19 October 1680, son of a Presbyterian minister. Educated at Glasgow University, which he entered at the age of thirteen, and at Edinburgh, where he studied divinity. His academic brilliance and social graces admitted him to the cultured society of Edinburgh. He was ordained for Antrim in 1703. Called to Dublin in 1717 and also to Belfast. The Synod assigned him to Dublin; Abernethy resolved that Antrim had first call on him, and decided to stay there. A controversy ensued, in which Abernethy disowned the sacerdotal assumptions of church courts. Presbyterians divided into two camps, subscribers and non-subscribers—now Unitarians—who followed Abernethy. In 1730 he accepted a call to Wood Street congregation in Dublin. In 1731 he became engaged in violent controversy arising out of the Test Act. Far in advance of his age, Abernethy stood firmly against all laws that excluded people of ability and integrity from serving their country merely on account of differences of religious opinion. He died suddenly in December 1740. A noted preacher, he published volumes of sermons and discourses. In collected *Tracts* he took issue with SWIFT.

ADAMNÁN, SAINT (*c.* 625–704). Little authentic information available. Said to have been born in Co. Donegal and elected Abbot of Iona in 679. He made a successful appeal in 686 to King of Northumbria for release of Irish captives. The Latin life of St Columba, *Vita Columbae*, now generally accepted as his work, throws valuable light on the social and religious conditions of the age. He took part in synods and conventions in Ireland, from which came rules called after him, including a law exempting women from military service. Died 23 September 704, his feast-day in old Irish and Scottish calendars. Tributes were paid to his piety and learning by his contemporary, Bede. The most scholarly edition of *Vita Columbae* is by DR WILLIAM REEVES, from an eighth-century codex in the library of Schaffhausen in Switzerland. *Lebor na hUidhri* in the RIA contains Fís Adamnáin (Adamnán's Vision), but this Old Irish vision of Paradise and Hell cannot be firmly attributed to him. A book on the Holy Land, *De Locis Sanctis*, was written down by Adamnán from a narration by a French bishop called Arculf.

ADAMS, ROBERT (1791–1875), surgeon. Born in Dublin. Educated TCD; elected fellow of Royal College of Surgeons 1818 and president three times. Surgeon to the Queen in Ireland 1861 and Regius Professor of Surgery in the University of Dublin. He served in Jervis Street and Richmond hospitals and had a high reputation as a surgeon. His *Treatise on Rheumatic Gout* (1857) became the classic work on the subject.

AE. See under RUSSELL, GEORGE.

AENGUS, SAINT (*c.* AD 824). Known as a *céile Dé* (anglicised 'culdee') or servant of God; was associated with a monastic reform movement that stressed rigid observance and intellectual pursuits, particularly the composition of devotional literature. He lived for a time at Clonenagh monastery in Co. Laois, where he was later abbot, and at Tallaght, Co. Dublin, and composed *Féilire Aengus,* a calendar in Old Irish in honour of the saints, with 365 quatrains, one for each day of the year. His feast-day is 11 March.

AIKEN, FRANK (1898–1983), revolutionary and politician. Born in Camlough, Co. Armagh, on 13 February 1898 and educated at Newry CBS. Joined the Irish Volunteers in 1914. Became commandant of Fourth Northern Division of IRA in 1921 and led many operations against the British forces. When the Civil War broke out in June 1922 he tried to bring about peace, and kept his own division neutral as long as he could. Succeeded Liam Lynch as Chief of Staff in April 1923, and on 24 May issued the order to 'cease fire and dump arms'. He was first elected TD for Louth in 1923. When Fianna Fáil won office in 1932 DE VALERA appointed him Minister for Defence. Subsequently he was Minister for Co-ordination of Defensive Measures 1939–1945, Minister for Finance 1945–1948, and Minister for External Affairs 1951–1954 and 1957–1969; Tánaiste 1959–1969. At the United Nations he won the confidence of the small states by his independent stance. He urged agreement on non-proliferation of nuclear weapons, and accepted Ireland's duty to contribute troops to UN peacekeeping forces. Supported by an exceptionally able staff, he won for Ireland a hearing out of proportion to its size or international importance. He retired from ministerial office in 1969 and from the Dáil in 1973 after fifty years' service. He received many decorations and honours, including honorary doctorates from NUI and TCD. He was a lifelong supporter of the Irish language. His wife died in a road accident in 1978. He died in a Dublin hospital on 18 May 1983, survived by a daughter and two sons.

AIKENHEAD, MARY (1787–1858), founder of the Irish Sisters of Charity. Born Cork, 19 January 1787. Brought up a Protestant like her father, Dr David Aikenhead, who on his death-bed became a Roman Catholic, as was his wife. Mary became a Catholic soon afterwards. After the death of her mother, the Archbishop of Dublin, Dr Murray, asked her to found a congregation of Sisters of Charity, the first in Ireland. After training in a convent in York, Mary and another woman opened their first house in North William Street, Dublin, Mary being appointed superior-general. Although in bad health, she succeeded in extending the order to ten houses and also founded St Vincent's Hospital, the first in Ireland served by nuns. Noted for her energy and generosity of spirit. Died 22 July 1858.

ALEXANDER, MRS. See under HECTOR, ANNIE FRENCH.

ALEXANDER, CECIL FRANCES (1818–1895), hymn-writer. Born Co. Wicklow. Began to write verse at an early age. Her *Hymns for Little Children* (1848) went into sixty-nine editions by 1896. 'There is a green hill far away' is her best-known hymn. Died in Derry, where her husband, William, was bishop, on 12 October 1895.

ALEXANDER, HAROLD RUPERT LEOFRIC GEORGE, first EARL ALEXANDER OF TUNIS AND ERRIGAL (1891–1969), field-marshal. Born 10 December 1891 on the family estate at Caledon, Co. Tyrone. Educated Harrow and Sandhurst. Served with the Irish Guards in France in First World War, wounded twice, once seriously. Awarded Military Cross, Legion of Honour, and the Russian Order of St Anne. After the war appointed to the Staff College, then the Imperial Defence College, and later served in India. By 1939, when Second World War broke out, he had risen to the rank of major-general. He was GOC Southern Command from 1940 to 1942 when he was made general and sent to Burma. He became Commander-in-Chief Middle East in 1942 and then Commander-in-Chief Eighteenth Army Group in North Africa when Rommel's forces were defeated. He commanded the Allied forces in Italy from 1943 to

1944 and then was made field-marshal and supreme Allied commander in the Mediterranean theatre until the end of the war. Governor-General of Canada 1946–1952. Minister of Defence 1952–1954. Received the Order of Merit in 1959. Alexander was regarded as the finest product in the Second World War of the British gentleman-soldier tradition, combining personal bravery and panache with military ability and a natural gift for leadership. Died in hospital near London, 16 June 1969.

ALEXANDER, HENRY. See under McALLISTER, ALEXANDER.

ALLEN, WILLIAM P. See under MANCHESTER MARTYRS.

ALLGOOD, MOLLY (1887–1952), actress. Stage name Máire O'Neill; sister of SARA ALLGOOD. Born Dublin, 12 January 1887. After her father's death she was sent to an orphanage and then apprenticed to a dressmaker. She joined the Abbey Theatre company in 1905. JOHN M. SYNGE was captivated by her and they became engaged. In January 1907 she played Pegeen Mike in *The Playboy of the Western World*. The Dublin audiences howled it down, but in London later that year it was received as a masterpiece, and her performance was a personal triumph. Synge died on 24 March 1909, and in June 1911 she married George Herbert Mair, drama critic of the *Manchester Guardian*. They had two children, Pegeen and John. Molly continued her career with great success, playing with the Liverpool Repertory Company, with Tree in Shakespeare in London and with J. B. FAGAN. Her husband died on 3 January 1926. Six months later she married Arthur Sinclair, an Abbey actor. They appeared together many times in the plays of SEÁN O'CASEY at home and on successful American tours. Her last years were clouded by divorce and money troubles; drink became a problem, though her versatility ensured that she seldom lacked parts. Her son was killed

in an air accident in 1942. She died on 2 November 1952.

ALLGOOD, SARA (1883–1950), actress. Born Dublin, 31 October 1883. Apprenticed to an upholsterer. Joined Inghinidhe na hÉireann, founded by MAUDE GONNE MacBRIDE. Their drama coach, WILLIAM FAY, enrolled her in the National Theatre Society. She had her first big success as Mrs Fallon in LADY GREGORY's *Spreading the News* on the opening night of the Abbey Theatre, 27 December 1904. In 1905 she became a full-time actress and showed her tragic power in *Cathleen ní Houlihan* and *Riders to the Sea*. Successful English and American tours followed. In 1915 she accepted the lead in *Peg o' My Heart*, a slight and amateurish comedy that was wildly successful, and in 1916 toured Australia and New Zealand with it. She married her leading man, Gerald Henson, in Melbourne in September 1916. In January 1918 she gave birth to a daughter who lived only an hour. In November 1918 her husband died at Wellington during an influenza epidemic. After a few seasons in London she returned to the Abbey. Her playing of Juno in 1924 on the first night of O'CASEY's *Juno and the Paycock* is part of Irish theatrical history. She gave another unforgettable performance in London in 1926 as Bessie Burgess in *The Plough and the Stars*. After many successful American tours she settled in Hollywood in 1940 and became an American citizen in 1945. The move was not a success. Film studios offered her only small 'quaint old Irishwoman' parts—cooks, barmaids, or landladies—and even these became scarce. Poor and lonely, she struggled on. Died in Hollywood, 13 September 1950.

ALLINGHAM, WILLIAM (1824–1889), poet. Born Ballyshannon, Co. Donegal, 19 March 1824. Entered the civil service as a customs officer. Made frequent visits to London and became a close friend of Leigh Hunt, Carlyle, and the Pre-Raphaelite circle. His first volume of poems appeared in 1850; a subsequent collection, *Day and Night Songs,* was illustrated by Millais and Rossetti. Many of his poems were sold widely in Ireland as halfpenny broadsheets. Granted a civil list pension of £60 in 1864, increased to £100 in 1870. He then retired to London where he became sub-editor and later editor of *Fraser's Magazine.* His most ambitious work, *Laurence Bloomfield in Ireland* (1864), has been described as an epic of Irish philanthropic landlordism. Died in London, 18 November 1889.

ALLMAN, GEORGE JAMES (1812–1898), botanist and zoologist. Born at Cork. Educated RBAI and TCD, graduating in medicine. He devoted himself to the study of natural science, especially marine zoology, of which he was one of the early pioneers. Professor of Botany at Dublin University 1844. FRS June 1854. Regius Professor of Natural History and keeper of the Natural History Museum in the University of Edinburgh 1855. His reputation rests on his investigation into the classification and morphology of the Coelenterata and Polyzoa. Most important work was *A Monograph on the Gymnoblastic or Tubularian Hydroids* (1871–1872). For his work on hydroids he received medals from the Royal Society of Edinburgh, RIA, and Linnean Society. Retired in 1870, died at Parkstone, Dorset, 24 November 1898.

AMORY, THOMAS (*c.* 1691–1788), author and eccentric of Irish descent. He lived for a time in Dublin where he knew SWIFT. In 1755 he published *Memoirs of Several Ladies of Great Britain,* a miscellany of biography, literary criticism, and observations on religious matters. *The Life of John Buncle, Esq.* (two volumes, 1756 and 1766) is a literary curiosity, an eccentric, idosyncratic variety of the English novel. Here are arts, sciences, ladies, wanderings, mansions, arguments, and adventures, with a defence of 'Christian deism' thrown in for good measure. He lived a very secluded life in London and died there at a great age on 25 November 1788.

ANDERSON, SIR ROBERT (1841–1918), official and writer. Born Dublin. Educated TCD. Called to Irish bar 1863. Appointed to secret service branch at Home Office 1867. Dealt with Irish affairs and advised on political crime. Investigated Fenian movement and supplied *The Times* with material for Parnell Commission. Appointed assistant commissioner and head of CID 1888. Investigated 'Jack the Ripper' murders. Made KCB on retirement 1901. Published *Sidelights on the Home Rule Movement* (1906), *Criminals and Crime* (1907), and *The Lighter Side of My Official Life* (1910). Was a Presbyterian lay preacher for fifty years and published some twenty books on religious subjects. Died in London.

ANDREWS, CHRISTOPHER STEPHEN ('TODD') (1901–1985), revolutionary and public servant. Born in Summerhill, Dublin, on 6 October 1901 and educated at St Enda's, Synge Street CBS, and UCD. He joined the Dublin Brigade, Irish Volunteers, at the age of fifteen. Arrested in April 1920 and released after ten days on hunger strike. Interned in the Curragh in June 1921 and tunnelled his way out with two companions. Took the Republican side in the Civil War, was wounded in the fighting in O'Connell Street, Dublin, and later appointed adjutant to General Liam Lynch. Interned by the Free State government until spring 1924, he then resumed his studies at UCD, graduating B.Comm. His first post was with the Irish Tourist Association; he then joined the ESB as chief accounts inspector. Shortly after the Fianna Fáil government took office in 1932 he was placed in charge of turf development. After trying co-operative methods, he decided to set up a properly managed modern enterprise, and headed a delegation to Germany and USSR to examine their production methods. Bord na Móna, as it was

4

named in 1946, was spectacularly successful under Andrews as managing director, increasing turf production to millions of tons yearly, establishing factories to produce briquettes and peat moss, and building model villages to house some of its thousands of workers. In September 1958 he was appointed chairman of CIE, the national transport system, which employed 20,000 workers, had 2,500 miles of railway, 7,000 lorries, 1,200 buses, 200 horses, and 450 miles of canal. It was losing millions of pounds yearly: the Transport Act, 1958, required CIE to pay its way within five years. He pruned the railway network drastically, reorganised the management, and reduced the deficit to £250,000. In June 1966 he was appointed chairman of the Radio Telefís Éireann Authority. He resigned in 1970, to avoid any conflict of interest when his son David was made chief whip of the Fianna Fáil parliamentary party. Honorary doctorates were conferred on him by NUI, TCD, and QUB. He was president of the Institute of Management and of the Institute of Public Administration, and a member of the Arts Council. He died at his home in Dundrum, Co. Dublin, on 11 October 1985, survived by his second wife, a daughter and three sons, two of them TDs. His first wife died in 1967. His nickname 'Todd', by which he was widely known, derived from his supposed resemblance to a character named Alonzo Todd who was featured in an English schoolboy magazine, the *Magnet*. His autobiography, a forthright account of his life and times, appeared in two volumes, *Dublin Made Me* (1979), and *Man of No Property* (1982).

ANDREWS, ÉAMONN (1922–1987), broadcaster and businessman. Born in Synge St, Dublin, on 19 December 1922 and educated at Holy Faith Convent in the Liberties and Synge St CBS. At eighteen he became a clerk in an insurance office. A keen amateur boxer, he won the Irish junior middleweight title in 1944. He had already got some part-

time work as a sports broadcaster, and in 1946 he left his job to become a full-time freelance broadcaster. He moved to London in 1950 and quickly made his name as presenter of a BBC Saturday evening sports programme. Further success followed in the very popular programmes 'What's My Line' and 'This is Your Life'. He won the *News Chronicle* award for top television personality in 1956 and 1957 and was reputed to be Britain's highest-earning television performer. His Irish business interests were connected with entertainment: recording studios, a dance hall, and the Gaiety Theatre. He was made a Knight of St Gregory in 1964 and an honorary commander of the Order of the British Empire in 1970. He died in a London hospital on 5 November 1987.

ANDREWS, JOHN MILLER (1871–1956), second Prime Minister, Northern Ireland. Born 17 July 1871. Educated RBAI. Flax-spinner and land-owner. Unionist MP in Northern parliament for Co. Down 1921–1929 and for Mid-Down 1929–1953. Minister of Labour 1921–1937. Minister of Finance 1937–1940. Succeeded CRAIG as Prime Minister in 1940 and held office until 1943. Grand Master of Orange Institution of Co. Down 1941, of All Ireland 1948, and of Imperial Grand Council of World 1949. Died 5 August 1956.

ANDREWS, THOMAS (1813–1885), chemistry professor. Born in Belfast, 19 December 1813. Educated at the RBAI and Universities of Glasgow, Dublin, and Edinburgh. He graduated in medicine in 1835, set up in private practice in Belfast, and also taught chemistry at his old school. Professor of chemistry, Queen's College, Belfast, 1849. He engaged in prolonged scientific research, and gained eminence for his work on ozone and on the continuity of the liquid and gaseous states. He showed that ozone is not a compound but oxygen in an altered and allotropic form. His work on carbon dioxide established the conceptions of critical temperature and critical pressure, and demonstrated his great skill as an experimentalist. FRS 7 June 1849, and president of the British Association 1876. He published numerous scientific papers and *The Church In Ireland* (1869), a plea in favour of the disestablishment of the Church of Ireland and the distribution of its assets. Died at Fort William Park, Belfast, 26 November 1885.

ANDREWS, THOMAS (1873–1912), master shipbuilder. Born in Comber, Co. Down. His uncle, Lord Pirrie, was chairman of Harland and Wolff's shipyard in Belfast. Andrews began work there at sixteen, rising at five a.m. to begin work at six. At night he studied machine and freehand drawing, applied mechanics, and naval architecture. He read neither books nor newspapers, regarding them as a waste of time. He became managing director in 1907 at the age of thirty-four. Chief designer of the *Titanic,* then the largest ship in the world. When the liner began to sink after hitting an iceberg in the North Atlantic on its maiden voyage to New York, in April 1912, Andrews showed courage and unselfishness in helping to save passengers, and went down with the ship. A memorial hall in Comber is named after him.

ANNESLEY, ARTHUR, first EARL OF ANGLESEY (1614–1686). Born in Dublin, 10 July 1614, son of Sir Francis Annesley, Lord Mountmorres. Educated at Magdalen College, Oxford, and Lincoln's Inn. MP for Radnor. During the Civil War he acquitted himself well in Ireland as a Commissioner. Aided the restoration of Charles II and appointed vice-treasurer and receiver-general for Ireland. Earl of Anglesey 1661; Lord Privy Seal 1673. He took an independent line in Parliament on Irish affairs. He strongly opposed the Cattle Act of 1666. During alleged Popish Plot alarms he dissented against the vote declaring an Irish plot and, according to his own testimony, interceded for OLIVER PLUNKETT. Had lucrative official posts and received large grants of

land and money from Ireland. He wrote many political tracts and collected a large library. In 1682 he was dismissed from government service when he published papers reflecting on James I and Charles I. Died at his country seat, Blechingdon, Oxfordshire, 26 April 1686.

ANNESLEY, JAMES (1715–1760). Born in Wexford, son of Lord Altham, a dissolute spendthrift who neglected the boy. Shortly after Altham's death the boy was kidnapped by his uncle who sent him to America, where he was sold as a common slave. Escaped in 1740, returned to England and claimed to succeed in place of his uncle, now Lord Anglesey. After a trial of fifteen days, he lost his case. His story was used in *Peregrine Pickle* by Smollett, in *Guy Mannering* by Scott, and in *The Wandering Heir* by Charles Reade.

ANSTER, JOHN (1793–1867), lawyer and writer. Born at Charleville (now Ráth Luirc), Co. Cork. Educated at TCD. Called to the Irish bar 1824. LL.D 1825. Registrar of the Admiralty Court 1837, and professor of civil law, University of Dublin, from 1850 until his death. A frequent contributor of prose and verse to the *Dublin University Magazine* and the *North British Review*. Best-known work is a translation of Goethe's *Faust,* which received favourable notice. Died in Dublin, 9 June 1867.

ARCHDALL, MERVYN (1723–1791), antiquary. Born Dublin, 23 April 1723. Educated TCD and took holy orders. Rector of Slane, Co. Meath. MRIA. Published *Monasticum Hibernicum* in 1786 after forty years' labour. Many mistakes in it were corrected by JOHN LANIGAN. Edited Lodge's *Peerage of Ireland* (seven volumes, 1789). Died at Slane, 6 August 1791.

ARCHDEKIN, RICHARD (1618–1693), Jesuit; also known as Arsdekin, and Mac Giolla Cuddy. Born Kilkenny, 16 March 1618. Studied theology at

Louvain. Entered Society of Jesus at Mechlin on 28 September 1642. Professor of philosophy, moral theology and scripture for many years at Louvain and Antwerp. Proficient in Irish, English, Latin, and Dutch. Published *A Treatise on Miracles* (1667), in Irish and English, perhaps the first book printed jointly in the two languages. His life of St Patrick (1671) included the prophecies of St Malachy concerning the succession of the Popes. His *Controversiae Fidei*, a theological work, went into thirteen editions between 1671 and 1718. Later editions, under the title *Theologia Tripartita Universa*, included lives of OLIVER PLUNKETT and PETER TALBOT, with other material on Ireland. Died at Antwerp, 31 August 1693.

ARCHER, JAMES (born *c.* 1550), Jesuit. Born at Kilkenny. Educated at Louvain; entered Society of Jesus in Rome 1581. Distinguished educationist, first rector of the Irish College at Salamanca. Between 1596 and 1603 he worked as a missioner in Ireland in conditions of great danger. Had many narrow escapes from capture by Crown forces. Died in Spain some time between 1617 and 1624.

ARCHER, WILLIAM (1830–1897), naturalist and librarian. Born 6 May 1830, Magherahamlet, Co. Down. About 1846 he came to Dublin and devoted his leisure to the study of natural history. Elected FRS in 1875 for his work on Protozoa. In 1877 became first librarian of National Library of Ireland and directed the preparation of an admirable dictionary catalogue. Cunningham gold medal of the RIA for his scientific attainments 1879. Resigned from the National Library 1895 and died at his house at 52 Lower Mount Street, Dublin, 14 August 1897.

ARMOUR, JAMES BROWN (1841–1928), 'Armour of Ballymoney', Presbyterian minister. Born Lisboy, Ballymoney, Co. Antrim, 20 January 1841. Educated Genaby School, a small local establishment; Ballymoney Model School, and the RBAI. Studied classics at Queen's Colleges, Belfast and Cork, teaching to support himself. Wanted to practise law but, deferring to family wishes, became Presbyterian minister at Ballymoney 1869. He married a widow with two sons in March 1883. In 1885, to supplement his income he became an assistant at Magee College, Derry, where he remained for twenty-three years. He built a new church, which was opened in 1885. His forthright statements on the great political questions of the day made him known throughout Ulster. In March 1893 a special General Assembly of the Presbyterian Church in Ireland was held to debate a resolution condemning the Home Rule Bill. Armour moved an amendment in favour of self-government with full protection of the rights and interests of the Presbyterian Church. His speech was interrupted by jeering and shouting. The official resolution was carried by a large majority. His congregation remained loyal to him, but elsewhere he was virtually ostracised for a while. Undaunted, he obtained the signatures of 3,535 Presbyterians supporting the Home Rule Bill, as a memorial to Gladstone. At the General Assembly of 1900 he opposed the adoption of a report condemning the proposed establishment of a Catholic University. He had consistently supported the Tenant Right movement and condemned landlordism, and in a controversy about this time with Dr Traill, later Provost of TCD, he argued against the ascendancy party in Ireland with great vigour. When the Liberals returned to power in 1906 he became the unofficial channel for representations to Dublin Castle, where a relative was Under-Secretary. In 1908 he was diagnosed as having a dangerous heart condition and advised to curtail his activities. The news drew tributes from all religious denominations. At the General Assembly of 1913 he moved an amendment to a Laymen's Memorial against Home Rule, to re-affirm the decision of the 1912 Assembly that politics should not be allowed to divide the Presbyterian Church. This evoked a storm of protest, to which he replied: 'If you deny the right of private judgement and of free speech, how much do you have of Protestantism worth keeping? Nothing at all.' The official resolution was passed by 921 votes to 43. He described the agitation fostered by CARSON as 'a wicked bluff', and said that partition would be ruinous to Ulster and to Protestantism. When the 1916 Rising broke out he said that the Northern Unionists were largely responsible, because of their actions in illegal gun-running and in encouraging the use of force to counter an Act of Parliament. During the First World War he was an honorary chaplain to the Lord Lieutenant and helped to recruit Irishmen to the British army. At the General Assembly of 1920 he spoke against the Government of Ireland Bill, which introduced partition, as divisive and anti-Unionist, as tending to accentuate racial and religious hatreds, and as ruinous to the moral and commercial prosperity of Ireland. To him, Unionism meant the unity of Ireland. Again the Assembly voted against him. He retired from the ministry on 2 September 1925 after fifty-six years' service, and died on 25 January 1928.

ARMSTRONG, SIR ALEXANDER (1818–1899), naval surgeon and explorer. Born Croghan Lodge, Co. Fermanagh. Educated TCD and Edinburgh University. Joined British navy 1842. Surgeon and naturalist on expedition to Arctic 1849–1854 under SIR ROBERT M'CLURE to search for Franklin, and was responsible for the good health maintained. Awarded Gilbert Blane gold medal for best journal kept by naval surgeons. Served in Baltic, on North American station, and in Malta. Director-general of medical department of navy 1869–1871. KCB 1871 and elected FRS 1873. Published *Personal Narrative of the Discovery of the North-West Passage* (1857) and *Observations on Naval Hygiene* (1858). Died 4 July 1899 at Sutton Bonnington, Leicestershire.

ARMSTRONG, EDMUND JOHN (1841–1865), poet. Born Dublin, 23 July 1841. Educated TCD. Gave promise of poetic gifts but died young at Kingstown (now Dún Laoghaire), 24 February 1865. *Poetical Works of Edmund J. Armstrong* and *Essays and Sketches* were collected and published by his brother in 1877.

ARMSTRONG, JAMES (1780–1839), Unitarian minister. Born Ballynahinch, Co. Down. Educated TCD. Ordained at Dublin 1806. A founder-member of the Irish Unitarian Society 1830. D.D. at University of Geneva 1834. Helped to found the Association of Irish Non-Subscribing Presbyterians 1835. He represented the association at Reformation tercentenary celebrations in Geneva 1835. His published works include sermons and an *Ordination Service* with an appendix on Irish Presbyterian biography based on his own extensive and scholarly research and of great value. He died suddenly at Stonehouse, Lanarkshire, 4 December 1839.

ASHE, THOMAS (1885–1917), revolutionary. Born at Lispole, Co. Kerry. Trained as a teacher in De La Salle College, Waterford. Principal in Lusk, Co. Dublin. Active in the Irish Volunteers and Gaelic League. Collected considerable sums for both organisations in the USA in 1914. In the Easter Rising, 1916, he commanded Volunteers in an engagement with armed RIC at Ashbourne, Co. Dublin, defeating them and capturing four police barracks and large quantities of arms and ammunition. He was arrested soon after, court-martialled, and sentenced to death. The sentence was commuted to penal servitude for life. In prison he wrote the poem 'Let me carry your cross for Ireland, Lord'. Released 1917. In August that year he was arrested, charged with 'speeches calculated to cause disaffection', and sentenced to one year's imprisonment with hard labour. With other Republican prisoners in Mountjoy Jail he demanded treatment as a prisoner of war. This was refused, and the prisoners went on hunger strike. Ashe died on 25 September 1917 as a result of forcible feeding. His funeral was followed by 30,000 people, led by armed Volunteers in uniform.

ASHFORD, WILLIAM (1746–1824), landscape painter. Born Birmingham. Settled in Dublin 1764 having obtained an appointment in the Ordnance Office through the surveyor-general, Ralph Ward. Exhibited flower pieces at Society of Artists 1767 and fruit and dead game 1770. His landscapes won second premium 1772 and first premium 1773. Regular contributor to society until 1780. He was in London 1789–1790 and exhibited at RA where he had first shown in 1775. He continued to exhibit there at intervals until 1811. President Irish Society of Artists 1813. He took active part in founding the RHA and was elected first president 1823. From 1780 he lived in Sandymount, Dublin, in house designed by his friend GANDON, and died there, 17 April 1824. Buried Donnybrook. Some of his landscapes were engraved, notably for Milton's Views.

ASTON, WILLIAM GEORGE (1841–1911), Japanese scholar. Born near Derry, 9 April 1841, son of a Unitarian minister and schoolmaster. After early education by his father, studied classics and modern languages at Belfast. In 1864 he joined the British consular service in Japan as a student interpreter, and served at Tokyo and Hyogo. From 1884 to 1886 he was consul-general in Korea and from 1886 until his retirement in 1889 Japanese secretary to the British legation in Tokyo. When he arrived in Japan, few Europeans had any practical knowledge of Japanese. There were no dictionaries or grammars either for Japanese or European students. Grammar was left entirely to philological specialists. He acquired a complete, accurate and fluent command of the spoken language and a facility in writing and reading Japanese. He compiled grammars (1869 and 1872) both for the spoken and written language (which differ in many important usages), and although these grammars have since been superseded they pioneered this branch of Japanese studies. He was the first European to complete a literal translation of the *Nihongi*, the *Ancient Chronicles of Japan* (1896), and his subsequent works *Japanese Literature* (1889) and *Shinto* (1905) became recognised textbooks: they have been translated into Japanese and used by leading native scholars in Japan. He contributed many articles to the *Transactions* of the Asiatic Society of Japan, the Japan Society, and the Royal Asiatic Society of London. On retiring in 1889 he was made a CMG. He settled at Beer, Devon, and died there, 22 November 1911. His collection of some 9,500 Japanese books, including many rare editions, was acquired by Cambridge University in January 1912.

B

BAGWELL, RICHARD (1840–1918), historian. Born 9 December 1840 at Clonmel, Co. Tipperary. Educated Harrow and Christ Church College, Oxford. Called to the bar. Commissioner of national education. Published two important works, *Ireland Under the Tudors* (three volumes, 1885–1890), and *Ireland Under the Stuarts* (three volumes, 1909–1910). Received D.Litt. from TCD and Oxford. Died Clonmel, 4 December 1918.

BALFE, MICHAEL WILLIAM (1808–1870), composer and singer. Born at 10 Pitt Street (later Balfe Street, now demolished), Dublin, 15 May 1808. Became proficient violinist at an early age. After his father's death in 1823 he went to London as apprentice under Charles Edward Horn, a noted singer, and played the violin in Drury Lane Theatre Orchestra to keep himself and his mother. In London he found a patron, a Count Mazzara, who took him to Italy. Was commissioned by La Scala in Milan to write the music for a ballet, *La Pérouse,* which won instant success. Went to Paris and met Rossini, who arranged tuition for him and an engagement to sing Figaro at the Théâtre des Italiens in 1827. Successful and retained for three years at a very generous salary. He returned to Italy in 1830 and met and married Lina Rosa, a beautiful and talented Hungarian singer. In 1833 he was back in England and wrote several operas for Drury Lane, the *Siege of Rochelle* being best-received. In 1838 his *Falstaff* was produced at Her Majesty's Theatre. Later that year he toured Ireland. In 1841 he started his own opera company in London but this proved a failure. Balfe then went to Paris where his *Puits d'Amour* was produced in 1843

and scored a remarkable triumph. When in London later that year for an English version he was asked to compose a new opera for Drury Lane. This was *The Bohemian Girl,* produced very successfully in 1843. The following years were spent mainly in musical tours. Balfe visited St Petersburg, Vienna, and the great cities of Italy. His only composition of importance during this period was the *Sicilian Bride* (Drury Lane 1852). In 1864 he bought Rowney Abbey, a small estate in Hertfordshire, where he wrote his last opera, *The Knight of the Leopard,* with libretto based on Scott's *Talisman.* He died there, 20 October 1870. He was buried at Kensal Green, and there is a tablet to his memory in Westminster Abbey.

BALL, FRANCIS ELRINGTON (1863–1928), historian. Born Portmarnock, Co. Dublin, 18 July 1863, son of the Lord Chancellor. Educated privately because of poor health. Stood unsuccessfully as Unionist for South Co. Dublin 1900. Turned to writing: *History of the County Dublin* (1902–20); *Correspondence of Jonathan Swift* (six volumes, 1910–1914), the first annotated edition, which gained him D.Litt. from TCD in 1911. *The Judges in Ireland, 1221–1921* (1926) is now an important source since the documents in the Irish Record Office on which it was based were destroyed in 1922. He settled in London in 1918. Died Dublin, 7 January 1928.

BALL, JOHN (1818–1889), scientist, politician and Alpine traveller. Born Dublin, 20 August 1818. Educated Oscott Jesuit College and Christ's College, Cambridge. Travelled in Europe for four years. Called to Irish bar 1845 but never practised. Liberal MP Carlow

1852. Under-Secretary for colonies 1855–1857. First president Alpine Club 1857. Left public life on being defeated for Limerick 1858. Published *The Alpine Guide* (1863–1868). Visited Morocco and South America and published *Journal of a Tour in Morocco* (1878) and *Notes of a Naturalist in South America* (1887). Contributed many papers on botany and physical science to learned journals. MRIA and fellow of the Linnean, Geographical and Antiquarian Societies of London. Elected FRS 1868. Died South Kensington, 21 October 1889.

BALL, SIR ROBERT STAWELL (1840–1913), astronomer and mathematician. Born Dublin, 1 July 1840. Educated at Tarvin Hall, Chester, and TCD, winning many prizes. Professor of mathematics, Royal College of Science, Dublin, 1867; professor of astronomy at TCD and Astronomer-Royal for Ireland 1874–1892; Lowndean Professor of Astronomy, Cambridge University, 1892–1913. Elected FRS 1873. He became known to a wide public through his many popular works on astronomy, particularly *The Story of the Heavens* (1886), and successful lecture tours. His published work on the theory of screw motions ranked him among the greatest mathematicians of his time. Knighted in 1886, died at Cambridge, 25 November 1913.

BALLANCE, JOHN (1839–1893), Prime Minister of New Zealand. Born Glenavy, Co. Antrim. At fourteen was apprenticed to an ironmonger in Belfast. When about twenty he emigrated to New Zealand and opened a small shop at Wanganui. He soon turned to journalism, and founded the *Wanganui Herald*. He served in the Maori war of 1867, and in 1875 entered the House of Representatives. He joined the Liberal party. Minister of Lands and Native Affairs 1884–1887. Leader of the Opposition 1889 and Prime Minister 1891. His policies were bold and progressive and won great popularity for his party. Died 27 April 1893, before he could see the fruits of his work.

BANIM, JOHN (1798–1842), novelist, playwright and poet. Born Kilkenny, 3 April 1798. Educated Kilkenny College and the drawing academy of the RDS. He became a teacher of drawing in Kilkenny in 1815. An engagement to one of his pupils was broken off, and the young woman died soon after. This tragedy had a shattering effect on him, and his health never recovered. In 1820 he moved to Dublin and, largely through his efforts, artists there obtained a charter of incorporation and a government grant. Banim received an address and a large sum of money. He then turned to literature, and his play *Damon and Pythias* was produced with success at Covent Garden. In 1822 he suggested to his brother MICHAEL that they should write a series of novels. Thus were begun the 'O'Hara Tales', which were immensely popular and on which the brothers' fame chiefly rests. John's contributions to the series included *The Boyne Water*, a political novel, and *The Nowlans*, a tragedy. He was now married and living in London where he befriended GERALD GRIFFIN. His health continued to fail and by 1835 he was semi-paralysed and was obliged to return to Kilkenny. Dublin gave him a benefit performance in the Theatre Royal. In Kilkenny he received an address of welcome and a large sum of money. He settled in a small cottage just outside the town, called 'Windgap Cottage'. In 1836 he was granted a civil list persion of £150 with a further £40 to educate his daughter. Banim's strength as a writer lay in his power to depict the real character of the Irish poor farmers and labourers, in contrast to the caricatures of now-forgotten hacks. He died 13 August 1842.

BANIM, MICHAEL (1796–1874), brother of JOHN BANIM. Born Kilkenny, 5 August 1796. Educated at Dr Magrath's Catholic school. Studied for the bar, but business reverses suffered by his father, a small shopkeepei and farmer, obliged him to give this up and take over the family business, which he restored to its former prosperity. With his brother John

11

he conceived the idea of a series of national tales and wrote the first, *Crohoore of the Billhook* (1825). Michael wrote about thirteen out of twenty-four works ascribed to the brothers. In 1840 he married. The next year brought serious business losses and illness. After the death of John, Michael continued to write, publishing *Clough Fion* in the *Dublin University Magazine* in 1852. He was appointed postmaster of Kilkenny in the same year. Failing health curtailed his writing and he resigned his post in 1873. He came to live at Booterstown, Dublin, and was given an allowance by the Royal Literary Fund. Died 30 August 1874. His widow was granted a civil list pension by the Prime Minister, Disraeli.

BARKER, FRANCIS (1773–1859), physician. Born Waterford. Educated TCD and Edinburgh medical school. Returned to Waterford and opened first fever hospital in Dublin. After five years, settled in Dublin. Senior physician, Cork Street Hospital, 1804. Professor of chemistry, TCD, 1808. Established the first Irish medical journal. Secretary to Irish board of health 1820–1852. Edited *Dublin Pharmacopia* 1826. Died Dublin.

BARLOW, JANE (1857–1917), writer. Born Clontarf, Dublin, daughter of Rev. James William Barlow, vice-provost TCD. Between 1892 and 1913 she published numerous volumes of stories of Irish life including *Irish Idylls*, which went into eight editions, and a volume of verse. Member of the National Literary Society, Dublin, and honorary D.Litt., Dublin University. She died at Bray, Co. Wicklow, 17 April 1917.

BARNARDO, THOMAS JOHN (1845–1905), philanthropist. Born Dublin, 4 July 1845, younger son of a wholesale furrier; educated privately. In 1862 during a Protestant religious revival he was converted, and began evangelising work in the slums. In 1866 he went to London to train as a medical missionary for China. While still a medical student, taught in a 'ragged school', and found that thousands of homeless waifs were sleeping out in the East End. He decided to devote himself to these children, and opened his first home for destitute boys in Stepney Causeway in 1870. The organisation grew with great rapidity but, despite occasional financial difficulties, never abandoned the cardinal principle, 'No destitute child ever refused admission.' 'Dr Barnardo's Homes' had as many as eight thousand children in their daily care before 1900. He died at Surbiton, 19 September 1905, survived by his wife and four children.

BARRALET, JOHN JAMES (*c.* 1747–1815), artist. Born Dublin, of French descent. Studied painting at school of Dublin Society. Worked and taught in Dublin until about 1770, when he went to London and opened a drawing academy. Exhibited drawings at RA, 1770–1776, and became a Fellow of the Society of Artists. Worked in Dublin 1779–1795 as illustrator of books on antiquities. In 1795 he went to America and settled at Philadelphia, where he worked as a book illustrator. Died there, 16 January 1815.

BARRET, GEORGE (1732–1784), landscape painter. Born in the Liberties of Dublin. Studied painting under Robert West of George's Lane. Lacking commissions in Dublin, he went to London in 1762 and won a premium of £50 that year from the Society of Artists for the best landscape. He continued to exhibit, his work was much admired, and he received many commissions. Active in founding of RA 1768, and exhibited regularly until 1782. Though reputed to be earning two thousand pounds a year he became bankrupt. Through EDMUND BURKE, an old friend, he obtained the lucrative post of Master Painter to Chelsea Hospital. Died at Paddington, 29 May 1784.

BARRETT, JOHN (1753–1821), professor and eccentric. Born Ballyroan, Co.

12

Laois, son of a clergyman. Educated at TCD. Took fellowship and became professor of oriental languages. Vice-provost in 1807. Publications include *An Enquiry into the Origin of the Constellations that Form the Zodiac,* and an essay on the early life of SWIFT. His most important work was the discovery in the college library of a palimpsest manuscript of the Gospel of St Matthew, which he edited and published. A noted eccentric, he scarcely ever left the college during the last fifty years of his life. Living in a garret on the library square, he allowed himself no fire, even in the coldest weather, and devoted himself to his two passions: reading, and the hoarding of money. Once some undergraduates had to resuscitate him with rum after finding him nearly frozen to death. He was short, with a huge head and small feet, and so mean and ragged in his appearance that the college servants objected to his presence when he stole into the kitchens to warm himself. He was a man of great acquirements and of tenacious memory, yet extraordinarily ignorant of the things of common life. He spoke Latin and Greek fluently, but had great difficulty in expressing himself in English. He died in 1821, leaving £80,000. His will stated, 'I leave everything I am possessed of to feed the hungry and clothe the naked.' The trustees of the will saw to it that his poverty-stricken brothers and sisters benefited generously.

BARRINGTON, GEORGE (born 1755), pickpocket and author. Born Maynooth, Co. Kildare, 14 May 1755, son of a silversmith named Henry Waldron. A clergyman, Dr Westropp, placed him at a free grammar-school in Dublin, but in May 1771, after being flogged for a misdemeanour, he ran away to join a company of strolling players under the name 'George Barrington'. He then went to England and became a 'genteel pickpocket'. In 1777 he was caught and sentenced to three years' ballast-heaving (hard labour on board convict hulks on the Thames at Woolwich). Released for good behaviour after twelve months, he was detected soon again and served several short sentences. Finally in 1790 was sentenced to seven years' transportation. His eloquence and gentlemanly bearing in court earned him considerable notoriety, and two contemporary accounts of his life and adventures sold widely. Sent to Botany Bay in New South Wales. In 1792 received first warrant of emancipation ever issued. Became superintendent of the convicts, high constable of Parramatta for a considerable period, and earned the regard of the governor. He published *A Voyage to Botany Bay* (1801), *A History of New South Wales* (1802), and a *History of New Holland* (1808). He lived to a very old age, and died at Parramatta, date not recorded.

BARRINGTON, SIR JONAH (1760–1834), judge and historian. Born Knapton, near Abbeyleix. Educated TCD. Called to the bar 1788. His abilities and social graces led to early preferment. He was returned to Irish House of Commons as member for Tuam 1790, lost his seat 1797, but sat for Clogher 1798–1800. He became judge to Admiralty 1798. He opposed Act of Union in 1800, although by his own account he was offered the post of solicitor-general for his support. Most inconsistently and inexplicably, he acted as agent for the government to bribe others to vote for the Union. He was knighted 1807. His extravagant habits led to frequent financial embarrassment, and he misappropriated court funds. A commission of inquiry revealed this, and in 1830 he was deprived of his judicial office by petition of both houses of Parliament. He left the country, never to return, and died at Versailles on 8 April 1834. His works include *Personal Sketches of His Own Time* (three volumes, 1827–1832), *Historic Memoirs of Ireland,* re-issued as *Rise and Fall of the Irish Nation* (1833). The *Personal Sketches* is the only work now remembered; it gives a vivid and racy account of life in the Irish society of his day.

BARRY, JAMES (1741–1806), painter. Born Water Lane, Cork, 11 October 1741, son of a shipmaster. Went to sea with his father but soon turned to painting. Studied at West's Academy in Dublin, where his 'St Patrick Baptising the King of Cashel' gained him a premium and the interest and friendship of EDMUND BURKE. Burke took him to London and gave him an allowance to enable him to study in Italy for four years. His 'Philoctes on the Isle of Lemnos' won him membership of the Clementine Academy in Bologna. Returned to England 1770. Exhibited 'Adam and Eve' at RA 1771. 'Venus Rising From the Waves' secured his election as associate 1772, and in 1773 he was elected RA. In 1773 he published a reply to the Abbé Winckelmann demolishing his theory that the genius of the English was limited by their climate. In 1777 he undertook to decorate, without payment, the Great Room of the Society for the Encouragement of the Arts in the Adelphi. Within six years, without assistance, he completed six huge pictures illustrating 'the Culture and Progress of Human Knowledge', 11½ feet (3.5 m) high and 140 feet (43 m) in length. To support himself while on this work, Barry sketched or engraved at night for print-sellers, and lived mainly on bread and apples. The society voted him 250 guineas and their gold medal. In 1782 Barry was appointed professor of painting to the Royal Academy but, after frequent quarrels with the academicians, was expelled in 1799. He lived solitary and poor until 1805 when, through the Society of Arts, £1,000 was subscribed to procure an annuity for him. He did not live to receive the first payment. Died 22 February 1806 and is buried in St Paul's.

BARRY, JOHN (1745–1803), commodore, United States navy. Born Tacumshane, Co. Wexford. He went to sea at fourteen, settled in Pennsylvania and became master of a merchant ship. He was given a naval commission by Congress early in the War of Independence. In 1776, in the brig *Lexington,* he seized the English ship *Edward,* the first warship captured by the American navy. In 1781, in command of the frigate *Alliance* of thirty-two guns, he carried the US agent to France and on the way back captured two English men-of-war. Severely wounded in the engagement. From 1782 until his death Barry superintended the progress of the US navy. Became Commodore in Navy List 1794. Has been called 'Father of the American Navy'. There is a statue of him in Wexford. Died Philadelphia, 13 September 1803.

BARRY, KEVIN (1902–1920), medical student. Born Dublin and educated UCD. Joined IRA and took part in raid for arms on military lorry in Church St in which six soldiers were killed. He was captured on the scene, court-martialled and hanged in Mountjoy jail on 1 November 1920. The making of the supreme sacrifice by a youth of eighteen aroused widespread feeling, and scores of his fellow-students joined the IRA that day. His execution was condemned by J. H. Thomas in the House of Commons.

BARRY, SPRANGER (1719–1777), actor. Born 20 November 1719, Skinner Row, Dublin. Took over the family business of silversmith. A few years' mismanagement brought bankruptcy. Took to the stage, first appearance at Smock Alley Theatre 15 February 1744. His fine voice and figure ensured a good reception. In October 1746 he played Othello at Drury Lane, London, and was highly successful. Rivalry developed between him and Garrick, and he left for Covent Garden in 1750. The critics said that his Romeo was superior to that of Garrick, and described him as 'the wonder and darling of every audience'. In October 1758 he and Henry Woodward opened a new theatre in Crow Street, Dublin, and in 1761 another in Cork. Heavy losses caused Woodward to retire in 1761, but Barry struggled on until 1767. He staged many splendid productions, and seems to have lived beyond his means, giving magnificent private parties. Financial difficulties forced him to return to London where he played at the Haymarket, Drury Lane, and Covent Garden. Died 10 January 1777. Buried in Westminster Abbey.

BARRY, GENERAL TOM (1897–1980), guerrilla leader in the War of Independence. Born in Roscarbery, Co. Cork, on 1 July 1897, and joined the British army in 1915, serving in Mesopotamia (Iraq) in First World War. On being demobbed in 1919 he joined the IRA and established himself as a military tactician, organising and training the West Cork Flying Column, a highly mobile and disciplined unit. In November 1920 he commanded an ambush at Kilmichael that virtually wiped out a company of Auxiliaries, and at Crossbarry in March 1921 his column routed a superior force from the Essex Regiment. He took the republican side during the Civil War and was imprisoned for some time in the Curragh. In 1927 he was appointed general superintendent with Cork Harbour Commissioners and held the post until his retirement in 1965. In 1938 he resigned from the IRA, as he disagreed with the proposed bombing campaign in England: he thought it had little prospect of success and would only cause the death of innocent civilians, and favoured instead action in the North. During the Second World War he served as operations officer with Southern Command. Published *Guerilla Days in Ireland* (1949). When Liam Deasy published his version of events in 1973, Barry issued a pamphlet contradicting it, *The Reality of the Anglo-Irish War, 1919–21* (1974). He died in a Cork hospital on 2 July 1980, survived by his wife, LESLIE BEAN DE BARRA.

BARTER, RICHARD (1802–1870), physician. Born Cooldaniel, Co. Cork, and qualified at London College of Physicians. Began as dispensary doctor at Inniscarra, a few miles west of Cork. During the cholera epidemic of 1832 he became impressed by the curative power of water. In 1842 he set up the St Anne's water cure establishment at Blarney, Co. Cork, which attracted many patients. On reading David Urquhart's description of hot-air baths in his *Pillars of Hercules,* he invited Urquhart to stay with him. He then set up the first modern hot-air bath in the British dominions. Later he set up vapourless baths, the so-called Turkish baths. Travelled to many countries to explain his system and promote its adoption. Died at Blarney, 3 October 1870.

BARTON, ROBERT CHILDERS (1881–1975), signatory of Anglo-Irish Treaty. Born Co. Wicklow, educated Oxford. An extensive landowner and a progressive agriculturist. Commissioned in the Dublin Fusiliers in 1914 and stationed in Dublin, Easter Week 1916. He immediately resigned his commission and joined the republican movement. Elected Sinn Féin MP for West Wicklow 1918. In February 1919 he was arrested for making seditious speeches. He escaped from Mountjoy jail on 16 March, leaving a note for the governor saying that he could not stay any longer as the service was not satisfactory. Re-arrested January 1920 and sentenced to three years' penal servitude. Released on declaration of Truce, July 1921. In the First Dáil he represented Kildare-Wicklow. Minister for Agriculture and later Minister for Economic Affairs. In October 1921 he was named as one of the plenipotentiaries sent to London to negotiate the Treaty. His cousin ERSKINE CHILDERS was secretary. He signed the Treaty in December 1921 with the others. Recommending it to the Dáil, he said that he had signed 'as the lesser of two outrages forced upon me, and between which I had to choose.' Although he had voted for the Treaty, he remained a supporter of DE VALERA. Elected to the Dáil in the general election of June 1922 but did not take his seat nor seek re-election later. Chairman, Agricultural Credit Corporation 1934–1954. Chairman, Bord na Móna for many years. Died at home at Annamoe, Co. Wicklow, 10 August 1975.

BAX, SIR ARNOLD EDWARD TREVOR (1883–1953), composer. Born London, 8 November 1883. Educated privately and at Royal Academy of Music, where he won prizes for composition and piano playing. In 1902 on reading *The Wanderings of Oisín* by W. B. YEATS said 'in a moment the Celt within me stood revealed.' He wrote a number of books and poems under the pen-name Dermot O'Byrne. These included *A Dublin Ballad-1916*, commemorating the Easter Rising, which was banned by the British authorities as seditious. Among his friends were PEARSE and other 1916 leaders. He had private means and devoted himself to musical composition, writing seven symphonies as well as concertos and chamber music. Knighted in 1937. Master of the King's Musick 1942. Extern examiner for UCC. Died in Cork, 3 October 1953. The college has dedicated a room to his memory.

BÉASLAÍ, PIARAS (1881–1965), revolutionary and writer. Born Liverpool, educated at local Jesuit College. He became a journalist and edited the *Catholic Times* in England. Came to Dublin 1904. Founded *An Fáinne*. President of Na hAisteoirí, a dramatic society. His motion proposing that the Gaelic League should stand for a free and Gaelic Ireland, independent of foreign influences, led to the resignation from the presidency of DOUGLAS HYDE at the 1915 congress. During the 1916 Rising he fought in the North King Street area, Dublin. Arrested and sentenced to penal servitude, he escaped from jail in Ireland and again from Strangeways prison in Manchester, to become director of publicity for the IRA. He voted for the Treaty in 1921 and in 1922 toured the United States on a publicity campaign to win Irish-Americans in favour of it. On his return he became chief of the press censorship department during the Civil War. TD for East Kerry 1918–1921, and commandant-general in the army. TD for Co. Kerry and West Limerick 1921–1923. Resigned from the army in 1924 and devoted himself to the language movement and literature. He was the author of plays, novels, and translations from English, French and German into Irish. Published life of Michael Collins, *Michael Collins and the Making of the New Ireland* (1925). Won gold medal for a play in Irish, Tailteann Games 1929. His works include *Fear na Milliún Punt* (1915), a play; *Astronar* (1928), a novel; *An Danar* (1929), a play; *Éigse Nua-Ghaedhilge* (1933–1934); and *Earc agus Áine agus Scéalta Eile* (1946). Died in Dublin, 22 June 1965.

BEATTY, SIR ALFRED CHESTER (1875–1968), mining engineer, philanthropist, art collector, and honorary citizen of Ireland. Born New York. Two grandparents were Irish. Educated at Westminister School, Dobbs Ferry, New York, the Columbia School of Mines, and Princeton University. He began his mining career in Denver, Colorado, and later moved to the Rocky Mountains. His major contribution to mining engineering was a new method of extracting copper from low-grade ore. His interests included projects in Mexico, Congo, Russia, Gold Coast (now Ghana), and Sierra Leone. In 1913 he visited Egypt, and was much impressed by the fine oriental manuscripts and copies of the Koran that he saw in the bazaars. This was the start of the greatest collection of oriental manuscripts ever made by a private collector. In 1953, having moved his home to Dublin, he built a special library building in Shrewsbury Road to hold his printed books and manuscripts. This collection, now the Chester Beatty Library, was left by him in trust to the Irish nation, and is open to the public. Its 13,000 volumes and other objects are reputed to be worth about £10 million; their artistic value is beyond price. The collection includes Babylonian clay tablets, some dating from 2500 BC, and Egyptian and

Greek papyri. Sir Alfred also made a gift to the National Gallery of paintings to the value of nearly £1 million, and presented his unique collection of oriental weapons to the Military College, Curragh Camp. He also made generous contributions to cancer research. Both TCD and NUI conferred honorary doctorates on him. He was made a freeman of Dublin, and an honorary citizen of Ireland, the first to receive this honour. He died in Monte Carlo, 20 January 1968, and was buried in Glasnevin, Dublin. As a mark of gratitude and respect he was given a state funeral.

BEAUFORT, SIR FRANCIS (1774–1857), admiral and hydrographer. Born Navan, Co. Meath, son of the rector. Joined the British navy in 1787 and served in the Napoleonic wars. Wounded off Málaga 1800. While recovering he helped his brother-in-law RICHARD LOVELL EDGEWORTH to establish a telegraph line from Dublin to Galway 1803–1804. Returning to active service, he was wounded again off Turkey 1812. Hydrographer to the navy 1829–1855. Published a survey entitled *Karamania; or A Brief Description of the South Coast of Asia Minor and of the Remains of Antiquity* (1817). He originated the Beaufort scale of wind velocities and a tabulated system of weather notation, both still in use. Elected FRS and served on royal commission on pilotage (1835) and on the harbours and rivers of the UK (1845). He received the KCB in 1848 for his civil achievements. Died in London, 17 December 1857.

BEDDY, JAMES P. (1900–1976), public servant. Born in Cóbh, Co. Cork, in 1900 and educated at O'Connell CBS (Dublin) and UCD. Joined the civil service and served as inspector of taxes in Tralee, where he learned to shoot snipe on the Kerry bogs. Joined the Industrial Credit Company as its first secretary in 1933 and became managing director in 1952. When the Industrial Development Authority was established in 1950 he

became chairman and was also first chairman of An Foras Tionscal, the grants board, from 1952. In these key posts he was responsible for much valuable and pioneering work in the financing and development of Irish industry. He retired from the IDA in 1965 and from the ICC some years later. He was awarded a doctorate in economic science by NUI for his thesis on *Profits: Theoretical and Practical Aspects,* published 1940, and lectured on economic geography for many years in UCD. He died in Dublin in September 1976.

BEDELL, WILLIAM (1571–1642), bishop. Born Black Notley, Essex. Educated Emmanuel College, Cambridge. Taking holy orders, he first ministered at Bury St Edmunds. Chaplain to Sir Henry Wotton, British ambassador to Venice 1607. Returned to parochial work in England 1610. Provost TCD, 1627. Bishop of Kilmore and Ardagh 1629. In 1633 he resigned Ardagh, as his principles were opposed to pluralities. He deplored the oppression of poor Catholics and the exactions levied on them. At TCD he had brought in a rule that divinity students of Irish birth should study Irish, so that they could better minister to their flock. He now pursued his study of the language, and had the Old Testament translated into Irish. In the war of 1641–1642 he sheltered many fugitives from the Confederate armies. At first the insurgents treated him well but he was imprisoned in Loughoughter Castle in 1641 and his house was taken over. Early in 1642 he was allowed to transfer to the house of a clergyman friend, Rev. Dennis Sheridan, at Dromlor, which was already crowded with English refugees. He died there of a fever on 7 February 1642 and was accorded military honours at his funeral by Confederate commanders. His Old Testament was printed in London in 1685, with translation by WILLIAM DANIEL of the New Testament, and became known as 'Bedell's Bible'.

BEHAN, BRENDAN (1923-1964), writer and talker. Born Holles St Hospital, Dublin, 9 February 1923. Educated Sisters of Charity, William St, and Brunswick St CBS, leaving school at fourteen to follow his father's trade of house painter. He received part of his education at home in Russell St, where he heard ballads and stories from Irish history, and listened to his father reading the English classics. In the family tradition, Brendan joined the IRA. Arrested Liverpool December 1939 and sentenced to three years' Borstal detention for possessing explosives. Released in December 1941, he returned to Dublin, was arrested in April 1942 and sentenced to fourteen years' penal servitude for shooting at a policeman with intent to kill. In prison in Mountjoy, Arbour Hill, and the Curragh, he learned Irish from native speakers interned with him, read omnivorously, and began to write. Released under a general amnesty in December 1946, he moved from Dublin to Kerry and Connemara, spent some time in Paris, had some further brushes with authority and short spells in prison, and eventually began to make his living in Dublin as a writer, contributing articles and stories to Radio Éireann and the *Irish Press*. In 1955 he married Beatrice Salkeld, daughter of the painter Cecil Salkeld. On 9 November 1954 his first play, *The Quare Fellow*, was produced by ALAN SIMPSON in the tiny Pike Theatre, Dublin. It made his name in Dublin. Produced by Joan Littlewood in May 1956 at the Stratford Theatre, London, it made him known internationally. His next play, *An Giall*, was first seen in June 1958 at Gael-Linn's theatre, the Damer. An English version, *The Hostage*, produced by Joan Littlewood in October 1958 was a runaway success: combining melodrama, farce, fantasy and ballad opera, it bore little resemblance to the moving and simple Irish original. The same month, the autobiographical *Borstal Boy* appeared and quickly became a best-seller. Television appearances and visits to New York, Paris, and Berlin for productions of *The Quare Fellow* added to Behan's international renown. The warmth and humour of his talk is shown in his later books, *Brendan Behan's Island*, *Brendan Behan's New York*, and *Confessions of an Irish Rebel*. *Richard's Cork Leg* is hardly more than a collection of music-hall sketches. Success and money brought their troubles. Drinking became a problem, compounded by diabetes, and his health finally gave way. He died, 20 March 1964, in the Meath Hospital, Dublin. His funeral to Glasnevin cemetery was the biggest in Dublin since the death of MICHAEL COLLINS.

BELLAMY, GEORGE ANNE (*c.* 1727-1788), actress. Born, according to her *Apology*, at Fingal, Co. Dublin, on St George's Day (23 April) 1733 (1727 seems a more probable date). Received her first names from a mishearing of 'Georgiana' at her christening. Daughter of Lord Tyrawley by a Quaker, Miss Seal, who eloped with him from boarding-school and later married a sea-captain called Bellamy. Tyrawley acknowledged her and had her educated at a convent in Boulogne. He would have done much for her but she disobeyed him by going to live with her mother. Made her first appearance at Covent Garden about 1744. Became one of Garrick's leading ladies at Drury Lane. Beautiful, arrogant, and extravagant, she was twice married, once bigamously. Her private adventures caused public scandal. At her best in romantic and tragic parts, her success owed a great deal to her youth and beauty, and when these left her she found difficulty in securing engagements. An appearance in Dublin in 1780 was a complete failure, although she had been a wild success there in 1760. On her retirement in 1785 a benefit was organised for her at Covent Garden. That year she published her *Apology*, a sensational six-volume account of her career. Her last years were spent in poverty and obscurity. Died in London, 10 February 1788.

BENN, GEORGE (1801-1882), historian of Belfast. Born 1 January 1801 at

Tandragee, Co. Armagh. Educated RBAI. Won a prize for an essay on the parish of Belfast 1819. It was published in 1823 with maps and engravings. With his brother Edward, engaged in distilling in Downpatrick and later farmed extensively at Ballymena, where he developed a derelict estate. Asked to complete his history of Belfast, he proposed instead a William Pinkerton, who collected some material but died in 1871 without having begun the history. Benn did not use any of Pinkerton's material but on his brother's death (1874) returned to Belfast, and published in 1877 *A History of the Town of Belfast from the Earliest Times to the Close of the Eighteenth Century*. Volume II (1880) covered the years 1799–1810. Died Belfast, 8 January 1882.

BENNETT, EDWARD HALLARAN

(1837–1907), surgeon. Born Charlotte Quay, Cork, 9 April 1837. Educated Hamblin's school in Cork, the Academical Institute, Harcourt St, Dublin, and TCD. Graduated in medicine 1859. University anatomist and surgeon at Sir Patrick Dun's hospital 1864. Professor of surgery TCD 1873. An authority on bone fractures, made a collection of fractures and dislocations for the pathological museum of the college. In 1881 he described a form of fracture of the base of the metacarpal bone of the thumb, which became known as 'Bennett's fracture'. President RCSI 1884–1886, and of Royal Academy of Medicine 1894–1897. Died 21 June 1907 at his home, 26 Fitzwilliam St, Dublin.

BENNETT, LOUIE (1870–1956), trade

unionist. Born Temple Hill, Dublin, daughter of a prosperous Anglo-Irish businessman. Educated Alexandra College, in England, and at Bonn, where she studied singing. In 1911 she helped start the Irishwomen's Suffrage Federation and was appointed its first secretary. She helped FRANCIS SHEEHY-SKEFFINGTON with the *Irish Citizen* and published several novels. Studied women's wages and conditions of employment, helped form the Irish Women's Reform League, which affiliated to the Suffrage Federation and drew attention to the social and economic plight of women workers. Active in peace propaganda activities during First World War. She represented Ireland on the International Executive of the Women's League for Peace and Freedom. Executive member of the Women Workers' Union and first woman president of the Irish Trade Union Congress, Cork 1932. Stood unsuccessfully for Labour in 1944 general election. Member of Administrative Council, Labour Party. Died November 1956, Killiney, Co. Dublin.

BERESFORD, JOHN CLAUDIUS

(1738–1805), statesman. Born Dublin, 14 March 1738. Educated Kilkenny College and TCD. Called to bar 1760 but never practised. MP for Waterford from 1760 until his death. Privy Councillor 1768. Commissioner of Revenue 1770. First wife died 1772. Married in 1774 a celebrated beauty, Barbara Montgomery, one of the 'Graces' in Reynolds's painting. First Commissioner of Revenue 1780. Introduced many reforms. With Lord Carlow, persuaded GANDON to come to Dublin in 1781 to build new Custom House. Under his auspices the quays were extended and Sackville St (now O'Connell St) opened up. When Pitt became Prime Minister, Beresford was virtually in charge of Irish affairs. Fitzwilliam came as Lord Lieutenant in 1795 to inaugurate a policy of conciliation and found Beresford 'virtually king of Ireland', and so unpopular with GRATTAN and his party that the new policy could not be carried out. He dismissed Beresford, though continuing his full salary of £2,000 a year. But in a few weeks Fitzwilliam was recalled and Beresford returned to office. A duel between them was prevented by the police. Beresford was a strong supporter of the Act of Union and remained in office to superintend the new fiscal arrangements. Died at his seat at Walworth, Derry, 5 November 1805.

BERESFORD, LORD JOHN GEORGE DE LA POER (1773–1862), primate of all Ireland. Younger son of the first marquis of Waterford, born Tyrone House, Dublin, 22 November 1773. Educated Eton and Christ Church, Oxford. Took holy orders, served in family livings and became successively bishop of Cork and Ross 1805, Raphoe 1807, and Clogher 1819. Archbishop of Dublin 1820. Archbishop of Armagh and primate of all Ireland 1822. Vice-chancellor of Dublin University 1829 and chancellor 1851. He made generous gifts to the library of the university, endowed a chair of ecclesiastical history and erected a campanile in the great quadrangle at a cost of £3,000. When St Columba's College was opened in Rathfarnham, Dublin, in 1844 'to furnish the gentry of Ireland with a school on the model of Eton', he made it a gift of £6,000. He also restored the cathedral of Armagh at a cost of £30,000. In politics he was a conservative and opposed the Catholic Relief Bill of 1829. He died at Woburn near Donaghadee, Co. Down, 18 July 1862. Buried in Armagh cathedral.

BERGIN, OSBORN JOSEPH (1873–1950), scholar. Born Cork, 26 November 1873. Educated Cork Grammar School and Queen's College, Cork, where he studied classics. He became interested in Irish, joined the Gaelic League soon after it was founded, and made many visits to the west Munster Gaeltacht. After teaching in his old school he was appointed lecturer in Celtic at Queen's College, Cork, in 1897. When the School of Irish Learning was founded in 1903 by KUNO MEYER, R. I. BEST and others, Bergin contributed to the first volume (1904) of their journal, *Ériu*, an event that marked the beginning of the scientific study of Modern Irish as a branch of general linguistics. Aided by a scholarship, due to the generosity of ALICE STOPFORD GREEN, he studied Early Irish in Berlin under Zimmer, and in Freiburg under Thurneysen, taking his doctorate at Freiburg in 1906. After the death of Strachan in 1907 he became professor in the School of Irish Learning. First professor of Early and Mediaeval Irish in UCD 1909–1940. First director of the School of Celtic Studies, DIAS, 1940. Resigned within a year without giving any reason: it was generally believed that his decision was due to disagreement with the Government over control of the school. Then devoted himself to research in Celtic philology. He contributed many learned articles to *Ériu* and *Studies*. His paper on 'Bardic Poetry' (*Journal of the Ivernian Society*, 1913) opened up new aspects of Irish literary history. His *Stories from Keating* (1909) became a standard textbook, and he edited Céitinn's *Three Shafts of Death* (1931), other mediaeval texts, and many previously unpublished poems. He was general editor of the RIA's *Dictionary of the Irish Language*, and he had an immense and accurate knowledge of Irish at its various stages of growth and neglect. As a student he often cycled eighty miles a day in the Munster Gaeltacht, 'baling out old women', as he described his collecting of words and phrases. The delightful lyric 'Maidean i mBéarra', composed for singing to the Derry Air and first published in 1901, conveys his affection for that wild and beautiful countryside and its people. Died in Dublin, 6 October 1950.

BERKELEY, GEORGE (1685–1753), metaphysical philosopher. Born at Dysart Castle, Co. Kilkenny, 12 March 1685. Educated TCD where he remained until 1713 as fellow and tutor. In 1709 he published his *Essay towards a New Theory of Vision*, a psychological analysis of visual perception, and developed his thought further in *A Treatise Concerning the Principles of Human Knowledge* (1710) and *Dialogues Between Hylas and Philonous* (1713). Between 1714 and 1721 he travelled widely in France and Italy. On return he wrote his *Essay Towards Preventing the Ruin of Great*

Britain, asserting that the depression following the South Sea Bubble was due to the decay of religion and public spirit. In 1724 he was appointed to the valuable deanery of Derry. He then advanced the project of a college in the Bermudas, to reform the English colonists and civilise the natives. He spent three years in London endeavouring to interest Walpole and finally was voted a government grant of £20,000. He sailed for the West Indies in 1728 and stayed for three years in Rhode Island among some American missionaries. His grant was withdrawn, and he returned in 1731 without ever reaching the Bermudas. However, he left his mark on American philosophy and gave an impetus to American university education. His *Alciphron,* written in Rhode Island, defends religion against freethinkers. In 1734 Berkeley was appointed Bishop of Cloyne but still devoted himself to philosophical speculation, to which he now added an interest in social reform. That year he published *The Analyst,* a critical examination of Newtonian mathematics, and in 1735 the first of three volumes of the *Querist,* containing in all some five hundred questions on the social and economic problems of Ireland 'with hints on legislation and political economy'. Further pamphlets on Ireland followed with appeals for religious toleration. The last of his philosophical works was *Siris* (1744), in which reflections on empirical medicine and the virtues of tar water lead to religious thought and an exposition of idealism. In 1752 failing health led to his resignation; he moved to Oxford, where he died in January 1753. He is buried in Christ Church Cathedral. Berkeley's first books, the *Essay* and the *Treatise,* contain some of the most penetrating and lucid analysis in the English language. Both Hume and Kant were moved by his ideas, although neither comprehended them properly. Berkeley showed the whole world from a new point of view, asserting that it is mind not matter that creates, and that even in the world of the senses we are living and moving and having our being in the Supreme Reason theologically known as God. The debate on his ideas has not yet ended, and his works have had a critical influence on European thought.

BERNAL, JOHN DESMOND (1901–1971), scientist. Born in Nenagh, Co. Tipperary, son of a farmer. Educated at Stonyhurst, Bedford College, and Emmanuel College, Cambridge. After graduation worked in Davy-Faraday laboratory at the Royal Institution, London. Returned to Cambridge in 1927 as lecturer in structural crystallography, and became a fellow of the Royal Society in 1937. During Second World War he worked with Solly Zuckerman investigating the effect of bombing on the British population. In 1942 he was assigned to Lord Mountbatten and studied the design of landing-craft and floating harbours for the invasion of Europe. Mountbatten acknowledged his work as a crucial element in the success of the invasion. In 1948 he became professor of physics at Birkbeck College, University of London. His work on the structure of proteins ranked among his greatest scientific achievements. Bernal joined the Communist Party of Great Britain in 1922 and remained deeply interested in the relation between science and politics. He published a number of books, including *The World, the Flesh and the Devil* (1929) and his most influential, *The Social Function of Science* (1939). He helped to establish UNESCO and the World Federation of Scientific Workers, and attempted to reduce the widening rift between eastern and western scientists. Awarded Lenin Peace Prize in 1953. Died on 15 September 1971 after a long illness.

BEST, RICHARD IRVINE (1872–1959), Celtic scholar. Born in the north of Ireland. Studied Old Irish in Paris where he met SYNGE and KUNO MEYER. Assistant director of the National Library 1904 and director 1924. Senior professor of Celtic studies, DIAS, 1940.

He was also chairman of the Irish Manuscripts Commission and an honorary fellow of the Bibliographical Society of Ireland. President RIA 1943–1946. Best's major work was the two-volume *Bibliography of Irish Philology and Manuscript Literature, Publications 1913–1941* (1942). His other publications include *The Irish Mythological Cycle and Celtic Mythology* (1903), *Bibliography of the Publications of Kuno Meyer* (1923), *The Martyrology of Tallaght* (1931), and *The Book of Leinster, formerly Lebar na Nuachongbála* (1954). Awarded the Leibniz Medal of the Royal Prussian Academy, one of the highest distinctions in international scholarship, 1914. Both NUI and TCD conferred honorary doctorates on him. He retired in 1947 and died at his house, 57 Upper Leeson St, Dublin, 25 September 1959.

BEWLEY, CHARLES (1890–1969), lawyer and diplomat. Born in Dublin to a well-known Quaker family. Educated at Winchester and New College, Oxford. Won the Newdigate Prize for English Verse 1910, the first Irishman to do so since OSCAR WILDE. Attracted to the Anglo-Catholic movement, became a Roman Catholic and regular contributor to the religious press in Britain and USA. Called to the Irish bar 1914 and practised successfully on the Western circuit. Appointed Minister at Berlin by the new Free State government 1922. Resumed practice at the Irish bar 1923, taking silk in 1926 and appearing for the state in many prosecutions. First Minister to the Holy See 1929. Grand Cross of St Gregory the Great 1933. Minister at Berlin from 1933 until his retirement in 1939. He then settled in Italy and died in Rome, 1 February 1969.

BIANCONI, CHARLES (1786–1875), promoter of the Irish road-car service. Born Lombardy, 24 September 1786. Came to Ireland at fifteen as apprentice to a fellow-Italian, a print-seller. He soon set up on his own account, accumulated a little capital, and started his first car service between Clonmel and Cahir, Co. Tipperary, in 1815, when the end of the Napoleonic wars and the carriage-tax had flooded the market with cheap horses and cars. The business prospered and Bianconi's cars were soon a familiar sight throughout the south and west of Ireland. In 1864 receipts from passengers and freight totalled £40,000 and the service covered nearly 4,000 miles (6,400 km) of road. A fervent Catholic, he was a strong supporter of O'CONNELL. He became a naturalised Irish citizen in 1831. Wisely he refused to oppose the establishment of the railways, taking shares in some of them. Retiring in 1865, he sold his business on liberal terms to his agents and employees, and passed the rest of his long life at his estate at Longfield, near Cashel, Co. Tipperary, where he died in September 1875.

BICKERSTAFF, ISAAC (*c.* 1735–*c.* 1812), dramatist. Born Dublin about 1735. Appointed page to Lord Chesterfield, then Lord Lieutenant, at eleven. Chesterfield obtained a commission for him in the marines. In London he became a prolific and successful dramatist and had more than twenty plays produced by Garrick. *Love in a Village* and *The Maid of the Mill* held the stage for many years. In 1772 he was accused of murder and fled to the Continent where he lived for many years in miserable exile, dying in poverty.

BIGGAR, JOSEPH GILLIS (1828–1890), nationalist. Born Belfast. Educated Belfast Academy. Joined his father's business of provision merchant and became head of the firm 1861. Home Rule MP for Co. Cavan, 1874 until his death. In the House of Commons he initiated the policy of obstruction, which was then taken up and pursued with success by PARNELL and the Irish Party. Joined IRB in 1875 but was expelled in 1877 for his refusal to abandon parliamentary activity. Of Presbyterian stock, Biggar joined the Catholic Church in 1877. He died in

London, 19 February 1890. Buried in Belfast.

BIGGER, FRANCIS JOSEPH (1863–1926), author and antiquary. Born in Belfast and educated at RBAI. Admitted solicitor 1888. Became involved in the literary revival and supported the Irish language movement. Edited *Ulster Journal of Archaeology* 1894–1914. Contributed to many periodicals at home and in England and America. Published historical, antiquarian and biographical works, best-known being *The Ulster Land War of 1770* (1910). MRIA and MA (QUB). At his own expense he restored ruined castles and churches, and re-erected ancient crosses and gravestones. His house 'Ardrigh' on the Antrim Road, now demolished, was a meeting-place for northerners of nationalist outlook. Died in Belfast, 9 December 1926. Left bulk of his extensive collection of books and manuscripts to Belfast Central Library.

BINDON, FRANCIS (died 1765), portrait painter and architect. Little is known of his life save that he was son of David Bindon, MP for Ennis, Co. Clare. He studied painting and architecture on the Continent, and on his return to Ireland devoted himself to portrait painting and the designing of large country houses. In demand as a portrait painter, and many noted contemporaries, including SWIFT, sat for him. Mansions erected to his design included Bessborough House and Woodstock House, Co. Kilkenny. He collaborated with Richard Cassels in designing Russborough House, Co. Wicklow. Succeeded to the family property in Co. Clare 1761. Died suddenly, 2 June 1765.

BING, GEOFFREY HENRY CECIL (1909–1977), lawyer and politician. Born Co. Down, 24 July 1909. Educated Tonbridge School, Lincoln College, Oxford, and Princeton University. Called to the bar, Inner Temple, 1934, Gibraltar 1937, Gold Coast (now Ghana) 1950, and Nigeria 1954. Served as signals officer in Second World War. Labour MP, Hornchurch, Essex, 1945–1955. Attorney-General in Ghana under President Nkrumah 1957–1961, returning to England after fall of Nkrumah. In the Commons he led a group of radicals and raised many questions about civil liberties in Northern Ireland. His *Tribune* pamphlet *John Bull's Other Island* (1950) indicted the Stormont administration and became a best-seller. Also published *Reap the Whirlwind* (1967), an account of Nkrumah's Ghana. CMG 1960. Consultant to Irish University Press from 1970. Died in London, 24 April 1977.

BIRMINGHAM, GEORGE A. See under HANNAY, JAMES OWEN.

BLACKBURN, HELEN (1842–1903), pioneer of women's suffrage. Born Valentia Island, Co. Kerry, 25 May 1842, daughter of a civil engineer who was manager of the Knight of Kerry's slate quarries on the island. The family moved to London in 1859, and Helen became interested in the movement for women's suffrage. Secretary National Society for Women's Suffrage 1874–1895. Editor, *Englishwoman's Review*, 1881–1890. In 1895 she gave up most of her public work to look after her father, who died in 1897 at eighty-five following a riding accident. Published *Women's Suffrage: a Record of the Movement in the British Isles* (1902), still a standard work. She also wrote several books on the position of women in industry. Died in London, 11 January 1903. Buried in Brompton cemetery.

BLACKBURNE, E. OWENS. See under CASEY, ELIZABETH.

BLACKLEY, WILLIAM LEWERY (1830–1902), cleric and social reformer. Born Dundalk, 30 December 1830. Educated Dr Friedlander's school, Brussels, and TCD. Took holy orders in 1854, and served in London, Surrey, and Hampshire. Vicar of St James the Less, Vauxhall Bridge Road, London, 1889.

Keenly interested in social questions. Published an essay advocating compulsory national insurance to prevent pauperism 1878. His scheme provided for payment in times of sickness and for old-age pensions at seventy. The National Providence League, with the Earl of Shaftesbury as president, was formed to advance this aim, and Blackley published a number of books expounding his schemes for insurance, thrift, and temperance. However, a select committee of the House of Commons reported adversely on 2 August 1887, on administrative and actuarial grounds, and he did not live to see his ideas accepted. Died at 79 St George's Square, London, 25 July 1902. (Old-age pensions were introduced in 1908 and national insurance in 1911.)

BLACKWELL, JAMES BARTHOLOMEW (1763-1820), colonel in the French army. Born in Ennis, Co. Clare. At the age of eleven he was sent to Paris to be educated at the Irish College. He studied medicine at the University of Paris until he was twenty, then became lieutenant in a hussar regiment. Became friendly with revolutionaries Danton and Desmoulins and was chosen by the Faubourg St Antoine to lead the attack on the Bastille on 14 July 1789. Took part in early campaigns with the revolutionary armies. He saved the lives of Colonel Wade of Worcester and his daughter Sophie who were travelling in France when war broke out with England, and afterwards married Sophie. Sailed with WOLFE TONE to Bantry Bay in 1796 and with NAPPER TANDY to Donegal in 1798. Although entitled to be treated as a prisoner of war, he was imprisoned for two years in Kilmainham Jail. On returning to France he was appointed *chef de bataillon* of the Irish Legion and fought under Napoleon in the Prussian and Austrian campaigns. Retired as colonel on half-pay and made commandant of the town of Bitche in Lorraine. Ill-health due to many wounds forced him to return to Paris and he died there in 1820 and was buried in the cemetery of Père La Chaise.

BLACKWOOD, FREDERICK, first MARQUIS OF DUFFERIN AND AVA (1826-1902). Born Florence, 21 June 1826. Educated Eton and Christ Church, Oxford. Spent ten years after graduation managing his Irish estates at Clandeboye, Co. Down. Favourite recreation was yachting. Published *Letters from High Latitudes* (1856), an account of his voyage to Iceland and Spitzbergen. Toured Middle East several times. After ministerial appointments became Governor-General of Canada 1872-1878, ambassador to Russia 1879-1880, to Turkey 1881-1882, to Egypt 1882-1884, and Governor-General of India 1884-1888. Ambassador to Italy 1889-1891, to France 1891-1896. Showered with public honours. Became chairman of London and Globe Finance Corporation on retirement 1897. It turned out to be a speculative mining venture in which he and many others lost heavily. This and the death of his eldest son in the Boer War clouded his last years. Died Clandeboye, 12 February 1902.

BLAKE, NICHOLAS. See under DAY-LEWIS, CECIL.

BLESSINGTON, MARGUERITE, COUNTESS OF (1789—1849), novelist, beauty, and gossip writer. Born Knockbrit, near Clonmel, Co. Tipperary, 1 September 1789, daughter of Edward Power, an unsuccessful merchant. Her father forced her at fifteen to marry a Captain St Leger Farmer, a man of ungovernable temper, from whom she fled after three months. He died in a drunken brawl in 1817, and a few months later she married Charles Gardiner, Earl of Blessington. Beautiful, hospitable, and witty, 'the most gorgeous Lady Blessington' drew a brilliant circle to her salon in St James's Square, and began to write sketches of London life. In 1822 the Blessingtons went on a Continental tour, accompanied by the young Count d'Orsay, who in 1827 married the earl's daughter by his first wife. They spent two months in Genoa in close friendship with Byron. On the death of the earl in Paris in 1829 Lady Blessington had to depend on a jointure of £2,000 a year and, returning to London accompanied by d'Orsay, whose marriage had broken up, she took to writing to maintain her position in society. Her first novel, *Grace Cassidy; or The Repealers* (1833) proved successful; she followed with books based on her experiences abroad. *Conversations with Lord Byron* appeared in 1834, *The Idler in Italy* in 1839–1840, and *The Idler in France* in 1841; all were welcomed for their easy, gossipy style and humour. She wrote several other novels, and edited two annuals, *The Book of Beauty* and *The Keepsake,* as well as contributing to magazines and newspapers. Her large earnings were not enough to maintain her lavish style of living and dazzling salon, and financial difficulties came to a head in 1849. To avoid ruin she fled to Paris with d'Orsay, and died there suddenly three months later on 4 June.

BLOOD, COLONEL THOMAS (1618–1680), adventurer. Little is known of his early life. Took Parliamentary side in the Civil War and received lands in Ireland, which were taken from him at the restoration. With other Cromwellians he attempted in 1663 to seize Dublin Castle and the Lord Lieutenant, Ormond. Betrayed, and fled to Holland. Fought with the Covenanters in Scotland at Pentland Hills 1666. Made another unsuccessful attempt on life of Ormond in London 1670. In May 1671 he stole the Crown jewels from the Tower of London and was caught red-handed. Insisted on being heard by the king, Charles II, who pardoned him and restored his Irish estates. Died at his house, Bowling Alley, Westminster, 24 August 1680.

BLYTHE, ERNEST (1889–1975), politician and theatre manager. Born Magheragall, near Lisburn, Co. Antrim,

son of a farmer, and educated locally. Began his working life at fifteen as a boy clerk in the Department of Agriculture in Dublin. Joined the Gaelic League and attended Irish classes where his teacher was Sinéad Flanagan, later BEAN DE VALERA. On invitation from SEÁN O'CASEY joined IRB. In March 1909 he became a junior reporter on the *North Down Herald* in Bangor and then in Newtownards. Went to the Kerry Gaeltacht about 1913 to improve his Irish and, to earn his keep, worked as a farm labourer. His activities as organiser for the Irish Volunteers led to years of arrests and imprisonments, and several hunger strikes. He was in prison during the 1916 Rising. Elected TD for North Monaghan 1918, and Minister for Trade and Commerce until 1922. He accepted the Anglo-Irish Treaty of 1921 and in 1923 became Minister for Finance under WILLIAM T. COSGRAVE, the first northern Protestant to become a government minister in the south. Also Minister for Posts and Telegraphs 1922–1932, and vice-president of the Executive Council. As Minister for Finance he reduced old-age pensions from 10 shillings (50p) to 9 shillings (45p) which aroused widespread indignation. Defeated in general election 1933. Senator until 1936, when he retired from politics. His devotion to the Irish language revival never faltered. He encouraged MAC LIAMMÓIR and EDWARDS to found an Irish-language theatre—the Taibhdhearc—in Galway, and founded An Gúm to publish books in Irish for the government. As Minister for Finance he gave the first direct grant, £1,000, to the Abbey Theatre. Managing director Abbey Theatre 1941–1967, retiring at seventy-seven. His policies drew sustained criticism: it was said that he engaged players for their knowledge of Irish rather than their acting ability, that he rejected good plays and put on bad, and favoured kitchen comedies in order to swell box-office receipts. On partition he held that spiritual reconciliation must come before there could be any realistic hope of political or institutional change in north-south relations. In 1957 he published *Trasna na Bóinne,* an account of his life until 1913. Died in Dublin, 23 February 1975.

BODKIN, THOMAS PATRICK (1887–1961), lawyer and professor. Born Dublin, 21 July 1887. Educated Belvedere College and Clongowes Wood College. He went to Paris for a year in 1905 and graduated RUI 1908. Called to the Irish bar 1911, and practised law until 1916, when he became secretary to the Commissioners for Charitable Donations and Bequests. Director of the National Gallery 1927–1935, then Barber Professor of Fine Arts and first director of the Barber Institute of Birmingham. When he retired in 1952, aged sixty-five, the trustees retained him as adviser on purchases for the collection on his full salary. His report on the arts in Ireland (1951), commissioned by the Government, led to the establishment of the Arts Council, An Chomhairle Ealaíon. Bodkin was invited to become the first director of the council, but declined. He had a life-long and consuming interest in the arts, especially painting. Took a leading part in the movement to secure for Dublin the collection made by SIR HUGH LANE, and in 1932 the Pegasus Press published, for the government, his *Hugh Lane and his Pictures.* He was a member of a government commission on coinage (1926) and of committees on the organisation of the National Museum (1927) and on art education (1927). Both NUI and TCD gave him honorary doctorates. Honorary RHA 1947. Papal Knight of St Gregory 1952. *Chevalier* of the Legion of Honour 1933, *officier* 1952. Many learned bodies invited him to lecture, and in his later years he became well known on radio and television programmes. Died in Birmingham, 24 April 1961.

BOLAND, FREDERICK HENRY (1904–1985), diplomat. Born in Dublin and educated at Merchant Taylors' School, London, Catholic University School, Clongowes Wood College, TCD, and King's Inns, where he was Victoria Prizeman and Brooke Scholar. Won a Rockefeller Research Fellowship in social science and studied from 1926 to 1928 at Harvard and the universities of Chicago and North Carolina. He joined the Department of External Affairs and rose to be secretary in 1945. Appointed ambassador to Britain in 1950. Ireland's first permanent representative at the UN in 1956, elected President of the General Assembly in September 1960. Retired from the diplomatic service in 1963 and elected Chancellor of Dublin University. Director of several leading companies. MRIA. Died in a Dublin hospital on 4 December 1985. Survived by his wife, Frances Kelly, artist, a son and four daughters, one being the poet Eavan Boland.

BOLAND, GERALD (1885–1973), politician. Born 25 May 1885 in Manchester of Irish parents who moved to Dublin almost immediately. The father was fatally injured in a fight between Parnellites and Healyites for possession of the offices of the *United Irishman.* The GAA launched a 'Boland Fund', and Mrs Boland opened a small shop in Wexford St. Gerald was educated at the O'Brien Institute, Fairview, and became a fitter on the Midland and Great Western Railway. He joined the Irish Volunteers, fought in Jacob's factory in the 1916 Rising, was arrested and interned. Some Russian crown jewels were held in safe keeping by the Boland family from 1920 to 1932, when they were handed over to the new Fianna Fáil government. They had been given to an IRA delegation seeking recognition of the Irish Republic, as security for a loan of £20,000, by one of the Russian envoys. He was TD for Roscommon 1923–1961. He helped to found Fianna Fáil in 1926. Minister for Posts and Telegraphs 1933; Minister for Lands 1936. In 1939 he became Minister for Justice, and to counter the threat posed by the IRA during the Second World War introduced strong measures including internment, military courts and special criminal courts. Three prisoners died on hunger strike, nine were executed after trial by the new courts, five men were shot in gun battles, and one was shot dead during a riot at the Curragh internment camp. Boland did not seek office after the general election of 1957, lost his Dáil seat in 1961 but remained in politics as a senator until 1969. When his son Kevin resigned as secretary of Fianna Fáil in 1970, because of disagreement with the party policy towards the Northern question, Gerald Boland resigned his posts as vice-president and trustee. Died Dublin, 5 January 1973.

BOLAND, JOHN PIUS (1870–1955), MP and Ireland's first Olympic gold medallist. Born in September 1870 at 135 Capel St, Dublin, son of a prosperous merchant, and educated at Catholic University School, the Oratory School, Birmingham, Bonn University, and Oxford University. Called to the bar in 1897 at Inner Temple, London. Nationalist MP for South Kerry 1900–1918 and whip to the party. A young Greek friend at Oxford invited him to the first modern Olympic Games in Athens in 1896. Impressed by his playing in friendly games of tennis, his friend, who was a member of the Olympic Committee, urged him to enter. He won the singles gold medal on 30 March 1896 and the doubles in partnership with an Austrian friend, also an Oxford man. After marriage he made his home in London. Died 17 March 1955.

BOND, OLIVER (1760–1798), United Irishman. Born in Ulster and settled in Dublin where he became a prosperous wool merchant. He joined the Society of United Irishmen on its foundation in 1791 and was active in promoting the resolutions in favour of Catholic emancipation and the reform of parliament. The House of Lords in Dublin deemed these to be libels and he was imprisoned for six months in 1793. When these objects could not be achieved by peaceful means, Bond and his associates formed an organisation to establish an Irish republic independent of England. He became a member of the Leinster directory, which met frequently at his house. In March 1798 he was arrested there with others and in July 1798 he was convicted of high treason and sentenced to be hanged. He died suddenly in prison in September. Buried in St Michan's Church, Dublin.

BOUCICAULT, DION LARDNER (c. 1820–1890), actor and dramatist. Born Dublin, 26 December 1820 or 20 December 1822, probably the natural son of Dr Dionysius Lardner, a boarder in his mother's house. Starting in the theatre in England as an actor, he then began to write plays and had a great success with a comedy, *London Assurance* (1841). He had the 'trick of the theatre', and is credited with about 150 plays, including translations and adaptations of novels. His three Irish plays, *The Colleen Bawn* (1860)—based on Gerald Griffin's novel *The Collegians*—*Arrah na Pogue* (1864), and *The Shaughraun* (1874), owed much of their popularity to his wife's portrayal of the heroines. Boucicault went to New York in 1853 and in 1859 created a sensation with *The Octoroon*, the first play to treat seriously of the American negro population. He returned to New York in 1872 where, in his later years, his fortunes declined, and he ended as a poorly paid teacher of acting. Died there, 18 September 1890.

BOURCHIER, JAMES DAVID (1850–1920), correspondent of *The Times* in the Balkan peninsula. Born Baggotstown, Bruff, Co. Limerick, 18 December 1850. Educated TCD and King's College, Cambridge, distinguishing himself in classics. After teaching at Eton for ten years he joined *The Times* and went to Athens in 1888 as their correspondent on Balkan affairs. Though deaf, he was a linguist and musician. He acted as intermediary between Cretan insurgents and the Greek government, and took a leading part in the secret negotiations that resulted in the Balkan alliance. He retired from *The Times* in 1918 and spent his final years working for a just and lasting settlement of the Balkan question, which proved unattainable. Died, in Sofia, 30 December 1920. Buried at Rilo monastery with every mark of honour.

BOURKE, PATRICK J. (1882–1932), actor and playwright. Born in Dublin. Long associated with the Queen's Theatre, Dublin, where his first play, *The Wexford Rose,* was performed in 1910. Other plays include *For the Land She Loved, The Northern Insurgent, In Dark and Evil Days.* He set various plays to music, including *Kathleen Mavourneen,* in which he acted.

BOURKE, RICHARD SOUTHWELL, sixth EARL OF MAYO (1822–1872), viceroy of India. Born Dublin, 21 February 1822. Educated at home and TCD. In 1845 he toured Russia and published an account of his experiences. He took an active part in relief work in the famine of 1846–1847. Chief Secretary for Ireland 1852, and again in 1858 and 1866. Suceeded to the earldom in 1867 on the death of his father. From 1847 to 1868 represented in succession Co. Kildare, Coleraine borough, and the English borough of Cockermouth. In Parliament he favoured a policy of conciliation towards Catholics. In 1868 he was appointed Viceroy and Governor-General of India. He cultivated the friendship of the neighbouring states, principally Afghanistan, Nepal, and Burma, so as to create in them networks of the British Empire. With those inside India he aimed at securing good government by their princes, with the minimum of interference. He reformed the public finances by a policy of decentralisation and by economies on defence and public works. He was assassinated on 8 February 1872 while inspecting a penal settlement at Port Blair in the Andaman Islands.

BOURKE, ULICK J. (1829–1887), priest and teacher. Born Castlebar, Co. Mayo, December 1829. Educated St Jarlath's, Tuam, and Maynooth College. While still a clerical student he wrote a *College Irish Grammar* (1856), chiefly for the use of his fellow students. Ordained 1858; professor of Irish, logic and humanities at St Jarlath's 1858–1878, and president 1865–1878. Parish priest of Kilcolman (Claremorris) 1878. He aimed to restore the use of Irish living speech as a literary medium and to preserve its purity by making a scientific study of its grammar. Through the *Nation* he issued a series of *Easy Lessons or Self-Instruction in Irish.* Other writings include *The Aryan Origins of the Gaelic Race and Language* (1875), and *Pre-Christian Ireland* (1887). First chairman of the Society for the Preservation of the Irish Language, founded in 1876; he left the society in 1880 to found the Gaelic Union with David Comyn and launched the *Gaelic Journal.* Died at Claremorris, November 1887.

BOWEN, ELIZABETH DOROTHEA COLE (1899–1973), novelist. Born Dublin, 7 June 1899, only child of Henry Cole Bowen of Bowen's Court, Kildorrery, Co. Cork. Educated at Downe House School, Downe, Kent. In 1918 she went to live in London, where her friends included Rose Macaulay, Virginia Woolf, and Edward Sackville-West. In 1923 she married Alan Charles Cameron, a Highland Scot who worked in the BBC schools broadcasting service, and they settled near Oxford. Her first book was a collection of short stories, *Encounters* (1923). Her first novel, *The Hotel,* appeared in 1927, and was followed by *The Last September* (1929), which describes life in a great house in Co. Cork during the 'Troubles'. *Bowen's Court* (1942) is a history of her family and their house, and *Seven Winters* (1942) includes reminiscences of her Dublin childhood. After she had inherited the family seat she spent a part of each year there, and also travelled a good deal in France and Italy and visited the United States. In all, she published about a dozen novels, as well as short stories and essays.

The Heat of the Day (1949), which she considered her best novel, was a Book Club choice in the United States, and became a best-seller. *Eva Trout* (1969), a novel of ironic fantasy, was awarded a prize by the Irish Academy of Letters in 1970. Her story 'A Summer's Night', set in Co. Cork, is said to be excelled only by Joyce's 'The Dead'. Her honours included CBE 1948, D.Litt. (Dublin University) 1949, and Lucy Martin Donnelly Fellow for 1956 at Bryn Mawr women's college. The scrupulous care of her writing and her consciousness as an artist have led to her being compared with Jane Austen, Henry James, and Virginia Woolf. After the Second World War she sold Bowen's Court and settled at Hythe, in Kent. Died in London, 22 February 1973.

BOWEN, GRETTA (1880–1981), artist. Born in Dublin on New Year's Day 1880. She married in her early twenties and moved to Belfast with her husband, Matthew Campbell, who died when she was forty-five. With little money and three sons to rear she took students as boarders in her house in the university district. Two of her sons, George and Arthur, became painters. Her own talent was discovered in her seventies when she used up some paint they had left lying around. She agreed to show publicly only under her maiden name, not wishing to be known as the mother of GEORGE CAMPBELL, then an established painter. She exhibited three times in Belfast under the Arts Council of Northern Ireland and her work attracted patronage in England, the USA, France and Morocco. In 1979, in her hundredth year, she was invited to contribute to the first international exhibition of naïve art, held in London. Her paintings of scenes recollected from early childhood inevitably brought comparison with her near-contemporary, the American primitive 'Grandma' Moses. She died on 8 April 1981 in her hundred-and-second year.

BOYLAN, DOM EUGENE (1904–1964), physicist, monk, and writer. Born in Bray, Co. Wicklow, and educated Derry CBS, O'Connell Schools, Dublin, and UCD. Studied atomic physics at Vienna University 1926–1928, and awarded a Rockefeller Scholarship 1928. A keen sportsman, he represented Ireland at the first Tailteann Games. Entered the Cistercian Order at Roscrea in 1933; professed 1938. Taught philosophy and moral and dogmatic theology to the community and students, and French and German in Roscrea College. He spoke at least a further five languages. He became known as a confessor and wrote several books on spiritual life, among them *This Tremendous Lover* (1946), which had a world-wide sale. Others were *Difficulties in Mental Prayer* (1943), *The Spiritual Life of the Priest* (1949), and *The Priest's Way to God* (1962). First Cistercian to set foot in Australia when he was sent in 1954 to found a house at Tarrawarra, outside Melbourne. For four years in the middle 1950s he was temporary superior at the Dominicans' Caldey Island priory; he put the community on a sound economic footing by developing the production of perfume. Returned to Ireland 1958; abbot of Mount Saint Joseph 1962. Died in January 1964.

BOYLE, HENRY, EARL OF SHANNON (1682–1764), Speaker, Irish House of Commons. Born at Castlemartyr, Co. Cork. MP for Midleton 1707–1713, for Kilmallock 1713–1715, Cork 1715–1753. In 1729 he successfully resisted the government's attempt to obtain a vote for a continuation of supplies to the crown for twenty-one years. He became a member of the Privy Council, Chancellor of the Exchequer and Commissioner of Revenue in Ireland. Speaker of Irish House of Commons 1733–1753. Gained great popularity for opposing government proposal to appropriate a surplus in the Irish exchequer and was dismissed from Crown office in 1756. He resigned the speakership and was given a pension of £2,000 for thirty-one years, with the titles Baron of Castlemartyr, Viscount

Boyle of Bandon, and Earl of Shannon. Sat for many years in House of Peers in Ireland and acted frequently as Lord Chief Justice. Died 'of gout in the head' in Dublin, 27 September 1764.

BOYLE, PATRICK (1905–1982), author. Born in Ballymoney, Co. Antrim, and educated at Coleraine Academical Institution. Joined the Ulster Bank and served for forty-five years, twenty of them in Donegal. Turned to writing late in life and achieved instant success with novel *Like Any Other Man* (1966), a satire on provincial social life, the principal character a hard-drinking bank manager. The bank retired him on pension in 1968, two years short of full service. Published collections of short stories, *At Night All Cats are Grey* (1966), *All Looks Yellow to the Jaundiced Eye* (1969), and *A View from Calvary* (1976), which show a wider range of sympathies than his novel. Died in Portmarnock, Co. Dublin, on 7 February 1982.

BOYLE, RICHARD VICARS (1822–1908), civil engineer. Born Dublin, 14 March 1922. Educated at private school. Articled to CHARLES BLACKER VIGNOLES. Employed as an engineer by WILLIAM DARGAN on the Belfast and Armagh, and Dublin and Drogheda, railways. District engineer on the East Indian railways 1853. For his services during the 'Indian Mutiny', when he defended his house with fifty men against 3,000 rebels, he received the Mutiny Medal and a grant of land near Arrah. Engineer-in-chief to the imperial Japanese railways 1872–1877, and laid out an extensive system. Died at 3 Stanhope Terrace, Hyde Park, London, 3 January 1908.

BOYLE, ROBERT (1627–1691), natural philosopher. Born 25 January 1627 at Lismore Castle, Co. Waterford, son of the 'great' Earl of Cork, and sent to Eton at eight. After four years he went abroad with a French tutor and became fluent in French and Italian. Studied 'the new paradoxes of the great star-gazer Galileo' in Florence, and in 1644 returned to live on an estate in Dorset inherited from his father. Moved to London 1668. He soon took a leading part in the 'invisible college' of contemporary philosophers, later to become the Royal Society. His first experiments on the properties of air were published in 1660, and in answer to criticism he enunciated the famous Boyle's Law, that the volume of gas varies inversely as the pressure. In physics, his work included the discovery of the part played by air in the transmission of sound, and investigations into specific gravities, refractive powers, crystals, electricity, and colour. His favourite study was chemistry; he propounded theories on the composition of matter and examined the chemistry of combustion and respiration. This scientific work was expounded in a steady flow of treatises between 1660 and 1691. Deeply religious, he learned Hebrew, Greek, and Syriac, the better to pursue his theological studies, and spent large sums to propagate the study of the Bible, including printing Bedell's Bible in Irish. He refused many honours, including a peerage and the provostship of Eton. Died in London, 31 December 1691.

BOYLE, WILLIAM (1853–1922), civil servant and writer. Born Dromiskin, Co. Louth. Educated St Mary's College, Dundalk. Entered the civil service 1874. His descriptions of Irish country life were published as *A Kish of Brogues*. Among the first to write for the Abbey Theatre, his plays include *The Building Fund* (1905), *The Eloquent Dempsey* (1906), *The Tale of a Town* (1906), and *The Mineral Workers* (1906). Died in London.

BRACKEN, BRENDAN RENDALL, VISCOUNT BRACKEN (1901–1958), publisher and politician. Born Templemore, Co. Tipperary, 15 February 1901. Educated at Jesuit College, Mungret, Co. Limerick. His father, John K. Bracken, a building contractor, was one of the founder-members of the GAA in 1884. Ran away from school at fifteen, and his widowed mother sent him to Australia to work on a sheep station. Returned to Ireland in 1919, found that his mother had remarried, collected a small legacy and left for England. Met J. L. Garvin, famous editor of the *Manchester Guardian,* who recommended him to Winston Churchill as an election worker. Joining the publishers Eyre and Spottiswode in 1924, his energy, judgment and self-assurance soon gained for him a directorship in the firm. He bought the *Financial News,* founded the *Banker,* and acquired control of the *Investors' Chronicle* and the *Practitioner.* All these enterprises flourished. MP for North Paddington 1929 with help from Churchill. On the outbreak of Second World War, Bracken became Parliamentary Private Secretary to Churchill, and one of his closest associates. Minister of Information in 1941, his informal approach delighted Fleet Street. After the war he devoted himself to his business interests, becoming chairman of the amalgamated *Financial News* and *Financial Times.* He declined office when Churchill was returned to power in 1951 but accepted a viscountcy in 1952. He died, in London, 8 August 1958.

BRADY, NICHOLAS (1659–1726), poet. Born Bandon, Co. Cork, 28 October 1659. Educated Westminster School, Oxford, and TCD. Took holy orders, served in Cork diocese and upheld Williamite cause. Received valuable preferment in England. Rector Stratford-on-Avon 1702–1705. With NAHUM TATE published metrical version of the Psalms (1696), his best-known work. Also wrote a tragedy, *The Rape,* and translated *Aeneid.* Died Richmond, 20 May 1726.

BRANDT, MURIEL (1909–1981), painter. Born in Belfast. She won a scholarship to the Royal College of Art, London, then settled in Dublin on marriage to Frank Brandt, artistic adviser to ESB. Her first important commission was a set of panels in Adam and Eve's church, Merchants' Quay, Dublin. She painted portraits of SIR ALFRED CHESTER BEATTY, GEORGE O'BRIEN, and other notables. Her picture of MÍCHEÁL MAC LIAMMÓIR, CHRISTINE LONGFORD and HILTON EDWARDS, directors of the Gate Theatre, sitting round a table, hangs in the foyer of the theatre. Member of the board of governors of the National Gallery and RHA. Died in Our Lady's Hospice, Dublin, on 10 June 1981, survived by son and two daughters, one, Ruth, also an artist.

BRANSFIELD, EDWARD (*c.* 1783–1852), sailor and explorer. Born in Cork about 1783 and became a merchant seaman. In 1803 he was pressed into the British navy, and took part in the blockade of French Atlantic ports during the Napoleonic wars. By 1815 he had risen to be master, the highest rank open to him. In 1816 he won a medal for bravery during the bombardment of the Corsair city of Algiers. From 1819 to 1821 he was engaged in exploring and charting the South Shetland Islands in the Antarctic, in command of the 216-ton brig *Williams.* He discovered Trinity Land, the north-western tip of the Antarctic peninsula, and claimed King George and Clarence Islands for Britain. Bransfield Strait, Bransfield Island, Bransfield Rocks and Mount Bransfield are named after him. He re-joined the merchant navy some years later and became master of several cargo vessels.

BREEN, DAN (1894–1969), republican. Born near Soloheadbeg, Co. Tipperary, son of a small farmer. Worked as a plasterer and later as a linesman on the Great Southern Railway. Joined the Irish Volunteers 1914. On 21 January 1919, the day the First Dáil met in the Mansion House, Dublin, he took part in the ambush, at Soloheadbeg, of a party of policemen escorting explosives to a quarry. Two policemen were killed. This was the first engagement with British forces since the Rising of 1916, and marked the beginning of the War of Independence. On the run with a price of £10,000 on his head, he quickly established a reputation as a leader in the IRA. In 1919 he rescued his comrade Seán Hogan at gun-point from a heavily guarded train at Knocklong station. He and Seán Treacy, surprised in a house in Drumcondra, Dublin, shot their way out through a heavy cordon of British military and escaped, though Breen was badly wounded. Elected TD for Tipperary 1923, and the first anti-Treaty deputy to take his seat, in January 1927. Defeated in general election, June 1927. Went to America for some years. Returned and represented Tipperary in Dáil 1932-1965. Published an account of his guerrilla days, *My Fight for Irish Freedom* (1924). Died Dublin, 27 December 1969.

BRENDAN, SAINT (*c.* AD 583). Was probably born near Tralee, Co. Kerry; founded a large monastery at Clonfert, and died at his sister's foundation at Annaghdown, Co. Galway. The story of his voyages, which led to his being called 'Brendan the Navigator', is told in a mediaeval publication, *Navigationis Brendani*, which was translated into many European languages. He is described as searching for the Isles of the Blest, reaching the Canaries, and even discovering America. It is reasonably certain that he sailed to the Scottish islands and possibly to Wales; the rest is conjecture.

BRENNAN, JOHN. See under CZIRA, SIDNEY.

BRENNAN, LOUIS (1852-1932), inventor. Born Castlebar, Co. Mayo, 28 January 1852. Went to Melbourne as a boy. Worked as watchmaker. Invented dirigible torpedo for coast defence. British government bought exclusive rights for £100,000 in 1886. Superintendent of government factory at Gillingham, Kent, to manufacture his torpedo, 1887-1896, and consulting engineer until 1907. Invented gyrostat monorail. Worked in Ministry of Munitions 1914-1918, and in Air Ministry 1919-1926 on development of helicopters. Died Montreux, 17 January 1932.

BRENNAN, ROBERT (1881-1964), diplomat and author. Born Wexford. Became a journalist. As commandant in the Irish Volunteers, he occupied Wexford with 600 men in the Rising of 1916. After the surrender ordered by PEARSE, he was sentenced to death, later commuted to penal servitude for life. On his release with the other prisoners, he organised the Department of External Affairs in the underground government until the Treaty of 1921, after which he took the Republican side. A director of the *Irish Press*, the newspaper founded by DE VALERA, 1930-1934. Then re-joined the diplomatic service. Minister to USA 1938-1947, including the difficult years of the Second World War, when Ireland was neutral. Returned to Ireland as Director of Broadcasting 1947-1948. Wrote plays and mystery stories, and in 1950 published his autobiography, *Allegiance*. Died Dublin, 12 November 1964.

BRENNAN-WHITMORE, WILLIAM JAMES (1886-1977), journalist and revolutionary. Born in Wexford, son of Thomas Whitmore. Orphaned as a child and reared by his uncle, John Brennan, on a farm at Clonee, Ferns. Joined British army and served in India with the Education Corps. Returned to Wexford, became a journalist, and joined the Irish Volunteers. In the Rising of 1916 he had the rank of commandant. Wounded, taken prisoner and interned in Frongoch, Wales. Released in December 1916. Served as intelligence officer under MICHAEL COLLINS. After the Treaty he joined the National Army. In the late 1920s he retired to Courtown, Co. Wexford, took up farming, and founded and edited a local newspaper, the *Record*. Died in Dublin 27 December 1977, aged ninety-one, the last surviving commandant of the 1916 Rising.

BRENON, ALEXANDER HERBERT REGINALD ST JOHN (1880-1958), film director. Born Dún Laoghaire, Co. Dublin, 13 January 1880. Educated in London, where his family had moved. Emigrated to USA at sixteen. Directed his first film for the Universal Company 1910. Between 1910 and 1914 he directed films in Europe, among them *Ivanhoe,* made in England. Spectacular film *Neptune's Daughter* (1914) starred the swimmer Annette Kellerman, whom he also directed in *A Daughter of the Gods* (1915). Other films from this early period include *The Kreutzer Sonata* with Nance O'Neil and Theda Bara, *The Fall of the Romanoffs, The Passing of the Third Floor Back* with Forbes Robertson, *War Brides,* which introduced Nazimova and Richard Barthlemess to the screen, and Benevente's *Passion Flower* with Norma Talmadge. Two of Brenon's most charming films were Sir James Barrie's *Peter Pan* and *A Kiss for Cinderella,* staring Betty Bronson. Made first version of *Beau Geste* (1926), with Ronald Colman, Neil Hamilton and Ralph Forbes. Directed many famous players including Pola Negri, Clara Bow, and Lon Chaney, before making his early talkies, *Lummox* and *The Case of Sergeant Grischa.* Returned to England 1935. Last film, Edgar Wallace's *The Flying Squad* (1940). He wrote or acted in many of his 300 films. Retired to Los Angeles, where he died, 21 June 1958.

BRENT, GEORGE (1904-1979), film actor. Born in Dublin. Raised in New York by an aunt after his parents died, returned to Dublin when sixteen to continue his education. Served as a courier for the IRA during the War of Independence. Fled to Canada in 1923 to escape arrest. Successful career in Hollywood, appearing in 110 films, including *Jezebel* (1938) and *Dark Victory* (1939). Died at his home in California.

BRIAN BÓRÚ (*c.* 941-1014), king of Ireland. Born in north Munster at a time when the Norsemen had secured many Irish seaports, and frequently plundered and harried the neighbouring countryside. In 976 he succeeded his brother Mathgamhain as king of Dál Cais and claimant of the kingship of Munster. In 978 he defeated and killed Mael Muad, king of the Eoghanacht, at Belach Lechtna in Cork and became king of Munster. He then waged war against Mael Sechnaill, king of Tara from 980. Brian sailed up the Shannon in 988 from his stronghold at Killaloe, and ravaged Connacht, Meath and Breifne. Counterattacks followed from Mael Sechnaill, but eventually he was forced to concede to Brian the mastery of the southern half of Ireland. In 997 they met at Clonfert and agreed to divide the country between them, Mael Sechnaill being recognised as king of the northern half. In 999 the Leinstermen revolted against Brian and allied themselves with the Norsemen in Dublin. Brian inflicted a crushing defeat on them at Glen Máma in Co. Wicklow, and then seized Dublin and plundered it. He married Gormlaith, mother of Sitric, king of the Dublin Danes, and gave his daughter in marriage to Sitric. He then felt strong enough to break with Mael Sechnaill and assert his claim to the northern half of the country. Mael Sechnaill failed to secure support from the northern Uí Néill and yielded to Brian, who then became king of all Ireland. In 1005 he marched with a large army through Meath to Armagh, gave twenty ounces of gold to the clergy and confirmed the primatial jurisdiction of the See. The following year he made a royal circuit of the north, and took tribute and hostages to ensure the continued submission of the Uí Néill. From this practice he got the name Brian Bórú (Brian of the Tributes). About 1012 the Leinstermen and the Uí Néill took the field against Brian. Late in 1013 Brian besieged Dublin with his son Murchad but, failing to take it, retired home at Christmas. The Leinstermen and their Norse allies realised that the attack would be renewed in the spring and they persuaded the Vikings of the Orkneys and Man to come to their assistance. The northern rulers stood aloof from this struggle. The opposing forces met on Good Friday, 23 April, 1014, in the battle of Clontarf, and the Leinstermen and their Norse allies were routed. Brian was slain in his tent by fleeing Norsemen. Clontarf was an important event in the internal struggle for leadership, and the Norsemen, whose power in Ireland had waned by then, played only a secondary role. Brian was buried at Armagh with great ceremony.

BRIGID, SAINT (*c.* AD 525). Little is known with certainty about this saint, save that she was born about the middle of the fifth century, probably at Faughart, near Dundalk, Co. Louth, and founded a great religious house at Kildare, where she died about the year 525. Many marvels are attributed to her in mediaeval hagiography. The tradition of St Brigid's Cross is still strong: according to legend, the saint converted a pagan on his deathbed by explaining the Redemption to him with a cross that she plaited from rushes from the floor. St Brigid, the 'Mary of the Gael', is one of the three patron saints of Ireland, Patrick and Colmcille being the others. Her feast-day is 1 February, the first day of spring.

BRISCOE, ROBERT (1894-1969), politician and businessman. Born Dublin. Son of a Lithuanian immigrant and brought up in strict orthodox Jewish tradition. Sent to USA by his father in 1914 for fear of conscription. Returned after the Easter Rising 1916, joined Fianna Éireann. Sent by MICHAEL COLLINS to Germany and USA to procure arms for the IRA. Took the anti-Treaty side in the Civil War. Founder-member of Fianna Fáil. TD Dublin City South 1927-1965. Elected to Dublin City Council 1930. Lord Mayor 1956 and 1961. Appointed to Council of State 1965. Led a delegation of the World Zionist Organisation to seek international support for the settlement of Jews in Palestine 1939. Toured the Middle East on a trade mission 1945, the first of many to publicise Irish goods

abroad. A television film of his life, *The Fabulous Irishman*, was circulated in the USA. Published his biography, *For the Life of Me*, written in collaboration with Alden Hatch, in 1959. Died in Dublin.

BRISTOL, EARL OF. See under HERVEY, FREDERICK AUGUSTUS.

BROCAS, HENRY, Sr (1762-1837), landscape painter and engraver. Born Dublin, and self-taught. Besides painting, mainly in watercolour, he was a prolific engraver and contributed to many Dublin periodicals. In 1801 he was appointed master of the Landscape and Ornament School of the RDS and held the post until his death in Britain St, 20 October 1837.

BROCAS, SAMUEL FREDERICK (*c.* 1792-1847), landscape painter. Son of HENRY BROCAS; born Dublin. Practised successfully, exhibiting at the RHA 1828-1847. A series of twelve views of Dublin drawn by him was engraved by his brother Henry and published in 1820. He died at his house, 120 Lower Baggot St, 14 May 1847.

BROCAS, WILLIAM (*c.* 1794-1868), portrait painter. Brother of SAMUEL FREDERICK BROCAS; born Dublin. Exhibited at RHA for nearly forty years. He became president of the Society of Irish Artists in 1843. RHA 1860. Died at his residence, 120 Lower Baggot St, 12 November 1868.

BROCK, LYNN. See under McALLISTER, ALEXANDER.

BROGAN, HARRY (1905-1977), actor. Born in Holywood, Co. Down. Family moved to Harold's Cross, Dublin, when he was an infant. Made his first stage appearance with CONSTANCE MARKIEVICZ in *Confederates* at Foresters' Hall, Parnell Square, in 1918. Followed his father's trade of stonemason but gave it up in early 1920s to join Billy Walsh and his Irish Players, a touring fit-up company. He had his first part in the Abbey Theatre in 1926 and became a permanent member of the company in

1936. He directed and played in many radio plays and was the first to read poetry from Radio Éireann, after obtaining permission from Mrs Pearse to broadcast the poems of PATRICK PEARSE. He starred in Synge's *Well of the Saints*, the first major dramatic work broadcast by Telefís Éireann. He appeared in almost every feature film made in Ireland, but refused many offers of work in the USA. Was associated also with Lyric Theatre, Parnell Square, and Torch Theatre, Capel St. Made a life member of Irish Actors' Equity in 1968 as a mark of respect for his long service to Irish theatre. In 1972 the Abbey made him a presentation as a tribute to his performance in the demanding role of Harry Hope in Eugene O'Neill's *The Iceman Cometh*. He died in Dublin, 20 May 1977, after a long illness.

BRONTË, PATRICK (1777–1861), clergyman, father of the Brontë sisters and Branwell Brontë. Born 17 March 1777, Ballynaskeagh, Co. Down, son of Hugh Brunty. At sixteen he opened a school in Drumgooland, Co. Down. The local vicar paid his way to Cambridge and on leaving Ireland he changed his name to Brontë. After graduating in 1806 he took holy orders and held curacies in various places in England until 1820. That year he secured the perpetual curacy of Haworth, a wild and lonely moorland district of Yorkshire, at a stipend of £200 a year and a house. He wrote a tract and some undistinguished verse and is chiefly remembered as the father of Charlotte, Emily and Anne Brontë, and for his eccentricties, moroseness, and spartan upbringing of his children. He remained in Haworth for forty-one years and died there, 7 June 1861, having survived all his children.

BROOKE, SIR BASIL, first VISCOUNT BROOKEBOROUGH (1888–1973), Prime Minister of Northern Ireland. Born Colebrook, Co. Fermanagh, 9 June 1888. Educated Winchester and Sandhurst. Military Cross and Croix de Guerre, First World War. About 1920 he resigned his regular commission in the Hussars to farm his large estates at Colebrook. He was elected to the Northern Ireland Senate in 1921 but resigned in 1922 to become Commandant of the Ulster Special Constabulary in their fight against the IRA. Unionist MP for the Lisnaskea division of Co. Fermanagh 1929. Minister of Agriculture 1933. Promptly dismissed all Roman Catholic workers on his estates, a quarter of the total, to set an example for other landowners. Minister of Commerce and Minister of Production 1941. Prime Minister 1943. He played an active role in linking the Orange Order, of which he was a leading member, with the government. In his twenty years as Prime Minister he had no official contact with trade unions or Roman Catholics. Viscount 1952. Resigned as Prime Minister 1963 after an illness. During his retirement he kept in close touch with Unionism and Orangeism, and opposed publicly the liberal policy of his successor, Terence O'Neill, towards the Irish Republic. Died at his home in Colebrook, 18 August 1973.

BROOKE, CHARLOTTE (*c.* 1740–1793), author. Daughter of HENRY BROOKE; born Co. Cavan. Educated by her father. After his death in 1783, she was reduced to poverty by unwise investment. In 1789 she published *Reliques of Irish Poetry*, consisting of odes, elegies and songs translated into English verse, with the original Irish. This and her edition of her father's works, published in 1792, repaired her fortunes to some degree. In 1791 she had published *School for Christians*, dialogues for the use of children. Died Longford, 29 March 1793. It is said that she was connected with *Bolg an tSoláir*, the earliest Irish-language magazine, but as the first and only number appeared in Belfast two years after her death, the connection is uncertain.

BROOKE, HENRY (*c.* 1703–1783), poet, dramatist and novelist. Born Co.

Cavan. Educated TCD. After some years in literary society in London he returned to Dublin and devoted himself to writing. A poem, 'Universal Beauty' (1735), won high praise from Pope. His play *Gustavus Vasa*, founded on incidents in Swedish history, was banned in London owing to the fancied resemblance of the villain to Sir Robert Walpole, but was performed in Dublin. His *Farmer's Letters to the Protestants of Ireland* (1745) were written with the avowed intention of rousing them to prepare against a Jacobite invasion. It was said that for these writings Lord Chesterfield made him Barrack Master at a salary of £400 a year. Of the many plays, pamphlets and novels he produced, *The Fool of Quality*, a curious amalgam of stories, adventure and argument (five volumes, 1766–1772), is the only work now remembered. A shortened version produced by John Wesley in 1781 under the title *The History of Henry, Earl of Moreland* was read by generations of his devout followers. Brooke survived his wife and all but one of his twenty-two children, and passed his last years in a state of mental depression. Died Dublin, 10 October 1783. His surviving daughter CHARLOTTE edited his works in 1792.

BROOKE, STOPFORD AUGUSTUS (1832–1916), divine and man of letters. Born Glendoen, near Letterkenny, Co. Donegal, 14 November 1832. Educated TCD. Ordained 1857 and won early renown as a preacher. After serving as a curate in London and at the British embassy in Berlin he became a chaplain-in-ordinary to Queen Victoria. He published volumes of sermons, and studies of Browning, Tennyson, Shakespeare, and Milton. His *Primer of English Literature* (1876) sold half-a-million copies during his lifetime. In 1880 he seceded from the Church of England but did not attach himself to any other denomination. Died Ewhurst in Surrey, 18 March 1916.

BROUGHAM, JOHN (1810–1880), actor and dramatist. Born Dublin on 9 May 1814. Educated TCD. Abandoned medicine for the stage, making first appearance in London, July 1830. Manager of Lyceum 1840. He went to America 1842 and opened his own theatre on Broadway in 1850, but this venture failed after two years. He continued to act on Broadway, spent several years in England, and returned to America to open his second theatre on site of present Madison Square Theatre. This failed after a few months. He continued to act with stock companies in New York until 1879 and died there. He wrote many farces, burlesques and adaptations but none have survived. Essentially a comedian, his best parts were the stage-Irishmen of tradition.

BROWN, CHRISTY (1932–1981), novelist and poet. Born in Crumlin, Dublin, son of a bricklayer. His mother bore twenty-one other children, of whom thirteen survived to adulthood. From birth he was almost completely paralysed by cerebral palsy. His mother taught him to read, and DR ROBERT COLLIS taught him how to co-ordinate his movements and his speech. He learned to type using his left foot and, encouraged by Collis, wrote an account of his early childhood, *My Left Foot* (1954). He expanded this into a best-selling autobiographical novel, *Down All the Days* (1970), the work of ten years, which was translated into fourteen languages. His first volume of poetry, *Come Softly to My Wake* (1971), was also a best-seller. In all, he wrote five novels and four volumes of poetry. In 1972 he married Mary Carr, a nurse from Tralee, Co. Kerry. The success of his books enabled him to acquire a bungalow in Ballyheigue, Co. Kerry, and another house in Parbrook, a village in Somerset. His friends found him gregarious and companionable, with a pungent turn of phrase. He died suddenly in Parbrook on 6 September 1981, aged forty-nine.

BROWN, STEPHEN JAMES MEREDITH (1881–1962), Jesuit priest and librarian. Born Holywood, Co.

Down. Educated Clongowes Wood. Entered Jesuits 1897, ordained 1914. His chief interest was in the development of libraries. Founded the Central Catholic Library 1922 and later director. Served on Hospital Library Council. Director of the Academy of Christian Art. Published *A Reader's Guide to Irish Fiction* (1910), *A Guide to Books on Ireland* (1912), and *Ireland in Fiction* (1916). Edited *Catalogue of Tales and Novels by Irish Writers* (1927). Died Dublin, 8 May 1962.

BROWN, WILLIAM (1777–1857), admiral in the Argentine navy. Born Foxford, Co. Mayo. Emigrated to America with his family in 1786. His father died soon after their arrival, and he shipped as a cabin boy on a merchant ship. In 1796 he was pressed into the English navy, but after some years succeeded in obtaining command of an English merchant ship and finally settled in Buenos Aires. In 1814 he accepted a command in the navy of the new Argentine Republic, and defeated the Spanish at the mouth of the Uruguay and at Montevideo. He was then made admiral and spent some years as a privateer, cruising in the Pacific to harass the Spaniards. He had been living in retirement in Buenos Aires for several years when, in December 1825, Brazil declared war against Argentina and blockaded the River Plata. Taking command again, he routed enemy squadrons twice in 1826 but was defeated by much larger forces in April 1827. Peace was then negotiated. He remained in the service until 1845, and then retired to a small estate near Buenos Aires, where he died, 8 May 1857.

BROWNE, FRANCES (1816–1879), poet, novelist and author of stories for children. Born in Stranorlar, Co. Donegal, on 16 January 1816 and was blind from infancy as a result of smallpox. Earned her living from writing, contributing to the *Irish Penny Journal, Hood's Magazine* and the *Athenaeum*. Settled in London in 1847 and became known as the 'blind poetess of Donegal'. Published an autobiography, novels and children's stories. Her collection of delightfully written fairy stories, *Granny's Wonderful Chair and the Stories It Told* (1857), became a world-wide best-seller. She received a small civil-list pension from Sir Robert Peel. Died in London 25 August 1879.

BROWNE, GEORGE COUNT DE (1698–1792), soldier of fortune. Born Camas, Co. Limerick, 15 June 1698. Educated at Limerick diocesan school. A Catholic and Jacobite, he had no opportunity of advancement in Ireland, and went to the Continent to make his career. Served under the Elector Palatine. Entered the Russian army in 1730, and distinguished himself in the Polish, French and Turkish wars. He had become a general, with command of 30,000 men, when he was taken prisoner by the Turks. Sold as a slave; obtained his freedom through the intervention of the French ambassador at Constantinople. While in slave's dress he discovered important state secrets, which he brought back with him to St Petersburg. For this service the Tsarina Anna made him a major-general under LACY. He gave distinguished service in the Seven Years' War, and was named field-marshal by Pyotr III. He was given chief command in the Danish war but, on his representing that the war was ill-advised, the tsar deprived him of his rank and ordered him into exile. Three days later, Pyotr repented this hasty decision and made him governor of Livonia (Latvia). He was confirmed in this office by Ekaterina II, and for thirty years ruled the province with great ability and fairness. Died 18 February 1792.

BROWNE, MICHAEL J. (1896–1980), bishop. Born in Westport, Co. Mayo, and educated at St Jarlath's College, Tuam, and Maynooth. Professor of theology at Maynooth 1921–1937, then appointed bishop of Galway. Member of Senate of NUI from 1934. Chairman of Commission on Vocational Organisation 1939–1944, which recommended

37

distribution of power among vocational groups as advocated in Pope Pius XI's encyclical *Quadragesimo Anno*. Elected with Cardinal WILLIAM CONWAY to represent Irish bishops at World Synod of Bishops in Rome in 1967, 1969, and 1971. He built sixty schools and thirty churches and commissioned a new cathedral in Galway, opened in 1966 to the accompaniment of criticism of its neo-Gothic style. His outspoken comments on public issues involved him in frequent controversy. He criticised Government policy for the amalgamation of small rural schools, and during the 'Mother and Child' debate in 1950–1951 asserted that education in regard to motherhood was a moral responsibility belonging to the church and outside the authority of the state. Of a Department of Education study 'Investment in Education' he said it included not a word about religion and might have been produced by a communist country. He attacked TCD as 'a centre for atheist and communist propaganda'. He died at his home in Galway on 23 February 1980.

BROWNE, MONSIGNOR PATRICK (PÁDRAIG DE BRÚN) (1889–1960), scholar. Born Grangemockler, Co. Tipperary. Educated at Rockwell College, Holy Cross College, Clonliffe, and NUI. Studied in Europe on a travelling scholarship in mathematics and mathematical physics. Ordained 1913 following a theological course at the Irish College, Rome. Graduated D.Sc. from the Sorbonne and later studied at Göttingen. Professor of mathematics, St Patrick's College, Maynooth, 1914–1945. In April 1945 he was elected president of University College, Galway, and in November 1959 he succeeded Seán Ó Faoláin as director of the Arts Council. Chairman of the council of the Dublin Institute for Advanced Studies. Member, governing body, School of Celtic Studies. Vice-chancellor NUI and member of NUI Senate. Published many translations into Irish from Greek, Latin, French, and Italian, including

Sophocles' *Antigone* (1926), *Oedipus Rex* (1928), *Oedipus at Colonus* (1929), Racine's *Athalie* (1930), and Plutarch's *Lives*. He also translated part of Dante's *Divine Comedy*; *The Inferno* was published posthumously in 1963. Honoured by the Italian and French governments. Domestic Prelate 1950. Died 5 June 1960.

BROWNE, VALENTINE EDWARD CHARLES, VISCOUNT CASTLEROSSE, sixth EARL OF KENMARE (1891–1943), columnist. Born Killarney, 29 May 1891. Educated Downside and Trinity College, Cambridge. Joined Irish Guards July 1914 and wounded in retreat from Mons. A good linguist, he made abortive attempts at a career in City of London. In 1926 his friend, Lord Beaverbrook, engaged him to write 'The Londoner's Log' for the *Sunday Express*. For fiteen years he filled this column with gossip and semi-philosophical reflections. His marriage in 1928 to Doris Delavigne ended in divorce ten years later. Published *Valentine's Days* (1934). A scratch golfer, in 1939 he had a magnificent course laid out on the family estate at Killarney. He worked with Carol Reed as adviser on film *The Young Mr Pitt* (1942). His first wife died 1942. Three weeks later he married Lady Enid Furness, an Australian widow. Died Killarney, September 1943.

BROY, COLONEL ÉAMONN (1887–1972), commissioner, Garda Síochána. Born in Rathangan, Co. Kildare. Joined DMP 1911. Assigned as sergeant to G division, the secret service of British administration in Ireland. Supplied MICHAEL COLLINS with valuable information, and hid him in College St police station when he was on the run. Arrested February 1921, jailed for six months, then dismissed. After the Treaty he was made adjutant of the Free State air force and promoted colonel. Appointed secretary of DMP in 1923 and chief superintendent 1925. Chief of detective division, February 1933. Appointed commissioner March 1933 to succeed

EOIN O'DUFFY. Formed 'Broy Harriers' to escort bailiffs seizing cattle from farmers who refused to pay rates during the 'Blueshirts' campaign 1933-1934. President Irish Olympic Council 1935. Retired 1938 and kept out of public eye. Died in Dublin, 22 January 1972.

BRUEN, JIMMY (1921-1972), golfer. Born Belfast. Spent most of his life as an insurance broker in Cork, where he was educated at the Presentation Brothers' College. Won British Boys' championship 1936. Picked for the British and Irish Walker Cup team to play America in 1938, and had to get a week's leave from school. Second World War cut short his golfing career, but in 1946 he won the British Amateur championship, the first Irishman ever to do so. Selected again for the Walker Cup team 1949 and 1951. Died in Cork on 3 May 1972 after short illness.

BRUGHA, CATHAL (1874-1922), revolutionary. Born 18 July 1874 at 13 Richmond Avenue, Dublin. Registered at birth as Charles William St John Burgess. Educated at Belvedere College. Obliged to leave at sixteen when his father's business failed, and became clerk in a church supplies firm. With Lalor brothers founded new firm, Lalor Ltd, in 1909, to manufacture candles. Joined Gaelic League 1899, and became lieutenant in the Irish Volunteers 1913. He was married in 1912. Second-in-command at South Dublin Union in Rising of 1916, severely wounded and lamed for the rest of his life. Took leading part in War of Independence. Chief of Staff, IRA, October 1917 to April 1919 and then Minister for Defence until January 1922. Represented Waterford in Dáil Éireann from 1918 until his death. In absence of DE VALERA and GRIFFITH, presided at first meeting of the Dáil, 21 January 1919. Voted against Treaty in January 1922 and replaced as Minister for Defence by RICHARD MULCAHY. Fought in O'Connell St, Dublin, on the Republican side in Civil War and died, 7 July 1922, from wounds received two days before.

BRYCE, JAMES (1838-1922), jurist, historian and politician. Born 10 May 1838, Arthur St, Belfast. Educated Belfast Academy, Glasgow University, Trinity College, Oxford, and Lincoln's Inn. His academic successes at Oxford included five major prizes and three first classes. His prize essay on the Holy Roman Empire, published when he was twenty-six, gained him a European reputation. Professor of civil law at Oxford 1870-1893. Joined the Liberal Party. MP for Tower Hamlets division of East London 1880-1885 and for South Aberdeen 1885-1906, and held junior posts. Chief Secretary for Ireland in 1905. He had previously supported Gladstone's policy on Home Rule for Ireland but, though sympathetic to Irish aspirations, he failed to win the confidence of the Irish leaders. In 1888 he had published *The American Commonwealth*, the most authoritative work extant on that subject and the fruit of many visits to the United States. In 1907 he was sent as ambassador to Washington. His mission was eminently successful, especially in promoting good relations between the United States and Canada, and on his retirement in 1913 he was created Viscount Bryce. He devoted the rest of his life to forwarding the founding of the League of Nations and to writing, his principal publication being *Modern Democracies* (1921). Died at Sidmouth, 22 January 1922. Buried in Edinburgh. Distinctions included Order of Merit and honorary degrees from thirty-one universities.

BULFIN, WILLIAM (1864-1910), writer. Born 1864 at Derrinlough, Birr, Co. Offaly. Educated at the Classical Academy and Presentation Schools, Birr, Royal Charter School, Banagher, at Cloghan, and Galway Grammar School. Emigrated to Argentina with his brother Peter 1884. Worked on the pampas at the estate of an Irish emigrant. Began to contribute to the

Southern Cross, a weekly paper in Buenos Aires, owned, edited and run for the Irish community by Michael Dinneen from Cork. After four years on the pampas, returned to Buenos Aires, became sub-editor on the *Southern Cross*, and shortly afterwards became proprietor and editor. Vigorous defender of the rights of Catholics and Irish immigrants. In 1902 he returned to Ireland. Sketches of his travels around the country on a bicycle appeared in the *Southern Cross* and later, partly because of his friendship with ARTHUR GRIFFITH, in the *United Irishman, Sinn Féin*, and the New York *Daily News*. They appeared in book form as *Rambles in Eirinn* (1907). He also published *Tales of the Pampas*. Bulfin returned to Argentina in 1904. Made Knight of St Gregory for his work on behalf of the Irish Catholic community. Returned to Ireland 1909 and sailed with the O'Rahilly to USA in an unsuccessful attempt to interest wealthy Irish-Americans in the founding of a Sinn Féin daily paper. Died at home at Derrinlough, January 1910.

BULL, LUCIEN (1876–1972), inventor. Born 8 January 1876 at Dublin. Son of owner of religious repository in Suffolk St. He became assistant to Dr Marey at his cinematography laboratory in Paris. Pioneered and developed ultra-rapid cinematography and as early as 1902 had recorded 500 images per second. In 1908 he invented the first electrocardiograph. Other achievements included research on optical illusions and acoustic phenomena, apparatus for the location of gun-batteries through sound, and photographic techniques of shock waves. In 1952 he recorded one million images per second. He was director, Institut Marey, 1914; in charge of research, National Office of Research and Invention, 1933; director, School of Higher Studies, 1937; president, Institute of Scientific Cinematography, 1948. His distinctions included *officier* of Legion of Honour, and commander of Order of the British Empire. On 16 March 1966 'Hommage à Lucien Bull' was mounted

at Conservatoire National des Arts et Métiers, Paris. He made all his own experimental apparatus. Died in Paris in August 1972.

BULLOCK, SHAN (1865–1935), novelist. Born Crom, Co. Fermanagh, 17 May 1865. His father was a bailiff on the Earl of Erne's estate, a magistrate, and a prosperous farmer in his own right. For two years after leaving school, Bullock worked on his father's farm, then joined the civil service in London, where he spent the rest of his life. *The Awkward Squad*, a collection of short stories, appeared 1893. This was followed during the next thirty years by a series of novels, including *By Thrasna River* (1895), *The Squireen* (1903), *Dan the Dollar* (1905), about Fermanagh life, and three less successful novels about London life, including *Robert Thorne* (1907). Wrote another book of short stories, *Ring o' Rushes* (1896). His last book of fiction was *The Loughsiders* (1924). Published autobiography, *After Sixty Years* (1931), and two volumes of verse, *Mores et Vita* (1923), and *Gleanings* (1927). Died at Cheam, Surrey, 27 February 1935.

BUNBURY, SELINA (1802–1882), novelist and traveller. Born in Kilsaran, Co. Louth. Her father went bankrupt when she was seventeen and her mother moved to Dublin with the children. Selina taught in a primary school and wrote books about Ireland: *A Visit to My Birthplace* (1820) and *Tales of My Country* (1833) are typical titles. The family moved to Liverpool, where she wrote many popular novels while keeping house for her twin brother. After his marriage in 1845 she visited most of the countries of Europe and published a number of travel books. Her output was very large but hardly reached the hundred titles sometimes attributed to her. She died in Cheltenham in 1882.

BUNTING, EDWARD (1773–1843), musician and antiquary. Born Armagh. After the death of his father in 1782 he went to live in Drogheda with his eldest brother, an organist and music teacher. His musical talent developed early under his brother's tuition and, when only eleven, he was appointed a sub-organist in Belfast. He gave music lessons and had his ears boxed, it is said, by one of his pupils because of his forthright comments on her performance. He became popular and successful as a professional musician. In 1792 a famous assemblage of harpers took place in Belfast. This awakened in Bunting a strong interest in old Irish music and he made many journeys throughout the country to collect material for a book on the subject. His *General Collection of the Ancient Irish Music* (1796) contained sixty-six airs. In 1809 he published another edition with an additional seventy-seven tunes, many being collected from a harper named Dennis Hempson, reputed to be over one hundred years old. In 1819 Bunting married a Miss Chapman and moved to Dublin where he became organist to St Stephen's, as well as teaching music. In 1840 he published a third collection of Irish music, containing 120 new airs. THOMAS MOORE drew on his first volume for many of his 'Melodies'. Bunting is buried in Mount Jerome cemetery.

BURGH, COLONEL THOMAS
(1670–1730), architect. Son of bishop of Ardagh. He served in the Williamite wars and became surveyor-general 1700. First known building is the Royal Barracks (now Collins Barracks), Dublin. His next important building, the old Custom House on Essex Quay, has not survived. He built the great library of TCD, begun in 1712 and opened in 1732 after his death. Other notable buildings were the Infirmary of the Royal Hospital (1711), St Werburgh's Church (1715), and Dr Steevens' Hospital (1721–1733). He bought an estate at Old Town, Naas, Co. Kildare, and built himself a fine mansion. Represented Old Town in Irish House of Commons 1715–1730. Died, probably at Old Town, 17 December 1730.

BURKE, EDMUND (1729–1797), political writer and orator. Born 12 Arran Quay, Dublin, 12 January 1729, son of a Protestant solicitor and a Catholic mother. Educated Quaker school in Ballitore, Co. Kildare, kept by Abraham Shackleton. He entered TCD 1744, and with three others founded the club that later became the College Historical Society. After graduating he studied law at the Middle Temple, London, but his failure to secure his call to the bar estranged him from his father. After a period of obscurity he published *A Vindication of Natural Society* in 1756. The same year, his essay *A Philosophical Inquiry into the Origin of our Ideas of the Sublime and Beautiful* attracted favourable attention. In 1757 he married June Nugent, the daughter of his Irish Catholic physician, and to support his family he became editor of the *Annual Register* in 1759 and retained his connection with it for nearly thirty years. By this time he was on friendly terms with Johnson, Reynolds, and Garrick, and in 1764 they founded their celebrated Club. He returned to Dublin in 1761 as secretary to W. G. Hamilton, 'Single-Speech Hamilton', Chief Secretary for Ireland, but after two years resigned this uncongenial post. Became secretary to Lord Rockingham, the new Prime Minister, and MP for Wendover in 1765. He soon made his mark, despite his harsh voice and awkward gestures, and his eloquence and power of thought went home to his listeners. The quarrel with the American colonies was gathering momentum, and Burke, by advocating conciliation rather than coercion, helped to delay the crisis. The Rockingham ministry lasted only a year, and he followed it into opposition. He was now very active in politics and besides speaking frequently and at length in the House of Commons published many pamphlets. *Thoughts on the Present Discontents* appeared in 1770, and was followed by his three great writings on the American struggle, his speech on *American Taxation* (1774), that on *Conciliation with the Colonies* (1775), and *A*

Letter to the Sheriffs of Bristol (1777). His Irish tracts are, unfortunately, not so well known. In the letters *To a Peer of Ireland on the Penal Laws* (1782), *To Sir Hercules Langrishe* (1792), and the earlier *Speech at the Guildhall, in Bristol* (1780), his theme is simple: stupidity has lost us America, stupidity will lose us Ireland. MP for Bristol 1774–1780. He claimed the right not to be a mere delegate, but the reasoning and independent representative of his constituents. His advocacy of a policy of conciliation and legislative independence for Ireland drew charges of 'Catholicism', and cost him his Bristol seat. He then became member for Malton, a pocket borough of Lord Rockingham's. In 1782 Rockingham was returned to power and Burke was made a Privy Councillor and Paymaster. He immediately secured the reduction of his own salary from £20,000 a year to £4,000, and then carried through other reforms affecting public offices. Lord Rockingham died in July 1786 and Burke resigned. Save for a second short period as Paymaster-General he never again held office in government. In 1788, largely at his instigation, Warren Hastings, Governor-General of India, was impeached, Burke opening the proceedings with a speech that lasted four days. The trial dragged on for eight years and ended with the acquittal of Hasting on all charges. In 1790 Burke published his best-known work, *Reflections on the Revolution in France*, which went into eleven editions and provoked many English replies, including Thomas Paine's *Rights of Man*. It was read all over Europe and brought Burke immense prestige and influence. His views were challenged by Charles James Fox and many of his Whig associates, and the long friendship with Fox came to a dramatic end in a bitter parliamentary debate in May 1791. After the end of the Hastings trial, in April 1795, Burke retired from Parliament, but continued to write in defence of his political views. As a 'new man' he had been opposed by the court and the landed aristocracy, and his integrity made him a difficult party man. Nevertheless he stood for tradition and inherited values and regarded society as a stable and orderly system moved by large historic influences, thus perhaps exaggerating the value of things as they were. In 1768 he had spent £20,000 on the purchase of a house and six hundred acres at Beaconsfield, twenty-four miles from London. This purchase had excited criticism and suspicion, as he was not a wealthy man. Died there, 9 July 1797.

BURKE, JOHN (1787–1848), genealogist. Born at Elm Hall, Tipperary. Although he was the elder son his younger brother succeeded to their father's estate under a family arrangement. He devoted himself to geneaolgical studies. Issued *Genealogical and Heraldic Dictionary of the Peerage and Baronetage of the United Kingdom* (1826). The *Peerage* was re-published at irregular intervals until its ninth edition (1847), now issued annually. *A General and Heraldic Dictionary of the Peerages of England, Ireland, and Scotland, Extinct, Dormant and in Abeyance,* was issued in 1831. *Official Kalendar for 1831* was intended to be the first of a series of annual handbooks, but the series was not continued. Between 1833 and 1838 he published *A Genealogical and Heraldic History of the Commoners of Great Britain and Ireland.* In later editions (1837 and 1843–1849) the title was altered to *A Dictionary of the Landed Gentry.* Burke was also the author of *The Portrait Gallery of Distinguished Females including Beauties of the Courts of George IV and William IV,* and editor of a short-lived periodical, the *Patrician.* Died Aix-la-Chapelle, 27 March 1848. Burke's *Peerage* has been described as 'a stud book of humanity, unmatched in Western Europe'.

BURKE, ROBERT O'HARA (1820–1861), explorer of Australia. Born St Clerans, Co. Galway. Educated in Belgium. Served in the Austrian army and the Irish constabulary. Emigrated to Australia in 1853, and became an inspector of police in Victoria. In 1860 he was given charge of an expedition to cross the Australian continent from south to north. The expedition left Melbourne on 20 August 1860, and reached Cooper's Creek on 11 November. After waiting for reinforcements, which failed to arrive owing to mismanagement, he made a dash for the Gulf of Carpentaria on 16 December, with three companions, Wills, Gray and King, leaving the bulk of his stores in charge of an assistant named Brahe, who was to wait up to four months for his return. They reached the tidal waters of the Flinders river on 12 February 1861, and were the first white people to cross the Australian continent. On the return journey, Gray died and they lost a day in burying him. When they reached Cooper's Creek on 21 April 1861 they found that Brahe had set off for home that day, leaving only a small store of provisions. Burke died of starvation on 28 June 1861, and Wills died about that time also. Their only surviving companion, John King, wandered off and was cared for by aborigines. He was reached by a relief expedition on 21 September.

BURKE, THOMAS (*c.* 1710–1776), historian of the Irish Dominicans. Born Dublin. Became a member of the Dominican order in Rome 1726. In 1731 he published in Rome, under the title of *Promptuarium Morale*, a Latin and enlarged edition of a Spanish work on moral theology by Francisco Larraga. He compiled offices for the festivals of Irish saints, published in Dublin in 1751 as *Officia Propria Sanctorum Hiberniae*. In 1752 Burke published in Dublin *A Catechism, Moral and Controversial*. Appointed historiographer of the Dominicans in Ireland 1753. In 1758 *Historical Collection out of Several Eminent Protestant Historians and the Strange Confusions Following in the Reign of Henry VIII, King Edward VI, Queen Mary and Queen Elizabeth* appeared. He became bishop of Ossory in 1759. His history of the Dominicans, *Hibernia Dominicana* (1762), was allegedly published in Kilkenny, actually in Cologne. Parts of it were later

removed as it was feared they would offend the English authorities. In 1775 Burke issued a pastoral letter condemning the Whiteboys. Died 27 September 1776.

BURKE, THOMAS NICHOLAS (1830–1883), Dominican friar. Born Galway, 8 September 1830, son of a poor baker. At seventeen he entered the Dominican order, and spent five years studying in Rome and Perugia. Ordained in England 1853. In 1857 he was sent to Ireland to found a novitiate at Tallaght, Co. Dublin. Became prior of San Clemente in Rome 1864. He returned to Ireland about 1870, and in 1872 he toured the USA as visitor to the Dominican houses there. He became immensely popular as a preacher and lecturer, and raised £100,000 for American charities. His most famous lectures were those delivered on the relations between Ireland and England, as a reply to the historian J. A. Froude. He returned to Tallaght at the end of his tour and died there, 2 July 1883.

BURKE, WILLIAM (1792–1829), criminal. Born Urney, Co. Tyrone. He probably started life as a labourer, and in 1818 went to Scotland to work on the canal at Mediston. In 1827 he was living in Log's lodging-house, Tanner's Close, Edinburgh, an establishment kept by another Irishman, William Hare, a native of Derry. When an old pensioner died in the house on 29 November 1827, Burke and Hare sold the body for £10 to Dr Robert Knox, for dissection. This easy money suggested to Hare that a profitable business could be operated by luring obscure wayfarers into the lodging-house, killing them, and selling the bodies. Aided by their wives, they disposed of at least fifteen persons, by first making them drunk and then suffocating them, so that no mark appeared on the bodies. The corpses were sold to Dr Knox's school of anatomy for prices ranging from £8 to £14. The neighbours became suspicious in October 1828 when a poor old woman called Margery

Campbell or Doherty disappeared, and they called in the police. The corpse was found in a box in the cellar in Dr Knox's house. Hare turned king's evidence, Burke was found guilty of murder and hanged in Edinburgh, 28 January 1829. He exonerated Dr Knox from all blame.

BURKE SHERIDAN, MARGARET (1889–1958), soprano. Born in Castlebar, Co. Mayo, on 15 October 1889. Orphaned at the age of four. Educated at Dominican Convent, Eccles Street, Dublin. Prizewinner at Feis Cheoil 1908. Proceeds of a benefit concert enabled her to study at the Royal Academy of Music, London. Further study in Rome was arranged by Marconi. She made her début there in 1918 as Mimi in *La Bohème.* Sang in La Scala, Milan, for the first time in 1920 and became extremely popular with Italian audiences, especially in Puccini's *Madame Butterfly.* She made many guest appearances in Covent Garden, London. Audiences were captivated by her beauty, expressive characterisation, and rich lyric soprano voice. Despite repeated requests she would never sing in Ireland or the USA. In 1936 she retired suddenly, at the height of her career and without explanation, and returned to Ireland. She died in Dublin on 16 April 1958.

BURTON, SIR FREDERICK WILLIAM (1816–1900), painter. Born Corofin House, Co. Clare, 8 April 1816, son of a wealthy landowner. He studied drawing under the BROCAS brothers in Dublin, and soon made his name as a painter of miniatures and watercolour portraits. Elected RHA 1839 and exhibited at RA. In 1851 he went to Germany and spent the following seven years studying German art as well as executing a number of drawings, which won high praise. In 1874 he was appointed director of the National Gallery in London, and gave up painting to devote himself completely to the duties of the post. During his twenty years' tenure of office, his well-judged purchases added some six hundred pictures of great value

to the collection. He was knighted in 1884. Died at his house in Kensington, 16 March 1900. Buried Mount Jerome, Dublin.

BURY, JOHN BAGNELL (1861–1927), classical scholar and historian. Born Monaghan, 16 October 1861. Educated Foyle College, Derry, and TCD, where he became professor of modern history in 1893, holding also the chair of Greek from 1898. In 1902 he was appointed to succeed Lord Acton as professor of modern history at Cambridge and held the post until his death. His reputation rests on his monumental work as a historian, beginning with his *History of the Later Roman Empire* (1889), which placed him, at the age of twenty-eight, among the leaders in historical studies at home and abroad. His later works on Roman and Greek history showed the range of his mature scholarship and his encyclopaedic knowledge. Died at Rome, 1 June 1927.

BUSHE, CHARLES KENDAL (1767–1843), chief justice. Born Kilmurry, Co. Kilkenny. Educated TCD, where he made a name as an orator in the College Historical Society. He was called to the Irish bar in 1790 and entered the Irish parliament in 1796 as member for Callan, Co. Kilkenny. An advocate of Catholic emancipation and a strong opponent of the Act of Union, he refused the post of Master of the Rolls, offered to keep him silent. Despite these differences with the government, he was made Lord Chief Justice in 1822 and held the post until his resignation in 1841. He died at his son's house, Furry Park, near Dublin, 6 November 1843. SIR JONAH BARRINGTON described him simply as 'incorruptible'. His great-grand-daughter EDITH SOMERVILLE published a biography, *An Incorruptible Irishman* (1932).

BUSHNELL, CATHERINE. See under HAYES, CATHERINE.

BUTCHER, SAMUEL HENRY (1850–1910), scholar. Born Dublin, 16

April 1850. Educated at Marlborough and Trinity College, Cambridge, winning many scholarships and prizes. In 1879 he published, with Andrew Lang, a translation of the *Odyssey*, which was greeted with acclaim as the best prose rendering that had yet appeared. In 1882 he was appointed to the chair of Greek at Edinburgh University, where he remained until 1903, resigning and moving to London after the death of his wife. His most important work, *Aristotle's Theory of Poetry and Fine Art* (1895), contains a critical text and translation of the *Poetics* with a commentary and analysis. He died in London, 29 December 1910, and was buried beside his wife in the Dean cemetery, Edinburgh.

BUTLER, LADY ELEANOR (1745–1829), recluse of Llangollen. Born probably in Dublin, sister of the seventeenth Earl of Ormond. About 1779 she and a friend, Sarah Ponsonby, resolved to live together in complete seclusion from the world. They settled in a cottage at Plasnewydd in the vale of Llangollen in Wales, accompanied by a maidservant, Mary Caryll. Here they lived for fifty years, neither leaving the cottage for a single night until their deaths. Their devotion to each other and their eccentric manners gave them wide notoriety. Tourists visited the vale especially to see 'the Ladies of Llangollen', and they received a number of orders from members of the Bourbon family. Prince Puckler-Muskace described them as 'the two most celebrated virgins of Europe', and said that they dressed invariably in semi-masculine fashion. The maidservant died first. Lady Eleanor died on 2 June 1829, and her companion on 8 December 1831.

BUTLER, JAMES, first DUKE OF ORMOND (1610–1688), statesman and soldier. Born in London, 19 October 1610. After the death of his father in 1619 he was made a royal ward and brought up as a Protestant. Married his cousin Elizabeth Preston, heiress of Earl of Desmond, in 1629 and so united the two families after a long feud. Succeeded his grandfather 1633. Supported Strafford and made commander-in-chief in 1640 during Strafford's absence. Rendered conspicuous service to the king during the rebellion of 1641. Arranged a 'cessation' with the Confederates in 1643 and in March 1646 made a treaty that granted religious tolerance to Catholics and removed various grievances. After the victory of OWEN ROE O'NEILL at Benburb, the Papal Nuncio, Rinuccini, denounced the treaty. Internal hostilities broke out between factions in the Confederates. In this confused situation Ormond transferred Dublin to the parliamentary forces and sailed for England. Later he returned and in 1649 arranged peace between Royalists and Confederates. On the execution of the king, Ormond proclaimed Charles II and was made Knight of the Garter. The rapid successes of Cromwell in Ireland forced Ormond to retreat to France in 1650, where he joined the court in exile. He was actively engaged in the negotiations for the Restoration and then became commissioner for the Treasury and the Navy and received other important places, with an English peerage, and dukedom of Ormond in the Irish peerage. Lord Lieutenant of Ireland again in 1662. Secured passage of the Act of Explanation (1665), which largely approved the Cromwellian land confiscations. He encouraged Irish manufactures, secured incorporation of the College of Physicians, and encouraged learning. Dismissed 1669 as a result of intrigue by Buckingham. Chancellor of Oxford University 1669. Restored to favour 1677 and reappointed Lord Lieutenant. Received English dukedom 1682. After the succession of James II in 1685 he retired from public life. Died at Kingston Lacy, Dorset, 21 July 1688. Buried Westminster Abbey.

BUTLER, JOHN, by courtesy **twelfth LORD DUNBOYNE** (1716–1800), bishop. Became bishop of Cork 1763. He succeeded his nephew unexpectedly as

Lord Dunboyne when he was seventy. Wishing to perpetuate his name and family, he resigned the bishopric and sought permission to marry from Pope Pius VI. This was refused. He then renounced Catholicism, turned Protestant, and married his cousin. They had no issue. When ill in 1800 he asked permission of the Pope to rejoin the Catholic Church and on his deathbed was received back by REV. WILLIAM GAHAN. In his will he left one of his Dunboyne estates to Maynooth College. This will was contested by his sister. A compromise settlement provided for the endowment of the Dunboyne Establishment, a department of the college. He died at Dunboyne Castle, 7 May 1800.

BUTLER, SIR WILLIAM FRANCIS (1838–1910), soldier and author. Born Suirville, Co. Tipperary, 31 October 1838. Educated Jesuit school, Tullabeg, Co. Offaly, and Dr Quinn's in Dublin. He joined the British army 1858 and served in Canada 1867–1873. His experiences with fur trappers and Indians on 'the glorious prairies' supplied him with material for *The Great Lone Land* (1872), which went into four editions. Later he took part in the Zulu wars in South Africa and in the expedition to relieve Gordon in Sudan. He rose steadily in the army, was knighted 1886, and retired to Bansha Castle, Co. Tipperary, in 1905 with the rank of lieutenant-general. He published biographies of Gordon and Sir Charles Napier as well as travel books. On retirement he became a Commissioner for National Education in Ireland, and supported the Gaelic League and Home Rule. Died at Bansha Castle, 7 June 1910.

BUTT, ISAAC (1813–1879), barrister and politician. Born 6 September 1813 at Glenfin, Co. Donegal, only son of Protestant rector. Educated Royal School, Raphoe, and TCD. A brilliant scholar, one of the founders of the *Dublin University Magazine* (1833) and editor 1834–1838. Professor of political economy 1836–1841. Called to the Irish bar 1838 and soon became a leader in his profession. In these early years his outlook was conservative and he wrote for the conservative press on both sides of the Irish Sea. He established in Dublin a weekly newspaper, the *Protestant Guardian*. The Great Famine and the idealism of the Young Irelanders won him over to nationalism. After the abortive rising of 1848 he defended SMITH O'BRIEN and others. MP for Harwich 1852. MP for Youghal 1852–1865. In the years 1865–1869 he defended many Fenians, sacrificing lucrative briefs to do so, although his financial position was precarious, as it remained throughout his life. He was president of the Amnesty Association in 1869. In 1870 he founded the Home Rule movement, aiming at a subordinate parliament with control over Irish domestic affairs. MP for Limerick 1871 and with the support of the Catholic middle classes he won half the Irish seats in the general election of 1874. But his failure to make progress with either of the large English parties made his followers impatient. With the rise of PARNELL and his new policy of obstruction, Butt's star waned and he lost control of the Home Rule party. Died Dundrum, Co. Dublin, 5 May 1879. Buried in Stranorlar, Co. Donegal.

BYRNE, CHARLES (1761–1783), giant. Born of parents of ordinary stature. At nineteen he was 8 feet (2.4 m) high. He travelled about the country giving exhibitions and visited Scotland and England. In London he created such a sensation that a pantomime was called after him: *Harlequin Teague; or The Giant's Causeway*. He died at Cockspur St, Charing Cross, London, 1 June 1783. His skeleton in the museum of the College of Surgeons, Lincoln's Inn Fields, measures exactly 92¾ inches (236 cm).

BYRNE, DONN. See under DONN BYRNE, BRIAN OSWALD.

BYRNE, MILES (1780–1862), United Irishman. Born Monaseed, Co.

Wexford, 20 March 1780, son of a farmer. He joined the Society of United Irishmen 1797. Fought at Vinegar Hill 1798. When the rising was defeated he hid for some time in the Wicklow mountains and then came to Dublin and worked as a clerk in a timber yard. Meeting ROBERT EMMET, he was sent by him to Paris to enlist the aid of Napoleon for another rising. Given a commission in the Irish Legion formed by the emperor with a view to a French expedition to Ireland. The expedition did not materialise, but Byrne served with distinction in the Napoleonic campaigns of 1804–1815, being made a *chef de bataillon* and *chevalier* of the Legion of Honour. In 1835 he resigned his commission and settled in Paris where he died, 24 January 1862. There is a monument over his grave in Montmartre cemetery.

His *Memoirs* were published in Paris in 1863: a facsimile edition was published by the Irish University Press in 1976.

BYRNE, SÉAMUS (1904–1968), lawyer and playwright. Born in Dublin 27 December 1904. Graduated LL.B. from NUI and practised law in Leitrim for nine years. Jailed in 1940 for involvement with IRA but released after nine months following a hunger strike of twenty-one days. *Design for a Headstone*, produced in the Abbey Theatre in 1950, deals with a proposed hunger strike by political prisoners in Mountjoy Jail. A right-wing Catholic organisation mounted a short-lived protest in the theatre. *Little City* (Dublin Theatre Festival, 1964) attacked social hypocrisies in Dublin. He died in Dublin in 1968.

C

CAIRNES, JOHN ELLIOTT (1823–1875), economist. Born 26 December 1823, Castlebellingham, Co. Louth; educated at Kingstown (now Dún Laoghaire), Co. Dublin. He was thought too dull for further study, but against the wishes of his father, who intended him for the family business, he went to TCD and graduated in 1848. Appointed Whately Professor of Political Economy 1856; the following year he published his lectures under the title *The Character and Logical Method of Political Economy*. Professor of political economy and jurisprudence at Queen's College, Galway, 1859. Published in 1862 *The Slave Power*, a defence of the position of the northern states in the American Civil War, which made his reputation and influenced the British to support the northern cause. In 1866 appointed professor of political economy at University College, London, and continued to write on politics and economics despite the crippling effects of a hunting accident in Galway in 1860. Published *Some Leading Principles of Political Economy Newly Explained* (1874). Died 8 July 1875 at Blackheath.

CALLAN, NICHOLAS JOSEPH (1799–1864), priest, scientist, and inventor. Born Darver, Dromiskin, Dundalk, Co. Louth, 20 December 1799. Educated Dundalk Academy under William Neilson, Presbyterian minister and philomath, and Navan seminary. Entered Maynooth 1816; ordained 1823. Doctor of divinity, Sapienza University, Rome, 1826. Returned to Maynooth as professor of natural philosophy. Pioneer in the development of electrical science; inventor of the induction coil, which led to the modern transformer. Constructed a giant battery of 577 cells producing enormous currents of electricity to the delight, astonishment and danger of his students. Like Cavendish before him, he made independent discovery of Ohm's Law. In applied science he devised several types of galvanic battery and influenced the study of high-tension electricity, exciting great interest with an exhibition of his apparatus in London in 1837, aided by his friend Sturgeon, inventor of the electric magnet. Wrote about twenty religious books, one of which influenced the conversion of Newman. Confessor to students and colleagues at Maynooth.

CALLANAN, JEREMIAH JOHN (1795–1829), poet. Born Cork. Intended by parents for priesthood but left Maynooth and studied at TCD for two years. His money ran out and he joined the British army but was bought out quickly by friends. Returned to Cork and taught in school kept by WILLIAM MAGINN, who introduced his early poems to *Blackwood's Magazine*. Most of his time was spent wandering in Munster collecting ballads and legends but unfortunately these were lost. His health failed and in 1827 he accepted a tutorship in Lisbon where he died of tuberculosis, 19 September 1829. His best lyric, 'Gougane Barra', appeared in 1826 and *Collected Poems* in 1861.

CAMPBELL, (FREDERICK) GEORGE, (1917–1979), artist. Born in Arklow, Co. Wicklow, grew up in Belfast, and settled in Dublin in the 1960s. He was encouraged to paint by his friend GERARD DILLON, and was associated with him in founding the Living Art Exhibition after the Second World War. He won many awards, including the President Hyde Gold

48

Medal (1966) and the Oireachtas prize for landscape (1969). Member of RHA. Spain, which he visited often, inspired many of his finest paintings, and the Spanish government gave him one of its highest cultural awards, Knight Commander of Spain. He also painted Belfast and the west of Ireland. His stained-glass work can be seen in Galway Cathedral and the Dominican Church in Athy. He also made a reputation as a classical guitarist, and broadcast frequently on BBC radio. He died suddenly in Dublin on 18 May 1979 and is buried in Laragh, Co. Wicklow. Survived by his wife, Madge, and his mother, GRETTA BOWEN.

CAMPBELL, JAMES HENRY MUSSEN, first BARON GLENAVY (1851-1931), lawyer. Born Dublin. Educated TCD. Called to Irish bar 1878 and became leading junior. QC 1892. Unionist MP for St Stephen's Green 1898-1900 and for Dublin University 1903-1916. Solicitor-general for Ireland 1901-1905, attorney-general 1905 and 1916. Member of provisional government formed by CARSON during Home Rule agitation. Lord Chief Justice of Ireland 1916-1918, baronet 1917, Lord Chancellor of Ireland 1918-1921, baron 1921. Chairman of first Irish Free State Senate 1922-1928. W. B. YEATS described him as 'handsome, watchful, vigorous, dominating'. Died Dublin, 22 March 1931.

CAMPBELL, JOSEPH (1879-1944), poet. Born Belfast. Attracted to the Irish literary revival, and in 1904, when Ulster Literary Theatre was founded, became one of its editors and contributed a short play, *The Little Cowherd of Slainge.* He collaborated with a young composer, Herbert Hayes, who was collecting traditional airs in remote parts of Co. Donegal. They published *Songs of Uladh,* which included 'My Lagan Love', later very popular. Campbell published several other volumes of poetry and then went to London where he spent several years and was secretary of the Irish National Literary Society.

On his return to Ireland he settled on a small farm at Glencree, Co. Wicklow. After the 1916 Insurrection he published a volume of poetry, *Earth of Cualann,* illustrated with his own line-drawings. Before the Civil War, Campbell was elected to Wicklow County Council and served as its chairman. When the war broke out he was arrested as a republican sympathiser, imprisoned in Mountjoy, and then interned in the Curragh for two years. On his release he emigrated to New York where he established a school of Irish studies. When the venture failed he became a lecturer in Anglo-Irish literature at Fordham University. After twelve years in the USA he returned to Glencree in 1935 and died there. *Poems of Joseph Campbell,* his collected poetry, was published in Dublin in 1963.

CAMPBELL, PATRICK, third BARON GLENAVY (1913-1980), author and broadcaster. Born in Dublin on 6 June 1913 and educated at Rossall, at Pembroke College, Oxford, in Germany, and at the Sorbonne. Succeeded to the barony on the death of his father in 1963. During the Second World War served as chief petty officer in the Irish Marine Service. Joined the *Irish Times* under R. M. SMYLLIE and as 'Quidnunc' wrote 'An Irishman's Diary'; readers delighted in the wry humour of his descriptions of untoward events. He then went to London and worked on the *Sunday Dispatch* 1947-1959 and as assistant editor of *Lilliput* magazine 1947-1953. Joined the *Sunday Times* 1961. Later he went to live in the south of France and turned to freelance work, writing film scripts and broadcasting on the BBC. 'From my earliest days,' he said, 'I have enjoyed an attractive impediment in my speech,' and he turned this to his advantage in BBC programmes, notably 'Call My Bluff', seen by millions. He wrote sixteen books, including an autobiography. The titles—e.g. *Life in Thin Slices* (1954) and *Rough Husbandry* (1965)—convey their Campbellian flavour. *How to Become a Scratch Golfer* (1963) reminds us he was

49

one himself. His first marriage, to Sylvia Willoughby Lee in 1941, was dissolved in 1947. His second, to Cherry Louise Monro in 1947, was dissolved in 1966. In November 1966 he married Mrs Vivienne Orme, a former film script writer and producer. In 1960 he was elected honorary president of the naval branch of the Organisation of National Ex-servicemen. He died at his house in Cannes on 10 November 1980. He had one daughter, Margaret Brigid, by his second wife.

CANTILLON, RICHARD (1680–1734), economist. Born Ballyheige, Co. Kerry. Became a merchant in London. Moved to Paris, established a banking house, entered society, and married the daughter of a Monsieur Omani, a rich merchant. Returning to London he settled in Albemarle Street, where on 14 May 1734 he was murdered by his cook, who ransacked the house, set fire to it, and made good his escape. Cantillon had been called the 'father of political economy' because of his one famous book, *Essai sur la Nature du Commerce en Général, Traduit de l'Anglais* (1755). The supposed English original has never been found. A very inferior English version appeared in 1759. The *Essai* is in three parts: an introduction to political economy, a treatise on currency, and a study of foreign commerce and exchange. Quoted by Adam Smith, Condillac, and Quesnay. Described by Professor Stanley Jevons as 'the cradle of political economy'.

CAOMHÁNACH, SEÁN (1885–1947), teacher and writer, brother of 'KRUGER' KAVANAGH. Born and educated in Dún Chaoin, Co. Kerry. Worked as a travelling teacher and then moved to Dublin in 1911, became friendly with ARTHUR GRIFFITH, and wrote regularly for *Sinn Féin*. He went to America in 1914, returned in 1921 and was interned in the Curragh for republican activities. From 1928 to 1937 he taught Irish in the Masonic Boys' School and St Andrew's, where he influenced DAVID GREENE. He

concentrated on conversation rather than grammar, and his headmasters were well satisfied. He published a novel, *Fánaí* (1927), based on his American experiences. In 1937 he was engaged by the Department of Education to compile words and phrases from the Kerry Gaeltacht and he spent eight years on the task, producing a collection of over two million words, to the consternation of the department. A dispute over terms of payment was eventually resolved, and manuscript and copyright were acquired for £4,608. The manuscript, still unpublished, is now in the National Library. He returned to Dublin and died there on 16 January 1947, and is buried in Dún Chaoin. From his wearing of a kilt he was known from boyhood as 'Seán a' Chóta'. An artist in life who lacked a Boswell, his friends WILLIAM CONOR, HARRY KERNOFF and SEÁN O'SULLIVAN all executed portraits of him.

CARBERY, ETHNA, pen-name of Anna MacManus, née Johnston (1866–1911), writer. Born Ballymena, Co. Antrim. Her writings did much to stimulate the early Sinn Féin movement. She wrote many poems for the *Nation*, *United Ireland*, etc., and with ALICE MILLIGAN founded a monthly paper, the *Northern Patriot*, in conjunction with a Belfast workingmen's club. Following disagreement with the club they founded the *Shan Van Vocht* in 1896. Publications include poetry, *The Four Winds of Eirinn* (1902), and collected short stories, *The Passionate Hearts* (1903) and *In the Celtic Past* (1904). She died 1911, survived by her husband, SÉAMUS MACMANUS.

CAREY, JAMES (1845–1883), Fenian and informer. Born James's St, Dublin. He followed his father's trade of bricklayer for eighteen years and then set up as a builder. His business prospered and he became a city councillor. He joined the Fenians and became a leader in the group calling themselves the Invincibles, pledged to violent action, who decided to assassinate T. H. Burke, Under-Secretary to the Lord-Lieutenant. Carey went with eight others to the Phoenix Park on 6 May 1882 and pointed out Burke to them. Burke was stabbed to death and with him the newly appointed Chief Secretary, Lord Frederick Cavendish, who was walking with Burke near his official residence. In 1883 Carey was arrested with sixteen others. He turned Queen's evidence, and five of his associates were condemned to death and executed in public. Carey and his family were sent secretly by the British authorities to South Africa. The Invincibles discovered this and one of their members, Patrick O'Donnell, a bricklayer, followed Carey and shot him dead on 29 July 1883 on board the *Melrose* shortly after the vessel left Cape Town for Natal. O'Donnell was brought to England and executed at Newgate, 17 December 1883. No mention was made by him or the prosecution of his Fenian connections.

CARLETON, WILLIAM (1794–1869), novelist. Born 4 March 1794 at Prillisk, near Clogher, Co. Tyrone, youngest of fourteen children of a small farmer who spoke Irish and English equally well, had a fund of folklore and a tenacious memory. Went to a hedge-school and later studied the classics under Rev. Dr Keenan. Intended for the church but after a visit to Lough Derg gave up the idea and went as a tutor to the family of a Co. Louth farmer. Here he read *Gil Blas* and determined to see the world. He went to Dublin with two shillings and ninepence (13¾p) in his pocket. After some vicissitudes he got employment as a tutor. The *Christian Examiner* accepted his sketch 'The Lough Derg Pilgrimage', and Carleton was launched on his career as a writer. *Traits and Stories of the Irish Peasantry* (1830) quickly went into several editions. In 1834 he published *Tales of Ireland* and in 1839 *Fardorougha the Miser*, a powerful and moving novel. Among the best-known of his many works are *The Black Prophet* (1847), a story of the Famine, *Willy Reilly and his Dear Colleen Bawn* (1855), and *Redmond Count O'Hanlon, the*

Irish Rapparee (1862). Despite his prolific output Carleton was beset with money troubles, but a memorial from many distinguished people including MARIA EDGEWORTH secured him a civil list pension of £200. The land war and secret societies figure in Carleton's novels and sketches. His *Traits and Stories* provides an excellent picture of nineteenth-century Irish rural life, revealing both the virtues and the faults of the small farmers, labourers and craftsmen of his time. He was a tutor when he married. He died in Dublin on 30 January 1869 and is buried in Mount Jerome. A biography by Benedict Kiely, *Poor Scholar*, appeared in 1947.

CAROLAN, TURLOGH (1670–1738), harper and composer. Born near Nobber, Co. Meath. About 1684 the family moved to Ballyfarnon, Co. Roscommon, where they were befriended by the MacDermott Roes, owners of a local iron-foundry. Turlogh was educated with their children and when he lost his sight from smallpox at fourteen, Mrs MacDermott Roe apprenticed him to a good harper. At twenty-one she provided him with a horse, a servant, and money, and he set out to travel Ireland as an itinerant harper. Received with honour and hospitality by rich and poor, he repaid them with songs and airs dedicated to his patrons. He spent most of his time in Connacht and Ulster, and the titles of his pieces read like a roll-call of the old Irish noble families that still survived there. Carolan married a Mary Maguire from Co. Fermanagh and built a house at Mohill, Co. Leitrim. She bore seven children before her death in 1733. He himself fell ill at Tempo, Co. Fermanagh, in 1738 and, making his way to his old friends, the MacDermott Roes, died at their house in Aldeford, Co. Roscommon, 25 March. He was buried at Kilronan, Lough Meelagh, after a wake lasting four days, attended by a huge crowd from all over Ireland. CHARLES O'CONOR said he was 'moral and religious', of convivial disposition but 'seldom surprised by intoxication'.

About fifty of his compositions were included by BUNTING in his collections; some show traces of the influence of the 'Italian School', which flourished in Dublin at the time.

CARROLL, PAUL VINCENT (1900–1968), playwright. Born Blackrock, near Dundalk, Co. Louth, 10 July 1900. Educated St Mary's College, Dundalk, and St Patrick's Training College, Dublin. Returned to teach in Dundalk but in 1921, disillusioned with Irish provincial life, emigrated to Glasgow. Taught English and mathematics in state schools in the poorer districts, and in his spare time wrote short stories and reviewed books. His first play, *The Watched Pot*, was produced at the experimental Peacock Theatre in 1930. *Things That Are Caesar's* (Abbey Theatre, 1932) launched him on his career as a playwright. In 1934 he won the Casement award of the Irish Academy of Letters. After the success of *Shadow and Substance* (Abbey Theatre, 1937) he became a full-time dramatist. This play won the New York Drama Critics' Circle award for the best foreign play of 1937/38. *The White Steed*, first produced in New York, received the same award in 1939. He had founded a neighbourhood theatre in Glasgow in 1933, and in 1943 he joined with James Bridie and others in founding the Glasgow Citizens' Theatre. In 1945 he moved to Kent to be near the British film industry, and for several years he wrote screenplays, later writing for television. Further plays appeared, including *The Wise Have Not Spoken* (1944) and *The Wayward Saint* (1955), and a number of short stories. After some years of poor health he died suddenly on 20 October 1968 at his home in Bromley, Kent. His portraits of clergymen and clerical life in his best plays have not been surpassed on the Irish stage.

CARSON, SIR EDWARD HENRY (1854–1935), lawyer and political leader. Born Dublin, 9 February 1854. Educated Portarlington School and TCD. Called to the Irish bar in 1877, soon built up a large practice and became solicitor-general for Ireland 1892. MP Dublin University 1892–1918. He was called to the English bar in 1893 and made a devastating cross-examination of OSCAR WILDE in Wilde's libel action against the Marquess of Queensberry. He joined the Unionist government in 1900 as solicitor-general and received a knighthood. In Parliament he vigorously opposed any move to weaken the links between England and Ireland, and became leader of the Irish Unionists in 1910. When Liberals under Asquith introduced the Home Rule Bill of 1912, Carson took a leading part in the formation of the Ulster Volunteers, who drilled openly to show that they were prepared to resort to force of arms rather than come under an Irish parliament in Dublin. A solemn Covenant of Resistance to Home Rule was signed by hundreds of thousands of northern Unionists. Carson told them, 'Don't be afraid of illegalities,' and in April 1914 the Ulster Volunteers landed guns at Larne, Co. Antrim, in defiance of the British government but with the open approval of the Conservative opposition. The Home Rule Bill received the royal assent in August 1914 but its operation was immediately suspended until after the war. The Ulster Unionists, led by Carson and JAMES CRAIG, were assured by Asquith that 'the coercion of Ulster was unthinkable.' Carson was appointed attorney-general in 1915 but resigned in 1916 in dissatisfaction with the conduct of the war. After the Easter Rising of 1916 he was assured by Lloyd George that the six north-eastern counties would be permanently excluded from the Home Rule Act of 1914, and he accepted office as first lord of the Admiralty. When the war was ended he became MP for the Duncairn division of Belfast. The Government of Ireland Act of 1920, setting up a parliament for Northern Ireland, was supported by the Ulster Unionists on Carson's advice as their only alternative, since there was no hope of repealing the Home Rule Act. In 1921 he was appointed Lord of Appeal in ordinary and took a life peerage as Baron Carson of Duncairn. He died in Kent on 22 October 1935 and after a state funeral in Belfast was buried in St Anne's Cathedral.

CARTY, FRANCIS (*c*. 1899–1972), author. Born Wexford. Served with IRA in War of Independence. Wrote novels, including *The Irish Volunteer* (1932) and *Legion of the Rearguard* (1934), and lives of the Irish saints. For many years editor of Parkside Publications, Dublin. Appointed editor of the *Irish Press* 1957. Editor of the *Sunday Press* from 1962 until his retirement in 1968. Died in Dublin, April 1972.

CARVE, THOMAS (1590–*c*. 1672), writer. Original name Carew. Born Mobarnan, Co. Tipperary. Became a priest in diocese of Leighlin. Left Ireland for Germany in 1626 as an army chaplain. In 1640 became chaplain-general to the English, Irish and Scottish forces in Thirty Years' War. In 1630 began his *Itinerarium RD Thomas Carve Tipperariensis* (first two parts published 1639 and 1641). Around 1643 Carve went to Vienna as Notary Apostolic and Vicar-Choral of St Stephen's Cathedral. Third part of *Itinerary* published at Spires in 1646, describes Wallenstein, the Civil War in England, and the Thirty Years' War. Other works include *Rerum Germanicarum ab anno 1617 ad annum 1641 gestarum Epitome* (1641), *Lyra, seu Anacephalaoesius Hibernica* (1651), *Galateus* (1669), *Enchiridion Apologeticum* (1670). Date of Carve's death is not known—still living at Sulzbach in 1672.

CARVER, ROBERT (*fl.* 1750–1791), landscape and scene painter. Born Dublin, studied painting under Robert West in George's Lane School. Practised landscape painting, then became scene painter for Smock Alley and Crow Street theatres. In 1769 Garrick invited him to London as principal scene painter, Drury Lane Theatre. When SPRANGER BARRY quarrelled with Garrick and moved to Covent Garden, Carver followed him and worked there until his death. Landscapes much admired; exhibited RA 1789 and 1790. Died at 13 Bow St, November 1791.

CARY, (ARTHUR) JOYCE LUNEL (1888–1957), author. Born Derry, 7 December 1888. Educated Tunbridge Wells and Clifton College. At seventeen he inherited £300 a year, and studied art at Edinburgh and Paris 1907–1909. Dissatisfied with his progress, he went to Trinity College, Oxford, and graduated in law 1912, although he spent most of his time writing and reading widely. He served in the Red Cross in the Balkan wars 1912–1913, then joined the Nigerian political service, and fought with the Nigerian Regiment in the Cameroons in First World War. Invalided home 1920, he settled with his wife and family at Oxford and devoted himself to writing. Ten years of hard endeavour passed before his creative powers could find satisfactory expression. His first novel, *Aissa Saved* (1932), like the three that followed, was based on his experiences in Africa. He planned to write three trilogies—on art, politics, and religion—but lived to complete only the first two. *The Horse's Mouth* (1944), life as viewed by the artist-narrator, Gulley Jimson, forms the triumphant close to the trilogy on art. He published in all sixteen novels, many short stories, and two long poems. His autobiographical novel, *A House of Children* (1941) (James Tait Black Memorial Prize), recalls the happiness of many boyhood summers spent in Inishowen, Co. Donegal. He revisited Africa in 1943 to work on a race relations film for the British government. He died in Oxford, 29 March 1957.

CASEMENT, SIR ROGER (1864–1916), patriot. Born Sandycove, Co. Dublin, 1 September 1864. Educated Ballymena Academy. He went to Africa in 1884 and joined the British colonial service there in 1892. In 1904 he made a notable report on the inhuman treatment of native workers in the Belgian

Congo. He was later promoted to consul-general at Rio de Janeiro and investigated conditions in the Peruvian rubber plantations along the Putamayo river. His report exposing the cruelties practised on the natives by the white traders created an international sensation on its publication in 1912. Casement was knighted in 1911 for his public services and retired from the colonial service in 1912. Always of strong nationalist sympathies, he joined the Irish Volunteers in 1913. When the First World War broke out he hoped to obtain German help to win Irish independence, and made his way to Berlin in November 1914. He tried to enlist Irish prisoners of war in a brigade for service in an Irish rising but without success. At length, in April 1916 the Germans despatched a ship, the *Aud*, with a cargo of arms to be landed in Kerry for use in the rising planned for Easter week. Casement followed in a submarine and landed on Banna strand, Tralee Bay. The *Aud* was captured by British warships and blown up by its crew. Casement was arrested and taken to England to stand trial. He was found guilty of high treason and sentenced to be hanged. Many influential people in England petitioned for a reprieve and in the USA there was strong feeling against the sentence. Copies of diaries alleged to be his, recording homosexual practices, were circulated, it is said, by the British government and had the inevitable effect on public opinion. Controversy surrounds these 'Black Diaries'. René MacColl, biographer of Casement, considers that they are authentic; the use alleged to have been made of them is another matter. Casement was hanged in Pentonville prison, 3 August 1916. His remains were returned to Ireland and reinterred in Glasnevin cemetery on 1 March 1965 after a state funeral.

CASEY, ELIZABETH (1845–1894), author, under pen-name E. Owens Blackburne. Born at Slane, Co. Meath, and educated at TCD. A severe eye ailment was cured in 1863 by SIR WILLIAM

WILDE. She moved to London in 1874, became a prolific journalist and also wrote about twenty novels. Her *Illustrious Irishwomen* (1877) was the first work of its kind. She returned to Ireland and was accidentally burned to death at Fairview, Dublin, 1894.

CASEY, JOHN KEEGAN (1846–1870), popular poet. Born at Mount Dalton, near Mullingar, Co. Westmeath, son of a peasant farmer. First poem published in the *Nation* when he was sixteen. Became a clerk in a miller's counting-house in Castlerea, Co. Roscommon, in 1865. Arrested in March 1867 on suspicion of being a Fenian and imprisoned in Mountjoy Jail. Released November 1867, settled in Dublin and became a journalist, contributing under pen-name 'Leo' to the *Shamrock, Irish People*, and *Boston Pilot*. Welcomed by Irish exiles on successful lecture tour in England. Published two collections of verse; remembered for poem 'Máire, My Girl' and rousing ballad 'The Rising of the Moon'. Died in Dublin of tuberculosis on 17 March 1870. It was said that his funeral was followed by 50,000 people.

CASEY, WILLIAM FRANCIS (1884–1957), editor of *The Times*. Born Cape Town, 2 May 1884, son of P. J. Casey, theatre owner, of Glenageary, Co. Dublin. Educated Castleknock College and TCD, and called to Irish bar in 1909. He had two plays, *The Suburban Grove* and *The Man Who Missed the Tide*, produced in 1908 at the Abbey Theatre with fair success. He secured a post on *The Times*, represented the paper in Washington and Paris 1919–1920 and, after serving as leader-writer and deputy editor, became editor in 1948. He died in London, 20 April 1957.

CASS, ANDREW. See under GARVIN, JOHN.

CASTLEREAGH, VISCOUNT. See under STEWART, ROBERT.

CASTLEROSSE, VISCOUNT. See under BROWNE, VALENTINE.

CAULFIELD, JAMES, fourth VISCOUNT AND first EARL OF CHARLEMONT (1728–1799), nationalist. Born Dublin, 18 August 1728. Educated privately. Made the grand tour of Europe 1746–1754. Succeeded to the peerage at six. Made an earl in 1763 for services against the French in defending Belfast. He had a house in London from 1764 to 1773 but decided to live in Ireland for patriotic reasons. In 1770 he began to build Charlemont House in Rutland (Parnell) Square, and in his demesne at Marino he built the Casino, often described as one of the most beautiful buildings of its kind anywhere. Charlemont House, now the Municipal Gallery of Modern Art, became a centre for the educated and upper classes, and he was a leader of the liberal and polite society of his day. He devoted himself to architecture, literature, and the affairs of the RIA, of which he was the virtual founder in 1785/86, but in middle age his Whig nationalism involved him in the Volunteer movement as an ally of GRATTAN. He became commander-in-chief of the Volunteers in July 1780, and prominent at the Dungannon Convention of 1782, which gave the final impetus to legislative freedom for the Irish parliament. The movement had then three aims to achieve: parliamentary reform, the removal of restrictions on Irish commerce, and Catholic emancipation. A Volunteer convention in Dublin on 10 November 1783 proposed certain reforms but these were defeated in the House of Commons almost immediately. Feelings ran high among the Volunteers, but Charlemont succeeded in persuading them to adjourn their meeting. Their political influence began to wane from then on. Charlemont was strongly opposed to the Union with England. He died on 4 August 1799, before the Union was enacted, and was buried in the family vault in Armagh cathedral.

CEANNT, ÉAMONN (1881–1916), revolutionary. Born Glenamaddy, Co. Galway, 21 September 1881. Educated at local national school, North Richmond St CBS, Dublin, and UCD. Joined the clerical staff of Dublin City Council. Joined the Gaelic League in 1900, taught classes in Irish and became a member of the governing body. Accompanied a group of Irish athletes to Rome for the jubilee of Pope Pius X, and played Irish airs on the uileann pipes at his request. Joined Sinn Féin in 1908, became a member of the Irish Republican Brotherhood, and was elected to the Provisional Committee of the Irish Volunteers on their formation in November 1913. As a Volunteer officer he helped in the Howth gun-running of July 1914. In command of the South Dublin Union in the rising of Easter week, 1916, one of the seven signatories of the Proclamation of the Republic. Court-martialled, condemned to death, and executed by firing squad in Kilmainham Jail on 8 May 1916.

CÉITINN, SEATHRÚN (GEOFFREY KEATING) (*c.* 1570–*c.* 1650), poet and historian. Born Burges, Co. Tipperary, of Norman stock. Educated at a local bardic school, and for the priesthood at an Irish college at Bordeaux, where he became a doctor in theology. He returned to Ireland about 1610 as curate in Tubrid near his birthplace. His fame as a preacher spread far; it is said that a local woman was so incensed at one of his sermons that she had him outlawed and that he hid in a cave in the Glen of Aherlow. About 1620 he began his most famous work, *Foras Feasa ar Éirinn* ('History of Ireland'), written to defend his country against writers such as Spenser and Giraldus Cambrensis. He travelled all over the country, consulting books and manuscripts in the possession of the gentry, who received him with honour. In contrast to the contemporary *Annals of the Four Masters*, which is a bare record of events and dates, Céitinn's history gives a connected narrative. Completed before 1634, it was written in early Modern Irish when it was still spoken by the educated classes and when the literary tradition was still unbroken. It was received with acclaim; many manuscript copies were made and circulated widely until well into the nineteenth century. Céitinn also wrote several theological works. *Trí Bior-ghaoithe an Bháis* ('The Three Shafts of Death') is a model of scholarly Irish. A defence of the Mass and a short tract on the Rosary are earlier works. 'Mo Bheannacht Leat, a Scríbhinn' is a charming lyric written while he was a student in France. His other poems, about eighteen in all, include laments for dead friends and for the departure of the nobles, as well as religious and didactic pieces. He was buried in Tubrid.

CENTLIVRE, SUSANNA (1667–1722), playwright. Born 1667 in Co. Tyrone, where her father, an English yeoman, had been given extensive grants of land in the Plantation of Ulster. She ran away from home at fifteen to escape from a tyrannical step-mother. By working as a servant she earned her passage to Liverpool. While walking to London she was befriended by a wealthy young gentleman named Arthur Hammond. He persuaded her to dress in boy's clothes and go with him as his houseboy-valet to Cambridge University. After some happy years in 'the Elysian fields of youth where mad-cap love dwells in sunlit ecstasy', her later description of Cambridge, she left for London, with money and letters of introduction from Hammond and a promise to marry her. But it was many years before they met again. In less than a year she was married to a rich young man. Within a year he was killed in a duel. She married again shortly after, but her second husband was also a duellist and she was a widow again before the year was out. She now turned to writing for the stage. She was very beautiful and spoke several languages, affecting a gentle, broken English-cum-French, which was said to be 'fetching in the extreme'. To secure a production for her first play, *The Perjured Husband*, she agreed to play the tragic heroine

opposite an actor-manager. They opened in Windsor and the entire staff of the Castle attended, including Queen Anne's chef, Joseph Centlivre, a Parisian. The play was a failure, but Centlivre fell in love with Susanna and they were married soon after. He had an important and well-paid position, and their house in Spring Garden St (now demolished) near Charing Cross became a meeting-place for distinguished men of letters. She wrote a number of highly successful comedies. *The Wonder! A Woman Keeps a Secret* (1714) gave Garrick one of his best parts, and *A Bold Stroke For a Wife* (1718), with its 'false' and its 'true Simon Pure' long held the stage. Her marriage was happy. She died at fifty-five, 'the lustre of her beauty scarcely touched by time'. She was buried in the church of St Martin-in-the-Fields: 'Here lies Susanna Centlivre (née Freeman) from Ireland. Playwright, 1st December, 1722.'

CHARLEMONT, EARL OF. See under CAULFIELD, JAMES.

CHESNEY, CHARLES CORNWALLIS (1826–1876), professor of military history. Born Kilkeel, Co. Down, 29 September 1826, in the house of his uncle, GENERAL FRANCIS CHESNEY. Educated Blundell's school, Tiverton, and Woolwich Military Academy. Appointed to the Royal Engineers in 1845. Served in the West Indies and New Zealand until delicate health forced him to return to England. Became professor of military history at Sandhurst and revolutionised the teaching of the subject, lecturing on the American Civil War while it was still in progress. *Campaigns in Virginia and Maryland* was published in 1863, *Waterloo Lectures* and *The Tactical Use of Fortresses* in 1868, and they all became military textbooks. Also wrote *Essays in Military Biography* (1874). Appointed colonel in command of the Royal Engineers in London in 1873 where he died of pneumonia, 19 March 1876.

CHESNEY, FRANCIS RAWDON (1789–1872), soldier and explorer. Born Annalong, Co. Down, 16 March 1789. Cadet Woolwich Academy. Appointed to the artillery in 1805. His army opportunities were confined to garrison duty, although he volunteered many times for active service. In 1829 he explored Egypt and Syria and descended the Euphrates. His report showed that a Suez canal was a practicable proposition, and de Lesseps, thus encouraged to undertake the project, called him 'the father of the Suez canal'. Chesney also reported the feasibility of a new route to India through Syria and the Persian Gulf. Parliament voted £20,000 for the expenses of a further expedition under his command. Chesney landed at the bay of Antioch in 1835, transported two small steamboats across the desert, and navigated the Euphrates to the Persian Gulf, charting the course carefully. He then explored the Tigris and Karum rivers, journeyed to India, and returned to London in 1837. In 1843 he was appointed commandant of Hong Kong, where he remained until 1847. In 1851 he retired to the family estate at Kilkeel, Co. Down, where he died on 30 January 1872. He published *Expedition for the Survey of the Euphrates and Tigris* (1850) and also wrote a book on firearms and an account of the Russo-Turkish campaign of 1828/29. The development of an overland route to India was prevented by international dissensions, although proved practicable by his surveys.

CHEYNEY, PETER (1896–1951), pen-name of Reginald Evelyn Peter Southouse-Cheyney, writer. Born Co. Clare, 22 February 1896. Educated Hounslow College, Middlesex, Mercer's School, London, and University of London. Clerk in a solicitor's office, then on the stage at sixteen. Joined the British army on the outbreak of First World War, severely wounded, and posted to the staff. Demobilised as a major, worked as a freelance journalist, and then set up and directed a literary agency. Editor of the *St John Ambulance Gazette* 1928–1943 and news editor of the *Sunday Graphic* 1933–1934. In 1932 he formed a private detective bureau, 'Cheyney Research and Intelligence'. His first thriller, *This Man is Dangerous* (1936), was an immediate success. He published in all more than fifty crime novels, of which millions of copies were sold. His tough transatlantic characters, Caution and Callaghan, struck a new note in English crime fiction. His legal knowledge, wartime intelligence work and the experience of running a detective agency gave him a sureness of touch that kept his books best-sellers for fifteen years. Despite prolonged illness he kept on writing until his death in London on 26 June 1951.

CHILDERS, ERSKINE HAMILTON (1905–1974), fourth President of Ireland. Born London, 11 December 1905, son of ROBERT ERSKINE CHILDERS. Educated Gresham School, Norfolk, and Trinity College, Cambridge. In 1928 he became European manager in Paris for an American travel organisation. In 1932 he returned to Ireland, where he had spent much of his boyhood at Glendalough House, Annamoe, Co. Wicklow, the home of his paternal grandmother, Anna Barton, and became advertising manager of the newly founded *Irish Press*. Some years later he was appointed secretary of the Federation of Irish Manufacturers. Elected Fianna Fáil TD for Athlone-Longford 1938. Parliamentary Secretary to the Minister for Local Government and Public Health 1944, and Minister for Posts and Telegraphs 1951. Liberalised the organisation of Radio Éireann, then a branch of the department, later established in June 1960 as a statutory corporation, Radio Telefís Éireann. Minister for Lands 1957, Minister for Transport and Power 1959–1969. Tánaiste and Minister for Health from July 1969 until defeat of Fianna Fáil in general election March 1973. Elected President of Ireland 30 May 1973, defeating T. F. O'Higgins, the Government candidate, by 635,867 votes to 578,771. A member of Dáil Éireann without a break for thirty-five years. A conscientious and hard-working minister, most successful as Minister for Health, with an abiding interest in the care of the underprivileged. In the Dáil he avoided any reference to the Civil War, in obedience to the injunction given him by his father the night before his execution not to do or say anything that might cause bitterness. He died suddenly in Dublin, 17 November 1974, from coronary thrombosis. Buried in Derrylossary, near Annamoe, Co. Wicklow. His first wife, Ruth Dow, daughter of an American general, had died in 1950. He was survived by his second wife, Rita, their daughter, and five children of his first marriage.

CHILDERS, ROBERT ERSKINE (1870–1922), author and patriot. Born London, 25 June 1870, educated Haileybury and Trinity College, Cambridge. Clerk in the House of Commons 1895–1910. His mother was a Barton of Glendalough House, Co. Wicklow, which was his only real home until his marriage. He volunteered for the Boer War in 1899 and wrote a vivid account of his experiences, *In the Ranks of the CIV* [*City Imperial Volunteers*] (1900). A skilled yachtsman, in 1903 he published *The Riddle of the Sands*, a fictional account of German preparations to invade England, based on his experiences on sailing holidays in the Baltic. In 1904 he married Mary Ellen Osgood of Boston; one of their wedding presents was the yacht *Asgard*. He resigned from the House of Commons in 1910 to devote himself to political work, and in July 1914 he sailed into Howth, Co. Dublin, in the *Asgard* with arms from Germany for the Irish Volunteers. In the belief that the Allies would support the claims of Irish nationality, Childers joined the British navy on the outbreak of the First World War and won the DSC. After demobilisation his earlier Home Rule sympathies hardened into full support for an Irish republic. Settling in Dublin in 1919, he was elected to Dáil Éireann

as member for Co. Wicklow in 1921, appointed Minister for Propaganda, and served as principal secretary to the Irish delegation in the Treaty negotiations of 1921. He opposed the Treaty, joined the Republican side in the Civil War, and was captured by Free State forces at Glendalough House. Court-martialled and sentenced to death, he was executed on 24 November 1922, having first shaken hands with each member of the firing squad. One of his two sons, ERSKINE CHILDERS, was later President of Ireland. The *Asgard* was used for some years as a sail training ship.

CHURCH, SIR RICHARD (1784–1873), 'liberator of Greece'. Born Cork, son of a Quaker merchant. Ran away from school to join the British army. After active service in Egypt and Italy joined an expedition to the Ionian Islands, met Greek leaders in exile, and became sympathetic to their aims. After the Napoleonic wars ended, Church pleaded for Greek independence in London and at the Congress of Vienna (1815), but to no avail. Entered the service of the Neapolitan government in 1816 but expelled by revolutionaries when commander-in-chief in Sicily in 1820. Knighted by King George IV of England in 1822. Invited to join the leaders of the Greek revolution of 1821, became commander-in-chief and led the campaign in western Greece. Settled in Greece and became a Greek citizen, a member of the Council of State and inspector-general of the army. Died in Athens, 30 March 1873.

CLANCY, WILLIE (1921–1973), musician, folklorist and master carpenter. Born in Milltown Malbay, Co. Clare. Spent many years in London and a short time in New York but lived in Milltown Malbay for most of his later years. He was the best-known traditional musician in Ireland and especially noted for his beautiful rendering of slow airs on the uileann pipes. Also excelled on the concert flute and the tin whistle. An Irish-speaker, he had an extensive repertoire of Irish songs and stories and was well-versed in local folklore. His concert appearances in Ireland, Britain, continental Europe and the USA drew large and enthusiastic audiences, and he was in constant demand as an adjudicator at competitions. He played a lament on the pipes at the funeral of his friend SEÁN Ó RIADA. A tradition of copying and preserving Irish-language manuscripts survived in the Clancy family, and he had in his house a manuscript of 'Cúirt an Mheán-Oíche' by MERRIMAN. He died suddenly in a Galway hospital, 24 January 1973.

CLARKE, AUSTIN (1896–1974), poet, dramatist, and novelist. Born Manor St, Dublin; educated Belvedere College and UCD, where he studied Irish under DOUGLAS HYDE. His first long poem, 'The Vengeance of Fionn', was published in 1917; that year he became a lecturer in English in UCD. In 1921 he went to London, wrote reviews for *The Times, Observer* and *Times Literary Supplement*, and worked as assistant editor of *Argosy*. His first novel, *The Bright Temptation* (1932), was banned in Ireland until 1954. In 1932 he won the national award for poetry at the Tailteann Games. In 1937 he returned to Ireland, 'determined not to become an exile'. In 1941 he formed the Dublin Verse-Speaking Society, which produced verse plays at the Peacock Theatre and the Abbey as the Lyric Theatre Company, including many of his own verse plays, notably *The Viscount of Blarney, The Son of Learning*, and *As the Crow Flies*. From 1942 to 1955 he broadcast a weekly programme of poetry on Radio Éireann and contributed critical essays and reviews to many periodicals, while continuing his astonishingly rich output of creative work in prose and poetry. In all, he published more than thirty works of poetry, drama, fiction and an autobiography, drawing largely for his themes on mediaeval Irish literature, and continuing to write until well into his seventies. He was a founder-member of the Irish Academy of Letters, president in

1952, and in 1968 was awarded the Gregory Medal, the academy's highest distinction. President of Irish PEN 1939–1942 and 1946–1948. Honorary D.Litt. from Dublin University 1966 as 'the outstanding literary figure in modern Ireland'. First literary award of the American-Irish Foundation 1972. He died at his house at Templeogue Bridge, Co. Dublin, in March 1974.

CLARKE, HARRY (1889–1931), artist. Born Dublin, 17 March 1889, son of an English father with a church decorating business at 33 North Frederick St. Educated Belvedere College. Apprenticed to his father's business 1905. In 1910 became a full-time student at the Metropolitan School of Art. Awarded gold medals for stained-glass design in national competitions of Board of Education 1911, 1912, and 1913. A travelling scholarship enabled him to visit France in 1914. His first stained-glass commission was to design windows for the Honan Chapel in UCC, which were finished in March 1917. He also worked as a book illustrator and was commissioned to illustrate Poe's *Tales of Mystery and Imagination*, Hans Andersen's *Fairy Tales*, Goethe's *Faust*, and books of poetry. His debt to Beardsley is shown in his decorative and fantastic manner. He designed many church windows, including those in Castleknock Church, in St Joseph's, Terenure, and in Castlehaven, Co. Cork, as well as executing a number of commissions from overseas. His masterpiece is generally considered to be the window commissioned in 1927 by the government for presentation to the ILO in Geneva, which shows scenes from the works of contemporary Irish writers. The window failed to receive government approval, and after repossession by the Clarke family was sold in 1988 to an American museum. During the 1920s he taught design in the Metropolitan School of Art, and he was elected RHA in 1926. In 1930 he established the Harry Clarke Studios at 33 North Frederick Street. He became seriously ill in 1928, spent a year in Switzerland, and returned there in 1931 to die at Coire.

CLARKE, THOMAS JAMES (1857–1916), revolutionary. Born of Irish parents in Hurst Castle, Isle of Wight, on 11 March 1857. The family emigrated to South Africa, where he spent his childhood until he was ten. They then settled in Dungannon, Co. Tyrone. At twenty-one he went to America, and joined Clan na Gael, the American wing of the IRB. In 1883 he was sent to England on a revolutionary mission, was arrested and sentenced to penal servitude for life. He served fifteen years under severe conditions and on his release and return to Ireland was made a freeman of the city of Limerick. Unable to get work in Ireland, he emigrated to America in 1899. In 1907 he returned to Ireland, and with his savings opened a tobacconists and news-agency at 75A Great Britain St (now Parnell St). He set about re-organising the IRB. With SEÁN MAC DIARMADA as manager, in 1910 he published *Irish Freedom*, a militant anti-English journal. In July 1911 he organised the first national pilgrimage to the grave of Wolfe Tone at Bodenstown, Co. Kildare, as a counterblast to the visit to Dublin of the new king of England, George V. In 1915 he became a member of the military council set up to plan a rising. He served in the GPO in Easter Week, 1916, and at the request of the other leaders was the first to sign the Proclamation of the Republic. He was executed on 3 May 1916.

CLIVE, KITTY (1711–1785), comic actress. Born Catherine Rafter in Ulster, daughter of William Rafter, a lawyer who settled in London. She got her first part at Drury Lane Theatre from the manager, Colley Cibber, and soon her singing and exuberant humour made her a favourite with London's theatregoers in high-spirited comedy and farce. Her ambition was to shine in tragedy, but for this she was quite unsuited. Most of her career was spent at Drury Lane, where she appeared with Garrick,

MACKLIN, and Cibber. She wrote four dramatic sketches, *The Rehearsal* being the most popular and the only one printed. Her acting was much admired by Johnson, Handel, and GOLDSMITH. In 1731 she married George Clive, a barrister, from whom she was soon separated. She retired from the stage on 24 April 1769, Garrick playing opposite her in her final appearance as a mark of his friendship, and went to live near Strawberry Hill, Surrey, in a small house, Clive's Den, presented to her by Horace Walpole. Here her sprightly humour and shrewd talk were relished by many visitors. She died there, 6 December 1785.

CLONMELL, EARL OF. See under SCOTT, JOHN.

CLOSE, FATHER LEO (1934–1977), paraplegic. Born Dublin. Educated at Belvedere College, Cistercian College, Roscrea and UCD. Studied for the priesthood at All Hallows' College, Dublin. At twenty-one he broke his back in an accident during a tour of shrines in France and was paralysed from the chest down. In 1959 he became the first priest to be ordained in a wheelchair. With others, he founded the Irish Wheelchair Association in 1960 and was the driving force behind it in its early years. He represented Ireland in the Paraplegic Olympic Games at Rome, 1960, Tokyo, 1964, and New Zealand at Tel Aviv, 1968, winning gold and silver medals in field and archery events. In 1964 he was appointed head of religious studies for New Zealand at Dunedin. He also founded a wheelchair association in New Zealand, was awarded the OBE, and became a national figure. He died in January 1977.

COFFEY, DENIS J. (1865–1945), physician and first president of UCD. Born Tralee, Co. Kerry. Educated Holy Cross Schools, Tralee, Cecilia Street Medical School, Dublin, and universities of Louvain, Madrid, and Leipzig. Professor of physiology at Cecilia Street

1893. Lecturer in Physiology at St Patrick's College, Maynooth, for some years. Registrar of the medical school in 1905, and in 1908 the first president of UCD. Represented the National University on the General Medical Council from 1919 until his death, Ireland's representative on the Health Council of the League of Nations. Between 1927 and 1945 he was chairman of the Medical Registration Council of Éire. A member of the Céitinn Branch of the Gaelic League and played a prominent part in the language movement. Distinctions included D.Sc. and LL.D., Dublin University, honorary member RCPI, *Croix de Chevalier* of the Legion of Honour, and Grand Cross of the Order of St Sylvester. He retired in 1940 and died in Dublin on 3 April 1945.

COIMÍN, MÍCHEÁL (1688–1760) (Michael Comyn), poet. Born Kilcorcoran, near Milltown Malbay, Co. Clare. The family lost their estates in the Cromwellian confiscations, but were granted a substantial farm in 1675, and lived in comfortable circumstances. It is said that Mícheál abducted a young woman, Harriet Stacpoole, in the fashion of the time for young bloods. He wrote *Laoi Oisín*, a poem describing Oisín's journey to the land of youth, Tír na nÓg, now studied as a classic. Circulated in manuscript copies for over a hundred years, as far afield as the Hebrides. His other best-known work is a wonder-tale, *Toirealach Mac Stairn.* When he died, his son Edward burned all his manuscripts. Only eight or nine of his poems survive, three of them on the abduction.

COLBERT, CON (1888–1916), revolutionary. Born Monalena, Co. Limerick. Educated at North Richmond St CBS after family moved to Dublin. Worked in Kennedy's bakery, Parnell St. Soon became interested in the movement for independence, became an Irish-speaker, and joined Na Fianna Éireann on its formation by MARKIEVICZ in 1909. Later joined the IRB and the Irish Volunteers.

In the 1916 Rising commanded the garrison in Watkins's brewery in Ardee St, moving to Jameson's distillery as the fighting increased. Court-martialled, sentenced to death, and executed at Kilmainham Jail on 8 May 1916.

COLGAN, JOHN (*c.* 1592–1658), hagiographer. Born near Carndonagh, Co. Donegal. Little is known about his early years. Probably left Ireland for Spain or Belgium about 1612, was ordained 1618 and entered the Franciscan order at Louvain 1620. Taught in Germany, then returned to Louvain. Joined Father Aodh Mac an Bhaird in compiling an ecclesiastical history of Ireland and lives of the Irish saints, *Acta Sanctorum*, containing lives of the Irish saints with feast-days in January, February and March, published Louvain 1645, and *Triadis Thaumaturgae*, lives of Sts Patrick, Brigid and Colmcille, 1647. A third volume remains unpublished. Published a life of JOHANNES DUNS SCOTUS (1655). Died at Louvain. Colgan was the first to apply the title *The Annals of the Four Masters* to the work of his contemporary MICHAEL O'CLERY and his associates.

COLLES, ABRAHAM (1773–1843), surgeon. Born Millmount near Kilkenny. Educated Kilkenny grammar school and TCD. Studied medicine at College of Surgeons, Dublin, Edinburgh, and London, returning to Dublin in 1797. Surgeon to Dr Steevens' Hospital 1799–1841 and professor of anatomy and surgery in the College of Surgeons 1804–1836. His name is remembered by 'Colles's fracture', a fracture of the radius just above the wrist, which he was first to describe precisely. President RCSI in 1802 and again in 1830; declined a baronetcy. Died in Dublin, 16 November 1843. Buried in Donnybrook cemetery.

COLLEY, GEORGE (1925–1983), politician. Born in Dublin in October 1925, son of Harry Colley (TD and former adjutant of IRA). Educated at Marino CBS, Dublin (where Charles

Haughey was a classmate), and UCD, and qualified as a solicitor. Elected TD for Dublin North-East 1961. Parliamentary Secretary to the Minister for Lands 1964, Minister for Education 1965, Minister for Industry and Commerce 1966. When SEÁN LEMASS announced his retirement in 1966, Colley and Haughey became candidates for leadership of Fianna Fáil, but when Jack Lynch belatedly agreed to go forward, Haughey withdrew. Colley was defeated by fifty-two votes to nineteen. In 1969 he became Minister for the Gaeltacht while retaining Industry and Commerce portfolio. Minister for Finance and the Gaeltacht 1970–1973. When Fianna Fáil returned to power in 1977 he became Tánaiste and Minister for Finance and the Public Service. On resignation of Lynch in 1979 he competed for the leadership against Haughey but was defeated by six votes. After the general election of 1982, Haughey refused to appoint Colley as Tánaiste. Colley insisted on a veto on the Justice and Defence portfolios. This was refused and he declined a ministerial post, retiring to the back benches. He died 17 September 1983, survived by his wife, Mary, three sons and four daughters. Political parties united in tributes to him as a man of honour and integrity, who remained faithful to the earlier republican traditions.

COLLIE, GEORGE (1904–1975), portrait painter. Born Carrickmacross, Co. Monaghan. Educated St Kevin's School, Blackpitts, Dublin, RHA, and Metropolitan School of Art. Won Taylor Art Scholarship 1927 and travelling scholarship awarded for exceptional merit. Continued his studies at Royal College of Arts in London under William Rothenstein and in Paris at Grande Chaumerie and Académie Colorossie. Returning to Dublin, taught in National College of Art, then opened his own studio and school in Schoolhouse Lane, Dublin. Became well known as a portrait painter in the academic style. Works included portraits of CARDINAL D'ALTON, other bishops, and prominent politicians, including PRESIDENT DE VALERA. He ran his school to within a few weeks of his death in Dublin on 1 July 1975.

COLLIER, PETER FENELON (1846–1909), pioneer subscription publisher. Born Myshall, Co. Carlow, 12 December 1846. Emigrated to USA 1866. Entered St Mary's Seminary, Cincinnati, Ohio, but did not become a priest, entering the publishing business instead. Started printing books from a basement store in New York, 1875. Sold on the instalment plan, the first publisher to use this method. In 1888 he launched a popular magazine, *Once a Week*, which became *Collier's, the National Weekly* in 1895. The business flourished from the start. *Collier's* grew to a paid circulation of 3,200,000. With his son Robert he published Dr Eliot's 'Five-Foot Shelf of Books', the Harvard Classics. More than 400,000 of these fifty-volume sets were sold by 1950. He raised funds to buy the old Lincoln farm in Kentucky and had a granite memorial erected at the site of the log cabin in which President Lincoln was born. Died in New York, 24 April 1909.

COLLINS, MICHAEL (1890–1922), revolutionary leader. Born 16 October 1890, Woodfield, Clonakilty, Co. Cork, son of a small farmer. Educated at Clonakilty NS. At sixteen went to London as a clerk, first in the Post Office and then with a firm of stockbrokers. Joined the IRB in London and came to Dublin to fight in the GPO in the 1916 Rising. Imprisoned until December 1916 and on release became prominent in Sinn Féin and Volunteer movements, and a member of the Supreme Council of the IRB, a position of considerable power. After victory of Sinn Féin in 1918 general election and establishment of Dáil Éireann, made Minister of Home Affairs and later Minister for Finance. Also director of organisation and intelligence for the Volunteers. Collins was responsible for the success of Dáil loans at home and in the USA, where they were heavily over-subscribed. He organised the supply of arms and ammunition for the Volunteers, and set up an intelligence system that kept him well informed of the plans of the British. With his organising ability went great physical energy, courage, and force of character. A member of the delegation that negotiated the Anglo-Irish Treaty of 6 December 1921; became chairman of the Provisional Government formed to implement it. After the outbreak of the Civil War in June 1922, he became Commander-in-Chief of the government forces. On 22 August 1922, at an ambush at Béal na Bláth, Co. Cork, he was shot in the head and died almost immediately. Buried in Glasnevin cemetery, Dublin.

COLLINS, THOMAS J. (1894–1972), co-editor of *Dublin Opinion*. Born Dublin, educated Rockwell College and UCD. Served in the Department of Education 1912–1934. In March 1922, C. E. KELLY, a colleague in the department, asked him to contribute to *Dublin Opinion*, a national humorous monthly just founded by Arthur Booth. Booth died in 1926, and Collins and Kelly formed a new company and continued the magazine. They were joint editors, 'both distinct and equal in all things', for forty-two years, until *Dublin Opinion* was voluntarily wound up by them in December 1968. (It was revived in 1987.) Collins contributed poems, stories, and articles, and set the tone: gentle humour rather than satire. Also co-author with Father Aindrias Mac Aogáin of two operettas, *Trághadh na Taoide* ('The Turning of the Tide'), and *Nocturne sa Chearnóg* ('Nocturne in the Square'), produced Gaiety Theatre, Dublin, in the 1940s. Died Dublin, 1 April 1972.

COLLIS, JOHN STEWART (1900–1984), author, brother of MAURICE and of WILLIAM ROBERT COLLIS. Born in Dublin, educated at Rugby and at Balliol College, Oxford. Devoted himself to country life in England and spent Second World War working as a farm labourer in Dorset. *While Following the Plough* (1946) and *Down to Earth* (1947) established his reputation among conservationists. Wrote other books on nature, an autobiography, *Bound Upon a Course* (1971), and studies of SHAW, Columbus, the Carlyles, and Tolstoy. His first wife died in 1970 after years of illness. He died in England in March 1984, survived by his second wife and two daughters.

COLLIS, MAURICE STEWART (1889–1973), author. Born Dublin, 10 January 1889. Educated Rugby School and Corpus Christi College, Oxford. Joined Indian civil service 1911. Served twenty-five years in Burma. District magistrate at Rangoon 1928. In First World War served in India and Palestine. His sympathy with Burmese nationalism did not help his career, and in 1936 he retired to England to write. Successful with his first book, *Siamese White*, a study of Samuel White, traveller and adventurer. Published some twenty-nine books, including novels, biographies, and historical works. They were translated into many European languages as well as Burmese and Thai. Some became best-sellers. In 1957, aged sixty-eight, he took up painting, and held one-man exhibitions in London. Became an art critic and founder-member of the International Association of Art Critics. Contributed art criticism to the *Observer, Sunday Telegraph*, and other periodicals, and wrote *The Discovery of L. S. Lowry* and a biography of Stanley Spencer. Died in London in January 1973.

COLLIS, WILLIAM ROBERT FITZGERALD (1900–1975), physician and author, brother of MAURICE. Born Killiney, Co. Dublin. Educated Aravon School, Bray, Rugby School, Trinity College, Cambridge, Yale University, and King's College Hospital, London. Joined the British army in 1918 as a cadet. Resigned after a year to study medicine. Appointed director of the Department of Pediatrics at Rotunda Hospital, Dublin, and in 1932 physician to National Children's Hospital. Contributed to medical journals and published a standard textbook on diseases of children. Played rugby for Cambridge, and for Ireland 1924-1926. Autobiography *The Silver Fleece* (1936). From his experiences of the life of the underprivileged in Dublin he wrote two plays, *Marrowbone Lane* and *The Barrel Organ*, both successfully produced in Dublin. After the Second World War, one of the first doctors to enter Belsen concentration camp, and led relief work for the child victims. In 1957 he went to Nigeria to establish the faculty of pediatrics in the University of Ibadan. Worked there for almost ten years as a doctor and teacher. From those experiences came two further books, *The Ultimate Value* (1951), on refugee children, and *A Doctor's Nigeria* (1960). He died, after a riding accident, at his home, Bo-Island, Newtownmountkennedy, Co. Wicklow, 27 May 1975. A second autobiography, *To Be a Pilgrim*, was published posthumously in 1975.

COLMCILLE, SAINT (521-597), one of the three patron saints of Ireland. Born Gartan, Co. Donegal, of royal blood from both parents. According to O'Donnell's *Life*, he was baptised Crimthann, and his name was changed to Colmcille, the 'dove of the church', by angelic intervention. He was educated at the great monastic schools of Moville and Clonard. After ordination he spent about fifteen years travelling around Ireland, preaching and founding monasteries, notably those at Derry, Swords, Durrow, and Kells. In 563 Colmcille sailed with twelve others to Iona Island, founded a monastery there, and set out to convert the Pictish tribes in Scotland. Missionary zeal was his inspiration, according to ADAMNÁN, his biographer, and to earlier sources, but tradition ascribes his exile to a quarrel with the high king of Ireland. Colmcille made a surreptitious copy of a psaltery, the property of St Finnian of Moville. The ensuing dispute over ownership was settled by a judgment from the high king,

Diarmuid, who said, 'To every cow its calf and to every book its copy.' Soon after, a hostage who had taken refuge from Diarmuid with Colmcille was seized and slain. Colmcille aroused his sept, the Uí Néill, and the high king was defeated at the battle of Cuildreimhne in 561. A synod at Teltown, Co. Meath, censured Colmcille and sentenced him to exile. Another account says that he sought counsel of St Molaise, who advised him to expiate his offence by winning for Christ as many souls as had perished at Cuildreimhne. Whatever his inspiration, Colmcille's mission to Scotland flourished, he founded numerous monasteries, and his influence spread from Dál Riada (Argyll) over most of Scotland. He kept in touch with Ireland, and in 575 he attended the Council of Druim Ceat in Co. Meath. Here he succeeded in preventing the abolition of the bardic order, whose members had grown arrogant and extortionate as a result of years of privilege, and defended the status of his Dál Riada kinsmen in Scotland. He died at Iona, probably in June 597, and was buried at the monastery. A rule he had drawn up for his monks was followed in many of the monasteries of western Europe until it was superseded by the milder ordinances of St Benedict. A large number of poems, in Latin and in Irish, have been ascribed to him; the few that can be accepted as authentic show that he had true poetic gifts. Tradition counts him as one of the great monastic scribes, and in the *Annals of Clonmacnoise* it is stated that he wrote three hundred books with his own hand. Tradition also ascribes to him the *Cathach*, a Latin manuscript of the psalms, probably the oldest surviving piece of writing in Ireland.

COLUM, MARY (1884-1957), writer. Born Collooney, Co. Sligo, 13 June 1884. Taught at St Enda's school under PEARSE. Married PÁDRAIC COLUM in 1912. Went with him to USA in 1914 and taught in Columbia University. Published *From These Roots* (1937), essays on modern literature; *Life and the Dream* (1947), an autobiography; and, in conjunction with her husband, *Our Friend James Joyce* (1958). Died New York, 22 October 1957.

COLUM, PÁDRAIC (1881–1972), poet and dramatist. Born 8 December 1881 in Longford, where his father was master of the workhouse, and brought up in Co. Cavan on the farm of his grandfather. Later his father became stationmaster at Sandycove, Co. Dublin. Colum's first job was a clerkship in the railway clearing-house in Kildare St, Dublin. He began to write for the theatre in 1903 when *Broken Soil*, later called *The Fiddler's House*, was produced, followed by *The Land* (1905), and *Thomas Muskerry* (1910), the story of a workhouse master. About this time he wrote his two best-known lyrics, 'She Moved Through the Fair' and 'A Cradle Song'. His first collection of poems, *Wild Earth*, appeared in 1907. With JAMES STEPHENS and THOMAS MACDONAGH he founded the *Irish Review*. In 1912 he married Mary Maguire (see COLUM, MARY), and in 1914 they moved to the USA, where they both became teachers of comparative literature at Columbia University, New York. He found additional remunerative work writing a series of folk tales, including legends of Hawaii, for the *New York Tribune*, and in 1923 the Hawaiian legislature invited him to make a survey of their native myths and folklore and edit them as stories for Hawaiian children. He continued to write and lecture in the USA, and his *Collected Poems* appeared in 1953. In 1954 he was awarded the Gregory Medal of the Irish Academy of Letters, presented every three years for outstanding literary work. UCD and Columbia University honoured him with doctorates in 1958. In 1958 he published *Our Friend James Joyce* in collaboration with his wife, and in 1960 a biography of ARTHUR GRIFFITH. The American-Irish Foundation presented him with a cash award and a scroll of appreciation to mark his ninetieth birthday. He was the last living link with YEATS, SYNGE, LADY GREGORY, and the early days of the Irish literary revival, and his great age did not impair his mental vigour. He made frequent extended visits to Ireland to renew friendships with writers and artists, and was president of the United Arts Club, Dublin, for many years until his death. He died in Enfield, Connecticut, 11 January 1972, and is buried in St Fintan's Cemetery, Sutton, Co. Dublin.

COLUMBANUS, SAINT (c. 543–615), missionary. Born in Leinster and while still young entered Bangor monastery, Co. Down, and studied there under Comgall for many years. Wishing to spread the Gospel, he went to Burgundy with twelve companions about 590, and journeyed through France, preaching to the Gauls. He founded monasteries at Luxeuil and Fontaines in the Vosges district. In 610 Theodoric II of Burgundy, angered at the saint's condemnation of the immorality of the court, banished him from the country. After travelling through Switzerland he settled at Bobbio in Italy where he founded a monastery on land granted to him by Agilulf, King of the Lombards, who held him in great honour. He died there in 615. A number of his writings, all in Latin, have survived; they include his Rule, letters, poems, and sermons.

CONGREVE, WILLIAM (1670–1729), dramatist. Born at Bardsey near Leeds. His father's regiment was posted to Ireland when he was four. Educated with SWIFT at Kilkenny School and TCD; they remained friends for life. Entered Middle Temple, London, 1691 but abandoned law for literature, encouraged by Dryden. His play *The Mourning Bride* was very successful, others moderately so. His masterpiece, *The Way of the World*, a witty comedy of manners, was a failure on the stage. He wrote little after that, living as a retired gentleman on government sinecures.

CONNELL, JAMES (c. 1850–1929), writer. Born Killskyre, Co. Meath. A

Fenian and a Land-Leaguer, had a varied career as sheep farmer, labourer, journalist, and self-taught lawyer. Went to London, joined the Social Democratic Federation, and became secretary of the Workmen's Legal Friendly Society. Wrote some political works and 'The Red Flag', which became the socialist anthem. Connell wrote the song during the great dock strike of 1889. It appeared in the socialist magazine *Justice*, and in 1895 was set by a Mr Headingly to an old German air, 'Tannenbaum', although Connell had in mind the air of the lively Jacobite song 'The White Cockade'. In 1924 Ramsay MacDonald, Labour Prime Minister, tried to oust it and had a competition to find a substitute, but the judges, JOHN MCCORMACK and Sir Hugh Roberton, said none of the 300 entries could match 'The Red Flag', and so it remained the socialist anthem, to the great delight of its then aged author. Died 8 February 1929, probably in London, where he had lived for years previously.

CONNELL, NORREYS. See under O'RIORDAN, CONAL.

CONNELL, VIVIAN (1905–1981), novelist and playwright. Born at Carrigaline, Co. Cork, son of a doctor. He said that he was taught to read and write by his father and gathered the rest of his education in pubs, on the hurling-field, and following the hounds. His first story was published by GEORGE RUSSELL in the *Irish Statesman*. He left Ireland when he was thirty and lived in England, Italy, France, Spain, and Cyprus. His most successful novel, *The Chinese Room* (1942), sold over three million copies, mostly in the USA; his most successful play was *The Nineteenth Hole of Europe* (1943). Several of his books were banned in Ireland. His marriage in England to a Cork woman, Anne Herrick, ended in divorce. She died in 1974. In 1969 he returned to Ireland. He lived alone in Bray, Co. Wicklow, for some years and died there in March 1981, survived by two sons and a daughter who live in the USA.

CONNELLAN, OWEN (1800–1869), scholar. Born Co. Sligo. First job was a scribe in the RIA, where he worked for twenty years, copying, among other manuscripts, the Books of Lecan and Ballymote. Appointed professor of Irish at Queen's College, Cork, about 1845, and held the chair until his death. Published *A Practical Grammar of the Irish Language* (1844). His most important work was an edition of *Imtheacht na Tromdháimhe* (1860), the story of the finding of the *Táin*. Died in Dublin.

CONNOLLY, JAMES (1868–1916), socialist. Born of Irish immigrant parents in the Cowgate, an Edinburgh slum, on 5 June 1868. Went to work at eleven. At fourteen he joined the British army and was stationed in the Curragh and Dublin, deserting to marry in Scotland a girl from Co. Wicklow. In Edinburgh he worked as a carter and became active in socialist and trade union affairs. In 1896 he came to Ireland as paid organiser of the Dublin Socialist Club, and founded *The Workers' Republic*, the first Irish socialist paper. From these beginnings he developed the Irish Socialist Republican Party, to secure 'the national and economic freedom of the Irish people'. He made a name for himself as a journalist and lecturer, and toured Britain and the USA in 1902. He returned to America in 1903 and stayed there seven years. He founded the Irish Socialist Federation in New York, published a monthly magazine, *The Harp*, and helped to found the 'Wobblies', the Industrial Workers of the World. He returned to Ireland in 1910 and became Ulster organiser for the Irish Transport Workers' Union. When the Dublin employers resorted to a lockout in 1913 in their fight against the unions, Connolly led the workers when LARKIN was sent to prison. The suffering of the workers and their families turned his mind to political action and he organised the Irish Citizen Army at Liberty Hall, the headquarters of the Transport Union. He saw capitalism as the great enemy to peace and social justice and, in

Larkin's absence in America in 1914, committed the labour movement to opposition to the Allies. When the secret military council of the IRB decided on an armed rising in 1916, Connolly took part in the preparations with PEARSE and MACDONAGH, and was appointed military commander of the Republican forces in Dublin, including his own Citizen Army. He was in command of the GPO during Easter week, and was badly wounded. One of the seven signatories of the Proclamation of the Irish Republic, he was executed by firing squad in Kilmainham Jail, 12 May 1916, while tied to a chair, as he could not stand. Connolly's writings, principally on labour and revolutionary socialism, appeared in a variety of periodicals over the years. *Labour in Irish History* (1910) is his most sustained work.

CONNOLLY, RODDY (1901–1980), politician. Served as a fifteen-year-old lieutenant with the Irish Citizen Army under his father, JAMES CONNOLLY, and took part in the 1916 Rising. Imprisoned for a short period. Joined the first Communist Party in Ireland and was editor of the party journal. Sent to Russia in 1920 to affiliate the party to the Communist International and met Lenin and Zinoviev. After the party broke up he joined the Labour Party in 1927. TD for Louth 1943–1944 and 1948–1951, senator 1975–77. Chairman of the Labour Party 1971–1978. Died 16 December 1980, survived by his wife, sons, and daughters.

CONNOR, BERNARD (*c*. 1666–1698), physician. Born Co. Kerry. At twenty he went to University of Montpellier to study medicine, then to Reims where he graduated doctor of physics in 1691, and to Paris. He was selected to take charge of the two sons of the High Chancellor of Poland, and travelled with them to Italy. At Venice he cured the fever-stricken William Legge, Earl of Dartmouth. Travelled through Bavaria and Austria, where he stayed at the court of the Emperor Leopold. In 1694,

at twenty-eight, he was appointed court physician by Jan Sobieski, king of Poland. Before returning to England in 1695, Connor accompanied the Polish king's daughter, Teresa Cunigunda, to Brussels to marry the Elector of Bavaria. In England he lectured on anatomy and physiology at Oxford and wrote *Dissertationes Medico-Physicae*. Elected FRS and in August 1696 became licentiate of College of Physicians, London. Became a member of the French Academy. Invited to lecture at Cambridge University. In *Evangelum Medici* (1697), Connor insists on the intrinsic probability of all miracles. His two-volume *History of Poland* was published in 1698. He died of fever in October 1698.

CONNOR, JEROME (1876–1943), sculptor. Born Patrick Jeremias Connor at Coomduff, near Anascaul, Co. Kerry, on 12 October 1876, son of a small farmer. The family emigrated to Holyoke, Massachusetts, when he was very young. In 1889 he ran away from home, and worked successively as sign painter, machinist, stone-cutter, and sculptor. He first exhibited sculpture in Philadelphia. From 1898 to 1903 he lived and worked with the Roycroft colony, a cultural centre for craftsmen at East Aurora, near Buffalo, New York. Connor did metal work, casting in plaster, and sculpture, in the workshops of the centre. He visited Italy about 1903 and then settled in Syracuse, New York, where he opened his own studio. His first big commission was the marble memorial to the American poet Walt Whitman. In 1912 he completed the Archbishop Carroll monument for Georgetown Catholic University, and in 1917 his statue of ROBERT EMMET was placed in the Smithsonian Institution in Washington. A cast of this statue is in St Stephen's Green, Dublin. He was a strong supporter of the Irish independence movement, and in 1921 exhibited a portrait head of ÉAMON DE VALERA at the Philadelphia Exhibition of Fine Arts. In 1924 his memorial sculpture 'Angels of the Battlefield' was completed, and placed in Washington. He returned to Ireland in July 1925 to work for an American committee on a memorial in Cóbh, Co. Cork, to those drowned when the *Lusitania* was torpedoed by a German submarine off the Old Head of Kinsale on 7 May 1915. This work occupied him on and off for the following fourteen years, with visits to the USA for consultation with the committee. In between, he submitted designs for a new Irish coinage and executed a series of relief portraits of the Irish Free State government. This series was exhibited at the RA in 1931, where he also showed in 1929 and 1930. In the early 1930s he worked on several commissions that proved abortive, including the 'Tralee Pikeman' and a memorial to the 'Four Kerry Poets' for Killarney. This latter involved him in a lawsuit, and in July 1936 he became a bankrupt. Between then and his death he made a living by selling small bronzes to his friends and acquaintances. He also exhibited these 'little pieces of free work', as he called them, at the New York World Fair and the RHA. He died in the Adelaide Hospital, Dublin, in August 1943 and is buried in Mount Jerome cemetery.

CONOR, WILLIAM (1881–1968), painter. Born Old Lodge Road, Belfast. Studied at Belfast College of Art. Joined the printing firm of David Allen as apprentice in the poster department, at 4 shillings and 6 pence (22½p) weekly. By painting in his spare time and selling where he could, he saved enough money to study further in Dublin and Paris. He first exhibited in Belfast in 1914, and during the First World War was commissioned by the British government to make official records of soldiers and munition workers. For fifty years he made studies in oil, charcoal and watercolours of the children, mill-workers and shipyard men of his native Belfast. Elected RHA in 1947 and in 1952 received the OBE. A retrospective exhibition of his work was held in 1957 in the Belfast City Art Gallery. That year he received an honorary MA from Queen's University. In the Conor Room at the Ulster Folk Museum fifty of his paintings and drawings are on permanent exhibition, a tribute to the commentary on the social life of Ulster made by his paintings. He said that he spelled his name with only one *n* because he 'could never make *n*'s meet'. He died in Belfast on 6 February 1968.

CONWAY, ARTHUR WILLIAM (1875–1950), mathematician and president of UCD. Born in Wexford, 2 October 1875. Educated at St Peter's College, Wexford, UCD, and Corpus Christi College, Oxford. Appointed professor of mathematical physics at UCD (then administered by the Jesuits) in 1901 and continued in same chair after establishment of UCD as constituent College of NUI. Registrar of UCD from 1908. Elected FRS in 1915. Became world authority on quaternions. Published the mathematical works of WILLIAM ROWAN HAMILTON, volume I (RIA, 1931) with J. L. Synge and volume II (RIA, 1940) with A. J. McConnell. Elected in 1939 to Papal Academy of Sciences to fill vacancy on death of Lord Rutherford. President RIA 1939–1940, and president RDS 1942–1945. Honorary fellow Corpus Christi College, 1940. He advised ÉAMON DE VALERA on the establishment of the Dublin Institute of Advanced Studies in 1940 and became chairman of the board of its School of Theoretical Physics. In April 1940 he was elected president of UCD. His willingness to delegate authority to college officers contrasted with the personal rule of his predecessor, Dr Denis Coffey, and his open, friendly style smoothed difficulties arising from rapid expansion. He was a familiar and genial figure at mathematical congresses abroad. Received honorary doctorates from TCD and St Andrew's University, Scotland. He retired in October 1947 and died in July 1950.

CONWAY, EDWARD JOSEPH (1894–1968), biochemist. Born 3 July

1894 in Nenagh, Co. Tipperary. Educated at Blackrock College and UCD, where he obtained his M.Sc. and graduated in medicine in 1921. After winning a studentship to the University of Frankfurt and taking his D.Sc., he became professor of biochemistry and pharmacology at UCD in 1932. For his studies of electrolytes he was elected FRS in 1947. In 1967 he received the Boyle Medal of the RDS, the premier award in science in Ireland. He contributed a number of papers to scientific journals in many countries, spoke at numerous international conferences, and was honoured by leading medical and scientific bodies at home and abroad. He died in Dublin on 29 December 1968.

CONWAY, CARDINAL WILLIAM (1913–1977), Archbishop of Armagh and Primate of All Ireland. Born 22 January 1913 at 108 Dover Street (now demolished), Belfast. Educated at Boundary Street Primary School, Barrack Street CBS, and QUB. Entered Maynooth seminary, ordained 1937; DD 1938. Studied canon law at Gregorian University, Rome, 1938–1941. Taught English and Latin at St Malachy's College, Belfast, 1941–1942. Appointed professor of moral theology at Maynooth 1942 and professor of canon law 1943, holding both chairs until 1958. Vice-president 1957. Edited *Irish Theological Quarterly* for a time. Contributed to it and other religious journals. Published *Problems of Canon Law* (1950). Titular bishop of Neve and auxiliary to CARDINAL D'ALTON 1958, and administrator of St Mary's parish, Dundalk, Co. Louth. Appointed archbishop of Armagh and primate of All Ireland 9 September 1963. Created cardinal 22 February 1965. He spoke frequently at Second Vatican Council and was one of three chairmen of the first Synod of Bishops, Rome, 1967. Member of four Vatican congregations, those for bishops, clergy, evangelisation of peoples, and Catholic education. 'Trócaire', the Catholic agency for development aid to the Third World,

was established mainly on his initiative. Member of the Pontifical Commission for the Revision of Canon Law, which is carrying out the first major revision since 1918. Died at his house in Armagh, 17 April 1977.

COOKE, HENRY (1788–1868), Presbyterian leader. Born Grillagh, Co. Derry, 11 May 1788. Educated locally and Glasgow College. Ordained in 1808, then studied at Glasgow, TCD, and Royal College of Surgeons. He was then called to Killelagh, Co. Down, and in 1829 to May Street, Belfast, where a church had been specially built for him. He became the architect and leader of a Protestant party in Ulster politics and the presiding spirit of Irish Presbyterianism. He opposed the Unitarians and had them expelled from the Synod of Ulster. His preaching drew immense crowds. When DANIEL O'CONNELL visited Belfast during his campaign for the repeal of the Union, Cooke inspired a huge anti-repeal meeting. His energy was phenomenal; he rose at four, needed little sleep, and poured out a constant flow of pamphlets, sermons, and magazine articles. When the new Board of National Education for Ireland was established, he saw a threat to Protestant education. The Synod, under his guidance, organised their own scheme, and in 1840 secured recognition from the Board. He was also instrumental in obtaining government endowment for a theological college in Belfast under the General Assembly. Presbyterian dean of residence, Queen's College, Belfast, 1849. Professor of rhetoric in the Theological College of the General Assembly 1855. He died at his house in Ormeau Road, Belfast, on 13 December 1868. His statue, erected in Belfast in 1875, was long regarded as a symbol of Protestantism in the North of Ireland.

COOPER, EDWARD JOSHUA (1798–1863), astronomer. Born St Stephen's Green, Dublin, in May 1798. Educated at Armagh, Eton, and Christ Church, Oxford. Left university without a degree and spent the next decade travelling. In 1820–1821 visited Egypt to obtain accurate copies of the Dendera and Esneh zodiacs and on his return published *Views in Egypt and Nubia* (1824). In 1830 succeeded his father at Markree Castle, Co. Sligo, and erected an observatory there. Between 1842 and 1843 determined the position of fifty stars within two degrees of the pole and made systematic meridian observations of minor planets. He kept meteorological records for thirty years from 1833. In 1844–1845, with his assistant, Andrew Graham, made an astronomical tour through France, Germany, and Italy. His *Catalogue of Stars Near the Ecliptic Observed at Markree* (Dublin, 1851–1856) contained approximate places of 60,066 stars, of which only 8,965 were already known. The *Cometic Orbits with Copious Notes and Addenda* (1852) contained data relative to 198 comets. Elected FRS 1853. Awarded the Cunningham Gold Medal of the RIA in 1858. Conservative MP for Co. Sligo 1830–1841 and 1857–1859. Died at Markree on 23 April 1863.

CORBET, WILLIAM (1779–1842), United Irishman. Born Ballythomas, Co. Cork, 17 August 1779. Educated at TCD. Joined the Society of United Irishmen and was expelled from college. Making his way to France, he joined NAPPER TANDY in his expedition to Ireland in 1798, but did not succeed in landing. On his return to the Continent he was arrested by the British in Hamburg and imprisoned in Kilmainham Jail in Dublin. He escaped in 1803 and, returning to France, joined the army and distinguished himself in campaigns in Portugal and Germany, being made a commander of the Legion of Honour. His last service was in Greece, where he helped to place King Otho on the throne and became commander-in-chief of the French forces in 1832, with the rank of general. He died at Saint Denis, 12 August 1842.

CORKERY, DANIEL (1878–1964), writer and teacher. Born 14 February 1878 at 1 Gardiner's Hill, Cork. Educated at the Presentation Brothers' school and then trained as a teacher at St Patrick's College, Dublin. His early years teaching were spent at St Francis' and St Patrick's schools in Cork. He resigned from St Patrick's in 1921 when he was refused the headmastership. He learnt Irish in his late twenties, and in 1908, with his friends TERENCE MACSWINEY and Con O'Leary, founded the Cork Dramatic Society, for which he wrote plays in Irish and English. Published a collection of short stories, *A Munster Twilight* (1916), and a novel, *The Threshold of Quiet* (1917). Between 1922 and 1925 he taught art for the Cork County Technical Education Committee. In 1925 the committee appointed him inspector in Irish, and in 1930 he became professor of English at UCC. On retirement in 1947 the NUI made him D.Litt. Member of the Arts Council 1950, and senator 1951–1954. Plays included *The Labour Leader,* performed by the Abbey in 1919, *The Yellow Bittern* (1920), and *Resurrection* (1924). He wrote several volumes of short stories, among them *The Hounds of Banba* (1920), *The Stormy Hills* (1929), and *Earth out of Earth* (1939). Other publications include *The Hidden Ireland* (1924), *Synge and Anglo-Irish Literature* (1931), and *The Fortunes of the Irish Language* (1954). By opening his readers' eyes to the forgotten riches of eighteenth-century Gaelic poetry and awakening a realisation of their ancient cultural heritage, *The Hidden Ireland* stimulated strong, sometimes aggressive, nationalist feelings. To a lesser extent he became known as a watercolour artist. He died at Passage West, Co. Cork, on 31 Decmeber 1964.

CORRIGAN, SIR DOMINIC (1802–1880), physician. Born in Thomas Street, Dublin, on 2 December 1802 and educated at a lay school attached to Maynooth College. He then studied medicine at Edinburgh University, qualifying in 1825. Returning to Dublin he became physician to Jervis Street Infirmary and to Maynooth College. He discovered a disease of the valves of the heart, characterised by a peculiar pulse, still known as 'Corrigan's pulse'. Elected president RCPI five times. In 1866 he was made honorary physician in Ireland to Queen Victoria, the first Catholic to receive the appointment, and was made a baronet the same year. Liberal MP for Dublin 1870–1874. His practice became enormous; it was said that his fees amounted to £9,000 yearly. He built himself a mansion at Dalkey, Co. Dublin, with an aquarium and a private harbour. He died at home on 1 February 1880.

CORRY, ISAAC (1755–1813), politician. Born at Newry, Co. Down, educated TCD. Elected MP for Newry in 1776 in succession to his father. At first he took the side of the Volunteers, but then became a professional politician and accepted public office. Surveyor-general 1788, Chancellor of the Exchequer 1798, and surveyor-general of Crown Lands 1799. He was the principal government speaker in favour of the Union. Wounded in duel with GRATTAN 1800. Defeated at Newry 1806 and 1807. A failure in the English House of Commons, he lived to repent the Union, which had destroyed his political importance. Died Merrion Square, Dublin, 15 May 1813.

COSGRAVE, WILLIAM THOMAS (1880–1965), first President of the Executive Council of the Irish Free State. Born 174 James's Street, Dublin, 6 June 1880. Educated at local CBS. He shared his father's keen interest in local and national politics, and attended the first Sinn Féin convention in 1905. He was elected to Dublin City Council in 1909, and joined the Irish Volunteers on their formation in 1913. In the 1916 Rising he served at the South Dublin Union under ÉAMONN CEANNT, and was sentenced to death. The sentence was commuted to penal servitude for life, and he was interned at Frongoch in Wales until January 1917, when he was released under a general amnesty.

Elected Sinn Féin MP for Kilkenny at a by-election, and re-elected in the 1918 general election. A member of the first Dáil Éireann, and Minister for Local Government, with the task of organising a policy of non-cooperation with the British authorities and establishing an alternative system. Like other members of the Republican government he was arrested and imprisoned several times. He supported the 1921 Anglo-Irish Treaty, and after the sudden death of ARTHUR GRIFFITH on 12 August 1922, he became acting chairman of the provisional government. Ten days later, MICHAEL COLLINS was killed, and Cosgrave found himself in charge. After the enactment of the constitution of the Irish Free State in October 1922, he was appointed President of the Executive Council, and held this office until 1932. He served also, for short periods, as Minister for Finance, and as Minister for Defence in 1924, when a threatened army mutiny created a crisis. After the defeat of his party, Cumann na nGaedheal, in the general election of 1932, he led the opposition in Dáil Éireann until his retirement from politics in 1945. He became a member of the Irish Racing Board that year and served as chairman over a long period. In 1925 he was made a Knight of the Grand Cross of the Order of Pius IX, and he received honorary degrees from universities of Ireland, England, and America. He died in Dublin on 16 November 1965.

COSTELLO, JOHN ALOYSIUS (1891–1976), lawyer and Taoiseach in the first two Coalition governments. Born Dublin, 20 June 1891. Educated at O'Connell Schools and UCD, graduating in modern languages, including Irish, and in law. At the King's Inns won the Victoria Prize in 1913 and 1914. Called to the bar 1914. Joined staff of attorney-general 1922. Attorney-general 1926–1932. As attorney-general represented the government at Imperial Conferences and League of Nations. Called to the inner bar in 1925 and in

1926 elected a Bencher of the Honourable Society of King's Inns. Elected to the Dáil in 1933 for Co. Dublin. Subsequently sat for Dublin Townships and Dublin South-East. By 1948 he had become a leading counsel but not prominent in politics. In February 1948 was asked to become Taoiseach of an Inter-Party government as the one man who could unite the diverse political elements involved. This first Coalition under him saw two significant and controversial events, the declaration of a republic, and the 'Mother and Child' health scheme, which later led to the break-up of the government. The declaration that the state was a republic and that the External Relations Act would be repealed was made by Costello at a press conference in Canada on 7 September 1948, and the Republic of Ireland was formally inaugurated on Easter Monday 1949. The government had other noteworthy achievements. A new record was set in house-building, the Industrial Development Authority was established, and the Minister for Health, Dr Noël Browne, brought about a spectacular advance in the treatment of tuberculosis. The same minister produced a 'Mother and Child' health scheme in 1950 with no means test or income limit, for maternity and child health. The scheme was strongly opposed by the Catholic hierarchy, on the principle that provision for the health of children was an essential part of the responsibilities of parenthood. Government support for Dr Browne melted away in face of this determined opposition, and he resigned in April 1951. The Baltinglass Post Office affair of December 1950 cost the government the support of two Independent deputies when the Minister, JAMES EVERETT, tried to supplant a postmistress, Helen Cooke, whose family had held the position since 1870. A dispute with the farming community over the price of milk was another of the apparently unrelated incidents that led Costello to seek a dissolution of the Dáil in May 1951. After the general election of June 1951, Fianna Fáil formed a government, although not having a majority. In the next general election, in May 1954, Fianna Fáil was defeated and Costello again headed a Coalition government. With a comfortable majority, it seemed set for the full term, but an outbreak of militant republican activity in Northern Ireland and Britain caused internal strains. The government took strong action against the republicans. SEÁN MACBRIDE, the leader of Clann na Poblachta, tabled a motion of no confidence, based on the weakening state of the economy. Then Fianna Fáil tabled their own motion of no confidence and, rather than face almost certain defeat, Costello again asked the President to dissolve the Dáil and Seanad. In the general election of March 1957, DE VALERA won a record number of seats, and Fianna Fáil took office again. Costello returned to the bar, and for the second time overcame the tradition that a practice could not be built up again after years of absence. In 1959, when GENERAL MULCAHY resigned the leadership of Fine Gael to JAMES DILLON, Costello retired to the back benches. He was a member of the RIA from 1948, and received honorary degrees from many American universities. In March 1975 he was made a freeman of the city of Dublin, along with his old political opponent Éamon de Valera. He practised at the bar up to a short time before his death in Dublin on 5 January 1976.

COSTELLO, LOUISA STUART (1799–1870), miniaturist and writer. Born in Ireland and taken by her mother to Paris in 1814 after the death of her father. She became a skilled miniaturist, supporting her mother and brother by her work. She moved to London after some years, and the success of her first volumes of poetry decided her to devote herself to writing. Her many novels and travel books were highly popular and sold widely. Retiring to Boulogne in 1865 she died there, 24 April 1870.

COSTELLO, GENERAL MICHAEL JOSEPH (1904–1986), soldier and public servant. Born in Cloughjordan, Co. Tipperary, where both his parents were schoolteachers. He left Nenagh CBS at sixteen to join the IRA. After the Treaty he joined the National Army; appointed Director of Intelligence 1923. In 1926 he was sent with other officers on a training course with the US army at Fort Leavenworth: their report led to the establishment of the Military College in the Curragh in 1930. He was Director of Military Training in 1931, then Assistant Chief of Staff. General officer commanding Southern Command during the Second World War. In 1945 he retired from the army and joined Comhlacht Siúcra Éireann (the Irish Sugar Company) as general manager. Under his direction worker-management relations improved dramatically and the company's activities were considerably expanded. He pioneered scientific methods of seed breeding and testing, and of increasing beet crop output. In 1966 he resigned because of disagreement with the Government about the financing of Erin Foods, an associated company formed to process and market convenience and other foods. He then farmed at Roscommon for a number of years with two sons. He lectured extensively at home and abroad on agriculture and the co-operative movement, and was vice-president of the Military History Society. Never slow to express strongly held views, he opposed participation by the army in Remembrance Day celebrations organised by the British Legion. He died in a Dublin hospital on 20 October 1986, survived by eight sons and a daughter; his wife predeceased him by several years.

COTTER, PATRICK (*c.* 1761–1806), giant. Born Kinsale, Co. Cork. Hired at eighteen by a showman for exhibition in England for £50 for three years. Quarrelled with showman and imprisoned for debt. On release, established himself at Bristol Fair and earned £30 in three days. Travelled and showed himself until 1804 under name of O'Brien. Died in lodgings at Clifton, 8 September 1806,

leaving £2,000 to his mother. Coffin plate gave his stature as 97 inches (246 cm). He was a pituitary giant who developed acromegaly.

COULTER, THOMAS (1793–1843), physician and botanist. Born in Dundalk, Co. Louth, and studied medicine at TCD and Paris. He went to Mexico in 1925 as physician to a mining company and then became a mine manager. He travelled extensively in the USA, fishing, shooting, and botanising. After the failure of an alum company he had founded in Mexico, he returned to Ireland in 1834, bringing with him a large collection of dried plants and the giant cone of a Californian pine. He presented his collection to TCD and was given rooms in the college, where he lived until his death on 26 November 1843. Among the plants he brought home was the beautiful white matilija or Californian tree poppy, *Romneya coulteri*, well known to Irish gardeners.

COUSINS, JAMES HENRY SPROULL (1873–1956), writer and teacher. Born 18 Cavour St, Belfast, on 22 July 1873. Educated at local national school. Left school at thirteen. Worked as errand boy, office boy, and filing clerk. Private secretary to Sir Daniel Dixon, Lord Mayor of Belfast. Moved to Dublin 1897 as ledger clerk. Began to write, and became friendly with YEATS, RUSSELL, HYDE, MOORE, and MARTYN. His play *The Sleep of the King* was the first production by the Irish National Dramatic Company, on 29 October 1902; the cast included Frank Fay and Máire Nic Shiubhlaigh, later well-known Abbey Theatre players. About this time he became a vegetarian, which he remained for the rest of his life. In 1903 he married Margaret Gillespie at the Methodist Church, Sandymount. Two years later he became assistant master at the High School, then in Harcourt St, Dublin. In 1908 he joined the Theosophical Society, following Yeats and Russell. In 1913 he went to Liverpool to work with a vegetarian foods firm. A turning-point came in 1915 when he went to Madras, India, to become literary sub-editor of *New India*, published by Annie Besant, a leading theosophist. From then on he lived and worked in India, save for visits to Japan, Europe, and America. In 1916 he became lecturer in English and in 1917 vice-principal of the Theosophical College at Madanapalle and principal 1920–1922 and 1933–1938. In 1938 full-time art adviser to the government of Travancore. From 1949 to 1956 he was vice-president of Kalakshetra at Adyar, an international academy of the arts. Apart from some poems, plays, and school textbooks, the mass of his output of over a hundred books was published in India. He wrote a great deal on education, art, theosophy, and philosophy generally, and contributed hundreds of articles to Indian periodicals. He formed the first public art gallery in India, at Travancore, and another collection at Mysore. Two of his poems appear in the *Oxford Book of Irish Verse* (1958), edited by DONAGH MACDONAGH. *We Two Together*, an autobiography written in collaboration with his wife, MARGARET, was published at Madras in 1950. He died at the Mission Hospital, Madanapalle, on 20 February 1956.

COUSINS, MARGARET, née GILLESPIE (1878–1954), teacher and worker for women's rights. Born 7 November 1878, Belmont, Boyle, Co. Roscommon. Educated at local national school, Boyle intermediate school, and Victoria High School for girls, Derry. Studied music at RIAM, Dublin. Took B.Mus. at RUI. Taught in a kindergarten. After marriage in 1903 to JAMES H. COUSINS taught music part-time. Treasurer of the Irish Women's Franchise League 1908. One of six Irish delegates to the Parliament of Women in London, November 1910, and sentenced to six months' imprisonment for throwing stones at 10 Downing Street. She accompanied her husband to India in 1915 and continued her work for women. First non-Indian member of the Indian Women's University at Poona 1916. One of seventy founder-members of the Women's Indian Association 1917. Founder-headmistress of National Girls' School in Mangalore 1919–1920. Also occupied in philanthropic and social work. First woman magistrate in India. A theosophist, in 1928 awarded the Founder's Silver Medal of the Theosophical Society for her services to the movement. In 1932 she was imprisoned for a year for having addressed a public meeting at Madras in protest against emergency ordinances being incorporated into the ordinary penal code. Contributed many articles on art, philosophy and education to Indian periodicals, and published a number of books and pamphlets. She was paralysed from 1943 until her death in 1954. Friends and admirers presented her with 7,000 rupees in 1944 in appreciation of her services to India. In 1949 the Madras government presented her with 5,000 rupees in recognition of her services as a political sufferer for Indian freedom, and in 1953 Pandit Nehru, Prime Minister of India, sent her a gift cheque for 3,000 rupees. *We Two Together*, a joint autobiography, was published at Madras in 1950. She died at Adyar on 11 March 1954.

COX, ARTHUR (1891–1965), lawyer and priest. Born in Dublin in 1891 and educated at Belvedere College and UCD. He qualified as a solicitor in 1915 and became the leading Irish practitioner in commercial law. His firm acted for Siemens-Schuckert in the Shannon Scheme, for the ESB, Bord na Móna, Irish Life Assurance Company, and many other large corporations. He was a director of many companies, a member of Seanad Éireann as a nominee of the Taoiseach 1954–1957, and received an honorary LL.D. from NUI in 1952. He had married the widow of his friend KEVIN O'HIGGINS, and after her sudden death in 1961 he retired from practice and entered Milltown Park to study for the priesthood. He was ordained a Jesuit priest on 15 December 1963, went on the missions in Zambia, and was seriously injured in a car crash on 8 June 1965. He died some days later and is buried in Zambia.

COYNE, JOSEPH STIRLING (1803–1868), playwright. Born Birr, Co. Offaly. Educated at Dungannon school. After success with light articles in Dublin periodicals, abandoned law studies. His first farce was *The Phrenologist* (Theatre Royal, Dublin, June 1835), and the following year he produced two further farces, *Honest Cheats* and *The Four Lovers*. In 1836 went to London, and, through WILLIAM CARLETON and CROFTON CROKER, obtained employment with *Bentley's Miscellany* and other magazines. That year his farce *The Queer Subject* was produced at the Adelphi, and he joined the literary staff of the short-lived *Morning Gazette*, the first cheap daily London paper. His farce *How to Settle Accounts with Your Laundress* was played in Paris (*Une Femme Dans ma Fontaine*) and Germany. Another of his well-known dramas was *Everybody's Friend* (1859), later renamed *The Widow Hunt*. While producing dramas for the Adelphi and Haymarket theatres he continued to contribute to newspapers and periodicals. He was one of the founders of *Punch* in June 1841 and contributed to its first number. In 1856 he was appointed secretary to the Dramatic Authors' Society. A prolific author, at the time of his death he had written fifty-five dramas, burlesques, and farces, as well as several plays written in collaboration with other authors. He also wrote a two-volume work, *Scenery and Antiquities of Ireland* (1842). He died in London on 18 July 1868.

CRAIG, JAMES, first VISCOUNT CRAIGAVON (1871–1940), Unionist leader. Born Belfast, 8 January 1871, son of a wealthy distiller. Educated privately and at Merchiston College, Edinburgh. Became a stockbroker and served in the British army in the South African war. MP East Down 1906. Second only to CARSON in leading Northern Unionist resistance against Home Rule. While Carson, a forceful speaker, promoted this cause at Westminster and at public meetings, Craig organised the Ulster Volunteers for armed resistance if necessary. Quartermaster-general in Ulster Regiment in France 1914–1916. After First World War he held minor office in British government as parliamentary secretary. Knighted 1918. He succeeded Carson as leader of the Northern Unionists in February 1921, and in June 1921 became first prime minister of Northern Ireland, constituted under the Government of Ireland Act, 1920. Following series of attacks on Catholics in Northern Ireland he made a pact with COLLINS in mid-January 1922 promising protection to that minority in return for agreement to settle the boundary between representatives of both sides. A formal pact was signed in March between Northern and Southern governments on similar lines. Created Viscount Craigavon of Stormont 1927. In 1929 he abolished the proportional representation voting system, saying that the people did not understand the danger of making mistakes under it. In 1934 he told the House of Commons, 'We are a Protestant parliament and a Protestant state.' Prime minister until his sudden death at Glencarrig, Co. Down, on 24 November 1940. Buried at Stormont.

CRAIG, MAY (*c.* 1889–1972), actress. Born Dublin. Played with MOLLY ALLGOOD in original production of *The Playboy of the Western World*, Abbey Theatre, 1907. Joined Abbey company 1916 shortly after marriage to a young American, Vincent Power-Fardy. Her husband died about 1930, leaving her with five young children. Remained with the Abbey all her life. Made six tours of USA. Her favourite part was Mrs Tancred in O'CASEY's *Juno and the Paycock*. Her playing of the medium, Mrs Henderson, in *The Words Upon the Windowpane*, YEATS's play about SWIFT, had an unforgettable uncanny power. Died in a Dublin nursing home on 8 February 1972.

CRAMPTON, SIR PHILIP (1777–1858), surgeon. Born Dublin, 7 June 1777. Graduated in medicine at Glasgow 1800. Surgeon to the Meath Hospital, and built up a large private practice. Surgeon-general to the forces in Ireland and surgeon-in-ordinary to Queen Victoria. Baronet 1839. An essay on the construction of the eyes of birds won him election as FRS in 1813. He took a leading part in founding Royal Zoological Society of Ireland and obtained a grant of land for it in the Phoenix Park. Died Dublin, 10 June 1858.

CRAWFORD, WILLIAM SHARMAN (1781–1861), politician. Born Co. Down, 3 September 1781. Sheriff of Down 1811. Recognised Ulster tenant-right custom on his extensive estates and campaigned to have it legalised and extended over Ireland. MP for Dundalk 1835. Advocated Catholic emancipation and supported Chartist movement in England. Refused to support repeal and lost seat in 1837. Accused O'CONNELL of sacrificing tenants' interests to Whig alliance by supporting Irish Tithe Bill. Elected MP for Rochdale, which paid his expenses, 1841. Condemned proclamation of O'Connell's Clontarf meeting. Formed Ulster Tenant Right Association 1846 which became Tenant League of Ireland in 1850. Defeated for Down 1852. Advocated federal parliamentary scheme rather than repeal. Died, 18 October 1861, at his home at Crawfordsburn.

CREAGH, RICHARD (c. 1525–1585), priest. Born Limerick. Educated Louvian with grant from Emperor Charles V. In Limerick 1557–1562, then to Rome at direction of Papal Nuncio, David Wolfe. There, on 23 March 1563, was appointed archbishop of Armagh. Towards the end of 1564 he landed in Ireland, probably at Drogheda. Arrested, and imprisoned in the Tower of London on 18 January 1565. Two months later he escaped to the Continent. He returned to Ireland and met Shane

O'Neill near Clondarell, Co. Armagh, in August 1566. In May 1567, he was arrested in Connacht, tried in Dublin for high treason and, though acquitted, was imprisoned. Escaped but was recaptured and sent to the Tower, where he died, possibly by poison, 14 October 1585. His writings include *De Lingua Hibernica, An Ecclesiastical History, A Catechism in Irish* (1560), *De Controversiis Fidei, Topographia Hiberniae,* and *Vitae Sanctorum Hiberniae.* A Latin account of his escape from the Tower in 1565 is included in Cardinal Moran's *Spicilegium Ossoriense.*

CREGAN, MARTIN (1788–1870), portrait painter. Born Co. Meath. In service of Stewart family of Killymon, Co. Tyrone, as a boy. When he showed aptitude for drawing they paid for his education as a painter in the Dublin Society's school, and in London under SIR MARTIN ARCHER SHEE. He exhibited at RA in 1812. In 1822 he settled in Dublin. One of the original members of the RHA, founded in 1823, and president 1832–1855. During his long career the leading portrait painter in Ireland; Strickland lists over three hundred of his paintings. Died at his house, 22 Lennox Street, Dublin, 10 December 1870.

CREMIN, CORNELIUS CHRISTOPHER (1908–1987), diplomat. Born 6 December 1908 in Kenmare, Co. Kerry. Educated at St Brendan's, Killarney, and UCC. Entered Department of External Affairs 1935, first secretary in Paris 1937 and saw German army enter. Appointed to Berlin in November 1943 as chargé d'affaires and was last foreign diplomat on the soil of the Third Reich. Ireland's first ambassador to France 1950–1954, ambassador to Vatican 1954–1956, to Britain 1956–1958, secretary of the department 1958–1963, and permanent representative at UN 1964–1974. Honorary LL.D. from NUI 1965. After retiring he remained chairman of the Irish delegation to the UN Conference on the Law of the Sea. After his first wife died he married again in

1979. Died in Kenmare on 19 April 1987, survived by his second wife, three daughters, and a son.

CROFTS, FREEMAN WILLS (1879–1957), detective-story writer. Born Dublin, son of a British army doctor. Educated Campbell College and Methodist College, Belfast. Became railway engineer. His first book, *The Cask* (1920), was a success. Became full-time author in 1929. He wrote some forty books, radio plays, and short stories. His detective stories featured Inspector French, a painstaking policeman, and gave the reader all the clues in meticulous detail. They were widely popular and were translated into many languages. Died in Worthing, 11 April 1957.

CROKE, THOMAS WILLIAM (1824–1902), archbishop. Born Ballyclough, Co. Cork. Educated Charleville and Irish Colleges, Paris and Rome. Ordained 1846 and, according to WILLIAM O'BRIEN MP, fought at the barricades in Paris during the revolution of 1848. President of St Colman's College, Fermoy, 1858. Parish priest of Doneraile 1865. Theologian to bishop of Cloyne at First Vatican Council in 1870. Met Cardinal Manning and formed a lasting friendship. Bishop of Auckland, New Zealand, 1870, and had great success. Promoted Archbishop of Cashel and Emly 1875. Croke's strong support of the GAA made it a great force in rural Ireland. Croke Park, the headquarters in Dublin, is named after him. He was also a forceful advocate of temperance, and threw his influence behind the Gaelic League from its foundation in 1893. He backed the Land League and the leadership of Parnell, incurring the anger and suspicion of successive British governments by his outspokenness. His influence in Ireland was immense, and of inestimable value to the nationalist cause. After the fall of Parnell in 1891 he withdrew from active participation in political controversy. He died at Cashel on 22 July 1902.

CROKER, JOHN WILSON (1780–1857), politician and essayist. Born Galway, 20 December 1780. Educated TCD and Lincoln's Inn. Called to the Irish bar 1802. In 1804 he published anonymously a verse satire, *On the Present State of the Irish Stage*, which became famous overnight. This was followed by an equally successful prose satire on Dublin society, *Intercepted Letters from Canton* (1804). *A Sketch of the State of Ireland Past and Present* (1808) was a serious study in which he advocated Catholic emancipation. MP for Downpatrick 1807, and made his mark in the House of Commons with an extempore maiden speech. The Duke of Wellington, then SIR ARTHUR WELLESLEY, Chief Secretary for Ireland, became his lifelong friend. Croker led Tory defence of Duke of York on charges of conniving at the sale of military appointments by his mistress, Mrs Clarke. Appointed Secretary to the Admiralty 1809, and quickly exposed a high official's misappropriation of £200,000 of public funds. During his twenty-two years there he built up the importance of the post, and encouraged nautical explorations. Croker was associated with the *Quarterly Review* from its foundation in 1809; conservative in literary matters as in politics, his severe criticism of Keats's *Endymion* showed a complete lack of sympathy with the Romantic movement. He wrote hundreds of articles on varied subjects for the *Review* and excited the enmity of political opponents, notably Macaulay and Disraeli. Macaulay retaliated with a slashing review of Croker's edition of Boswell's *Life of Johnson*, and Disraeli by caricaturing him as Rigby in his novel *Coningsby*. Croker opposed the Reform Bill, and retired from public life when it was passed. Peel's conversion to the repeal of the Corn Laws ended their association, but Croker maintained a close friendship with the other Tory leaders. He advised Lord Hertford on the management of his vast estates and refused payment for his services. Hertford, however, left him £20,000 in his will. Croker's other works included editions of *Lady Suffolk's Letters* and of *Walpole's Letters*. His *Memoires, Diaries and Correspondence* were published in 1884 after his death. He was the first to apply the term 'Conservative' to the Tory party. He died at Hampton, Middlesex, on 10 August 1857.

CROKER, RICHARD (1841–1922), 'Boss' Croker of Tammany Hall. Born Clonakilty, Co. Cork, 23 November 1841. His family emigrated to New York when he was three. Educated at New York public schools and began work at thirteen as a machinist. Entered local politics, joined Tammany Hall, and became alderman in 1868. Appointed coroner in 1873 at $25,000 a year. Succeeded 'Honest John' Kelly as Tammany leader in 1886 and held power for seventeen years. Held other lucrative public offices as fire commissioner and city chamberlain. Retired to England with a large fortune about 1903. From 1907 to 1919 he lived at Glencairn, Co. Dublin (now residence of British ambassador), and maintained racing stables there. His horse Orby won the English Derby in 1907 with odds 10 to 1 against. After death of his first wife in 1914 he married Bewla Benton Edmundson, a Cherokee Indian from Oklahoma. His last years were embittered by litigation with his family concerning property. He died in New York, 29 April 1922.

CROKER, THOMAS CROFTON (1798–1854), antiquary. Born Cork, 15 January 1798. Limited education, and apprenticed to a local merchant. Spent his spare time collecting stories and songs in the south of Ireland. Sent many songs to THOMAS MOORE. Although no relation, JOHN WILSON CROKER secured for him a clerkship in the Admiralty in London in 1818. His *Fairy Legends and Traditions of the South of Ireland* (1825) went into several editions, the second illustrated by MACLISE, and was translated into German by the brothers Grimm, and into French. *Legends of the Lakes* appeared in 1829, and *The Popular*

Songs of Ireland in 1839. In 1852 he wrote two popular humorous stories, *The Adventures of Barney Mahony*, and *My Village versus Our Village*. Member of the Society of Antiquaries and many other learned societies, and registrar of the Royal Literary Fund 1837–1852. Retired from the Admiralty 1850. Died at Old Brompton, 8 August 1854.

CRONE, JOHN SMYTH (1858–1945), physician and editor. Born Belfast, 25 November 1858. Educated RBAI and QUB. Qualified in medicine, Apothecaries Co. and RCPI. Practised in Willesden, London, for forty years and received many honours from local authority. Founded *Irish Book Lover* 1909 and edited it until 1924. MRIA 1916 and president, Irish Literary Society, London, 1918–1925. Published *Concise Dictionary of Irish Biography* (1928), the first since WEBB of 1878. Died, probably in London, 6 November 1945.

CROSS, ERIC (1903–1980), scientist and writer. Born in Newry, Co. Down. His father worked in the British diplomatic service and he was reared and educated in England. Studied medicine in Manchester and chemistry in London. Worked as a research chemist for fifteen years. He invented a synthetic marble, and after the Second World War set up a factory to make knitting-needles from bicycle spokes. In 1942 he published *The Tailor and Ansty*, an affectionate account of the fireside conversation of Tim Buckley (the Tailor), his wife Anastasia (Ansty) and their friends and neighbours in their cottage near Gougane Barra, Co. Cork, which he had been visiting since the 1920s. FRANK O'CONNOR described the Tailor as a rural Dr Johnson, and the book is now a minor classic. It was banned by the Censorship Board, a bitter controversy followed, and the ban was debated for four days in Seanad Éireann, which upheld it. The old couple were boycotted locally, and priests forced the Tailor to burn his copy of the book on his own hearth. The ban was removed some twenty years later.

Eric Cross contributed stories and sketches to RTE and the BBC and in 1978 published *Silence is Golden and Other Stories*. Since 1953 he lived as a virtual recluse near Westport, Co. Mayo, and he died there on 5 September 1980.

CROZIER, FRANCIS RAWDON (1796–1848), explorer. Born Banbridge. Entered British navy 1810. Accompanied Captain Parry on three Arctic voyages 1821–1827. Promoted lieutenant 1826. Voyaged to Antarctic 1839–1843 with Captain (later Sir) James Ross. Promoted captain 1841. Commanded *Terror* on Franklin's expedition to Arctic, sailing from England 1845. Fate unknown until their record was found by MCCLINTOCK 1859. They discovered the North-West Passage, but were ice-bound in 1846. Franklin died June 1847, leaving Crozier in command. With provisions running low, they landed in April 1848 and made for Back's Fish River, but all perished on the way.

CULLEN, PAUL (1803–1878), cardinal. Born Prospect, Co. Kildare, 29 April 1803. Educated Shackleton Quaker school at Ballitore, Carlow College, and College of Propaganda, Rome. Ordained Rome 1829, rector of Irish College 1832. As agent for the Irish bishops, sought to counteract British influence at Vatican. On his advice, Pope Gregory XVI condemned the Queen's Colleges and urged the Irish bishops to establish a Catholic university. Archbishop of Armagh and apostolic delegate 1850. Summoned and presided over first national synod held in Ireland since the twelfth century (Thurles, 1850). Transferred to Dublin as archbishop 1852. Used his influence to improve social conditions by constitutional means, and abhorred the Young Ireland and Fenian movements. Nevertheless his petition to the Crown saved Thomas F. Burke, the Fenian leader, from hanging. The founding of the Catholic University in 1854 and the appointment of Newman as first rector

were largely due to his support. He was a strict disciplinarian and worked hard to improve the morale and education of the clergy. Clonliffe College, the Dublin diocesan seminary, was founded by him in 1859. A frequent visitor to Rome, he took a leading part in the First Vatican Council and is said to have drafted the dogma on papal infallibility. Cardinal 1866. Died Dublin, 24 October 1878. Buried at Clonliffe College.

CUMING, WILLIAM (1769–1852), portrait painter. Studied painting in the Dublin Society's school. Soon established himself as a historical and portrait painter. One of the original members of the RHA 1823, president 1829–1832. He had private means, travelled abroad a good deal, and ceased to paint after 1832. Died at his house, 31 Lower Abbey Street, Dublin, 5 April 1852.

CURRAN, JOHN PHILPOT (1750–1817), lawyer and nationalist. Born Newmarket, Co. Cork. Educated Midleton School, TCD, and Middle Temple. Called to the Irish bar 1775, king's counsel 1782. He first won fame by appearing at Cork for a Catholic clergyman who had been horsewhipped by Lord Doneraile. Curran, a Protestant, gained the verdict and popularity both for religious and political reasons. Fond of talk and drink, he was at this time 'prior' of the 'Monks of the Screw', a literary and convivial club with GRATTAN and CHARLEMONT as members, and he wrote their charter song. In 1783 he was given a seat for Kilbeggan in the Irish House of Commons but, refusing to be subject to his patron's views, he bought another seat for Rathcormack, Co. Cork, at his own expense, and held it until 1797. In parliament he was a strong advocate of Catholic emancipation and a severe critic of government patronage and corruption. After 1798 he defended the United Irishmen HAMILTON ROWAN and WOLFE TONE. He opposed the Act of Union of 1800 with vigour and eloquence; yet after the rising of 1803, when he discovered that his daughter SARAH was secretly engaged to ROBERT EMMET, he behaved so harshly to her that she was obliged to leave his house, the Priory, Rathfarnham. Her attachment to Emmet cast suspicion on Curran, and he was examined by the Privy Council, but cleared. Master of the Irish Rolls 1806, with a seat in the Privy Council. Retired 1814 with a pension of £2,700 a year and moved to London where he joined the congenial company of THOMAS MOORE, RICHARD BRINSLEY SHERIDAN and Byron. Died at Brompton, Middlesex, 14 October 1817. Buried in Glasnevin Cemetery.

CURRAN, SARAH (died c. 1808), youngest daughter of JOHN PHILPOT CURRAN. Secretly engaged to ROBERT EMMET. When her father discovered this after the rising of 1803, he behaved so harshly to her that she was obliged to take refuge with friends in Cork. Here she met and married in 1805 a Captain Sturgeon. She died in England three years later. MOORE's song 'She is Far From the Land' was inspired by her story.

CURTIN, JEREMIAH (1838-1906), writer. Born in Detroit of Irish parents. Joined US government service as translator. Served in St Petersburg (Leningrad) 1864-1870. On staff of Bureau of Ethnology, Smithsonian Institution, 1883-1891. Became one of the best-known collectors of Irish folk tales, and made many visits to Ireland, using an interpreter, as his own Irish was poor. Published *Myths and Folklore of Ireland* (1890-1911), *Hero Tales of Ireland* (1894), and *Tales of the Fairies and the Ghost World* (1893). Also collected American and Mongolian folk tales, and wrote *The Mongols: a History* (1908). Died Vermont, USA.

CUSACK, MARGARET ANNE (1832-1899), the 'Nun of Kenmare'; in religion, Sister Mary Frances Clare. Born Dublin. Joined Anglican sisterhood in London. Became a Catholic 1858. Joined the Irish Poor Clares in Newry in 1860 to work with friendless girls. Sent to Kenmare, Co. Kerry, in 1861 to open foundation at request of parish priest. Collected funds for relief of poor in famine year 1879-1880. Difficulties arose with the community and she left Kenmare in 1881. Proposed to open a convent at Knock, Co. Mayo, but episcopal consent was withdrawn. In 1884 she obtained the approval of Pope Leo XIII to found the Sisters of Peace and went to the USA to organise training and guidance for Irish emigrant working girls. American bishops and clergy cold-shouldered her and she was forced to abandon the project. In her autobiography, *The Nun of Kenmare* (1889), she made bitter attacks on the Catholic clergy. According to CRONE she reverted to her former faith. She published biographies of O'CONNELL, FATHER MATHEW, SAINTS PATRICK, COLUMBA and BRIGID, local histories, and pamphlets on women in modern society. Died Leamington, Warwickshire, 5 June 1899.

CUSACK, MICHAEL (1847-1906), founder of GAA. Born Carron, Co. Clare. Teacher in west of Ireland and tutor to family of Lord Gough. Spent some years in America, then taught at Newry, Blackrock College, and Clongowes Wood. Opened the Civil Service Academy, a cramming establishment in Dublin, which prospered and gave him a large income. With Maurice Davin of Carrick-on-Suir called a meeting in Hayes's Commercial Hotel, Thurles, Co. Tipperary, on 1 November 1884 and founded GAA. Others present included John Wyse-Power of Naas, Co. Kildare, editor of the *Leinster Leader*; P. J. O'Ryan, Callan, Co. Kilkenny, solicitor; John McKay, reporter, *Cork Examiner*; J. K. Bracken (father of BRENDAN) of Templemore, Co. Tipperary, building contractor; and St George MacCarthy, Templemore (an inspector in the RIC). Davin was elected president, and later DR CROKE, PARNELL, and DAVITT became patrons. Cusack liked to be called 'Citizen Cusack'. Died 27 November 1906.

CZIRA, SIDNEY, née GIFFORD (1889–1974), journalist, pen-name John Brennan. Born Dublin, youngest of twelve children of well-to-do solicitor. Educated Alexandra College, Dublin. Of her family she said, 'half became socialists, great admirers of Bernard Shaw; the other half went to Sinn Féin.' On leaving school she followed her older sisters, Muriel and Grace, into the national movement. She became a member of Inghinidhe na hÉireann with HELENA MOLONY, MAUD GONNE, and CONSTANCE MARKIEVICZ, and contributed lively articles to *Sinn Féin* and other nationalist journals. She adopted the pen-name John Brennan thinking that a man's name would carry more weight. In 1914 she went to America, hoping that it would be easier for a woman to make a career there as a journalist, married a Hungarian émigré, and continued to write and campaign vigorously for Irish independence. The 1916 Rising brought widowhood to her sisters Muriel, who had married THOMAS MACDONAGH, and Grace, who had married JOSEPH PLUNKETT. Her activities in association with JOHN DEVOY and other notable Irish-Americans led to her being blacklisted by the British authorities, but she returned to Ireland before the end of the First World War with her infant son, travelling on a borrowed passport. In Dublin she continued to work as a journalist, and also broadcasted frequently from Radio Éireann. She died in Dublin on 15 September 1974. Her recollections, *The Years Flew By*, appeared in 1975.

D

DALTON, GENERAL EMMET (1898–1978), revolutionary. Born on 4 March 1898 and joined the British army in 1915 after he left school in Dublin. He rose to the rank of major and won the Military Cross. Returned to Ireland in 1919, joined the IRA and became special adviser and aide to MICHAEL COLLINS. Later he became director of military training. Dressed in his old British army uniform he led an abortive attempt to rescue SEÁN MACEOIN from Mountjoy Jail. He supported the Treaty and was in charge of the bombardment of the Four Courts on the morning of 28 June 1922, which signalled the beginning of the Civil War. He was with Collins when their party was ambushed at Béal na Bláth and Collins was killed. When the Civil War ended he became Clerk of Seanad Éireann for a short time, then resigned and made a career in the film industry in Hollywood and London. Died in Dublin on 4 March 1978.

D'ALTON, JOHN (1792–1867), historian. Born at his father's mansion, Bessville, Co. Westmeath. Educated at TCD and King's Inns. Called to the Irish bar 1813. Won Cunningham gold medal of the RIA in 1827 for essay on early Irish society. Contributed a series of articles on antiquities to *Irish Penny Journal* with illustrations by SAMUEL LOVER. Published *Memoirs of the Archbishops of Dublin* (1838), *History of the County of Dublin* (1838) and *History of Drogheda* (1844), *Annals of Boyle* (1845), and *King James II's Irish Army List, 1689* (1855), a valuable source for family history. He died on 20 June 1867.

D'ALTON, JOHN FRANCIS (1883–1963), cardinal. Born Claremorris, Co. Mayo. Educated Blackrock College, Dublin, RUI, and Clonliffe Diocesan College, Dublin. Received his doctorate in divinity, *summa cum laude*, in Rome 1908, then spent some time at the universities of Oxford and Cambridge. A classical scholar of distinction, professor of ancient classics, Maynooth, 1912, president of the college 1936. Bishop of Meath 1943, Archbishop of Armagh and Primate of All Ireland 1946 in succession to CARDINAL MACRORY. Made cardinal by Pope Pius XII in January 1953. He published a number of scholarly works, including *Horace and his Age* (1917), and *Roman Literary Theory and Criticism: a Study in Tendencies* (1931). In 1960 Pope John XXIII appointed him a member of the Central Preparatory Commission of the Second Vatican Council. Died in Dublin on 1 February 1963. Buried in the grounds of Armagh Cathedral.

D'ALTON, LOUIS (1900–1951), playwright and theatrical producer. Son of Charles D'Alton, comedian and theatremanager. As a child he toured England, Scotland and Ireland with his father's company. Formed his own company, for which he wrote and produced plays. His first play for the Abbey Theatre, *The Man in the Cloak*, was based on the life of JAMES CLARENCE MANGAN. This was followed by *The Spanish Soldier* (1940); others include *Lovers' Meeting, This Other Eden, The Devil a Saint Would Be*, and *The Money Doesn't Matter*. One of the Abbey's leading producers. Took their second company on tour of the provinces 1940. Published a novel, *Death is So Fair*, based on events between 1916 and 1921. Died in a London hospital, 16 June 1951.

DALY, EDWARD (1891–1916), one of the sixteen leaders executed after the 1916 Rising. Born Frederick St,

Limerick, 25 February 1891. Educated at local CBS. He came from a noted republican family: his father had taken part in the Fenian Rising of 1867, his uncle John Daly had served twelve years in English jails, and his sister Kathleen was married to THOMAS CLARKE. He worked in a local bakery, then as a clerk, moving to Dublin in 1912 to work with May Roberts, wholesale chemists. He joined the Irish Volunteers on their formation in 1913, and commanded the Four Courts garrison in 1916. He was court-martialled, sentenced to death, and executed in Kilmainham Jail, 4 May.

DALY, RICHARD (died 1813), actor and theatre manager. Born Co. Galway. Educated TCD. Having run through his inheritance, he went on the stage, and played in Dublin with success. He then married a Mrs Lister, a popular actress and singer of good reputation, who owned considerable property. In 1781 he bought Smock Alley Theatre and then Crow St Theatre, Dublin, and some provincial theatres. In 1788 opened the Theatre Royal in Crow St but it failed to prosper, owing partly to attacks on him in Dublin newspapers and partly to competition from Astley's Amphitheatre and from a private theatre established by some of the principal nobility and gentry. It was represented to the authorities that the decay of the drama in Ireland was due to Daly's mismanagement, and in 1798 he agreed to transfer his interests in the Dublin theatres to one F. E. Jones, in return for an annuity for himself and his children. Died Dublin, September 1813.

DANBY, FRANCIS (1793–1861), landscape painter. Born 16 November 1793 at St John's, near Killinick, Co. Wexford. The family moved to Dublin in 1799, and he studied art in the Dublin Society's school. In 1813, after selling a picture for fifteen guineas, he went to England and, after some vicissitudes, settled in Bristol. Exhibited RA 1822–1823. In 1824 he moved to London, was elected an associate of the RA 1825, and was well on the road to success when he was involved in a scandal. His wife deserted him for another artist and he, in turn, left for the Continent with a Welsh woman, Helen Evans. For the following ten years he lived chiefly in Switzerland, yachting and boat-building on Lake Geneva, and supporting himself by the sale of drawings. He returned to England about 1841 and became a regular exhibitor at the RA, but was never admitted to full membership, although he showed more than forty pictures. The refusal of this honour embittered his later years. Died at his home, Shell House, Exmouth, 10 February 1861. Took out a patent for a new form of ship's anchor, the 'Danforth', 1861.

DANIEL or Ó DOMHNUILL, WILLIAM (died 1628), archbishop. Born Kilkenny. Educated TCD; fellow 1593; DD and treasurer of St Patrick's Cathedral 1602. Translated New Testament into Irish 1602. John Francke printed it with type presented by Queen Elizabeth to John Kearney in 1571 and used by him to print a catechism, the first work printed in Irish. Translated the Book of Common Prayer into Irish and had it printed by Francke 1608. Archbishop of Tuam 1609, and restored the cathedral. Died there, 11 July 1628.

DARGAN, WILLIAM (1799–1867), railway contractor. Born Carlow, 28 February 1799. Educated in England. He joined a surveyor's office and was employed under Telford on the construction of the Holyhead road in 1820. He then returned to Ireland to start his own contracting business, and in 1831 constructed the first railway in Ireland, the line from Dublin to Kingstown (Dún Laoghaire). The business prospered, and by 1853 he had constructed over 600 miles (965 km) of railway, as well as the Ulster Canal, connecting Lough Erne and Belfast. He organised and financed the Dublin Exhibition of 1853, losing £20,000 on the promotion. The National

Gallery was built to commemorate his services, and his statue stands on the lawn. He declined the offer of a baronetcy from Queen Victoria, who visited him at his house, Mount Anville, now a convent. Subsequent business ventures outside construction work did not prosper. In 1866 he was injured in a fall from his horse, and his inability to attend to his affairs brought acute financial difficulties. Died at 2 Fitzwilliam Square, 7 February 1867.

DARLEY, GEORGE (1795-1846), poet and mathematician. Born Dublin. Educated TCD. Going to London, he worked for the *London Magazine* and the *Athenaeum* as a drama critic. Edited *The Works of Beaumont and Fletcher* (1840). His poems include some fine songs. His prose tragedies and stories are largely forgotten save for *Lillian of the Vale*, a story after the manner of Washington Irving. From 1826 to 1828 he published a series of popular treatises on algebra, geometry, and other branches of mathematics. Died London, 23 November 1846. Complete poems published London 1908.

DAVIES, CHRISTIAN (1667-1739), woman soldier. Born Dublin. At twenty-one she inherited an inn in Dublin from an aunt, and married Richard Welsh, one of the waiters. He disappeared suddenly, and a year later wrote that he had been pressed into the army in Flanders. She set out in search of him, and enlisted as a man under the name of Christopher Welsh. She fought at Nijmegen, Blenheim, and other battles, and after a separation of thirteen years found her husband. She accompanied him as his acknowledged wife for three years until he was killed at the battle of Malplaquet. She then married Hugh Jones, a grenadier, but he was mortally wounded in 1710 at the siege of St Venant. She went to England, was presented to Queen Anne, and received from her a pension of a shilling a day for life. She then returned to Dublin and married a soldier called Davies. After twenty-five years of obscurity, poverty, and illness, she died at Chelsea on 7 July 1739. That account of her life is given in the autobiography *The Life and Adventures of Mrs Christian Davies* (1740), which does not seem to be genuine. However, a contemporary record dated 7 July 1739 notices her death on that day, and says that she served for several years as a dragoon in the Royal Inniskilling Regiment but, receiving a wound in King William's wars in Ireland, was discovered, and that she then married and accompanied her husband to Flanders as his wife.

DAVIS, THOMAS OSBORNE (1814-1845), poet and nationalist. Born Mallow, Co. Cork, 14 October 1814, son of a British army surgeon. Educated TCD. Called to the bar 1838. Joined Repeal Association 1839. Pleaded for Irish historical studies in famous speech to Historical Society, TCD, 1840. Became the leader of the younger men who were impatient of O'CONNELL's constitutional methods. With GAVAN DUFFY and JOHN BLAKE DILLON founded the *Nation* in 1842. His spirited contributions in prose and verse captured the national imagination and inspired his contemporaries with his vision of an Ireland free to pursue its own destiny. His ballads 'A Nation Once Again' and 'The West's Asleep' are popular to this day. He died of fever in his mother's house, 67 Baggot Street, Dublin, on 16 September 1845. Buried Mount Jerome cemetery. His influence on movements for political freedom persisted long after his death. ARTHUR GRIFFITH described him as 'the prophet I followed throughout my life, the man whose words and teachings I tried to translate into practice in politics.'

DAVITT, MICHAEL (1846-1906), founder of the Irish National Land League. Born at Straide, Co. Mayo, son of a small farmer. The family was evicted in 1850 and emigrated to Haslingden in Lancashire. Here, at eleven, Michael lost his right arm while working in a cotton mill. In 1865 he joined the Fenians, became organising secretary of the IRB in 1868, and in 1870 was sentenced to fifteen years' penal servitude. His release from Dartmoor after seven years was mainly due to agitation by BUTT and PARNELL. Davitt then went to America and in co-operation with JOHN DEVOY worked out a new policy for the national movement, with the two great aims of self-government and land reform. Back in Ireland in 1878 he found both the IRB and Parnell slow to accept this 'new departure'. His chance came when crop failure and falling prices in 1879 faced the rural population with disaster. He persuaded Parnell to speak in Westport on 8 June and a huge meeting heard from Parnell the historic words, 'Hold a firm grip of your homesteads and lands.' Four months later Davitt founded the Land League with Parnell, a Protestant landlord, as president. It combined in one great agrarian movement all nationalists from moderates to revolutionaries and received strong backing and financial help from America. In the ensuing land war a new word was added to the English language when an evicting landlord's agent, Captain Charles Boycott of Lough Mask, was ostracised. The Land Act of 1881 gave the tenants the 'three F's'—fair rent, fixity of tenure, and free sale—but the league fought on for tenant ownership. Gladstone arrested the leaders and suppressed the league, but eventually the British government yielded and in 1885 began the process of ending landlordism. Ironically 'the land for the people' meant to Davitt the nationalisation of the land, whereas to the tenants it could mean only one thing, ownership by themselves. He was elected MP for Co. Meath 1882, for North Meath 1892, and for South Mayo 1895-1899. Both Davitt and Parnell saw the winning of the land war as a step to ultimate independence. The fall of Parnell and the split in the Irish Party set that cause back for generations. From 1899 Davitt devoted himself to travel and journalism. He visited America and South Africa, and published six books, including *Leaves From a Prison Diary* (1884) and *The Boer Fight for Freedom* (1902). Died Dublin, 31 May 1906. Buried at Straide.

DAY-LEWIS, CECIL (1904-1972), poet and critic. Born 27 April 1904 in Ballintubber, Co. Mayo. Educated at Sherborne and Wadham College, Oxford, where Auden and Spender were his contemporaries and friends. His first volume of poetry, *Beechen Vigil*, appeared in 1925. His many succeeding collections established him as a lyric poet of vision and assured technique. Left-wing sympathies brought him into the Communist Party in the thirties, but he left it in 1938. Worked as a teacher, then in British Ministry of Information during Second World War. Turning to academic life, he lectured at Cambridge, was professor of poetry at Oxford 1951-1956, and at Harvard 1964-1965. Poet Laureate 1968, and member Irish Academy of Letters. His most important critical work, *The Poetic Image*, combines practical criticism with an exploration of the nature of poetic experience. Under the pen-name Nicholas Blake wrote many successful murder mysteries, featuring a civilised and witty detective, Nigel Strangeways, who seemed to his friends to be a reflection of the author himself. Published his autobiography, *Buried Day* (1960). Died in Hertfordshire, 22 May 1972, after a long illness.

DEANE, SIR THOMAS NEWENHAM (1828-1899), architect. Born Dundanion, near Cork, 15 June 1828. Educated Rugby and TCD. He was trained in his profession by his father, and became head of the family firm in 1871. The National Library and National Museum in Kildare St, Dublin, constitute his best-known work. He was knighted at the public opening of the buildings in 1890. On the passing of legislation in 1882 and 1892 to protect the national monuments of Ireland, Deane became inspector under the Act and did much valuable work. Died suddenly in Dublin, 8 November 1899.

DE BARRA, LESLIE, née PRICE
(1893–1984), revolutionary and Red
Cross official. Born and educated in
Dublin. Qualified as a teacher at St
Mary's College, Belfast, in 1915.
Returned to Dublin and became active
in Cumann na mBan. Carried dispatches in Easter week 1916. After the
rising she became Director of Organisation for Cumann na mBan and
travelled the country organising the
resistance movement. Thus she met
GENERAL TOM BARRY whom she
married in 1921. They settled in Cork
and she devoted the rest of her life to the
relief of human suffering at home and
abroad. Joined Irish Red Cross Society
at its inception in 1939; chairwoman
from 1950. Decorated by the Irish, West
German and Italian governments for her
services to the society. In 1978 she
received the International Committee's
highest award, the Henri Dunant medal.
National president of 'Gorta' until her
resignation in 1968. Active worker in
Conradh na Gaeilge. Honorary LL.D.
(NUI). Died 9 April 1984, aged ninety-
one.

DE BLÁCAM, AODH (1890–1951),
journalist. Born in London, of Ulster
parents. Joined the staff of the *Enniscorthy
Echo* 1915. Wrote nationalist propaganda during War of Independence.
Interned in 1922. An active member of
Sinn Féin. Published *Towards the Republic*
(1919); other books included *The Story of
Colmcille* (1929), *Gaelic Literature Surveyed*
(1929), *The Life of Wolfe Tone* (1935), *The
Black North* (1938), and the lives of
several Irish saints. Two of his best-
known plays are *King Dan* and *Two
Kingdoms.* He edited *Commonweal,* a short-
lived literary journal, and was a regular
contributor to daily and weekly papers
and periodicals. On the staff of the *Irish
Times,* writing leaders and reviewing
books; left to become editor of the
Standard, and later joined the *Irish Press*
as writer of a daily feature under the
name 'Roddy the Rover'. He was a
member of the Fianna Fáil executive
until December 1947, when he resigned
to join Clann na Poblachta. Defeated for
Co. Louth 1948. A member of the Emigration Commission. Succeeded FRANK
GALLAGHER as Director of Publicity of
the Department of Health 1949. Died in
January 1951.

DEEVY, TERESA (1894–1963), playwright. Born 31 January 1894 in Waterford. Despite deafness, began to write for
the theatre. Her first play, *Temporal
Powers,* was performed at the Abbey in
1932. She contributed three other plays
to the Abbey, *The King of Spain's Daughter,
Katie Roche,* and *The Wild Goose,* but after
1936 concentrated on radio plays. Elected to Irish Academy of Letters 1954.
Died January 1963 in Waterford.

**DE HINDEBERG, FATHER
RISTEARD** (Richard Henebry)
(1863–1916), scholar. Born Waterford.
Educated St John's College, Waterford,
St Patrick's College, Maynooth, and the
universities of Griefswald and Freiburg.
Ordained in 1892. For some years he was
professor of Irish at the Catholic Univer-
sity of Washington, returning to Ireland
in 1906 to teach in the Irish college,
Ring, Co. Waterford. Professor of Celtic
studies, UCC, 1908. His books include
Sounds of Munster Irish (1898), *Greas Fuir-
seoireachta* (1910), and *Handbook of Irish
Music,* published posthumously in 1928.
Died at Portlaw, Co. Waterford, on 17
March 1916.

DELANEY, PATRICK (1685/86–
1768), dean of Down. Educated as a poor
scholar at TCD, where he took holy
orders and became a senior fellow. In
1730 he became chancellor of St
Patrick's Cathedral, Dublin. In 1732 he
married a rich widow and was able to
pay his debts and entertain his friends,
including SWIFT. His wife died in 1741
and two years later he married another
wealthy widow, a Mrs Pendarves.
Through her influence he was appointed
Dean of Down. He was renowned as a
preacher and published a number of
miscellaneous pieces on religious and
biblical subjects, besides a defence of
Swift (1754) that gives an interesting and

valuable account of Swift in his prime. The Delaneys' house, Delville, at Glasnevin, Dublin, drew many famous contemporaries to it for its hospitality and good company. He died in Bath, where he had gone for the waters, 6 May 1768.

DELARGY, JAMES HAMILTON (1899–1980), folklorist. Born at Cushendall, Co. Antrim, on 26 May 1899. His father, a sea captain, died when he was two, and the family moved to Dublin. He was educated at Castleknock College and UCD, where he graduated in Celtic studies. His interest in folklore was awakened from listening to storytellers while on holiday in Antrim, and he devoted his life to collecting and preserving the oral folklore tradition. He became a lecturer in Irish language and literature at UCD and professor of folklore in 1946. He helped to found the Folklore of Ireland Society in 1925. Co-founder in 1927 with PÁDRAIG Ó SIOCHFHRADHA of its journal, *Béaloideas*, which he edited for forty-six years. The Irish Folklore Institute (1930) gave way in 1935 to the Irish Folklore Commission, financed by the Government. Delargy was seconded to the commission, and under his direction a band of dedicated workers travelled the country, recording and transcribing the stories and folklore of the dying oral tradition and amassing a store of material unrivalled in any other country. He published *The Gaelic Storyteller* (1945), *Leabhar Sheáin Í Chonaill* (1948)—stories taken down by him from a monoglot Irish-speaker in south Kerry—and *Seanchas ón Oileán Tiar* (1956), a collection made by Robin Flower on the Great Blasket. The commission was absorbed into the Department of Irish Folklore of UCD in 1977. Delargy lectured in many countries and was decorated by the governments of Sweden and Iceland. He received honorary doctorates from universities in Scandinavia, Nova Scotia, Wales, and the three Irish universities. He died in Dublin on 25 June 1980, survived by a son and a daughter.

DELL, PEGGY (*c*. 1905–1979), pianist and entertainer. Born in Dublin as Peggy Tisdall and formed her own band in her late teens. Played principal boy in pantomime at the Queen's Theatre (now demolished). Sang with Roy Fox's band in London, its first woman singer, and toured USA with Jack Hilton's dance band. Returned to Ireland on outbreak of Second World War and performed at the Metropole Ballroom with Phil Murtagh's band. A head injury in a taxi accident in 1970 seemed to have ended her career but her appearance in December 1973 on RTE's 'Late Late Show', celebrating the birthday of NOEL PURCELL brought her fame again. She won a Jacob's Award in 1974 for her performance in RTE's 'Peg o' My Heart'. Died in Dublin, 30 April 1979.

DENHAM, SIR JOHN (1615–1669), poet and playwright. Born in Dublin. Educated at Oxford and Lincoln's Inn. He took the Royalist side in the Civil War and, as governor of Farnham Castle, surrendered to the Parliamentary forces. After the restoration of 1660, Charles II rewarded him with a knighthood and the office of Surveyor of the Royal Works. He wrote a number of verse plays and a long poem, 'Cooper's Hill' (1642), describing in elegant heroic couplets the countryside around his home near Windsor. Buried in Poets' Corner, Westminster Abbey.

DENVIR, JOHN (1834–1916), editor and author. Born in Bushmills, Co. Antrim, of an old Norman family. He spent most of his life in England, starting as a builder in Liverpool. He then went into the printing business and became manager and editor of the *Catholic Times*, the *United Irishman* and the *Nationalist*, all published in Liverpool. In 1870 he founded his 'Illustrated Irish Penny Library', a series dealing with Irish history, poetry, songs, and biography, which became immensely popular, selling by the million. He contributed to the *Library*, and wrote a novel, *The Brandons* (1903), and some plays, but is best-remembered by *The Irish in Britain* (1892) and his autobiography, *Life Story of an Old Rebel* (1910). He died in London on 1 December 1916.

DERMODY, THOMAS (1775–1802), poet. Born Ennis, Co. Clare, in January 1775, son of a schoolmaster. He showed precocious talent, and at nine taught the classics in his father's school. When about fifteen he ran away to Dublin where he was befriended by many distinguished people. Rev. Gilbert Austin, rector of Maynooth, arranged the publication of his first poems in 1792. Shortly afterwards he enlisted in the British army, was commissioned as a second lieutenant, and served abroad with distinction. He was wounded, and returned to England on half-pay. His intemperate habits wrecked his health and his career, and he died in a hovel at Sydenham, Kent, on 15 July 1802. Buried in Lewisham churchyard. His collected poems were published in 1807 under the title *The Harp of Erin*.

DERMOTT, LAURENCE (1720–1791), freemason. Born Co. Roscommon. Went to London about 1750. Elected grand secretary of the 'Antient Masons' in 1752. This organisation later became the Grand Lodge of England. In 1771 the Duke of Atholl appointed him deputy grand master, a position he retained until 1787. The success of the Antient Masons has been ascribed to Dermott's zeal. In 1756 he published *Ahiman Rezon or Help to a Brother*, a remarkable book, setting out the laws of masonry and explaining its origin. Died in London.

DE VALERA, ÉAMON (1882–1975), revolutionary, politician, and President of Ireland. Born in Manhattan, New York, on 14 October 1882, son of Catherine Coll from Knockmore, Bruree, Co. Limerick, and Vivion Juan de Valera, a Spaniard whose father was engaged in the sugar trade between Cuba and Spain and the United States. His father died when he was two years old, and his widowed mother sent him to Ireland to be reared by his grandmother, Elizabeth Coll, who lived in a labourer's cottage at Knockmore. He went to the national school at Bruree, a mile distant, and said many years later that the 'Land League' parish priest, Father Eugene Sheehy (an uncle of Dr Conor Cruise O'Brien), 'taught me patriotism'. From there he went to Christian Brothers' school at Charleville (now Ráth Luirc) at the age of fourteen, walking the seven miles there and back every day, since the Colls could not afford a bicycle. At sixteen he won a scholarship to Blackrock College, Co. Dublin. He won further scholarships and exhibitions, and in 1903 was appointed professor of mathematics at Rockwell College, Co. Tipperary. He graduated in mathematics in 1904 from the Royal University, and then went back to Dublin to teach at Belvedere College. In 1906 he secured a post as professor of mathematics at Carysfort Teachers' Training College for women in Blackrock, Co. Dublin. His applications for professorships in colleges of the National University were unsuccessful, but he obtained a part-time appointment at Maynooth, and also lectured in mathematics at various Dublin colleges. At school and later he was a keen rugby footballer.

In 1908 he joined the Ard-Chraobh of the Gaelic League, the beginning of his life-long devotion to Irish. One of his teachers was Sinéad Flanagan, herself a teacher and four years his senior. They were married on 8 January 1910 at St Paul's Church, Arran Quay. In those early years of the century, Sinn Féin, the Gaelic League, the GAA and the Irish literary revival had brought about an awakening of the national consciousness. On 25 November 1913 a public meeting was held in the Rotunda, Dublin, to found a volunteer force. De Valera attended, joined, and was soon elected captain of the Donnybrook company. Preparations were pushed ahead for an armed rising, and he was made commandant of the Third Battalion and adjutant of the Dublin Brigade. He was sworn by THOMAS MACDONAGH into the oath-bound IRB, which secretely controlled the central executive of the Volunteers, but refused to attend meetings, preferring to concentrate on his duties as a Volunteer officer. He took part in the landing of guns from the *Asgard* in July 1914.

On 24 April 1916 the rising began, and de Valera occupied Boland's Bakery, his task being to cover the south-eastern approaches to the city. After a week of fighting the order came from PEARSE to surrender. De Valera was court-martialled, convicted, and sentenced to death, but the sentence was immediately commuted to penal servitude for life. There is no evidence that his American birth saved him from the firing squad. Neither he nor THOMAS ASHE were tried until 8 May, after the execution of five of the signatories of the Proclamation of the Republic. In the interval a revulsion of feeling against the executions had begun in England and Ireland. Ashe and he were reprieved on 9 May. After imprisonment in Dartmoor, Maidstone, and Lewes, he and his comrades were released in June 1917. Shortly after, he contested a by-election in East Clare, standing as a declared Republican against the Irish Party nominee, Patrick Lynch KC, and winning easily. He was clearly emerging as a leader, and at this early stage showed his adroitness as a politician by evolving a formula to avoid a split between Sinn Féin as a political movement and the militant Volunteers. 'Sinn Féin', he declared, 'aims at securing the international recognition of Ireland as an independent Irish Republic. Having achieved that status, the Irish people may, by referendum, freely choose their own form of government.' At a convention in October 1917 he was elected President of the 'new' Sinn Féin, ARTHUR GRIFFITH having magnanimously agreed to withdraw and to propose de Valera. A presidential salary of £500 a year left him, a married man now with four children, free to devote all his energies to the struggle for independence. Shortly after his release from jail, he had discontinued his membership of the IRB.

In March 1918 the British government decided to extend conscription to Ireland, and the resulting public outcry was led by Sinn Féin. De Valera was arrested in May and interned in Lincoln jail. In the general election in December 1918 Sinn Féin won seventy-three seats, although forty-five of their candidates were in prison, and the Irish Party was reduced to six seats. De Valera was returned for East Mayo; his seat in Clare was not contested. On 21 January 1919 the constituent assembly, or Dáil Éireann, promised in the Sinn Féin election manifesto, met in the Mansion House, Dublin, and formally established the Government of the Irish Republic. De Valera made an audacious escape from Lincoln jail, and on 1 April 1919 he was unanimously elected by the First Dáil as Príomh-Aire or President. In pursuance of the aim of securing international recognition, SEÁN T. Ó CEALLAIGH had been sent as envoy to Paris to present the Irish case to the Peace Conference convened by the Great Powers at the end of the First World War. When it became clear by May 1919 that this mission could not succeed, the President decided to visit the United States. He had three objectives: to ask for official recognition of the independent Irish republic, to float a loan to finance the work of the government, and to secure the support of the American people for the republic. His visit lasted from June 1919 to December 1920 and had mixed success. A loan of six million dollars was raised, a sum that far exceeded the hopes of the Dáil, and he won wide public support, but official recognition was not forthcoming and he had difficulties with the Irish-American leaders JOHN DEVOY and Judge Daniel Cohalan, who resented the dominant position he took up and wished to retain their control over Irish affairs in the United States. An open breach finally resulted.

He returned to Ireland in December 1920 to find the War of Independence at a grim stage, with the regular British forces being assisted by the notorious Auxiliaries and the 'Black and Tans'. The Republican army meanwhile was using guerrilla tactics to make British government impossible in Ireland. But public opinion in Britain and the United States was becoming increasingly uneasy, as reprisals were followed by counter-reprisals, towns were burned, and civilians shot dead. The first overt move towards peace came on 22 June 1921 when, at the opening of the Stormont parliament set up in Belfast under the Government of Ireland Act of 1920, King George V made a moving appeal 'to all Irishmen, to pause, to stretch out the hand of forbearance and conciliation, to forgive and forget.' A truce was declared on 11 July, and negotiations were opened with the English Prime Minister, Lloyd George, and his government, culminating in the signing of the Anglo-Irish Treaty on 6 December 1921. This provided not for an Irish republic but for a divided Ireland, with an oath of allegiance to the king. Partition, of course, had been a reality since the Act of 1920. De Valera, who had not been one of the pleni-potentiaries who negotiated the Treaty, announced that he could not recommend acceptance of the terms either to the Dáil or to the people. However, after a long and often bitter debate in the Dáil, the Treaty was accepted on 7 January 1922, the voting being 64 in favour and 57 against. ARTHUR GRIFFITH was elected President in place of de Valera, and a Provisional Government was appointed to set up the new Irish Free State.

A period of confusion followed, with de Valera striving to maintain the objective of a republic, and the gap rapidly widening between those who shared his view, and upholders of the Treaty, who were being subjected to intense pressure from Britain to implement its terms. A general election on 16 June 1922 indicated that public opinion was definitely in favour of the Treaty, with 58 seats going to pro-Treaty candidates, 35 to anti-Treaty and 35 to others who were to some extent committed to accepting it. Six days later SIR HENRY WILSON was assassinated on his door-step in London. On 28 June the forces of the Provisional Government opened fire on the Four Courts, which had been occupied by anti-Treaty Republicans under Rory O'Connor. The Civil War had begun, two days before the new Dáil was to meet. Before it ended, almost 800 had died. De Valera issued a statement appealing for public support for Rory O'Connor and his comrades, 'the men who have refused to forswear their allegiance to the Republic'. He then enlisted as a private in his old battalion of the Volunteers, and at no time did he rank as a military leader during the Civil War. In the 'war of the brothers' many died who had fought tenaciously for Irish freedom, but now fell on different sides, and the fate of MICHAEL COLLINS, Harry Boland, ERSKINE CHILDERS, CATHAL BRUGHA and others brought bitterness that lasted for generations. In May 1923 the chief of staff of the Republicans ordered the army to cease fire and dump their arms. The war was over, and de Valera had reached the nadir of his fortunes.

A general election was held on 27 August 1923 and he stood for Clare. He was arrested on 15 August and imprisoned until July 1924, but Clare again returned him at the head of the poll. In April 1926 he formed a new party, Fianna Fáil, and in the general election of June 1927 this party won 44 seats out of 155. Since 1922, Republican deputies had refused to take the oath of allegiance required under the constitution of the Free State. De Valera said that he saw no alternatives but taking their seats or giving up political action. Led by him, the Fianna Fáil deputies signed the book containing the oath, but maintained that this was an empty formality, as they neither read nor repeated the words of the oath. At a snap general election in September of that year the party gained a further 13 seats, bringing their numbers up to 57. He now decided to press ahead with plans, mooted as early as 1924, to found a republican daily paper, and made missions to America in 1928 and 1929 to raise funds. The first number of the *Irish Press* appeared on 5 September 1931 under the editorship of FRANK GALLAGHER, and the paper proved of immense assistance to Fianna Fáil in finally winning power. In the general election of February 1932 they secured 72 seats and became the largest party in the Dáil, although without a majority. De Valera was elected president of the Executive Council, and proceeded to form the first Fianna Fáil government. He at once initiated steps to fulfil his election promises to abolish the oath and withhold the land annuities. In retaliation, the British imposed economic sanctions against Irish exports, and the resulting economic war caused much distress. On his advice, the appointment of JAMES MACNEILL as Governor-General was terminated by King George V on 1 November 1932 and a 1916 veteran, DOMHNALL UA BUACHALLA, was appointed Seanascal in his place. Thus another symbol of monarchial authority was virtually removed. To strengthen his position against the opposition in the Dáil and Senate, he called a general election in January 1933 and won 77 seats, giving him an overall majority. In the remaining years of his first period of office, which lasted until 1948, the significant events were the enactment of a new Constitution in 1937, and the Anglo-Irish Agreement of 1938, which ended the economic war and handed back the ports that Britain had held under the Treaty for use in time of war. The full significance of this latter achievement did not become apparent until he was faced with the delicate task of maintaining Ireland's neutrality during the Second World War. He was Minister for External Affairs as well as President, and in that capacity attended meetings of the League of Nations. He was president of the Council of the league on his first appearance at Geneva in 1932 and, in a speech that made a worldwide impression, appealed for genuine adherence by its members to the principles of the Covenant of the league. In September 1938 he was elected nineteenth president of the Assembly of the league, a tribute to the international recognition he had won by his independent stance on world questions. At this stage in his career he had gained an authority unequalled by an Irish leader since the fall of Parnell nearly fifty years before.

The Second World War tested his powers of patient diplomacy to the utmost, as he resisted pressure and sometimes threats, open or veiled, from Germany, Britain and the USA against his policy of neutrality. And at home, the IRA presented another threat, which was met by the sternest of measures. Over a thousand of its members were interned or imprisoned, nine were executed, three died on hunger strike, and another six were shot in armed encounters with detectives. After the war the position of Fianna Fáil began to weaken, and in 1948 they were ousted from power by the first Coalition government, with JOHN A. COSTELLO as Taoiseach. De Valera, as leader of the opposition, embarked on a world campaign on the partition question. In 1951 he was back in power but without an overall majority. He had had trouble with his eyes in the 1930s, and in 1936 underwent an operation in Zürich. This was successful, and his sight, with the proper glasses, became very good. A second operation was necessary in 1940. In 1952 his sight failed again, due to detachment of the retina. After six operations, carried out in Utrecht by Professor Weve, the retina was re-attached, but he was left with only peripheral sight and unable to read.

In 1954 his party was again defeated in a general election and the second Coalition government took office, but this, like the first, lasted only three years. At the general election of 1957, de Valera, then in his seventy-fifth year, won a majority of nine seats over all the others combined, the greatest number he had ever secured. His last bid at constitutional reform failed when the people, by referendum, rejected his proposal that the proportional representation system of election should be changed to the direct vote. On the same day in June 1959 he was elected President of Ireland in succession to SEÁN T. Ó CEALLAIGH, defeating GENERAL SEÁN MAC EOIN by a comfortable majority. As President he received many distinguished visitors, including Presidents Charles de Gaulle and John Kennedy. In 1964, at the age of eighty-one, he visited Washington and addressed Congress, speaking for twenty-five minutes without notes. He was re-elected President in 1966, when he was eighty-three, but this time his majority was only 10,000 votes.

Space does not permit more than a mention of the honours he received during his long career, which spanned sixty-three years in public life. He was elected Chancellor of the National University in 1921 and held the post until his death. Pope John XXIII bestowed on him the Order of Christ. He received honorary degrees from universities in Ireland and abroad, and in 1968 was elected FRS, a recognition of his lifelong interest in mathematics. During his parliamentary career he was MP for Down from 1921 to 1929 and for South Down from 1933 to 1937, but did not take his seat. He retired from office in June 1973, having served for fourteen years, the longest period allowed under the Constitution. Éamon de Valera died on 29 August 1975 at the age of ninety-two, eight months after the death of his wife. He was buried in Glasnevin cemetery after a state funeral. An assessment of his achievements and failures must be left to historians, but it may be said that his two great aims, the restoration of Irish and the ending of partition, seem no nearer achievement today than when he first put them forward as national objectives.

DE VALERA, SINÉAD, née FLANAGAN (1878–1975), born Bal-briggan, Co. Dublin, 3 June 1878. She trained as a teacher, and took up her first post in a national school in Dorset St, Dublin. In her spare time she taught Irish at the Leinster College of the Gaelic League in Parnell Square, and took part in amateur dramatics. She played in *The Tinker and the Fairy* by DOUGLAS HYDE in the garden of GEORGE MOORE's house in Ely Place. When she asked his advice about making the stage her career, Moore replied: 'Height, five feet four; hair, red; name, Flanagan—no, my dear.' One of her pupils at the Leinster College was ÉAMON DE VALERA, then a teacher of mathematics. They were married on 8 January 1910. There were five sons and two daughters of the marriage, and she devoted herself to her home and family, taking no part in public life. During the years after the 1916 Rising she saw little of her husband, who was either serving prison terms in English jails, or in America working for the republican cause. In 1920 she was smuggled into America on a false passport to visit him. After Éamon de Valera had become head of the Irish government, in 1932, and with her family growing up, she began to write for children, in Irish and English. She published plays, poems, and fairy stories, including translations from English and French. During her husband's period of office as President of Ireland from 1959 to 1973 she seldom appeared in public, but was a regular attender at children's drama competitions in Irish and at Gaelic League functions. She died in a Dublin nursing home on 7 January 1975, on the eve of her sixty-fifth wedding anniversary, survived by her husband and all her children, save Brian, her third son, who had been killed in a riding accident in the Phoenix Park in February 1936.

DE VERE, SIR AUBREY (1788–1846) (originally HUNT), poet. Born Curragh Chase, Adare, Co. Limerick, 28 August 1788. Educated at Harrow, where Byron was a contemporary. He lived a quiet life as a country gentleman, avoided politics, and was a good landlord. His publications included verse tragedies, long poems, and sonnets; these latter won high praise from Wordsworth. He died at Curragh Chase, 5 July 1846.

DE VERE, AUBREY THOMAS (1814–1902), poet, son of SIR AUBREY. Born Curragh Chase, 10 January 1814. Educated at home and at TCD. Visiting England frequently, he formed a close friendship with Newman, Wordsworth, and Tennyson. In the famine of 1846–1847 he worked with practical energy on relief committees. In 1851 he was received into the Catholic Church, and thereafter lived quietly in his family home until his death, unmarried, on 21 January 1902. Published many volumes of poetry and some political pamphlets, in which criticism of English misrule of Ireland was tempered by support of the Union. His early poems treated of classical subjects; later he turned to Irish legend and history for inspiration. He published his *Recollections* in 1897.

DEVLIN, ANNE (*c.* 1778–1851), patriot. Was a niece of MICHAEL DWYER and the devoted servant of ROBERT EMMET. When Emmet was in hiding in the Dublin mountains after the failure of his rising in 1803, she carried messages between him and his friends in Dublin. She was arrested, but despite imprisonment and torture refused to give any information. Released after two years, she spent the rest of her life in great poverty in the slums of Dublin. She was befriended by RICHARD MADDEN towards the end of her life, and he had a monument erected over her grave in Glasnevin cemetery.

DEVLIN, DENIS (1908–1959), poet and diplomat. Born Greenock, Scotland, on 15 April 1908. Educated at Belvedere College, UCD, Munich University and the Sorbonne. Entered the Irish diplomatic service in 1935 and served in Italy, New York, Washington and London, before being appointed minister plenipotentiary to Italy in 1950; accredited also to Turkey 1951; ambassador to Italy 1958. His first book of poems, in conjunction with Brian Coffey, was published in Dublin in 1930. Further collections were *Intercessions* (London, 1937), *Exile* (1949), *Lough Derg* (New York, 1946), and *The Heavenly Foreigner* (Dublin, 1950). He also published *Memoirs of a Turcoman Diplomat* (Rome, 1959). In his last years he devoted himself to a poetic commentary on the *Via Crucis*. His friend Ignazio Silone observed his habitual sadness at that time, presaging his death in Dublin on 21 August 1959. The Denis Devlin Memorial Award for Poetry is administered by the Arts Council.

DEVLIN, JOSEPH (1871–1934), nationalist. Born Hamill St, Belfast, 13 February 1871, son of a car-driver. Educated Divis St CBS. He worked as a pot-boy in a public-house, then became a journalist on the nationalist *Irish News*. He soon showed gifts as a public speaker. Returned unopposed as MP for North Kilkenny 1902; won the West Belfast seat 1906. He re-established the Ancient Order of Hibernians, and was president from 1905 until his death. When CARSON formed the Ulster Volunteers to resist Home Rule, Devlin took a prominent part in organising the National Volunteers in opposition and was offered the chairmanship of the Irish Party on the death of JOHN REDMOND in 1918, but gave way in favour of JOHN DILLON. Defeated ÉAMON DE VALERA in the Falls division of Belfast 1918 and held the seat until 1922. With short breaks, he sat in the new Northern parliament until his death and also represented the constituency of Fermanagh and Tyrone at Westminster from 1929. Belfast people called him affectionately 'Wee Joe', and T. M. HEALY described him as 'the duodecimo Demosthenes'. He founded a holiday home for working women near Belfast. Died in Belfast, 18 January 1934.

DEVOY, JOHN (1842–1928), Fenian. Born Kill, Co. Kildare, 3 September 1842, son of a smallholder and labourer.

The family moved to Dublin after the Famine, and the father obtained a job in Watkins' brewery. John attended evening classes for a short while in the Catholic University, worked as a clerk, and then joined the Fenians. In 1861 he enlisted in the French Foreign Legion and spent a year in Algeria in order to learn soldiering. On his return to Ireland he was placed in charge of Fenian organisation in the British army in Ireland. He was arrested in February 1866 and sentenced to fifteen years' penal servitude. After five years' imprisonment in Millbank, Portland, and Chatam, he was released in 1871 on condition that he live outside the United Kingdom. He went to America and worked as a journalist in New York and Chicago, eventually settling in New York. He joined Clan na Gael, the foremost Irish-American organisation, and soon became one of its most influential leaders. The aims of Clan na Gael were to keep a firm grip on Irish-American opinion, organise anti-English views, send help, mainly financial, to those working in the cause in Ireland, and keep in constant touch with all involved in the movement for Irish freedom. In 1879 he made a secret visit to France and Ireland, and when DAVITT came to America shortly after, Devoy threw the influence of Clan na Gael behind the 'new departure', the policy by which revolutionary and constitutional nationalists formed a common front on the two great issues of self-government and the land question. He was chairman of the committee that organised the rescue of six Fenian prisoners from Fremantle, Australia, in 1876 on board the whaler *Catalpa*, an exploit that brought great prestige to Clan na Gael. He founded his own newspaper, the *Irish Nation*, and then in 1903 founded a weekly, the *Gaelic American*, which he edited until his death. Clan na Gael had a stormy existence, marked by many splits, factions, and internal controversies, but he kept his dominant position in the organisation, with Judge Daniel Cohalan, who joined it about

1900 and became his closest associate. Devoy personified exiled Ireland, and in his small office in New York was visited through the years by thousands of supporters of the Irish cause. Through his influence the Clan helped every Irish movement of note, subscribing funds to the *United Irishman*, edited by ARTHUR GRIFFITH; to St Enda's, the school founded by PEARSE; and to the Irish Volunteers. Between the death of PARNELL and the rise of Sinn Féin, the Clan used every opportunity to drive a wedge between America and England, and tried to keep the USA neutral in the First World War. When DE VALERA began his mission in America in 1919 to gain support and funds, he was at first well received by Devoy, but strained relations soon developed, and ended in a complete break. The Irish-Americans wanted to retain their control in America and resented the dominant position being taken by the leader from Ireland. After the Anglo-Irish Treaty of 1921, Devoy supported the Irish Free State. He visited Ireland in 1924 for the revival of the Tailteann Games, and was feted and honoured by the government and public representatives. On his return to America he published his *Recollections of an Irish Rebel* (1929). He had previously published *The Land of Éire* and *The Irish Land League* (both 1882). He died at Atlantic City on 29 September 1928, unmarried and virtually penniless. His remains were taken to Ireland and buried in Glasnevin cemetery. His letters were edited by William O'Brien and Desmond Ryan and published in Dublin in 1948 under the title *Devoy's Post Bag*.

DILL, SIR JOHN (1881–1944), field-marshal. Born Lurgan, Co. Armagh, 25 December 1881. Educated Cheltenham College and Sandhurst Military College. After service in South Africa and the First World War he became commandant of the British Army Staff College and then Director of Military Operations at the War Office, reaching the rank of lieutenant-general. Passed over in 1937 for the post of Chief of the

Imperial General Staff in favour of Lord Gort, and went to France as corps commander. Appointed chief of staff April 1940, but as chief military adviser to British government often found himself in conflict with Churchill, who regarded him as over-cautious. Sent to Washington in 1942 to lead the British military mission there, and by his integrity, ability and charm soon gained great prestige in US military and official circles, winning the trust and friendship of Roosevelt and General Marshall. Died in Washington, 4 November 1944. Buried in Arlington Cemetery.

DILLON, GERARD (1916–1971), painter. Born Belfast. Educated at CBS. At fourteen apprenticed to a painting and decorating contractor. Studied art at Belfast Technical School for a short time. Moved to London in 1934, and two years later began to paint seriously. Spent the war years in Belfast and Dublin, and exhibited with the White Stag group in Dublin. Went back to London 1945, and worked for a while with demolition gangs to earn a living. About this time he began to exhibit regularly at RHA, the Exhibition of Living Art, and commercial galleries in Dublin and London. His early primitive oils included many landscapes of Connemara, which he visited often. He experimented with various media in his middle period and designed many tapestries and murals. He visited Italy and Spain and in 1958 he represented Ireland at the Guggenheim International and Britain at the Pittsburgh International Exhibition. About this time he taught in several London art schools. In the early sixties he visited America as a member of an Irish trade and culture delegation. Returned to live in Dublin 1968. Joined Dublin Graphic Studios and made etchings. Commissioned by Bord Fáilte to design a wall hanging, finished in 1970. He helped to design sets and costumes for an Abbey Theatre production of O'CASEY's *Juno and the Paycock*. In his final phase he was absorbed by the theme of the clown and the human con-

dition. He wrote a collection of short stories about his childhood and made a record of folk songs he had heard and remembered. Died in Dublin; buried in Belfast.

DILLON, JAMES MATTHEW (1902–1986), politician. Born in Dublin on 26 September 1902, fourth son of JOHN DILLON. Educated at Mount St Benedict's, Gorey, UCG, and King's Inns. Called to the bar in 1931. He studied business methods in Selfridge's of London and Marshall Fields of Chicago before becoming manager of the family's general merchant business in Ballaghadereen, Co. Roscommon. TD for West Donegal 1932–1937 and for Monaghan 1937–1969. Became deputy leader of Fine Gael under WILLIAM COSGRAVE. Resigned from Fine Gael early in 1942 after making a speech in Dáil Éireann opposing the all-party policy of neutrality in the Second World War. Was appointed Minister for Agriculture as an independent TD in the inter-party government 1948–1951. Re-joined Fine Gael in 1953 and was Minister for Agriculture 1954–1957. Became leader of Fine Gael in 1959 and president of the party in 1960. Resigned as leader in 1965 on grounds of age and retired to the back benches, retiring from politics in 1969. He was regarded in Dáil Éireann as an outstanding parliamentarian and a colourful orator. He died on 10 February 1986, survived by his wife and son.

DILLON, JOHN (1851–1927), nationalist, son of JOHN BLAKE DILLON. Born Blackrock, Co. Dublin, 4 September 1851. Educated at Catholic University medical school, qualified as a surgeon but soon turned to politics, and became one of PARNELL's most prominent supporters in the Land League. Elected MP for Tipperary in 1880; his health suffered from several terms of imprisonment but he resumed his activities in 1885. Was elected MP for East Mayo and, with WILLIAM O'BRIEN, began the 'plan of campaign', under which tenants offered a fair rent, and if this was refused, paid nothing. The cry 'Remember Mitchelstown' originated when the police, prevented from reaching the platform, fired and killed three people in a huge crowd being addressed there by Dillon. After the split in the party in 1891 following the O'Shea divorce case, Dillon became chairman of the anti-Parnell group; but when moves were begun to heal the breach, he insisted on resigning, leaving the way clear for REDMOND to become leader in 1900. Dillon distrusted A. J. Balfour's policy of conciliation, which he regarded as 'killing Home Rule with kindness', and his attacks on the 1903 Land Act led to permanent estrangement between himself and O'Brien. The formation of the Irish Volunteers in 1913, the stand taken by Redmond in support of the Allies when the First World War broke out and the 1916 Rising marked a gradual erosion of the support the Irish Party had enjoyed. He showed independence and moral courage in his opposition to conscription and in a famous speech in the House of Commons in defence of the leaders of the rising. On Redmond's death in 1918 Dillon became leader. In the general election of that year the party was virtually wiped out, and Dillon himself was defeated in East Mayo by DE VALERA. He retired from politics and died in London, 4 August 1927.

DILLON, JOHN BLAKE (1816–1866), nationalist. Born Ballaghadereen, Co. Mayo. Educated TCD, where he formed a close friendship with THOMAS DAVIS. Called to the Irish bar 1841. Joined Davis and GAVAN DUFFY in founding the *Nation* in 1842. He was active at Killenaule, Co. Tipperary, in the unsuccessful rising of 1848 and afterwards escaped to France and thence to America, where he practised law until 1855 when an amnesty allowed him to return to Ireland. MP for Tipperary 1865, supported the Repeal movement but was opposed to Fenianism. Died suddenly of cholera in Killarney, 15 September 1866. Buried Glasnevin cemetery.

DILLON, MYLES (1900–1972), Celtic scholar. Born Dublin, son of JOHN DILLON. Educated Mount St Benedict, UCD, and University of Bonn. Reader in English at the Sorbonne 1925. Lecturer in comparative philology and Sanskrit, TCD, 1928, and UCD 1930–1937. Professor of Irish at the University of Wisconsin 1937; professor of Celtic philology and comparative linguistics, Chicago University, 1946. Later joined the American Office of War Information. Attached to the American embassy in London for some time. After a short period as professor of Celtic at Edinburgh University, Dillon joined the DIAS as senior professor in the School of Celtic Studies. Director of the school 1960–1968. Published numerous scholarly works on Irish, Celtic studies, and Sanskrit. In 1931 he was the first to translate and edit a Sanskrit text on Indian theatre. In 1956 he edited the third volume of the *Celtica Äuss-Memorial*. Council member of Irish Texts Society; president of RIA 1966. In 1953 visited a number of universities in Australia, lecturing in several cities in India en route home. Honorary doctorate, University of Rennes, 1962. O'Donnell Lecturer in Celtic Studies at Oxford University 1970–1971. Died Dublin, 18 June 1972.

DILLON, WENTWORTH, fourth EARL OF ROSCOMMON (*c.* 1633–1685), writer. Nephew of the great Earl of Strafford. Born in Ireland; educated University of Caen. After making a tour of the continent he returned to England after the Restoration of 1660, and had his extensive estates in Ireland restored to him. He wrote poetry, translated Horace's *Art of Poetry*, and tried to set up a literary society on the model of the French Academy 'to refine and fix the standard of our language'. Died in London in January 1685. Buried in Westminster Abbey. His *Poetical Works* went into many editions.

DOGGETT, THOMAS (*c.* 1660–1721), actor. Born in Castle St, Dublin, and became a travelling actor. He first appeared at Drury Lane in 1691 and made his reputation as a comic actor. He wrote one play, *The Country Wake* (1690), which was well received and often revived. A good businessman, he became part-proprietor of the Haymarket Theatre and made a comfortable fortune. He was a strong Hanoverian, and on 1 August 1716, to honour the accession of King George I, he gave funds for a coat and badge 'to be rowed for by six watermen from London Bridge to Chelsea, and to be continued annually on the same day for ever'. He died at Eltham, Kent, in September 1721.

DOHENY, MICHAEL (1805–1863), Young Irelander. Born Brookhill, near Fethard, Co. Tipperary, 22 May 1805, son of a small farmer. He educated himself, entered Gray's Inn, and by the age of thirty had become a well-known barrister. He became legal adviser to the borough of Cashel, and in 1842 joined the Repeal movement. When the association came under the influence of English Whigs he left to join the Young Irelanders. At the failure of the 1848 insurrection he fled to the USA with JAMES STEPHENS, and in 1849 published there *The Felon's Track: History of the Attempted Outbreak in Ireland*. With JAMES STEPHENS and JOHN O'MAHONY he founded the Fenian brotherhood in the United States. Doheny continued to practise as a lawyer, and died in the USA in April 1863.

DONELLAN, NEHEMIAS (died 1609), archbishop. Born Galway, and educated Cambridge University 1579–1582. Archbishop of Tuam 1595. An Irish-speaker, he added to an Irish translation of the New Testament begun by John Kearney and Nicholas Walsh, bishop of Ossory. WILLIAM DANIEL published a complete translation 1602, claiming to have worked from the original Greek. What use he made of his predecessors' work is not known.

DONN BYRNE, BRIAN OSWALD (1889–1928), novelist, pen-name Donn Byrne. Born New York, 20 November 1889, of Irish parents, and brought to Armagh as an infant. Spoke Irish, and known locally as Brian O'Beirne. Educated at UCD, Sorbonne, and Leipzig. Returned to New York about 1911 and after some years' literary hack work contributed short stories to *Harper's, Smart Set,* and *Ladies' Home Journal*. First novel, *The Stranger's Banquet*, published 1919. Further novels—*The Foolish Matrons* (1920), sold for filming, *Messer Marco Polo* (1922), and *Blind Raftery* (1924)—were highly successful. Travelled extensively in Europe, then settled at Montrose (now RTE headquarters), Dublin, 1922–1925. Other successful novels were *Hangman's House* (1926), *Brother Saul* (1927), and *Destiny Bay* (1928). Bought Coolmain Castle, Kilbrittain, Co. Cork, in 1928. Drowned in Courtmacsherry Bay, 19 June 1928, when his car ran off the road. Buried Rathclarin, Coolmain.

DONNELLY, CHARLES (1910–1937), poet and republican. Born near Dungannon, Co. Tyrone, and educated at O'Connell Schools, Dublin, and UCD. Formed a left-wing group, Student Vanguard, and contributed poems to the university magazine, *Cothrom Féinne*. Failed his examinations and went to London where he worked for the Republican Congress and for a news agency. Went to Spain in January 1937 to fight for the republic with the International Brigade against Franco. Killed at the Jarama on 27 February 1937.

DONNELLY, DAN (died 1820), pugilist. Born Dublin, son of a carpenter, and followed same trade. Fond of drink and company, he led a wild and extravagant life. Lived in Ringsend, and became noted for his strength in encounters with sailors. Some Irish and London gentlemen arranged a match with a famed English pugilist, Hall. Donnelly was taken to Kilcullen some weeks beforehand to train away from drinking companions. He beat Hall at the Curragh on

14 September 1814 after seventeen rounds; 40,000 attended the fight. Donnelly received 100 guineas, which he spent in a fortnight. His next match was against the English champion, Cooper, in 1815. He defeated him in eleven rounds at 'Donnelly's Hollow' in the Curragh, now marked by a small obelisk. A timber merchant set him up as a publican in Capel St and he got married. He neglected the business, moved to Poolbeg St, but business stagnated and debts accumulated. He went to England to give sparring exhibitions and was matched with one Oliver, whom he beat at Crawley Downs, near London, in thirty-two rounds, 21 July 1819. At that time a round lasted until one or other was thrown or knocked to the ground. He returned to Dublin, opened a public-house in Pill Lane at the corner of Greek St and did a roaring business. He had never taken care of his health, often leaving a public-house to sleep out in the rain. He died in his house, of a sudden chill, on 17 February 1820.

DOWDEN, EDWARD (1843–1913), critic. Born Cork, 3 May 1843. Educated Queen's College, Cork, and TCD. Appointed to the newly founded chair of English literature in TCD in 1867, four years after he had graduated there, and held the post until his death. Made his reputation as a critic with his first work, *Shakespeare, His Mind and Art* (1875). Many other critical works followed, and a *Life of Shelley* (1886). Though tolerant in his views, he disliked Irish nationalism and opposed home rule. Died Dublin, 4 April 1913.

DOWLAND, JOHN (1562–1626), musician. Born Dalkey, Co. Dublin. Became the greatest lutanist of his age. He travelled extensively on the Continent and was for some time court lutanist to the king of Denmark, at a princely salary equal to that of the Admiral of the Realm. His melodies, which were often based on well-known folk-songs, were published by his own account in Paris, Antwerp, Cologne, Hamburg, Leipzig, and Amsterdam, and he was mentioned by many of the poets and dramatists of his day. His songs, which were mostly intended to be sung either in four parts or as solos with lute accompaniment, were the most celebrated of their time, and became widely known again on being republished this century. He spent his money freely and seems to have fallen into neglect in his later years. He died in London and was said to have been poor and embittered, and to have contrasted his 'kingly entertainment in a forraine climate' with his inability to 'attaine to any place at home'.

DOWNEY, RICHARD JOSEPH (1881–1953), archbishop. Born Kilkenny, 5 May 1881. Educated Enniscorthy CBS and St Joseph's seminary, Upholland, near Wigan, being ordained in 1907. He joined the Catholic Missionary Society in London and spent fifteen years preaching and lecturing. When in 1928 he was appointed archbishop of Liverpool at the age of forty-seven he became the youngest Roman Catholic archbishop in the world. He completed a new seminary at a cost of £250,000 and commissioned Sir Edwin Lutyens to design a cathedral, but the Second World War intervened and this project was never finished. Spokesman for the English hierarchy on educational matters, he was a strong champion of the voluntary schools. His influence was largely responsible for ending sectarian strife in Liverpool. Although only 5 feet 4 inches (163 cm) tall, reached 18 stone (114 kg) in 1932. By a system of dieting and exercise he reduced his weight to 9 stone (57 kg) by 1939, and received letters from all over the world asking how he had achieved this. He was made a freeman of Kilkenny, his native town. Died in Woolton, 16 January 1953.

DOYLE, HENRY EDWARD (1827–1892), painter. Born Dublin. In early life worked as a draughtsman and wood-engraver in London, while also painting some portraits. On the recommendation of Cardinal Wiseman, he was appointed Commissioner for Rome in the London International Exhibition of 1862, and was created a knight of the Order of Pius IX. In March 1869 he was elected director of the National Gallery of Ireland, and by judicious purchases during his twenty-three years of office added many fine pictures to the gallery. Though exhibiting only occasionally, he became a member of the RHA in December 1874. Died suddenly in London, 17 February 1892.

DOYLE, JACK (1913–1978), boxer, wrestler, singer and playboy. Born in Cóbh, Co. Cork, and joined the British army in his teens. He took up amateur boxing and became famous for his lethal right-hand punch. An Irish trainer, Dan Sullivan, bought him out of the British army and he turned professional. A string of wins brought him a meeting in July 1933 with Jack Peterson for the British heavyweight title. He was disqualified in the second round for a low blow. He then left for the USA where he was defeated by Buddy Baer in the first round. His marriage to a minor Hollywood actress, Judith Allen, ended quickly in divorce. He then married a Mexican starlet, Movita, and returned to England where they enjoyed success as a double singing act. They came to Ireland and were married again in a blaze of publicity at St Andrew's Catholic Church, Westland Row, Dublin. Movita left him in 1945 to marry Marlon Brando. He returned to London and drew crowds as an all-in wrestler. Later days saw him living there in poor circumstances in a basement flat. He died in a London hospital on 13 December 1978. A long-time friend said that he had survived on two remittances, of £25 a month from Movita under their divorce settlement, and £100 a month from the wealthy Dodge family on condition that he never see their daughter Delphine again. She had been cited by Doyle's first wife in her divorce petition.

DOYLE, JAMES WARREN (1786–1834), bishop of Kildare and Leighlin.

Born near New Ross, Co. Wexford. As a young boy saw the atrocities that followed the 1798 Rising. Educated Augustinian seminary, New Ross, and University of Coimbra, Portugal. When the Peninsular Wars interrupted his studies in 1806, he joined Sir Arthur Wellesley's army as a volunteer interpreter, and the ability he showed during peace negotiations in Lisbon is said to have elicited tempting offers from the Portuguese. He remained true to his vocation, however and, returning to Ireland, was ordained in the Augustinian order in 1809. After some years teaching in New Ross and in Carlow College, he was appointed bishop of Kildare and Leighlin in 1819. The new bishop actively identified himself with the social struggles of the oppressed Catholics. He gave open support to O'CONNELL and became a formidable opponent of the established Protestant Church and of the administration generally. His pamphlet *A Vindication of the Religious and Civil Principles of the Irish Catholics* (1824), and his *Letters on the State of Ireland* (1824–1825), published under the initials JKL (James of Kildare and Leighlin) were widely read; his trenchant style and forceful arguments impressed opponents and allies alike. He was called to London in 1825, 1830 and 1832 to give evidence on Irish affairs before parliamentary committees. In his pastoral work he reformed discipline in the diocese, built schools, opened libraries, and strove to improve the standard of education. Died at his house, Braganza, Carlow, 16 June 1834.

DOYLE, JOHN (1797–1868), caricaturist. Born Dublin. Studied drawing at the school of the Dublin Society. He first made his name as a painter of horses. In 1821 he went to London and, after indifferent success as a portrait painter, found his true métier as a political caricaturist. Over a period of twenty-two years he published a series of lithographs on contemporary politicians under the signature HB (formed of two JDs one over the other). These drawings, 917 in all, constitute a remarkable record of public events between 1829 and 1851, and were immensely popular. He retired from active work in 1851. Died 2 January 1868.

DOYLE, LYNN. See under MONT-GOMERY, LESLIE A.

DOYLE, MARTIN. See under HICKEY, WILLIAM.

DOYLE, PASCHAL VINCENT (1923–1988), hotelier and builder. Born in Dublin and educated at Westland Row CBS. He left school at an early age and joined his father's building business. At twenty-two he built the County Club, a public-house in Churchtown, Dublin, and then moved into the hotel business, building and operating first the Montrose and then the Skylon, Tara Tower, Green Isle and Burlington. He was quick to see the opportunity created by the emergence of a new affluent middle class, and set out to capture that market. In his own words, Dublin hotels were until then still catering for the ascendancy. When these hotels had been firmly established he moved 'up-market', building the luxury Berkeley Court in 1978 and Westbury in 1984. He became the most successful hotelier in the history of the industry in Ireland, employing two thousand people. He also owned hotels in Britain and the USA and built a number of houses and apartment blocks. He was appointed chairman of Bord Fáilte in 1973 and retained in the post by successive Governments. He served as chairman of the Dublin Diocesan Finance Committee and on the Board for the Employment of the Blind. He was also a board member of the Meath Hospital and of the Central Council of the Federated Dublin Hospitals. He died in a Dublin hospital on 6 February 1988.

DRENNAN, WILLIAM (1754–1820), poet. Born Belfast, 23 May 1754. Educated Glasgow University (M.A. 1771), and Edinburgh (M.D. 1778). Practised as a doctor in Belfast for two or three years and then moved to Newry. In 1789 he settled in Dublin, where he soon built up a good practice. Joined the Society of United Irishmen, became one of the leaders, and wrote their original prospectus. Tried for sedition June 1794 and acquitted. After this he withdrew from active participation in the society. He wrote a great deal of popular poetry, including 'Memories of William Orr' or 'The Wake of William Orr', and was probably the first to call Ireland the Emerald Isle. In 1800 he married a wealthy Englishwoman and in 1807 moved to Belfast, where he founded the Academical Institution and the *Belfast Magazine*. He died Belfast, 5 February 1820.

DU CROS, SIR ARTHUR PHILIP (1871–1955), pioneer of the pneumatic tyre industry. Born Dublin, 26 January 1871. Educated at a national school and entered the civil service in the lowest grade at fifteen. Left in 1892 to join his father and brother in a company formed to devolop the pneumatic tyre invented by John Boyd Dunlop. Founded the Dunlop Rubber Company 1901, and devoted himself during the following twenty-five years to a successful world-wide expansion of the business. In the economic depression of the late 1920s the company suffered heavy losses and Du Cros lost much of his personal fortune. He wrote the history of the industry in *Wheels of Fortune: a Salute to Pioneers* (1938). Died at his home in Hertfordshire, 28 October 1955.

DUFF, FRANK (1889–1980), lay apostle. Born in Dublin and educated at Blackrock College. He joined the civil service in 1908. Became an active member of the Society of St Vincent de Paul and with another social worker, Matt Lalor, who owned a chain of tobacconists, he founded the Legion of Mary in 1921. It grew rapidly and is now an international organisation with over a million members, all voluntary workers who devote themselves to apostolic and social work especially among the poor and underprivileged. In 1928 the Legion founded the Morning Star hostel in Dublin for down-and-out men and in 1931 a hostel nearby for destitute women and unmarried mothers, taking in mother and child together. He retired from the civil service in 1933 to devote himself full-time to the work of the Legion, and wrote several books on Marian theology as well as the Legion Handbook. Received honorary LL.D. from NUI and the papal Order of St Gregory the Great. He died in the Morning Star hostel on 7 November 1980, aged ninety-one.

DUFFERIN AND AVA, MARQUIS OF. See under BLACKWOOD, FREDERICK.

DUFFY, SIR CHARLES GAVAN (1816–1903), nationalist. Born Monaghan, 12 April 1816, son of a shopkeeper. Save for a few months at a local school he was self-educated, reading omnivorously. He entered journalism, working in Dublin and Belfast, and was called to the bar in 1845 but did not practise. With THOMAS DAVIS and JOHN BLAKE DILLON he founded the *Nation*, a weekly journal, in 1842. Duffy was editor, and his talented contributors included the leading Young Irelanders. The aim of the *Nation* was 'to create and foster public opinion in Ireland and make it racy of the soil,' and it soon gained immense popularity and influence. A collection of songs and ballads, *The Spirit of the Nation*, was received with enthusiasm all over Ireland. The Young Irelanders soon broke away from O'CONNELL. The Paris revolution of 1848 inspired them to plan a rising, but in July that year Duffy was arrested and the *Nation* suppressed. He was discharged in 1849, revived the *Nation*, and flung himself into the land reform agitation, being elected MP for New Ross in 1852. Attempts at reform were blocked by the House of Lords, and Duffy, in despair and his health impaired, emigrated to Australia in 1855 to practise law. Entering politics, he became prime minister of Victoria in 1871 and was knighted in 1873 for his services to the colony. He retired to the south of France in 1880 and devoted himself to literary work, including a life of Davis, histories of the Young Ireland movement, and an autobiography, *My Life in Two Hemispheres* (1898). Died at Nice, 9 February 1903. Buried Glasnevin cemetery, Dublin.

DUFFY, GEORGE GAVAN (1882–1951), solicitor and politician. Born October 1882, son of SIR CHARLES. Educated in France. He qualified as a solicitor and practised in London until 1917 when he was called to the Irish bar and came to live in Dublin. As a solicitor he was engaged in some important political cases: he prepared the defence for his friend ROGER CASEMENT. He represented South Dublin in the Dáil from 1918 to 1923. Two years after coming to Ireland he was appointed Irish envoy extraordinary in Paris and, with SEÁN T. Ó CEALLAIGH, was there for some time as the Sinn Féin representative. In September 1920 he was given twenty-four hours to leave the country for failing to cease anti-British propaganda. Duffy was the Republican envoy in Rome in 1920 and was a member of the Irish Peace Delegation to London in 1921. He was one of the five Irish signatories of the Treaty in 1921 and voted for it in the Dáil. He recommended the Treaty reluctantly—he was the last to sign it—but he saw no alternative. In January 1922 he became Minister for Foreign Affairs in the provisional government of the Irish Free State. He resigned in August 1922 in protest against a government decree abolishing the Republican courts. In 1923 he resigned his Dáil seat, resumed his legal practice, and was engaged in some notable constitutional cases. Called to the inner bar 1929; chairman, Greater Dublin Commission, 1935–1938. Member of commission on setting up of second house of the Oireachtas 1937. Judge of the High Court 1936, and president of the court 1946. Died Dublin June 1951.

DUFFY, JAMES (1809–1871), bookseller and publisher. Born Monaghan. Educated at hedge school. Became bookseller's assistant in Anglesea St, Dublin. Started his own business about 1830 with twopenny edition of *Boney's Oraculum*, a dream book also called *Napoleon's Book of Fate*, which had a huge sale. Then launched his Popular Sixpenny Library, books of devotional and national interest, and fireside tales, well bound and printed. This venture broke new ground, and the books sold widely. Published work of the Young Irelanders, including *Spirit of the Nation* and the 'Library of Ireland' and works of CARLETON, the BANIMS, and MANGAN. Employed 120 workers. Never took a regular holiday nor allowed one to his staff, although otherwise an excellent employer. Died in Dublin, 4 July 1871.

DUFFY, LOUISE GAVAN (1884–1969), teacher and revolutionary, daughter of CHARLES GAVAN DUFFY. Born in Nice, and came to Ireland for the first time in 1903 for her father's funeral. She resolved to learn Irish, and graduated from UCD in 1911. Taught in Scoil Íde, the girls' school founded by PATRICK PEARSE. Joined Cumann na mBan and served in the GPO in the 1916 Rising, escaping capture after the surrender. In 1917 with Annie McHugh, who later married ERNEST BLYTHE, she founded Scoil Bhríde, an Irish-language secondary school for girls, in Dublin. The school prospered and moved from St Stephen's Green to larger premises in Oakley Road in 1965. She died in Dublin on 12 October 1969.

DUGGAN, ÉAMONN (1874–1936), lawyer and nationalist. Born Longwood, Co. Meath. Admitted a solicitor in 1914 and built up a large practice. Became a supporter of Sinn Féin and fought in the 1916 Rising. Court-martialled and sentenced to three years' penal servitude, but released after serving a year. Acted as solicitor for next-of-kin at the inquest of THOMAS ASHE, and was for a time IRA Director of Intelligence. At the end of 1920 he was re-arrested and not released until the Truce of July 1921. Elected to the First Dáil as the member for South Meath 1918 and re-elected 1921. After the Truce he was appointed chief liaison officer for Ireland. In October 1921 he was appointed as one of the five envoys plenipotentiary to negotiate and conclude a treaty with the British Commonwealth. He signed the Treaty, not at Downing Street but at 22 Hans Place. In the post-Treaty provisional government he was appointed Minister for Home Affairs and later became parliamentary secretary to the Minister for Defence and to the Executive Council. He declined to go forward in the 1933 general election, but was elected to the Senate and in 1933 became the last citizen of the Free State to take the oath as a member of the Oireachtas. He was the first chairman of Dún Laoghaire Borough Council. Died suddenly at Dún Laoghaire on 6 June 1936.

DUGGAN, GEORGE CHESTER (1887–1969), civil servant. Born Greystones, Co. Wicklow. Educated High School, Dublin, and TCD. Entered the civil service in 1908 and, after serving in the Admiralty, and the Chief Secretary's Office, Dublin Castle, joined the Northern Ireland civil service. Comptroller and Auditor-General from 1945 until his retirement in 1949. A series of articles that he contributed to the *Irish Times* in 1950, 'Northern Ireland, Success or Failure?', drew strong criticism in the Northern houses of parliament. Died at his home at Mullagh, Co. Cavan, 15 June 1969.

DUNBOYNE, LORD. See under BUTLER, JOHN.

DUNCAN, ELLEN, née DOUGLAS (*c.* 1850–1937), patron of the arts. Born in Dublin. Educated at Alexandra College and RIAM. Appointed by SIR HUGH LANE as first curator of Municipal Gallery of Modern Art, Dublin, which opened on 18 January 1908. The city council found they had no legal power to maintain the gallery, and Lane met these expenses until 1913. She contributed articles to Irish periodicals and the *Burlington Magazine, Athenaeum, Studio,* etc. Married James Duncan, a civil servant who later retired to the south of France. With CONSTANCE MARKIEVICZ founded the United Arts Club in 1907. Organised the first exhibition in Ireland of Post-Impressionist paintings, in the Arts Club in 1911. Took part in campaign for return of Lane pictures.

DUNLAP, JOHN (1747–1812), printer. Born Strabane, Co. Tyrone. Served his apprenticeship at Gray's printing press in the town. Emigrated to America and in 1771 founded the *Philadelphia Packet*, the first daily newspaper in the USA. He also printed the Declaration of Independence. During the Revolution he subscribed £4,000 to supply Washington's army, and was a member of the general's bodyguard. Died in Philadelphia.

DUNRAVEN, EARL OF. See under QUIN, W. T. W.

DUNS SCOTUS, JOHANNES (c. 1266–1308), mediaeval schoolman. Has been claimed by both Ireland and Scotland. Little is known for certain about his life. LUKE WADDING stated that he was born in Dún (Down) in Ulster, and it appears that while still young he entered the Franciscan order and studied at Merton College, Oxford. He succeeded William Verron in the Oxford chair of divinity in 1301, and attracted great crowds to his lectures on philosophy and theology. According to tradition he was recommended by Consalvo, general of the Franciscans, to the warden of the University of Paris, then the intellectual centre of Europe. In public disputation there he maintained the dogma of the Immaculate Conception with such ingenuity and resource as to be called 'Doctor Subtilis'. From Paris he went to Cologne, where he died about 1308. He wrote extensively in Latin on grammar,

logic, metaphysics, and theology. The only complete edition of his works was made by Luke Wadding, and published in twelve volumes at Lyon in 1639. His principal theological treatise is said to have been written at Oxford, and is called *Opus Oxoniense*. In the sixteenth century, humanists and reformers ridiculed his followers as enemies of learning, and 'dunce' came to mean one slow at learning.

DUNSANY, LORD. See under PLUNKETT, EDWARD.

DURNFORD, ANTHONY WILLIAM (1830–1879), soldier. Born 24 May 1830, Manorhamilton, Co. Leitrim. Entered the Royal Military Academy at Woolwich in 1846. Commissioned in the Royal Engineers June 1848. After service in Ceylon (Sri Lanka), Malta, and at home stations, he was posted to South Africa. He disapproved of the policy of the colonial government towards the natives, by whom he was highly regarded. After the annexation of the Transvaal and the 'Kaffir War', a dispute about boundaries broke out with the Zulus. War was declared against their chieftain, Cetehwayo, and his people. Durnford, who was then a colonel, was surprised by the Zulus at Rorke's Drift, and killed with all his men on 22 January 1879.

DWYER, MICHAEL (1771–1826), insurgent leader. Born Glen of Imaal, Co. Wicklow. Took part in the rising of 1798, and for five years evaded all attempts by the British forces to capture him. Supported the abortive rising of 1803 organised by ROBERT EMMET but arrived from his hideout in the Wicklow mountains too late to be of assistance. He surrendered voluntarily on 17 December 1803. On account of the humanity he had shown in various engagements, he was spared execution and instead sentenced to transportation to New South Wales, Australia. Became high constable of Sydney 1815, and died there.

E

EASON, JOHN CHARLES MALCOLM (1880–1976), businessman. Born in Dublin and educated at TCD. He joined the family firm of wholesale newsagents and stationers in 1901 and spent his working life there. He was managing director of Eason and Son from 1926 to 1950, chairman until 1958, and remained on the board until eighty. Received the OBE in 1920 for his work in 1918 as joint secretary of the War Savings Committee in southern Ireland. Active in the Civics Institute, Chamber of Commerce, and Statistical and Social Inquiry Society of Ireland. He played a prominent part in reconciling the mainly Protestant Dublin business community to the new state. As president of Dublin Chamber of Commerce in 1927 he influenced the chamber, previously hostile, to support the establishment of the ESB. Member of Currency Commission 1927–1933 and of Banking Commission 1934–1938. Honorary M.Comm. (TCD) 1960. He died in Dublin in 1976, aged ninety-six.

EATON, TIMOTHY (1834–1907), merchant. Born Clogher, Ballymena, Co. Antrim, posthumous son of a farmer. Emigrated to Canada about 1854 and went into partnership with two of his elder brothers in general shop at St Mary's, Ontario. Moved to Toronto in 1868 and opened a dry-goods store. By selling at fixed price and for cash he revolutionised commercial methods and built up one of the largest department stores in North America, supplying everything except alcohol. He was the first 'early closer', and took personal interest in welfare of his employees. Died Toronto, 31 January 1907.

EDGEWORTH, HENRY ESSEX (1745–1807), confessor to Madame Elizabeth of France. Born Edgeworthstown (Mostrim), Co. Longford, son of the Protestant rector. Cousin of RICHARD LOVELL EDGEWORTH. His father converted to Catholicism while on a visit to Toulouse, and Henry was educated at the Jesuit College and at the Sorbonne. Ordained priest and joined the Séminaire des Missions Étrangères in the Rue du Bac, Paris, about 1769. Took the name 'de Firmont', after the family home in Ireland, because Edgeworth was too difficult for the French to pronounce. Devoted himself to the poor of Paris for about ten years, until his health failed, then ministered only to the Irish and English in Paris. In 1791 he became spiritual director to Madame Elizabeth, sister of King Louis XVI. The king, condemned to death two years later, asked for the Abbé de Firmont, who heard his confession and was with him when he was guillotined on 21 January 1793. The abbé went into hiding and, after some narrow escapes, made his way to England. Pitt offered him a pension and from Ireland came an offer of the presidency of Maynooth. He declined both, as he had already declined Irish bishoprics. In 1796 he set out for Blanckenburgh in Brunswick, bringing letters for Louis XVIII. Louis persuaded him to stay as his chaplain. The exiled court moved to Mitau (Jelgava), near Riga, in 1798. Sent to St Petersburg (Leningrad) with the Order of the Holy Spirit from Louis to Tsar Pavel. The tsar, deeply impressed by him, knelt for his blessing, and settled on him a pension of 500 rubles. While ministering to French prisoners of war he contracted fever and died at Mitau on 22 May 1807.

EDGEWORTH, MARIA (1767–1849), novelist. Born at Black Bourton, Oxfordshire, on 1 January 1767, second child of RICHARD LOVELL EDGEWORTH. Educated in England. The family went back to Edgeworthstown (Mostrim), Co. Longford, in 1782. Became her father's chief assistant in running the property and educating his numerous other children. First publication *Letters to Literary Ladies* (1795), much influenced by father's ideas on women's education. *The Parent's Assistant* was published in 1796. Her first novel, *Castle Rackrent* (1800), was an immediate success. Scott said in the original edition of *Waverley* that his aim was 'in some distant degree to emulate the admirable Irish portraits drawn by Miss Edgeworth.' Another novel, *Belinda*, followed in 1801. *Essays on Irish Bulls* (1802) was written by herself and her father. Visited Brussels and Paris 1802. Received a proposal of marriage from a M. Edelcrantz, a Swedish count. Refused from a sense of duty to her family. Back at Edgeworthstown in 1803 she wrote sitting at a table in the family sitting-room, undisturbed by surrounding talk and activity. Her father encouraged her, provided plots, and sometimes inserted long passages of his own composition. *Tales of Fashionable Life* (six volumes, 1809–1812) earned her considerable royalties. *The Absentee* (1809) and *Ormond* (1817) are novels of Irish life. The family spent some time in London in 1813. According to a contemporary account, Maria was 'courted by all persons of distinction'. Wrote further books for and about children. Collaborated with her father in *Practical Education* (1798), which anticipated Froebel in recommending play and spontaneous activity. Wrote little after her father's death in 1817. Made further visits to London and Paris, and to Abbotsford in 1823, where Scott gave her a princely welcome, and they formed a lasting friendship. Showed considerable business ability in managing the estate for her brother after her father's death, and worked hard to relieve the sufferings of the poor during the Great Famine of 1845–1847. Her last novel, *Helen*, was published in 1834. Died at Edgeworthstown, 22 May 1849.

EDGEWORTH, RICHARD LOVELL (1744–1817), landlord, inventor, and father of MARIA. Born at Bath on 31 May 1744. Educated TCD and Corpus Christi College, Oxford. Married four times and had twenty-two children, nineteen surviving infancy. Reclaimed bogs and improved roads on his large estate at Edgeworthstown (Mostrim), Co. Longford. Invented a semaphore that transmitted messages from Dublin to Galway in eight minutes, a velocipede, and a pedometer. 'I am not', he said, 'a man of prejudices. I have had four wives. The second and third were sisters, and I was in love with the second in the lifetime of the first.' Sat in GRATTAN's parliament, advocated Catholic emancipation and parliamentary reform. Strong supporter of Lord Charlemont and the Volunteers. Voted against the Union. Wrote *Practical Education* (1798) in collaboration with Maria. *Professional Education* (1809), in advance of its time, dealt with what is now called vocational education. Founder-member RIA. His *Memoirs* were completed by Maria after his death on 13 June 1817 at Edgeworthstown.

EDWARDS, HILTON ROBERT HUGH (1903–1982), actor and producer. Born in London and educated at St Aloysius School, Highgate. He toured Ireland with Doran's Shakespearian company in 1920 and then joined the Old Vic theatre, London. He also sang baritone with the Old Vic Opera Company. He came to Ireland in 1927 to play with ANEW MCMASTER and met MÍCHEÁL MAC LIAMMÓIR. They decided to found a new theatre in partnership and opened on 19 October 1928 in the 102-seat Peacock in Abbey Street, Dublin, with *Peer Gynt*. In 1930 they moved to the Gate Theatre, Parnell Square. Edwards directed more than 400 productions there and played in many of them. He introduced methods of production, décor and lighting that brought new life and excitement to drama in Dublin. The company made many successful tours abroad. In 1951 he directed a short film, *Road to Glenascaul*, which was nominated for an Academy Award. He was head of drama in RTE for some years from 1961. Distinctions included life membership of Irish Actors' Equity (1972), the freedom of the city of Dublin (1973), and honorary doctorates from NUI and TCD. He died in a Dublin hospital on 18 November 1982.

EGLINTON, JOHN. See under MAGEE, WILLIAM KIRKPATRICK.

EMBURY, PHILIP (1728–1773), founder of American Methodism. Born Ballingrane, Co. Limerick, 21 September 1728, son of German refugees from Palatinate. Educated at the village school and apprenticed to a carpenter. Became an itinerant preacher and helped to build Methodist church at Court Matrix. Emigrated to New York 1760 where he worked as a carpenter and schoolmaster. Began preaching again in 1766 and in 1768 built the first John Street Methodist Church, the beginning of now widespread American Methodist Episcopal Church. Migrated to Washington County, New York, 1770. Died Camden, Washington County, August 1773.

EMMET, ROBERT (1778–1803), United Irishman. Born St Stephen's Green West, Dublin, youngest son of Dr Robert Emmet, physician to the viceroy. Educated at private schools. Entered TCD 1793. Soon distinguished himself as an orator in the Historical Society. Became one of the leaders of the United Irishmen in the college. In April 1798 the Lord Chancellor made a visitation to find the extent of student support for the United Irishmen. In protest on being summoned before the Visitors, Emmet removed his name from the college books, so ending his prospects of a professional career. Warrant for his arrest issued in April 1799 but not enforced. Went to the Continent, met his brother THOMAS. Canvassed with him the possibility of a rising in Ireland. In 1802 dis-cussed Irish independence with Napoleon and Talleyrand, but doubted the sincerity of Napoleon's professed interest in Ireland's welfare. Irish leaders in France were not agreed on course to pursue. Emmet returned to Dublin in October 1802 determined to organise a rising, though with little hope of military help from France. Pressed ahead with his plans, establishing several depots of arms, mainly pikes, in the city, and hoping for support from neighbouring counties. War with France was renewed in May 1803. He intended to time the rising to coincide with Napoleon's expected invasion of England in August. Explosion in one of his depots forced his hand. Decided to act on 23 July. Plan included attacks on Dublin Castle, Pigeon House fort, and Islandbridge (now Clancy) Barracks. The rising was confused and ineffective. Help from outside Dublin failed, treachery was suspected, and leaders were at odds. In the late evening, Emmet put on his uniform of green coat, white breeches and cocked hat, and from his depot in Marshalsea Lane led a hundred undisciplined followers to attack Dublin Castle. On their way they met ARTHUR WOLFE, Lord Kilwarden, the lord chief justice. Dragging him and his nephew from their coach, they murdered them. Emmet fled to the Dublin mountains. Returned to a hiding-place in Harold's Cross to see SARAH CURRAN, to whom he was secretly engaged, hoping to escape with her to America. Arrested in his hiding-place by MAJOR HENRY SIRR, tried for treason, and found guilty. He ended his speech from the dock with the famous words: 'When my country takes her place among the nations of the earth, then, and not till then, let my epitaph be written.' Hanged at Thomas Street, Dublin, on 20 September. Many ballads were written about 'bold Robert Emmet'. His love affair with Sarah Curran inspired THOMAS MOORE's songs 'She is Far From the Land' and 'O Breathe Not his Name'. A commemorative statue by JEROME CONNOR stands directly opposite his birthplace.

EMMET, THOMAS ADDIS (1764–1827), elder brother of ROBERT EMMET. Born Cork; educated TCD. Studied medicine at Edinburgh University and visited the principal medical schools in Europe. On the death of his elder brother, Temple, a barrister of great promise, changed to law. Studied at the Temple in London. Called to the Irish bar in 1790. First brief was to defend NAPPER TANDY, and soon gained recognition as the leading nationalist counsel. Took the oath of the United Irishmen in 1795 in open court to show publicly that he considered it legal. Elected secretary of the Supreme Council of the society that year. When the plans for the rising of 1798 were being prepared, Emmet advised waiting for aid from France. Government spies were at work: he was arrested March 1798 with other leaders and imprisoned. To save further bloodshed, he and his friends agreed to give 'honourable information' and consented to exile, and in 1799 he was sent to Fort St George in Scotland, where his wife and family joined him. Released in 1802, went to France and was in Paris when he heard of his brother Robert's abortive rising and execution. He tried to interest Napoleon in an invasion of Ireland but, making little headway, decided to try his fortunes in the United States. Landing in 1804, joined the New York bar. Built up a large practice. Distinguished himself by eloquent pleading for the liberty of slaves who had taken refuge in New York. Died suddenly in court in New York and was buried at St Mark's, Broadway.

ERIUGENA, JOHANNES SCOTUS (*c.* 810–877), philosopher and theologian. Born in Ireland (Ériu, hence 'Eriugena') about 810. About 851 was at the court of the West Frankish king, Charles II (the Bald), as master of the palace school. Took part in theological disputes arising from the doctrines of Gottschalk. Wrote *De Praedestinatione*, which was condemned at the Council of Valence (855): described as 'pultes Scotorum' or Irish porridge. At the request of Charles, translated into Latin the works of the pseudo-Dionysius the Areopagite, which influenced thereafter the development of mediaeval mystical thought. Chief work, *De Divisione Naturae*, condemned in 1225 by Pope Honorius III and placed on the Index in 1685. According to tradition, he was forced to leave France under suspicion of heresy after the death of Charles the Bald in 877, called to England by Alfred the Great and when abbot of Malmesbury, killed by his students. It seems probable that he never left France, and died there in 877.

ERVINE, ST JOHN GREER (1883–1971), dramatist, novelist, and critic. Born in Ballymacarret, Belfast. Started work at fourteen in an insurance office. Three years later emigrated to London. Had several plays produced and two novels published before the First World War. Served as lieutenant in the Dublin Fusiliers; severely wounded and lost a leg. In 1915 became manager of the Abbey Theatre, Dublin, for a short period. At that time a nationalist, but within a few years became a strong unionist. Wrote adulatory biographies of CARSON and CRAIGAVON. Settled at Seaton in Devon, and maintained a steady output of literary work, publishing seven novels. *God's Soldier*, a biography of William Booth, founder of the Salvation Army, appeared in 1934. An unsympathetic study of OSCAR WILDE followed in 1951, and a massive biography of GEORGE BERNARD SHAW in 1956. Drama critic for the *Observer* until 1939. Plays include *The First Mrs Fraser* (1928) and *Boyd's Shop* (1935). Became one of the first members of the Irish Academy of Letters, with YEATS and Shaw. From 1933 to 1936 professor of dramatic literature, Royal Society of Literature. Died at Seaton, Devon, on 24 January 1971.

'EVA' OF THE 'NATION', pen-name of MARY EVA KELLY (1826–1910). Born Headford, Co. Galway. Contributed verse to the *Nation, Irish Tribune*, and other nationalist papers under the

pen-name 'Eva'. Engaged to KEVIN IZOD
O'DOHERTY before his conviction in
1849. Declined his offer to release her.
Married him in 1855 in Kingstown (Dún
Laoghaire), Co. Dublin. Died in
Brisbane, May 1910.

EVERETT, JAMES (*c.* 1890–1967),
Labour politician. Born Wicklow. On
leaving school, became an organiser
with Co. Wicklow Agricultural Union,
which later merged with the Irish Transport and General Workers' Union.
Served as a Sinn Féin justice in Republican courts from 1919 to 1922. Elected
to Dáil in 1921 for Kildare and Wicklow.
Represented Wicklow until his death.
Key figure in the split in Irish labour and
trade union circles 1943. Formed six-
member National Labour Party in the
Dáil. Minister for Posts and Telegraphs
1948 in the first Coalition government.
Split healed in 1949 when his party
merged with the official Labour Party.
Central figure in the 'Battle of Baltinglass' in 1950, when he appointed one
Michael Farrell as sub-postmaster. The
office had been run by Miss Helen Cooke
for her invalid aunt whose family had
held the post since 1870. Local feeling
ran high in support of Miss Cooke; telegraph poles were cut. Public interest was
roused at home and abroad. Farrell
resigned in December 1950. Everett
bowed to the storm and appointed Miss
Cooke. Widely believed that the 'Battle
of Baltinglass' was a factor in defeat of
the government in the general election of
June 1951. Minister for Justice
1954–1957 in second Coalition government. 'Father of the House' when he
died.

F

FAGAN, JAMES BERNARD (1873–1933), actor-manager and playwright. Born Belfast, 18 May 1873. Educated at Clongowes Wood and Trinity College, Oxford. He read for the bar but abandoned law to join the company of Sir Frank Benson in 1895, later acting with Beerbohm Tree. In 1899 he turned to writing plays, and did not resume his career as actor and producer until 1913. He founded the Oxford Playhouse in 1923 with a young company that included Flora Robson, John Gielgud, and TYRONE GUTHRIE, and became director of the Festival Theatre, Cambridge, in 1929. Fagan was responsible for many noteworthy productions on the London stage, including *Juno and the Paycock* by SEÁN O'CASEY. His own plays were well received, particularly *And So To Bed,* a Pepysian comedy (1926), and *The Improper Duchess* (1931). Died at Hollywood, California, 17 February 1933.

FAHY, FRANCIS ARTHUR (1854–1935), song-writer. Born Kinvara, Co. Galway, 29 September 1854. Educated local national school. Joined civil service in London, 1873. Founded Southwark Junior Literary Club 1881, where Irish children learned history, songs and legends of Ireland. Founded Southwark Irish Literary Club 1883; from this grew the London Irish Literary Society 1891. A native Irish-speaker and president of London Gaelic League. *Songs and Poems* (1887) included the 'Ould Plaid Shawl' and 'The Donovans'. Wrote *A Child's Irish History* in verse, contributed to many periodicals, and lectured extensively. Died Clapham.

FAIR, JAMES GRAHAM (1831–1894), miner and millionaire. Born near Belfast, 3 December 1831. Taken to Illinois at twelve. Joined California gold rush of 1849, then went to the Nevada silver mines. Described as canny and acquisitive; established Bank of Nevada with associates Mackay, Flood, and O'Brien, also Irishmen. They found and developed immense deposits of gold and silver, which yielded 100 million dollars in six years. Elected senator for Nevada 1881–1887. Led gaudy and irregular life, divorced his wife, and was estranged from his children. Died San Francisco, 28 December 1894.

FALCONER, EDMUND (1814–1879), actor and dramatist, real name Edmund O'Rourke. Born Dublin, and went on the stage at an early age. Manager Lyceum Theatre, London, 1858–1859 and 1861–1862. Joint lessee Drury Lane 1862–1866. Opened Her Majesty's at Haymarket with his play *Oonagh* 1866. It failed, and he went to America 1866–1869. He wrote many plays, best-received being *Peep o' Day,* founded on *John Doe* and *The Nowlans,* novels by JOHN BANIM. Dramatised *Charles O'Malley* by LEVER as *Galway-go-Bragh.* Other plays were *The Cagot, or Heart for Heart* (1856) and *A Husband for an Hour* (1857). Created part of Danny Mann in *Colleen Bawn* by BOUCICAULT at Adelphi 1860. Wrote famous song 'Killarney', and published two volumes of verse. Died at his house in Russell Square, London, 29 September 1879.

FALLON, GABRIEL (1898–1980), theatre critic and actor. Born in Dublin, educated at O'Connell CBS. Joined the civil service in 1914, retiring in 1958. Became a part-time actor in the Abbey Theatre and played in original production of first plays by SEÁN O'CASEY.

Left the Abbey about 1930. Drama critic *Irish Monthly* (1926-1957), *Catholic Standard* (1938-1954) and *Evening Press*. Director of the Abbey Theatre 1959-1974. Extra-mural lecturer in theatre arts and public speaking, UCD, 1950-1959. Guest producer and actor with Radio Éireann. Published *Seán O'Casey, the Man I Knew* (1965) and *The Abbey and the Actor* (1969). Died at home in Dublin on 10 June 1980, survived by his wife and six children.

FALLON, PÁDRAIC (1905-1974), poet and playwright. Born Athenry, Co. Galway. Educated St Joseph's College, Roscrea, and Garbally Park, Ballinasloe. Joined Customs and Excise in Dublin. Befriended by GEORGE RUSSELL and SEUMAS O'SULLIVAN, who published his first poems. Transferred to Wexford 1930, and spent the rest of his official career there. He lived in an eighteenth-century house on twenty acres of land on the outskirts of the town, and described himself as 'a poet and armchair farmer'. Old Irish sagas and folk myths gave him inspiration and provided many of his themes. His first verse play for radio, *Diarmuid and Gráinne*, was broadcast in 1950 by Radio Éireann. Later verse plays, also broadcast, included *The Vision of Mac Conglinne* (1953), *Steeple Jerkin*, and *The Poplar*. In all, he wrote seventeen plays for radio. He also wrote two plays for the stage, *The Seventh Step*, produced in Cork 1954 after rejection by the Abbey Theatre, and *Sweet Love Till Morn*, also staged in Cork some years later. His poems appeared in many Irish, English and American periodicals. A collected edition was issued by the Dolmen Press 1974. He retired from the civil service 1970 and went to live in Kinsale, Co. Cork. Died in hospital in Kent, England, 9 October 1974.

FALLS, CYRIL BENTHAM (1888-1971), military historian and journalist. Born in Dublin on 2 March 1888. Educated at Portora Royal School, Enniskillen, at Bradfield

College, and London University. Served with the British army in the First World War. From 1923 to 1939 he worked on the team writing the official history of the war. Military correspondent of *The Times* 1939-1953. Published many books, including *The History of the 36th (Ulster) Division* (1922), in which he described vividly from his own experiences the realities of war on the western front, *Elizabeth's Irish Wars* (1950), and *Mountjoy: Elizabethan General* (1955). Contributed a weekly commentary on political affairs to the *Illustrated London News*. Died at Walton-on-Thames, 23 April 1971.

FARQUHAR, GEORGE (1678-1707), dramatist. Born in Derry, educated TCD. He abandoned his studies to go on the stage but, after accidentally stabbing another player, gave up acting, moved to London, and turned to writing comedy. His first plays, *Love and a Bottle* (1698) and *The Constant Couple* (1699), were well received at Drury Lane theatre. Receiving a commission as lieutenant from Lord Orrery, he went to the midlands on a recruiting campaign, and drew on his experiences in writing *The Recruiting Officer*, produced successfully in 1706. His last play, *The Beaux' Stratagem*, was an equally vigorous and entertaining comedy, but he did not live to benefit from its success. It is said that he had sold his commission to pay his debts, and he died in April 1707 in great poverty.

FARRELL, MICHAEL (1899-1962), novelist. Born in Carlow and studied medicine at UCD. Imprisoned for six months in Mountjoy Jail during the War of Independence, then went on a long walking-tour in France before taking a job as a marine superintendent in the Belgian Congo (Zaïre). Returned to Ireland after a few years and in 1930 married Frances Cahill, who ran the Crock of Gold, a hand-weaving business. Resumed his medical studies, this time at TCD, but soon abandoned them for journalism, contributing to the *The Bell* and Radio Éireann. Later he left journalism and took over management of the Crock of Gold. Remembered for his one book, a novel, *Thy Tears Might Cease*—his life's work, written at enormous length, which he could not bring himself to edit. After his death MONK GIBBON reduced it by 100,000 words for publication (1963), and it achieved great success both here and in America. Farrell died in June 1962.

FARREN, ELIZABETH, COUNTESS OF DERBY (*c.* 1759–1829), actress. Born Cork, where her father was an apothecary and surgeon. After his early death, probably due to hard drinking, his widow went on the stage in the English provinces to support herself and her three children. Elizabeth made her first appearance in London in 1777 as Miss Hardcastle in *She Stoops to Conquer* and was well received. Her tall, slim figure was unsuited to 'breeches' parts, and after one unfortunate appearance she wisely left these roles to PEG WOFFINGTON. Her natural elegance, wit and refinement made her popular in London society. Lord Derby, who was separated from his wife, became her friend, and she often took part in private theatricals in great houses. Her character was irreproachable and her private life free from scandal. Her success on stage continued, and she played leading parts at Drury Lane and the Haymarket for twenty years. Lord Derby's wife died on 14 March 1797, and Elizabeth married him the following 1 May. She was received at court with special favour by Queen Charlotte. Died Knowsley Park, Lancashire, 29 April 1829, survived by her husband and their three children.

FAULKNER, (ARTHUR) BRIAN DEANE (1921–1977), politician. Born in Helen's Bay, Co. Down. Educated at St Columba's College, Rathfarnham, Co. Dublin, and joined family business of shirtmaking. Youngest ever MP in Northern Ireland parliament when elected to East Down 1949. Government chief whip 1956, Minister of Home Affairs 1959, and Minister of Commerce 1963. Showed marked ability in attracting industry from abroad. Later became deputy Prime Minister. Firmly identified with right-wing Unionism, and in 1969 helped to bring down the more moderate Prime Minister Terence O'Neill. Became Prime Minister in March 1971. His introduction of internment led to increased violence and filled the Catholic population with feelings of deep-seated bitterness. This, and his acceptance of assurances from the British Prime Minister, Edward Heath, that the Stormont parliament would not be suspended, were seen as major mistakes. Direct rule from Westminster was introduced on 25 March 1972. In December 1973 he committed his party to the Sunningdale agreement, providing for power-sharing and a Council of Ireland, and became chief of the Executive, made up of Unionists, SDLP and Alliance members. Most Unionists detested this move and the Executive was brought down after five months by an Ulster Workers' Council strike. His following dwindled to five members of his Unionist Party of Northern Ireland. He resigned from politics in mid-1976. Made Baron Faulkner of Downpatrick, January 1977. Patronised by Northern Ireland landed gentry as 'the little shirtmaker', he lived in a Co. Down mansion, was a Deputy Lieutenant, and rode to hounds. He was killed in a riding accident on 3 March 1977 in a stag hunt in Co. Down.

FAULKNER, GEORGE (*c.* 1699–1775), printer. Born Dublin. Educated at Dr Lloyd's school and apprenticed to a printer. Opened his own printing and bookselling shop in 1726. Printed *Dublin Journal* and many English works, mostly pirated, which made him wealthy. Lost a leg in an accident in London that occurred, he said, when he fled from a jealous husband. A friend of SWIFT, who called him 'the prince of Dublin printers'. The first to issue a collected edition of Swift's works (1735). His shop at the corner of Essex Street was a resort for the notables of Dublin. Lord Chesterfield, when viceroy, listened to his unofficial advice and offered a knighthood, which he declined. Became a Roman Catholic 1758 and spoke against the penal laws. Alderman 1770. Died Dublin, 30 August 1775.

FAY, WILLIAM GEORGE (1872–1947), actor and producer. Born Dublin, 12 November 1872. Educated Belvedere College, Dublin. With his elder brother, Frank, he set out to make a career on the stage, and formed his own small company, playing in Dublin and the country. The brothers joined W. B. YEATS and LADY GREGORY in founding the Abbey Theatre and evolved the style of acting identified with it, a style marked by economy of gesture and movement, admirably suited to the realistic yet poetic dialogue of the plays. After a difference with the Abbey directors in 1908 the Fays went to the USA and produced a repertory of Irish plays. William went to London in 1914 and had a distinguished career on the English stage, also appearing in a number of films. Published *The Fays of the Abbey Theatre* (1935). Died London, 27 October 1947.

FEIRITÉIR, PIARAS (*c.* 1600–1653), poet. A chieftain of Norman descent whose castle stood near Ballyferriter in the Dingle peninsula. In the rising of 1641 he took the side of the native Irish and led an attack on Tralee castle in which he was badly wounded. The castle was taken and he continued the struggle until the fall of Ross castle in 1653. He was induced to go to Killarney to arrange terms, and when the negotiations broke down he was promised safe conduct by Brigadier-General Nelson. He was seized at Castlemaine, brought back to Killarney, and publicly hanged with a priest and a bishop. He was highly regarded by his fellow poets and is still a folk hero in Kerry. The sophistication of his courtly love poems pleased many of the new Elizabethan colonists. His poems were edited in 1903 by PÁDRAIG Ó DUINNÍN.

FERGUSON, HARRY GEORGE (1884–1960), engineer and inventor. Born 4 November 1884, Growell, Hillsborough, Co. Down. At sixteen he started his own garage business in Belfast, raced successfully, and in 1909 became the first person to fly in Ireland, in a monoplane he designed and built himself. After years of experiment he designed a revolutionary new farm tractor with mounted ploughs and other implements. In a 'handshake' agreement with Henry Ford in 1939 he became the only partner Ford ever had, selling millions of pounds worth of tractors made to his design by Ford. This unwritten contract was repudiated by Ford's grandson in 1947, and Ferguson took legal action against him, winning nine million dollars compensation after a four-year suit. Died at his home, Stow-in-the-Wold, 25 October 1960.

FERGUSON, SIR SAMUEL (1810–1886), poet and antiquary. Born Belfast, 10 March 1810. Educated RBAI and TCD. Called to the Irish bar 1838, took silk 1859. In 1867 he retired from practice on his appointment as first deputy keeper of public records of Ireland. His work in making a thorough re-organisation of this neglected department was recognised by a knighthood 1878. He wrote many essays on Irish antiquities for the RIA, of which he was president 1882. His most important work in this field, *Ogham Inscriptions in Ireland, Wales and Scotland* (1887) was edited after his death by his widow. Ferguson's collected poems, many based on the Irish mythological cycles, were published in 1865 as *Lays of the Western Gael*. In 1872 he published *Congal, An Epic Poem in Five Books.* His fine 'Lament for Thomas Davis', and his graceful translations from the Irish, appear in many anthologies. An early work was a satire in verse on Irish education, *Father Tom and the Pope* (1838). His house in North Great George's St, Dublin, was open to everyone interested in Irish art, literature, or music. Died Howth, Co. Dublin, 9 August 1886.

FERRIS, RICHARD (1754-1828), soldier of fortune, priest, lawyer, and secret agent. Born at Ballymalis, Co. Kerry, and went to France at sixteen to join Berwick's regiment of the Irish Brigade. He then studied at the Irish College and the University of Paris. Ordained priest 1778. Became doctor of civil and canon law and chaplain at the court of Louis XVI and Marie Antoinette. *Avocat* at the Palais de Justice and administrator of Montaigu Royal College of the university. After the revolution he refused to take an oath as a state priest and in 1790 re-joined his old regiment. He took part in the abortive invasion of France by royalist, Austrian and Prussian forces in 1792. Disappeared for some years, emerging in London in 1794 as a secret agent for the French. He tried to become a double agent but the English suspected him. In 1799 he was back in Paris and was arrested and charged with espionage. His old friend from his days at court, Talleyrand, whom he rivalled in his ability to survive all shifts in power, was then foreign minister, and he was soon released. Ferris now set up as a lawyer in Paris, with great success. He became head of the Irish College in 1814 and then rector and administrator of the 'British Colleges', English, Scottish, and Irish. Made a Chevalier of France 1817. After a long feud with the Irish hierarchy he was dismissed from the rectorship of the Irish College in October 1820. He resumed his legal practice and amassed a fortune. He moved to the cathedral town of Soissons when his health began to fail and died there on 16 June 1828.

FIELD, JOHN (1782-1837), composer. Born Dublin, 26 July 1782, son of a theatre violinist. Taught music by his father and grandfather, an organist. At twelve made his first public appearance in London, then apprenticed to Muzio Clementi, who gave him further tuition in return for services as pianoforte demonstrator and salesman. In 1802 Clementi brought him to Paris, Vienna, and St Petersburg (Leningrad). Field soon secured recognition as a pianist and composer, and settled in Russia. He gave concerts throughout Europe during the following thirty years and was in great demand as a fashionable teacher. He returned to London in 1832, and scored a great success with his E flat piano concerto at a Philharmonic Society concert. After visits to France and Italy he returned to Moscow in poor health, and died there on 11 January 1837. He wrote about twenty nocturnes, as well as seven concertos, four sonatas, and a number of shorter pieces. In the delicate noctures he anticipated Chopin in his style, technique, and spirit.

FIGGIS, DARRELL (1882-1925), poet, novelist, playwright and journalist. Born Rathmines, Dublin. Began career as tea buyer and broker in London and Calcutta 1898. Gave up business 1910 and until 1913 worked as literary adviser to publishers Dent and Sons, and as free-lance journalist. Involved with ERSKINE CHILDERS in the Howth gun-running in 1914. Arrested several times for his political activities 1916-1918. Honorary secretary of Sinn Féin 1917-1919. Edited *The Republic* from June to September 1919, when it was suppressed along with other Sinn Féin newspapers. Secretary 1919-1922 to the Commission of Inquiry into the Resources and Industries of Ireland set up by Dáil Éireann. Was acting chairman of the 1922 committee that framed the Irish Free State Constitution. TD for Co. Dublin 1922. Committed suicide in London. He published some twenty books, including several novels and studies of GEORGE RUSSELL and WILLIAM CARLETON, using the pen-name Michael Ireland.

FINNERTY, PETER (1766-1822), journalist. Born Loughrea, Co. Galway. Became a printer in Dublin. In 1797 he published *The Press*, a nationalist newspaper, and was sentenced to two years' imprisonment for seditious libel for printing a letter on the execution of WILLIAM ORR. On his release he went to London and joined the staff of the

Morning Chronicle. Sailed with the Walcheren expedition as special correspondent 1809, but his dispatches were so critical that the government shipped him home in a man-of-war. He blamed Lord Castlereagh for his recall, and in 1811 he was sentenced to eighteen months' imprisonment for libelling Castlereagh. His courage and wit at his trial brought him a public subscription of £2,000. He memorialised the House of Commons on his treatment, and his pamphlet *The Case of Peter Finnerty* went into four editions in 1811. Died Westminster, 11 May 1822.

FITZGERALD, BARRY (1888–1961), actor, stage-name of William Joseph Shields. Born in Dublin, educated at Merchant Taylor's School. Joined civil service 1911. Started acting with amateur group, the Kincora Players. Played at Abbey Theatre 1916–1929 in his spare time, taking name Barry Fitzgerald because of his civil service post. Resigned 1929 to become full-time actor. Toured USA in 1934 when New York critics, led by George Jean Nathan, voted him best character actor of the year for his performance as Fluther Good in *The Plough and the Stars.* Acclaimed for his Captain Jack Boyle in *Juno and the Paycock.* Lived in USA from 1936, touring until 1937, when he went to Hollywood, where he remained for over twenty years. Appeared in many films and won an Oscar for his Father Fitzgibbon in *Going My Way.* Played in *The Quiet Man,* directed in Ireland by John Ford, with John Wayne and Maureen O'Hara. Spent many summers sailing in Dublin Bay. Returned to Ireland about 1959. Died in Dublin, 4 January 1961.

FITZGERALD, DESMOND (*c.* 1888–1947), revolutionary and statesman. Born and brought up in London. Joined 'Imagist' group of young English poets, which included Richard Aldington and Harold Munro and was later joined by Ezra Pound. Married about 1911, lived in France until 1913, then moved to Ventry, Co. Kerry.

Joined IRB in September 1914 and organised Irish Volunteers in Kerry. Imprisoned for six months in 1915 for making political speech. Expelled from Kerry by police orders and moved to Bray, Co. Wicklow. Fought in GPO in 1916 Rising. Escaped to his house in Bray but was arrested, court-martialled, and sentenced to life imprisonment, later commuted to twenty years' imprisonment. Jailed in Dartmoor and Maidstone. Elected Sinn Féin MP for Pembroke, Dublin, 1918 and released later that year. Appointed director of publicity for Dáil Éireann April 1919 and edited the underground news-sheet, the *Bulletin.* Arrested again March 1921 but released when the Truce was arranged in July. Supported the Anglo-Irish Treaty of 6 December 1921. As Minister for External Affairs 1922–1927 he represented Ireland at League of Nations and at Imperial Conferences in 1923, 1926 and 1930. Minister for Defence 1927–1932, TD for Dublin County 1922–1932 and for Carlow-Kilkenny 1932–1937. Senator from 1938 to 1943, when he retired from politics. His play *The Saints* was produced at the Abbey Theatre in 1919. In 1939 he published *Preface to Statecraft,* on the philosophy of politics. Lectured in USA on Thomism. He died in Dublin on 9 April 1947. He was the father of Garret FitzGerald (Minister for Foreign Affairs 1973–1977 and Taoiseach 1981–1987).

FITZGERALD, LORD EDWARD (1763–1798), United Irishman. Born Carton House, Co. Kildare, 15 October 1763, twelfth child of first Duke of Leinster and Emilia Mary, daughter of Duke of Richmond. After the death of his father the family lived in France in a house lent by the Duke of Richmond. Edward showed a liking for a military career. Joined the Sussex Militia 1779. Went to America on active service, severely wounded at battle of Eutaw Springs 1781. Returned to Ireland and sat for Athy in the Irish parliament, voting with the minority led by GRATTAN and CURRAN. Rejoined British army in

114

Canada 1788. Made an adventurous journey to Québec through unexplored territory. Returned to Ireland, became MP for Kildare and, attracted by the new thinking inspired by the French Revolution, visited Paris in 1792, staying with Thomas Paine and attending the debates of the Convention. At a dinner of British residents he joined in a toast to the abolition of all hereditary titles and was cashiered from the army as a result. On 27 December 1792 he married Pamela, a beautiful girl of 19, ward of Madame de Genlis and probably her daughter by the Duke of Orléans. He returned to Dublin with his young wife in 1793 and quickly showed parliament where his sympathies lay by denouncing the government for prohibiting a meeting of Volunteers. At this time he was living at Frascati House, Blackrock, Co. Dublin. Losing hope of constitutional reform, he joined the United Irishmen, who now openly aimed at an independent republic. In 1796 he accompanied Arthur O'Connor to Basel to negotiate with General Hoche for French help, but the Directory declined to treat with Fitzgerald because of Pamela's connection with the royalists. Back in Ireland he told the Kildare electors that he would not stand again for parliament as free elections were impossible under martial law. By now he had committed himself to armed revolution and headed a military committee of the United Irishmen. Their plan was to co-operate with a French invasion or, failing that, to rise themselves, confident that the organisation could count on 280,000 men ready under arms. Delays by the French decided the committee to rise in May 1798, but the English authorities had infiltrated the movement with spies, and the members of the Leinster committee were arrested in March at the house of OLIVER BOND in Bridge St, Dublin. Fitzgerald had been warned and was not there. He was now 'on the run', a reward of £1,000 was offered, an informer came forward, and Fitzgerald was seized by MAJOR HENRY SIRR in a house in Thomas St on 19 May.

In the fierce struggle he killed one of his attackers and was himself shot in the arm. Died of his wounds in Newgate prison, 4 June. Buried in St Werburgh's. William Cobbett, who served under him in Canada, described him as the only really honest officer he had ever known. Cheerful, courageous, and skilled in arms, his death was a heavy blow to the United Irishmen.

FITZGERALD, GEORGE FRANCIS (1851-1901), natural philosopher. Born Dublin; educated TCD. Became fellow 1877, and Erasmus Smith Professor of Natural and Experimental Philosophy 1881. Developed electromagnetic theory of radiation and made researches into electric waves and electrolysis. FRS 1883; president of Physical Society 1892-1893; Commissioner of Education 1888. His *Scientific Writings* (1902) were collected by SIR JOSEPH LARMOR.

FITZGERALD, GEORGE ROBERT (c. 1748-1786), 'Fighting Fitzgerald'. A descendant of the Desmond branch of the great Geraldine family. Educated Eton; left to join the British army. His first station was Galway, and he soon became noted for his gallantry, his recklessness, and his duelling. Against the wishes of her parents he married a cousin of the Duke of Leinster, who brought him a fortune of £10,000. Soon afterwards he went to the Continent, where his wife died, leaving an only daughter. He married again, his second wife being the only daughter and heiress of Mr Vaughan of Carrowmore, Co. Mayo. He then began to take an interest in politics, became a strong supporter of legislative independence for Ireland, and assisted in the formation of companies of Volunteers. He introduced many improvements on his Mayo estate. His eccentricities included a habit of hunting at night. Having no male heir, he became jealous of his younger brother, whose children would ultimately inherit the family property, and carried him off to his house at Turlough. The brother brought an action against him for forcible abduction, and he was found guilty and sentenced to three years' imprisonment and a fine of £1,000. He evaded justice for a time, but his father, with whom he had quarrelled over money matters, tricked him into going to Dublin. He was arrested and kept in prison until a serious illness induced the authorities to release him. He then became involved in a quarrel between a retainer of his, one Murphy, and a Patrick Randal McDonnell. McDonnell was waylaid on the road from Castlebar by Fitzgerald and his associates and taken prisoner. A member of his escort was killed in the attack. A company of Volunteers came along and arrested Fitzgerald. He was tried for murder, found guilty, and executed at Castlebar 11 June 1786.

FITZGERALD, GERALD, eighth EARL OF KILDARE (died 1513), the 'Great Earl'. Succeeded to title 1477. Appointed deputy by Edward IV in 1481 and retained by Richard III and Henry VII. Suspected of plotting against the king, he was attainted at a parliament in Drogheda in 1494 by Sir Edward Poynings, and sent to the Tower of London. After two years he was pardoned and made deputy, the king saying: 'If all Ireland cannot rule this man, let him rule all Ireland.' In 1498 he presided over the first parliament held in Ireland under Poynings' Law. He defeated southern chiefs at Knockdoe, Co. Galway, 1505. Made knight of the Garter that year. Continued in office under Henry VIII. Died from wounds received in engagement against O'Carroll of Offaly.

FITZGERALD, GERALD, ninth EARL OF KILDARE (1487–1534), 'Garret Óg'. Spent his youth at English court as pledge of his father's loyalty. Allowed to return to Ireland about 1504 and appointed lord high treasurer. Succeeded his father as lord deputy 1513. Wolsey came to power soon after; his animosity to Kildare was unconcealed. Kildare was summoned to London in 1515 on charges of maladministration but satisfied the king. He was called to account again in 1519 and 1526, being sent to the Tower the second time. He was released in 1530 and reappointed deputy 1532. That year he was wounded in battle and 'never after enjoyed his limbs' (STANIHURST). There was a long-standing feud between the Butlers, earls of Ormond, and the Fitzgeralds. Allegations of treason, partly originating with Ormond, resulted in Garret Óg being summoned yet again to London. He gave the sword of state to his son THOMAS. He was confined in the Tower, and died in December 1534.

FITZGERALD, KATHERINE (died 1604), the 'old' Countess of Desmond. Daughter of Sir John Fitzgerald, lord of Decies. Became the second wife of Thomas Fitzgerald, twelfth Earl of Desmond, some time after 1505. He died in 1534 at the age of eighty, leaving a daughter by her, so that her marriage was unlikely to have taken place after 1524. Sir Walter Raleigh, in his *History of the World* (1614), stated that the 'old countess' was living in 1589 'and many years since'. That her death occurred in 1604 is stated in a manuscript of Sir George Carew's that is preserved in Lambeth Library. In his *Itinerary* (1617), Fynes Morison states that 'in our time' she had lived to the age of 'about' one hundred and forty years, and was able in her last years to go on foot three or four miles to the market town and that only a few years before her death all her teeth were renewed. Sir John Harrington, speaking in 1605 of the wholesomeness of the country, said 'where a man hath lived to above 140 years, a woman, and she a countess, above 120, the country is likely to be healthy'. The story of her death being due to a fall from an apple, cherry or walnut-tree is almost certainly apocryphal. That she lived to one hundred and forty is, of course, highly unlikely, but it may be reasonably concluded that she reached at least one hundred and four, and may very well have lived well beyond that age.

FITZGERALD, PERCY HETHER-INGTON (1834-1925), writer, sculptor and painter. Born Fane Valley, Co. Louth. Educated Stonyhurst and TCD. Called to the bar; Crown prosecutor on the north-eastern circuit, then settled in London to a literary life. Published fiction, biography, history, plays, and books on Catholic religious subjects. Over a hundred of his titles listed in National Library. A friend of Dickens, he executed a bust of him at Bath, a statue of Johnson in the Strand, and of Boswell at Lichfield. Died London.

FITZGERALD, LORD THOMAS, LORD OFFALY, tenth EARL OF KILDARE (1513-1537), 'Silken Thomas'. He spent a considerable part of his early life in England. In February 1534, when his father, the ninth earl, was summoned to London, he appointed Thomas deputy-governor of Ireland in his absence. In June Thomas heard rumours that his father had been executed in the Tower and that the English government intended the same fate for him and his uncles. He summoned the council to St Mary's Abbey, Dublin, and on 11 June, accompanied by one hundred and forty horsemen with silken fringes on their helmets (from which he was called 'Silken Thomas'), rode to the Abbey and publicly renounced his allegiance to the king. In July he attacked Dublin Castle, but his army was routed. By this time his father had taken ill and died in London, and he had succeeded as tenth earl. He retreated to his stronghold at Maynooth, Co. Kildare, but in March 1535 this was taken by an English force under Sir William Skeffington while Thomas was absent gathering reinforcements to relieve it. The garrison was given the 'Maynooth Pardon', that is, they were all executed. In July Lord Leonard Grey arrived from England as marshal of Ireland; Kildare, . seeing his army melting away and his allies submitting one by one, asked pardon for his offences. He was still a formidable opponent, and Grey, wishing to avoid a prolonged conflict, guaranteed his personal safety and persuaded him to submit unconditionally to the king's mercy. In October 1535 he was sent as a prisoner to the Tower. Despite Grey's guarantee, he was hanged, drawn and quartered, with his five uncles, at Tyburn, 3 February 1537.

FITZGIBBON, EDWARD (1803-1857), angler and writer. Born Limerick, son of a land agent. Became devoted to angling at an early age. His father died when he was fourteen and, after periods of teaching in England and a stay of six years in Marseille, he joined the staff of the London *Morning Chronicle* and became their parliamentary reporter. Wrote on angling for many years for *Bell's Life in London*. His style and knowledge made his articles celebrated among fishermen. Also published a *Handbook on Angling* (1847), long regarded as a classic; *The Book of the Salmon* (1850), with A. Young; and the best extant edition of Izaak Walton's *Compleat Angler* (1853). He once killed fifty-two salmon and grilse in fifty-five hours' fishing on the Shin river in Scotland. His writing gave a great impetus to the sport and led to many improvements in fishing tackle. A man of great charm, Fitzgibbon appears to have been an alcoholic, and his health became impaired some years before his death in London, 19 November 1857.

FITZGIBBON, JOHN, EARL OF CLARE (1749-1802), Lord Chancellor of Ireland. Born near Donnybrook, Dublin. Educated TCD and Christ Church, Oxford, gaining high academic distinction in Dublin. Called to the Irish bar in 1772, and soon had a large and lucrative practice. Between 1783 and 1789, when he became Lord Chancellor, he received £36,939 in fees. MP for Dublin University 1778-1783; later sat for Kilmallock. Attorney-General 1783. In 1789 he became Lord Chancellor of Ireland, became a viscount 1793, Earl of Clare 1795, and in 1799 a peer of Great Britain as Lord Fitzgibbon of Sidbury

(Devonshire). In politics he resisted all reforms, especially those designed to ameliorate the position of Catholics, and took a leading part in securing the passage of the Act of Union with Great Britain in 1800. He is said to have been the author of a pamphlet published in 1799 in which 'Paddy Whack', writing to his mother Sheelagh of Dame St, Dublin, advises her to marry 'the rich, and generous, and industrious, and kind, and liberal, and powerful, and free, honest John Bull'. When Lord Fitzwilliam, a conciliatory viceroy, was recalled in 1795, mainly because of Clare's influence, a Dublin mob attacked his house. Died Dublin, 28 January 1802. His funeral was followed by a jeering Dublin mob.

FITZHENRY, MRS (died 1790?), actress. Was the daughter of one Flannigan, who kept the Ferry Boat tavern in Abbey St, Dublin. She worked as a seamstress, and then married a Captain Gregory, who commanded a vessel trading between Dublin and Bordeaux. After his death by drowning and then the death of her father, she went to London in 1753, and made her first appearance on the stage at Covent Garden on 10 June 1754. At the end of the season she secured an engagement to play at the Smock Alley Theatre, Dublin, at £400 a year. From then until her retirement, about 1774, she played with success in Dublin, with periods at Drury Lane and Covent Garden. About 1757 she married a lawyer named Fitzhenry, by whom she had a son and a daughter. Her principal parts included the Queen in *Hamlet*; Lady Macbeth; and Emilia in *Othello*. The date and place of her death are uncertain, but it seems that she died in Ireland about 1790.

FITZMAURICE, GEORGE (1878–1963), playwright. Born Co. Kerry, son of a Church of Ireland clergyman. Joined staff of Department of Agriculture, Dublin. His earliest play, *The Toothache,* was not discovered until 1965, and was first produced some years later in Listowel. His first play to be seen in public, *The Country Dressmaker*, was produced at the Abbey Theatre 1907 and was well received. His next two plays, *The Pie Dish* (1908) and *The Magic Glasses* (1913), were also produced at the Abbey. A London production of *The Magic Glasses* was praised above the plays of YEATS and LADY GREGORY in a small repertoire presented by the Abbey. No other play of his appeared at the Abbey until 1923, when *Twixt the Giltinans and the Carmodys* was played there. On the outbreak of the First World War he joined the British army and after the Armistice returned to the department, in the words of AUSTIN CLARKE, 'without bodily harm, medal or stripe'. He wrote a number of other plays and fantasies, some of which were published in the *Dublin Magazine* by his friend SEUMAS O'SULLIVAN. *Five Plays* was published by Maunsel in Dublin in 1914. He retired from the civil service in 1943 and led a secluded life on a very small pension, spending his mornings reading the newspapers in a public library and his evenings in a pub over a quiet drink with some cronies. His plays were revived by the Lyric Theatre Company, directed by Austin Clarke. Productions included *The Dandy Dolls* (1945) and *The Linnaun Shee* (1949), both in the Abbey. His works were published by the Dolmen Press under the titles *Dramatic Fantasies* (1967) and *Plays* (1969). Died Dublin.

FITZMAURICE, COLONEL JAMES C. (1898–1965), aviator. Born Dublin, 6 January 1898. Co-pilot on first east-to-west flight across the Atlantic. Joined the Cadet Company of the 7th Leinsters 1914; sent home when his age was discovered. Waited three months and then joined the 7th Lancers, landing in France early in 1915. Eighteen months later he was wounded and transferred to the infantry, where he saw heavy fighting on the Somme and at Arras. Obtained commission in the 8th Irish (King's) Liverpool Regiment; wounded, and transferred to the Royal Flying Corps 1917. Selected to pilot the first night mail flight from Folkestone to Cologne 1919. Later picked as pilot for a proposed Cairo-to-Cape Town flight, eventually abandoned. He re-joined the Royal Air Force 1920, but resigned his commission on the signing of the Anglo-Irish Treaty and came home. He cycled out to Baldonnel airfield outside Dublin when he heard that officers were being selected for a new Army Air Corps. After a hair-rising display of aerobatics he was signed on as lieutenant. He was sent to Fermoy to restore the old RFC base. During the Civil War was engaged on transport duties, and dropped amnesty leaflets over Cork and Kerry. When the Fermoy airport closed he was sent back to Baldonnel to take charge of flying training, but the humdrum life bored him. With his friend DR OLIVER ST JOHN GOGARTY he unsuccessfully tried to raise money for piloting an Irish plane east-to-west across the Atlantic. In September 1927 as co-pilot with Captain R. H. MacIntosh on the *Princess Zenia,* he took part in an unsuccessful attempt. The North German Lloyd Shipping company's publicity manager, Baron Von Hünefeld, saw a successful attempt as a means of rehabilitating world opinion of his country after the First World War. He invited Fitzmaurice to join him, and on 12 April 1928 the *Bremen* left Baldonnel with Fitzmaurice, Captain Köhl and Von Hünefeld as crew. They carried two copies of the *Irish Times,* the first European newspaper to cross the Atlantic; and 36½ hours later landed on a frozen lake on Greenly Island, off Labrador. Fitzmaurice was ordered to ignore film and writing offers and to act as 'an Irish officer and gentleman'. When his efforts to interest the Government in air services between Britain and Ireland failed he resigned in disillusionment. He persuaded the Irish Hospitals' Sweepstakes to enter a plane in the 1934 air race to Melbourne, but the specially built plane was disqualified and did not take part. Fitzmaurice then went to America for some years. He returned to England in 1939 and during the war years ran a London club for servicemen.

Took up residence in Ireland again 1951. In 1953 went to Bremen for the twenty-fifth anniversary celebration of his flight. Died Dublin September 1965.

FITZPATRICK, WILLIAM JOHN (1830–1895), biographer. Born Thomas St, Dublin, 31 August 1830. Educated Clongowes Wood. His father, a successful merchant, left him well off, and he devoted his life to biographical studies. In a pamphlet published in 1856 he attempted to prove that many of the Waverley novels had been written by Thomas Scott, a brother of Sir Walter. His most successful biographies were *Life and Times of Bishop Doyle* (1861) and *The Sham Squire* (1866), dealing with the betrayal of LORD EDWARD FITZGERALD. He published the results of his further investigations into the history of Ireland in *Ireland Before the Union* (1867) and *The Secret Service Under Pitt* (1892), showing persistence and skill in piecing scattered evidence together to form a connected narrative. He wrote biographies of LADY MORGAN, CHARLES LEVER, FATHER TOM BURKE and others, with varying success. In 1888 he published *The Correspondence of Daniel O'Connell with his Life and Times*, a valuable and important study. Pope Leo XIII honoured him with the order of St Gregory the Great in recognition of this work. Died at his house, 48 Fitzwilliam Square, Dublin, 24 December 1895.

FLANAGAN, OLIVER J. (1920–1987), auctioneer and politician. Elected independent TD for Laois-Offaly 1943. Joined Fine Gael 1952. Parliamentary Secretary for Fisheries 1954–57 and for Local Government 1975–76, then Minister for Defence until 1977. Noted for his extreme right-wing views, trenchantly and colourfully expressed. He was a Knight of Columbanus and urged politicians to accept the teachings of the Catholic Church. In 1978 he was created Knight of the Grand Order of St Gregory the Great, the highest church honour open to a layman. Died at home on 28 April 1987, survived by his wife, three daughters, and a son, Charles, who had succeeded him as TD in February 1987.

FLEMING, JOHN (1814–1896), scholar. Born Ballyneil, parish of Mothel, Co. Waterford. Educated at Kill village school and became schoolmaster, first at Carrickbeg, then at Rathcormac from 1849 to 1881. On retirement due to poor health he compounded his pension for a lump sum; it was soon exhausted. Employed by the RIA at £80 a year to 1893 as assistant to Dr Atkinson, and then received a small allowance from Rev. Maxwell Close, a Protestant clergyman. He contributed to the *Gaelic Journal* from 1882, and succeeded David Comyn as unpaid editor in 1884. Published Irish lessons in *National Teacher's Journal* 1872–1877. Published life of DONNCHADH RUA MAC CON MARA in *The Irishman* 1881, and an edition of Mac Con Mara's poems in *Gaelic Journal* 1884. Died at 33 South Frederick Street, Dublin, 28 January 1896.

FLOOD, HENRY (1732–1791), statesman and orator. Illegitimate son of Warden Flood, Chief Justice of the King's Bench in Ireland. Born Co. Kilkenny; educated TCD and Christ Church, Oxford, and the Inner Temple, London. Returned to Ireland 1759. MP for Kilkenny in Irish House of Commons, and later for borough of Callan. He soon became leader of the opposition, whose policy included independence for the Irish legislature, and was accounted the finest orator of his day. In 1769 he killed James Agar, an electioneering opponent, in a duel, and was brought to trial but acquitted. In October 1775 he accepted the post of vice-treasurer of Ireland, a sinecure worth £3,500 a year, on the mistaken grounds that by taking office he would be better able to influence policy for the good of the country. He continued to hold nationalist views, made no attempt to support the government against opposition attacks, and was removed from office in 1781. When he resumed his seat on the opposition benches he found his popularity gone and his place as leader taken by GRATTAN. He advocated sweeping reforms as against the conciliatory approach favoured by Grattan, and their differences culminated in a quarrel on the floor of the house, marked by bitter personal invective. A duel was prevented only by both being arrested. In 1783 he purchased a seat for Winchester in the English House of Commons, but was a failure there. In the general election of 1790 he was not returned to parliament, and retired to his seat at Farmley, Co. Kilkenny, where he died on 2 December 1791.

FLOOD, WILLIAM HENRY GRATTAN (1859–1928), musician and historian. Born Lismore, Co. Waterford. Educated Mount Melleray and Catholic University. Took doctorate in music, became organist in Belfast 1879 and at Enniscorthy Cathedral 1895. Wrote *History of Irish Music* (1905), which became a university textbook. Also published *Story of the Harp* (1905), *The Story of the Bagpipes* (1911), *The Diocese of Ferns* (1916), *John Field of Dublin* (1920), *History of Enniscorthy* (1920), and *Early Tudor Composers* (1925). Was Irish correspondent of *The Tablet*. Made Knight of St Gregory 1922. Died at Enniscorthy.

FOLEY, DÓNAL (1922–1981), journalist. Born in Ring, Co. Waterford, and educated at Ferrybank national school, where his father was a teacher, and St Patrick's secondary school, Waterford. After temporary jobs he emigrated to London in 1944 and worked with the London, Midland and Scottish Railway. Contributed freelance items to the *Irish Press*, then joined their London office in the late 1940s. Joined London staff of the *Irish Times* in mid-1950s. Returned to Ireland as news editor of the *Irish Times* 1963, became deputy editor 1977, and played a leading part in the development and modernisation of the paper. He wrote a weekly column, 'Man Bites Dog', which became a steady best-seller for ten years when published annually in book form. An autobiography, *Three Villages*, appeared in 1977. He was a strong supporter of the Irish language and Gaelic games. He had a sure instinct for talent and recruited women journalists whose reporting made them household names. He died in a Dublin hospital on 7 July 1981, survived by his wife, two daughters and two sons.

FOLEY, JOHN HENRY (1818–1874), sculptor. Born 6 Montgomery St, Dublin, 24 May 1818. Studied modelling and drawing at the RDS school. Joined his brother Edward in London 1834 and studied at RA, where he won a silver medal. Began to exhibit at the academy in 1839, and soon received many commissions for busts and statues. TCD commissioned from him the statues of BURKE and GOLDSMITH now outside its front gate, and he executed the figures of the Prince Consort and of Egeria for the Albert Memorial in London. He did work for London Corporation and executed a statue of Hampden for St Stephen's Hall, Westminster; a statue of HENRY GRATTAN, now in College Green, Dublin; and many portrait busts and church monuments. RA 1858; RHA 1861. By the age of forty, his great industry and ability had secured his recognition as the leading sculptor in Ireland and Britain. In 1866 he was commissioned to execute the O'Connell Monument in Dublin, but he died while still working on the full-size clay models. The work was completed by Brock, his assistant. Died at his house, the Priory, Hampstead, 27 August 1874.

FORD, PATRICK (1837–1913), journalist and politician. Born Galway, 12 April 1837. His parents emigrated to Boston when he was four and he was educated there. He became a journalist and edited the *Boston Sunday Times*. In 1870 he founded the *Irish World*, a New York weekly, which soon became the voice of the Irish who had settled in America. It had great influence, and promoted the organisation of 2,500 branches of the Land League in the USA. Ford conducted and edited the *Irish World* for forty-three years, and he was described by DAVITT as 'the most powerful support on the American continent of the struggle in Ireland'. In his later years, Ford favoured home rule and the constitutional movement. He published two books, *The Criminal History of the British Empire* (1881) and *The Irish Question and American Statesmen* (1885). Died Brooklyn, 23 September 1913. It is said that the subscriptions collected by the *Irish World* in support of successive Irish movements amounted to half-a-million dollars.

FOSTER, JOHN, BARON ORIEL (1740–1828), last speaker of the Irish House of Commons. Born Collon, Co. Louth. Educated TCD, called to the Irish bar 1766. MP for borough of Dunleer in Irish parliament 1761–1769, and then represented Co. Louth until he became a peer in 1821. Chancellor of the Exchequer in Ireland 1784, and that year secured the passage of his Corn Law, which, by granting large bounties on the export of corn and imposing heavy duties on its import, encouraged a substantial change in Irish farming from pasture to tillage. Unanimously elected Speaker of the House of Commons 1785 and held the office until the Act of Union of 1800. As a convinced supporter of the Protestant ascendancy, he was opposed to Catholic emancipation, and also a strong opponent of the Act of Union. When the house met for the last time on 2 August 1800 he refused to surrender the mace, and it was preserved by his descendants with the speaker's chair at Antrim Castle for many years. (The mace is now in the Bank of Ireland, formerly the Parliament House; the chair was destroyed in a fire.) He was one of the few anti-unionists to secure a seat in the united parliament, and in July 1804 was again appointed Chancellor of the Irish Exchequer. He retired in 1811, and in 1821 was created Baron Oriel of Ferrard (Co. Louth). Died at his seat at Collon, Co. Louth, 23 August 1828.

FOSTER, VERE HENRY LEWIS

(1819–1900), philanthropist and educationist. Born 25 April 1819 at Copenhagen, where his Irish-born father was British minister. Educated Eton and Christ Church College, Oxford. He entered the British diplomatic service, and was attached to missions in South America from 1842 to 1847. He visited Ireland in 1847, the worst year of the Great Famine, and the misery he saw decided him to work for the social betterment of the Irish people. He made three passages to America on emigrant ships to get first-hand knowledge of the conditions endured by the Irish passengers, and his evidence to parliamentary committees helped to secure reforming legislation. He then turned to education, and gave grants to assist in building several hundred new parish school-houses. When famine threatened again in 1879 he promoted the emigration of women to America and the British colonies, and paid most of the cost out of his own pocket. Both Catholic and Protestant clergy supported his scheme. He devised for school use a series of copy-books giving instructions in handwriting, drawing, and watercolouring. The 'Vere Foster copy-book' remained in use in schools throughout Ireland to the 1920s. His last years were spent in Belfast, working for the relief of the sick poor. He died there, unmarried, on 21 December 1900, having spent virtually his entire personal fortune in philanthropy.

FOWKE, FRANCIS (1823–1865),

architect. Born Ballysillane, near Belfast, 7 July 1823. Educated Dungannon College and Royal Military Academy, Woolwich. Became captain in Royal Engineers and served in Bermuda and Paris. In 1857 he was appointed architect and engineer, Art and Science Department, London. He designed the Museum of Science and Art, Edinburgh, as well as the National Gallery, Dublin, and International Exhibition buildings 1862. His design for South Kensington Museum won first prize 1864, but his death prevented its adoption. In 1865 he designed the Royal Albert Hall. Died at his official residence, South Kensington, 4 December 1865.

FOX, CHARLOTTE MILLIGAN

(1864–1916), folk music collector. Born Omagh, Co. Tyrone, 17 March 1864, sister of ALICE MILLIGAN. Founded Irish Folk Song Society 1904. Travelled all over Ireland collecting folk songs and airs on gramophone records. Published *Annals of the Irish Harpers* (1911) from the papers of BUNTING. Died London, 25 March 1916.

FRANCIS, SIR PHILIP (1740–1818),

reputed author of the 'Letters of Junius'. Born Dublin, 22 October 1740. Educated at a private school kept there by a Mr Roe, and at St Paul's School, London. On leaving school he was appointed to a junior clerkship in the office of the secretary of state, and became a principal clerk in the War Office 1762. His chief claim to fame as a writer is his supposed authorship of the 'Letters of Junius', which appeared in the *Public Advertiser* between January 1769 and January 1772 and made bitter attacks on the ministries of Grafton and North. No conclusive evidence of his authorship has yet been found, but he remains the most likely of those to whom the letters have been ascribed. In 1773 Lord North appointed him a member of the newly constituted Supreme Council of India at Fort William, Calcutta, at a salary of £10,000 a year. The reason for this spectacular promotion is almost as great a mystery as the identity of 'Junius'. He reached Bengal in October 1774 and with his colleagues on the council began a long and bitter struggle with Warren Hastings, the Governor-General. Their enmity culminated in 1780 in a duel in which Francis was wounded, and he returned to England the following year. He then embarked on a campaign to turn public opinion against Hastings, and succeeded in having the Governor-General impeached at the bar of the House of Lords in 1788. It was a bitter blow to him when Hastings was acquitted in 1795. When the Whigs returned to power in 1806 he hoped to realise his life-long ambition and become Governor-General of Bengal, but instead he was offered the governorship of the Cape at £10,000 a year. He refused this offer and also refused a peerage, but did accept knighthood. Died London, 23 December 1818.

FRENCH, NICHOLAS (1604–1678), bishop of Ferns. Born Wexford town. Educated at Louvain Irish college and became president. Parish priest of Wexford about 1641 and bishop of Ferns about 1646. Represented Wexford at Confederation of Kilkenny, 1645. He first supported the peace of 1648 but in 1650 condemned it and Ormond's proceedings. Went to Brussels in 1651 in an unsuccessful bid for assistance from the Duke of Lorraine. Became coadjutor to archbishop of Santiago until 1666, then to the archbishop of Paris, and finally to the bishop of Ghent, where he died. He published historical works dealing with his own times, notably *The Unkind Deserter* (1676), which prompted Clarendon to write his *History of the Rebellion and Civil Wars in Ireland* (1720) in defence of Ormond.

FRENCH, (WILLIAM) PERCY (1854–1920), entertainer and painter. Born Cloonyquin, Co. Roscommon. Educated at Windermere College, Foyle College, and TCD. He graduated in civil engineering in 1881, and joined the Board of Works as a surveyor of drains in Co. Cavan. He had already begun to make some money writing songs, 'The Mountains of Mourne' being especially popular, and when the board reduced its staff about 1887 and he lost his capital in an unwise investment in a distillery he turned to journalism, as editor of the *Jarvey*, a weekly comic paper. This failed after a year, and he then joined a Dr Collisson in writing and producing a musical comedy, *The Knights of the Road*, at the Queen's Theatre, Dublin. This was the beginning of a long and successful career as songwriter and entertainer,

with Collisson as partner. They toured Canada, the USA, and the West Indies, as well as playing in England. His song about the West Clare Railway, 'Are ye right there, Michael?' led to a libel action with the directors. He was a talented watercolourist, and as a young engineer spent his spare time painting the scenery of the midlands. 'Friends and relatives', he said, 'often urge me to grow up and take an interest in politics, whiskey, race meetings, foreign securities... but no, I am still the small boy messing about with a paintbox.' Moved to London in 1890. Died at Formby, Lancashire.

FRYE, THOMAS (1710–1762), painter, mezzotint engraver, and china manufacturer. Born near Dublin. As a young man, went to London to work as a portrait painter in oil, crayon, and miniature. In 1734 he painted a full-length portrait of Frederick, Prince of Wales, for the Saddlers' Company, which attracted favourable notice and brought him a large practice. In 1734 he took out, with Edward Heyleyn, a merchant of Bow, a patent for a new method of making china, using earth produced by the Cherokees in America. He became manager of a factory at Bow, which he called New Canton, for producing this china. For fifteen years he devoted all his energies to the business, which proved very successful, but the time spent at the furnaces impaired his health, and he retired from the management in 1759. After a tour in Wales to restore his health he settled at Hatton Gardens, London, and resumed his profession as a portrait painter, specialising in mezzotints. His chief work was a series of life-size portraits, which were unnamed, and engraved and published as fancy subjects, although done from life. Died London, 2 April 1762.

FURNISS, HARRY (1854–1925), caricaturist. Born Wexford, 26 March 1854. Educated Wesley College, Dublin, where he produced *The Schoolboy's 'Punch'*, a manuscript magazine. Contributed to *Zozimus* (the 'Dublin *Punch*') at seventeen. Went to London 1873; became regular contributor to *Illustrated Sporting and Dramatic News*. Joined staff of *Illustrated London News* 1876. His first sketch for *Punch* appeared in 1880, and he was on its staff from 1884 to 1894. Made many successful lecture tours, visiting the USA 1892. Founded *Lika Joka*, a humorous weekly, in 1894, and *New Budget* in 1895, but these ventures failed. In 1912 he worked with Edison in New York as film writer, actor, and pro-ducer. Illustrated a complete edition of Dickens (1910) and Thackeray (1911). Published *Confessions of a Caricaturist* (1901), *Poverty Bay*, a novel (1905), *Some Victorian Women* (1922), and *Some Victorian Men* (1924), and illustrated the last two. Also published several manuals of instruction. In his last thirty years he maintained an untiring and prolific output as cartoonist, illustrator, journalist, author, and lecturer. Died at his home in Hastings, 14 January 1925.

G

GAHAN, REV. WILLIAM (1730–1804), author. Born Dublin; joined Augustinian order and studied at Louvain 1747–1758. Returned to Dublin 1761, appointed curate in St Paul's parish, then retired to Augustinian priory to write devotional books. He received JOHN BUTLER, Lord Dunboyne, back into the Catholic Church, and in 1802 was imprisoned for a few days for refusing to reveal Dunboyne's statements on his death bed, pleading secrecy of the confessional. Died in his priory, 6 December 1804.

GALL, SAINT (*c.* 550–*c.* 645), apostle of Switzerland. The earliest extant life, written about 771, survives only in fragmentary form. Its authenticity is doubtful since it was written so long after his death. According to this and later sources he was educated at Bangor under ST COLUMBANUS and accompanied him to the Continent about 590. He remained in Bregenz after Columbanus left in 610 and later established a hermitage at the source of the Steinach, where he was joined by twelve disciples. This was the origin of the famous monastery from which the present town and canton of Sankt Gallen get their name. The monastery was suppressed in 1805; the library and archives, now in public ownership, contain many valuable Irish and other early manuscripts.

GALLAGHER, FRANK (1898–1962), journalist. Born Cork. Started career as journalist on *Cork Free Press*. Joined the Irish Volunteers. From 1919 to 1921 worked with ERSKINE CHILDERS on publicity staff of Republican government. The underground *Irish Bulletin*, which they edited, never missed an issue. Took the Republican side after the Treaty, was imprisoned, and survived a lengthy hunger strike. First editor of the *Irish Press*, founded by DE VALERA, 1931. Went to Radio Éireann as deputy director 1936. Director of the Government Information Bureau 1939–1948. On de Valera's return to office in 1951 he again became director of the bureau until 1954. From then until his death he was on the staff of the National Library working on preparations for a dictionary of Irish biography. Published *Days of Fear* (1928) on his hunger strike, and *The Four Glorious Years* (1953) on the War of Independence, under the name David Hogan. Died in Dublin in July 1962.

GALLAGHER, PATRICK (1873–1964), 'Paddy the Cope'. Born Cleendra, Co. Donegal, Christmas Day 1873, the eldest in a family of nine on twenty acres of reclaimed bog. Educated as far as the 'second book' at Roshine school. At ten he was sent to the hiring-fair at Strabane where his labour for six months was bought for £3. Until he was sixteen he hired out to farms on the Lagan, then he went to Scotland and England for a few years, working as a farm labourer, building labourer, and coalminer. Shortly after his marriage he became a member of the Pumperstown Co-operative Store in Scotland and with his savings bought a farm at Cleendra. He was the first in the district to use a plough. After hearing GEORGE RUSSELL on the benefits of a Co-operative Agricultural Bank he joined local merchants as a subscriber and founding committee member. His first venture, the bulk ordering of fertilisers, met with resistance from the merchants. He then invited the Irish Agricultural Organisation Society to send an organiser to Cleendra, and the Templecrone Co-operative Society was set up in 1906 with the backing of fourteen half-crown (12½p) subscribers. Initially the society bought staple goods such as tea and sugar and sold eggs. In 1906 he was appointed Justice of the Peace and invited to give evidence at an enquiry under Lord Dudley into the working of the Congested Districts Board. The Templecrone Society and Paddy Gallagher met with continuing opposition from the traders or 'gombeen men'. Rumours were circulated that the society was subsidised by Orange Lodge grants, and Gallagher was jailed after an action brought by traders and put under a rule of bail to be of good behaviour. Elected to Donegal County Council in 1911. Under his direction 'the Cope' (Co-op) continued to diversify and expand its activities. Donegal-made woven and knitted goods were exported to England and the USA, a pier was built at Dungloe, and a ship, the *Glenmay*, bought to overcome the British blockade of supplies to west Donegal during the Black and Tan period. A glove factory employing 150 women was set up, and the society's generator supplied electricity to the town of Dungloe. It was free to the Catholic and Protestant churches and to the main street. Gallagher travelled to England, the USA and Netherlands to buy and sell the co-operative's produce. Published his autobiography, *My Story*, in 1939. Died in Donegal.

GANDON, JAMES (1743–1823), architect. Born in London, 29 February 1743. His father, a French Protestant, dissipated his fortune on Rosicrucianism and alchemic experiments. James determined to fit himself to earn his own living, applied himself to the classics, mathematics, and drawing, and attended evening classes at Shipley's Academy. At fifteen he became an apprentice to William Chambers, and about eight years later set up on his own. His first connection with Dublin came in 1769 when he won second prize of £60 in a competition to design the Royal Exchange (now the City Hall). Princess Dashkov, introduced to him by his friend Paul Sandby, invited him to Russia to build in St Petersburg (Leningrad), offering him an official post with military rank. Instead, he accepted an offer from JOHN BERESFORD and Lord Carlow to come to Ireland and build a new Custom House. He arrived in Dublin on 26 April 1781 to face opposition from the Dublin merchant princes to the project. In September a mob led by NAPPER TANDY broke down the paling round the new works. Nevertheless the building was completed in 1791, with sculpture by EDWARD SMYTH. Meanwhile Gandon had been commissioned in 1782 to make extensions to the Parliament House designed by PEARCE, and in 1785 to design the new Four Courts, not finished until 1802. The third of his great Dublin buildings was the King's Inns, begun 1795. Irritated by interference from the Lord Chancellor, he resigned from the project in 1808, and it was completed by his partner, Baker. He retired from active professional life and built himself a house at Canonbrook, Lucan, Co. Dublin, where he died in 1823. Buried in Drumcondra churchyard. His Custom House has been described as one of the noblest buildings in Europe.

GARVIN, JOHN (1904–1986), civil servant and Joycean scholar. Born in Sligo and educated at UCG and UCD. Appointed administrative officer in Department of Local Government 1925, and rose to be Secretary 1948; retired 1966. Dublin city commissioner 1969. He wrote and lectured widely at home and abroad on Anglo-Irish literature and Irish local history. An acknowledged international authority on JAMES JOYCE, sometimes writing under the pen-name Andrew Cass, and delivered the memoral lecture in the University of Zürich on the re-interment of Joyce in Fluntern cemetery in 1966. Received D.Litt. from NUI in 1972. Died at home in Dublin on 9 February 1986, survived by his wife, daughter and two sons.

GIBBINGS, ROBERT JOHN (1889–1958), wood-engraver, book designer, and author. Born Cork, 23 March 1889. Educated UCC. After two years' medical studies he turned to art and studied at the Slade School in London and the Central School of Arts and Crafts. Served with the Royal Munster Fusiliers in the First World War; wounded at Gallipoli. In 1918 he started engraving, and from 1924 to 1933 he was proprietor of the Golden Cockerel Press, which produced a notable series of books, many illustrated by his engravings. In 1940 he published *Sweet Thames Run Softly*, an account of his exploration of the river in a punt, with his own illustrations. This was the first of a highly successful series, which included *Lovely Is the Lee* (1945) and *Sweet Cork of Thee* (1951), as well as books about his travels in France, Italy, and the South Seas. His eight 'river' books contain nearly five hundred engravings in all and show the full flowering of his remarkable talents as writer, book designer, and illustrator. Died at Oxford, 19 January 1958.

GIBBON, (WILLIAM) MONK (1896–1987), poet and man of letters. Born in Dublin on 15 December 1896 and educated at St Columba's College, Rathfarnham, and Keble College, Oxford. Served in the British army in the First World War. Invalided out 1918, he taught in Wales and Switzerland before returning to Ireland about 1930. He published poetry, a novel, biography, travel books, criticism, and six volumes of autobiography; won a silver medal for poetry at the Tailteann Games 1928; was a fellow of the Royal Society of Literature and MIAL. He died at home in Sandycove, Co. Dublin, on 29 October 1987.

GILBERT, SIR JOHN THOMAS (1829–1898), historian and antiquary. Born 23 Jervis Street, Dublin, 23 January 1829. Educated Bective College, Dublin, and Prior Park College, Bath. In 1855 he became joint honorary secretary, with J. H. TODD, of the Irish Celtic and Archaeological Society, which published many works of historical importance. His *History of the City of Dublin* (1854–1859) became the standard work on the subject. His criticisms of the official treatment of historical documents led to the founding of the Public Record Office by the government in 1867; Gilbert was appointed secretary. Librarian, RIA for thirty-four years and initiated the publication, under his own editorship, of their notable collection of Irish manuscripts. He lived at Villa Nova, Blackrock, Co. Dublin, for nearly fifty years and there amassed a valuable collection of historical and archaeological works, which was acquired by Dublin City Council after his death. His works included a *History of the Viceroys of Ireland* (1865) and his edition of *A Contemporary History of Affairs in Ireland from 1641 to 1652* (1879–1880). Gilbert married the novelist ROSA MULHOLLAND in 1891, and was knighted in 1897. Died 23 May 1898. A biography by his widow was published in 1904.

GILBERT, MARIE DOLORES ELIZA ROSANNA. See under MONTEZ, LOLA.

GILDEA, SIR JAMES (1838–1920), philanthropist. Born Kilmaine, Co. Mayo, 23 June 1838. Educated St Columba's and Pembroke College, Cambridge. Served with ambulance company in Franco-Prussian War (1870–1871). Raised large sums for homes for widows and daughters of officers; also raised funds for widows and orphans of soldiers. One of the founders of St John's Ambulance Association; published books on the association and the order. CB 1898, and knighted 1908. Died 11 Hogarth Road, London, 6 November 1920.

GILL, MICHAEL HENRY (1794–1879), master printer. Born 1794, son of Henry Gill, a woollen-draper and member of the Dublin Society of United Irishmen. Apprenticed to Dublin University Press 1813. By 1842 had become the sole lessee of the press. Under his direction it produced such notable works as the seven volumes of the *Annals of the Four Masters*, edited and translated by JOHN O'DONOVAN. His work for the RIA equalled the most outstanding academic printing in Europe. In 1856 he purchased the stock, copyrights and premises of a publisher, James McGlashan, and founded the publishing house of McGlashan and Gill, which in 1876 changed its name to M. H. Gill and Son and which, through association with Macmillan of London, became Gill and Macmillan in 1968. Acknowledged as 'the father of his profession, the grand old printer of Dublin'.

GILMORE, GEORGE (1898–1985), republican socialist. Born in Belfast, brought up in Howth and Foxrock, Dublin. His father was a leading Dublin accountant. George joined the IRA and after the Treaty was arrested many times for republican activities. He led a raid on Mountjoy jail in 1926 and released nineteen prisoners. Visited the USSR in 1930 in an abortive attempt to secure aid for the training of IRA officers. Sentenced to five years' imprisonment 1931 but released 1932 when Fianna Fáil took office. In 1934 with PEADAR O'DONNELL and FRANK RYAN he left the IRA and set up the Republican Congress to establish a workers' republic. Though supported by some trade unions and the Communist Party it was dissolved in 1935 after meeting bitter opposition from the IRA. He recruited volunteers to fight on the Republican side in the Spanish Civil War. He died at home in Howth on 20 June 1985, survived by his brother, Charlie.

GILMORE, PATRICK SARSFIELD (1829–1892), bandmaster. Born near Dublin, 25 December 1829. Shopboy in Athlone. Taught cornet by conductor of garrison band, and went to Canada with regiment in 1848. Established Gilmore's Band in Boston, and toured the USA. Served in Civil War. In New Orleans in 1864 organised the 'monster band concert'. At World Peace Jubilee, Boston, 1872, conducted a concert with an orchestra of 2,000, chorus of 20,000, a battery of cannon and fifty anvils. Later he declared he was 'through with tornado choruses'. He toured the USA, Canada and Europe with the band of the New York National Guard. Composed military band numbers, dance-pieces and songs, including 'When Johnny Comes Marching Home'. Died at St Louis, 24 September 1892.

GLENAVY, LORD. See under CAMPBELL.

GLOVER, JULIA (1779–1850), actress. Born Newry, Co. Down, on 8 January 1779, daughter of an actor called Betterton or Butterton. After appearing with her father in the English provinces she secured an engagement at Covent Garden, London, in October 1797 at the then high salary of £20 per week. Her father took her salary and treated her badly. After the death in 1798 of James Biggs, an actor whom she had loved, he forced her to marry Samuel Glover, supposed heir to a large fortune. Glover treated her as badly as her father had. Her stage career was very successful, and she was the leading comic actress of her day. Macready called her 'a rare thinking actress'. She made her last appearance at her benefit at Drury Lane on 12 July 1850 in the part of Mrs Malaprop, but was so ill that she could hardly speak. Died 16 July 1850.

GLYNN, PATRICK MACMAHON (1855–1931), lawyer and politician. Born Gort, Co. Galway, 25 August 1855, son of a successful merchant. Educated Gort Convent and the French College (now Blackrock College), Co. Dublin. Studied law at TCD. Qualified as a solicitor. Called to the bar, April 1879. Finding progress slow at the bar he decided to try his luck in Australia, where he had a number of relatives, and arrived at Melbourne in October 1880. On his first day in court he heard Ned Kelly, the bandit, being condemned to death. He failed to secure even one brief, and after much hardship and misery took a job selling insurance to save himself from starvation. In July 1882 he was asked to go to Kapunda, 48 miles (77 km) north of Adelaide in South Australia, to open an office for a firm of solicitors who wanted a Catholic Irishman for the position. Life there so depressed him that within a year it nearly drove him out of the colony. He persevered, became editor of the *Kapunda Herald* in 1883, bought out the legal practice in 1886, and proved a hard rider to hounds. He became interested in politics and was elected MP for West Adelaide in the South Australian parliament 1887. Defeated 1890; re-elected at by-election 1895. In the summer of 1894/95 he met Abigail Dynon just once and suggested, half-jokingly, that she should wait for him. In September 1897 he wrote to her proposing marriage. She accepted him by telegram the following day and they were married the day after. Elected delegate for South Australia to the Federal Convention 1897. The commonwealth was inaugurated on 1 January 1901 and he was elected to the commonwealth parliament in Melbourne. Attorney-general 1909, and Minister for External Affairs 1913. He was one of three Liberal MPs selected to visit England in 1916 at the invitation of the Empire Parliamentary Association. Minister for Home and Territories 1917, but lost his seat at the election of 1919. His practice had grown steadily and had become one of the largest in Adelaide. Died 28 October 1931.

GODKIN, EDWIN LAWRENCE (1831–1902), editor and author. Born 2 October 1831 at Moyne, Co. Wicklow. Educated Queen's College, Belfast, and Lincoln's Inn. Published *History of Hungary* in 1853. Special correspondent for *Daily News* in Crimea 1853–1855. Went to USA 1856; admitted to New York bar 1858; toured Europe for his health 1860–1862. In 1865 he founded in New York *The Nation*, a weekly journal speaking for the independents or 'Mugwumps'. Its contributors included many distinguished writers, and it had a great influence on public opinion. He denounced Tammany Hall and was responsible for its temporary defeat in 1884. Opposed the Spanish-American War, the Boer War, and the annexation of Hawaii and the Philippines by the USA. Supported Home Rule for Ireland. Declined professorship of history at Harvard 1870. Made honorary DCL, Oxford, 1897. Published several works on politics. Returned to England 1900. Died Devonshire, 21 May 1902. The 'Godkin Lectures' on government were established at Harvard in his memory.

GODLEY, ALFRED DENIS (1856–1925), classical scholar and writer. Born Ashfield, Co. Cavan, 22 January 1856. Educated Harrow and Balliol College, Oxford. Returned to Oxford in 1883 as a tutor and fellow of Magdalen College, and remained in that post until his retirement in 1912. He was joint editor of the *Classical Review* 1910–1920, edited and translated Herodotus, Tacitus, and Horace, and edited the poems of W. M. Praed and THOMAS MOORE. A regular contributor to the *Oxford Magazine*, his first collection, *Verses to Order*, appeared in 1892, followed by *Lyra Frivola* (1899), *The Casual Ward* (1912), and other volumes of light verse. 'Motor Bus' and the political ballad 'The Arrest' are his best-known single pieces. He died at Oxford, 27 June 1925, from a fever contracted on a tour in the Middle East.

GOGARTY, OLIVER ST JOHN (1878–1957), surgeon, wit, and writer. Born 5 Rutland (now Parnell) Square, Dublin, on 17 August 1878. Educated at Clongowes Wood and TCD. Graduated in medicine 1907. He was a close friend of JAMES JOYCE for a while and is described in *Ulysses* as 'stately plump Buck Mulligan'. Gogarty twice won the Vice-Chancellor's Prize for English verse, and went to Oxford for two terms in a vain attempt to emulate OSCAR WILDE by winning the Newdigate. His enthusiasm for the classics won him the favour of Trinity dons MAHAFFY and TYRRELL. He quickly built up a large practice as a nose and throat surgeon. His reputation for irreverent wit was established at sessions in the Bailey restaurant in Duke Street where he forgathered with ARTHUR GRIFFITH, SEUMAS O'SULLIVAN, SIR WILLIAM ORPEN and James Montgomery. In the Civil War his sympathy with the Free State side led to his capture by Republicans. He escaped by swimming the Liffey, and presented two swans to the river in gratitude. He was nominated to the first Senate, organised the Tailteann Games, and won a gold medal for his book of verse *An Offering of Swans* (1924). His house at Renvyle in Connemara was burned down in the Civil War, but he rebuilt it as a hotel, run on rather eccentric lines, where he invited his friends, who now included Augustus John and W. B. YEATS. He developed an obsessive hatred of ÉAMON DE VALERA and an increasing dislike for the conservative Ireland of the thirties, ill-suited to his flamboyant personality. In 1937 he lost a libel action arising from his reminiscent *As I Was Going Down Sackville Street* and moved to London and then to America in 1939. There he continued to write, publishing some further volumes of reminiscences, several novels, and his *Collected Poems* (1951). He died in New York on 22 September 1957.

GOLDSMITH, OLIVER (1728-1774), author. Born Pallas, Co. Longford, 10 November 1728. Son of a clergyman. Educated at local schools and TCD. Having been rejected by the church, he went to Edinburgh to study medicine, left after two years for Leiden and, after wandering around Europe on foot, arrived in London virtually penniless but with a dubious medical degree. He tried various ways of earning a living, and then turned to authorship. After some years of hack work he was invited to write for the *Public Ledger* and in 1761 produced his *Chinese Letters*, afterwards published as *The Citizen of the World* (1762). He was now becoming known in literary circles, and was one of the original members of Samuel Johnson's famous 'Club'. His first important poem, 'The Traveller', added to his growing reputation. From then on he alternated between journey-work and creative literature. *The Vicar of Wakefield* (1766) remains a classic of unfeigned charm. He tried the stage, had moderate success with *The Good-Natur'd Man* (1768), and in 1773 triumphed with *She Stoops to Conquer*. His finest work in verse, *The Deserted Village* (1770), with 'The Haunch of Venison' and the unfinished 'Retaliation', completes the catalogue of his poetry. Most of his life was passed in poverty and hardship. He died in London, of a fever, on 4 April 1774. Goldsmith seemed improvident and ineffectual in ordinary life, yet the shrewd and easy humour of his essays, and the unforced charm and ease of his style, are the product of no ordinary mind. His range was wide; he reached the first rank as essayist, dramatist, novelist, and poet, and his works have the enduring quality of undoubted classics.

GONNE, MAUD. See under MACBRIDE.

GORE-BOOTH, EVA (1870-1926), poet. Second daughter of Sir Henry Gore-Booth of Lissadell, Co. Sligo, and sister of CONSTANCE MARKIEVICZ. Between 1904 and 1918 she published some ten volumes of verse, including *Unseen Kings* (1904) and *The Death of Fionavar* (1916). Her best-known lyric is probably 'The Little Waves of Breffny'. At twenty-two she moved to Manchester and was active in trade union organisation for women. Died at Hampstead, 30 June 1926. Her *Complete Poems* were published 1929.

GORHAM, MAURICE ANTHONY CONEYS (1902-1975), journalist and author. Born London, son of Dr. J. J. Gorham of Clifden, Co. Galway. Educated Stonyhurst College and Balliol College, Oxford. On staff of *Westminster Guardian* and *Weekly Westminster* 1923-1926. Joined the *Radio Times* 1926, art editor 1928 and editor 1933-1941.

130

Director North American BBC services 1941-1944. Director Allied Expeditionary Forces programme 1944/45. In charge of the BBC's new Light Programme in 1945/46 and then made head of their television service. He resigned from the BBC in 1947 and returned to journalism. On 1 January 1953 he was appointed director of Radio Éireann, which he described as having three main functions: entertainment, information, and education. In September 1959, shortly before the disclosure of the Government's decisions concerning the organisation of the Irish television service, he announced his resignation. No reason was given, but it seemed clear that he did not agree with the Government proposals. He wrote a number of books, two on broadcasting, *Sound and Fury* on his twenty-one years in broadcasting with the BBC and *Forty Years of Irish Broadcasting* (1967), an officially sponsored history of Radio Éireann. He delighted in pub life, its talk and bonhomie, and wrote two books on taverns, *The Local* and *Back to the Local*. Among his last works were two books on Ireland, *Ireland from Old Photographs* and *Dublin from Old Photographs*. He continued to live in Ireland after his retirement from Radio Éireann. Died Dublin, 9 August 1975.

GOUGH, SIR HUBERT DE LA POER (1870-1963), general. Born at Gurteen, Co. Waterford. Educated at Eton and Sandhurst and commissioned in the British army in 1889. Served in India and the Boer War, relieving Ladysmith against orders. Returned to Ireland in 1911 as brigadier-general commanding 3rd Cavalry Brigade at Curragh. In 1914 with fifty-seven other officers he determined to resign rather than take part in military operations in Ulster to impose Home Rule. Alarmed at prospect of a 'Curragh Mutiny', the British government gave them assurances that the army would not be used for that purpose. Gough was promoted lieutenant-general in the First World War but was replaced and sent home in March 1918 after a German breakthrough. Retired 1922. Published memoirs, *Soldiering On* (1954). Died in London on 18 March 1963.

GRALTON, JIM (1886-1945), radical. Born at Effernagh, Co. Leitrim, son of a small farmer. He joined the British army young but, refusing to serve in India, deserted, worked on the Liverpool docks and in Welsh coal-mines, then went to sea in a tramp steamer. He settled in the USA, worked as a bartender and taxi-driver and became an American citizen in 1909. He joined the American Communist Party and became active in the trade union movement. He raised money for unfortunate fellow workers and for the republican cause in Ireland. He returned to Leitrim in 1921 and with voluntary local labour built the Pearse-Connolly Hall on his father's land, conducting there a court to settle local grievances, usually disputes about land. He was denounced by the local clergy as a professed communist leading a campaign of land agitation, and went back to New York in 1922. When Fianna Fáil came to power in 1932 he returned to Leitrim, took over the family farm and re-opened the hall for social events. He came under clerical attack again and the hall was burnt down on Christmas Eve 1932. He was served with a deportation order as an undesirable alien with effect from 4 March 1933, went on the run and addressed meetings asking for a fair trial, supported by GEORGE GILMORE and PEADAR O'DONNELL. He was arrested on 10 August 1933 and put on board ship for America, where he spent the rest of his life. He was married shortly before his death, which took place in a New York hospital on 29 December 1945.

GRANT, ALBERT (1830-1899), company promoter. Born Albert Gottheimer in Dublin. Educated in London and Paris. He took the name Grant and embarked on a career as a company promoter. He obtained lists of clergy, widows, and other small and sanguine investors, who took up shares in his companies as fast as he could float them. An example was the Emma Silver Mine, with a capital of £1 million in £20 shares. The prospectus was issued in 1871 and profits were estimated at £800,000 a year. The mine was virtually valueless, and the investors eventually received only a shilling for their £20 shares. He floated companies to a total market value of £24 million; of this sum, £20 million was lost by the subscribers. Elected MP for a London borough 1865, re-elected 1874. He bought Leicester Fields, converted the space into a public garden, and presented it to the London authorities. In 1874, when no public funds were available, he paid 800 guineas for a portrait of Sir Walter Scott, by Landseer, and presented it to the National Portrait Gallery. A series of actions in the bankruptcy courts started about this time and soon reduced him to comparative poverty. He died at Aldwick Place, Bognor, 30 August 1899.

GRATTAN, HENRY (1746–1820), patriot and orator. Born Dublin, 3 July 1746. Educated TCD and Middle Temple, London. Called to Irish bar 1772. MP for borough of Charlemont in Irish parliament 1775. HENRY FLOOD had lost his popularity by accepting the office of vice-treasurer, and Grattan soon took his place as leader of the opposition. His first success was the repeal of the restrictions on Irish trade, and he then campaigned for legislative independence for Ireland. This demand was advanced with vigour at the Dungannon Convention in 1782, and the repeal of the Declaratory Act and other important legislation soon followed. The Irish parliament voted £50,000 to Grattan to show their gratitude, but before long Flood, who was now no longer in the government service, led a movement that agitated for 'simple repeal' rather than the concessions on which Grattan hoped to build, and their differences erupted into a dramatic and bitter quarrel on the floor of the house. 'Grattan's Parliament', as it was called, could not become the organ of statesman-

ship of which Grattan himself dreamed. The large majority of the population had no representation, two-thirds of the seats were held at the nomination of patrons, and corruption was rife. Demands for parliamentary reform put forward in 1783 at a Dublin Convention were rejected. Grattan, a Protestant, had now become a strong advocate of Catholic emancipation, but there seemed little hope of progress by parliamentary reform. The influence of the French Revolution had generated support for the United Irishmen. His health weakened, Grattan retired from parliament to his house at Tinnehinch, Co. Wicklow, in 1797. After the rising of 1798 he returned to the parliament as member for Wicklow to fight against the Act of Union, but his eloquence and courage were of no avail. He retired again to private life, but emerged in 1805 to sit for Malton and subsequently for Dublin in the English House of Commons. He devoted the rest of his life to the cause of Catholic emancipation, which he maintained was both the price of the Union and intrinsically just. In 1819 his health finally began to give way but his responsibility for this cause weighed more heavily on him. In May 1820 he left Dublin for London; he was so ill that he travelled by canal from Liverpool, as he was unable to bear the jolting of a carriage, and he died in London on 4 June. He is buried in Westminster Abbey. His son Henry published a collection of his speeches in 1820 and a biography in 1839–1846.

GRAVES, ALFRED PERCEVAL (1846–1931), author and educationist. Born 12 Fitzwilliam Square, Dublin, 22 July 1846, son of CHARLES GRAVES. Educated Windermere College and TCD. After a brilliant academic career he joined the civil service and became an inspector of schools in England. He published *Songs of Old Ireland* in 1882 and *Songs of Erin* in 1892, both in collaboration with SIR CHARLES STANFORD. Graves wrote the words to old Irish folk tunes derived from the collection of GEORGE PETRIE. *Songs of Old Ireland* included 'Father O'Flynn', which became famous, but Graves had sold the copyright for a small sum and had no share in the profits. He contributed to *Punch* and was active in the Irish Literary Society in London. His autobiography, *To Return to All That* (1930), followed close on *Goodbye to All That* (1929) by his son Robert. Died at Harlech, Wales, 27 December 1931, and is buried there.

GRAVES, CHARLES (1812–1899), bishop and mathematician. Born Dublin, 6 November 1812. Educated at private school near Bristol and TCD. Graduated with distinction in mathematics and mathematical physics. Fellow 1836; professor of mathematics 1843. Dean of the Castle Chapel, Dublin, 1860, dean of Clonfert 1864, and bishop of Limerick, Ardfert and Aghadoe 1866. He held this office until his death thirty-three years later. President RIA 1861, and FRS 1880. His only mathematical book was a translation of Charles's two memoirs *On the General Properties of Cones*, with extensive notes giving a number of new theorems. He studied ogham writing and made renderings of a number of ogham inscriptions on cromlechs and other stone monuments. As a result of his representations, a government commission was established to edit and translate the Brehon Laws, and he became a member of this commission. Died Dublin, 17 July 1899. One of his sons was A. P. GRAVES, and Robert Graves, the poet, is a grandson.

GRAVES, ROBERT JAMES (1796–1853), physician. Born Dublin. Educated TCD, graduating in medicine 1818. He then studied in London and Edinburgh and on the Continent, where he travelled through the Alps with Turner, the painter. On his return to Dublin in 1821 he became physician to the Meath Hospital. President RCPI 1843–1844 and FRS 1849. He contributed many essays to the *Dublin Journal of Medical Science*, which he helped to found and edit. His reputation rests on his *Clinical Lectures* (1843), which were translated into German and Italian, and on his diagnosis of 'Graves' disease'(hyperthyroidism). One of his greatest reforms was the substitution of adequate nourishment and stimulants for the traditional 'lowering treatment' in cases of fever. He advocated a network of medical observatories to record the rise, progress and character of diseases. Died Dublin, 20 March 1853.

GRAY, BETSY (died 1798), heroine. Born Killinchy, Co. Down. Carried a green flag for insurgents at battle of Ballynahinch, 13 June 1798. Fought beside her brother and her lover who stayed by her in the retreat although they could have outridden their pursuers. All three were cut down by the yeomanry. She is remembered in song and story.

GRAY, EDMUND DWYER (1845–1888), journalist, second son of SIR JOHN GRAY. Born in Dublin; and on the death of his father succeeded him as proprietor of the *Freeman's Journal*. Also became proprietor of the *Belfast Morning News*. When only twenty he saved five people from drowning in Dublin Bay and was awarded the Tayleur Medal, the Royal Humane Society's highest honour. A young woman who saw his bravery became his wife shortly afterwards. He was elected to Dublin City Council and promoted reform in the municipal health system. MP successively for Tipperary, Carlow and St Stephen's Green (Dublin) divisions 1877–1888, and became a strong supporter of PARNELL. Lord Mayor of Dublin 1880, High Sheriff 1882. Was imprisoned for six weeks in 1882 for comments in the *Freeman's Journal* on the composition of the jury at the murder trial of Francis Hynes (later executed). He died in Dublin on 27 March 1888.

GRAY, EILEEN (1879–1976), designer and architect. Born Enniscorthy, Co.

Wexford, and educated privately. Studied painting at Slade School, London, while apprenticed to Sugawara, a Japanese lacquer craftsman. In 1907 she settled in an apartment in Rue Bonaparte, Paris, which she occupied until her death. Designed furniture and carpets. In the First World War she drove an ambulance. About 1919 she opened a gallery at 217 Faubourg St Honoré. Her furniture, made by her own craftsmen, became famous. In 1925 she built two houses at Roquebrune. One was featured in a special issue of *Architecture Vivante* and decorated by Le Corbusier; the other became the home of Graham Sutherland. *Wendingen*, a leading Dutch review, devoted an issue to her work in 1924. She was made honorary fellow of the Royal Institute of Architects of Ireland, April 1975. She loved flying, accompanied Latham on unsuccessful Channel crossing 1909, and in the early 1920s flew on first air-mail service in America from New Mexico to Acapulco. She died in Paris, 31 October 1976.

GRAY, SIR JOHN (1816–1875), journalist. Born Claremorris, Co. Mayo. Graduated in medicine from Glasgow University 1839. Settled in Dublin that year and began to contribute to the newspapers, while practising medicine. Became joint proprietor of the *Freeman's Journal* and political editor in 1841. A Protestant nationalist, he supported the Repeal movement led by O'CONNELL. In 1843 he was sentenced to nine months' imprisonment for conspiracy, but the sentence was reversed. In 1850 he became sole owner of the *Freeman's Journal* and increased its circulation. Elected to Dublin City Council 1852 and promoted the Vartry water supply scheme against strong opposition; knighted in 1863 when the scheme was inaugurated. MP for Kilkenny 1865–1875. In Parliament he advocated disestablishment of the Irish Protestant Church, reform of the land laws, and free denominational education. Through his paper he instituted a commission on

disestablishment, and in 1868 published its report, *The Church Establishment in Ireland*. A testimonial of £3,500 was presented to him in recognition of his work in this cause. Elected Lord Mayor of Dublin 1868, but declined office. Died Bath, 9 April 1875.

GREATRAKES, VALENTINE (1629–1683), also GREATOREX, 'stroker' or faith-healer. Born on his father's estate at Affane, Co. Waterford, 14 February 1629. Educated at free school, Lismore, and afterwards privately in England. He served under Cromwell in his Irish campaign, but at the Restoration of 1660 was deprived of his offices of magistrate and clerk of the peace. He first began to 'touch for the king's evil', or scrofula, in 1662 and, encouraged by his success, extended his treatment to ague, rheumatism, and other diseases. His fame spread, and hundreds came for his cure. In 1666 he was invited to England and spent several months in London, treating a great number of patients with varying success. He would say 'God Almighty heal thee for his mercy's sake', told his patients to give God the praise if they were cured, and refused any payment. He returned to his Irish estate in May 1666 and died there, 28 November 1683. In 1666 he published in London an autobiographical defence of his cures, in the form of a letter to ROBERT BOYLE, accompanied by fifty-three testimonials from notable contemporaries.

GREEN, ALICE STOPFORD (1847–1929), historian. Born Kells, Co. Meath, 31 May 1847. Educated at home. After the death of her father, Archdeacon Stopford, in 1874 the family moved to London, where she married the historian John Richard Green in 1877. He died seven years later; she had become virtually his collaborator, and produced new and revised editions of his works. Her own first noteworthy book was *Town Life in the Fifteenth Century* (1894). She then turned to Irish history, and formed strong anti-imperialist views as a result of her studies. In 1908 she published *The*

Making of Ireland and its Undoing, which was violently attacked for alleged inaccuracy by English reviewers. She followed this with *Irish Nationality* (1911), which had great vogue and influence with the new Irish generation then emerging in the national and literary resurgence. She conducted at her London house one of the most interesting salons of the day, but after 1916 she decided that her place was in Ireland and she moved to 90 St Stephen's Green, Dublin, which quickly became an intellectual centre. In the pamphlet *Ourselves Alone in Ulster* (1918) she attacked CARSON's policy. A strong supporter of the Treaty of 1921, she was nominated to the first Irish Senate in December 1922. Her last major work, *A History of the Irish State to 1014*, was published in 1925. Died Dublin, 28 May 1929.

GREENE, DAVID WILLIAM (1915-1981), scholar. Born in Dublin and educated at St Andrew's College and TCD, where he combined academic brilliance with activity in student societies. A travelling scholarship took him to Oslo to study under Carl Marstrander, an outstanding scholar in Celtic and general linguistics. He was an assistant lecturer in Glasgow University 1939-1940, returned to Ireland to become an assistant librarian in the National Library 1941-1948, professor in the Dublin Institute for Advanced Studies 1948-1955, professor of Irish, TCD, 1955-1967, and senior professor, School of Celtic Studies, DIAS, from 1967 until his death. He was president RIA 1973-1976, received honorary doctorates from NUU, Glasgow University and NUI, and was a visiting professor at Harvard University. He made many important contributions to learned journals; to the general reader his best-known work is *A Golden Treasury of Irish Poetry* (1967), which he edited with FRANK O'CONNOR. He was strongly influenced by Marstrander's outstanding scholarship and background of Norwegian independence and political sophistication. SEÁN CAOMHÁNACH

(Seán a' Chóta) taught him Irish in St Andrew's, brought him to Dún Chaoin on holidays, and made Gaelic Ireland a reality to him. David Greene was tall, burly, bearded, vigorous in debate and of daunting erudition. He died suddenly on 13 June 1981, survived by a daughter of his first marriage. His second wife, HILARY HERON, predeceased him in 1977.

GREENE, HARRY PLUNKETT (1865-1936), singer. Born Old Connaught House, Bray, Co. Wicklow, 24 June 1865. Educated Clifton College. He was intended for the bar, his father's profession, but he had such a fine voice that he decided to become a professional singer, and studied at Stuttgart, Florence, and London. He made his first public appearance in the *Messiah* in London on 21 January 1888, and was soon engaged at all the most important concerts. From 1893 onwards he gave recitals with the pianist Borwick in the classical repertory of German lieder and Brahms songs. He took part in the first production of most of the cantatas and oratorios written by Hubert Parry. SIR CHARLES VILLIERS STANFORD wrote many of his finest songs for him. His powers of interpretation and the beauty of his English diction were special features of his performances. In his later years he lectured and wrote on his art, publishing *Interpretation in Song* in 1912. He also wrote a book on dry-fly fishing, *Where the Bright Waters Meet* (1924), reminiscences under the title *From Blue Danube to Shannon* (1934), and a life of Stanford (1935). Died London, 19 August 1936.

GREGG, JOHN ROBERT (1867-1948), inventor of Gregg shorthand. Born 17 June 1867 at Rockcorry, Co. Monaghan. Educated at Glasgow. Studied theory and practice of many systems of stenography. Based his own system on the natural motion of the hand. It appeared first at Liverpool in a twenty-eight page pamphlet, now a collector's item. He went to the USA in

1893 and soon after published a revised version, *Gregg Shorthand Manual*. Settled in Chicago in 1895, founded his own publishing company, and wrote many books on commercial education. Edited *American Shorthand Teacher* from 1920. Received award of New York Academy of Public Education in 1938. His system is widely used in North America and has been adapted to more than thirteen languages. He died in New York, 23 February 1948.

GREGORY, LADY (ISABELLA) AUGUSTA (1852–1932), playwright. Born Roxborough, Co. Galway, 15 March 1852. Educated privately. In 1880 she married SIR WILLIAM GREGORY, a widower whose estate at Coole Park, Gort, was not far from that of her father, Dudley Persse. Her husband died in 1892. Lady Gregory had taken little interest in the theatre, but after meeting W. B. YEATS in London in 1898 she became his friend and patron. He encouraged her to collect folklore, and their association resulted in the formation of the Irish Literary Theatre, which had its first production, Yeats's *The Countess Cathleen*, in May 1899. The Irish literary renaissance was just beginning, and the leading figures— SYNGE, Yeats, MARTYN, and others—were frequent visitors to Coole Park, where they found 'a scene well set and excellent company' (Yeats). She learned Irish, and published English versions of the old heroic sagas under the titles *Cúchulain of Muirthemne* (1902) and *Gods and Fighting Men* (1904). The Abbey Theatre was opened in 1904 with Lady Gregory as co-director with Yeats and Synge. She devoted her energies and considerable administrative abilities to the theatre for the rest of her life. At this time she suddenly emerged as a gifted dramatist and wrote in all twenty-seven original plays, mostly short comedies based on her sympathetic observation of Irish rural life. The best-known, *Spreading the News* (1904), *The Rising of the Moon* (1907), and *The Workhouse Ward* (1908), are often revived. Her rendering

of the speech of Irish country people became known as 'Kiltartan' after a village on her estate. The collection *Seven Short Plays* contains the best of her work, and shows her mastery of construction and of vivid dialogue. Her later and longer comedies and 'folk history' plays were less successful. In *Our Irish Theatre* (1914) she described the early years of the movement and set out its ideals. 'We went on giving what we thought good until it became popular,' she said. She died at Coole on 22 May 1932. Her only son, Robert, was killed in the First World War.

GREGORY, SIR WILLIAM HENRY (1817–1892), Governor of Ceylon (Sri Lanka). Born in under-secretary's lodge, Phoenix Park, Dublin, 12 July 1817. Educated Harrow and Christ Church, Oxford. Conservative MP for Dublin 1842–1847 and Liberal MP for Co. Galway 1857–1871, then appointed Governor of Ceylon. He proved a successful administrator, but resigned in 1877 and retired to the family estate at Coole Park, Co. Galway. He took a keen interest in the arts, and was a trustee of the National Gallery from 1867 until his death. LADY AUGUSTA GREGORY was his second wife. He died London, 6 March 1892.

GRIFFIN, GERALD (1803–1840), dramatist, novelist, and poet. Born 12 December 1803 at Limerick, and educated there. After writing for local journals, he went to London in 1823 to make a career in literature. JOHN BANIM helped him to place contributions with the *Literary Gazette* and other periodicals. His first success came with *Holland Tide* (1826), a collection of stories. The privations he had undergone impaired his health and he returned to Limerick in 1827. His next work, *Tales of the Munster Festivals*, was followed by a novel, *The Collegians*, issued anonymously in 1829. It was based on the notorious Scanlon murder case, and achieved wide popularity. He continued to write, publishing further novels and collections of stories until 1838, when he burned his manuscripts, entered the Christian Brothers, and devoted the rest of his short life to teaching in the North Monastery, Cork, where he died on 12 June 1840. His play *Gissippus*, which had failed to find acceptance in his lifetime, was produced at Drury Lane in 1842 and when published that year reached a second edition immediately. DION BOUCICAULT based his highly successful play *The Colleen Bawn* (1860) on *The Collegians*.

GRIFFITH, ARTHUR (1871–1922), political leader. Born 61 Upper Dominick Street, Dublin, 31 March 1871. Educated Strand Street CBS. He worked for a time as a printer, and joined the Gaelic League and the Irish Republican Brotherhood. In 1896 he went to South Africa, where he worked in the gold mines. He returned to Ireland in 1898 at the request of his friend WILLIE ROONEY to edit a new weekly paper, *The United Irishman*. The fall of PARNELL in 1890 had dimmed hopes of winning Irish independence by constitutional means, and the new generation were turning to new methods. In a series of articles Griffith outlined a new policy advocating abandonment of parliamentary action at Westminster and passive resistance to English rule in Ireland. Irish members of parliament should form a national assembly in Dublin, and the courts would be superseded by tribunals set up by the national assembly. These articles, which cited the example of the Hungarians under Deák after 1848, were published in 1904 as a pamphlet with the title *The Resurrection of Hungary*. At a convention in Dublin in 1905 Griffith expounded this policy under the name Sinn Féin ('ourselves'), chosen to emphasise the idea of national self-reliance. The *United Irishman* ceased publication in 1906 as a result of a libel action, and Griffith started a new paper, *Sinn Féin*. The Home Rule Bill of 1912 conceded so little to Irish aspirations that it strengthened the new movement. The Ulster Volunteers were established that year to resist home rule and when, in

reply, the Irish Volunteers were formed in 1913, Griffith supported them and took part in the landing of arms at Howth in July 1914. On the outbreak of the First World War in August 1914 thousands of young Irishmen, responding to REDMOND's call, joined the British army to fight 'for small nations'. Griffith urged them against this course, and his paper was suppressed. He took no part in the 1916 Rising. This impaired his standing with the dominant, militant wing of the Volunteers, but the British government realised the effect of his writings in reviving the national spirit, and he was imprisoned along with those who had fought in the Rising. After the executions of the leaders, public opinion, until then either lukewarm or antagonistic, turned in favour of Sinn Féin, and a convention in Dublin in October 1917 showed the strength of the movement. Although most republicans disagreed with Griffith's Sinn Féin policy, in the popular mind the term Sinn Féin included all fighters for Irish freedom. Griffith stood down as president in favour of ÉAMON DE VALERA and in the general election of 1918 Sinn Féin had an overwhelming victory. Griffith retained the East Cavan seat he had won at a by-election earlier that year. The elected members assembled as Dáil Éireann, proclaimed themselves the legitimate parliament of Ireland, and declared a republic, thus going further than Griffith, who had not envisaged complete constitutional separation from England. De Valera was elected president of the republic and Griffith vice-president. While de Valera was in the USA from June 1919 to the end of 1920 to enlist American support Griffith acted as head of the republic. His policy was now put into practice: town and county councils ignored the British authorities in Dublin, Sinn Féin courts were set up, and functioned with remarkable success. Over large parts of the country British rule ceased to operate. This civil resistance was buttressed and accompanied by guerrilla warfare under the leadership of MICHAEL COLLINS and RICHARD MULCAHY. Griffith was arrested in November 1920 and imprisoned in Mountjoy jail until July 1921. Pressure of public opinion in America and Britain led to a Truce in July 1921, and Griffith was chosen to lead the Irish plenipotentiaries to the negotiations that resulted in the Anglo-Irish Treaty of 6 December 1921. In the long and often bitter debate that followed in the Dáil, he defended the Treaty as giving Ireland the opportunity to advance to full freedom. The Treaty was ratified by 64 votes to 57, and de Valera, who had opposed it, resigned. Griffith was elected President in his place. In the general election of June 1922 the Treaty party won 58 seats, the anti-Treaty side 36, with the remaining 34 shared by Farmers, Labour, and Independents. Civil War began with the shelling of the Four Courts (held by anti-Treaty forces) on 28 June 1922. Griffith died suddenly in Dublin, 12 August 1922, and is buried in Glasnevin cemetery. He had married in 1910 and was survived by his wife, a son, and a daughter.

GRIFFITH, SIR RICHARD JOHN (1784-1878), geologist and civil engineer. Born Hume Street, Dublin, 20 September 1784. Educated for the army, became a lieutenant in the Royal Irish Artillery 1799, but after the Union resigned his commission to study civil engineering in London and Edinburgh. In 1808 he returned to Ireland; he surveyed the coalfields of Leinster for the RDS and reported on the bogs of Ireland for a government commission. Mining engineer and professor of geology to the RDS 1812, and also became government inspector of mines for Ireland. Commissioner of valuation after the passing of the Irish Valuation Act of 1827, and based his land valuation on a method he had observed in Scotland, relying on an examination of the active soil and subjacent rock. 'Griffith's valuation' has remained the basis for county rate assessment to the present day. From 1830 he was involved in almost every public

work of importance, including the improvement of the Shannon navigation. Chairman, Board of Works, 1850-1864, baronet 1858. The Geological Society awarded him the Wollaston Medal for his geological map of Ireland on its publication in final form in 1855. Died 22 September 1878 at his house in Fitzwilliam Place, Dublin.

GRIMSHAW, BEATRICE (1880-1953), writer. Born Cloona, Co. Antrim. Educated in Belfast, London, and France. Became journalist in Dublin. Edited the *Social Review* for four years. Tiring of this work, she began to travel to remote areas. In 1906 she went to Papua New Guinea and was commissioned by the Australian government to publicise the development of the country. The result was several travel books, including *From Fiji to the Cannibal Islands* (1907). Also published several novels, including *When the Red Gods Call* (1910) and *Guinea Gold* (1912).

GRUBB, THOMAS (1800-1878), optician. Born Kilkenny. Opened an engineering shop in Dublin. Here he designed a machine for engraving, printing and numbering bank-notes for the Bank of Ireland. He became a practical optician, and made reflecting and refracting equipment for the observatories at Armagh, Dunsink, Markree, and Glasgow, and for many magnetic stations. He assisted Lord Rosse (WILLIAM PARSONS) in constructing his great telescope at Parsonstown. His last work was a reflector for Melbourne, Australia, which was described by a committee of the Royal Society as 'a masterpiece of engineering'. FRS 1864, fellow Royal Astronomical Society 1870, MRIA 1839. Contributed many papers to these societies. Died at his house in Rathmines, Dublin, 19 September 1878.

GUBBINS, JOHN (1838-1906), breeder and owner of racehorses. Born 16 December 1838 at Kilfrush, Co. Limerick. Educated privately. Inherited fortune and property and settled at

Bruree in 1868, where he spent about £40,000 building kennels and stables and buying horses and hounds. A fine rider, he won many steeplechases at Punchestown and elsewhere. Bred Galtee More, which won the 2,000 Guineas, the St Leger and the Derby in 1897 and made him the highest-winning owner, with a total of £22,739; also Ard Patrick, which won the Eclipse Stakes in 1903. He died at Bruree, 20 March 1906.

GUINNESS, ARTHUR (1725–1803), founder of Guinness's Brewery. Born at Celbridge, Co. Kildare. Leased a brewery at Leixlip in September 1756. At the age of thirty-four he came to Dublin intending to begin brewing there. At the time export restrictions and a heavy tariff prevented the development of the Irish brewing industry, so Guinness first surveyed the possibility of setting up at Caernarvon or Holyhead in Wales. He failed to find a ready-built brewery there and instead in 1759 bought a brewery on twenty-four acres at St James's Gate from Mark Rainsford, later Lord Mayor of Dublin. The purchase included 'a dwelling-house, a brewhouse, two malt houses, and stables'. There, nineteen years later, he began to brew porter as distinct from ale. Known as 'Guinness's black Protestant porter' after the proprietor's opposition to the United Irishmen, it became the sole product of the brewery in 1799. At that time the threat of a popular boycott encouraged Guinness to develop what became a prosperous export trade to England. For many years Guinness was involved in a dispute with Dublin City Council over water rights. It culminated in May 1775 when the waterworks committee, with some labourers, set out to fill in the watercourse from which the brewery drew its supply. When Guinness confronted the sheriff with a pickaxe the party withdrew. The matter was finally settled by agreement in May 1785. Guinness became successively warden and master of the Dublin Corporation of Brewers and their representative on the

city council. He founded Ireland's first Sunday school in 1786. He died in 1803.

GUINNESS, SIR ARTHUR EDWARD, BARON ARDILAUN (1840–1915), philanthropist. Born St Anne's, Clontarf, Dublin, 1 November 1840. Educated at Eton and TCD. He was head of the family brewing business 1868–1877, MP for Dublin 1868–1869 and 1874–1880. Dublin remembers him for his generosity. He restored Marsh's Library; extended the Coombe Hospital; bought, laid out and presented to the city the public park of twenty-two acres now known as St Stephen's Green. In 1899 he bought the Muckross estate, beside the Lakes of Killarney, to save the area from commercial exploitation. President RDS 1892–1913 and sponsored the publication of its history. Died at St Anne's, 20 January 1915.

GUINNESS, SIR BENJAMIN LEE (1798–1868), brewer. Born Dublin, 1 November 1798. Joined his father, Arthur, in the family business at an early age. On the death of his father in 1855 he became sole owner. He attended personally to the smallest details, extended the home market, and built up a large export trade. In 1851 he was elected the first Lord Mayor of Dublin under the reformed corporation. In 1860 he undertook at his own expense the restoration of St Patrick's Cathedral, then in a dangerous state of disrepair, and personally superintended the work, which cost £150,000. Conservative MP for Dublin 1865–1868; baronet 1867. He was engaged in the restoration of Marsh's Library at the time of his death, which took place at his London home, Park Lane, on 19 May 1868.

GUINNESS, EDWARD CECIL, first EARL OF IVEAGH (1847–1927) philanthropist. Born St Anne's, Clontarf, Co. Dublin, 10 November 1847. Educated TCD. The family business was formed into a public company in 1886 and he became chairman; applications for shares exceeded a hundred million pounds in a heavy over-subscription. His benefactions to his native city ran into hundreds of thousands of pounds, devoted chiefly to hospitals and housing for the poor. After 1900 he lived mainly in England. Died London, 7 October 1927, leaving an estate estimated at £11 million.

GUINNESS, REV. HENRY GRAT-TAN (1835-1910), evangelist. Born Kingstown (Dún Laoghaire), Co. Dublin, 11 August. His mother was the widow of D'Esterre, killed in a duel by O'CONNELL. He was educated privately and went to sea at seventeen. He experienced 'religious conversion' at eighteen, was ordained as undenominational evangelist in 1857 and devoted the rest of his life to evangelical work. As 'boy preacher' he drew huge crowds in London. Toured Ireland, the Continent and America. Founded East London Institute for Home and Foreign Missions 1873, and extended his work to Africa, Peru, Argentina, and India. Made world tour in 1903. Published sermons, works on prophecy, and grammar of the Kongo language. Died at Bath, 21 June 1910.

GUINNESS, RUPERT EDWARD CECIL LEE, second LORD IVEAGH (1874-1967), brewer and philanthropist. Born London; educated Eton and Trinity College, Cambridge. Won the Diamond Sculls at Henley Regatta 1895 and 1896. In 1900 he served in the Boer War with the Irish Hospital Corps. Unionist MP 1908-1910 and 1912-1927. In 1927 he succeeded his father, the first Lord Iveagh, as chairman of the family brewing business in Dublin and for thirty-five years directed its consolidation at home and expansion abroad with the establishment of breweries in London and in Nigeria and Malaya. A keen agriculturist, he transformed a barren shooting estate at Elveden in Suffolk into a highly productive farm. He donated generous sums to Dublin hospitals, and in 1939 presented to the government his Dublin

residence, Iveagh House (80 St Stephen's Green), now the headquarters of the Department of Foreign Affairs, and gave the gardens to University College, Dublin. Chancellor of Dublin University 1927-1963. His only son, Viscount Elveden, was killed in action in 1945. He retired from Guinness in 1962 in favour of his grandson, Lord Elveden. Elected FRS in March 1964 at ninety, for his services to science and agriculture. Died in his sleep at his house in Woking, Surrey, 14 September 1967.

GUNNING, MARIA, COUNTESS OF COVENTRY (1733-1760) and **GUNNING, ELIZABETH, DUCHESS OF HAMILTON AND ARGYLL** (1734-1790), celebrated beauties. Daughters of John Gunning of Castlecoote, Co. Roscommon, and so poor that on presentation to the lord lieutenant in Dublin Castle they were obliged to borrow their dresses from the actress PEG WOFFINGTON. Their beauty created a sensation when they went to London in 1751. In 1752 Elizabeth married the Duke of Hamilton, and three weeks later Maria married the Earl of Coventry. Hamilton died in 1758 and the following year Elizabeth married the Marquis of Lorne, later Duke of Argyll. Maria had five children and died at twenty-seven. It is said that her health was impaired by her excessive use of white lead paint as a cosmetic. Unlike her younger sister, she had little sense, and once told King George II that the sight she most wished to see in London was a coronation. Elizabeth had three children by her first husband and five by her second. During the Wilkes riots, when a mob attacked her London house in her husband's absence, she showed courage and calmness. A contemporary said that 'she seemed composed of a finer clay than the rest of her sex.' At her presentation the courtiers climbed on chairs and tables to see her. Seven hundred people sat up all night to see the sisters entering their chaise in the morning, and Maria was given a guard of soldiers to protect her from being mobbed in Hyde Park.

Elizabeth died in London on 20 May 1790.

GUTHRIE, SIR TYRONE (1900–1971), theatre producer. Born Tunbridge Wells, Kent, son of a doctor. His mother was a granddaughter of the actor TYRONE POWER. Educated at Wellington College and St John's College, Oxford. Invited by J. B. FAGAN to join the Oxford Playhouse 1923 but stayed only a few months. Began to work in broadcasting at Belfast. Spent two years at Glasgow as director of Scottish National Theatre Society. Worked for the BBC in London, at the Festival Theatre, Cambridge, and with the Canadian Broadcasting Corporation. Directed the inaugural production of Bridie's *The Anatomist,* Westminster Theatre, London, 1931. Play director at the Old Vic and Sadler's Wells in 1933. Introduced Laurence Olivier as Hamlet. Administrator from 1937 to 1945 and director of the Old Vic in 1951 and 1952. He had many productions in England, the USA, Australia, Finland, and Israel, and in 1962 became the first director of the Old Minnesota Classical Theatre in Minneapolis. Received honorary degrees from DU, QUB, and several North American universities. Chancellor, QUB, 1963–1970; chairman, Ulster Theatre Council. Knighted for his services to the theatre 1961. Among the books he published was *A Life in the Theatre* (1960). In 1962, concerned at the high rate of emigration from Co. Monaghan, he helped to start a jam and preserves factory at Newbliss. It went into liquidation in the year of his death. He died on 15 May 1971 at his Newbliss home, Annaghmakerrig House. His will provided that after the death of his wife the house would pass to the government to be used as a retreat for artists and writers.

GWYNN, STEPHEN LUCIUS (1864–1950), author and nationalist, grandson of WILLIAM SMITH O'BRIEN. Born 13 February 1864 at St Columba's College, Rathfarnham, Co. Dublin, where his father was warden. Educated there and Brasenose College, Oxford. He became a schoolmaster and then a journalist and, joining REDMOND's Irish Party, was MP for Galway 1906–1918. Although over fifty on the outbreak of the First World War, he served in France as a captain with the Connaught Rangers, and was made a *chevalier* of the Legion of Honour. Leaving politics after the war, he published verse, novels, and volumes of biography, including studies of SWIFT and GOLDSMITH, and made himself an authority on eighteenth-century Ireland. He was honoured by the Irish Academy of Letters shortly before his death in Dublin, 11 June 1950.

141

H

HALIDAY, CHARLES (1789–1866), antiquary. Born Dublin; became merchant 1812 and amassed large fortune. Became consul for Greece, secretary of Dublin Chamber of Commerce, and director, Bank of Ireland. MRIA 1847; formed a large collection of books and tracts, presented to RIA by his widow. Wrote pamphlets on social questions and on history of Dublin. Published *Scandinavian Kingdom of Dublin* (1881). Died Monkstown, Co. Dublin, 14 September 1866.

HALIDAY, SAMUEL (1685–1739), presbyterian. Born probably at Omagh, Co. Tyrone. Educated Glasgow and Leiden. Ordained at Geneva 1708 and became army chaplain. Called to Belfast 1719. Refused to subscribe to Westminster Confession of Faith, hence arose the division of presbyterians into 'subscribers' and 'non-subscribers', controversy in the Synod and press, and a pamphleteering war in which he joined. Died Belfast, 5 March 1739.

HALIDAY, WILLIAM (1788–1812), grammarian, brother of CHARLES HALIDAY. Born Dublin. Became a solicitor. Learned Irish, thinking it prudent to assume the name 'O'Hara' for the purpose, so low was Irish esteemed. Published *Grammar of the Irish Language* (1808) under another assumed name, Edmond O'Connell. Was one of the founders of Gaelic Society of Dublin in 1807. In 1811 published first volume of a translation of *Foras Feasa ar Éirinn* by CÉITINN. Had begun an Irish dictionary when he died, 26 October 1812.

HALL, ANNA MARIA (1800–1881), author. Born Anne St, Dublin, 6 January 1800. Went to London with her mother, Mrs Fielding, in 1815. Married Samuel Carter Hall 1824. Published *Sketches of Irish Character* (1829); further *Sketches* followed, and nine novels. She had four plays produced successfully, including *The Groves of Blarney* (1838), in which TYRONE POWER appeared. With her husband published *Ireland, its Scenery, Characters, etc.* (1840), her best-known work and a valuable record of pre-famine conditions. Her books were popular in England but little regarded in Ireland. Edited *St James Magazine* 1862–1863. Granted civil list pension of £100 a year in 1868. Founded the Hospital for Consumption at Brompton, the Governesses' Institute, the Home for Decayed Gentlewomen, and the Nightingale Fund. Died East Moulsey, 30 January 1881.

HALPIN, CAPTAIN ROBERT CHARLES (1836–1894), master mariner. Born in the Bridge Hotel, Wicklow, and went to sea on a coasting vessel at the age of ten. He rose to officer rank and in 1855 transferred from sail to steam, and soon was given command of Atlantic mail ships. In 1866, as navigating officer, he brought the *Great Eastern*, then the largest ship in the world, to the exact spot where an Atlantic cable had parted and sunk in deep water. The cable was raised and new cable laid to complete the connection between Valentia, Co. Kerry, and Heart's Content, Newfoundland, the first transatlantic link. In 1868 he was made master of the *Great Eastern*. In 1869 he successfully laid the then longest cable, from Brest to Newfoundland, and later connected Bombay with Aden and Suez, and Madras with Singapore and Penang. In 1871 he laid cables from Australia to Indonesia and in 1874 joined

Madeira by cable to St Vincent, Cape Verde Island and Recife. Emperor Pedro II of Brazil made him a knight of the Order of the Rose. In all, he was responsible for the laying of cables 26,000 miles long, equal to the circumference of the earth. No crew member ever suffered serious injury under his command. An infected toe-nail led to gangrene, causing his death on 20 January 1894 at fifty-seven. He is commemorated by a monument in Wicklow town.

HAMILTON, ANTHONY (1645–1719), soldier and writer. Born Roscrea Castle, Co. Tipperary. Son of Sir George Hamilton, Governor of Nenagh. Went to France with his parents 1651 after his father had surrendered Nenagh to the Cromwellians under Ireton. Attached to the court of Charles II. Returned to Ireland after the restoration of Charles, and became responsible for raising men in Ireland for the service of Louis XIV in the Régiment d'Hamilton. With his two brothers he fought in France under Turenne in 1673—as Catholics they were debarred from service in England. Returned to Ireland 1674 and collected 900 men at Dingle but had difficulty in getting them away. When James II succeeded to the English throne, Hamilton was given a commission as lieutenant in a regiment stationed at Roscrea in 1685 and became Governor of Limerick. Major-general in James's Irish army and fought at Lisnaskea against the Williamites, suffering a heavy defeat for which he was tried by court-martial but acquitted. After the first siege of Limerick he was sent to France with dispatches for King James. He never returned—supposedly because he left in debt—and thereafter attended James in France. His description of the exiled court appeared in 1696 and was later used extensively by the historian Macaulay. His principal work, a French classic, *Mémoires de Grammont*, is mainly concerned with the amorous intrigues at the court of Charles II during 1662–1664. Also wrote a series of *Contes* designed to satirise the fashionable

stories of the marvellous. Accompanied the 'Old Pretender' on the abortive expedition of 1706. Died St Germain, 21 April 1719.

HAMILTON, HUGH DOUGLAS (1739–1808), portrait painter. Born Dublin. Studied drawing in ROBERT WEST's school in George's Lane, then practised successfully as a portrait painter in crayon, his pictures being usually ovals about $9\frac{1}{2}$ by $7\frac{1}{2}$ inches (240 by 190 mm). Went to London about 1764 and soon built up a fashionable and extensive practice; King George III and his queen sat for him. Went to Rome 1778 and, on the advice of John Flaxman, took up painting in oils. In 1791 he returned to Dublin, and was soon in great demand as a portrait painter, chiefly working in oils. Many of his paintings of the leading Irishmen of the time are in the National Gallery of Ireland. Died at his house, Lower Mount St, Dublin, 10 February 1808.

HAMILTON, SIR WILLIAM ROWAN (1805–1865), mathematician and astronomer. Born 36 Lower Dominick St, Dublin, 4 August 1805. Educated by his uncle, a clergyman, at Trim, Co. Meath. At twelve he had a good knowledge of modern European and oriental languages as well as Latin and Greek. He was largely self-taught in mathematics and while still in his teens mastered Newton's *Principia* and had detected an error in Laplace. He entered TCD in 1823 and showed such prodigious intellectual powers that in 1827, while still an undergraduate, he was appointed professor of astronomy and superintendent of Dunsink Observatory. Soon afterwards he was made Astronomer Royal for Ireland. Knighted 1835. Published a treatise on the *Theory of Systems of Rays* in 1828. In 1834 his *General Method in Dynamics* made a profound impression, especially on continental mathematicians. For these researches he was made an honorary member of the Academy of St Petersburg (Leningrad), a rare and coveted distinction. Twice honoured with the gold medal of the Royal Society. President RIA 1837, and an honorary member of most of the great scientific academies of Europe. He published a large number of papers on mathematical problems, including his *Lectures on Quaternions*, which appeared in 1853. *The Elements of Quarternions*, probably his greatest work, was published posthumously in 1866 and ranked him with Descartes in originality and insight. Died Dublin on 2 September 1865. A modest man of simple tastes, Hamilton was the friend of MARIA EDGEWORTH, Wordsworth, and Southey. He wrote a number of poems himself.

HANLEY, MARY (died 1979), teacher and literary historian. Born Mary Nealon at Carron, Co. Clare; became a primary teacher and, after her marriage, director of a kindergarten in Limerick. In 1961 she founded the Kiltartan Society to foster interest in the literary history of the area and especially in the works of YEATS, LADY GREGORY, and EDWARD MARTYN. The society successfully undertook the restoration of Thoor Ballylee, where Yeats had lived for a while, and it was declared open in 1965 by PÁDRAIC COLUM. She remained president of the society and a director of Thoor Ballylee until her death in September 1979.

HANLON, FATHER JACK (1913–1968), priest and artist. Born Dublin; educated Belvedere College, Clonliffe Diocesan College, and UCD. Ordained Maynooth 1939. Served as curate in archdiocese of Dublin. Won the Taylor Art Scholarship and studied painting in Paris under André Lhote in the early 1940s. He later won the Douglas Hyde Gold Medal and Arts Council prize for a historical subject, and an Olympic bronze medal for a painting of yachts on the Boyne. He worked mainly in soft watercolours and flower pieces. One of the founders of the Living Art Exhibition, which gave a new direction to Irish painting after the Second World War. Curate at Churchtown, Co. Dublin, when he died, 12 August 1968.

HANNAY, JAMES OWEN (1865–1950), novelist, under pen-name George A. Birmingham. Born Belfast, 16 July 1865. Educated Haileybury and TCD. He entered the church and became rector of Westport, Co. Mayo, in 1892. His first half-dozen novels produced little stir. In 1908 he published *Spanish Gold*, featuring a red-haired curate, the Rev. Meldon, of unusual boldness and eloquence. The reading public welcomed this new sort of humorous novel, and Hannay responded by writing a 'George Birmingham' novel almost every year. His *General John Regan* when produced as a play in Westport in 1913 led to a riot and the boycotting of Hannay when the townspeople discovered that he was the author. He left Westport and, after service as an army chaplain, settled at Mells rectory, Somerset, in 1924. Later he took charge of a small parish in London where he died on 2 February 1950. Besides his novels, he published *A Padre in France* (1918), *An Irishman Looks at his World* (1919), *A Wayfarer in Hungary* (1925), and some religious works.

HARDIMAN, JAMES (*c.* 1790–1855), historian. Born in Connacht, studied law in Dublin. Became subcommissioner of public records in Dublin Castle and active member of the RIA. Published a *History of Galway* (1820). *Irish Minstrelsy, or Bardic Remains of Ireland* (1831) is his best-known work. Became librarian of Queen's College, Galway, soon after it was founded, and died there in November 1855.

HARDMAN, EDWARD TOWNLEY (1845–1887), geologist. Born Drogheda, 6 April 1845. Educated Royal College of Science, Dublin, and joined staff of Geological Survey 1870. Wrote papers on coalmining in Co. Tyrone and on the chemical analysis of minerals. Appointed in 1883 by Colonial Office to report on the mineral resources of West Australia, and discovered an extensive gold-field at Kimberley. Returned to duty in Ireland. Died of typhoid fever, 30 April 1887, after exposure while surveying in Wicklow mountains. A range of mountains in West Australia is named after him.

HARMSWORTH, ALFRED, VISCOUNT NORTHCLIFFE (1865-1922), journalist and newspaper proprietor. Born Chapelizod, Co. Dublin, 15 July 1865. Educated Stamford Grammar School and Henley House. Beginning as a freelance journalist, he became editor of *Bicycling News* in Coventry and conceived the idea of a popular paper on the lines of *Tit-Bits* to cater for the vast reading public created by the Education Act of 1870. The result was *Answers to Correspondents*, founded in 1888 and soon shortened to *Answers*. Its phenomenal success was due to his flair for sensing the public taste, and the financial acumen of his brother Harold (later Lord Rothermere), who had joined him in the venture. Other cheap periodicals followed and were the beginnings of Amalgamated Press, the largest publishing empire of its kind at that time. Branching into the newspaper world, Harmsworth bought the struggling *London Evening News* in 1894 and made it profitable. On 4 May 1896 he launched the *Daily Mail*, inaugurating a new style of journalism, with sensational success. 'Explain, simplify, clarify,' he told his staff. The new formula was used with equal success in the *Sunday Dispatch* and *Daily Mirror*. He reached the peak of his career as a newspaper proprietor when he took control of *The Times* in 1908. Harmsworth deluded himself that his achievements as a populariser of genius gave him the right and the power to mould public opinion, but he made little impact on public events and his influence with politicians was slight. In his later years his autocracy and megalomania became a byword, and a complete breakdown led to his death in London, 14 August 1922.

HARRINGTON, TIMOTHY CHARLES (1851-1910), nationalist. Born Castletown Bearhaven, Co. Cork. Educated at national school. After some years teaching, founded and edited the *Kerry Sentinel*, the first issue appearing in 1877. Entering politics, he became secretary of the Land League in 1882 and was twice imprisoned under the Coercion Acts for his activities. He was mainly responsible for devising the 'Plan of Campaign' during the land war. MP for Co. Westmeath 1883 and for Harbour division of Dublin from 1885 until his death. Called to the bar in 1887, he appeared for many political prisoners. Counsel for PARNELL under SIR CHARLES RUSSELL in the Parnell Commission of 1888/89, and was fined £500 for contempt of court for an article that had appeared in the *Kerry Sentinel*. He supported Parnell after the split in the Irish Party in 1891 but served under REDMOND after the death of Parnell. Lord Mayor of Dublin 1901-1904. Died at his house in Harcourt Street, 12 March 1910.

HARRIS, JAMES THOMAS (FRANK) (1856-1931), editor, author, and adventurer. Born Galway, probably on 14 February 1856, son of a naval commander in the revenue service. Educated Royal School, Armagh, and an English grammar-school. At fifteen he ran away to the USA where, after working as a bootblack, hotel clerk, and cowpuncher, he attended the State University of Kansas. Returned to Europe, travelled for a while, studied at Heidelberg, and at twenty-seven descended upon London to begin his literary career, editing successively the *Evening News*, the *Fortnightly Review* and, as proprietor, the *Saturday Review*. His marriage in 1887 to a wealthy widow, Mary Edith Clayton, failed, and in 1894 he eloped with Helen O'Hara, whom he later married. From 1894 to 1899 he made the *Saturday Review* the most brilliant literary and political weekly of the time. Of his several plays, *Mr and Mrs Daventry* was the most successful; he also wrote some novels and volumes of short stories. The 'new' psychoanalytical approach in his own favourite critical work, *The Man Shakespeare*, neither pleased nor impressed Shakespearian scholars. Harris sold the *Saturday Review* in 1899, and his subsequent journalistic enterprises were a series of disasters, ending in imprisonment for contempt of court in a libel suit. On release from jail in 1914 he went to the USA, where he bought and edited *Pearson's Magazine*, with declining success. He then began a series of books on famous people he had known, published as *Contemporary Portraits* (1915–1920), and wrote biographies of OSCAR WILDE and GEORGE BERNARD SHAW. And finally he produced his autobiography, *The Life and Loves of Frank Harris* (five volumes, 1923–1927). Besides detailed descriptions of his sexual prowess, it gives a picture of Edwardian society, high and low, that has a ring of authenticity despite his evident conceit and disregard for exactitude. Harris lived in Europe, often in dire financial straits, for some years before his death at Nice, 26 August 1931. Shaw has been quoted as saying of him: 'He is neither first-rate nor second-rate nor tenth-rate. He is just his horrible, unique self.'

HARRISON, FRANCIS LLEWELLYN (1905–1987), musicologist. Born in Dublin on 29 September 1905 and became a boy chorister in St Patrick's Cathedral. He studied music at TCD, graduating Mus.B. 1926 and Mus.D. 1929. He earned his living for a while as pianist in a Dublin cinema. Assistant professor of music, Queen's University, Kingston, Canada, 1935–1946, spending his last year of tenure as postdoctoral fellow of Yale University. Professor of music, Colgate University, 1946–1947 and Washington University, St Louis, until 1952 when he was appointed lecturer at Oxford University, later becoming senior lecturer and reader in the history of music. Left Oxford 1970 to become professor of ethnomusicology at University of

Amsterdam until 1976. Visiting professor at Yale, Princeton, and Utrecht. Elected fellow of the British Academy 1965. Contributed important papers to many journals; edited *Now Make We Merthe* (1968), mediaeval and Renaissance carols older than previously available. His most valuable work is *Music in Medieval Britain* (1958), a pioneering study that soon became a standard reference book and brought a new understanding of mediaeval music. He researched the social history of western music and folk music of Ireland, Scotland, Wales, and Latin America, and showed a rare breadth of insight in all his studies. He died in Canterbury, England, on 29 December 1987.

HARRISON, HENRY (1867–1954), nationalist and writer. Born Holywood, Co. Down, 17 December 1867. Educated Westminster and Balliol College, Oxford. Developed an interest in Irish politics. Secretary of the Oxford Union Home Rule group. His courageous intervention in a Donegal eviction in 1889 was followed in 1890 by his election as Nationalist MP for mid-Tipperary. He took the side of PARNELL in the split of that year and lost his seat in 1892. Although nearly fifty, he joined the Royal Irish Regiment in 1915 and won the MC and bar. Captain Harrison, as he was known afterwards, then plunged again into Irish affairs, becoming associated with SIR HORACE PLUNKETT and later became Irish correspondent of the *Economist*. He then embarked on his real life work, the rehabilitation of the 'Chief', his beloved Parnell. In 1931 he published *Parnell Vindicated: the Lifting of the Veil*, based partly on information he had obtained from Mrs Parnell many years previously and partly on original research. He continued to defend Parnell in a second book, *Parnell, Joseph Chamberlain and Mr Garvin*, in which he successfully attacked Garvin's treatment of the Irish leader in his *Life of Joseph Chamberlain*. He was responsible in 1952 for securing amendments to the account of the Pigott forgeries in the *History of*

'*The Times*', and published an account of his intervention in *Parnell, Joseph Chamberlain and 'The Times'* (1953). Dublin University honoured him with the LL.D. that year. Died Dublin, 20 February 1954.

HARTY, SIR (HERBERT) HAMIL-TON (1879-1941), musician. Born Hillsborough, Co. Down, 4 December 1879, son of an organist, by whom he was trained to be a musician. Became an organist himself in Belfast and then in Dublin, where he was helped by Esposito. Going to London in 1900 he soon made a reputation as an accompanist and composer. Married the soprano Agnes Nicholls in 1904, and gave many recitals with her. About 1907 he began to appear as a conductor with the London Symphony Orchestra. Conductor Hallé Orchestra, Manchester, 1920-1933. This latter post brought him international fame and led to tours in the USA and Australia. Knighted 1925. His compositions include a tone poem *With the Wild Geese,* an *Irish Symphony*, and songs and orchestral arrangements of pieces by Handel and JOHN FIELD. Died at Hove, Sussex, 19 February 1941.

HARVEY, (BEAUCHAMP) BAG-ENAL (1762-1798), United Irishman. Born Bargy Castle, Co. Wexford. Educated TCD. Called to the bar 1782; practised with success and became known as a supporter of Catholic emancipation and parliamentary reform. On the death of his father in 1792 he inherited estates worth £3,000 a year. In 1793 he presided at meetings of the United Irishmen in Dublin. When the rising of 1798 broke out in Wexford, the insurgent leaders unanimously agreed to appoint him their commander-in-chief. He accepted the post with reluctance, and issued orders prohibiting plunder and other excesses, on pain of death. After their defeat at New Ross in June, he was deposed from his command and took refuge in a cave on the Great Saltee Island. He was discovered, court-martialled, and sentenced to death. He was hanged on Wexford bridge on 26 June 1798.

HAUGHTON, SAMUEL (1821-1897), scientist. Born Carlow, 21 December 1821. Educated Carlow and TCD, graduating in mathematics. Fellow 1844; professor of geology 1851-1881; senior fellow 1881-1897. His first publications were papers on mathematical physics and on polarised light. He then turned to geology, and published a number of papers on the mineralogy of Ireland and Wales. In 1854 he undertook a study of Irish tidal movements, and was then commissioned to report on observations made on the tides of the Arctic seas. His studies of fossils aroused his interest in medicine, and he entered Trinity medical school in 1859, at the age of thirty-eight. On graduating in 1862 he became medical registrar of the school, and carried through much-needed reforms. In the cholera epidemic of 1866 he organised a voluntary nursing staff among the students. In 1873 he published *Animal Mechanics*, a study of the mechanical principles of muscular action. From 1860 he took an active part in the work of the Royal Zoological Society of Ireland and was president in 1883. FRS 1858; president RIA 1887. Received many academic honours. Died at his home, 12 Northbrook Road, Dublin, 31 October 1897.

HAVERTY, JOSEPH PATRICK (1794-1864), portrait and subject painter. Born Galway, and began career there. Moved to Dublin 1815 and contributed to RHA 1826-1861. Elected RHA 1829 but resigned 1837. He also worked in Limerick and London and showed twenty-seven portraits at RA between 1835 and 1858. Executed portraits of O'CONNELL for the Catholic Association, one now in the Reform Club, the other in Limerick Town Hall. His 'Limerick Piper' was engraved and sold widely. Died at his home, 44 Rathmines Road, Dublin, 27 July 1864. Buried Glasnevin Cemetery.

HAYDN, JOSEPH (1786–1856), compiler of dictionaries. Born Limerick, educated abroad. Became journalist and edited the *Dublin Evening Mail*. Founded the *Statesman* 1828. Moved to Limerick and founded the *Limerick Star and Evening Post* 1834 and later the *Limerick Times*. Worked as journalist in London from 1839. Edited Lewis's *Topographical Dictionary* (eight volumes, 1849). Published his great work, *A Dictionary of Dates*, in 1841 and *A Dictionary of Dignities* in 1851. Later employed in records department of Admiralty, and received a small pension. Died London, 17 January 1856.

HAYES, CATHERINE (1825–1861), soprano. Born of poor parents at 4 Patrick Street, Limerick, 29 October 1825. Through the influence of Bishop Knox of Limerick she was sent to Dublin 1839 to study under Antonio Sapio. Her success at public concerts enabled her to go to Paris in 1842 for further study, and then to Milan, where her teacher was Felici Ronconi. On her first appearance at La Scala, in 1845, she received an ovation. After a tour of Italy she went to England in 1849 and was engaged for Covent Garden at a salary of £1,300. In 1851 she went to New York and met an electioneering agent, William Avery Bushnell, whom she made manager of her American tour. As much as a thousand dollars was paid for a ticket to one of her concerts in California. She then went on a world tour, singing in South America, Australia, and India. She returned to England in 1856, and the following year married Bushnell in London. He soon fell into poor health, and died in Biarritz on 2 July 1858, aged thirty-five. She continued to appear in London, where her ballad-singing was very popular. She died in the house of a friend, Henry Lee, at Sydenham, Kent, 11 August 1861.

HAYES, CANON JOHN M. (1887–1957), founder of Muintir na Tíre. Born 11 November 1887 at Murroe, near Limerick, son of an evicted farmer. Educated Murroe NS, Crescent College, Limerick, St Patrick's College, Thurles, and the Irish College, Paris. Ordained Paris 1913. Ministered in Liverpool until 1924, then assigned to the parish of Castleiny, near Templemore, Co. Tipperary. Confrontation with the difficulties besetting rural Ireland prompted him, in 1931, to found Muintir na Tíre, a society open to all prepared to work for the rural community. The essence of the movement was co-operation based on Christian charity within each parish, and the rules laid stress on adherence to the social principles laid down in the papal encyclicals *Rerum Novarum* (Leo XIII) and *Quadragesimo Anno* (Pius XI). Church and state leaders gave their approval to the new organisation, and guilds were established in 420 parishes. A feature of the movement was the Rural Week, when prominent people from many avocations gathered for wide-ranging discussions. The local guilds were encouraged to undertake various tasks, such as providing community halls, repairing cottages and roads, and organising social functions. Appointed parish priest of Bansha, Co. Tipperary, 1946. Much in demand in Ireland as a preacher, and also lectured in the USA and South America. In July 1954 Pope Pius XII sent him an Apostolic Letter in praise of Muintir na Tíre and its work for rural Ireland.

HAYES, MICHAEL (1889–1976), politician and professor. Born Dublin, 1 December 1889. Educated Synge St CBS and UCD. Became lecturer in French at UCD. Joined Irish Volunteers in 1913 and fought in Jacob's factory in 1916 Rising but escaped capture. Arrested and interned in Ballykinlar 1920. Elected TD for NUI 1921; Minister for Education 1922. Voted for the Treaty. Elected Ceann Comhairle of first Free State Dáil 1922 and held post until 1932. Lost Dáil seat in general election 1933; elected to Seanad 1938 and held seat until 1965. Chairman of Civil Service Commission 1922–1932. Called to the bar 1929. Successively leader of government and opposition in Seanad. Became professor of Irish at UCD in 1951. Died Dublin, 11 July 1976.

HAYES, MICHAEL ANGELO (1820–1877), painter. Born Waterford, 25 July 1820. Taught by his father, Edward, also a painter. Exhibited at RHA 1837. Became military painter-in-ordinary to Lord Lieutenant 1842. He spent the following few years in London, exhibiting at New Society of Painters in Water Colours and at the RA in 1848. Elected RHA 1854 and secretary 1856. He reorganised the affairs of the academy, especially its finances, but antagonised older members. After a bitter quarrel he was expelled, but returned as member in 1860 under a new charter. Elected secretary again 1861; retired 1870. He continued to exhibit until 1874, then resigned membership. Appointed City Marshal of Dublin 1867. Involved in libel action for caricaturing Sir W. Carroll MD, ex-Lord Mayor. He was noted for his military and sporting pictures and executed the BIANCONI car-travelling prints. While inspecting a water tank on top of his house at 4 Salem Place, Dublin, on 31 December 1877, he fell in and was drowned.

HAYES, RICHARD (1882–1958), physician, author, and film censor. Born in Bruree, Co. Limerick. Qualified from Catholic University Medical School and became dispensary doctor in Lusk, Co. Dublin. Joined the Irish Volunteers and was commander of the Fingal Battalion. Attended the wounded at engagement at Ashbourne in Easter Week 1916. Arrested, court-martialled and sentenced to death but sentence commuted to twenty years' penal servitude. Released in June 1917 under general amnesty. Re-arrested 1918, and elected MP for Limerick while in Reading Jail. Took the Treaty side in 1922. Resigned from the Dáil in 1924 to devote himself to his medical practice and to historical scholarship. Served as dispensary doctor for Donnybrook district, Dublin. Film

censor 1944–1954. He made himself an authority on the Wild Geese, publishing *Ireland and Irishmen in the French Revolution* (1932), *Irish Swordsmen of France* (1934), *The Last Invasion of Ireland* (1937), *Old Irish Links with France* (1940), and *Biographical Dictionary of Irishmen in France* (1949). He was a director of the Abbey Theatre from 1934 and vice-president of the Military History Society. Distinctions included MRIA, Legion of Honour, and honorary D.Litt. from NUI. Married Mrs Hilda Shaw in 1939. Died in Dún Laoghaire, Co. Dublin, on 16 June 1958.

HAYES, RICHARD JAMES (1902–1976), librarian and bibliographer. Born Abbeyfeale, Co. Limerick. Educated Clongowes Wood and TCD. At Trinity he achieved a unique feat in taking three honours degrees simultaneously: in Celtic studies, modern languages, and philosophy. Some years later he took a doctorate in law. Joined staff of National Library 1926; became director 1940. In 1927 he published *Comparative Idiom*, an introduction to the study of modern languages. In 1938–1940 he published the first of his great bibliographical works, *Clár Litrídheachta na Nua-Ghaedhilge*, in three volumes, covering 1,000 books, 7,000 poems, and 18,000 essays in modern Irish. During the Second World War he held a phantom commissioned rank in the army in the counter-intelligence branch. He was a brilliant cipher breaker and played a leading part in the interception and decoding of messages, which frustrated German attempts to establish an intelligence network in Ireland. During his period as director, the National Library acquired the Ormond papers from Kilkenny Castle, the Lawrence collection of thousands of old photographic plates, and the records of the former Office of Arms, which, as the Genealogical Office, became part of the National Library in 1943. He secured the manuscripts of the early novels of GEORGE BERNARD SHAW in response to his letter: 'Dear Bernard

Shaw, I can think of no better place than the National Library of Ireland for your manuscripts and first editions. Can you?' After the war he organised the location and copying on microfilm of documents of Irish interest that had been scattered throughout the world for reasons of history. The cataloguing of this material and of the manuscripts in the library formed the basis for his next monumental bibliographical work, *Manuscript Sources for the History of Irish Civilisation* (eleven volumes, 1965). It contains more than 300,000 entries, describing material assembled from 678 libraries in thirty countries and in over 600 private collections. In recognition of this work, both Dublin University and NUI conferred honorary doctorates on him. He retired from the National Library in 1967, and in 1970 published a companion to the earlier work, *Sources for the History of Irish Civilisation: Articles in Periodicals,* containing about 270,000 entries describing articles from some 200 learned periodicals published in Ireland from 1800 to 1969. QUB then conferred a further doctorate on him. When SIR ALFRED CHESTER BEATTY founded his library and art gallery in Dublin, Hayes became honorary librarian and, on his retirement, librarian and chairman of the trustees. He was for some time a director of the Abbey Theatre and a member of the Arts Council, and of the cultural experts committee of the Council of Europe. Died Dublin, 21 January 1976.

HEALY, CAHIR (1877–1970), nationalist politician. Born Mountcharles, Co. Donegal, 1877. Moved to Enniskillen at an early age and lived there for the rest of his life. Worked as a journalist with the *Fermanagh News,* but politics were his main interest. Joined Sinn Féin about 1905 and worked in election campaigns, and in May 1922 was arrested and interned in Belfast Lough on board the prison ship *Argenta,* and later moved to Larne workhouse. The *Sunday Express* published a series of articles by him on prison conditions, which were smuggled out of Larne workhouse and helped to secure the release of the internees. Elected Sinn Féin MP for Westminster constituency of Fermanagh and Tyrone, November 1922, but kept in custody until the general release of prisoners in 1924. Elected Nationalist member for South Fermanagh at Stormont 1925. Held the seat for forty years until he retired. In 1941 he was again arrested, interned at Brixton prison, and held for two years despite a storm of protest from Nationalist MPs. He became a member of Westminster parliament in 1950 but did not seek re-election there in 1955. He was a prolific contributor to newspapers, as book reviewer and writer of articles and letters to the editor. As a young man he produced a volume of poems, *The Lane of the Thrushes* (1907), with Cathal O'Byrne, and also wrote a novel and a story for children. Died, 8 February 1970, in the Erne Hospital, survived by two sons and a daughter. His wife predeceased him in 1948.

HEALY, JOHN EDWARD (1872–1934), journalist. Born Drogheda, 17 March 1872. Educated at local grammar-school and TCD, where he graduated in classics and modern literature with distinction, winning many prizes. He entered journalism, became editor of the Dublin *Daily Express,* was called to the bar, and then in 1907 was appointed editor of the *Irish Times.* MAHAFFY had been his tutor at Trinity and remained his friend and counsellor. Healy was an opponent of Irish nationalism and used all his influence to keep Ireland within the British Empire. He was associated with the work of SIR HORACE PLUNKETT in developing agricultural co-operation. His twenty-seven years as editor and principal leader writer of the *Irish Times* made him well known in Britain. Died Dublin on 30 May 1934, survived by his wife, sister of Dr Alton, Provost of Trinity College, and two sons.

HEALY, MICHAEL (1873–1941), stained-glass artist and painter. Born 14

November 1873 at 40 Bishop Street, Dublin. His father died when he was a child and, after elementary schooling, he went to work at fourteen in a sugar boiler's and then with a spirit bonder. In 1897 he joined the School of Art, and the following year obtained a post as illustrator for the *Irish Rosary*, published by the Dominican order. The editor, Father Glendon OP, recognised his talent and arranged that he should visit Florence for further study. He stayed in Florence from the autumn of 1899 until May 1901. On his return be became art teacher in the Dominican College at Newbridge (Droichead Nua), Co. Kildare, but resigned in 1903 to join An Túr Gloine, a stained-glass studio at 24 Upper Pembroke St, Dublin, at the invitation of SARAH PURSER. In this studio the artist took undivided responsibility for the design of windows and their execution. He worked there for the rest of his life. Examples of his work may be seen in Blackrock and Clongowes Wood colleges and in Letterkenny cathedral. Loughrea cathedral contains some of his finest work, spanning the period 1907–1940. Glowing colour, strong composition and expressive line characterised his windows. He also executed commissions for New York, Chicago, and Wellington, New Zealand. Besides stained glass, he contributed sketches and cartoons to the *Leader*, and exhibited at the RHA 1912–1914. He painted many watercolours, mostly street scenes and characters in Dublin, but few were ever exhibited. He lived almost as a recluse. Died Mercer's Hospital, Dublin, 22 September 1941.

HEALY, TIMOTHY MICHAEL (1855–1931), politician and first Governor-General of the Irish Free State. Born Bantry, Co. Cork, on 17 May 1855. Educated Fermoy CBS, but left school at thirteen and became a railway clerk in Newcastle-on-Tyne. Moving to London in 1878 he became parliamentary correspondent of the *Nation*. His intelligence and industry impressed the Irish MPs, and he was called to

Canada by PARNELL to organise his political mission there. He then took an active part in the agrarian agitation in Ireland, was arrested for intimidation but acquitted on trial shortly after. Returned unopposed as member for Wexford in 1880, he soon made himself a master of parliamentary procedure, aided by his prodigious memory. He secured the adoption of the 'Healy' clause in the Land Act of 1881, protecting tenants from rent increases on improvements. MP for Monaghan 1883 and south Londonderry 1885. Called to the bar 1884 and built up a practice in land law. When the crisis arose in 1890 over Parnell's involvement in the O'Shea divorce case, Healy bitterly opposed Parnell's continuance as leader, taking the view that Gladstone's support was more important to the home rule cause. His political career thereafter was marked by frequent quarrels with the party, and he was expelled in 1902. The support of the Catholic church and William Martin Murphy enabled him to hold North Louth from 1891 to 1910, when he found a seat in North-East Cork with the help of WILLIAM O'BRIEN. That year he became a KC and a bencher of Gray's Inn; in Parliament he now had an established reputation as a witty and trenchant speaker. A strong critic of the policy of JOHN REDMOND, he declared his sympathy with the ideals of Sinn Féin, excluding the element of force, after 1916, and in 1918 resigned his seat in Cork in favour of a Sinn Féin prisoner. In 1922, after the signing of the Anglo-Irish Treaty, he was appointed Governor-General of the Irish Free State on the recommendation of Lord Birkenhead and KEVIN O'HIGGINS, his own cousin. Republicans and Parnellites joined in criticising the choice. He retired in 1928 and died at Chapelizod, Co. Dublin, on 26 March 1931, leaving three sons and three daughters. His wife predeceased him in 1927.

HEARNE, JOHN J. (1893–1969), constitutional lawyer and diplomat. Born in Waterford and educated at Waterford

CBS and UCD. He studied for the priesthood at Maynooth for some years but left to enter King's Inns. Was called to the bar and became assistant parliamentary draftsman 1923-1929 and legal adviser to the Irish delegation to the Imperial Conferences of 1926, 1929, and 1930. He gained international recognition as an authority on constitutional law. Legal adviser to the Department of External Affairs 1929-1937. In 1935 he was instructed by ÉAMON DE VALERA to draft the heads of the new Constitution of Ireland. On 29 December 1937, when the new constitution came into operation, de Valera dedicated a copy to Hearne as 'Architect-in-Chief and Draftsman... in testimony of the fundamental part he took in framing this the first Free Constitution of the Irish People.' Hearne became high commissioner to Canada 1937-1950 and ambassador to the USA 1950-1960. He was called to the inner bar in 1939 in special recognition of his work on the Constitution. He died in 1969.

HECTOR, ANNIE FRENCH (1825-1902), novelist, under name Mrs Alexander. Born Dublin, 23 June 1825. Educated by governesses. The family moved to England when she was nineteen, and at thirty-three she married Alexander Hector, a wealthy merchant. Widowed at fifty, she settled down to novel writing, publishing over forty titles with steady success, the last when she was seventy-seven. The best known are *The Wooing O't* (1873) and the semi-autobiographical *Kitty Costello* (1902). Died in London, 10 July 1902. Buried in Kensal Green cemetery.

HELY-HUTCHINSON, JOHN (1724-1794), lawyer. Born John Hely at Gortroe, Co. Cork. Educated TCD, and called to the bar 1748. Married an heiress in 1751 and adopted her name. MP Lanesborough 1759 and Cork 1761-1790. For his support of the government he received a sinecure of £1,000 a year and later was made principal secretary of state. His appointment as provost of TCD in 1774 by favour of government aroused violent criticism in letters to the *Freeman's Journal*, some of which were later published as *Pranceriana*. He tried unsuccessfully to turn the university into a pocket borough for his family. Yet he supported claims for independence, political liberty for Catholics, and free trade. He published anonymously *Commercial Restraints of Ireland* (1779), which was considered seditious and burnt by the common hangman. MP Taghmon, Co. Wexford, 1790-1794. His wife was made Baroness Donoughmore in 1785. He died at Buxton, 4 September 1794.

HENDERSON, JOHN (1757-1788), eccentric student. Born at Ballygarran, near Limerick, son of a Wesleyan preacher. Educated at Wesleyan school at Kingswood, near Bristol. He later assisted in a school opened by his father, also near Bristol. A clergyman, Dean Tucker, was so impressed by the young man's learning that he paid his way to Pembroke College, Oxford. Henderson had an exceptional memory and became a remarkable linguist, with a good knowledge of Persian, Arabic, Hebrew, Greek, and Latin, as well as Spanish, Italian, and German. He gradually became very eccentric, dressing strangely, going to bed at daybreak and rising in the evening. He smoked incessantly, took opium, and drank heavily. He took the degree of B.A. in 1786 and then became a recluse, devoting himself to study. He died while on a visit to Pembroke College, 2 November 1788.

HENN, THOMAS RICE (1901-1974), Yeatsian scholar. Born in Sligo, where his father was resident magistrate. Educated Manor School, Fermoy, at Aldenham, and St Catherine's College, Cambridge, where he studied modern languages. Lecturer and fellow of the college 1926, senior tutor 1945-1957, and president 1951-1961. On the outbreak of the Second World War he joined the British army, and held the rank of brigadier on demobilisation in 1945. Awarded the military CBE, American Legion of Merit, and twice mentioned in despatches. He became deeply interested in Anglo-Irish literature, published studies of W. B. YEATS and JOHN M. SYNGE, and in 1960 was invited to lecture for the newly formed Yeats Society in Sligo. At his suggestion the society organised a Yeats Week on the lines of the Stratford and Cambridge summer schools, and this quickly developed into the Yeats International Summer School. He was director of the school until 1969, saw it expand tenfold, and became patron in 1972 after the death of PÁDRAIC COLUM. In 1966 he was made a freeman of the borough of Sligo. His ambition to secure a permanent base in Sligo for the school was realised in 1972 when Allied Irish Banks presented the society with the old Royal Bank building. His publications ranged from *Longinus and English Criticism* to *Practical Fly Tying*, for his favourite relaxation was angling. He was also interested in shooting, and produced manuals on automatic rifles and machine-guns. He died in Cambridge in December 1974.

HENNESSY, PATRICK (1915–1980), painter. Born in Cork and educated in Glasgow. Took an arts diploma at Dundee College of Art. Painted in France and Italy before returning to Ireland, where he was soon elected to the RHA. About 1970 he went to live in north Africa. He was a consummate craftsman with a love of texture and a feeling for light. His work is represented in permanent collections in Dublin, Cork, Limerick, and Waterford. He died in a London hospital on 30 December 1980.

HENNESSY, RICHARD (1720–1800), soldier and distiller. Born Ballymoy, Killavullen, Co. Cork, where members of the family still live. In 1740 he went to France, where relatives had settled with others of the Wild Geese after the defeat of the Jacobite cause in 1691. He became an officer in Dillon's regiment and fought at Dottingen 1743, Fontenoy 1745, and other battles in the War of the Austrian Succession. After being wounded he retired from military service. In 1763 he married his cousin Ellen, widow of James Hennessy of Brussels and a cousin of EDMUND BURKE. Two years later he settled in Cognac in the department of Charente and established the distillery that produces the famous Hennessy brandy. He died in 1800 leaving a son, James who, after military service like his father, carried on the business.

HENRY, AUGUSTINE (1857–1930), physician and botanist. Born in Cookstown, Co. Tyrone, son of a flax buyer. Educated Cookstown Academy and Queen's Colleges, Galway and Belfast, graduating in medicine 1879. Acquired a working knowledge of Chinese and in 1881 joined customs service in China, first at Shanghai and then to Ichang for seven years. His first collection of a thousand plants was sent to Kew Gardens and regarded as one of the most important to come out of inland China. In 1888 he published a list of Chinese plants with their colloquial names at Ichang in the journal of the Chinese Royal Asiatic Society. Elected a fellow of the Linnean Society of London 1888. He served on the islands of Hainan and Formosa (Taiwan). The first to publish an account of the flora of Formosa, and compiled a dictionary of the language of the Lolos, a national minority in southwest China, hitherto unknown to Europeans. While in Formosa he studied law and became a member of the Middle Temple. On his return to Europe in 1900 he began to study at the National School of Forestry at Nancy in France and in 1903 he began his collaboration with H. J. Elwes on the seven-volume *Trees of Great Britain and Ireland*. Appointed reader in forestry at Cambridge in 1908 and developed the university's School of Forestry. Appointed professor of forestry at the College of Science, Dublin, 1913. Awarded honorary M.A. by Cambridge 1908. Member of the forestry institutions of many European countries and of the Royal Horticultural Society. Died in Ranelagh, Dublin, in March 1930.

HENRY, JAMES (1798-1876), physician and classical scholar. Born in Dublin on 18 December 1798, son of a woollen-draper, and studied classics and medicine at TCD. He soon built up a large practice, infuriating fellow doctors by charging a fee of five shillings instead of their professional guinea. At eleven he had bought a copy of Virgil's *Aeneid* and in 1845, when he received a large legacy, he gave up medicine and devoted the rest of his life to Virgilian studies. He travelled on foot all over Europe with his wife and daughter, visiting the great libraries of Dresden, Florence, Heidelberg, the Vatican and elsewhere, and crossed the Alps seventeen times. He searched out and collated all existing Virgil manuscripts, and his commentaries were highly praised by other scholars. His writings, including a number of poems, were published privately. His wife died in the Tyrol in 1849. His daughter, who continued to travel with him and assist him, died in December 1872. He then returned to Dublin, spent his last years on research in TCD library, and died in Dalkey, Co. Dublin, on 14 July 1876.

HENRY, PAUL (1877-1958), painter. Born Belfast, the son of a Baptist minister. Educated at RBAI. He spent a year with the Broadway Damask Company in Belfast as an apprentice designer, and then entered the Belfast School of Art. About 1900 he went to Paris for a year, studied at the Académie Julien and in Whistler's studio, and came under the influence of the Post-Impressionists, particularly Cézanne, Gauguin, and Van Gogh. From Paris he moved to London, and shared rooms with ROBERT LYND there and in Guildford, Surrey, until about 1912. He then went to Achill, Co. Mayo, on a visit, and stayed for seven years. He first discovered his abilities as a landscape painter when living in Surrey. He turned from charcoal drawings of English water meadows to oil paintings of the rugged scenery and personalities of the west of Ireland for which he is best known. The influence of Whistler is discernible in the subtle colouring of his work at this period. In 1920 he moved to Dublin and held many exhibitions. Elected RHA 1929. He designed travel posters for the London, Midland and Scottish Railway and for the Irish Tourist Board, of which many thousands were sold. He gave dates to very few of his paintings, and his autobiography, *An Irish Portrait* (1951), shows the same lack of interest in chronology. He lost his sight in 1945 and went to live in Bray, Co. Wicklow, where he died in 1958. His first wife, Grace Mitchell, who had become well known as a painter under her married name, Grace Henry, had died in 1953. He was survived by his second wife, Mabel Young.

HERON, ARCHIE (1894-1971), socialist and trade union organiser. Born Portadown, Co. Armagh. Educated at the local school. He came to Dublin in 1912 and became a full-time organiser with the IRB. Later he was associated with JAMES CONNOLLY in the Irish Transport and General Workers' Union, and became one of its first organisers. He married a daughter of Connolly about this time. Labour TD for Dublin North-West 1937, but lost his seat in general election 1938. General secretary, Local Government Officers' Union, 1940; labour relations officer, Department of Local Government, 1950. His post was transferred to Industry and Commerce, and then to the Department of Labour. Died in Dublin on 10 May 1971.

HERON, HILARY (1923-1977), sculptor. Born in Dublin. Spent most of her childhood in New Ross, Co. Wexford, and Coleraine, Co. Derry. Educated at a one-teacher school and the National College of Art, Dublin. Won three of the Taylor Prizes. Awarded the first Mainie Jellett Memorial Travelling Scholarship, 1947, for work in carved wood, limestone, and marble. Helped to found the Irish Exhibition of Living Art, and first exhibited there in 1943. Represented Ireland with Louis Le Brocquy at the Venice Biennale, 1956. She travelled in Asia, America, and Europe, and her works are in private and public collections in many countries. Died in Dublin, 28 April 1977, survived by her husband, PROFESSOR DAVID GREENE.

HERVEY, FREDERICK AUGUSTUS, fourth EARL OF BRISTOL (1730–1803). Educated Westminster School and Corpus Christi College, Cambridge, and took holy orders. Interested in art, and toured the Continent. Made bishop of Cloyne 1767 and bishop of Derry 1768. Constructed roads and bridges at his own expense. Built princely residences at Downhill and Ballyscullion, Co. Derry, to house his art treasures. He succeeded to earldom of Bristol and rental of £20,000 in 1779. Opposed tithe system and advocated relaxation of penal laws. Favoured parliamentary reform and Catholic emancipation, and took prominent part in Irish Volunteers 1782–1783. Made freeman of Derry and Dublin. He spent much time on the Continent because of ill-health, and in late life had a scandalous affair with Countess Lichtenau, mistress of Friedrich Wilhelm II of Prussia. CHARLEMONT described him as 'a bad father, a worse husband, a determined deist, very blasphemous in his conversation and greatly addicted to intrigue and gallantry.' He died at Albano, 8 July 1803.

HEUSTON, SEÁN (1891–1916), one of the sixteen leaders executed after the 1916 Rising. Born in Dublin. Educated at CBS. Employed by the Great Southern and Western Railway. Posted in Limerick, where he became active in organising Na Fianna Éireann, the boy-scout movement founded by MARKIEVICZ in 1909. On his transfer to Dublin in 1913 he continued his work in the movement, became director of training

for the Fianna, and joined the Irish Volunteers at their inception that year. He led a contingent of the Fianna who brought a trek-cart of rifles, unloaded from the *Asgard* in July 1914, from Howth to Dublin. In the 1916 Rising he was commandant in charge of the Volunteers in the Mendicity Institute on Usher's Island. He was court-martialled, condemned to death, and executed in Kilmainham jail on 8 May.

HEWITT, JOHN (1907–1987), poet. Born in Belfast in October 1907 and educated at Methodist College and QUB. He was keeper of art at the Ulster Museum 1930–1957, and director of the Herbert Art Gallery and Museum, Coventry, 1957–1972, then retired and returned to Belfast. He was a director of the Lyric Theatre and poetry editor of their periodical, *Threshold*. His *Collected Poems* appeared in 1968 and he published two further volumes, *Out of My Time* (1974) and *Time Enough* (1976), which won the Poetry Book Society Award. He also edited the poems of WILLIAM ALLINGHAM and published a monograph on the painter COLIN MIDDLETON. He described himself as 'an Irishman of planter stock, by profession an art gallery man, politically a man of the left,' and his poems reflect this self-assessment. He died at his family home in Belfast on 27 June 1987. His wife, Roberta, had predeceased him by over ten years and they had no children.

HEWSON, GEORGE H. P. (1881–1972), musician. Born in Dublin. Educated at Cathedral Grammar School and TCD; Mus. Doc. 1914. He started to play the organ when he was twelve; became organist and choirmaster at St Patrick's Cathedral, professor of organ at the RIAM, and in 1935 professor of music at TCD. He gave many organ recitals, and composed four services and a well-known setting for Tennyson's 'Crossing the Bar'. He was appointed an honorary fellow of the Royal College of Organists in London, and was organist at TCD from 1927 until his death in Dublin on 22 November 1972.

HICKEY, WILLIAM (1787–1875), philanthropist. Born at Murragh, Co. Cork. Educated at TCD and St John's College, Cambridge. He became curate at Bannow, Co. Wexford, in 1820, and with Thomas Boyce founded the South Wexford Agricultural Society, the first of its kind in Ireland. Under the pen-name Martin Doyle he published a long and popular series of books and pamphlets on practical farming, vegetable-growing, poultry-keeping, and any subject he thought might help the struggling small farmers of Ireland. With Edmund Murphy he conducted the *Irish Farmers' and Gardeners' Magazine* 1834–1842. He became rector of Kilcormick, and then of Wexford and of Mulrankin. Died on 24 October 1875.

HIGGINS, BRYAN (1741–1818), physician and chemist. Born Collooney, Co. Sligo. Graduated M.D. at Leiden and began practice in London. Opened a school of practical chemistry in Greek Street, 1774. Involved in a dispute with Priestley, whom he accused of having plagiarised his experiments on air, 1775. Published part of his course of lectures under the title *A Philosophical Essay Concerning Light* (1776). Obtained letters patent for a cheap and durable cement 1779 and in 1786 published his best-known work, *Experiments and Observations Relating to Acetous Acid, Fixable Air . . . Oils and Fuels, etc.* Some time between 1780 and 1790 he visited Russia, apparently at the invitation of the Empress Ekaterina. In December 1796 he was appointed to assist committees set up by the Jamaican House of Assembly to improve the manufacture of muscovado sugar and rum: he lived at Spanish Town, Jamaica, 1797–1799, and the results of his work were published in 1800 and 1803 as *Observations and Labours.* Died Walford, Staffordshire.

HIGGINS, FRANCIS (1746–1802), the 'Sham Squire'. Born of poor parents who migrated from Downpatrick, Co. Down, to Dublin. He became an attorney's clerk, converted to Protestantism and, by posing as a landed gentleman, induced a lady of means to marry him. He became an attorney in 1780 and made himself wealthy by operating shady gaming-houses. He bought the *Freeman's Journal,* and in its pages continually denounced opponents of the government, particularly the United Irishmen. He became a government informer and is almost certainly the 'F.H.' recorded as receiving £1,000 'for the discovery of Lord Edward Fitzgerald'. He died at his house, 82 St Stephen's Green, Dublin, 19 January 1802.

HIGGINS, FREDERICK ROBERT (1896–1941), author. Born at Foxford, Co. Mayo, but grew up in Co. Meath. At fourteen he began work in a building provider's office, then became an official of the labour movement. He began to contribute articles to literary and economic reviews and edited various journals, including a trade journal and a women's periodical called *Welfare* that ran for two issues. Joint editor with YEATS of a series of broadsheets published by the Cuala Press 1935. His one-act play *A Deuce o' Jacks* was produced at the Abbey Theatre, 1935. He became a director of the theatre in 1936 and managed the company during its 1937 American tour; he later became the company's business manager. During the Second World War he encouraged an Abbey policy based on his belief that 'enough plays are being written to enable the Abbey to continue almost indefinitely without ever repeating anything more than a year old.' Founder-member and honorary secretary of the Irish Academy of Letters, which awarded him its Casement Medal for his book of poems, *Arable Holdings* (1933). Professor of literature to the RHA. In 1940 he published *The Gap of Brightness*, his most widely acclaimed volume of poetry. He died in Dublin in January 1941.

HIGGINS, JOHN (1670-1729), physician. Born in Limerick in 1670; after the defeat of the Jacobite cause and the Treaty of Limerick went to Montpellier, where he studied at the medical school, then one of the most famous in Europe. In 1700 the Duke of Berwick, generalissimo of the allied French and Spanish forces, persuaded him to accompany him to Spain as chief medical officer of his army. He saw active service in the ten years of the War of the Spanish Succession, in which various regiments of the Irish Brigade were prominent. His reputation grew, and in 1718 Philip V of Spain appointed him to be his chief physician. The following year the king had a serious illness and attributed his successful recovery to the skill of Dr Higgins. The king made him a royal councillor, and he was also elected president of the Royal Academy of Medicine. In 1723 James III of England (the 'Old Pretender') made him a baronet in recognition of his devotion to the Jacobite cause. In 1721 the Duc de Saint Simon came to Madrid as French ambassador and contracted smallpox immediately after his arrival. The king sent Higgins to him, and the ambassador was cured. In his memoirs the latter speaks in glowing terms of the qualities of the Irish doctor as a physician and as a person: 'one of the best and most skilful physicians in Europe, who is also capital company.' He died in Madrid in October 1729.

HIGGINS, WILLIAM (*c.* 1763-1825), chemist. Claimed to be the originator of the atomic theory in its nineteenth-century form. Born at Collooney, Co. Sligo, but as a boy went to his uncle, BRYAN HIGGINS, in London. Educated at Magdalen Hall and Pembroke College, Oxford. Published *Comparative View* (1789), in which he applied an atomic theory to the explanation of chemical phenomena, thus refuting the current phlogiston theory. After working with his uncle he returned to Ireland in 1792 as chemist to the newly instituted Apothecaries' Hall of Ireland. Later, as chemist to the Irish Linen Board, he devised a new, more economical bleaching process. At the suggestion of RICHARD KIRWAN he was employed by the RDS, to which he became professor of chemistry. MRIA, and a founder-member of the Kirwinian Society; elected FRS 1806. Died in June 1825 at 71 Grafton Street, Dublin.

HINCKS, EDWARD (1792-1866), orientalist. Born at Cork, 19 August 1792; educated at TCD. In 1825 he was made rector of Killyleagh, Co. Down, and lived there the rest of his life. From this remote country rectory he established a reputation as a pioneer in the deciphering of cuneiform writing. He contributed many articles on Egyptian hieroglyphics to the *Transactions* of the RIA, and studied also Assyrian, Median, Persian and Babylonian inscriptions. At Killyleagh he rediscovered the Persian cuneiform vowel system at the same time as Rawlinson discovered it independently at Baghdad. He died at Killyleagh. His bust has been placed at the entrance to Cairo Museum.

HINKSON, KATHARINE. See under TYNAN, KATHARINE.

HINKSON, PAMELA (1900-1982), writer, only daughter of KATHARINE TYNAN. Born 19 November 1900 in London. Educated privately in Ireland. Became a journalist and travelled widely in Europe and America. Contributed to the *Observer, New Statesman* and *Manchester Guardian* among others. Published *The Ladies' Road* (1932), which was very successful, *Seventy Years Young* (1937), in collaboration with Lady Fingall, and *Irish Gold* (1939). After a visit to India as guest of the Viceroy in the late 1930s she published *Indian Harvest* (1941). During the Second World War she made a lecture tour of the USA for the British Ministry of Information. Other books were *The Deeply Rooted* (1934), *Golden Rose* (1944), and *The Lonely Bride* (1951). She returned to Ireland in 1959 and died on 26 May 1982.

HITCHCOCK, REGINALD IN-GRAM MONTGOMERY (1893-1950), film director, known as Rex Ingram. Born 18 January 1893 at 58 Grosvenor Square, Rathmines, Dublin, son of Rev. Francis Montgomery Ryan Hitchcock, a Donnellan Lecturer at TCD, and later rector of Kinnitty, Co. Offaly. Educated at St Columba's College, Dublin. At eighteen he emigrated to the USA, studied sculpture at Yale School of Fine Arts, and in 1913 joined the young film industry, working for the Edison, Vitagraph and Fox companies as actor and scriptwriter. At the early age of twenty-three he directed *The Great Problem*, from his own story, for Universal. Later films for this company included *Black Orchids, Reward of the Faithless, The Flower of Doom*, and *Under Crimson Skies*. Joined the Metro Company 1920 and launched *The Four Horsemen of the Apocalypse* (1921), distinguished for its pictorial beauty and its introduction of Rudolph Valentino and Alice Terry, who was to become Ingram's wife and the star of many of his films. It was a great financial success and the basis of the fortunes of Metro, which later became the major partner in Metro-Goldwyn-Mayer. *The Conquering Power, The Prisoner of Zenda* (1922), *Trifling Women* and *Scaramouche* (1923) followed, the latter three films introducing the young Mexican actor Ramón Novarro. Tired of the regimentation of Hollywood, Ingram turned to North Africa and Europe for backgrounds to his films, and founded the Victorine Studios of Nice. There, in 1926, he made *Mare Nostrum*, based on a Blasco Ibañez story, *The Magician*, and the *Garden of Allah*. He made one sound film, *Baround*, a romance of Morocco, in which he played the lead. He retired from film-making in 1933 to devote himself to sculpture, writing, and travel. The director of twenty-seven films, he is regarded as one of the three most important film-makers in Hollywood during the 1920s. Received honorary degree from Yale University, Cross of the Legion of Honour from the French government, and Order of Nichan Iftkar from the Bey of Tunis. At one stage he embraced Islam. He left two novels, *The Legion Advances* (1934), a story of North Africa, and *Mars in the House of Death* (1939), a tale of bullfighting in Spain and Mexico. Died in Hollywood on 22 July 1950.

HOBAN, JAMES (*c.* 1762-1831), architect of the White House, Washington. Born outside Callan, Co. Kilkenny, and studied drawing under THOMAS IVORY at the school of the Dublin Society. In 1780 he won a premium for drawings of 'brackets, stairs, roofs, etc.' He was then employed, probably as a joiner, on Dublin buildings including the Royal Exchange (now City Hall) and the Custom House. Seeing little opportunity for advancement in Ireland he emigrated to America in 1785. He settled first at Philadelphia and then moved to South Carolina, where he won the design for the State Capitol at Columbia, completed successfully in 1791. In 1792 he won a competition for a design for the President's House at Washington, later called the White House. The finished building shows striking similarities to Leinster House in Dublin. He was retained to supervise the construction work at £315 a year. At the laying of the cornerstone by President Washington on 13 September 1793, he assisted as master of the Federal Masonic Lodge, which he had helped to organise. He designed and built the Great Hotel at Washington (1793-1795) and the Little Hotel (1795). Captain in the Washington Artillery 1799. When the city was incorporated in 1802 he was elected a member of the council and retained his seat until his death. After the destruction of the White House by the British in 1814 he was retained to rebuild it. He also designed and built the State and War offices. Died in Washington on 8 December 1831, leaving an estate valued at £60,000.

HOBSON, BULMER (1883-1969), revolutionary and writer. Born at

Holywood, Co. Down, of Quaker stock settled in Ireland for several generations. Educated at the Friends' School in Lisburn. Came into contact with nationalist societies and left school a convinced disciple of Wolfe Tone. In 1900, while working in the printing business in Belfast, he started a club for boys, the Ulster Debating Club, and with one of its members, William McDonald, later set up the Protestant National Society to recruit young Ulster Protestants into the national movement. In 1901 he joined the Tír na nÓg branch of the Gaelic League and shortly afterwards became secretary of the first Antrim County Board of the GAA. He resigned from the GAA when it refused to help the junior hurling clubs, and started Na Fianna Éireann, a local boys' organisation. In 1909 he and CONSTANCE MARKIEVICZ expanded it to a national boy scouts' organisation that was also a drilled military corps. Hobson was one of the founders of the Ulster Literary Theatre, for which he wrote a poetic drama, *Brian of Banba*, produced in 1905. He joined Cumann na nGaedheal, the first association founded by ARTHUR GRIFFITH but, dissatisfied with its lack of activity, Hobson and Denis McCullough, a prominent young IRB leader, started the Dungannon Club in Belfast in March 1905. For this, Hobson wrote his first publication, *To the Whole People of Ireland: the Manifesto of the Dungannon Club* (1905). The club was particularly active in campaigning against recruiting, and other Dungannon Clubs were set up throughout Ireland and in London. In December 1906 he founded a weekly paper called the *Republic*, which six months later merged with the *Peasant* in Dublin as a result of financial difficulties. In 1907 he went to America at the invitation of JOHN DEVOY to introduce the Sinn Féin movement to America; his visit helped to strengthen the activist alliance between Clan na Gael in America and the IRB in Ireland. On his return later that year Hobson was instrumental in arranging an amalgamation of the Dungannon Clubs and Cumann na nGaedheal. He became a vice-president of Sinn Féin. In 1909 he edited a short-lived weekly, the *County Dublin Observer*. At this time living in Dublin, Hobson also helped F. J. BIGGER to prepare a series of volumes on prominent northern United Irishmen but only one, on WILLIAM ORR, was published. In 1909 he also issued a small volume entitled *Defensive Warfare: a Handbook for Irish Nationalists*, published by the West Belfast Branch of Sinn Féin. In 1910 Hobson, with a number of others, including P. S. O'HEGARTY and Denis McCullough, left Sinn Féin, chiefly because of policy disagreements with Arthur Griffith. He thereafter devoted his time to the IRB—he was a member of its Supreme Council—and to the Fianna, and formed a number of 'Freedom Clubs'. In 1911 he started a paper, *Irish Freedom*, the property of the IRB, and edited it until May 1914. Hobson was a founder-member of the Irish Volunteers in 1913 and their first secretary, and with THOMAS MACDONAGH organised the landing of arms at Howth in July 1914. This episode is described in his book *A Short History of the Irish Volunteers: Vol. 1* (1918; a second volume never appeared). Hobson resigned from the Supreme Council of the IRB in 1914 when his decision to accede to JOHN REDMOND's demand that his nominees make up half the Provisional Committee of the Volunteers alienated him from militant members such as TOM CLARKE and SEÁN MAC DIARMADA. He made the decision in order to prevent a 'tragic split' in the Volunteer movement. In 1916 he joined EOIN MACNEILL in opposing the Easter Rising. It was Hobson who conveyed to MacNeill that a rising was imminent, and it was to him that MacNeill, in one of his countermanding orders, virtually handed over command of the Volunteers. Hobson's own IRB members arrested him, and only released him when the rising had started. He had been opposed to using the Volunteers except against an attack by the British government or in resistance to conscription. He had maintained that the Volunteers should be held in reserve and used to reinforce the Irish national claim to an all-Ireland parliament after the war. After the rising he withdrew from the revolutionary movement and interested himself in afforestation, theories of social credit, support of the Dublin Gate Theatre, and publications of a non-political character. After the establishment of the Free State in 1922 he was appointed chief of the Revenue Commissioners' Stamp Department, Dublin Castle. On retiring in 1948 he went to live in Roundstone, Co. Galway, and later in Limerick. Among his publications were *The Life of Wolfe Tone* (1919), *A National Forests Policy* (1923), and *Ireland Yesterday and Tomorrow* (1968). He died in August 1969.

HOGAN, AUSTIN (1907–1974), trade unionist. Born Co. Clare, son of an RIC constable named de Loughrey. Educated North Monastery CBS, Cork, Crawford Technical School, and London Institute for Mechanics. Joined Fianna Éireann during the Civil War. Emigrated to USA in the late 1920s and studied engineering at Columbia University. Worked as civil engineer in California and New York. With Michael Quill, a Kerryman, he founded the Transport Workers' Union of America, and adopted his mother's name, Hogan, to protect his engineering job. Quill and he were militantly left-wing and made the union a strong force. They split in 1947/48, and Hogan, who had never been a transport worker, was expelled from the union as a communist. He was commissioned a captain of engineers in the US army in the Second World War and was badly wounded in the Pacific. He returned to Ireland in poor health about 1968. In 1972 the union paid his fare back to the USA and gave him a welcoming reception. He returned to Ireland in 1974, and died at Cork, 26 December.

HOGAN, DAVID. See under GALLAGHER, FRANK.

HOGAN, EDMUND (1831–1917), scholar. Born Great Island, Cork, 25 January 1831. Joined the Society of Jesus and studied in Rome. Edited many important Irish manuscripts. Published *Distinguished Irishmen of the 16th Century* (1894), *Irish Phrase-Book* (1899), and other books on Irish subjects. Undertook his last and greatest work at seventy, *Onomasticon Goedelicum: an Index to Gaelic Names of Places and Tribes* (1910). Was professor of Irish language and history at UCD and Todd Professor of Celtic at the RIA. Died Dublin, 26 November 1917.

HOGAN, JOHN (1800–1858), sculptor. Born Tallow, Co. Waterford, on 14 October 1800. At fourteen he began work as a lawyer's clerk in Cork, but after two years became apprenticed to Thomas Deane, builder and architect. He first worked as a carpenter, but with encouragement from Deane took up sculpture and secured some church work from Dr Murphy, bishop of Cork. His work attracted notice, and a public subscription was raised to send him to Rome, where he studied at the School of St Luke and the Galleries of the Vatican and the Capitol. In 1837 he was elected a member of the Virtuosi del Pantheon, a society founded in 1500. He received many commissions from Ireland, married an Italian, and stayed in Rome until the revolution of 1848 obliged him to return home. There were few patrons of art in Ireland at that time, but after some years of struggle he received important commissions including statues of FATHER MATHEW for Cork and of O'CONNELL for Limerick. His best-known works in Dublin are a statue of O'Connell in City Hall, the 'Dead Christ' in Clarendon St Church, and the 'Drunken Faun' in UCD. He died at his house, 14 Wentworth Place, Dublin, 27 March 1858.

HOGAN, MICHAEL (1832–1899), the Bard of Thomond. Born Limerick, and worked as wheelwright. Published *Light of Munster* (1852), *Anthems to Mary* (1859), and contributed further verse to the

Nation and *Irishman*. These were collected as *Lays and Legends of Thomond*, which went into three editions between 1865 and 1880. *Shawn-a-Scoob*, his satire in verse, founded on an old legend, was published in eight parts at a shilling (5p) each (1868–1876) and had a large sale. He also wrote some election squibs, equally popular. He was in New York in 1888, returned to Limerick 1889 and died there.

HOGAN, PATRICK (1886–1969), politician. Born Kilmaley, Co. Clare. Joined the Gaelic League as a young man and became an Irish-speaker; then joined the Volunteers in Limerick and was deported to England. While in jail he wrote the song 'Shawl of Galway Grey', which became very popular in nationalist circles. During the War of Independence he fought against the Black and Tans in Co. Clare. After the Treaty he became an official of the Irish Transport and General Workers' Union. Elected Labour TD for Co. Clare in 1923; he held his seat until 1938, sat in the Seanad 1938–1943, and then entered the Dáil again. Ceann Comhairle 1951 to 1967. Called to the bar 1936 and practised when not in the Dáil. He wrote many articles, and published a collection of short stories, *The Unmarried Daughter*. Died in Mullingar, 24 January 1969.

HOLLAND, JOHN PHILIP (1841–1914), inventor of the submarine. Born Castle Street, Liscannor, Co. Clare, 24 February 1841, son of a coast-guard, and educated at Limerick CBS. Poor eyesight prevented him from going to sea, as he wished, and he joined the Christian Brothers, taking initial vows in June 1858. He taught in their schools in Cork, Portlaoise, Enniscorthy, Drogheda, and Dundalk. In 1872 he was dispensed from his vows, and went to the USA, and taught in Paterson, New Jersey. After years of experiment he built a small submarine, helped by funds from Irish friends, and operated it successfully. JOHN DEVOY, through Clan na Gael, secured £60,000 for him in the early

stages of his trials, hoping that the submarine could be used against England. To develop his invention he formed a company in 1895 and secured a contract to build a submarine for the US navy. The first ship was a failure but the second, the *Holland*, passed the navy's tests. The British navy soon ordered several Holland vessels, and the submarine won a place in naval warfare. Holland is now generally recognised as the 'father' of the modern submarine. Died Newark, New Jersey, 12 August 1914.

HOLLOWAY, JOSEPH (1861–1944), theatre-goer. Born March 1861, son of a baker, in Lower Camden Street, Dublin. Educated St Vincent's College, Castleknock, and School of Art, Dublin. At nineteen he entered the office of T. T. O'Callaghan, architect, and remained until 1896 when he set up his own office: he ceased practising architecture at the outbreak of the First World War. Became known as a Dublin 'character', attending every theatre performance in the city, and joining every society connected with theatre. Accumulated a vast collection of material relating to the theatre: playbills, prompt-sheets, etc., and adorned the walls of his house with paintings and sketches of theatrical personalities. Kept a journal in which he wrote some twenty-eight million words on Dublin's theatre world; selections from it were published under the title *Joseph Holloway's Abbey Theatre* in 1967. All his material is now in the National Library. Died in Dublin.

HOLT, JOSEPH (1756–1826), insurgent. Born at Ballydaniel, Co. Wexford, son of a well-to-do farmer. He, also, prospered as a farmer. He was a Protestant, with little interest in politics, but when the rising of 1798 broke out, his landlord, who had become his enemy, denounced him as a United Irishman. In his absence his house was burned down by the yeomen, and this treatment turned him into a rebel. Many others joined him, and at Ballyellis in June 1798 he won a complete victory over the government forces. Thousands more then joined him, and at one time he had 13,000 men under his command. After the collapse of the rising he avoided capture for some time, but surrendered on 10 November. He was sentenced to transportation to Botany Bay in New South Wales. There he worked first as a bailiff, and then was able to buy some land. His energy and ability brought prosperity, but in 1812 he decided to sell out and return to Ireland. He embarked for England on 1 December 1812 with his wife and youngest son. On 8 February 1813 their ship was wrecked on Eagle Island, one of the Falkland group. He took over the leadership, built cabins, organised hunting and fishing parties, and stored provisions for the future. In April the *Namina*, an American vessel, arrived at Eagle Island and offered to rescue them, although England was then at war with America. An English cruiser then arrived, captured the *Namina*, and sent her as a prize to Rio de Janeiro. In October 1813 Holt left Rio for Liverpool, and on 5 April 1814 arrived in Dublin, and set up in business as a publican. After heavy losses, he sold the public-house and retired to Kingstown (Dún Laoghaire). There he lived out his life on the rent of a few houses he built there, always regretting that he had left the prosperity he had enjoyed in New South Wales. Died on 16 May 1826.

HOLWELL, JOHN ZEPHANIAH (1711–1798), survivor of the 'Black Hole of Calcutta'. Born Dublin, 17 September 1711; studied medicine at Guy's Hospital, London, and went to India in 1732 as a surgeon. In 1756 he helped to defend Calcutta against the Nawab of Bengal, and when it surrendered on 20 June he claimed to have been imprisoned with 145 others in a room only 15 by 18 feet (4.5 by 5.5 m). Only Holwell and twenty-two others were alive the next morning. After rescue by Clive and a short visit to England, he returned to India and became Governor of Bengal.

In 1761 he resigned and returned to England, where he wrote a number of books on Indian history and religion. His *Genuine Narrative of the Deaths... in the Black Hole* appeared in 1758. Grave doubts have been cast by modern historians on the whole episode. He died at Pinner near Harrow on 5 November 1798.

HONE, EVIE (1894–1955), artist. Born at Roebuck Grove, Co. Dublin, 22 April 1894. Poliomyelitis early in life left her a semi-invalid. Determining to be an artist, she studied in London and Paris between 1915 and 1931 with her devoted friend and fellow artist MAINIE JELLETT. In Paris they worked first under Lhote, and then became pupils with Gleizes. She began to exhibit her abstract paintings in Dublin in 1924. Her interest in the work of Rouault, and her deeply religious nature, inspired her to turn to stained-glass work. Her first window consisted of three small panels for the Protestant church at Dundrum, Co. Dublin. Recognition came quickly and she received many commissions. Her best-known works are 'My Four Green Fields' (CIE office, Dublin), five windows for the Jesuit college at Tullabeg, and a large window depicting the Last Supper and the Crucifixion for the chapel at Eton College. Despite ill-health, she produced over one hundred and fifty small stained-glass panels and a number of oils and watercolours. She died in Rathfarnham, Co. Dublin, on 13 March 1955.

HONE, JOSEPH MAUNSEL (1882–1959), literary historian. Educated at Wellington and Cambridge. Went to Persia (Iran) with Page L. Dickinson in 1909. Published his first book, *Persia in Revolution* (1910), an account of the country on the eve of the deposition of the Kajar Shahs. Translated Daniel Halévy's *Life of Nietzsche*, with an introduction by T. M. KETTLE (1911). Hone continued to translate the works of French and Italian writers and to contribute to periodicals in England. In

1929, in collaboration with Dr Rossi, he published a biography of the Irish philosopher BERKELEY. His later works were mainly biographical, and included *Thomas Davis* (1934), *The Moores of Moore Hall* (1939), *The Life of Henry Tonks* (1939), and *W. B. Yeats: 1865–1939* (1942). President, Irish Academy of Letters, 1957. Died in Dublin.

HONE, NATHANIEL (1718–1784), portrait painter. Born Dublin, 24 April 1718. Nothing is known of his early training as an artist, but as a young man he went to England and earned his living as an itinerant portrait painter. He married 1742; his wife had property, which enabled them to settle in London. In 1750 he went to Italy and studied and painted there for two years. On his return to London he soon established a reputation as a portrait painter in oils and in miniature. One of the original members of the RA, 1768; between then and 1784 showed sixty-nine pictures in all. In 1775 his picture 'The Conjuror' was removed from the academy on the grounds that it ridiculed the president, Sir Joshua Reynolds, whom Hone disliked, and also contained an indecent caricature of Angelica Kauffmann. Hone then painted out the objectionable figure. The picture is now in the National Gallery of Ireland. Died at 44 Rathbone Place, London, 14 August 1784.

HONE, NATHANIEL (1831–1917), painter, and descendant of Berkeley Hone (a brother of NATHANIEL HONE). Born Fitzwilliam Place, Dublin, on 26 October 1831. Educated at TCD, where he studied engineering. Worked with the Midland Great Western Railway until 1853, when he decided to become a painter. He spent two years in Paris, studying first under Adolphe Yvon and then with Thomas Couture. He then moved to Barbizon, where he spent the following twenty years, with short visits to Italy. At Barbizon he worked in close contact with Millet and Harpignies and painted landscapes only. He exhibited at the RA in 1869, and at the Salons during the sixties. In 1875 he returned to Ireland and settled at Malahide, Co. Dublin, where he spent the rest of his life painting and farming. He had sufficient private means to be able to live without selling his work. Elected RHA 1880 and exhibited there from 1876 until his death. In 1894 he succeeded SIR THOMAS JONES as professor of painting at the RHA and held the appointment until his death. In 1901 he held an exhibition in Dublin with JOHN BUTLER YEATS, and it was this event that first aroused the interest of SIR HUGH LANE in Irish art. Apart from a lunette of 'St Patrick and his Companions' for Sir Patrick Dun's Hospital, Dublin, he confined himself generally to landscapes and seascapes. His widow presented over 500 of his oil paintings and some 900 watercolours and drawings to the National Gallery. His paintings display the subtle play of light and colour of the Irish landscape with assured mastery. Died, 14 October 1917, at St Dolough's Park, north Co. Dublin.

HOPE, JAMES (JEMMY) (1764–*c.* 1846), United Irishman. Born Templepatrick, Co. Antrim, 25 August 1764, son of a fugitive Covenanter. Left school at ten and became a linen-weaver. The movement for civil and religious freedom for all classes attracted his support, and in 1795 he joined the Society of United Irishmen. The following year he was sent to Dublin to enlist members for the society, and worked as a cotton-weaver in the Liberties. In 1798 he went back to Belfast and took part in the battle of Antrim during the rising that year. In November 1798 he succeeded in making his way to Dublin, where he was joined by his family and where he lived in constant fear of arrest. After the political amnesty of 1806 he returned to Belfast and resumed work as a linen-weaver. The date of his death is uncertain, but he seems to have been alive in 1846, when MADDEN published his memoirs.

163

HORAN, MONSIGNOR JAMES (1912–1986), priest and airport builder. Born in Partry, near Ballinrobe, Co. Mayo, and educated at St Jarlath's College, Tuam, and at Maynooth. Ordained 1935 and served as curate in Scotland for three years. Curate in Bally-glunin, Co. Mayo, and Lettermullen, Co. Galway, then went to Toureen, where he first showed his business ability, building a hall that became a dancing centre in the West. He was appointed to Knock, Co. Mayo, in 1963 and became parish priest in 1967. Although it had been a place of pilgrimage since 1879, when villagers had reported an apparition of the Virgin Mary, facilities for visitors were scanty. Father Horan provided a hostel and a rest and care centre for invalids and built a large church. Later he established a social services centre, including a marriage bureau. He was made monsignor when Pope John Paul II visited Knock in 1979 to mark the centenary of the shrine. In 1981 the Government approved his plans for an airport to serve Knock shrine and business interests in the west. The project ran into difficulties when a later Government refused further funding after £9 million had been spent. Monsignor Horan pressed on, raising money to complete the runway, and the airport was opened by the leader of the opposition, Charles Haughey, in May 1986. He died on 1 August 1986 while on a pilgrimage to Lourdes.

HORGAN, JOHN JOSEPH (1881–1967), solicitor. Born Cork; educated Presentation College, Cork, and Clongowes Wood. Qualified as a solicitor in 1902 and soon began to take a prominent part in public affairs. An enthusiastic supporter of the Gaelic League and of the Irish Party under JOHN REDMOND. Member of Cork Harbour Commissioners 1912–1961, and of many other public bodies, and sat as coroner at the inquest into the victims of the sinking of the *Lusitania* by a German submarine in May 1915. A friend of artists and patron of the arts; chairman of Cork Opera Co.

for many years. A strong advocate of the city managerial system, and inspired the Cork City Management Act, which set a precedent for other cities. Publications included *Great Catholic Laymen* (1908), *Home Rule, a Critical Consideration* (1911), *The Complete Grammar of Anarchy* (1918), and an autobiography, *Parnell to Pearse* (1948), as well as many contributions to newspapers. Died Cork, 21 July 1967.

HUGHES, MOST REV. JOHN (1797–1864), first archbishop of New York. Born Annaloghlan, Co. Tyrone, 24 June 1797. Educated locally. His father emigrated to USA 1816 and John joined him in 1817. Worked as a gardener at seminary in Emmitsburg, Maryland; was accepted as a student, and ordained 1826. Became noted for vigorous defence of Catholicism in writings and sermons. Coadjutor, New York diocese, 1838, and bishop 1842; archbishop 1850 when New York was made an archdiocese. Supported the Union in the Civil War and sent by US government on mission to Europe to promote their cause. Founded college at Fordham, now Jesuit university, and laid foundation stone of St Patrick's Cathedral, New York. Died New York, 3 January 1864.

HUGHES, JOHN (1865–1941), sculptor. Born 30 January 1865 at 21 Portland Place, Dublin, the son of a carpenter. Educated North Richmond St CBS and Metropolitan School of Art. In 1890 he won a scholarship to the South Kensington Art School, London, where he studied under Édouard Lantéri. Another scholarship in 1890 took him to the Académie Julien and Collarossi's Academy in Paris, after which he visited Italy. Second art master in Plymouth Technical School 1893. Appointed instructor in modelling at the Metropolitan School of Art in Dublin 1894, and professor of sculpture in the RHA school. Held both these posts until he gave up teaching in 1901. Elected RHA 1900. His first important commission came in 1901 when he executed his 'Man of Sorrows' and 'Madonna and Child' for Loughrea Cathedral. From 1903 to 1906 he was engaged on a large memorial to Queen Victoria, which stood for many years in front of Leinster House. Other important works included a monument of CHARLES KICKHAM in Tipperary, and the Gladstone monument in Hawarden, Clwyd. He also executed portrait busts of prominent Dublin people. In the Dublin International Exhibition of 1907 he was represented by a marble sculpture 'Orpheus and Eurydice'. He also showed at the Irish exhibitions in Paris in 1922 and in Brussels in 1930. He was a founder-member of the Royal Society of British Sculptors. From 1903 he lived abroad, settling first in Paris and then about 1920 moving to Florence, where he lived with a sister until 1926. In the 1930s he spent a good deal of time in Italy, finally settling in 1939 in Nice, where he died on 6 June 1941 and is buried. A plaque has been erected to his memory on his last Dublin home, 28 Lennox St.

HULL, ELEANOR (1860–1935), historian and journalist. Born in England, of Co. Down parents. Educated at Alexandra College, Dublin. An Irish scholar, in 1899 she founded the Irish Texts Society for the publication of early manuscripts, and acted as honorary secretary for nearly thirty years. Among her publications are *The Cúchulain Saga in Irish Literature* (1898), *Pagan Ireland* (1904), *Early Christian Ireland* (1904), *A Textbook of Irish Literature* (1906–1908), *The Poem-Book of the Gael* (1912), *The Northmen in Britain* (1913), *Folklore of the British Isles* (1928), and *A History of Ireland* (1931).

HUNT, JOHN (1900–1976), mediaevalist. Born in Limerick on 25 May 1900. The family moved to London when he was in his teens but he returned in 1940 to live by Lough Gur, Co. Limerick. He acquired a world-wide reputation as an expert in mediaeval art, especially religious art. He was conferred M.A. (NUI) in 1946 for his thesis 'Medieval Armour in Ireland'. As an archaeological field-worker he took part in the excavation of the famous Sutton Hoo ship-burial. He was responsible for the restoration of Bunratty Castle and the establishment of a 'folk park' there. Under his guidance, Craggaunowen Castle was restored, a replica of a crannóg built in the grounds at the lake edge and a ring-fort and souterrain built in the woods. He then presented the castle and grounds to the nation. He also presented to the nation his private collection of antiques and archaeological treasures, now housed in the Hunt Museum, Plassey House, Limerick. He contributed many articles to antiquarian and art journals and was a member of the Arts Council. His major work, *Irish Medieval Figure Sculpture*, appeared in two volumes in 1974. He died in 1976, survived by his wife, Gertrude.

HUSSEY, THOMAS (1741–1803), bishop and first president of Maynooth College. Born Ballybogan, Co. Meath; studied with distinction at Salamanca, and became a Trappist monk. By order of the Pope he left the monastery, was ordained, and was assigned to the Spanish court. About 1767 he became chaplain to the Spanish embassy in London. Here he met Johnson and BURKE. Was elected FRS in 1792. When Spain allied itself to France on the side of the American colonies, Hussey stayed on at the embassy after the ambassador had returned to Madrid, and was then sent to Madrid by George III to detach Spain from the alliance. His mission failed, but his abilities as a diplomat were recognised, and in 1794 he was sent to Ireland to investigate unrest among Catholics in the English army there. He helped to establish a Catholic seminary at Maynooth, Co. Kildare, and became first president in 1795. Two years later he was appointed bishop of Waterford and Lismore. It is said that he helped to frame the Concordat of 1802 between Napoleon and Pope Pius VII. Died at Tramore, Co. Waterford, 11 July 1803.

HUTCHESON, FRANCIS (1694–1746), philosopher. Born 8 August 1694, probably at Saintfield, Co. Down. Educated Glasgow University. Returned to Ireland in 1716, and started a private academy in Dublin. Following his publication of several treatises on the philosophical theories of Hobbes and Mandeville, he was invited in 1729 to take the chair of moral philosophy at Glasgow, and spent the rest of his life there. In addition to university lectures on morals and jurisprudence, he devoted his Sunday evenings to discourses on the proofs of Christianity, and attracted students from every faculty. He helped poor students with money, and admitted them free to his lectures. In 1745 he was offered the chair of moral philosophy at Edinburgh, but declined, although the salary was higher than at Glasgow. Adam Smith was among his pupils, and Hume corresponded with him on ethical questions. His principal works were *An Enquiry into the Original of Our Ideas of Beauty and Virtue* (1725), and *A System of Moral Philosophy*, published by his son in 1755. He was one of the first exponents of a decided utilitarianism as distinguished from 'egoistic hedonism', and coined the phrase 'the greatest happiness of the greatest number', usually attributed to Bentham. His theology differed little from the optimistic deism of his day. Died at Glasgow.

HYDE, DOUGLAS (1860–1949), scholar and first President of Ireland. Born at Castlerea, Co. Roscommon, 17 January 1860. Son of Rev. Arthur Hyde, rector of Tibohine, Frenchpark. Educated at TCD. Won prizes for English verse and prose. To his command of Latin, Greek and Hebrew he added fluency in French, German, and Irish. Took his LL.D. in 1888. In 1891 he went to Canada for a year as interim professor of modern languages in the University of New Brunswick. Returning to Ireland, settled at Ratra Park in Roscommon and devoted himself to literary pursuits and the revival of Irish, which he had learned from the old people in the countryside around his father's rectory, and he collected folklore and poetry from them. *Beside the Fire* (1889) was his first collection of folk-tales. *Love Songs of Connacht* followed in 1893 with his own verse translations. That year saw the foundation of the Gaelic League, with Hyde as moving spirit and first president. The league flourished and by 1905 had 550 branches, which organised lessons in Irish and encouraged Irish dances and games. He went to the USA in 1905 on a successful fund-raising tour, and on his return was made a freeman of Dublin, Cork, and Kilkenny. The league took a dominant part in the successful agitation to make Irish an essential subject for entrance to the new NUI, founded in 1908. By this time it had become a vital force in the movement for national revival. Hyde became the first professor of Modern Irish in UCD, in 1909, and held the chair until his retirement in 1932. He was a Free State senator 1925–1926. He had always insisted that the Gaelic League must remain a non-sectarian and non-political organisation, but its very success in reviving the national spirit helped to inspire the separatist movement, and it became clear that the language and the political struggle could not be kept apart. Hyde resigned the presidency in 1915 and, avoiding political activity, confined himself to academic pursuits. Characteristically, he showed no animosity towards his successors. When the office of President of Ireland was created under the Constitution of 1937, Hyde was unanimously selected by all parties, and held office until his term expired in 1945. He died in Dublin, 12 July 1949. His wife, whom he married in 1893, predeceased him in 1939. They had two daughters. Hyde's verse translations from the Irish have appeared in many anthologies. He adopted the Irish pen-name 'An Craoibhín Aoibhinn', 'the delightful little branch'. His folk-tales kindled the imagination of YEATS, LADY GREGORY and others prominent in the Irish literary revival. The Irish Academy of Letters awarded him the Gregory Medal in 1937. His other publications included *Religious Songs of Connacht* (1906), *A Literary History of Ireland* (1899), and some one-act plays. His play *Casadh an tSúgáin*, produced by the Irish Literary Theatre, October 1901, was the first play in Irish to appear on a professional stage.

I

INGRAM, JOHN KELLS (1823–1907), scholar and poet. Born at the rectory, Temple Carne, Co. Donegal, 7 July 1823. Educated at Dr Lyons's school, Newry, and TCD. Fellow of the college 1846, and remained associated with it for fifty-five years, as professor of oratory 1852–1866, professor of Greek 1866–1877, librarian 1879–1887, senior lecturer 1887, and finally as vice-provost 1898–1899. His intellectual energy ranged over mathematics, classics, poetry, religious speculation, and economics, but he is best remembered for his poem 'Who Fears to Speak of Ninety-eight?' written when he was nineteen and published anonymously in the *Nation* in April 1843 under the title 'The Memory of the Dead'. His authorship was an open secret in Dublin, but despite this poem Ingram showed no nationalist sympathies at any time, maintaining that Ireland was not ready for self-government. He published many studies in economics, sociology, and religion, the most important being *History of Political Economy* (1888), which was translated into eight languages. In 1873 he founded and edited *Hermathena*, a series of papers on science, philosophy and literature by members of the college. Helped to found Dublin Statistical Society 1847, president 1878–1880; and president RIA 1892–1896. Died at his home, 38 Upper Mount Street, on 1 May 1907. Buried in Mount Jerome cemetery.

INGRAM, REX. See under HITCHCOCK, REGINALD.

IRELAND, DENIS (1894–1974), author and senator. Born Belfast; educated RBAI and QUB. He broke off his medical studies in 1914 to join the Royal Irish Fusiliers and served in France and Macedonia before being invalided home with the rank of captain. He then joined the family linen firm and represented it in Britain, Canada, and the USA. In the 1930s he gave up his career in business to devote himself to writing. Apart from a period as a talks assistant with the BBC he was a freelance writer and broadcaster for nearly forty years. Much of his writing was in support of his ideal of a united and independent Ireland. His many articles, pamphlets and books advocating his political aims were written from his own independent standpoint and without regard for the policies of any party. Nominated to Seanad Éireann 1948 by the then Taoiseach, JOHN A. COSTELLO, the first resident of Northern Ireland to become a member of the Oireachtas. He thanked Clann na Poblachta, one of the parties in the Coalition government, for having him nominated and giving him the opportunity to carry on his work for a united Ireland in a wider sphere. He was not nominated again when DE VALERA returned to power in 1951. He maintained that his political views were in the true tradition of Ulster Presbyterianism. In *Red Brick City* he expounded his view that Ulster Presbyterians were the only natural republicans in Ireland, and analysed the cause of the changes in the Presbyterian outlook from the days when they were pioneers of republicanism. Other books included *From the Irish Shore* (1936), an autobiography, *Patriot Adventurer* (1936), a short life of Wolfe Tone, *The Age of Unreason* (1942), and *Six Counties in Search of a Nation* (1947). Died in a Belfast nursing home, 23 September 1974.

IRELAND, MICHAEL. See under FIGGIS, DARRELL.

ÍTE, SAINT (otherwise MIDA) (died *c.* 570). Born near Drum, Co. Waterford, and is said to have been of royal descent and to have been first named Deirdre. She was a virgin and a contemplative, and founded a school and convent at Killeedy (Cill Íde) near Newcastle West, Co. Limerick. By tradition, ST BRENDAN attended her school, and heard from her the three things God loved most: true faith in God with a pure heart, a simple life with a religious spirit, and open-handedness inspired by charity; and the three things he most detested: a face that scowls on mankind, obstinacy in wrongdoing, and putting entire trust in the power of money. St Íte died at Killeedy about 570.

IVORY, THOMAS (*c.* 1720–1786), architect. Born Cork, and started probably as cabinet-maker. Designed bridge over Blackwater at Lismore, probably for Duke of Devonshire. Went to Dublin and was employed as gunstock maker by Alderman Truelock, gunsmith. Studied drawing and made reputation as architectural draughts-man. Appointed master of Dublin Society's Architectural School 1759 and held the post until his death. Was also Surveyor of the Revenue Buildings. He designed the Blue-Coat School, after-wards King's Hospital, Blackhall Place, now owned by the Incorporated Law Society of Ireland, one of Dublin's most beautiful buildings (1773–1780), and Newcomen's Bank (1781), now city council offices. They have been described as gentle and urbane, like Ivory himself. He died in Dublin.

J

JACKSON, ROBERT WYSE (1908–1976), bishop and writer. Educated at Abbey School, Tipperary, Bishop Foy School, Waterford, and TCD. Called to the bar in London but decided on holy orders, and was ordained in 1935. Served in Killaloe, Tipperary, and Limerick. Dean of Cashel 1946 and bishop of Limerick, Ardfert and Aghadoe 1961. Retired in 1970 for health reasons, and was made freeman of Limerick. Published books on law, local history, and the life and times of JONATHAN SWIFT, as well as two novels and a play. Died in Greystones, Co. Wicklow, on 21 October 1976, survived by his second wife, five sons and two daughters.

JACKSON, REV. WILLIAM (c. 1737–1795), United Irishman. Born Dublin. Went to London, became a tutor, and took holy orders. Curate of St Mary-le-Strand. Became secretary to the notorious Duchess of Kingston some time before 1775. Made a name as a radical journalist. Edited the *Public Ledger* and *Morning Post*, and gave strong support to the American revolutionaries. Went to France about 1792 and was commissioned to ascertain the chances of success of a French invasion of England. Back in London he renewed acquaintance with Cockayne, former attorney to the Duchess of Kingston, who accompanied him to Dublin and informed on him. CURRAN defended him at his trial for high treason. He was found guilty, and poisoned himself in the dock on 30 April 1795.

JACOB, ARTHUR (1790–1874), oculist. Born Knockfin, Maryborough (Portlaoise), 13 or 30 June 1790. Studied medicine in Dr Steevens' Hospital, Dublin, in Edinburgh, Paris, and London. Became demonstrator of anatomy at TCD in 1819. Discovered a previously unknown membrane of the eye, named after him 'membrana Jacobi'. Professor of anatomy, RCSI, 1826–1869, and president three times. In 1832, with Benson and others, he established the City of Dublin Hospital (Baggot St). With Dr Henry Maunsell he founded the weekly *Dublin Medical Press* and edited it until 1859. Chief publications: *A Treatise on the Inflammation of the Eyeball* (1849) and *On Cataract and the Operation for its Removal by Absorption* (1851). Died Barrow-in-Furness, 21 September 1874.

JACOB, JOSHUA (1805–1877), 'White Quaker'. Born Clonmel, Co. Tipperary. Prospered as a grocer in Dublin. Disowned by Society of Friends in 1838 and formed his own society. The members wore undyed garments, hence their name. He was imprisoned for two years for contempt of court, arising out of a suit against him concerning his use of orphans' funds for his society. About 1849 he established a community at Clondalkin, Co. Dublin, whose members lived in common, abstained from meat, and rejected the use of newspapers and clocks. When it broke up he went into business again at Celbridge, Co. Kildare. Published *The Truth as it is in Jesus* (1843–1844), an account of the proceedings of the White Quakers, with prayers, hymns, and letters; also other tracts. Died in Wales, 15 February 1877.

JELLETT, MAINIE (1897–1944), artist. Born Mary Harriet Jellett at 36 Fitzwilliam Square, Dublin. Attended National College of Art 1917–1919, then moved to London with her friend EVIE

170

HONE and studied at the Westminster School under Sickert and Meninski. They went to Paris in 1920 where they worked, first at the Académie Lhote, and then as pupils of Albert Gleizes, a 'cubist integral'. She returned to Ireland in 1930 and was commissioned by the government to design murals for the Irish pavilion at the Glasgow Fair. In 1943, with Evie Hone and others, she founded the Irish Exhibition of Living Art. Examples of her austere abstract paintings are in the Municipal Gallery of Modern Art, Dublin. Died in Dublin.

JERVAS, CHARLES (*c*. 1675-1739), portrait painter. Born Shinrone, Co. Offaly. Studied painting under Kneller in London, and with the help of friends went to Italy for further training. Returned to England in 1709 and soon became fashionable as a portrait painter. Pope, Addison, SWIFT and other celebrities sat for him. He married a widow with a fortune, and entertained lavishly at his house in Hampton. Succeeded Kneller as principal painter to George I, 1723, and retained the post under George II. Died in London, 2 November 1739.

JOCELYN, ROBERT, third EARL OF RODEN (1788-1870), of 'Dolly's Brae' fame. MP Dundalk 1810-1820, then succeeded his father as earl. Created peer of UK and knight of St Patrick 1821. Became grand master of the Orange Society. On 12 July 1849 the local Orangemen gathered to celebrate the Battle of the Boyne. They paraded through a Catholic district, Dolly's Brae near Castlewellan, Co. Down, and were then entertained by Roden on his grounds at Tullymore Park. The government had dispatched troops and dragoons to the area and these escorted the Orangemen on their return, which they chose to make again through the 'Brae'. In an encounter with a gathering of Catholics, including armed Ribbonmen, six or seven Catholics were killed, many were wounded, and the Orangemen set fire to

their houses. Only one or two Orangemen were wounded seriously. A government commission was set up to investigate the affair: Roden was censured and dismissed from the magistracy. He died in Edinburgh, 20 March 1870.

JOHNSON, THOMAS (1872-1963), first parliamentary leader of the Irish Labour Party. Born in Liverpool. Left school at twelve to become a messenger-boy. At nineteen he got a job with an Irish fish merchant, and spent half the year in Liverpool and the other half at the fishing-villages of Kinsale, Co. Cork, and Dunmore East, Co. Waterford. In 1900 he obtained a post as a commercial traveller in Belfast and began his connection with the labour movement. Vice-president Irish Trade Union Congress 1913, president 1916. Joint secretary of the Mansion House conference that organised the anti-conscription movement, and helped to organise an anti-conscription strike in 1918. A member of the small group that drafted the Democratic Programme of the First Dáil. Secretary Irish Trade Union Congress 1920-1928. TD Co. Dublin 1922-1927, and leader of the Parliamentary Labour Party until 1928. Senator 1928-1936; foundation member of the Labour Court 1946-1956. Died in Dublin in January 1963.

JOHNSON, SIR WILLIAM (1715-1774), pioneer and soldier. Born Co. Meath. The family emigrated to America in 1737, and he became an Indian trader in the Mohawk valley, now in New York State. By his fairness and industry he won the friendship of the Indians, and was called their 'benevolent dictator'. During the Anglo-French wars his influence prevented the 'Six Nations' from going over to the French. He was given 'sole management and direction of the Six Nations', and made a major-general in 1755. That year he defeated the French at Lake George and was rewarded with a grant of £5,000 and a baronetcy. For his services against the French in Canada in

1760 he was granted 100,000 acres on the north bank of the Mohawk river. Here he built himself a new house, called Johnson Hall, where he kept open house, entertaining in princely style. He induced a large number of Irishmen to settle in the district, and opened it up for the development of agriculture. His first wife died young and he then took to his house Molly Brant, sister of Joseph Brant, a Mohawk war chief, who became known as the 'Indian Lady Johnson'. In his will he styled their offspring his 'eight natural children'. He died suddenly in July 1774 after delivering an address to the Council of the Six Nations.

JOHNSTON, ANNA. See under CARBERY, ETHNA.

JOHNSTON, FRANCIS (1760–1829), architect. Son of William Johnston, architect, of Armagh. After practising in Armagh for some years, he moved to Dublin about 1793 and became architect and inspector of civil buildings to the Board of Works. He rebuilt the House of Commons, designed St George's Church, the cash office of the Bank of Ireland, the Chapel Royal in Dublin Castle, and the GPO, O'Connell Street. Mainly through his efforts the Royal Hibernian Academy of Painting, Sculpture and Architecture was incorporated in 1823, and he was president for many years. He provided the academy buildings in Lower Abbey Street at a cost of £14,000 paid out of his own pocket, and granted the academy a lease in perpetuity. The buildings were destroyed during the 1916 Rising. Died Dublin on 14 March 1829.

JOHNSTON, JOSEPH (1890–1972), professor of economics. Born Castlecaulfield, Co. Tyrone. Educated in Dungannon, TCD, and Lincoln College, Oxford, graduating in classics and ancient history. Elected to Albert Cahn Fellowship 1914 and spent a year travelling and studying social and economic phenomena in India,

America, Java, China, and Japan. Returning to TCD he lectured first in ancient history and then turned to economics. Rockefeller Fellow for Economic Research in Europe 1928–1929; professor of applied economics at TCD, 1939, a chair created specially for him; senator, 1938–1943, 1944–1948, 1951–1954. Served on many government commissions. During his earlier years he managed small farms in Meath and Louth. One of the first in the country to specialise in agricultural economics. A prolific writer, he published his first book, *Civil War in Ulster*, in 1914. His subsequent writings were mainly concerned with economics. *Berkeley's Querist in Historical Perspective* (1970) gained him the degree of D.Litt. from TCD. Died in Dublin in August 1972.

JOHNSTON, (WILLIAM) DENIS (1901–1984), playwright. Born in Dublin on 18 June 1901, son of William Johnston, later a judge of the Supreme Court, and educated at St Andrew's, Dublin, Merchiston School, Edinburgh, and Cambridge University, where he studied law. He was called to the bar in Dublin, Belfast and London and practised for ten years. When his first play, *Shadowdance*, was rejected by the Abbey Theatre with the words 'The Old Lady says No' written on the title page, he retitled it *The Old Lady Says 'No'* and it was successfully produced at the Gate in 1928 by MAC LIAMMÓIR and EDWARDS. *The Moon in the Yellow River* was produced at the Abbey in 1931 to a mixed reception. In the mid-1930s he joined the BBC in Belfast as a script-writer and in 1936 became a drama producer in London for the new BBC television service. During the Second World War he was a war correspondent for BBC radio in north Africa, Italy, the Balkans and Germany, and received the OBE for his services. *Nine Rivers to Jordan* (1953) is an account of his wartime experiences. In 1950 he embarked on a new career as professor in American universities, teaching at Mount Holyoke, Amherst and Smith and later becoming visiting professor in California and New York. Distinctions included a Guggenheim fellowship (1955), Allied Irish Banks award for literature (1977), and an honorary doctorate from NUU (1979). In all, he had nine plays produced, five at the Gate and four at the Abbey. They owed nothing to any school, and their originality in conception and outlook baffled many audiences. *In Search of Swift* (1959) and *The Brazen Head* (1977), an autobiography, are equally Johnstonian. He died in Ballybrack, Co. Dublin, on 8 August 1984, survived by his first wife, SHELAH RICHARDS, three sons, and a daughter, the novelist Jennifer Johnston. His second wife, Betty Chancellor, had predeceased him.

JOLY, CHARLES JASPER (1864–1906), astronomer. Born St Catherine's Rectory, Tullamore, Co. Offaly, 27 June 1864. Educated Galway grammar school and TCD, where he took fellowship in 1894. Appointed astronomer-royal for Ireland at Dunsink 1897. Edited *Quaternions* of ROWAN HAMILTON (1899–1901). Accompanied expedition to Spain in 1900 to view eclipse. MRIA, and elected FRS 1904. Published *Manual of Quaternions* (1905). Died at Dunsink, 4 January 1906.

JOLY, JASPER ROBERT (1819–1892), book collector. Born Clonsast, Co. Offaly, 26 May 1819. Educated at home, and entered TCD at thirteen, graduating 1837; LL.D. 1857. Called to the bar but never practised. Appointed vicar-general of Diocese of Tuam, an office abolished by the Irish Church Act (1869). Received an annuity of £106 in compensation. A lover and collector of books from childhood, in 1863 he donated a collection of 23,000 printed volumes and unbound papers and prints to the RDS, to be transferred to a national library when such was established. It is now in the National Library, its chief glory. Particularly valuable are the Napoleonic literature and the books on Irish history, topography, and biography. He died in Dublin, Christmas Day 1892. Buried Clonbulloge, Co. Offaly.

JOLY, JOHN (1857–1933), engineer, geologist, and physicist. Born Hollywood, Co. Offaly, on 1 November 1857. Educated Rathmines School and TCD. Studied modern literature and engineering, and on graduation in 1883 secured a teaching post in the school of engineering; professor of geology 1897–1933. He maintained a constant flow of inventions, including a photometer, and a steam calorimeter. In 1899 he measured the age of the oceans by estimating the rate of deposit of sodium, and also devised a method of estimating the age of rocks. He carried out pioneer work on the cooling of the earth, on radium extraction, and on the radium treatment for cancer. Elected FRS in 1892 and received many other distinctions from learned bodies. Died in Dublin on 8 December 1933.

JONES, FREDERICK EDWARD (1759–1834), theatre manager. Born Vesington, Co. Meath. Educated TCD. He was a man of wealth and position and spent some time on the Continent as the associate of people of rank. In 1796 he leased Crow Street Theatre from RICHARD DALY on very onerous terms. He spent £1,200 on it, but was soon obliged to close down because of the disturbed state of the country. In 1808 he sold a quarter of his shares for £10,000, but Crampton, who had bought one-eighth and taken over the management, proved so incompetent that Jones had to resume control. Riots and disturbances between 1814 and 1819, and the refusal of a patent in 1819, led to his retirement. In his heyday he was a member of Daly's, the most aristocratic club in Ireland, and lived in magnificent style in a house in Fortick's Grove, rented from Lord Mountjoy at £1,000 a year and called Clonliffe House. Jones's Road is called after him. He died in retirement.

JONES, HENRY (1721–1770), poet and playwright. Born at Beaulieu, near

Drogheda, Co. Louth. Apprenticed to a bricklayer but contrived to study privately. Complimentary verses to Drogheda Corporation and lines *On Mr Pope's Death* attracted the attention of Lord Chief Justice Singleton of Beaulieu. In 1745, while working on repairs to the Parliament House in Dublin, Jones celebrated the arrival of Lord Chesterfield as lord lieutenant of Ireland in a poem presented to Chesterfield by Singleton. Chesterfield rewarded the poet liberally, and at his request Jones followed him to England in 1748. With his assistance Jones published *Poems on Several Occasions* (1749). His tragedy *The Earl of Essex*, produced at Covent Garden 1753 with SPRANGER BARRY in the lead, was highly successful, as were subsequent plays. He began to lead a dissipated life and was eventually rejected by his patron. In April 1770, while intoxicated, he was run over by a wagon in St Martin's Lane, London, and died soon after in the parish workhouse.

JONES, HENRY MACNAUGHTEN (1845-1918), surgeon. Born Cork. Educated Queen's College, Cork, and became professor of midwifery. In 1868 he founded Cork Ophthalmic Hospital and was first physician there. With Dr Cummins he founded Cork Maternity Hospital in 1872. Had a large part in founding the County and City of Cork Hospital (now Victoria Hospital) in 1874. He moved to London in 1883. His *Manual of Diseases of Women* (1884) went into nine editions. He published several volumes of verse privately. Died at Barnet, near London.

JONES, JOHN EDWARD (1806-1862), sculptor. Born Dublin on 2 May 1806. Trained as a civil engineer under Nimmo. After working in Ireland he settled in London, and in 1840 began to practise there as a sculptor. Success came quickly. Exhibited at the RA each year from 1844 and also at the RHA. In great demand for portrait busts; his sitters included Queen Victoria, Prince Albert, Wellington, and O'CONNELL. Died near

Finglas, Co. Dublin, while on a visit, on 25 July 1862.

JONES, SIR THOMAS ALFRED (*c.* 1823-1893), portrait painter. Of unknown parentage, was found and reared by the charitable Archdale family of Kildare Place, Dublin. He began to study art at the RDS school at ten, then entered TCD in 1842. He left without taking a degree, and spent the years 1846-1849 in travel on the Continent. In 1849 he returned to Dublin, began to practise as a portrait painter, and became a regular exhibitor at the RHA. Elected RHA 1860, president 1869. Knighted by the lord lieutenant, the Duke of Marlborough, 1880, the first president of the academy to be so honoured. He had great success as a portrait painter, and also worked hard to advance the interests of the academy. Died at his house, 41 Morehampton Road, Dublin, 10 May 1893.

JORDAN, DOROTHY (1761-1816), actress. Born near Waterford, the illegitimate daughter of an actress, Grace Phillips, and a gentleman called Francis Bland. In 1777 she was assistant to a milliner in Dame Street, Dublin, and in 1779 she made her first recorded appearance on the stage at Crow Street Theatre. She later played in Cork and Waterford. She was seduced by her manager, Richard Daly, and fled to England with her mother and sister. Taking the name Mrs Jordan, she joined a company playing the Yorkshire circuit. In 1785 she went to Drury Lane Theatre, London, and quickly won a great name in comedy, especially 'breeches parts'. Hazlitt described her as 'all exuberance and grace, a child of nature whose voice was cordial to the heart,' and she was also highly praised by Leigh Hunt, Lamb, Byron, and Sir Joshua Reynolds. She remained at Drury Lane until 1809 and then went to Covent Garden, retiring from the stage in 1815. She had a daughter by her first manager, Daly, and then bore four children to Richard (afterwards Sir

Richard) Ford. In 1790 she became mistress of the Duke of Clarence, afterwards King William IV, and bore him five sons and five daughters, all of whom took the name Fitzclarence. The duke gave her an allowance of £1,000 a year, and when he proposed to reduce it to £500 she sent him the bottom part of a playbill reading 'No money returned after the rising of the curtain.' They were separated in 1811, and it appears that the duke made reasonable provision for her and her children. Nevertheless her later years were overshadowed by money troubles. She made a great deal of money from her acting, but said herself that most of it went to support her mother and family. In August 1815 she went to France and settled secretly in a large and dilapidated house at St Cloud. She died there on 3 July 1816 and was buried in the cemetery of St Cloud.

JOY, FRANCIS (c. 1697–1790), printer and papermaker. Born Belfast. Described by R. R. MADDEN as 'a conveyancer and notary public who was given a printing works to pay off a debt.' He founded the Belfast *News Letter*, the oldest newspaper in Ireland, in 1737. He founded a paper mill at Randalstown, Co. Antrim, the first in Ireland. He retired in his fifties 'upon an easy fortune'. Died Randalstown in June 1790.

JOY, GEORGE W. (1844–1925), painter. Born in Dublin on 7 July 1844, son of a physician and grand-nephew of Chief Baron Joy, a distinguished lawyer. He was educated at Harrow and intended for a career in the British army but an injury to his foot ended that ambition. He was sent to Kensington Art School, won many prizes and went on to the Royal Academy schools, studying under Millais, Leighton, and Watts. He spent some time in the Paris studio of Jalabert, a pupil of Delaroche, and became a successful exhibitor at the RA. His 'St Joan' was bought by the French government and is now in the museum at Rouen. A very popular painting showed the last moments of General Gordon; prints sold widely, and Queen Victoria showed her pleasure by commissioning a portrait of Princess Alice. His boyhood studies of Nelson and Wellington endeared him to the Victorian public. The New London Museum houses 'The Bayswater Omnibus', which drew from a French critic the tribute, '*M. Joy est le Pickwick de la palette*,' in admiration of its delineation of character. Joy proclaimed his Irish identity by representing Ireland on six occasions at Wimbledon and Bisley as a rifleman from the Artists' Corps. He died in 1925 at Purbrook in Hampshire.

JOYCE, JAMES AUGUSTINE (1882–1941), poet, novelist, and playwright. Born at 41 Brighton Square, Dublin, on 2 February 1882, the son of John Stanislaus Joyce, an official in the Tax Office. He was sent at six as a boarder to Clongowes Wood, a Jesuit foundation, but his father lost his post and James had to leave Clongowes because of straitened family finances. He then went to Belvedere College and University College, where he studied languages and read deeply in St Thomas Aquinas and Aristotle. His first published work, an essay on Ibsen, appeared in the *Fortnightly Review* in April 1900. On graduating in 1902 he went to Paris on borrowed money, but with neither position nor regular income came near to destitution. In 1903 the death of his mother brought him back to Dublin. In 1904 he entered a Feis Cheoil competition but refused to sing at sight. He met OLIVER ST JOHN GOGARTY, but apart from occasional teaching failed to find a job. In 1904 he met and fell in love with a Galway woman, Nora Barnacle, and left with her for Zürich, later living in Pola and Trieste, where he existed by teaching English in the Berlitz school. In 1909 he returned to Dublin on a short visit and ventured into business, opening the Volta cinema in Mary Street. This failed, and his next visit to Dublin was in 1912 to arrange for publication of his book of short stories, *Dubliners*; but disagreement with his publishers thwarted that project also, and he returned to Trieste, never to visit Dublin again. He spent the greater part of the war years 1914-1918 in Zürich. While still at college he had resolved to become a writer, but without inherited wealth he found great difficulty in supporting his family. His financial difficulties were relieved by a grant from the Royal Literary Fund, then by an allowance from Mrs McCormick, daughter of J. D. Rockefeller, and finally, and most generously of all, by an allowance from Miss Harriet Weaver, editor of the *Egoist*. In 1904 he had begun writing a novel, *Stephen Hero*, mainly autobiographical. Deciding that it lacked form, he rewrote it under the title *Portrait of the Artist as a Young Man*. This, his first full-length work, was published in the USA in 1916. In it he wrote: 'I go to forge in the smithy of my soul the uncreated conscience of my race.' The favourable reception accorded to it, and to *Dubliners*, published in 1914, encouraged Joyce to proceed with his major project, *Ulysses*. His eyes had begun to trouble him in 1917, and between then and 1930 he endured twenty-five operations in all for iritis, glaucoma, and cataract, being completely blind for short periods. He showed great fortitude under this trial and pressed on with his writing. In 1920 he went to Paris at the invitation of Ezra Pound and in 1922 his masterpiece, *Ulysses*, was published there by Sylvia Beach, owner of the bookshop 'Shakespeare and Company'. It was banned in the USA and Britain for some years, but by 1936 was freely available in both countries. Curiously, it was never banned in Ireland. *Ulysses* brought international fame to Joyce and has had great influence on later writers. It related the incidents of one day in Dublin, 'Bloomsday', 16 June 1904, when Leopold Bloom left his house in the morning and, after a series of misadventures, returned to his wife, Molly, late that night. Joyce familiarised his readers with the 'stream of consciousness' technique, which he claimed to have borrowed from a forgotten French writer, Édouard Dujardin (1861-1949). The technique is at least as old as the novel form, but nobody before Joyce had used it so continuously. *Ulysses* owes its strength to its ironic humour, its mastery of language and its marvellous portrayal of character rather than to any literary technical device. No work of this century has received so much continuous notice as *Ulysses*. It has been praised extravagantly, condemned, translated into many languages, and been the subject of countless critical studies. Nor is interest in it on the wane. It has a vigour and a creative and sustained energy that must be accounted the work of a genius. Joyce immortalised Dublin in it, the shabby-genteel, down-at-heel, rakish Dublin of the early 1900s, a Dublin that he had never really left. In Paris he worked for seventeen years on the book he himself regarded as his magnum opus, *Finnegans Wake*, published in 1939, a treasure of curious scholarship, a philological *divertissement*, and a work for the studious minority. It begins with the end of a sentence left unfinished on the last page, to show that Joyce regarded history as a cycle. Ostensibly the story of a Chapelizod publican, Mr Humphrey Chimpden Earwicker, his wife Mrs Anna Livia, and their three children, Shem, Shaun, and Isobel, it is written in an amalgam of languages, living and dead, into which are packed thousands of allusions, literary and historical. Joyce expected his readers to spend their lives on this book, and a small army of American scholars have taken him at his word. His remaining works were *Exiles*, a play (1918), *Pomes Pennyeach*, published in Paris in 1927, and an early volume of poems, *Chamber Music* (1907). The Joyces had two children, George and Lucia; Joyce married Nora in 1931. In 1940 he took his family back to Zürich, where he died on 13 January 1941 and where he is buried.

JOYCE, PATRICK WESTON (1827-1914), historian and music collector.

Born near Glenosheen, Co. Limerick, and educated in local hedge schools. He became a teacher and principal of the Model School, Clonmel. In 1856 he was one of fifteen teachers selected and trained to reorganise the national school system. Meanwhile he studied at TCD and graduated BA 1861, MA 1864. Principal, Training College, Marlborough Street, Dublin, 1874–1893. Member, Society for the Preservation of the Irish Language, and published an Irish grammar 1878. Wrote a number of books of value to teachers, and published many history books, including *Origin and History of Irish Names of Places* (1869), *Old Celtic Romances* (1879), *A Child's History of Ireland* (1898), *A Social History of Ancient Ireland* (1903), and *English as we Speak it in Ireland* (1910). He was a noted collector of Irish music and acted as adjudicator at the first Oireachtas organised by the Gaelic League. MRIA, and president, Royal Society of Antiquaries, 1906. Died at his Rathmines, Dublin, home in November 1914.

JOYCE, ROBERT DWYER (1830–1883), physician and songwriter. Born in Glenosheen, Co. Limerick. Educated in local hedge schools. Trained as a teacher and succeeded his brother, PATRICK WESTON JOYCE, as principal of Clonmel Model School. Resigned 1857 and studied medicine at Queen's College, Cork, and graduated in 1865. To earn his college fees he contributed poems, stories and articles to the *Nation, Harp,* etc. He published *Ballads, Romances and Songs* in 1861. Shortly after completing his medical studies he became professor of English literature in the Catholic University, Dublin, and MRIA. Disappointed that the Fenian rising failed to eventuate in 1865, he emigrated to the USA in 1866. Settled in Boston, continued to publish poetry and prose with much success, and became closely associated with the Fenian movement in the USA. Also lectured in Harvard Medical School. Returned to Ireland in September 1883; died in Dublin the following month.

JOYCE, WILLIAM (*c.* 1906–1946), 'Lord Haw-Haw'. Born in Brooklyn, USA, of Irish father and English mother. Brought to Galway in 1914 and educated at St Ignatius' Jesuit College. The family emigrated to England in 1922. In 1933 he joined Sir Oswald Mosley's British Union of Fascists. Expelled from it in 1937, and founded his own British National Socialist Party, which supported Hitler. He went to Germany before the outbreak of the Second World War. From September 1939 to April 1945 he broadcast Nazi propaganda from Radio Hamburg with the call-sign, 'Germany calling, Germany calling'. His upper-class British accent earned him the nickname 'Lord Haw-Haw'. Goebbels, Hitler's propaganda minister, made special arrangements for his escape at the end of the war, but he was captured by British officers at Flensburg, despite a disguise: his distinctive voice betrayed him. He was convicted of treason at the Old Bailey, London, and hanged in Wandsworth jail, 3 January 1946. His defence was his American birth; the prosecution relied on his British passport, valid until July 1940, which, it was alleged, he had obtained in the 1930s by falsely claiming to have been born in Galway. He was reburied in Galway, November 1976.

JUDGE, PETER (1889–1947), actor, under the stage-name F. J. McCormick. Born at Skerries, Co. Dublin. After a brief civil service career in Dublin and London, during which he acted in amateur dramatic societies, he became a member of the Abbey Theatre Company in 1918. During his early acting career in Dublin he was tutored by Frank Fay, brother of WILLIAM FAY. McCormick acted in over five hundred plays at the Abbey, and was particularly noted for his performances in plays by SEÁN O'CASEY. He toured America five times, and played three major film roles, the last being in *Odd Man Out* (1947). Died in April 1947.

K

KANE, SIR ROBERT JOHN (1809-1890), scientist. Born in Dublin in September 1809. Educated at TCD. Appointed professor of chemistry, Apothecaries' Hall, Dublin, 1831. Published *Elements of Practical Pharmacy* (1831). Founded the *Dublin Journal of Medical Science* in 1832. Professor of natural philosophy, RDS, 1834. Editor of the *Philosophical Magazine*, 1840; published *Elements of Chemistry* 1841. Delivered a course of lectures on the development of industries in Ireland in 1843, published as *Industrial Resources of Ireland* (1844). In 1846, at his suggestion, the government established, at St Stephen's Green, a Museum of Irish Industry, of which he became director. Appointed president of Queen's College, Cork, 1845 (opened in 1849); spent some time on the Continent studying methods of university education. Member of the Commission appointed in 1845 to inquire into the potato blight and the relief of Irish distress. Knighted in 1846; FRS 1849. Appointed Commissioner of National Education in 1873, when he resigned his post at Queen's College. President RIA 1877. In 1880 he was made vice-chancellor of the newly created Royal University of Ireland. Died in Dublin on 16 February 1890.

KAVANAGH, ARTHUR MAC-MORROUGH (1831-1889), landlord and MP. Born Borris House, Co. Carlow, 25 March 1831. Educated privately. He was born severely handicapped, with only rudimentary arms and legs but, showing great resolution, he learned to ride, shoot, and fish, and became a fair painter using the stumps of his arms with extraordinary dexterity. He rode to hounds strapped to a chair saddle and, despite the dangers of a fall, took fences boldly. With his eldest brother and a tutor he travelled to India through Russia and Persia (Iran), and showed prowess in tiger hunting. He returned to Ireland in 1853, succeeded to the family estates that year, and married a cousin from Termonfeckin, Co. Louth, in 1855. SIR CHARLES RUSSELL called him 'a landlord of landlords'. He rebuilt the villages of Borris and Ballyragget, subsidised and managed the railways from Borris to Bagenalstown (Muine Bheag) and, though a Protestant, had New Ross poorhouse provided with a Catholic chapel, the first of its kind in Ireland. Conservative MP for Co. Wexford 1866-1868 and for Co. Carlow 1868-1880. An enthusiastic and experienced yachtsman, in 1865 he published *The Cruise of the RYS Eva*, an account of a cruise off the coast of Albania. Died at his London town house in Chelsea, 25 December 1889. Buried in Borris.

KAVANAGH, MUIRIS 'KRUGER' (1894-1971), innkeeper. Born in Dún Chaoin in the Kerry Gaeltacht. At the local school he was leader of the Boer faction and got the nickname 'Kruger' by which he was known for the rest of his life. He emigrated to America in 1913 and attended night school for three years and Fordham University briefly. He became publicity manager for Metro-Goldwyn-Mayer and was well known to impresarios Samuel Goldwyn and Adolph Zukor as well as film stars Al Jolson and Mae West. He toured the USA as advance representative for tenor Walter Scanlan, and he selected girls to dance for the Ziegfeld Follies. When ÉAMON DE VALERA visited the USA, Kavanagh was one of his bodyguards. In 1920 he returned to Ireland and opened

178

a guest-house in Dún Chaoin. Scholars, politicians, writers, artists and actors became habitués of 'Kruger's'; BRENDAN BEHAN wrote a song to celebrate the granting of his publican's licence. He was a natural host and innkeeper and a leader in promoting the welfare of his native district. He died on 15 April 1971, survived by his wife, Cáit.

KAVANAGH, PATRICK (1904–1967), poet. Born Iniskeen, Co. Monaghan, 21 October 1904, and educated locally. He worked on his father's small farm and for a time as a shoemaker. In 1938 he published his first book, *Ploughman and Other Poems*, and *The Green Fool*, which he later described as a 'stage-Irish autobiography'. The following year he went to Dublin and supported himself precariously as a literary journalist, contributing articles and poems to *The Bell, Envoy,* and the *Dublin Magazine.* As 'Piers Plowman' he wrote film criticism for the *Irish Press.* Through his friendship with John Betjeman, then British press attaché in Dublin, he obtained some work with the BBC. *The Great Hunger,* a long poem with a harsh view of rural life, appeared in 1942. A further collection of poems, *A Soul for Sale* (1947), was followed by a novel, *Tarry Flynn* (1948). In 1952 with his brother Peter he published *Kavanagh's Weekly,* a journal of politics and literature, which survived for sixteen issues. The same year the *Leader,* a weekly paper, published a profile of him in a series on notable contemporaries, and he sued for libel. After a ferocious cross-examination by J. A. COSTELLO, former Taoiseach, he agreed to a settlement. A long illness followed. In 1957 Costello secured for him a post as lecturer in extramural studies in UCD and he began to write again. 'Come Dance with Kitty Stobling' and other poems appeared in 1960, and a short *Self-Portrait* in 1962. With the appearance of his *Collected Poems* (1964), his full stature as a poet became recognised outside Ireland. *Collected Pruse* [*sic*] appeared in 1967. He died in Dublin, 30 November 1967, survived by his wife,

Kathleen Barry Maloney, whom he married the previous April. A novel, *By Night Understood,* was published posthumously in 1977.

KEAN, CHARLES JOHN (1811–1868), actor, second son of Edmund Kean. Born Waterford, 18 January 1811. Educated at Eton College. When he was sixteen his father's marriage broke up, he was withdrawn from Eton, and after a quarrel with his father he went on the stage. His first engagement was at Drury Lane for three years at a salary rising from ten to twelve pounds per week. In 1828 he was reconciled with his father and they acted together for a season. He made a successful tour in America in 1830 and in 1833 played Iago at Drury Lane to his father's Othello. His father died shortly after. Further successful American tours followed, and then in 1850 he took over management of the Princess's Theatre in London with Robert Keeley, becoming sole manager in 1851. Here he embarked on a series of spectacular revivals. After a heavy loss in 1858 he retired from management the following year. A public banquet was held in his honour in 1859 and in 1862 he was presented with a silver vase said to be worth £2,000. He had married an Irish actress, Ellen Tree, in Dublin in January 1842 and they went on a world tour in 1863. Made his last appearance on the stage at Liverpool, May 1867. Died at Queensborough Terrace, Chelsea, 22 January 1868.

KEARNEY, PEADAR (1883–1942), author of the national anthem. Born in Dublin, an uncle of BRENDAN BEHAN; grew up in the Dolphin's Barn area. Educated at Model School, Schoolhouse Lane, and Marino CBS. Left school at fourteen to work in a bicycle puncture mending business during the day; in the evenings he took suppers to the performers in the Gaiety Theatre. Worked in a variety of odd jobs for three years, then became a house painter and joined their union. Joined the Gaelic League 1901; became a member of the IRB in

1903. In 1907 he wrote the words of 'A Soldier's Song', and a friend, Patrick Heeney, wrote the music. It was published by BULMER HOBSON in *Irish Freedom* in 1912. It became the marching-song of the Irish Volunteers, and in 1926 the national anthem. He wrote other popular songs, including 'The Tri-Coloured Ribbon' and 'Down by the Glenside'. Connected with the Abbey Theatre as an odd-job man and small-parts actor, and when the company toured England in March 1916 he went with them as property man. Returned to Ireland at Easter and fought in the Rising, at Jacob's factory. Arrested in 1920 and interned for twelve months. On his release he returned to his house-painting employment. Died at his home in Inchicore, Dublin, in November 1942.

KEATING, GEOFFREY. See under CÉITINN, SEATHRÚN.

KEATING, SEÁN (1889–1977), painter. Born in Limerick on 29 September 1889 and educated at St Munchin's College, Limerick, and the Limerick Municipal School of Art. At twenty he won a scholarship to the Metropolitan School of Art, Dublin, where he won the Taylor Scholarship. He then spent four years in the Aran Islands, where, he said, he found the Ireland he could paint. He went to London and studied under SIR WILLIAM ORPEN for some years. He then returned to Ireland, settled in a house in the Dublin mountains and later moved to a house in Ballyboden that he designed himself. He was elected to the RHA 1923 and was president 1949–1962. He first exhibited at the RHA in 1914 and showed every year for sixty-one years. He was professor of painting in the National College of Art for about twenty years. He made many visits to the USA and in 1939 he painted a large canvas for the New York World's Fair. In 1961 he was commissioned by the Government to execute a mural for the main hall of the International Labour Office in Geneva. Freeman of the city of Limerick 1948. Over a long period he spent half of every year in Aran, and his fine draughtsmanship is seen in his portraits of Aran people. He was a traditionalist and disliked modern trends. He died in a Dublin hospital on 21 December 1977.

KELLY, CHARLES E. (1902–1981), artist and cartoonist. Born in Dublin and joined the civil service, serving in the Department of Education. In 1926 he joined THOMAS COLLINS in editing *Dublin Opinion*, a national humorous monthly, and contributed cartoons signed 'CEK'. He was appointed deputy director of Radio Éireann 1942 and director 1948–1952, when he was appointed director of savings. He was a well-known water-colourist. In 1979 he received an honorary doctorate from NUI. He died on 20 January 1981, survived by his second wife (his first wife died in 1965), three sons and three daughters. After forty-two years, *Dublin Opinion* was voluntarily wound up by its editors in 1968 but was revived in 1987 and continues the founders' tradition of gentle humour.

KELLY, GEORGE (1688–1762), Jacobite. Born in Connacht. Educated at TCD and took deacon's orders. About 1718, after preaching a sermon in Dublin in support of the 'Old Pretender', he was threatened with prosecution and forced to fly to Paris. There, under the alias James Johnson, he became involved with John Law's Mississippi Scheme and acted as secretary to Atterbury in the latter's correspondence with the 'Old Pretender'. Went to London in 1722 and was arrested on a charge of treason. His defence was printed and went into four editions. In October 1736 he escaped to France from the Tower, and in Paris rejoined Jacobite circles. Entered Prince Charles Edward's service, one of the seven companions who sailed with him from Nantes to Eriskay in June 1745, and carried messages between the Jacobites in the field and sympathisers in Paris.

After Culloden and the Prince's escape, Kelly rejoined him in Paris and in 1747 became his only secretary. Translated Castelnan's *Memoirs of the English Affairs* (1724), and Morabin's *The History of Cicero's Banishment* (1725). Died Rome.

KELLY, HUGH (1739–1778), playwright and journalist. Born in Killarney, Co. Kerry, and brought up in Dublin where his father opened a public house. He served his apprenticeship as a staymaker, moved to London at twenty-one and became a successful hack writer, editing in succession the *Court Magazine*, the *Ladies' Museum* and the *Public Ledger*. In 1767 he published a sentimental novel, *The History of a Magdalen*. His first play, *False Delicacy*, produced by Garrick in 1768 at Drury Lane, was a great success and was translated into French, German, and Portuguese. Later plays were less successful. He quarrelled with GOLDSMITH but wept over his grave. He died at thirty-eight, possibly from drink.

KELLY, MARY EVA. See under 'EVA' OF THE 'NATION'.

KELLY, MICHAEL (1764–1826), actor, singer, and composer. Born in Dublin. Appeared on the Dublin stage at an early age. In 1779 he sailed for Italy for further training. Principal tenor at Vienna 1783–1787. He then went to England and appeared successfully in opera at Drury Lane Theatre and at many concerts in London and the provinces. He became musical director at Drury Lane and in 1797 began a long and successful series of musical settings of plays. About 1802 he opened a shop for his own compositions, but this venture into business led to his bankruptcy in 1811. He appeared for the last time at Drury Lane on 17 June 1808, and the last time in Dublin on 5 September 1811. After years of suffering from gout he died at Margate, 9 October 1826.

KELLY, OISÍN (1915–1981), sculptor. Born in Dublin on 17 May 1915 and educated at St James's National School,

Mountjoy School, TCD, and at Goethe University, Frankfurt. Originally Austin Ernest, he was called Oisín when he went to school. He attended the National College of Art as a schoolboy and studied intermittently there for thirty years; he also spent a year studying under Henry Moore at Chelsea Polytechnic, London. He became a teacher but gave it up in 1966 to become a full-time artist with the advent of the Kilkenny Design Workshops, where he worked twice a week on designs suitable for commercial reproduction. Apart from church work, he received few commissions until the 1970s. His best-known sculptures are 'The Children of Lir' in the Garden of Remembrance and his statue of JIM LARKIN in O'Connell Street, Dublin. He died on 12 October 1981 at his home near Tallaght, Co. Dublin. In 1942 he married Ruth Olive Gwynn who died early in 1981. They had seven children, one of whom died as a teenager.

KELLY, SÉAMUS (1912–1979), journalist. Born in Belfast in August 1912 and educated at St Mary's CBS and QUB, where he was a boxing champion. He then worked his way through UCC, supporting himself by part-time journalism and canvassing for the ESB. He joined the army in 1940 and was commissioned lieutenant on the Intelligence Staff in September 1941. In November 1945 R. M. SMYLLIE engaged him as drama critic of the *Irish Times* in succession to John Weldon (BRINSLEY MACNAMARA). He was also ballet critic. He left the army in 1946 to become public relations officer for Aer Lingus. In August 1949, again at Smyllie's request, he became 'Quidnunc' of 'An Irishman's Diary', the former identity of PATRICK CAMPBELL, while remaining as drama and ballet critic. He continued in this dual capacity for nearly thirty years, an astonishing performance, especially in the demanding job of writing a daily column. He had a break in 1954 when he took a seven-month sabbatical to play the part of Flask, the third mate, in John

Huston's film of Melville's *Moby Dick*. He refused further offers of film work and returned to the *Irish Times*. As drama and ballet critic he was guest contributor to *The Times, Observer, New York Times* and other prestigious newspapers and journals. His interests, reflected in his column, included sailing in Dublin Bay, Spain, and Irish inland waterways. He died in Dublin on 10 June 1979, survived by his wife, Aileen, two sons and a daughter.

KELLY-ROGERS, CAPTAIN J. C. (1905–1981), aviation pioneer. Born in Dún Laoghaire, Co. Dublin, in 1905 and educated at Presentation College, Glasthule, at Clongowes Wood College and on the British cadet training ship *Conway*. Joined the Royal Naval Reserve as midshipman 1921. Became a pilot in the RAF 1927; joined Imperial Airways (later BOAC, now British Airways) 1935. In 1938 he conducted the first flight refuelling tests and used the system when commanding the first British transatlantic air-mail flight. During the Second World War he commanded the aircraft used by Winston Churchill on his transatlantic journeys. Awarded OBE 1941. Chief north Atlantic pilot for BOAC that year and in 1946 inaugurated the first British land-plane service between London and New York. Joined Aer Lingus as technical manager 1947, and became deputy manager 1952; retired 1965. He was mainly responsible for establishing the Irish Aviation Museum, of which he was honorary curator. He was a freeman of the city of London and a fellow of the Royal Aeronautical Society. Died in Dublin on 29 January 1981, survived by his wife, son and daughter.

KELVIN, WILLIAM THOMSON (1824–1907), scientist and inventor. Born on 26 June 1824, College Square East, Belfast. He entered Glasgow University, where his father had become professor of mathematics, at eleven, left for Peterhouse, Cambridge, at seventeen, and graduated 'second wrangler' (first-class honours) in 1845. He accepted the chair of natural philosophy at Glasgow in 1846 and held it for fifty-three years. His principal scientific achievement was the discovery of the second law of thermodynamics, but his work on electric currents is more widely known. This work, of great value in submarine telegraphy, ensured the success of the Atlantic cables and earned him a knighthood in 1866. A keen yachtsman, he devised tide gauges and predictors, invented depth-sounding apparatus, and reconstructed the mariner's compass. He invented numerous instruments for measuring electricity and published more than three hundred papers on aspects of physical science. Created Baron Kelvin in 1892; received Order of Merit 1902. His golden jubilee as professor was celebrated by scientists from all over the world. An exhibition of his inventions was held as part of the celebrations. Died at his house near Largs in Scotland on 17 December 1907. Buried in Westminster Abbey.

KENDRICK, MATTHEW (*c.* 1797–1874), marine painter. Born in Dublin and went to sea as a young man. On his return to Dublin his fine seamanship brought him employment as sailing master in yacht races in Dublin Bay. In 1825 he entered the Dublin Society's school to study painting. He first exhibited at the RHA in 1827 and he was a constant contributor of marine paintings and drawings until 1872. Elected RHA 1850, and was keeper from 1850 to 1866. He also exhibited at the RA and the Society of British Artists. In 1872 he became paralysed in the right hand and moved to London, where he died 1 November 1874.

KENEALY, EDWARD VAUGHAN (1819–1880), barrister and writer. Born Cork, 2 July 1819. Educated TCD. Called to the bar 1840 and to English bar 1847, became QC and bencher, Gray's Inn, 1868. Imprisoned for a month in 1850 for cruelty to his natural son, aged six. Appeared in several famous criminal cases. Became leading counsel for Orton, the Tichborne claimant, in 1873, and protracted the trial inordinately by long and violent addresses. Started a scurrilous paper, the *Englishman*, which gained wide circulation, to plead Orton's case. This, with his conduct at the trial, brought his disbenchment and disbarment in 1874. He then founded the Magna Carta Association and stumped the country to avenge the grievances of himself and his client. Elected MP for Stoke 1875 but lost his seat 1880. A voluminous writer of prose and verse, and claimed to have translated from eleven languages. Died 6 Tavistock Square, London, 16 April 1880.

KENNEDY, HUGH (1879–1936), first Chief Justice of the Irish Free State. Born in Dublin on 11 July 1879. He was educated privately and at University College, where he founded the student magazine *St Stephen's* with Felix Hackett and was its first editor. He studied law at King's Inns, was called to the bar in 1902, and took silk in 1920. His father, Surgeon Kennedy, was an Irish-speaker from Co. Donegal, and Hugh Kennedy joined the Gaelic League and was honorary secretary of the Ard-Chraobh; fellow committee members were PATRICK PEARSE, EOIN MACNEILL, and ÉAMONN CEANNT. He was legal adviser to the Department of Local Government under the First Dáil and a member of the committee that drafted the Constitution of the Irish Free State. He became first Attorney General in 1922 and was elected TD for South Dublin in 1923. In June 1924 he became the first Chief Justice of Saorstát Éireann and held the position until his sudden death in December 1936. He was a fellow and vice-president of the Royal Society of Antiquaries of Ireland, vice-president of the Statistical Society, MRIA, and a governor of the National Gallery.

KENNEDY, JIMMY (1903–1984), song-writer. Born in Omagh, Co. Tyrone, brought up in Portstewart, Co. Derry, and educated at TCD. He taught for a while in England before taking up song-writing. He was prolific and successful. His first big success was 'The Teddy Bears' Picnic', followed by others many of which are still popular today. His songs include 'Red Sails in the Sunset', 'South of the Border', 'Play to me, Gypsy' and 'Love is like a Violin'. He also wrote the 'Cokey-Cokey', which later became the 'Hokey-Cokey'. Bing Crosby recorded nine of his songs and became a great friend. He composed more than a thousand airs and won two Ivor Novello awards for his contribution to British music. He was awarded an honorary degree from NUU, and the OBE. He lived in Greystones, Co. Wicklow, for some years in the 1970s, and died in hospital in Cheltenham, England, on 6 April 1984, survived by his wife, Elaine, two sons and a daughter.

KENNEDY, JOHN PITT (1796–1879), engineer and agriculturist. Born at Carndonagh, Co. Donegal, 8 May 1796. Educated at Foyle College, Derry, and Royal Military Academy, Woolwich. Commissioned in the Corps of Engineers 1815 and served until 1831, when he returned to settle in Ireland as estate manager in Co. Tyrone. In 1837 he was appointed inspector-general in national education, with particular responsibility for practical instruction in agriculture. He acquired sixty acres at Glasnevin, Dublin, with a large house and garden, to form a central model farm and training establishment for teachers. His plans for extending agricultural education throughout the country received little support from the authorities, and he resigned in 1839. From 1843 to 1845 he acted as secretary to the Devon Commission on land law in Ireland, and in 1846 he became agent for large estates in Co. Limerick. In 1849 he re-joined the army on the invitation of Sir Charles Napier, commander-in-chief in India, and built a great military road, which bears his name, from the plains of Simla towards Tibet. He settled in England in 1852 and became one of the founders and managing directors of the Bombay, Baroda and Central Indian Railway. Died 28 June 1879 at his house in St George's Square, London.

KENNEDY, PATRICK (1801–1873), author. Born Co. Wexford. Educated by Carew family. Became assistant in Kildare Place training school, Dublin, 1823 and subsequently opened a bookshop and library in Anglesea Place, which he conducted until his death. He studied Irish mythology and antiquities. His regular contributions to the *Dublin University Magazine* were published in book form as *Legendary Fictions of the Irish Celts* (1866), *The Banks of the Boro* (1867), *Evenings in the Duffrey* (1869), *The Bardic Stories of Ireland* (1871) and, under the pseudonym Harry Whitney, *Legends of Mount Leinster* (1855). Died 28 March 1873.

KENNY, SEÁN (1933–1973), stage designer. Born Portroe, Co. Tipperary; studied architecture in Dublin. An admirer of the American architect Frank Lloyd Wright, he sailed across the Atlantic from Dublin with three fellow students in the *Ituna*, a converted Morecambe Bay shrimper, and was accepted by Wright, with whom he studied for two years. After an adventurous period hunting wolves in Canada, searching for gold in Arizona, and a scientific expedition in the Pacific, he returned to Ireland. Failing to secure architectural commissions he left for London, and had his first major success in the theatre in 1958 with the design for the production of *The Hostage* by BRENDAN BEHAN. In 1963 he redesigned the Old Vic Theatre for its occupation by the National Theatre Company. Outside the theatre his successes included the 'Gyroton', a roller-coaster ride at Canada's Expo '67; an all-glass underwater restaurant in Nassau; and a multi-layer stage for a Las Vegas night-club. He had achieved international fame as a designer and had begun to show brilliant insight as a stage director when he died suddenly in London on 11 June 1973.

KENT, THOMAS (*c.* 1867–1916), revolutionary. Born at Bawnard House, Castlelyons, Co. Cork, where his family farmed 200 acres. Emigrated to Boston for some years, and on his return about 1889 became active in the national movement and in the Gaelic League, following the strong family tradition. Joined the Irish Volunteers about 1913, arrested, and imprisoned for short periods. On Easter Sunday 1916 he received word from Dublin that the projected rising had been cancelled. He remained at home with his brothers, awaiting further instructions. On 2 May 1916 the house was surrounded by an armed force of the RIC, and after a gun-battle lasting three hours, during which a head constable and one of the brothers was killed, the Kents surrendered. Thomas was executed in Cork military detention barracks on 9 May, the only leader executed in Ireland outside Dublin.

KEOGH, JOHN (1740–1817), Catholic leader. Born in poor circumstances, and began life as a small tradesman in Dublin. His business prospered and he gained wide influence among his fellow-Catholics. Joining the Catholic Committee, he led a delegation to London in 1792 to press for alleviation of Catholic grievances. His persistent work led to the Catholic Convention of 1792 in the Tailors' Hall, Dublin, which in turn was largely instrumental in securing the Relief Act of 1793. Among other limited concessions the Act enabled Catholics to vote in the election of MPs and admitted them to the outer bar, although imposing a humiliating oath. This Act was the great triumph of Keogh's life. He was on friendly terms with WOLFE TONE and other United Irishmen who visited his mansion at Mount Jerome. He was arrested in 1796 but released shortly afterwards. Subsequently he took little part in public affairs. Died in Dublin, 13 November 1817.

KEOGH, WILLIAM NICHOLAS (1817–1878), judge. Born Galway, 7

December 1817. Educated Mountjoy School, Dublin, and TCD. Called to the bar 1840 and acquired good practice; QC 1849 and MP for Athlone 1847–1856. One of the founders of the Catholic Defence Association, and supported tenant-right movement. Made Solicitor General 1852 and denounced by GAVAN DUFFY and LUCAS. Made Attorney-General 1855 and judge 1856. Tried the Fenian leaders 1865. In the Galway election petition of 1872 his verdict unseated the Home Ruler, Colonel John Nolan, on grounds of undue influence and intimidation by the Catholic clergy. There was a popular outcry, and he was attacked by the Home Rule party for the rest of his life. His health failed, and at Bingen am Rhein he attacked his valet and then cut his own throat, 30 September 1878.

KERNOFF, AARON or HARRY (1900–1974), artist. Born in London, 9 January 1900, son of a Russian Jewish father and a Spanish Jewish mother. Attended an elementary school in London until 1914, when the family moved to Dublin. Studied at Dublin Metropolitan School of Art and won the Taylor Scholarship in 1923. He began his working life as a woodworker in his father's furniture business, and later this led him to the production of woodcuts. He painted mainly in oils, and exhibited at the RHA every year from 1926. Elected RHA, 1936. In the 1950s he began to paint on a small scale, on canvasses 6 by 8 inches (150 by 200 mm), and produced many hundreds of miniature oil paintings. His work was exhibited in Paris, Chicago, Amsterdam, and Toronto, and at World Fairs in Glasgow (1938) and New York (1939). He spent the summer of 1958 painting in Nova Scotia. During his career of more than fifty years he painted most of the noteworthy literary figures of Dublin, including JOYCE and YEATS, and also many of the people of Dún Chaoin and the Blasket Islands. Collections of his woodcuts were published in limited editions in 1942 and 1951. Died,

unmarried, in the Meath Hospital, Dublin, on Christmas Day 1974.

KETTLE or KYTELER, DAME ALICE (*c.* 1324), reputed witch. Lived in Kilkenny in the fourteenth century. It is said that she married four times and that her first husband and her favourite son were bankers. Holinshed's *Chronicle of Ireland* relates that she was accused by the bishop of Ossory with two accomplices of holding 'nightly conference with a spirit called Robert Artisson to whom she sacrificed in the high waie nine red cocks and nine peacocks' eies.' One of her accomplices, her maid Petronilla, was burned at the stake. Some of the nobility took Alice's part and conveyed her to England, where no more was heard of her. In her closet was found a sacramental wafer, with a print of the devil and a 'a pipe of ointment wherewith she greased a staffe, upon which she ambled and galloped through thick and thin.' It is possible that the accusation arose from her wealth, or a dispute with the church. A Latin manuscript account of the affair was edited in 1843 for the Camden Society by Thomas Wright. Her house, the oldest in Kilkenny, has been restored and reopened as Kyteler's Inn.

KETTLE, THOMAS (1880–1916), nationalist. Born north Co. Dublin, son of Andrew J. Kettle, one of the principal founders and organisers of the Land League. Educated North Richmond Street CBS, Dublin, Clongowes Wood College, and University College. Called to the bar 1905, and practised law until his appointment in 1908 as the first professor of national economics at UCD. He developed strong nationalist sympathies. Elected MP for East Tyrone by sixteen votes in 1906. Made a successful tour of the USA on behalf of the Nationalist party. Resigned his seat 1910 to devote himself to his university duties. Joined the Irish Volunteers on their formation in 1913 and in July 1914 was sent to Belgium to obtain arms. After the outbreak of the First World War he became convinced that England was on the side of the small nations and would not go back on its Home Rule legislation but would in fact enlarge its scope. He returned to Ireland, applied for a commission in the Dublin Fusiliers, and took part in the campaign to recruit Irishmen for the British forces. The 1916 Rising came as a complete surprise to him. He said that it had spoiled his dream of a free, united Ireland in a free Europe. He asked to be sent to France, and was killed in September 1916 when leading his men in an attack on Givenchy in the battle of the Somme. His body was never recovered. A memorial to him in St Stephen's Green, Dublin, bears these lines from a sonnet he wrote to his daughter:

> Died not for flag, nor King, nor Emperor,
> But for a dream, born in a herdsman's hut,
> And for the secret scripture of the poor.

His wife, Mary Sheehy, daughter of David Sheehy MP, was a sister of Mrs Sheehy Skeffington and of Mrs Cruise O'Brien, mother of Dr Conor Cruise O'Brien, a member of the third Coalition government.

KICKHAM, CHARLES JOSEPH (1828–1882), novelist. Born at Mullinahone, Co. Tipperary, son of a prosperous shopkeeper. Intended for the medical profession, but an accident with gunpowder at the age of thirteen injured his sight and hearing. Joined the Young Ireland movement and became a Fenian about 1860. JAMES STEPHENS appointed him with LUBY and O'LEARY to the supreme executive of the movement and co-editor of their newspaper, the *Irish People*. Kickham was arrested in 1865 and sentenced to fourteen years' penal servitude, but was released in poor health after four years and thereafter confined himself to writing. *Sally Cavanagh* (1869) was written while he was in prison. *Knocknagow or The Homes of Tipperary*, considered his best work, appeared in 1879. His poems and stories were published in collected form in 1870. Died at Blackrock, Co. Dublin, 21 August 1882.

KIERNAN, THOMAS J. (1897–1967), diplomat and author. Born Dublin; educated at St Mary's College, Rathmines, and UCD. Became inspector of taxes in 1919. Appointed secretary of the High Commissioner's office in London 1924. Returned to Dublin in 1935 as Director of Broadcasting. In 1941 he became Minister to the Holy See, and in 1946 went to Australia to open Ireland's first mission there as High Commissioner, becoming ambassador in 1950. Subsequently he served as ambassador in West Germany, Canada, and the USA. After his retirement in 1964 he remained in America to administer the Irish-American Foundation, which was established after the visit of President Kennedy to Ireland in June 1963. He was author of *British War Finance, A Study in National Finance,* and *A History of the Financial Administration of Ireland to 1817*. Other works were *The Irish Exiles in Australia*, a literary portrait of Pope Pius XII, and a historical novel. Died in Dublin in December 1967. His wife was a popular ballad-singer under her maiden name, Delia Murphy.

KILLEN, REV. WILLIAM DOOL (1806–1902), historian. Born Ballymena, Co. Antrim, 5 April 1806. Educated RBAI. Ordained Presbyterian minister of Raphoe, Co. Donegal, 1829. Appointed professor of church history, Presbyterian College, Belfast, by the General Assembly 1841, and held the post for forty-eight years. Appointed president of the college 1869. Received D.D. and LL.D. from University of Glasgow. He completed Reid's *History of the Presbyterian Church in Ireland* (1853), published *The Ecclesiastical History of Ireland* (two volumes, 1875), and numerous other works on church history. *Reminiscences of a Long Life* appeared in 1901. Died Belfast, 10 January 1902.

KILWARDEN, VISCOUNT. See under WOLFE, ARTHUR.

KING, CECIL (1921-1986), painter. Born in Rathdrum, Co. Wicklow, and educated at the Church of Ireland school in Ranelagh, Dublin, and at Mountjoy School. He embarked on a business career with a printing firm in Dundalk and became active in 'An Óige' (the Irish Youth Hostels Association), serving as national honorary treasurer and national honorary secretary. In 1963 he gave up his business career to become a full-time painter. As his reputation grew, he held one-man exhibitions in France, Sweden, West Germany, and Spain, as well as in Ireland. The rich texture of his painting illumined his personal version of the hard-edge school. He was a founder-member of the Contemporary Irish Art Society and of 'Rosc'. He was generous in his support of younger artists and acted as assessor for final-year students in colleges of art throughout the country. He received an award of $4,000 from the Irish-American Cultural Institute in 1977. He died suddenly in hospital in Dún Laoghaire, Co. Dublin, on 7 April 1986.

KING, EDWARD, VISCOUNT KINGSBOROUGH (1795-1837), author. Born Cork, 10 November 1795; educated Exeter College, Oxford. MP for Co. Cork 1818-1826, resigning in favour of a younger brother. The sight of a Mexican manuscript in the Bodleian Library determined him to devote his life to the study of Mexican antiquities. He promoted and edited a magnificent work, *Antiquities of Mexico* (nine volumes, 1830-1848). Four copies were printed on vellum with the plates coloured. It cost him £32,000, and his life: unable to pay his paper-maker, he was arrested, and died of typhus in the sheriff's prison, Dublin, 27 February 1837. Had he lived another year he would have inherited estates worth £40,000 annually.

KING, WILLIAM (1650-1729), archbishop. Born Antrim, 1 May 1650. Educated Dungannon and TCD. Ordained 1674; rector of St Werburgh's parish, Dublin, 1679. Founder-member of Dublin Philosophical Society 1683, a forerunner of the RIA. Dean of St Patrick's Cathedral 1688. Took Williamite side and was imprisoned. Released after Battle of the Boyne 1690 and made bishop of Derry. Published *State of the Protestants of Ireland Under the Late King James's Government* (1691), a vindication of the revolution, which quickly went into three editions. Promoted archbishop of Dublin 1703. He encouraged the teaching of Irish at TCD to supply clergymen who could minister to the native Irish. Supported penal legislation against Roman Catholics. Encouraged SWIFT in the agitation against 'Wood's halfpence'. An indefatigable correspondent, letters preserved in TCD and British Museum throw much light on the state of Ireland at the time. Published sermons and *De Origine Mali* (1702), a theological work. Died Dublin, 8 May 1729.

KIRKWOOD, MAJOR THOMAS WILLIAM (1885-1972), soldier and polo player. Born in Co. Roscommon and served in the Indian Cavalry for twenty-one years, reaching the rank of major. An excellent linguist. He commanded an officers' training camp at Omsk in 1919. Later served as an intelligence officer in Japan, and was awarded the Order of the Rising Sun. After leaving the army he married a member of the Jameson distilling family and settled in Dublin. He was a polo player of international standing and did much to keep the game alive in Dublin, where it provided a free spectacle in the Phoenix Park. He represented Ireland abroad in many tournaments and continued to play until he was seventy. Died in Dublin in January 1972.

KIRWAN, RICHARD (1733-1812), chemist. Born at Cloghballymore, Co. Galway. Educated at Poitiers and at a Jesuit novitiate in the Netherlands. Abandoned his studies for the priesthood in 1755, returned to Ireland and was called to the bar in 1766. In order to enter the legal profession he had to conform to the established church. Practised law for only two years and then, having ample private means, went to London. His career as a chemist began in 1777. Elected FRS 1780, and received its highest honour, the Copley Medal, for his first scientific publications, the fruit of 18 years' experimental work and dealing with the subject of chemical affinity. His *Elements of Mineralogy* (1784) became a standard treatise, and his *Essay on Phlogiston* was considered the most authoritative exposition and defence of that theory. During his lifetime the Kirwinian Society of Dublin was founded as a tribute to him and to spread his ideas. President RIA 1799–1812; president, Dublin Library Society, inspector-general of His Majesty's Mines in Ireland, and perpetual member of the Amicable Society of Galway. Elected to many foreign academies including those of Berlin, Dijon, Stockholm, and Philadelphia.

KIRWAN, WILLIAM BOURKE (born *c.* 1814), miniature painter. Born in Dublin and worked as an anatomical draughtsman for surgeons, and as a picture cleaner. He exhibited miniatures and watercolours at the RHA 1836–1846. In 1852 he was the central figure in a famous trial when he was condemned to death for the murder of his wife at Ireland's Eye, near Howth. For many years previously he had maintained a separate establishment at Sandymount, where he had a mistress by whom he had eight children. His sentence was commuted to transportation for life and his subsequent fate is uncertain.

KITCHENER, HORATIO HERBERT, first EARL KITCHENER (1850–1916), field-marshal. Born Crotter House, Ballylongford, Co. Kerry, 24 June 1850. Educated Switzerland and Royal Military Academy, Woolwich. Commissioned in the Royal Engineers 1871. Saw much service in the Near East. Sirdar of Egyptian army 1892. Routed Khalifa Abdullah at Omdurman 1898 and won back the Sudan for Egypt. Raised to peerage 1898. Successively chief of staff and commander-in-chief in Boer War 1900–1902. He received a grant of £50,000, was made viscount, and received the Order of Merit. Commander-in-chief India 1902–1909, and made field-marshal 1909. Appointed agent and consul-general for Egypt 1911 and made earl 1914. Appointed Secretary of State for War on outbreak of First World War and organised a large army. He was lost when HMS *Hampshire* struck a mine off the Orkneys, June 1916.

KNOWLES, JAMES SHERIDAN (1784–1862), actor and author. Born Cork, 12 May 1784, son of a schoolmaster and lexicographer, James Knowles who was a first cousin of RICHARD BRINSLEY SHERIDAN. The family moved to London and James graduated in medicine at Aberdeen University. He soon abandoned medicine and took to the stage. Finding that this only gave him a precarious living, he opened a school at Belfast and later at Glasgow. He wrote a number of plays, two novels, and some poetry. Two of his plays in particular, *The Hunchback* (1832) and *The Love Chase* (1837), were extremely popular, and he was considered the most successful dramatist of his day. In 1844 he became a Baptist preacher and denounced Catholicism, but avoided preaching against the stage. He received a civil list pension of £200 in 1848 and died at Torquay, 30 November 1862.

KUSS, GERALD V. (1920–1969), journalist. Born Navan, Co. Meath. Served for some time in the British merchant navy. At the outbreak of the Finnish-Russian War in November 1939 he volunteered for the Finnish army. On repatriation to Ireland in 1942 he became a freelance journalist, later joining Radio Éireann and then Bord Fáilte. He wrote several books on angling, on which he was recognised internationally as an expert. A speaker of Finnish, Swedish, and German, he wrote and broadcast regularly for Scandinavian media. Died in Dublin, 9 June 1969.

KYAN, JOHN HOWARD (1774–1850), inventor. Born Dublin, 27 November 1774. Educated to help in management of his father's copper mines in Co. Wicklow. The mines failed and, after his father died in 1804, he went to England. Worked in vinegar brewery in London. Patented a method of preserving wood 1832: Faraday praised it highly. Sold his rights for large sum to Anti-Dry-Rot Company 1836. The timber used in building the British Museum, College of Surgeons, London, Temple Church and Ramsgate harbour works was 'Kyanised'. The process was superseded by the discovery of creosote. He also patented ship propulsion by jet of water ejected at the stern 1833. Died 5 January 1850 in New York, where he was planning the filtering of the water supply.

KYTELER, DAME ALICE. See under KETTLE.

L

LACY, COUNT PETER (1678–1751), field-marshal. Born at Killedy, Co. Limerick, 29 September 1678. At thirteen he served as an ensign in the defence of Limerick against the Williamite forces. After the treaty of 1691 he left Ireland with Sarsfield's troops and joined the Irish Brigade in the service of France. His father and two brothers fell in that service; Lacy fought in Italy until 1696, and when the regiment was disbanded after the peace of Rijswijk he entered the service of Peter the Great of Russia. The emperor placed him in command of a company called the Grand Musketeers, a hundred Russian nobles armed and horsed at their own expense. In 1708 he was appointed colonel, and distinguished himself in the war against Sweden. At the battle of Poltava he commanded a brigade and was wounded. Between 1709 and 1721 he served in many campaigns against the Danes, Swedes, and Turks. By 1728 he was a general and governor of Livonia (Latvia). In 1733 he made an expedition to Poland at the head of 30,000 men to establish Augustus of Saxony on the throne, and entered Warsaw in triumph in 1735. Created field-marshal 1736. He saw further active service against the Turks and Swedes and received many marks of favour from the Empress Anna. After more than fifty years' campaigning he retired to his estates in Livonia in 1743. Died there on 11 May 1751.

LALOR, JAMES FINTAN (1807–1849), Young Irelander. Born at Tinnakill, Co. Laois. Son of a gentleman-farmer and MP. Educated at Carlow Lay College. He was shortsighted, deaf, and ungainly, and had to leave school after a few years because of continual ill-health. He led a secluded life for many years but seems to have become deeply interested in agrarian reform. In 1845 he wrote to the prime minister, Peel, urging that the agitation for repeal of the Union could be suppressed if a settlement of the land question were first made. His views caused a rift with his father, who supported O'CONNELL's policy on Repeal as an essential first step before land reform or any other reform. He left home and lived precariously in Dublin and Belfast but ill-health brought him back in 1846. In 1847 he contributed to the *Nation* a series of letters advocating 'the land of Ireland for the people of Ireland', and founded a tenant-right league in Co. Tipperary with the help of MICHAEL DOHENY, but his attempt to organise a rent strike failed. After the arrest of MITCHEL and JOHN MARTIN, Lalor took charge of the *Irish Felon*, successor to the suppressed *United Irishman*. He was arrested in July 1848 but released in bad health the following November. He continued to work towards organising a rising, undeterred by the failure earlier that year, but his health became worse. Died, 27 December 1849.

LALOR, PETER (1823–1889), colonial politician, younger brother of JAMES FINTAN LALOR. Born at Tinnakill, Co. Laois. Educated at TCD; he became a civil engineer, and in 1852, shortly after the discovery of gold in Australia, he sailed for Melbourne. He took up rich claims at Ballarat in the Eureka lead and gravel pits. When the miners refused to continue paying licence fees to the government, a force of soldiers and police were sent to collect the money. In an encounter at Eureka Stockade on 3 December 1854 twenty-two miners were killed, twelve wounded, and one hundred and twenty-five taken prisoner. Lalor, who was in command of the miners, lost an arm but succeeded in escaping. Subsequently the gold fields were granted parliamentary representation, and he was elected member for Ballarat. He held a number of government posts, including commissioner of customs and trade, and postmaster-general. Speaker of the House 1880 to 1888, and on his resignation because of ill-health was given a vote of thanks and a grant of £4,000. Died in Melbourne, 10 February 1889.

LAMB, CHARLES (1893–1964), painter. Born in Portadown, Co. Armagh, elder son of a painter and decorator. Apprenticed to his father, went to the local technical school, and in 1913 attended the evening life drawing class of the Belfast School of Art. In 1917 he won a scholarship to the Metropolitan School of Art in Dublin. He began to exhibit at the RHA in 1922; elected RHA 1938. He first visited Carraroe in the Connemara Gaeltacht in 1921 and returned frequently to paint landscapes and portraits of local characters, for which he became well known. In 1935 he built a house and settled there permanently. He visited Brittany in 1926/27 and spent nearly a year painting in Aran in 1928. He first exhibited in New York in 1929 and was represented in the Irish Exhibition in Brussels in 1930. In the 1930s he also showed in Los Angeles and Chicago and at the RA. He illustrated *Cré na Cille* (1949), the classic by MÁIRTÍN Ó CADHAIN, with line drawings.

LANE, SIR HUGH PERCY (1875–1915), art collector and critic. Born 9 November 1875 at Ballybrack, Co. Cork, where his father was rector, and spent his boyhood travelling on the Continent with his mother. He joined Colnaghi's, the London picture dealers, in 1893 and also worked for a time with the Marlborough Gallery, before setting up for himself at 2 Pall Mall Place. He was twenty-three and had virtually no capital. His success was immediate, and his flair had made him a wealthy man within ten years. He was knighted in 1909, and acted as adviser to the galleries at Johannesburg and Cape Town. In 1901, after meeting YEATS at the house of his mother's sister, LADY GREGORY, he visited a joint exhibition in Dublin of paintings by the poet's father and NATHANIEL HONE, which awakened his interest in the Irish art scene. He lent a very fine collection of modern paintings, mainly French impressionists, to the Dublin Municipal Gallery, then in temporary premises in Harcourt St, and with typical generosity offered them as an outright gift on condition that a permanent gallery be provided. However, Dublin City Council rejected Sir Edwin Lutyens's design for a building on a bridge over the Liffey. Lane withdrew his loan, and in a will made in 1913 bequeathed the paintings to the English National Gallery. In 1914 he was appointed director of the National Gallery of Ireland and made many improvements there. In February 1915 he added an unwitnessed codicil to his will, restoring his collection to Dublin. When returning from America on the *Lusitania* he was drowned when the ship was torpedoed on 7 May 1915. He was unmarried. A controversy over the ownership of the Lane Collection dragged on until 1959 when an agreement was made between the Government and the English National Gallery. The pictures were divided into two groups; the groups are lent alternately to Dublin, each group for five years.

LANE, TIMOTHY O'NEILL (1852–1915), lexicographer. Born Templeglentan, Co. Limerick, and became a teacher there. Secured a clerical post in London 1877 and later went to Paris as a newspaper correspondent. In 1904 he published his *English–Irish Dictionary*. A second and enlarged edition was published in Dublin 1922. Lane said he spent twenty years collecting material, at a cost of £2,500, and acknowledged generous donations from bishops and clergy. He also obtained a grant of £250 from the British government. Died Tournafulla, Co. Limerick.

LANGRISHE, SIR HERCULES (1731–1811), politician. Born Knocktopher, Co. Kilkenny. Educated TCD. MP for Knocktopher from 1761 until the Union. Virtually sole proprietor of that borough, which made him independent. Held posts as Commissioner of Revenue 1774–1801 and of Excise 1780–1801. Friend of EDMUND BURKE, and supported Catholic claims for relaxation of penal laws. Attacked the government in 'The History of Barataria Continued', published in the *Freeman's Journal*, April–May 1771. Prompted by Burke's *Letter to Sir Hercules Langrishe* (1792), he introduced the Catholic Relief Bill that year. Supported the Union and received £13,862 for his interest in the borough of Knocktopher. Retired from politics 1801. Died at his house in St Stephen's Green, Dublin, 1 February 1811.

LANIGAN, JOHN (1758–1828), ecclesiastical historian. Born at Cashel, Co. Tipperary. Educated by his schoolmaster-father at a local seminary. Studied at the Irish College in Rome, and after ordination was appointed professor of Hebrew, ecclesiastical history and divinity at the University of Pavia. In 1796 Napoleon's troops captured the duchy of Milan, the university staff was dispersed, and Lanigan returned to Ireland. The bishop of Cork suspected him of Jansenism and raised difficulties about his proposed appointment to the chair of Hebrew and Sacred Scripture in Maynooth College. He became an editor and translator on the staff of the RDS at £1.50 a week, which was raised to £3 in 1808 when he became librarian. He remained in the post until mental illness incapacitated him in 1813. Died 7 July 1828 in Dr Harty's private asylum, Finglas, Co. Dublin. His principal work is *An Ecclesiastical History of Ireland* (four volumes, 1822). With the scholar EDWARD O'REILLY he founded the shortlived Gaelic Society of Dublin in 1808.

LARCHET, JOHN F. (1884–1967), musician. Born in Sandymount, Dublin, into a musical family. Educated at Catholic University School and TCD. He was a prominent member of the musical profession in Dublin for over forty years. Senior professor at the Royal Irish Academy of Music 1920; professor of music, UCD, 1921–1958, and director of music at the Abbey Theatre for nearly thirty years. As director of music examinations in secondary schools he did much to raise standards of teaching. Musical adviser to the army in 1923, and president and musical director of the Dublin Grand Opera Society for many years. As a composer he is remembered for his adaptations of folk music, notably 'An Ardglass Boat Song' and 'Diarmuid's Lament'. Died in Dublin, 10 August 1967.

LARDNER, DIONYSIUS (1793–1859), scientific writer. Born Dublin, 3 April 1793. Educated TCD; LL.B. and LL.D. 1827, and won many prizes. Married 1815 and separated by mutual consent 1820. Elected professor of natural philosophy and astronomy, London University, 1827. In 1829 initiated the *Cabinet Cyclopaedia*, 133 volumes, completed 1849, and secured as contributors the most eminent writers of the day. Also edited *Dr Lardner's Cabinet Library* (nine volumes, 1830–1832), and *Edinburgh Cabinet Library* (thirty-eight volumes, 1830–1844), and published many popular scientific works. All the while he carried on an affair with Mary Heaviside, wife of a cavalry officer, and ran away with her in 1840. Captain Heaviside obtained £8,000 damages. The marriage was dissolved by Act of Parliament in 1845. From 1840 to 1845 Lardner lectured in the USA and Cuba and is said to have made £40,000 on his tours. He settled in Paris in 1845. He was a fellow of the Linnean, Zoological and Astronomical societies, FRS, and MRIA. Died Naples, 29 April 1859.

LARKIN, JAMES (1876–1947), labour leader. Born in Liverpool, 21 January

1876, the second son of impoverished Irish parents. He spent his early childhood with his grandparents in Newry, Co. Down, returning to Liverpool at nine to begin work at half-a-crown (12½p) a week. Later, after a period as a seaman, he became a foreman on Liverpool docks. He lost his job for joining the men under him in a strike, and then became an organiser for the National Union of Dockers. During the Belfast disputes of 1907 he organised sympathetic strikes, introduced the weapon of 'blacking' goods, and even succeeded in bringing the police out on strike. His militant methods alarmed his union, and in 1908 he came to Dublin to found his own organisation. The Irish Transport and General Workers' Union, launched by him in 1909, catered for unskilled workers such as carters, dockers, labourers, and factory hands, who lived in conditions of great misery in the slums of Dublin, then probably among the worst in Europe. With his magnetic personality and gifts of oratory, 'Big Jim' soon had thousands of workers enrolled. His success caused apprehension among the employers, who, led by WILLIAM MARTIN MURPHY, banded into a federation and insisted that all employees should leave 'Larkin's Union'. When they refused, the great lock-out of 1913 followed. Other unions supported their fellow-workers, and about 100,000 were thrown out of employment. Despite being reduced to starvation they kept up the struggle for eight months, and although the result was, in CONNOLLY's words, 'a drawn battle', the workers had established rights that could never again be denied them. Larkin then went to America to raise funds to re-build the union, but found employers there even more antagonistic. In 1920 he was sentenced to ten years' penal servitude for what the court called 'criminal syndicalism'. He had served three years when he was released by order of Governor Al Smith in 1923. He returned to Ireland to a tumultuous welcome, but was soon at odds with the committee of his union, which he

thought was not acting forcefully enough in the cause of socialism. The dispute ended in his expulsion, but he soon founded a new organisation, the Workers' Union of Ireland, and won his way back into public life, becoming a Dublin city councillor, and a deputy in Dáil Éireann from 1927 to 1932 and again in 1937–1938 and 1943–1944. He led a campaign in the 1940s against the Wages Standstill Order and forced a modification of its terms. His last main achievement was to secure a fortnight's annual leave for manual workers, after a fourteen-week strike. His habits were sober and his wants were few: when he died on 30 January 1947 he left only £4.50 and a few personal belongings.

LARKIN, MICHAEL. See under MANCHESTER MARTYRS.

LARMINIE, WILLIAM (1849–1900), civil servant and writer. Born in August 1849 at Castlebar, Co. Mayo, into a family descended from Huguenot émigrés. Educated at Kingstown School and TCD. He subsequently worked for many years in the India Office, retiring about seven or eight years before his death. Published in London *Glanua and Other Poems* (1889) and *Fand and Other Poems* (1890). In 1893 he published a volume of stories recorded in Donegal, Mayo and Galway as *West Irish Folk-Tales and Romances*. His translation of JOHANNES SCOTUS ERIUGENA's *De Divisione Naturae* remains unpublished. Died at Bray, Co. Wicklow, 19 January 1900.

LARMOR, SIR JOSEPH (1857–1942), physicist. Born at Magheragall, Co. Antrim, 11 July 1857. Educated RBAI, Queen's College, Belfast, and St John's College, Cambridge, where he was 'senior wrangler' and first Smith's prizeman. Professor of natural philosophy at Queen's College, Galway, 1880. Returned to St John's in 1885 as a lecturer in mathematics, and in 1903 was appointed Lucasian Professor of Mathematics in Cambridge, in succession to

SIR GEORGE STOKES. He contributed three extensive papers to the *Philosophical Transactions* of the Royal Society (1894-1897) on 'A Dynamical Theory of the Electric and Lumeniferous Medium', which he later revised and extended in book form under the title *Aether and Matter* (1900). He is remembered principally for this work and as the first to give the formula for the radiation of energy from an accelerated electron. He was also the first to give an explanation of the effect of a magnetic field in splitting the lines of the spectrum into multiple lines. Elected FRS 1892, and was honoured by it with a Royal Medal and the Copley Medal in 1921. Secretary of the society 1901-1912, knighted 1909. Unionist MP for University of Cambridge, 1911-1922. He received many honorary degrees and the freedom of the city of Belfast. Shortly after retiring in 1932 he returned to Ireland and died, unmarried, at Holywood, Co. Down, on 19 May 1942.

LA TOUCHE, JAMES DIGGES (1788-1827), banker and philanthropist. Son of WILLIAM GEORGE. Born Dublin, 28 August 1788. Educated TCD. Became manager of family banking business. Secretary, Sunday School Society of Ireland, 1809, and connected with many charitable activities. Esteemed for his practical wisdom and elected to boards of public companies. Stood firm during run on Dublin banks in 1820 after failure of provincial banks, despite 'the frenzy and alarm of the whole community' (his journal). Died in Dublin.

LA TOUCHE, WILLIAM GEORGE (1747-1803), banker, grandson of David Digges La Touche, Huguenot refugee and founder of first Dublin bank. William was born in Dublin, 24 August 1747. Educated at St Paul's, London. Apppointed British resident at Basra, Iraq, 1764. Gained good will of travellers and natives. When Zohier was captured by the Persians he ransomed the inhabitants at his own expense, saving them from slavery. Returned to Dublin 1784, married a daughter of Puget, a London banker, and entered family business. By his integrity and London connections expanded the business. Built family mansion in St Stephen's Green. Died Dublin, 7 November 1803.

LAVERTY, MAURA (1907-1966), writer. Born Maura Kelly in Rathangan, Co. Kildare, and brought up there. Studied teaching at Brigidine Convent, Carlow, then in 1926 went to Spain as a governess. Was secretary to Princess Bibesco, became a foreign correspondent and then a journalist in Madrid. Returned to Ireland in 1928 and worked in Dublin as a journalist and broadcaster. She wrote a number of novels, a play, cookery books, and books for children. 'Tolka Row', a popular television serial, was based on her novel *Lift Up Your Gates* (1946). She died in Dublin in 1966.

LAVERY, CECIL (1894-1967), Supreme Court judge. Born in Armagh, 6 October 1894. Educated at St Patrick's College, Armagh, St Vincent's College, Castleknock, and UCD. Called to the bar 1915 and won the Brooke Scholarship. He became a member of the Irish Volunteers at their first meeting in 1913 and joined the Armagh Division. He helped in the Howth gun-running in July 1914. When the rising broke out in Easter Week 1916 he stood by with the Armagh Division waiting for instructions that never came. He acted as a judge in the Dáil Courts 1921-1922 and after the Treaty took the Free State side. He took silk in 1927 and became a bencher of the King's Inns in 1933. TD North Co. Dublin 1935-1938; attorney-general in the first Coalition government 1948, and was elected to the Seanad. He helped to draft the Convention of Human Rights for the Council of Europe in 1949. He drafted and advised on the Republic of Ireland Bill, 1949, and later attended a meeting in Paris of the United Kingdom and Commonwealth Ministers, presided over by Dr Evatt,

Australian Minister of External Affairs, when the essential provisions regarding the relations of Ireland with the Commonwealth were settled. Appointed to the Supreme Court in April 1950. His interests included horse racing, and he was a steward of the Turf Club. Died in Dublin, 16 December 1967.

LAVERY, SIR JOHN (1856-1941), painter. Born in Belfast, exact date uncertain, son of an impoverished publican. His father was drowned when he was three, and his mother died soon after. He was sent to relatives in Scotland, apprenticed to a painter-photographer in Glasgow at seventeen. After studying at the Glasgow School of Art he set up as an independent artist at twenty-three. He then studied in London and Paris. His first success came with the showing of his 'Tennis Party' at the RA in 1886; it was much admired and, better still, bought for the Neue Pinakothek in Munich. Two years later he received a commission to paint the state visit of Queen Victoria to the Glasgow Exhibition, and this gave him social connections that brought him valuable commissions for the next fifty years. His career from then on was one of uninterrupted success. Knighted 1918, elected RA 1921; he was also a member of the RHA, Royal Scottish Academy, and the academies of Rome, Antwerp, Milan, Brussels, and Stockholm. He received honorary degrees from QUB and TCD, and was made a freeman of Belfast and Dublin. At eighty-four he published his autobiography, *The Life of a Painter* (1940). Died at Rosenarra House, Kilkenny, 10 January 1941. His works are on exhibition in galleries all over the world. He followed the movement for Irish independence with sympathetic interest, and painted dramatic pictures of the trial of SIR ROGER CASEMENT and of the lying-in-state of TERENCE MACSWINEY. His conversation pieces showed famous contemporaries such as GEORGE MOORE and Ramsay MacDonald at ease in their homes and, with his portraits, are of great historical interest. The Government commissioned his portrait of Hazel, his American-born wife, which appeared on Irish banknotes from 1928.

LAWLESS, HONOURABLE EMILY (1845-1913), author. Born at Lyons Castle, Co. Kildare, daughter of Sir Nicholas Lawless, later third Lord Cloncurry. Spent a great deal of her youth in the west of Ireland with her mother's people, Kirwans of Castlehacket, Co. Galway. Published a number of novels, including *Hurrish* (1886), a tale of the Land League, *With Essex in Ireland* (1890), and *Maelcho* (1894), historical romances. Her *Story of Ireland* appeared in 1887, and a biography of MARIA EDGEWORTH in 1904. Her volume of poems, *With the Wild Geese* (1902), contains her best-known work. 'After Aughrim' and 'Clare Coast' evoke the heartbreak of defeat and emigration. On medical advice she moved in later life to the south of England, and died at Gomshall, Surrey.

LAWLESS, MATTHEW JAMES (1837-1864), painter. Born in Dublin, son of a solicitor. Educated at Prior Park School, Bath. He decided to become a painter, and studied at the Langham School and under Henry O'Neill RA. Exhibited at the RA in 1858, and each year afterwards until 1863. In great demand as an illustrator, and contributed many drawings to the leading periodicals of the day, including *Good Words, London Society, Once a Week,* and *Punch.* His promising career was cut short by ill-health, and he died in London on 6 August 1864. His picture 'The Sick Call' is in the National Gallery of Ireland.

LAWLESS, WILLIAM (1772-1824), general in French army. Born Dublin, 20 April 1772. Became a surgeon and professor of anatomy RCSI. Joined the United Irishmen, became close friend of LORD EDWARD FITZGERALD, was outlawed and fled to France. Joined French army and appointed captain in the Irish Legion 1803. Decorated personally by Napoleon with Legion of Honour for bravery at siege of Flushing 1806, and promoted lieutenant-colonel. Lost a leg at battle of Lowenberg, 21 August 1813. Promoted to rank of general of brigade and retired from active service to his country house at Tours. On the restoration of the Bourbons in 1814 he was placed on half-pay with rank of brigadier-general. With other Irish Catholic officers in France signed protest to French government against proposed transfer of funds of Irish College at Paris to Maynooth College. Died Paris, 25 December 1824. Buried at Père Lachaise.

LAWLOR, JOHN (1820-1901), sculptor. Born Dublin; received his art training at school of RDS. Exhibited 'Boy and Dog' at RHA 1844. Went to London 1845 and soon gained recognition. Modelled many of the statues for the new Houses of Parliament. One of eight artists chosen to execute plaques at corners of Albert Memorial, Kensington, and also executed the large group 'Engineering'. Exhibited at RA 1848-1879 and at intervals at RHA; elected ARHA 1861. His 'Bather', shown RHA 1851, was bought by Prince Albert and executed in marble for Osborne House. He visited the USA 1886-1888, then worked in Cork on statue of Bishop Delaney. Executed statue of SARSFIELD for Limerick and made busts of O'CONNELL, SMITH O'BRIEN and many other distinguished contemporaries. He worked only when he felt inclined or when necessity compelled him, and made little provision for his old age. Died in London, unmarried.

LEADBEATER, MARY (1758-1826), writer. Born in Ballintore, Co. Kildare, daughter of a Quaker family named Shackleton. Her grandfather, Abraham, taught EDMUND BURKE. Went to London with her father 1784 and met Burke, the EDGEWORTHS, George Crabbe, and Sir Joshua Reynolds, with all of whom she later maintained a corres-

pondence. Married a local landowner, William Leadbeater, in 1791, and during her married life kept the village post office. Her *Poems* appeared in 1808, followed by *The Cottage Dialogues* (1811), an annotated edition of which was published by the Edgeworths in England; *The Landlord's Friend* (1813), *Tales for Cottagers* (1814), *Cottage Biographies* (1822), *Memoirs of Richard and Elizabeth Shackleton* (1822), and *The Pedlar, a Tale* (1824). *The Annals of Ballytore*, an account of events in the years 1766 to 1824 including the 1798 Rising, was published in 1862 as *The Leadbeater Papers*. Died at Ballitore, 27 June 1826.

LECKY, WILLIAM EDWARD HARTPOLE (1838-1903), historian. Born at Newtown Park, Co. Dublin, 26 March 1838. Educated at Armagh School, Cheltenham, and TCD. Having private means, he travelled widely on the Continent after graduating in 1859. His first publications—essays, poems, and the anonymous *Leaders of Public Opinion in Ireland* (1861)—went unnoticed, but his *History of Rationalism* (1865) met with great success, and with his next book, *History of European Morals* (1869), his reputation was assured. His great work, *A History of England in the Eighteenth Century*, appeared between 1878 and 1890 in eight volumes and devoted nearly half its space to Ireland, Lecky's object being 'to refute the calumnies of Froude against the Irish people'. He declined the chair of history at Oxford in 1892 and was elected MP for Dublin University in 1895. He published two further works, *Democracy and Liberty* (1896) and *The Map of Life* (1899). In politics he was a liberal unionist and opposed home rule. He favoured the release of the Fenian prisoners and the establishment of a Roman Catholic University. He received the Order of Merit in 1902. Died in London, 22 October 1903, having lived there since 1871. He was buried in Mount Jerome Cemetery, Dublin, and his widow endowed the Lecky chair of history at TCD in his memory and left all his manuscripts, published and unpublished, to the college. They had no children.

LEDWIDGE, FRANCIS (1887–1917), poet. Born 19 August 1887 at Slane, Co. Meath, the son of an evicted tenant. He left the local national school at the age of twelve and earned his living as a farm labourer, and later as a road-overseer. His early poems were published in the *Drogheda Independent*. In 1912 he sent some verses to Lord Dunsany, who encouraged him to continue writing. Although he became known as a poet, Ledwidge remained working as before, became secretary of the Co. Meath farm labourers' union, and served on the Navan district council. In October 1914, although a convinced nationalist, he joined the Royal Inniskillings, to fight 'neither for a principle nor a people nor a law, but for the fields along the Boyne, for the birds and the blue skies over them.' He survived the Gallipoli landing, but was killed in Belgium on 31 July 1917. His first collection, *Songs of the Fields*, was published in 1916, and the *Complete Poems* in 1919.

LEECH, WILLIAM JOHN (1881–1968), painter. Born at 45 Rutland (Parnell) Square, Dublin. Educated at St Columba's College, Rathfarnham, Co. Dublin. Went to the Metropolitan School of Art and from 1899 to 1901 studied at the RHA under WALTER OSBORNE. In 1901 he went to Paris and studied in the Académie Julien under Bougereau and Laurens. He won the Taylor Scholarship in 1905 with 'A Lesson on the Violin' and again in 1906 with 'The Toiler'. He began to exhibit at the RHA in 1899 and was elected RHA in 1910. He lived in Brittany from 1902 to 1916 but continued to exhibit in Dublin. From 1907 to 1910 he was a member of a group that included the Markieviczes and GEORGE RUSSELL. In 1914 he was awarded the bronze medal of the Société des Artistes Françaises at their Paris Salon for 'Le Café des Artistes, Concarneau'. After 1916 he settled first in London and later in the south of England, continuing to exhibit with the RHA, the New English Art Club, and the RA. In 1922 and 1930 he was represented at the Irish exhibitions in Paris and Brussels. His paintings are remarkable for their treatment of light and shade and for his innovation in basing the picture plane on the diagonal and not on the horizontal of the canvas. Died in Guildford, Surrey, 16 July 1968.

LE FANU, JOSEPH SHERIDAN (1814–1873), novelist and journalist. Born at 45 Dominick Street, Dublin, on 28 August 1814. Educated by his father, a clergyman, and at TCD. While an undergraduate he became a contributor to the *Dublin University Magazine*, and about 1837 wrote two stirring ballads, 'Paudrig Crohoore' and 'Shamus O'Brien', which won wide popularity. Called to the bar 1839, but soon abandoned law to devote himself to journalism. He bought three Dublin newspapers, the *Warder*, *Evening Packet*, and *Dublin Evening Mail*, and amalgamated them as the *Evening Mail*; it flourished for over one hundred years. Gregarious and witty until the death of his wife in 1858, he withdrew from society and took to writing the novels by which he is remembered. *The House by the Churchyard* (1863) and *Uncle Silas* (1864) made his reputation as a master of the mysterious and the uncanny. *In a Glass Darkly* (1872), a collection of his stories, includes 'The Watcher', the most spine-chilling. From 1869 to 1872 he was editor and proprietor of the *Dublin University Magazine*. He published a further dozen volumes before his death on 7 February 1873 at his home, 18 (now 70) Merrion Square, Dublin.

LEMASS, SEÁN FRANCIS (1899–1971), Taoiseach. Born 15 July 1899 at Ballybrack, Co. Dublin, where his family were on holiday. Educated at O'Connell Schools, Dublin, winning a first-class exhibition in the Junior Grade Intermediate examination. At 15½ he joined the Irish Volunteers, serving first in Captain ÉAMON DE VALERA's company. He fought in the GPO in the

1916 Rising, but escaped deportation and went back to school. At eighteen he went to work in his father's drapery shop in Capel Street, Dublin, but was soon back in the Volunteers as a full-time officer. He was arrested in December 1920 and interned for a year in Ballykinlar. After the Treaty of 1921 he took the Republican side, fought in the Four Courts during the Civil War, and was captured and interned in the Curragh Camp and Mountjoy jail from December 1922 to December 1923. In prison he read every book he could find on history and economics. Elected TD 1925 and represented his constituency in Dublin city without a break until his retirement in 1969. A founder-member of Fianna Fáil; Minister for Industry and Commerce in de Valera's first government in March 1932 at the age of thirty-two. He held that portfolio—combining it with that of Supplies from 1941 to 1945—in subsequent Fianna Fáil governments until his election as Taoiseach in June 1959. He succeeded de Valera, who had nominated him Tánaiste in 1945. With characteristic drive and energy he had built up the country's industry behind a tariff wall and promoted state boards to develop turf resources (Bord na Móna) and to provide Ireland with a national airline (Aer Lingus) and shipping company (Irish Shipping). Then in 1965 he re-established free trade with England, seeing this as a prelude to a joint entry into the Common Market. In January that year he won wide praise for his initiative in visiting, in Belfast, the Premier of Northern Ireland, Captain Terence O'Neill (now Lord O'Neill of the Maine). At this and other such meetings, measures of practical co-operation between both parts of Ireland were initiated. He received many honorary degrees from universities in Ireland and the USA, and held the Grand Cross of the Order of Gregory the Great, of the Pian Order, and of the Order of Merit of the Federal Republic of Germany. Resigned as Taoiseach 10 November 1966. Died in Dublin, 11 May 1971.

LENIHAN, MAURICE (1811–1895), journalist and historian. Born 5 February 1811 in Waterford. Educated at St Patrick's College, Carlow. He became a reporter on the *Tipperary Free Press* in 1831, then editor of the *Waterford Chronicle* from 1833 and editor of the *Limerick Reporter* 1841–1843. He knew O'CONNELL, SHEIL, FATHER MATHEW and other public figures. Encouraged particularly by O'Connell, he founded the *Tipperary Vindicator* in Nenagh in 1844, to advocate repeal and disestablishment. In 1849 he bought the *Limerick Reporter* and published an amalgamated paper under the two names. He moved to Limerick shortly after and in 1866 published his large *Limerick: Its History and Antiquities*. Though published by subscription it cost him money he could ill afford, and he was obliged to work into his old age to support his family. Elected MRIA 1869 and Mayor of Limerick 1883–1885. His 'Reminiscences' appeared in the *Limerick Reporter* 1866–1869 but never appeared in book form. Died in Limerick, Christmas Day 1895.

LESLIE, SIR SHANE (1885–1971), writer. Born John Randolph Leslie on the family estate at Glaslough, Co. Monaghan. Educated at Eton, Paris University, and King's College, Cambridge. In 1907 he visited Russia and became friendly with Tolstoy, whom he described as 'the greatest influence on my life'. He entered the Catholic Church in 1908, became interested in the Irish revival movement, and espoused the nationalist cause. He contested two elections in Derry for the Nationalist Party and in 1911 toured the USA to raise funds. His first publications were collections of verse. He later turned to prose works on religious and philosophical themes and also wrote biographical studies of SWIFT, King George IV, Mrs Fitzherbert, Cardinal Manning, and others. He succeeded Wilfred Ward as editor of the *Dublin Review* in 1916, and in 1933 was made an associate member of the Irish Academy of Letters. He was honoured by Pope Pius XI, who made him a Privy Chamberlain. In 1944 he succeeded his father as baronet; that year he presented a family treasure, a ninth-century manuscript of the Féilire or calendar of AENGUS THE CULDEE, to the University of Notre Dame, Indiana, where he had been made Rosenbach Fellow of Bibliography. Died at Hove, Sussex, 13 August 1971.

LESTER, SEÁN (1888–1959), secretary-general of the League of Nations. Born at Carrickfergus, Co. Antrim. Educated at Methodist College, Belfast. He began as a journalist on the *North Down Herald* and later the *Freeman's Journal.* Active in the independence movement, he joined the new Department of External Affairs in 1922. In 1929 he was appointed Irish representative at Geneva and in 1936 High Commissioner for the League of Nations in Danzig (Gdańsk), where he showed great courage in protests against the Nazi persecution of the Jews. In 1940 he was made acting secretary-general of the league but found himself increasingly isolated in Geneva as the war ground on and the position of the league deteriorated. Victory for the Allies brought disillusionment and the end of the league. The USA had never been a member, the USSR had been expelled as an aggressor, and when in 1945 the Charter of the United Nations was adopted at San Francisco, the league was ignored. Lester had the mournful task of winding it up, and he retired to the west of Ireland in 1947, dying at Galway in 1959. He set a high standard of courage and integrity as an international civil servant and his services were recognised by the Woodrow Wilson Award and honorary doctorates from TCD and the NUI.

LEVENTHAL, ABRAHAM JACOB ('CON') (1896–1979), literary critic. Born in Dublin and educated at Wesley College and TCD. His college career was interrupted by a year spent in Palestine working for the first Zionist Commission and helping to found the *Palestine Weekly.* He succeeded Samuel Beckett in 1931 as lecturer in French literature at TCD. In 1923 he submitted a perceptive review of *Ulysses* to the *Dublin Magazine*; the printers refused to touch it and he published it in a one-issue magazine, the *Klaxon.* A friendship with SEUMAS O'SULLIVAN resulted, and for fifteen years he contributed to the *Dublin Magazine*, in a 'Dramatic Commentary', a valuable diary of Dublin theatre from 1943 to 1958. He published another magazine, *To-Morrow*, which lasted two issues. Assistant editor of the university magazine *Hermathena*, and a regular broadcaster on Radio Éireann and the BBC. On retirement from TCD he went to live in Paris and contributed to the *International Herald Tribune* and the *Financial Times*, writing much on the work of his friend Beckett. He died in Paris.

LEVER, CHARLES JAMES (1806–1872), novelist. Born in Dublin, 31 August 1806. Educated at TCD and Göttingen, where he studied medicine. After graduation he spent four or five years in the backwoods of North America. Returned to Ireland, he practised medicine in Kilrush, Co. Clare, and other country towns, collecting material for his stories of rural life. His experiences included working through the cholera epidemic of 1832. Then, after a few years in practice in Brussels he returned to Dublin and edited the *Dublin University Magazine* from 1842 to 1845. He had already published several novels, including *Harry Lorrequer* (1840) and *Charles O'Malley* (1841), for which he is now best remembered. He then went again to the Continent, eventually settling at La Spezia, and writing all the time. In 1852 he was appointed vice-consul at La Spezia by Lord Derby, and in 1867 promoted to consul at Trieste, where he died on 1 June 1872. Lever met a number of Peninsular and Waterloo officers in his wanderings on the Continent, and their experiences enabled him to give great life and colour to his army stories. His Irish novels helped to create the tradition of the rollicking devil-may-care young Irishman overflowing with animal spirits.

LEWIS, CLIVE STAPLES (1898–1963), novelist and critic. Born in Belfast, 29 November 1898, son of a solicitor. Educated at Malvern College and University College, Oxford. His studies were interrupted by service in the First World War with the Somerset Light Infantry. He graduated with a triple first, and became a fellow and tutor of Magdalen College, Oxford, from 1925 to 1954, when he was elected professor of medieval and Renaissance literature at Cambridge. *The Allegory of Love* (1936), a critical work, won him the Hawthornden Prize, and was followed by other literary criticism that presented wide information in a very readable form. He also wrote allegorical fantasy fiction and a number of religious works. *The Problem of Pain* (1940) and *The Screwtape Letters* (1942) attracted a wide readership. His autobiography, *Surprised by Joy* (1955), relates his conversion to Anglo-Catholicism. He also wrote a number of books for children. Died at Cambridge.

LEYDON, JOHN (1895–1979), public servant. Born on 17 January 1895 on a small farm at Arigna, Co. Roscommon, and educated at St Mel's, Longford, and Maynooth. He left Maynooth after two years, deciding that he had no vocation. He joined the British civil service in London in 1915 and came to Dublin in 1923 to help establish the civil service of the Irish Free State. His work in the Department of Finance in settling claims for compensation for damage caused before the Treaty and during the Civil War marked him out for advancement. In 1932 he declined the secretaryship of the Department of Industry and Commerce offered by the outgoing Cosgrave government. The offer was renewed by SEÁN LEMASS when he took office and Leydon accepted. Their dynamic partnership generated the industrial

expansion of the 1930s and the establishment of state companies such as Aer Lingus and Bord na Móna. On the outbreak of the Second World War he was put in charge of the Department of Supplies, again with Lemass as minister, and their energies and ability were applied with remarkable success to maintaining essential supplies and services. He secured the formation of Irish Shipping and then the Insurance Corporation of Ireland, to counter the excessive rates charged by London marine insurers. Both enterprises flourished for forty years. Lemass described him as the ablest man he had ever met. He retired from the civil service in 1955 and became director and later chairman of the National Bank. Distinctions included Knight Commander of St Gregory the Great, and LL.D. (DU). He died on 2 August 1979, survived by a daughter.

LOGAN, JAMES (1674–1751), colonial statesman and scholar. Born 20 October 1674 at Lurgan, Co. Armagh, the son of a Quaker schoolmaster, and educated by his father. The family moved to Bristol, and he began to trade on his own account with Dublin. He made the acquaintance of William Penn, became his secretary, and sailed with him for Pennsylvania in September 1699. Penn appointed him secretary of the province and clerk to the provincial council. On Penn's return to England in 1700 he became also commissioner of property and receiver-general. His career of fifty-two years in Pennsylvania was one of increasing responsibility and honour. He became president of the council and acted as chief executive from 1736 to 1738. His judicial career began in 1726 as a judge in Philadelphia County and in 1731 he was appointed Chief Justice of the Supreme Court. An attempt by opponents of the Penn family to impeach him for usurpation of authority dragged on from 1706 to 1712, but then petered out. His official duties did not absorb all his energies and he made a fortune in land investment and in trade with the

Indians. He lived in princely style on his estate of 500 acres at Germantown, near Philadelphia, and there received ceremonial visits from chiefs of the Indian tribes, with whom he always enjoyed friendly relations. He amassed a library of three thousand volumes and devoted his later years of retirement to the study of natural science and botany. His botanical investigations received recognition from Linné, who named the Loganiacae for him. He contributed a number of papers on scientific subjects to the Royal Society, and published a translation of Cicero's *De Senectute*, said to be the best specimen of printing from Franklin's press. Died 31 October 1751 on his estate at Germantown.

LOGUE, MICHAEL (1840–1924), cardinal. Born at Carrigart, Co. Donegal, 1 October 1840. Educated at a hedge school, a private school at Buncrana, and Maynooth. A brilliant student, he was appointed professor of dogmatic theology at the Irish College in Paris in 1866, the year of his ordination. In 1874 he returned to Donegal as a curate at Glenswilly, but was back in Maynooth in 1876 as dean and professor of Irish and theology. He became bishop of Raphoe in 1879, archbishop of Armagh in 1888, and was created a cardinal in 1893. While bishop, he raised funds in America to relieve the famine of 1880. The completion of Armagh Cathedral in 1904 was due to his energy in raising a fund of £50,000 for the purpose. When the O'Shea divorce case precipitated a crisis in the Irish Party, Logue denounced PARNELL and afterwards remained suspicious of the party. He supported the Gaelic League wholeheartedly, being himself a native Irish-speaker. Sinn Féin aroused his opposition when it resorted to physical force. He accepted the Treaty of 1921 although protesting vigorously against partition. Died in Armagh, 19 November 1924.

LONG, JOHN ST JOHN (1798–1834), painter and quack. Born at Newcastle West, Co. Limerick. Studied drawing at the Dublin Society's school. In 1825 he went to London and had some success as a painter. He exhibited in the British Institution and with the Society of British Artists and won a silver medal from the Society of Arts for a landscape. In 1827 he abandoned art and set up as a specialist in 'consumption' (tuberculosis), rheumatism, and other diseases, which he treated by liniments and friction. His patients besieged his house in Harley St, and he took £13,000 in fees in one year. In 1830 he was found guilty of the manslaughter of a patient who had died, but received only a heavy fine. In 1831 he was tried again for another death and acquitted. Died in London, 2 July 1834.

LONGFORD, CHRISTINE, COUNTESS OF (1900–1980), playwright and novelist. Born Christine Patti Trew in Cheddar, Somerset, and educated at Wells High School and Somerville College, Oxford. In 1925 she married EDWARD PAKENHAM, sixth Earl of Longford, and in 1927 came to live in Ireland, which became her adopted country. She wrote more than twenty plays for the Gate Theatre and for her husband's company, and helped him to run his theatre, continuing to manage it for some years after his death in 1961. She also wrote a number of successful novels and received an honorary doctorate from NUI. Died in a Dublin hospital on 14 May 1980.

LONGFORD, LORD. See under PAKENHAM, EDWARD.

LOVER, SAMUEL (1797–1868), novelist and painter. Born in Dublin and trained as a painter. He established himself as a marine painter and miniaturist. Elected RHA in 1828. One of the founders of the *Dublin University Magazine*. After writing ballads and sketches, he published his first book, *Legends and Stories of Ireland* (1831), with his own illustrations. He settled in London in 1835 and wrote *Rory O'Moore*

201

(1836) and the successful *Handy Andy* (1842). When his eyesight began to fail in 1844 he devised a stage entertainment called *Irish Evenings* featuring his own songs and sketches, and toured England and the USA, making a great hit with songs such as 'The Low-backed Car' and 'Molly Bawn'. In all he wrote over 300 songs. In 1856 he received a civil list pension. Died at St Helier, Jersey, on 6 July 1868. Lover's name is often coupled with that of his contemporary LEVER as an exploiter of the 'stage-Irishman', and this has caused the real merits of much of their work to be overlooked.

LOWE, SIR HUDSON (1769–1844), governor of St Helena. Son of a Miss Morgan of Galway and an army surgeon, Hudson Lowe. Born 28 July 1769 at Galway, where his father was stationed. He went to school at Salisbury, and joined the British army as an ensign before he was twelve. He served in various parts of the Mediterranean, learned Italian, French, Spanish, and Portuguese, and rose to the rank of lieutenant-colonel. During the Napoleonic wars he was for some time attached to Blücher's Prussian army. When Napoleon was banished to St Helena, then a possession of the East India Company, Lowe was appointed governor at a salary of £12,000 a year. He was made a KCB in January 1816, and instructed to permit every indulgence to Napoleon compatible with the entire security of his person. Shortly after his arrival at St Helena in April 1816, Napoleon took a violent dislike to him, and relations between the governor and Napoleon's staff became extremely strained. Napoleon died on 5 May 1821, and Lowe returned to England the following July. In 1822 BARRY O'MEARA published his *Napoleon in Exile*, castigating Lowe for his treatment of the ex-emperor. From 1825 to 1831 Lowe was attached to the staff at Ceylon (Sri Lanka) as second-in-command. He retired to London in 1831 and from then until his death was ceaselessly engaged in memorials and petitions to the govern-

ment to vindicate his actions in St Helena and to defend his character as a public servant whose conduct it had approved. He died at Charlotte Cottage near Sloane Street, Chelsea, on 10 January 1844, having dissipated his fortune on that fruitless campaign.

LUBY, THOMAS CLARKE (1821–1901), Fenian. Born in Dublin, son of a Church of Ireland clergyman. Educated at TCD. He became involved in the Young Ireland movement with SMITH O'BRIEN, and after the abortive rising of 1848 was imprisoned for a short time. About 1853 he travelled around Ireland with JAMES STEPHENS to sound out the feelings of the people, and in 1858 took a leading part in founding the Irish Republican Brotherhood or Fenian movement, and formulated the oath by which the members were bound. He was sent to America by Stephens in 1863 to collect funds, but without great success, and he returned the same year to find the movement languishing. He then became co-editor with KICKHAM and O'LEARY of the *Irish People*, a newspaper founded by Stephens in 1863 to advance the Fenian cause, which won a wide circulation. Arrested with other leaders in November 1865 and sentenced to twenty years' penal servitude. Released in 1871, but forbidden to return to Ireland, he settled in New York and took up journalism. Published a *Life of Daniel O'Connell* (1872) and *The Lives and Times of Illustrious and Representative Irishmen* (1878). Died at New York, 1 December 1901. His reminiscences are incorporated in O'Leary's *Recollections*.

LUCAS, CHARLES (1713–1771), patriot. Born 16 September 1713, probably at Ballingaddy, Co. Clare, and became an apothecary in Charles St, Dublin. In 1735 he published a pamphlet on abuses in the sale of drugs, which led to an Act for the inspection of medicines. Elected to the council, he campaigned with his friend La Touche against corruption in the city administration and advocated parliamentary independence for Ireland. Threatened with imprisonment, he fled to the continent in 1749. He graduated in medicine at Leiden in 1752 and conducted a successful practice in London from 1753 to 1761. That year he returned to Dublin, was elected MP for the city, and held his seat until his death ten years later. When the *Freeman's Journal* was founded in 1763 he became a frequent contributor. He published a number of political pamphlets, translated and printed *The Great Charter of the City of Dublin* (1749), and never hesitated to attack a system or practice that he thought unjust. He died at his house in Henry St, Dublin, on 4 November 1771. There is a statue of him in City Hall.

LUCE, ARTHUR ASTON (1882–1977), professor of philosophy. Born in Gloucester, 21 August 1882. Educated at Eastbourne College and TCD: BD 1908, DD 1920. Ordained 1908; elected fellow 1912. Chaplain, St Columba's School, 1907–1909. Served in First World War with 12th Royal Irish Rifles 1915–1918, and awarded MC 1917. Professor of moral philosophy, TCD, 1928–1949. Canon, St Patrick's Cathedral, 1930–1936, chancellor 1936–1953 and precentor 1953–1977. Vice-provost, TCD, 1946–1951. He became internationally known as an authority on GEORGE BERKELEY and published *Berkeley's Philosophical Commentaries* (1944), *The Works of George Berkeley* (with T. E. Jessop) (nine volumes, 1948–1957), and *Life of George Berkeley* (1949). Also lectured extensively and contributed to many learned journals on Berkeley's philosophy. Other publications included *Bergson's Doctrine of Intuition* (1922), *Teach Yourself Logic* (1958), and *The Dialectic of Immaterialism* (1963). Appointed Berkeley Professor of Metaphysics, TCD, 1953, with life tenure for himself only. His recreation was fishing, and his *Fishing and Thinking* (1959) was regarded highly by anglers. His wife and daughter were accidentally drowned in the Liffey at Celbridge, Co. Kildare, in May 1940. He died in a Dublin hospital on 28 June

1977, following an assault a few days previously. His 65-year tenure of fellowship was a record.

LUNDY, ROBERT (*c.* 1689), governor of Derry. After service abroad, was sent to Derry in 1688 and took command of the small Protestant garrison. With them he declared allegiance to William III and opposition to James II. When Jacobite forces approached the city, he recommended immediate surrender. REV. GEORGE WALKER and Major Henry Baker, with the support of the apprentice boys, called on the people to resist, and removed him from office. The siege was abandoned on 31 July 1689, after 105 days, when relief ships burst through booms on the river Foyle. Lundy was allowed to escape in disguise to Scotland, where he was captured. He was imprisoned for a short time in the Tower of London; his fate after his release is not known. His name was made a synonym for treachery, and his effigy is burnt each year at the commemoration of the siege.

LUTTRELL, HENRY (1655–1717), colonel. Born about 1655, probably at the family estate, Luttrellstown, Co. Dublin. He served in the French army for some time. He then joined the army of James II and served with distinction under SARSFIELD in Connacht 1689–1690. After the surrender of Limerick he brought his regiment over to the Williamites and received a pension of £500 a year from William III. These circumstances tend to confirm the contemporary belief that he betrayed the Jacobites and gave information that led to their defeat at Aughrim and to the surrender of Limerick. In 1693 he enlisted 1,500 Irish Catholics to serve for the Venetian government against the Turks, and in 1702 became a major-general in the Dutch army. While in his sedan chair in Stafford Street, Dublin, on 3 November 1717 he was shot dead; the assassins were never traced.

LYNAM, WILLIAM FRANCIS (*c.* 1845–1894), soldier and writer. Born probably in Co. Galway. Lieutenant, Royal Lancashire Militia, 1867; major 1881. Lived at Churchtown House, Co. Dublin, 1863–1887, then at 2 Warrenpoint, Clontarf, where he died. Wrote many serials, including extremely popular *Mick McQuaid*, which ran in the *Shamrock* from 1867 until his death. Also wrote a play, *Darby the Dodger*.

LYNCH, CHARLES (1906–1984), pianist. Born on 22 October 1906 in Parkgariff, Cork, son of a colonel in the British army, and educated at boarding-school in Sussex. He gave his first public recital at nine, and won a scholarship to the Royal Academy, London, at fifteen. By the 1930s he had won an international reputation. In addition to concert recitals he broadcast regularly with the BBC, and in 1937 acted as assistant to Sir Thomas Beecham at Covent Garden. SIR ARNOLD BAX, Master of the King's Musick, dedicated his fourth sonata to him, and Lynch played it for the first performance. At Rachmaninov's request he gave the first performance in England of the composer's first sonata, and in 1938 he was invited to play Stravinsky's own arrangement of *Petruchka*. The Second World War interrupted his career. He returned to Ireland, conducted ten operas with the Dublin Grand Opera Society and gave many recitals at the RDS. He also gave master classes at the Cork School of Music, giving his advice and knowledge freely to young pianists. Although his reputation still stood high, he did not regain his place as a musician of international importance. He died in hospital in Cork on 15 September 1984.

LYNCH, HENRY BLOSSE (1807–1873), explorer. Born 24 November 1807 at Partry House, Ballinrobe, Co. Mayo. Became a midshipman in the Indian navy at sixteen. He served on the survey of the Persian Gulf, learned Persian and Arabic, and on promotion to lieutenant in 1829 was made interpreter to the Gulf squadron. In 1834 he was appointed second-in-command to COLONEL F. R. CHESNEY on an expedition to explore the Euphrates route to India. When Chesney returned to England in 1837, Lynch was placed in command, and ascended the Tigris to Baghdad, a feat of navigation never before accomplished. He was stationed at Beles, on the Euphrates, and at Baghdad, until 1851. From 1851 to 1853 he commanded a small squadron of the Indian navy during the Second Burmese War. He retired in 1856 and settled in Paris. At the end of the Persian War of 1856–1857 he was delegated to conduct the negotiations with the Persians, which resulted in the Treaty of Paris of March 1857. In recognition of his services the Shah nominated him to the highest class of the Order of the Lion and Sun, an order he had first received in 1837. Died at his home in the Rue Royale, Faubourg St Honoré, 14 April 1873.

LYNCH, REV. JOHN (*c*.1599–*c*. 1673), historian. Born Galway; educated by Jesuits. Became a priest about 1622 and taught classics in Galway. Appointed archdeacon of Tuam. Fled to France after fall of Galway to Parliamentarians in 1652. Translated *Foras Feasa ar Éirinn* by SEATHRÚN CÉITINN into Latin. Wrote *Cambrensis Eversus* (1662), a valuable work on the history of Ireland including a refutation of Giraldus, and other treatises. Died probably at St Malo.

LYNCH, PATRICIA (1898–1972), author of stories for children. Born in Cork. The family moved to London after her father's death, and she was educated at schools in England, Scotland, and Bruges. She became active in the women's franchise movement and was sent to Ireland in 1916 by Sylvia Pankhurst to report the Rising for the *Workers' Dreadnought*. Described as the first authentic and sympathetic account of affairs in Ireland, her report was published as a pamphlet, *Rebel Ireland*, and circulated in Europe and the USA. Her first story had been published when she was eleven, and her first book, *The Cobbler's Apprentice*, won the Tailteann silver medal for literature in 1932. *The Turf Cutter's Donkey* (1934) was serialised in the *Irish Press* with illustrations by JACK B. YEATS. In all she published more than fifty books, and they were translated into many European languages. In 1920 she married the writer R. M. Fox and settled in Dublin, where she died in September 1972.

LYNCH, THOMAS KERR (1818–1891), explorer. Younger brother of HENRY BLOSSE LYNCH. Born Partry, Co. Mayo; educated TCD. Joined his brother on Euphrates expedition 1837–1842. Established steamer service on Tigris linking Baghdad with India. Travelled extensively in Mesopotamia (Iraq) and Persia (Iran). Appointed consul-general for Persia in London and made knight of the Lion and Sun by the Shah. Died London, 27 December 1891.

LYND, ROBERT WILSON (1879–1949), essayist. Born in Belfast, 20 April 1879, son of a Presbyterian minister. Educated at RBAI and QUB. In 1901, determining to be a writer, he went to London, where he shared a studio with PAUL HENRY, and made a precarious living for some years as a freelance journalist. In 1908 he joined the staff of the *Daily News* (the *News Chronicle* from 1930), and remained there until near the end of his life, being literary editor from 1912. To this paper he contributed essays and descriptive articles on sporting and other public events. His best work, however, appeared in the *New Statesman* from 1913 to 1945, where week after week he delighted readers with his whimsical and engaging essays signed 'Y.Y.' These were collected in book form at intervals; he also published *Home Life in Ireland* (1919), *Ireland a Nation* (1919), *The Art of Letters* (1920), and *Dr Johnson and Company* (1927). His wife, Sylvia, was a novelist and poet, and their hospitable house in Hampstead became a meeting-place for writers and artists. He died there, 6 October 1949.

LYONS, FRANCIS STEWART LELAND (1923–1983), historian. Born in Derry on 11 November 1923 and educated in St Stephen's School, Tunbridge Wells, High School, Dublin, and TCD. He lectured in history at Hull University and TCD, became professor of history in Kent University in 1964 and master of Eliot College there in 1969. In 1974 he became Provost of TCD, relinquishing the post in 1981, three years ahead of term, to devote himself to completing a biography of W. B. YEATS commissioned in 1974 by Oxford University Press. His reputation as a historian and biographer with an exceptionally lucid and elegant style rests on a succession of distinguished books: *The Fall of Parnell, 1890–91* (1960), *John Dillon* (1968), *Ireland Since the Famine* (1971), *Charles Stewart Parnell* (1977), and *Culture and Anarchy in Ireland, 1890–1939* (1979), which was awarded the Ewart-Biggs Memorial Prize and the Woolfson Literary Award. He was awarded honorary doctorates by five universities: Pennsylvania, Kent, Hull, QUB, and NUU. He was visiting professor at Princeton University and a fellow of the Royal Society of Literature and of the British Academy. He died on 21 September 1983, after a short illness, survived by his wife and two sons.

LYSAGHT, ANDREW. See under RYNNE, MICHAEL.

LYTTON, LADY ROSINA (1802–1882), novelist. Born Rosina Doyle Wheeler, Co. Limerick, 4 November 1802. Her parents were separated and she lived in London with her uncle, General Sir John Doyle. She married Edward Bulwer Lytton, first Baron Lytton, against his mother's wishes. They became estranged, and were legally separated in 1836. In her first novel, *Chevely, or the Man of Honour* (1839), her husband figures as the villain; she renewed her attack on him in some of her succeeding novels. In 1858 she was confined in a mental asylum for a short time. She lived for various periods in Paris, Florence, and Geneva. Returned to England 1857. Died Upper Sydenham, 12 March 1882.

M

**MacALISTER, ROBERT ALEX-
ANDER STEWART** (1870-1950),
archaeologist. Born in Dublin; educated
at Rathmines School, in Germany, and
Cambridge University. Member, Royal
Society of Antiquaries, 1895. Edited the
society's journal 1910-1918, and president 1924-1928. Director of
excavations for the Palestine
Exploration Fund 1900-1909. The
results of his work there were embodied
in over fifty publications. First professor
of Celtic archaeology, UCD, 1909-1943.
President, RIA, 1926-1931; chairman,
National Monuments Advisory Council, 1930-1943. At his instigation
the archaeological survey of Ireland was
undertaken. *The Archaeology of Ireland*
appeared in 1927. Among his most
important works is a monograph on
ancient settlement in the barony of
Corkaguiney, Co. Kerry. He was particularly interested in the epigraphy of
Irish monuments, especially ogham
inscriptions, and published *The Secret
Languages of Ireland* in 1937. Died at his
Cambridge home in April 1950.

McALLISTER, ALEXANDER (1877-
1944), playwright and novelist. Born in
Dublin; educated at Clongowes and the
Royal University. Chief clerk and librarian, NUI, 1908-1914. Began writing
plays in 1900, using the pseudonyms
Henry Alexander and Anthony P.
Wharton. They included *Irene Wycherly*
(1906) and *At the Barn* (1912), his two
most successful plays. During the First
World War he served in the machine-
gun corps. After 1918 he lived in
England, and under the name Anthony
Wharton wrote novels such as *The Man
on the Hill* (1923). In 1925 he began
writing novels under another
pseudonym, Lynn Brock, beginning

with *The Deductions of Colonel Gore. The
Two of Diamonds* was published in 1926
and followed by a long series of successful
detective novels. In 1943 his last play,
The O'Cuddy, was produced at the Abbey
Theatre.

MACAN, SIR ARTHUR VERNON
(1843-1908), gynaecologist and obstet-
rician. Born 9 Mountjoy Square,
Dublin, 30 January 1843. Educated at St
Columba's College, Rathfarnham, Co.
Dublin, and TCD, graduating in
medicine 1868. Studied medicine at
Berlin 1869-72, interrupting his studies
to serve as a volunteer in the Prussian
army in 1870. Assistant physician at the
Rotunda Hospital 1872, then gynaecologist to the Royal City of Dublin
Hospital (Baggot St), and finally he was
appointed master of the Rotunda in
1882. He instituted the necessary
reforms to bring obstetric practice up to
the standard he had observed on the
Continent, and was one of the first to
apply Listerian principles in midwifery.
Later he substituted aseptic for antiseptic
methods, as far as possible. By these
means the heavy mortality from
puerperal sepsis was dramatically
reduced. These reforms met strong
opposition from the medical profession,
and he and other progressives were
called 'the German Band'. King's Professor of Medicine at TCD 1889, and
gynaecologist to Sir Patrick Dun's
Hospital. President, RCPI, 1902-1904.
Knighted in 1903, and honoured by the
leading medical societies of Ireland and
England. Although he did not publish a
book, he made many contributions to
the *Dublin Journal of Medical Science* and
other medical journals. Died at his
home, 53 Merrion Square, Dublin, on 26
September 1908. His wife predeceased

him in 1886, dying of puerperal sepsis, a disease that he had done so much to combat.

McARDELL, JAMES (*c.* 1728–1765), mezzotint engraver. Born in Cow Lane, Dublin. Apprenticed to John Brooks, engraver, as a boy. In 1746 he went with Brooks to London, and was soon working on his own account. He engraved plates after Reynolds, Van Dyck, Gainsborough, and other leading artists, and became the foremost engraver of his day. Died in London on 1 June 1765.

MACARDLE, DOROTHY (1899–1958), historian, novelist and drama critic. Daughter of Sir Thomas Macardle KBE, DL, head of the well-known Dundalk brewing family. Educated UCD; became teacher at Alexandra College, Dublin. Influenced by MAUD GONNE, she became involved in the republican movement, was arrested, and went on hunger strike. Her position at Alexandra College was kept open until she could resume work. Worked as a publicist during the War of Independence and for the Republican side during the Civil War. At the request of ÉAMON DE VALERA she wrote her best-known work, *The Irish Republic* (1937), a history of the years 1916–1923. Other works include *Tragedies of Kerry* (1946), an account of incidents during the Civil War, and *Children of Europe* (1949), on the subject of refugee children. Two of her novels, *Uneasy Freehold* (1944) and *The Uninvited*, were made into films; she also wrote two plays, *Asphara* and *Dark Waters*. During the early years of the *Irish Press* she was the paper's drama critic. Between 1939 and 1945 her concern was for refugees. Also keenly interested in youth movements. President, Irish Association of Civil Liberties, 1951. Died in December 1958 in the Medical Missionaries of Mary Hospital, Drogheda.

McATEER, EDWARD (1914–1986), politician. Born in Coatbridge, Scotland, where his father, an Irish-speaker

from Fanad, Co. Donegal, worked as a labourer. The family moved to Derry when Edward was two. In 1949 he was returned unopposed to Stormont as MP for Mid-Derry. Elected for Foyle as the anti-partition candidate in 1953 and became leader of the Nationalist Party. When Terence O'Neill and SEÁN LEMASS exchanged visits in 1965, McAteer responded positively by accepting the role of leader of the opposition at Stormont. He abandoned this position after the civil rights marches of 1968. In the general election of February 1969 he was defeated for Foyle by John Hume, then vice-chairman of the Derry Citizens' Action Committee, presaging the eclipse of his party by the SDLP and Sinn Féin. In June 1970 he was defeated by the sitting unionist for the Derry City seat at Westminster, and retired from active politics. He died in a Derry hospital on 28 March 1986, survived by his wife, Rose, and ten children.

McAULEY, CATHERINE (1778–1841), founder of the Order of Mercy. Born at Stormanstown House, Dublin, 29 September 1778. Her parents died when she was young, and at eighteen she was adopted by Mr and Mrs Callahan of Coolock House. She converted them both to Catholicism, and on his death in 1822 Callahan left her his large fortune. She bought a site in Lower Baggot Street, and in 1827 built a school for poor children and a residence for working women, called the House of Our Blessed Lady of Mercy. In 1829 with two others she entered the Presentation Convent at George's Hill, Dublin, and when they took simple vows of poverty, chastity and obedience on 12 December 1831, the Sisters of Mercy came into existence. ARCHBISHOP MURRAY supported her aims, 'to educate poor little girls, to lodge and maintain poor young ladies who are in danger, that they may be provided for in a proper manner, and to visit the sick poor.' Her rule was approved by Pope Gregory XVI on 24 March 1835 and given final confirmation by him in June 1841. The order became the largest religious congregation ever founded in the English-speaking world, with houses in England, Australia, New Zealand, and the USA. She died on 10 November 1841, and is buried at the convent in Baggot Street.

MacBRIDE, CATALINA (1901–1976), revolutionary. Daughter of WILLIAM BULFIN, born in Buenos Aires and brought up in Ireland from 1902. From her earliest years, 'Kid' Bulfin, as she was known, was involved in the struggle for independence. Secretary to AUSTIN STACK; opposed the Treaty and joined the Four Courts garrison in 1922. Imprisoned for a year in Kilmainham Jail and went on hunger strike. On 26 January 1925 she married SEÁN MACBRIDE at University Church, Dublin, in great secrecy, as both were on the Free State government's 'wanted' list. Continued to support the republican movement and campaigned for the release of prisoners and the abolition of capital punishment. Died in Dublin on 12 November 1976.

MacBRIDE, JOHN (1865–1916), leader in the 1916 Rising. Born in Westport, Co. Mayo, on 7 May 1865. Studied medicine for a while but gave it up and worked with Hugh Moore and Co., a Dublin firm of wholesale chemists. As a young man he joined the IRB and was associated with MICHAEL CUSACK in the formation of the GAA. In 1896 he was sent by the IRB on a mission to the USA. Shortly afterwards he emigrated to London and then to South Africa. When the Boer War broke out in 1899 he joined an Irish Brigade formed to fight the British, and became second-in-command with the rank of major. He then settled in Paris, and there, in 1903, married MAUD GONNE. The marriage was a failure and he returned to Dublin and became a minor official in the Dublin waterworks. He did not join the Irish Volunteers, but on Easter Monday 1916 he offered his services to THOMAS MACDONAGH and was made second-in-command of the garrison in Jacob's factory. After the rising he was court-martialled, sentenced to death, and executed in Kilmainham jail on 5 May.

MacBRIDE, MAUD GONNE (1865–1953), revolutionary. Born at Aldershot, daughter of a wealthy army officer of Irish descent and an English mother. Educated by a governess in France, after her mother's early death. Her father was posted to Dublin in 1882 and she acted as his hostess there until his death some years later. Sent to Royat in the Auvergne to recuperate after a tubercular haemorrhage, she fell in love with Lucien Millevoye, a politician and journalist, whose marriage had broken down. He proposed that they should work together for Irish freedom and the regaining of Alsace and Lorraine for France. She returned to Ireland, led protests against evictions in Donegal, and helped to secure the release of Irish political prisoners from Portland jail. In 1890 her doctor sent her to the south of France, where she again met Millevoye, also threatened with tuberculosis. Between 1893 and 1895 she bore two children; the first died in infancy, the second, a girl, was named Iseult. In 1899 she broke off their affair on discovering that Millevoye had no real interest in the Irish cause. She spent the 1890s in ceaseless nationalist activities, visiting France, England, Scotland and America to lecture and collect funds. In Paris she published a news-sheet, *L'Irlande Libre,* to enlist French sympathy for the Irish cause. On Easter Sunday 1900 she founded a revolutionary women's society, Inghinidhe na hÉireann ('Daughters of Ireland'), which organised a patriotic treat for 30,000 schoolchildren the following July as a counter-attraction to an official treat celebrating a visit to Ireland by Queen Victoria. In 1908 the Daughters founded a monthly magazine, *Bean na hÉireann* ('The Irishwoman'), with HELENA MOLONY as editor. W. B. YEATS had unsuccessfully proposed marriage to her in 1891. On 2 April 1902 she took the leading role in his play, *Cathleen ní*

Houlihán. She had 'the walk of a queen'; her beauty and the power of her acting created a sensation. About this time she joined the Catholic Church. On 21 February 1903 she married JOHN MACBRIDE in Paris; their son, SEÁN, was born in 1904. The marriage was a failure, and MacBride returned to Ireland. She remained in Paris until 1917. In 1918 she was arrested in Dublin, and interned in Holloway jail for six months. During the War of Independence she worked with the White Cross for the relief of victims and their dependants. She opposed the Anglo-Irish Treaty of 1921, and in 1922 settled at Roebuck House on the outskirts of Dublin and organised the Women's Prisoners' Defence League to help Republican prisoners and their families. In 1938 she published *A Servant of the Queen*, a vivid account of her life until her marriage. She died on 27 April 1953 and was buried in the Republican Plot in Glasnevin cemetery, Dublin.

MacBRIDE, SEÁN (1904–1988), patriot and world statesman. Born in Paris on 26 January 1904, son of JOHN MACBRIDE and MAUD GONNE MACBRIDE. His first language was French, but after early schooling in Paris he was sent to Mount St Benedict's, Gorey, a Benedictine establishment. He joined the Irish Volunteers, saw active service in the War of Independence, and opposed the Treaty of 1921. He remained a member of the IRA, served terms in prison, and went on the run for several years. Earned his living as a journalist in Paris and London, then returned to Dublin and became chief of staff of the IRA in 1936. He was called to the bar in 1937 and resigned from the IRA on enactment that year of the new Constitution of Ireland, which, he said, made it possible to achieve national objectives by political means. He soon made his mark as a barrister, especially in defending republican prisoners. In 1946 he founded Clann na Poblachta and joined the first inter-party government in February 1948 as Minister for External Affairs.

Under his guidance Ireland rejected NATO and acceded to the Council of Europe, thus affirming Ireland's neutral stance. His presence in the Government undoubtedly influenced the repeal of the External Relations Act and the formal declaration of a republic, symbolically, on Easter Monday 1949. A crisis over the 'Mother and Child' health scheme, proposed by Dr Noël Browne, Clann na Poblachta Minister for Health, and opposed by the Catholic hierarchy, who had MacBride's support, prompted Browne's resignation in April 1951. In the general election of June 1951 Clann na Poblachta was reduced from ten seats to two. MacBride held his seat, was re-elected in 1954, but was defeated in the 1957 and 1961 general elections, and left Irish politics.

While continuing his career at the bar and contesting important cases in constitutional law, MacBride became increasingly prominent on the world stage as a defender of human rights and campaigner for peace. He took the Lawless case on internment to the European Commission on Human Rights, the first case to be heard by that body. He was a founder-member of Amnesty International and international chairman 1961–1974. Secretary-general of the International Commission of Jurists 1963–1971, which monitored the observance of human rights around the world. Executive chairman, International Peace Bureau, Geneva, 1969, and president 1974. Member of many other international bodies devoted to the cause of peace. United Nations Commissioner for Namibia 1973–1976, with rank of assistant secretary-general. In 1974 his work was recognised by the award of the Nobel Prize for Peace. In 1977 he received the Lenin Peace Prize and in 1978 the American Medal for Justice. He was chairman of UNESCO's international commission for the study of communication problems, which published its report in 1980 under the title *Many Voices, One World*. He was responsible for proposing the 'MacBride Principles', aimed at eliminating discrimination by employers in Northern Ireland against Catholics, and won support for these principles in the USA in his last public campaign. He died at his home, Roebuck House, Clonskea, Dublin, on 15 January 1988 after a short illness and was buried in the republican plot in Glasnevin cemetery with his mother and his wife, CATALINA MACBRIDE.

MAC CÁBA, ALASDAIR (1886–1972), teacher, politician, and founder of the Educational Building Society. Born 5 June 1886 at Keash, near Ballymote, Co. Sligo. Educated Summerhill College, Sligo. Trained as a teacher at St Patrick's, Dublin, and returned to Sligo to become principal of Drumnagranchy NS. Elected member of the Supreme Council, IRB, 1914 and active in recruiting members. Acquitted by Dublin jury on charge of possessing explosives 1915. Jailed for six months in 1917, released after thirty days' hunger strike. Further jail periods in Lincoln and the Curragh. Supported the Treaty and was adjutant in Free State army during the Civil War. Sinn Féin TD for South Sligo 1918–1921, East Mayo–Sligo 1921–1923, and Leitrim–Sligo 1923–1924. Resigned his seat 1924, retired from politics, and returned to teaching. Founded Educational Building Society in 1935 with £500 capital. Continued to teach while managing the society in the evening. Became full-time managing director 1941. With support of teaching profession the society flourished and now has assets exceeding £100 million. He retired in 1970. Died 31 May 1972.

McCABE, EDWARD (1816–1885), cardinal, and archbishop of Dublin. Born in Dublin. Educated at Father Doyle's School on the quays, and at Maynooth College. Ordained 1839. Curate in Clontarf, then parish priest of St Nicholas Without, and of Kingstown (Dún Laoghaire). Bishop of Gadara 1877, and assistant to CARDINAL CULLEN, archbishop of Dublin. Succeeded Cullen as archbishop, March 1879. Created a cardinal March 1882. A town-dweller all his life, he had little sympathy for the Land League, continually denounced agrarian outrage, and disapproved strongly of the 'no rent' manifesto. Died at his house in Eblana Avenue, Kingstown, 11 February 1885.

McCALL, PATRICK JOSEPH (1861–1919), song-writer. Born on 6 March 1861 at 25 Patrick Street, Dublin, where his father ran a public house and grocery, and educated at the Catholic University. He contributed sketches and verses to the popular press and is best-remembered for his ballads 'Boolavogue' and 'Kelly, the Boy from Killane'. He died in Dublin on 8 March 1919.

McCANN, JOHN (1905–1980), politician and playwright. Born in Dublin and educated at Synge Street CBS and Kevin Street and Bolton Street technical schools. He became an engineer in the Post Office, joined the Irish Volunteers and was dismissed from his job for his republican activities. Founder-member of Fianna Fáil; TD for Dublin South City 1939–1954, Lord Mayor 1946–1947 and 1964–1965. He wrote a number of very popular plays for the Abbey Theatre company, then playing in the Queen's Theatre, Pearse Street. *Twenty Years A-Wooing* was the most successful, and broke box-office records. He died in a Dublin hospital, survived by his wife, Margaret, a son, the actor Dónal McCann, and a daughter.

McCARRISON, SIR ROBERT (1878–1960), medical scientist. Born in Portadown, Co. Armagh, 15 March 1878. Studied medicine at Queen's College, Belfast, and Richmond Hospital, Dublin. Joined the Indian Medical Service in 1900 and served at Chitral, Gilgit, and Kassauli. He made a special study of goitre and cretinism, and in 1913 began a wider investigation into the nature of deficiency diseases. His studies were interrupted by active service in the First World War. He returned to India in 1918 and resumed his researches, working in the Pasteur Institute at Coonoor with only two untrained assistants and little equipment. Director of the Nutrition Research Laboratories at Coonoor 1929, and held this position until he retired from the Indian Medical Service in 1935 with the rank of major-general. During this period, with encouragement from the viceroy, Lord Linlithgow, he built up one of the finest institutes of its kind in the world. The importance of his work lay in his combination of laboratory experiments with observations in the field. In 1935 he went to live in Oxford. An official medical adviser during the Second World War, and from 1945 to 1955 the first director of postgraduate medical education at Oxford. On his seventy-fifth birthday he was presented with a festschrift entitled *The Work of Sir Robert McCarrison*, which included all his important papers, and an assessment of his work. His distinctions were numerous, including various academic prizes and medals. Awarded the Kaisar-i-Hind gold medal for public service in India 1911, and in 1914 the Prix Amussat of the Academy of Medicine of Paris for original researches on goitre and cretinism. Honorary physician to the king of England 1928–1935. Knighted in 1933. When on leave in 1921 he made a tour of the USA, giving lectures at the leading universities and medical foundations. A McCarrison Society has been founded in London. Died at Oxford, 18 May 1960.

McCARTHY, JUSTIN (1830–1912), politician, historian and novelist. Born near Cork on 22 November 1830. Family poverty frustrated his wish to read for the bar, and at seventeen he turned to journalism with the *Cork Examiner*. In 1854 he joined the *Northern Daily Times* in Liverpool, and in 1859 he went to London and joined the *Morning Star*, becoming editor in 1864. He then published a number of successful novels, and was so well received on a visit to the USA that he contemplated settling there, but returned to London in 1871 to serve in the Irish Party under PARNELL while earning his living as leader-writer on the *Daily News*, and by writing novels and biographies. His *History of Our Own Times* (1879) established him as a popular historian. MP for Co. Longford 1879, and then vice-chairman of the party. When the party split following the O'Shea divorce case, McCarthy led the anti-Parnell group, but avoided personal recriminations and remained on friendly terms with Parnell. The strain of political life combined with unremitting literary activity undermined his constitution, and he became almost blind in 1897. He left political life in 1900 and continued to dictate novels and memoirs until 1911, but with diminished success. In 1903 he was awarded a civil list pension of £300 a year for his service to literature, at the instance of the prime minister, Balfour. Died at Folkestone on 24 April 1912. His novels include *Dear Lady Disdain* (1875), and *Mononia* (1901), depicting life in Munster in his youth.

McCAUGHEY, SIR SAMUEL (1835–1919), the 'Sheep King'. Born near Ballymena, Co. Antrim, 30 June 1835. Emigrated to Australia 1856. Worked as a 'jackeroo' or apprentice on a sheep station in Victoria; became manager in two years. In 1860 bought a station in New South Wales with two partners and built up a famous Merino stud. Acquired other stations. Introduced irrigation methods and spent large sums to improve yield and quality of wool. At one stage was shearing one million sheep a year. Became wealthiest man in the state. Member of Legislative Council 1899–1919; knighted 1905. Presented twenty warplanes to the government in First World War. Bequeathed nearly two million pounds for education and charitable purposes. Died, unmarried, at North Yanco, 25 July 1919.

McCLINTOCK, SIR FRANCIS LEOPOLD (1819–1907), admiral and explorer. Born in Dundalk on 8 July 1819. Entered the British navy in 1831;

211

lieutenant 1845. In 1848 and again in 1850 he was chosen to serve on voyages of discovery to the Arctic. In 1852 he was in command of the *Intrepid* on a further expedition. He made several long journeys by sledge in the Arctic regions, and introduced many improvements in this method of travelling. In 1855 Lady Franklin asked him to command an expedition to search for her husband, Sir John Franklin, presumed lost in the Arctic. He sailed in the *Fox*, a yacht bought by Lady Franklin and fitted out at her expense. On his return in 1859 he published an account of this expedition, confirming the death of Franklin and his companions, entitled *The Voyage of the Fox in the Arctic Seas; a Narrative of the Fate of Sir John Franklin and his Companions.* It went into a number of editions, and he was knighted in 1860 for his services. M'Clintock Channel, Canada, is named after him. From 1861 until his retirement in 1884 he served in the Mediterranean, the North Sea, North America, and the West Indies, with a five-year spell as admiral superintendent of Portsmouth dockyard. KCB 1891. Died in London, 17 November 1907.

M'CLURE, ROBERT JOHN LE MESURIER (1807–1873), explorer. Born in Main Street, Wexford, 28 January 1807. Educated by General Le Mesurier, who adopted him as a son and sent him to Eton and Sandhurst. He entered the British navy in 1824, served in an Arctic expedition in 1836, and in 1848 was first lieutenant to Sir John Ross's expedition that went in search of Sir John Franklin and his crew, who had set out in 1845 to find the North-West Passage and had disappeared in the Arctic regions. This was one of the first of fifteen expeditions despatched with this object between 1848 and 1854. In 1850 he again went in search of Franklin as second-in-command of another expedition. M'Clure's ship, the *Investigator*, parted from its companion and was ice-bound until the following spring. M'Clure discovered Baring's Island, penetrated Barrow Strait into the Atlantic Ocean, and discovered the North-West Passage. The ship being trapped again in ice for two years, M'Clure with his men completed the journey on foot and were rescued eventually by Captain Kellett. On his return to England in 1854 he was knighted and voted a reward of £10,000 by Parliament. M'Clure Strait, Canada, is named after him. After further service in Chinese waters, he was made an admiral. He published the story of his Arctic expeditions in *Voyages* (1884). Died in England, 17 October 1873.

MAC CON MARA, DONNCHADH RUA (1715–1810), poet. Born at Cratloe, Co. Clare. As a young man he was sent to Rome to study for the priesthood, but was expelled for misconduct. On his return to Ireland he became for a while a schoolmaster at Sliabh gCua, near the Comeragh mountains, Co. Waterford, where a school of poetry still flourished. His *Eachtra Ghiolla an Amarráin* (The Adventures of a Luckless Fellow), a long mock-heroic poem, sometimes called 'The Mock Aeneid', recounts an attempt to make a new start in life by emigrating to Newfoundland. Thousands sailed there from Waterford every year, but it is not certain that Mac Con Mara ever made the voyage, although its vivid description of the miseries and hazards of shipboard life seem to come from first-hand experience. He led a wandering life, seldom settling for long anywhere, and *Bán-Chnoic Éireann Óigh* (The Fair Hills of Holy Ireland), a classic lyric of exile, is said to have been written while he was in Hamburg. About 1765 he was in dire straits from his rakish way of life, and turned Protestant to secure the parish clerkship of Rossmire. Little is known of his subsequent career. The *Freeman's Journal* announced his death thus: 'On October 6th 1810 at Newtown, near Kilmacthomas, in the 95th year of his age, Denis MacNamara, commonly known by the name of Ruadh or Redhaired, the most celebrated of the modern bards.'

McCONNELL, ADAMS ANDREW (1884–1972), surgeon. Qualified in medicine at TCD in 1909. Joined the staff of the Richmond Hospital, Dublin, in 1911, and worked there for over sixty years, specialising in brain surgery, in which he gained an international reputation. President RCSI 1935–1937. Regius Professor of Surgery in Dublin University, 1946–1956. Died in the Richmond Hospital on 5 April 1972.

McCORMACK, JOHN (1884–1945), operatic and concert tenor. Born at Athlone, Co. Westmeath, 14 June 1884. Educated at the Marist Brothers, Athlone, and Summerhill College, Sligo. In 1902 he won a gold medal in the tenor competition at the Feis Cheoil in Dublin. After a short tour in the USA in 1903 he studied in Italy under Sabatini and made his operatic début in 1907 at Covent Garden in *Cavalleria Rusticana.* In 1909 he appeared at the Manhattan Opera House, New York, in *La Traviata,* and afterwards sang with the Chicago and Boston opera companies and the Metropolitan Opera Company. His success continued, and in 1911 he toured Australia with Melba in Italian opera. After two further operatic seasons he turned to the concert stage where he achieved extraordinary popularity, and was acclaimed as the greatest lyric tenor of his time. He made more than five hundred recordings, which sold steadily in great numbers. In recognition of his services to Catholic charities, he was made a hereditary Papal count in 1928. He became an American citizen in 1919. Died at his house, 'Glena', Booterstown, Co. Dublin, 16 September 1945, survived by his wife, the former Lily Foley, a Dublin singer, and three children.

McCORMICK, F. J. See under JUDGE, PETER.

McCRACKEN, HENRY JOY (1767–1798), United Irishman. Born in High Street, Belfast, of Huguenot ancestry on 31 August 1767. At twenty-two he was put in charge of a cotton factory. In 1791 he joined with THOMAS RUSSELL in founding the first Society of United Irishmen in Belfast. He was arrested in 1796 and imprisoned in Kilmainham jail for thirteen months. Released on bail, he took a leading part in planning a rising and was appointed to command the insurgents in Co. Antrim. An attack on Antrim town led by him was defeated by the British troops. He hid for some months in the Slemish mountains, but when about to escape to America he was seized, tried by court-martial, and hanged at Belfast market-house on 17 July 1798.

MAC CUILLEANÁIN, CORMAC (836–908), king-bishop of Munster. Succeeded to the kingship in 902, and was soon embroiled with Flann mac Mael Sechnaill, king of Tara. Flann made several expeditions into Munster and took hostages, but in 907 Cormac marched northwards and defeated Flann in a battle at Mág Léna. The following year, after an extensive campaign in Connacht, he was defeated and slain in the battle of Belach Mughna. Tradition ascribed to him the authorship of Sanas Cormaic ('Cormac's Glossary'), which, as well as commenting upon obsolete and difficult words, gives by way of illustration much information about ancient customs and beliefs. The Saltair or Psalter of Cashel is also attributed to him, although it appears to be the work of more than one hand. It gives the genealogies of the leading families of the period, and includes the Book of Rights, a chronicle of the stipends and tributes paid to the provincial kings, written partly in prose and partly in verse. These works are among the most valuable to have survived from mediaeval Ireland, and have been edited and published by WHITLEY STOKES, JOHN O'DONOVAN, and KUNO MEYER.

McCULLAGH, JAMES (1809–1847), mathematician. Born Upper Badoney, Co. Tyrone, son of a poor farmer. Educated TCD; took fellowship 1832. Professor of mathematics 1836, professor of natural philosophy 1843. Introduced studies of electricity, galvanism, heat and terrestrial magnetism into fellowship course. Secretary RIA 1842–1846. Received Cunningham Medal 1838. Elected FRS and received Copley Medal 1843. Wrote papers on geometry, wave theory of light, and surfaces of the second order. Unsuccessfully contested Dublin University in nationalist interest. He committed suicide in October 1847, probably in a fit of temporary insanity due to overwork.

MacCURTAIN, TOMÁS (1884–1920), nationalist. Born at Ballyknockane, Co. Cork, in March 1884. Educated at Bunfort NS and the North Monastery School, Cork. Joined the Blackpool branch of the Gaelic League, 1901, and became its secretary 1902. Joined the Cork branch, National Council of Sinn Féin, 1907 and became a member of the IRB. From 1911 he was involved in the running of Na Fianna Éireann, and he became a Volunteer in 1914. Contributed to *Fianna Fáil*, a weekly paper published by TERENCE MACSWINEY, in 1914. With MacSwiney he dispersed the Volunteers in Cork in obedience to MACNEILL's countermanding order at Easter 1916. Served prison terms in 1916 and 1917 in Wakefield, Frongoch, and Reading. Elected as Sinn Féin councillor for Cork North-West in the 1920 local government elections. On 30 January 1920 he was elected Lord Mayor of Cork. In the early morning of Saturday 20 March he was murdered in his home. A coroner's jury returned a verdict of wilful murder against the RIC.

MacCURTIN, HUGH (c. 1680–1755), poet and lexicographer. Born Kilmacreehy, Corcomroe, Co. Clare. Educated by his cousin, Andrew McCurtin, whom he succeeded as chronicler to the O'Briens of Thomond. Studied in France. Tutor in household of Dauphin for seven years. Returned to Ireland about 1714 and led wandering life of poet. Wrote laments for deaths of

Donagh O'Loughlin of Burren and Lewis O'Brien, and other poems. Published at Louvain *Elements of the Irish Language* (1728). With Conor O'Begley published in Paris in 1732 an *English-Irish Dictionary*, incomplete, but a valuable record of the vernacular of the day. He kept a school in his native parish in his later years, and died there.

MacDERMOT, FRANK (1886–1975), politician and journalist. Born Dublin, youngest son of twelve children of the Right Honourable The MacDermot KC, of Coolavin, Co. Sligo. Educated at Downside and Queen's College, Oxford. Called to the English bar in 1911 and became active in politics, campaigning for home rule in two Westminster general elections. On the outbreak of the First World War he joined the British army and served in France and Belgium, ending with the rank of major. In 1919 he joined Huth and Co., bankers, in New York but retired in 1927 and went to live in France. He began to take an interest in Irish politics and in 1929 stood unsuccessfully in West Belfast as a Nationalist candidate for Westminster. In 1932 he won a seat for Roscommon as an independent in the Dáil general election, and later that year he formed the National Centre Party, which had as its aims the elimination of antagonism between North and South and the establishment of good relations with Britain as a basis for unity. In the general election of 1933 the Centre Party won eleven seats, and shortly afterwards agreed to merge with Cumann na nGaedheal to form the United Ireland Party, a name suggested by MacDermot. Although he accepted GENERAL EOIN O'DUFFY as leader of the new party and became vice-president, he was unhappy with O'Duffy's leadership, and resigned from the party in 1935. He sat as an independent until the general election of 1937. Did not seek re-election, but was nominated to the Seanad in 1938 by DE VALERA. That year he became Irish correspondent in Dublin for the *Sunday*

214

Times, but moved to New York soon after the start of the Second World War when wartime censorship made his task frustrating. When the war ended he transferred to Paris, and was the chief *Sunday Times* correspondent there until his retirement in 1950. He continued to live quietly in Paris until his death, which took place in London on 24 June 1975 while he was visiting his family. His only book, a biography of WOLFE TONE, was published in 1939.

MAC DIARMADA, SEÁN (1884–1916), revolutionary. Born in Kiltyclogher, Co. Leitrim, on 28 February 1884, emigrated at sixteen to Glasgow, where he worked as a gardener and later as a tramway conductor. In 1902 he moved to Belfast, and worked as a tramcar conductor and then as a barman. He joined the Gaelic League and became an Irish-speaker. In the league he met BULMER HOBSON, who asked him to act as organiser for the Dungannon Clubs, set up by the IRB to promote republicanism in Ulster. In 1906 he joined the Belfast Circle of the IRB and was later appointed treasurer of the Supreme Council. In 1907 he became a full-time organiser for Sinn Féin at a salary of £1.50 a week, and set up branches all over Ireland. In 1910 he was appointed manager of *Irish Freedom*, a monthly journal launched by the IRB and edited by Dr Patrick McCartan. An attack of poliomyelitis crippled him in 1912 but he continued his work in the republican movement, was elected to the Provisional Committee of the Irish Volunteers in 1913, and in 1915 became a member of the military council set up by the IRB to plan a rising. He fought in the GPO in Easter Week 1916 and was one of the seven signatories of the Proclamation of the Republic. Court-martialled, sentenced to death, and executed on 12 May.

MAC DOMHNAILL, SEÁN CLÁRACH (1691–1754), poet. Born Charleville (Ráth Luirc), Co. Cork. Was trained for the priesthood and may have taken holy orders. He knew Latin and Greek well and began a translation of Homer into Irish verse. He was undisputed chief poet in the Munster of his day and presided over the Courts of Poetry that met in his house. About 1738 he wrote a merciless satire on the death of a local landlord, Colonel Dawson, and had to take refuge abroad for some years. Only a handful of his poems survive, including lines on Philip of Orléans and on the European wars of 1740-1748. Ó DUINNÍN published an edition in 1902.

MacDONAGH, DONAGH (1912–1968), poet, dramatist and lawyer. Born in Dublin, 22 November 1912, son of THOMAS MACDONAGH. Educated at Belvedere College and UCD. Called to the bar 1935; practised until 1941, when he was appointed a district justice. Had a varied literary career as poet, dramatist, ballad writer, broadcaster, and editor. His most successful play was the exuberant *Happy as Larry* (1946), later described as 'a ballad opera without music', which has been translated into a dozen European languages. He also wrote *God's Gentry*, a play about tinkers, *Step-in-the Hollow* (1957), and *Lady Spider*, a re-telling of the Deirdre legend. With LENNOX ROBINSON he edited the *Oxford Book of Irish Verse* (1958). His own poetry appeared in two volumes, *The Hungry Grass* (1947) and *A Warning to Conquerors* (1968). He was a justice of the Dublin Metropolitan Courts when he died in Dublin on 1 January 1968.

MacDONAGH, THOMAS (1878–1916), poet and revolutionary. Born 1 February 1878 in Cloughjordan, Co. Tipperary. Educated at Rockwell College, Cashel. Taught in Kilkenny and Fermoy and, while in Aran to improve his Irish, met PATRICK PEARSE. In 1908 he came to Dublin and helped Pearse found St Enda's School at Cullenswood House, Ranelagh, becoming the first teacher on the staff. He then graduated from UCD and was appointed assistant in the English department. When the Irish Volunteers were founded in November 1913 he joined at once, and became Director of Training the following year. He joined the IRB in 1915 and was a member of the military council set up to plan a rising. He was in command of Jacob's factory during the 1916 Rising, signed the Proclamation of the Republic, and was executed by firing squad on 3 May 1916. A British officer said, 'They all died well, but MacDonagh died like a prince.' With JOSEPH PLUNKETT he edited the *Irish Review*, and helped to found EDWARD MARTYN's Irish Theatre in Hardwicke Street in 1914. He published several volumes of poems, and *Literature in Ireland, Studies Irish and Anglo-Irish* (1916); his play *When the Dawn is Come* was produced at the Abbey Theatre in 1908.

McDONALD, WALTER (1854–1920), theologian. Born in June 1854 at Mooncoin, Co. Kilkenny. Educated St Kieran's College, Kilkenny, and Maynooth seminary. Ordained 14 October 1876. Taught philosophy and English in St Kieran's until 1881 when he was appointed professor of theology at Maynooth. Prefect of Dunboyne Establishment at Maynooth 1888, continuing as professor. His *Motion: Its Origin and Conservation* (1898) aroused doubts about his orthodoxy. The Irish bishops referred it to Rome, and the Sacred Congregation of the Index condemned it in December 1898, but said that out of regard for the author, whose piety was not in doubt, and for Maynooth, the decree should not be published. Dr McDonald wrote five further volumes of theology but all were refused an imprimatur and so could not be published. However, *Principles of Moral Science* (1903), a statement of ethical principles handed down by tradition, passed the censor. In 1906 he initiated the *Irish Theological Quarterly*, but episcopal pressure forced him to withdraw from the editorial committee. He supported DR O'HICKEY in his appeal to Rome against his dismissal from

Maynooth. Largely responsible for changing the system of appointment to Maynooth to favour candidates who had published work of exceptional merit, and for provision of adequate libraries and reading-rooms. *Some Ethical Questions of Peace and War, with Special Reference to Ireland* (1919) and *Ethical Aspects of the Social Question: Suggestions for Priests* (1920) were published in London, under imprimatur from the Westminster censor. At no time did the bishops attempt to dismiss him. He died at Maynooth on 2 May 1920 after a long illness. His *Reminiscences of a Maynooth Professor,* edited by Denis Gwynn, appeared in 1925.

MacDONNELL, ALEXANDER (1798–1835), chess player. Born at Belfast. Became a merchant at Demerara in the West Indies. About 1830 appointed London secretary to the West India Committee of merchants, with the duty of watching the progress through Parliament of bills connected with the West Indies. He became the leading player at the Westminster Chess Club, which was founded at Bedford St, London, in 1833. In 1834 a chess master from Paris, Louis de Labourdonnais, engaged him in a famous series of matches at the Westminster Club. As MacDonnell spoke no French and Labourdonnais no English, the only word that passed between them was 'check'. After eighty-eight games the Frenchman held the lead, winning forty-four to MacDonnell's thirty, fourteen being drawn. The contest was interrupted by Labourdonnais's recall to Paris, and before they could meet again MacDonnell died, 14 September 1835, in a boarding-house in Tavistock Square, where he had lived for many years. He was regarded as one of the great masters of his day, and a selection of his games was published by W. G. Walker in 1836.

MacDONNELL, ANTONY PATRICK, BARON MacDONNELL OF SWINFORD (1844–1925), statesman. Born at Shragh, Co. Mayo, on 7

March 1844. Educated at Summerhill College and Queen's College, Galway. Joined the Indian civil service, and received rapid promotion in the provincial government at Calcutta. He was largely responsible for the Bengal Tenancy Act of 1885, designed to protect the tenant-farmers from rackrenting and arbitrary eviction. In 1893 he was created knight commander of the Star of India, and in 1895 became Lieutenant-Governor of the United Provinces, ruling over a population of forty million. His health suffered from his unremitting hard work and he resigned in 1901. In 1902, though a Roman Catholic and a Liberal, he was offered and accepted appointment as permanent under-secretary at Dublin Castle, having indicated that he thought Ireland not yet ready for home rule, though he favoured it in principle. He gave valuable service to Wyndham, the Chief Secretary for Ireland, in preparing the Land Act of 1903, which dramatically accelerated the long process of transfer of ownership from landlord to tenant. His attempt to secure a measure of devolution of powers to Dublin angered the Unionists, and was opposed by the Nationalists, who feared it might weaken the home rule cause. Another project, to reform university education, eventually succeeded with the establishment of the NUI and QUB in 1908, but by that time he had resigned, a disappointed man. Created Baron MacDonnell of Swinford in 1908 and spoke frequently in the House of Lords on Irish and Indian questions. Died in London, 9 June 1925.

McDONNELL, SORLEY BOY (*c.* 1505–1590), chieftain. Born probably at Ballycastle, Co. Antrim. Imprisoned in Dublin Castle 1551–1552, and in retaliation seized the constable at Carrickfergus Castle and exacted a heavy ransom. In 1564–1565 he was captured by SHANE O'NEILL, who had attacked him and his Scots followers. Two years later O'Neill was slain by the McDonnells. Sorley Boy was defeated at Castle Toome in 1575 by Essex. He had sent his wife and children and those of his followers to Rathlin Island for safe-keeping, but they were butchered by Captain John Norris while Sorley Boy looked on helplessly from the mainland. He 'was likely to run mad for sorrow', Essex reported to Elizabeth. He retrieved his position with fresh support from Scotland and dominated north-east Ulster until 1586. He then submitted on good terms. He died at Dunanyane Castle.

McDYER, CANON JAMES (1911–1987), priest and community leader. Born at Kilraine, Glenties, Co. Donegal, on 14 September 1911, son of a small farmer, and educated at St Eunan's College, Letterkenny, and Maynooth. He was ordained in 1937 and served in London and Brighton during the Second World War, working largely with Irish immigrants. He was then transferred to Tory Island, Co. Donegal, and in 1951 to Glencolumbkille, where he remained as curate until 1971. When he arrived the area had no electricity, no piped water, no industry, no dispensary, and no paved roads. He initiated a number of co-operative projects, including vegetable processing, craft work, a knitwear factory, a holiday village, and a folk museum. Hundreds of young people came yearly for summer work. He secured piped water and paved roads, and built a community hall and park. Electricity was brought to the glen in 1954, well before most rural areas. Not all his projects were successful, but he brought confidence and hope to a remote and depressed area. The folk museum still attracts many visitors, and a fish processing plant now employs 150. He published *The Glencolumbkille Story* (1962) and his autobiography, *Father McDyer of Glencolumbkille* (1982). He was appointed parish priest of Carrick and Glencolumbkille in 1971 and died at home on 25 November 1987.

McELLIGOTT, JAMES J. (1893–1974), public servant. Born Tralee, Co. Kerry. Educated at UCD, graduating with honours in classics and economics. Entered the civil service at administrative level 1913, and was assigned to the Irish Local Government Board. Joined the Irish Volunteers on their formation that year, and served in the GPO in the 1916 Rising. Deported to England and interned in various jails, winding up in Stafford jail in the next cell to MICHAEL COLLINS. On release in 1917 he became a freelance financial journalist. From 1921 to 1923 he was managing editor of the *Statist*, a financial weekly published in London. Invited back to Ireland in 1923 to help establish the new Department of Finance. Appointed secretary of the department and head of the civil service in 1927. Held this post for twenty-six years, until his appointment in 1953 as governor of the Central Bank, and played a key role in the formation of the economic policies of the new state. Conservative in outlook, he favoured the doctrines of Adam Smith and Gladstone rather than the new theories of Keynes and his followers. Served on the Banking Commissions of 1926 and 1934–1938. Chairman of the Tariff Commission from 1926 to 1930, and first president of the Economic Research Institute. Also represented Ireland at many international conferences. Retired from the governorship of the Central Bank in 1960, but continued to serve as a director until his death, which occurred suddenly at his house in Blackrock, Co. Dublin, on 23 January 1974.

MacENTEE, SEÁN (1889–1984), politician and poet. Born in College Square, Belfast, educated at St Malachy's and Belfast Municipal College of Technology and qualified as an electrical engineer. He joined the Irish Volunteers and was sentenced to death for his part in the Easter Rising of 1916. The sentence was commuted to life imprisonment. After penal servitude in Dartmoor, Lewes and Portland prisons, he was released under amnesty in June 1917.

Elected Sinn Féin MP for Monaghan in 1918 general election. Opposed the Treaty, arguing passionately that it would perpetuate partition. Imprisoned by the Free State government; after the Civil War in 1923 he became a partner in a firm of consulting engineers. Founder-member Fianna Fáil 1926 and TD for Dublin constituencies 1927–1969. Minister for Finance in first Fianna Fáil government 1932 and held that portfolio eleven times. Also served as Minister for Local Government, for Industry and Commerce, and for Health. Tánaiste 1959–1965. Retired 1965. Honours included honorary doctorate (NUI) and Knight Grand Cross of the Pian Order. His *Poems* (1918) showed genuine poetic quality; his total commitment to public life took precedence over writing. He died in Dublin on 10 January 1984, survived by a son and two daughters: one is the poet Máire Mhac an tSaoi, second wife of Dr Conor Cruise O'Brien. His wife predeceased him.

MAC EOIN, GENERAL SEÁN (1893–1973), soldier. Born at Bunlahy, Granard, Co. Longford. Worked as a blacksmith and farmer before coming into prominence in the War of Independence as leader of the North Longford Flying Column, IRA. Became known as 'the Blacksmith of Ballinalee' after holding the village of Ballinalee against superior British forces in February 1921. Captured the following month and sentenced to death. While in prison he was elected to Dáil Éireann in the general election of May 1921. After the Truce had been arranged, all imprisoned deputies save Mac Eoin were released, but following an ultimatum from DE VALERA he was freed at once. In the Dáil he seconded the motion, proposed by ARTHUR GRIFFITH, that the Treaty be accepted. Joined the Free State army as a senior officer. Chief of Staff 1928–1929. In 1929 he resigned from the army to enter the Dáil as deputy for Sligo-Leitrim, and afterwards represented Longford-Westmeath until his defeat in the 1965 general election. He stood unsuccessfully as Fine Gael candidate for the presidency in 1945 and again in 1959. Minister for Justice in the first Coalition government 1948–1951; Minister for Defence 1954–1957. Died in St Bricin's Military Hospital, Dublin, 7 July 1973.

McFADDEN, CANON JAMES
(1842–1917), the 'fighting priest of Gweedore'. Came to Gweedore, Co. Donegal, from Doochary in 1873 and became parish priest two years later. He ruled his parish strictly, built schools and selected the teachers, and put down cross-roads dancing and merrymaking, principally because of the poteen-drinking that accompanied these amusements. Though a small, stocky man, his fearless enforcement of his own rules made him known as An Sagart Mór, 'the big priest'. He was not averse to fisticuffs or to using his blackthorn stick in encounters with transgressors, and once made a group of children walk barefoot to school for a week in winter as a penance. He became famous for his defence of the small farmers of Gweedore against rackrenting landlords and evictions. When the bailiffs set out to seize goods and cattle, warning was given by the blowing of horns from house to house across the valleys, and often as many as a thousand men and women assembled to harass police and bailiffs and prevent a seizure. He was saying Mass in Derrybeg chapel on 3 February 1889 when a force of police under District Inspector Martin arrived, escorting a number of bailiffs. A scuffle took place when he emerged, and Martin was thrown to the ground. He struck his head against a stone and died shortly afterwards. Some of the Donegal men who were present escaped by taking to the mountains and bogs, where they eluded the police. Others walked to Derry and took passage to America. Thirty men, including Father McFadden, were arrested and lodged in Maryborough (Portlaoise) jail. On 18 October 1889 the trial of the priest and twelve others began, the chief charge being the murder of Martin. The prosecutor was the attorney-general, PETER O'BRIEN, 'Peter the Packer', and the jury was selected from neighbouring rich landowners and merchants. TIM HEALY was counsel for the defendants. After the trial had proceeded for two weeks, an arrangement was made between Healy and O'Brien that all should plead guilty, that nobody should be condemned to death, and that Father McFadden should be released immediately. The others received sentences ranging up to thirty years, and in a bitter article the *Freeman's Journal* accused Healy and Father McFadden of reneging on them. He was never again to place himself on the wrong side of the law. Subsequently he became parish priest of Iniskeel, and lived in Glenties, where he died.

MAC FIRBISIGH, DUBHALTACH
(*c.* 1585–1670), antiquary and scribe. Born at Lackan Castle, Co. Sligo, of a family of hereditary historians. He studied law and history at the schools kept by the MacEgan family in Co. Tipperary and the O'Davorens in Co. Clare, and about this time copied the Annals of Ossory and Leinster. After the death of his father in 1643 and the loss of the family estate in the wars of 1641–1643, he moved to Galway. Here he compiled a valuable treatise on the genealogy of Irish families. From 1655 to 1666 he was employed in Dublin by SIR JAMES WARE, for whom he translated and transcribed many important manuscripts, including *Chronicum Scotorum: a Chronicle of Irish Affairs from the Earliest Times to 1135* (published 1866). While resting in an inn at Dunflin, Co. Sligo, on his way on foot to Dublin he was stabbed to death by a man called Crofton who was making advances to the servant-girl and resented the presence of the old man.

McGEE, THOMAS D'ARCY
(1825–1868), writer and nationalist. Born at Carlingford, Co. Louth, 13 April 1825. Emigrated to Boston in 1842 and became editor of the *Boston Pilot* in 1846.

His growing reputation and his political activities brought him to the notice of the Young Irelanders, and he was appointed London correspondent of the *Nation*, to which he contributed many poems. After the abortive rising of 1848 he went back to Boston and founded the *American Celt*. His views changed in favour of constitutional methods, and he was bitterly attacked by former associates. Moving to Montreal, he founded another paper, the *New Era*, became an MP, held government office, and took a leading part in promoting the federation of the Canadian provinces. He denounced a threatened Fenian invasion of Canada, and on 7 April 1868 he was shot dead outside his house in Ottawa. His publications included a *Popular History of Ireland* (1862), as well as biographies and speeches.

MacGILL, PATRICK (1891–1963), author. First of eleven children of a small farmer in the Glenties, Co. Donegal. Left the local school when he was ten, and at twelve was hired out at the Strabane hiring-fair. After two years he went to work on the Scottish potato fields and was later the first to publicise the dreadful conditions there. He worked as a farm hand and then as a navvy, endeavouring to educate himself by joining circulating libraries. His first publication, *Gleanings from a Navvy's Scrapbook* (*c.* 1911), included translations of La Fontaine's fables and Goethe's poems. The success of the collection brought him an invitation to join the editorial staff of the *Daily Express*. Routine reporting did not appeal to him, so he accepted a job editing ancient manuscripts in the Chapter Library of Windsor Castle. His appointment at twenty-three by the archivist, Canon Dalton, caused a sensation. Meanwhile, he published two further volumes of poetry, *Songs of a Navvy* (1911) and *Songs of the Dead End* (1912). His first novel, the semi-autobiographical *Children of the Dead End* (1914), sold 35,000 copies in England in the week of publication. Regarded as 'anti-clerical', it had less

success in Ireland. A year later *The Rat Pit* was published, followed by seventeen other novels, including *Glenmornan* (1919) and *Moleskin Joe*. His experiences at the front during the 1914–1918 war were recorded in *The Great Push*. He wrote one play, *Suspense*. In 1930 he went to the USA, intending to stay for a short period. However, illness prevented him from leaving; he wrote no more, and died there in November 1963. He is buried at the Notre Dame cemetery, Fall River, Massachusetts.

McGILLIGAN, PATRICK (1889–1979), politician and lawyer. Born in Coleraine, Co. Derry, on 12 April 1889, son of an Irish Party MP, and educated at St Columb's, Derry, Clongowes Wood College and UCD. Called to the bar 1921. He joined Sinn Féin and stood unsuccessfully for North Derry in 1918. Elected TD for NUI in 1923. Minister for Industry and Commerce 1924–1932. In 1927 he pushed through the legislation to set up the ESB and harness the Shannon, despite strong opposition from the financial and commercial establishment. After the assassination of KEVIN O'HIGGINS in 1927 he was given the additional portfolio of External Affairs. He played a leading part at the Committee on the Operation of Dominion Legislation in 1929 and at the Imperial Conference of 1930. The Statute of Westminster, which emerged from these meetings, gave greater independence to Commonwealth countries and opened the way for further constitutional change. Represented Dublin constituences in Dáil Éireann 1937–1965. Minister for Finance 1948–1951 in first inter-party government, initiated measures to promote exports and stimulate industry, and introduced the Keynesian concept of the dual budget. While in opposition 1932–1948 he built up a practice at the bar and became professor of constitutional and international law at UCD. Senior counsel 1946, Attorney-General in the second inter-party government 1951–1954. An incisive and witty speaker, his work in the three ministries he held earned for him from commentators the title 'nation builder'. He died in a nursing home in Dalkey, Co. Dublin, survived by his wife, Ann, a daughter and three sons.

MAC GIOLLARNÁTH, SEÁN (1880-1970), author. Born at Gurteen, Ballinasloe, Co. Galway. On leaving school, joined the British Revenue Department in London. There he joined the IRB and the Gaelic League. He came to Dublin at the beginning of the century and became editor of *An Claidheamh Soluis*, the organ of the Gaelic League. From 1909 to 1916 he taught at St Enda's, the school founded by PEARSE. He was a courier for the IRA during the War of Independence. In 1920 he qualified as a solicitor, began to practise at Athenry, Co. Galway, and presided at Sinn Féin courts. In 1925 he was appointed a district justice for Galway and served until 1950. He explored all parts of Connemara in search of folklore, and published several books of folk-tales and local history. Wild birds and their haunts were the inspiration for *Saoghal Éanacha* (1925) and *Féilire na nÉan*. His last book, *Mo Dhúthaigh Fhiáin*, won the Craoibhín Prize at the Oireachtas. It gives a memorable description of the wild places of Connemara: Cúdar, the lake-dweller, is a character of Wordsworthian simplicity. He died in Galway in January 1970.

MacGONIGAL, MAURICE (1900-1979), landscape painter. Born in Dublin in January 1900 and educated at Synge St CBS. He became an apprentice at the stained-glass studios of his cousin HARRY CLARKE. He joined Fianna Éireann and then the IRA and was interned in Kilmainham Jail and later at Ballykinlar Camp before the Treaty. He studied at the Metropolitan School of Art, Dublin, and in the Netherlands, won the Taylor Scholarship in painting, and in 1928 won the silver medal for landscape and the bronze medal for drawing at the Tailteann exhibition.

Assistant professor of painting, National College of Art, 1937 and succeeded SEÁN KEATING as full professor. In 1969 he resigned in protest against what he saw as the erosion of the professional authority of the college. Became Keeper of the RHA 1950 and moved with his family into the Keeper's house in Ely Place, Dublin, formerly the residence of OLIVER ST JOHN GOGARTY. President, RHA, 1962-1978. Honorary member RA and Scottish RA. Honorary LL.D. (NUI) in 1970. He died in a Dublin hospital on 31 January 1979, survived by his wife, Aida, and sons Muiris and Ciarán.

McGOWRAN, JACK (1918-1973), actor. Born in Dublin; educated at Synge Street CBS. He started his working life as a clerk in an insurance office. After some years of amateur acting he turned professional and played at the Gate and Abbey Theatres, and with the Radio Éireann Repertory Company. He went to London about 1953 and acted with success in West End plays produced by independent companies. Film work came from directors John Ford, Paul Rotha, Walt Disney, and Roman Polanski. In the 1950s he began a notable series of interpretations of the plays of Samuel Beckett. In 1961 he was named British Television Actor of the Year for his performance as Vladimir in *Waiting for Godot*, and in 1971 became the New York Critics 'Actor of the Year' for his playing in Beckett's *Beginning to End*; he was the first non-American actor to receive this award. He died in New York in January 1973.

McGRATH, JOSEPH (1887-1966), revolutionary and founder of Irish Hospitals Sweepstakes. Born in Dublin. Joined firm of accountants. Enrolled in IRB and fought in Marrowbone Lane in 1916 Rising. Arrested, and jailed in Wormwood Scrubs and Brixton. Elected Sinn Féin member for St James division, Dublin, in general election, December 1918. TD for North-West Dublin 1921-1923. Minister for Labour,

January–August 1922, and for Industry and Commerce, August 1922 to April 1924. TD for North Mayo 1923. Resigned from office April 1924 because of dissatisfaction with government attitude to army officers and 'government by a clique and by officialdom of old regime'. Resigned Dáil seat, October 1924. In 1925 he became labour adviser to Siemens-Schuckert, German contractors for the Shannon hydro-electric scheme. Founded Irish Hospitals Sweepstakes in 1930. Its great success made him a wealthy man. He launched into other extensive and successful business interests and became Ireland's best-known racehorse owner and breeder. Won all the Irish classic races and, with Arctic Prince, won the Epsom Derby in 1951. Member of Turf Club 1951; member of Racing Board 1945–1966 and chairman 1956–1962; president Bloodstock Breeding Association of Ireland, 1953. Died at his house in Cabinteely, Co. Dublin, March 1966.

MacGREEVY, THOMAS (1893–1967), poet and critic. Born at Tarbert, Co. Kerry. Commissioned in the Royal Field Artillery in First World War and twice wounded. On being demobilised he entered TCD and graduated in history and political science. He worked for a while with LENNOX ROBINSON in organising libraries, and then in 1926 was appointed English reader at the University of Paris. Through friendship with JAMES JOYCE he secured a post on the art review, *Formes*. When Joyce died he was at his bedside, and was his executor. In the 1930s he moved to London, where he became chief critic on *The Studio*, lectured on the history of art in the British National Gallery, and contributed to the *Times Literary Supplement*. In 1934 he published a book of poems. In 1941 he settled in Dublin, and was appointed Director of the National Gallery in 1950. He published essays and monographs on the works of JACK B. YEATS, T. S. Eliot, Richard Aldington, and Nicholas Poussin. In 1948 the French government made him a *chevalier*

of the Legion of Honour. He retired from the gallery in 1964, and died in Dublin, 16 March 1967.

McGUINNESS, NORAH (1903–1980), painter. Born in Derry, daughter of a coal merchant and shipowner, and studied at the National College of Art, Dublin, and the Chelsea Polytechnic, London. In London she married the poet Geoffrey Phibbs; they were divorced in 1929. She continued her studies in Paris under André Lhote. She was in New York just before the Second World War, exhibited at the Sullivan and Reinhardt galleries and designed windows for leading department stores. Returning to Ireland, she was president of the Living Art Exhibition 1944–1972, was elected to the RHA in 1957, illustrated books by W. B. YEATS and designed sets for the Abbey and Peacock theatres and for Longford Productions. For over twenty years she designed windows and displays for a Grafton Street store. In 1950 with NANO REID she represented Ireland at the Venice Biennale; her paintings, mostly landscapes, were also shown in London and Paris and are in many public collections at home and abroad. She travelled widely, visiting many European countries, Egypt and India. A retrospective exhibition was held in the Douglas Hyde Gallery, TCD, in 1968. She died in a Dublin hospital in November 1980.

McGUIRE, EDWARD (1932–1986), painter. Born in Dublin and educated at Downside School, Somerset, and the Slade School of Art, London. He travelled widely in France and Italy and lived off and on in London. At home he soon won recognition as a portrait painter, particularly of literary figures. His subjects included Séamus Heaney, PATRICK KAVANAGH and Francis Stuart. He was represented in the 'Rosc' exhibition 1971 and the Delighted Eye exhibition in London 1980. He delighted to paint owls and hawks, with masterly craftsmanship. He died in a Dublin hospital on 26 November 1986, survived by his wife, Sally.

MacHALE, JOHN (1791–1881), Archbishop of Tuam. Born 6 March 1791 at Tobbernavine, Tirawley, Co. Mayo, and baptised by a Father Andrew Conroy, who was hanged after the rising of 1798. MacHale went to a local hedge school and then to Maynooth, where he was ordained in 1814. He remained in Maynooth teaching theology until 1825 when he was named coadjutor bishop of Killala. In a series of public letters begun in 1820 and signed 'Hierophilos', he attacked the tithe system, which obliged Catholics to contribute to the established Church of Ireland, and appealed for Catholic emancipation and the repeal of the Union. These letters attracted the attention of O'CONNELL, and MacHale became one of his chief supporters. He was appointed Archbishop of Tuam in 1834 despite strong government opposition aroused by his uncompromising nationalist views. He continued to denounce the maladministration of Ireland by English governments, supported the agitation for reform of land tenure, and opposed the plans for national schools and Queen's Colleges put forward by Peel and Russell between 1847 and 1850. He succeeded in gaining the support of the hierarchy for his strongly held views against the education together of Catholic and Protestant children; in 1869 Pope Pius IX ratified their decision to condemn mixed education. Though approving of the plan to establish the Catholic University in Dublin, MacHale was opposed to the selection of Newman, an Englishman, as first rector; this opposition, and his differences with CARDINAL CULLEN over the issue, did much to prevent the success of the plan. After this controversy in 1854 his influence with the hierarchy declined as that of Cardinal Cullen grew, and he withdrew from national affairs. A native Irish-speaker, MacHale was all his life an enthusiastic advocate of Irish culture and the language. He published poems, textbooks, a diocesan catechism and devotional works in Irish; his most important publications were a translation of the Pentateuch (1861) and of Homer's *Iliad* (1844–1871). At ninety he preached regularly at Sunday Mass; not until he was eighty-eight did he receive a coadjutor to assist him. He died at Tuam, 7 November 1881.

McHUGH, ROGER (1908–1987), professor, author and playwright. Born in Dublin on 14 July 1908 and educated at UCD. Lecturer in English, UCD, 1947–1965; professor of English 1965–1967 and professor of Anglo-Irish literature and drama 1967–1978. He was Mellon professor, University of Pittsburgh, 1969–1970, Berg professor, New York University, 1977 and visiting professor at various times at universities in England, Scandinavia, Iceland, Japan, and the USSR. Member of Seanad Éireann 1954–1957 and of the Senate, NUI, 1954–1972. His plays *Trial at Green Street Courthouse* (1941) and *Rossa* (1945) were produced at the Abbey Theatre; *Rossa* won the Abbey Theatre prize for 1945. He edited *Carlow in '98* (1949), *Letters of W. B. Yeats to Katharine Tynan* (1953), *Dublin, 1916* (1966), and *Ah, Sweet Dancer: W. B. Yeats and Margot Ruddick, a Correspondence* (1970). Wrote *Henry Grattan* (1936) and, with Maurice Harmon, *A Short History of Anglo-Irish Literature* (1982). He died in Dublin on 2 January 1987, survived by his wife, Patricia, three daughters and two sons.

McINERNEY, MICHAEL (1906–1980), journalist. Born in Limerick and educated at Limerick Vocational School. Became a clerk with the London and North-Western Railway in London. Was co-founder of the London Connolly Club and joined the Communist Party of Great Britain. Freelance contributor to the *Daily Worker* and editor of *Irish Front*, the journal of the Connolly Association, 1939–1941. Was refused permission to re-enter Britain after a holiday in Dublin 1941, and became a clerk in the Great Northern Railway in Belfast. While there he was editor of the Communist Party of Ireland newspaper, *Unity*, and an active trade unionist. Moved to

Dublin 1946 as a reporter with the *Irish Times* and appointed political correspondent 1951. Wrote widely praised profiles of prominent politicians, published biographies of ERSKINE CHILDERS and PEADAR O'DONNELL, and contributed articles on historical and political subjects to university publications in Ireland and Britain. Active member of National Union of Journalists, president of Irish branch, and elected honorary life-member in 1974 on retirement from the *Irish Times*. Continued to contribute to the paper until his death in his Dublin home on 26 January 1980. Survived by his wife, Nancy, and a daughter.

MACKEN, WALTER (1916–1967), actor, dramatist, and novelist. Son of a carpenter who was killed in France in the First World War. Born in Galway. Educated there by the Patrician Brothers. Started acting in the Taibhdhearc Theatre at seventeen, and also worked as producer and stage manager, before going to London where he worked for some years as an insurance salesman. In the 1940s he joined the Abbey Theatre company. His first published work was a play, *Oidhreacht na Mara*. His first play in English, *Mungo's Mansion*, was produced at the Abbey in 1946, and was followed by more plays and a number of novels. *Rain on the Wind* (1950) was accounted one of his best novels; his greatest success came with his historical trilogy, *Seek the Fair Land* (1959), *The Silent People* (1962), and *The Scorching Wind* (1964). Many of his plays had long runs at the Abbey, particularly *Home is the Hero* (1953), which was later filmed. Died suddenly at his house in Menlo, Galway, on 22 April 1967.

MacKENNA, JOHN or JUAN (1771–1814), Chilean general. Born at Clogher, Co. Tyrone, 26 October 1771. His kinsman, Alexander O'Reilly, a general in the Spanish service, arranged his entry to the Royal Academy of Mathematics at Barcelona in 1784. In 1787 he was appointed a cadet in the Irish corps of military engineers in the Spanish army. Irked by slow promotion, he sailed for Perú in 1796, with recommendations to the Spanish viceroy, AMBROSE O'HIGGINS. He gave distinguished service as a military engineer in Chile, and was appointed governor of Osorno in 1797. In 1810 he joined the revolutionary party under Carrera, and was appointed commander-in-chief of artillery and engineers. A rift with Carrera led to his banishment to Rioja in 1812, but he was recalled in 1813, promoted brigadier-general, and appointed military commander of Santiago. He then allied himself with Carrera's rival BERNARDO O'HIGGINS, and when O'Higgins supplanted Carrera as commander-in-chief after the republican defeat on the banks of the Roble in October 1813, MacKenna became second-in-command. A military revolution restored Carrera to power in 1814, and MacKenna was arrested and banished to Mendoza. On 21 November 1814 he was killed in a duel in Buenos Aires with Luís Carrera, brother of the revolutionary leader.

McKENNA, SIOBHÁN (1923–1986), actress. Born in Belfast on 24 May 1923. When she was five her father was appointed professor of mathematics at UCG and the family moved to Galway. She was educated at the Dominican Convent there, St Louis Convent, Monaghan, and UCG. She acted in the Taibhdhearc, the Irish-language Galway theatre, then joined the Abbey Theatre 1944. There she met DENIS O'DEA and they were married in 1946. She enjoyed great success on stage, screen and television, being specially acclaimed for her performances as St Joan in Shaw's play and as Pegeen Mike in Synge's *Playboy of the Western World*. She appeared in eight films, including *Dr Zhivago* (1965). In 1958 the *Evening Standard* (London) named her actress of the year. Her one-woman show, *Here Are Ladies*, was a great hit in London and the USA; it included Molly Bloom's soliloquy, which ends Joyce's *Ulysses*. She received many honours in recognition of her service to the arts, including the Gold Medal of the Éire Society of Boston 1971, honorary D.Litt. (DU) 1971 and life membership, RDS, 1983. President CEARBHALL Ó DÁLAIGH appointed her to the Council of State 1975. She died in a Dublin hospital after a short illness on 16 November 1986, survived by her son, Donncha, a former Irish swimming champion.

MacKENNA, STEPHEN (1872–1934), translator of Plotinus. Born Liverpool, 15 January 1872. Worked in Dublin as a bank clerk, became a journalist in London, then moved to Paris, where he met SYNGE, JOHN O'LEARY and MAUD GONNE. He joined an international brigade to fight for Greece against Turkey in 1897. Thus began his life-long love for Greek literature. After periods in London, New York, and Paris, he was appointed European correspondent of the *New York World*, a well-paid post. Disliking the 'yellow journalism' it demanded, he resigned and returned to Dublin, where he worked for a time on the *Freeman's Journal*, and became an enthusiastic worker for the language revival. He tried to join the GPO garrison in the 1916 Rising but was refused because of his obvious poor health. After his wife died in 1923 he went to England and made a poor living by casual journalism. His great work was a translation (1917–1930) of the works of the Greek philosopher Plotinus, founder of neo-Platonism. He died in England, 8 March 1934.

McKENZIE, REV. JOHN (*c.* 1648–1696), Presbyterian. Born near Cookstown, Co. Tyrone. Ordained minister of Cookstown 1673. Took refuge in Derry in 1688 and became chaplain of Walker's regiment. Published *Narrative of the Siege of Londonderry* (1690), giving a totally different version from 'Governor' Walker's and stripping him of much of his self-attributed glory. McKenzie read his account to officers who had served in the siege and who corroborated it. He returned to his ministry in Cookstown and died there.

MACKLIN, CHARLES (*c.* 1697–1797), actor and dramatist. Born in Ulster and educated at a school at Island Bridge, Dublin. After various vicissitudes he joined a strolling company in Bristol. His acting ability brought him to Drury Lane Theatre in London, where he played leading parts for many years. His performance of Shylock, his favourite character, made him famous, and drew from Pope the comment: 'This is the Jew, that Shakespeare drew.' In a quarrel in the green room in 1755 he killed a fellow-actor, and was found guilty of manslaughter but managed to escape punishment. He wrote and produced a number of plays with varying success. The comedies *Love à la Mode* (1759) and *The Man of the World* (1766) were well received both in London and Dublin, where he played at Smock Alley and Crow St theatres. He made his last appearance on the stage at Covent Garden on 7 May 1789 in the part of Shylock. Died at 4 Tavistock Row, Covent Garden, 11 July 1797, reputedly one hundred years old.

MacLAINE, or McLEAN, JAMES (1724–1750), gentleman highwayman. Born at Monaghan, second son of a Presbyterian minister. He quickly went through the inheritance he received in 1742 on the death of his father. He then entered domestic service in London, and in 1746 married well and set up as a grocer and chandler in Cavendish Square. His wife died in 1748, and with an accomplice called Plunkett, an apothecary who had attended his wife, he took to the road. His victims included Horace Walpole, and his takings enabled him to pass in society as an Irish squire. In July 1750 he was arrested and sent for trial at the Old Bailey. At his lodgings were found twenty-three purses, a quantity of clothes and wigs, and 'a famous kept mistress'. His arrest created great excitement, troops had to conduct him to and from the court, and great ladies 'shed tears in abundance' at his trial. He was found guilty, and hanged at Tyburn on 3 October 1750.

McLAUGHLIN, THOMAS A.

(1896–1971), engineer. Born in Drogheda, Co. Louth, in 1896 and graduated from UCD in mathematics and physics 1914. Joined UCG as assistant lecturer in physics, studied engineering in his spare time and took a degree in electrical engineering 1922. He went to Berlin in 1922 to train with the electrical engineering firm Siemens-Schuckert and studied the design of power plant and methods of transmission of electricity. He devised a scheme for a hydro-electric generating plant based on the Shannon, secured the support of Siemens-Schuckert, and in 1923 put his plan to the Government. By that time his salary with Siemens-Schuckert was £5,000 a year, equivalent to £100,000 or more today. PATRICK MCGILLIGAN, Minister for Industry and Commerce, became an enthusiastic supporter and in 1925 the Government decided to proceed with McLaughlin's scheme despite strong opposition from banking and commercial interests. The ESB was established in 1927, McLaughlin became managing director at a fraction of his German salary, and the Ardnacrusha power station was officially opened on 29 July 1929. Conflict developed between McLaughlin and the other directors and McGilligan, and in May 1931 he left the board. He was reappointed in August 1932 by the Fianna Fáil government, this time as a full-time director, but after some years of boardroom tension he retired in 1958 and became a director of Irish Steel and other companies. He had an international reputation as the architect of the Shannon Scheme, and its success owed much to his prophetic zeal in promoting it, inspired by his far-seeing conviction that electric power at an economic price was essential to the development of the new state. He died on 15 July 1971 while on holiday in Benidorm, Spain.

MACLEAR, SIR THOMAS (1794–1879), astronomer. Born on 17 March 1794 at Newtownstewart, Co. Tyrone.

Educated at Guy's and St Thomas's hospitals in London. Became house surgeon at Bedford Infirmary in 1815, and began to study astronomy and mathematics. In 1823 he entered into a medical partnership with his uncle at Biggleswade in Bedfordshire, and in 1833 was appointed royal astronomer at the Cape of Good Hope. His work on Lacaille's arc, published in 1866, earned him the Lalande prize and a royal medal in 1867. His industry was unflagging and he made observations of many thousands of southern stars. He instructed the explorer Livingstone in the use of the sextant. Knighted in 1860, and on retirement in 1870 went to live near Cape Town. Went blind in 1876. Died on 14 July 1879.

MAC LIAMMÓIR, MÍCHEÁL (1899–1978), actor, writer, and painter. Born in Cork on 25 October 1899. The family moved to London and he became a child actor with Herbert Beerbohm Tree's company, appearing with Noël Coward in *Peter Pan*. He spent two years in Spain, determined to become a painter, and studied at the Slade School, London. Joined the London Gaelic League. Made a 'grand tour' of Europe, wandering around for several years studying painting and languages in Germany, Italy, Switzerland, and France. Came back to Ireland 1927, toured with ANEW MCMASTER and met HILTON EDWARDS. On 27 August 1928 Taibhdhearc na Gaillimhe opened with a performance of his *Diarmaid agus Gráinne* in which he played the lead; he also designed and painted the sets. On 19 October 1928 Edwards and he launched the Gate Theatre with a production of Ibsen's *Peer Gynt* in the 102-seat Peacock Theatre. The company moved to the present Gate Theatre in 1930 and brought to Dublin most of the major European plays of the time. Many notable Irish plays had their first production there. The partnership brought a great sense of style and a demanding professionalism to each production. They made many successful tours abroad, visiting Egypt, Greece, Malta, and the USA. Mac Liammóir

excelled in Shakespearian parts; he received the Kronberg Gold Medal for his playing of Hamlet at the Theatre Festival in Helsingør (Elsinore), Denmark. His creative output was prodigious. He wrote ten plays, three one-man shows, and nine books on the theatre and his life in it, three of them in Irish. His faithfulness to the language never faltered: he wrote his diary in Irish every night. His ideal was an Ireland Gaelic and European rather than Anglo-American. He received many honours: the Lady Gregory Medal of the Irish Academy of Letters and election to the academy 1960, honorary LL.D. (DU) 1962, honorary membership of Irish Actors' Equity 1972, freedom of the city of Dublin 1973, and French Legion of Honour 1973. He died at his home, 4 Harcourt Terrace, Dublin, on 6 March 1978.

MACLISE, DANIEL (1806–1870), painter. Born in Cork on 2 February 1806. Educated at a day-school. Entered Newenham's Bank in Cork but soon left to study art, and opened a studio in Patrick St, where he executed small portraits in pencil. When Sir Walter Scott visited Cork in 1825, Maclise sketched him in a bookshop, and won praise for the portrait. By 1827 he had saved enough money to go to London, where he entered the RA school, and won silver and gold medals. He first exhibited at the academy in 1829; associate member 1835. Between 1830 and 1838 he contributed to *Fraser's Magazine* a series of character portraits of literary celebrities, including his lifelong friend Charles Dickens. By 1850 he had become well established in his profession, being especially noted for his narrative pictures, and his career continued in unbroken prosperity until his death. Between 1859 and 1864 he executed two very large frescos for the Houses of Parliament, 'The Meeting of Wellington and Blücher' and 'The Death of Nelson'. The National Gallery of Ireland has two large paintings by him, 'The Marriage of Strongbow and Aoife'

and 'Merry Christmas in the Baron's Hall'. In 1866 he refused the presidency of the RA, and he also refused a knighthood. Died at his house, 4 Cheyne Walk, Chelsea, London, 25 April 1870.

MacLYSAGHT, EDWARD ANTHONY EDGEWORTH (1887–1986), genealogist. Born at sea on 6 November 1887 and brought up on his father's farm at Raheen, Co. Clare. Educated at Rugby School, Corpus Christi College, Oxford, and UCC. Member of Irish Free State Senate 1922–1925. Worked as a journalist in South Africa 1936–1938, returned to Ireland and became an inspector with the Irish Manuscripts Commission 1939, travelling the country on his bicycle and rescuing manuscripts from big houses and small. Awarded Litt.D. (NUI) 1941. Joined staff of National Library 1942, Keeper of Manuscripts 1949–1955, Chief Herald and Genealogical Officer 1943–1955. Chairman, Irish Manuscripts Commission, 1956–1973. While working in Dublin he made frequent visits to Clare to oversee the family farm at Raheen, which he had inherited. He wrote two novels, one in Irish—*Cúrsaí Thomáis* (1927)—three volumes on Irish families, their origins and coats of arms, a valuable *Guide to Irish Surnames* (1964), the scholarly *Irish Life in the Seventeenth Century* (1939), and an autobiography, *Changing Times* (1978), as well as editing important manuscripts. Received honorary LL.D. (NUI) 1972. He died at his home in Blackrock, Co. Dublin, on 4 March 1986 in his ninety-ninth year, survived by his second wife, Mary, three sons and a daughter.

MacMAHON, HEBER (1600–1650), bishop and general. Born at Farney, Co. Monaghan. Educated at the Irish College, Douai, and at Louvain, where he was ordained in 1625. Returned to Ireland and served for many years in the diocese of Clogher, where he became vicar-general. In 1642 he was appointed bishop of Down and Connor. He took a prominent part at the Confederation of

Kilkenny and became counsellor to OWEN ROE O'NEILL. He opposed the Ormond Peace of 1646, since he could not accept any settlement that did not provide religious freedom and the restoration of confiscated Catholic property. After the death of O'Neill in November 1649 he was chosen to lead the Ulster army, and was defeated at Scarrifhollis, near Letterkenny, Co. Donegal, on 21 June 1650. He was wounded, captured by Cromwellian troops, and executed at Enniskillen on 17 September 1650.

MacMANUS, ANNA. See under CARBERY, ETHNA.

MacMANUS, FRANCIS (1909–1965), author. Born in Kilkenny. Educated there at CBS and at UCD. Trained as a teacher at St Patrick's College, Drumcondra, Dublin, and followed that profession until 1948, when he joined Radio Éireann to take charge of talks and features. Published his first novel, *Stand and Give Challenge* (1935), at twenty-five. It told the story of the poet DONNCHADH RUA MAC CON MARA, and was the first of a trilogy, completed with *Candle for the Proud* (1936) and *Men Withering* (1939). All three have been translated into a number of European languages. *The Greatest of These* followed in 1943. He wrote thirteen novels in all, as well as short stories, essays, and biographies. His *Boccaccio* (1947) was very well received. In Radio Éireann his outstanding contribution was the Thomas Davis series of lectures, delivered at his invitation by leading figures in Ireland's cultural life. Member, Irish Academy of Letters. Died in Dublin, 27 November 1965.

MacMANUS, SÉAMUS (1869–1960), poet, historian, and novelist. Born on a small farm near Mountcharles, Co. Donegal. Educated at Glencoagh NS. Became a teacher, and in 1888 was appointed principal of his old school at Glencoagh. Shortly afterwards he won a prize offered by the *Weekly Irish Times* for an article 'A Ride in an Irish Jaunting Car'. He continued to contribute articles to local papers and about this time discovered the wealth of folklore in the mountains of his native parish. He resigned his badly paid teaching post in 1899 and went to the USA, where he found a ready market for his stories of local traditions. From fairy-tales he turned to poetry and novels, humorous plays and sketches. While he continued to be based in the USA he returned to Donegal each year. Married ETHNA CARBERY. Published an autobiography, *The Rocky Road to Dublin* (1938). Died in New York 1960.

MacMANUS, TERENCE BELLEW (1811–1861), revolutionary. Born probably in Co. Fermanagh and became a successful shipping agent in Liverpool. He returned to Ireland about 1843 and joined the Young Ireland movement. He was with SMITH O'BRIEN and JOHN BLAKE DILLON at the engagement at Ballingarry in July 1848, and was arrested in Cork on board a vessel bound for the USA. He was sentenced to death for high treason, but the sentence was commuted to transportation for life, and he was sent to Van Diemen's Land (Tasmania) in 1849. He escaped with MEAGHER in 1852, and settled at San Francisco. He tried to resume his former business as a shipping agent but failed, and spent his last years in poverty, and died in San Francisco on 15 January 1861. His body was brought to Ireland and, despite CARDINAL CULLEN's opposition, was buried in Glasnevin cemetery, Dublin, on 10 November 1861, after a huge funeral organised by the Fenian movement.

McMASTER, ANEW (1894–1962), actor. Born in Monaghan. First appeared on stage in 1911 in *The Scarlet Pimpernel* in Fred Terry's company. Leading man to Peggy O'Neill in *Paddy the Next Best Thing* 1920. Toured Australia in 1921. In 1925 he founded a company to present Shakespeare on tour, managing, acting and directing himself. Outstanding as Shylock,

Richard III, and Coriolanus. Appeared as Hamlet at Shakespeare Memorial Theatre, Stratford-on-Avon, 1933, and then took his company on a tour of the Near East. His insistence on taking Shakespeare to less favoured localities meant that he was less well known in London than he deserved. During the Second World War he toured the Irish provinces with Shakespearian plays and then made a two-year tour of Australia. Returned to Dublin 1951. Tall and handsome, he was the last of the Irish actor-managers. Married a sister of MÍCHEÁL MAC LIAMMÓIR. Died in Dublin, 24 August 1962.

MacMURROUGH, DIARMUID
(1110–1171), king of Leinster. Succeeded his father as king of Leinster about 1126. He is remembered for abducting Dervorgilla, wife of Ó Ruairc of Breifne, and inviting the Normans to Ireland. Varying accounts are given of these events. According to Giraldus Cambrensis and SEATHRÚN CÉITINN, Dervorgilla went willingly enough in her husband's absence. Diarmuid was banished from his kingdom for this misdemeanour, and invited Henry II to Ireland. The Four Masters say that in a raid on Ó Ruairc's territory MacMurrough 'carried off Dervorgilla with her cattle and furniture,' and that she was restored to her husband the following year. They add that she survived her husband by twenty-one years and died in the abbey of Mellifont in her eighty-fifth year, in 1193. As to the Normans, they say that following his defeat by his enemies, of whom the principal was Ó Ruairc, he sought the aid of Henry II to recover his kingdom, promising to hold it as Henry's vassal. Pope Adrian IV had some time previously issued a bull authorising the king to take Ireland. Henry II was too engaged with other affairs to take part himself but he gave Diarmuid letters patent authorising any of his subjects to help him. Diarmuid persuaded Richard de Clare, called Strongbow, to join him, promising him his daughter Aoife in marriage and the succession to the kingdom. So began the Norman invasion of Ireland. After advance contingents had landed in May 1169, Strongbow landed in August 1170, took Waterford, and married Aoife. Diarmuid captured Dublin later that year. He died at Ferns about 1171, the Four Masters say, 'without a will, without penance, without unction, as his evil deeds deserved.' The Book of Leinster says that 'he died after the victory of unction and penance; thenceforward is the miserable reign of the Saxons, amen, amen.' Henry II, on his arrival in person at the close of 1171, received the submission of natives and invaders alike, the beginning of that subjection of Ireland to England which was the inevitable outcome of Diarmuid's appeal to the English king.

McNAGHTEN or MacNAUGHTON, JOHN
(d. 1761), criminal. Born at Benvarden, near Ballymoney, Co. Antrim. Inherited an estate worth £500 a year at six. Educated at TCD but left without taking a degree. He gambled away most of his inheritance, but restored his fortunes by marrying an heiress. After some years he started gambling again, and after an attempt was made to arrest him for debt his wife died in childbirth. By the influence of Lord Massereene he obtained a post as collector of the King's duty in Coleraine, but soon lost it when he gambled away the money he had collected. At this low ebb in his fortunes, he was befriended by Andrew Knox, of Derry, MP for Donegal. He paid court to Knox's only daughter, Mary Anne, whose fortune was worth £5,000. The daughter was willing, but the father opposed the marriage. He persuaded her to read over the marriage service with him in the presence of a youth named Hamilton, and then claimed her as his wife. He was wounded in a duel with a friend of the Knox family, and had £500 damages awarded against him in court on account of the pretended marriage. He fled to England, but returned in November

1761, and with some accomplices attacked the Knox family near Cloughhean, when they were travelling to Dublin by coach. In the struggle Miss Knox was fatally wounded. MacNaughton was wounded, captured, and tried for murder. He was found guilty, condemned to death, and hanged at Strabane jail on 15 December 1761.

McNAGHTEN, SIR WILLIAM HAY (1791–1841), diplomat. Born Dundarave, Bushmills, Co. Antrim. Educated Charterhouse School. Entered service of East India Company as cadet in 1809. Learned Hindustani, Persian, and other languages. Held various legal posts in Bengal civil service. Appointed envoy to Kabul 1838. Largely responsible for policy of intervention in Afghanistan, which led to deposition of Dost Mohammed and restoration of Shah Soojah to throne of Kabul. Created baronet 1840; governor of Bombay 1841. When the Afghan chiefs mounted a revolt at Kabul in November 1841, McNaghten agreed, among other terms, that the British would evacuate Afghanistan and restore Dost Mohammed. Unfortunately he then parleyed with the Dost's son and agreed other terms with him. At a meeting on Seeah Sung plain, this was proclaimed as treachery to the chiefs, and McNaghten was shot dead by the Dost's son.

McNALLY, LEONARD (1752–1820), playwright and informer. Born in Dublin, and kept a small grocery shop in St Mary's Lane. Called to the bar 1776, and to the English bar 1783. One of the first members of the Society of United Irishmen, fought a duel with SIR JONAH BARRINGTON in defence of their honour and appeared in court on behalf of TONE, EMMET, TANDY and other leaders. He wrote a number of comedies and comic operas, some of which were produced at Covent Garden. His best-known song, 'Sweet Lass of Richmond Hill', was written in praise of his first wife, who came from Richmond, Yorkshire. He died at his house, 22 Harcourt Street, Dublin, on 13 February 1820. His heir claimed continuance of a secret service pension of £300 a year that his father had enjoyed since 1798. It then emerged that while taking fees to defend the United Irishmen, McNally had also accepted large sums from the government to betray them.

MacNAMARA, BRINSLEY (1890–1963), writer, pen-name of John Weldon. Born near Delvin, Co. Westmeath. Joined the Abbey Theatre Company in 1909 and toured USA with it. Turned to writing in 1912. *The Valley of the Squinting Windows* (1918) established him as a novelist. A study of a rural community and of the power of gossip, its publication caused a storm. Published three books of short stories, two other novels, and wrote many plays for the Abbey, of which he was a director for some years. His best-known comedies are *The Glorious Uncertainty* (1923) and *Look at the Heffernans* (1926). A founder-member and president, Irish Academy of Letters. Succeeded JAMES STEPHENS in 1924 as registrar, National Gallery of Ireland. Died in Dublin, February 1963.

MacNEICE, LOUIS (1907–1963), poet. Born in Belfast, son of a Church of Ireland clergyman who became a bishop. Educated at Marlborough, and Merton College, Oxford. Lectured in classics at Birmingham 1930–1936 and in Greek at Bedford College, University of London, 1936–1940. He then joined the BBC as a feature writer and producer, and stayed there until his death, save for a year in Athens with the British Institute. His first volume of poems, *Blind Fireworks*, appeared in 1929 while he was still at Oxford, and in the 1930s he was associated with a group that included C. DAY-LEWIS, Spender and Auden. He wrote a number of radio plays, *The Dark Tower* (1947) being regarded as the best; travel books, and two long poems, *Autumn Journal* (1939) and *Autumn Sequel* (1954), which were inspired by his travels in India and the Middle East. Later volumes of poetry included *Visi-*

tation (1957) and *Solstices* (1961). He died on 3 September 1963. His autobiography, *The Strings are False*, recounting his life to 1940, was published posthumously in 1965.

MacNEILL, EOIN (1867–1945), scholar and patriot. Born at Glenarm, Co. Antrim, 15 May 1867. Educated at St Malachy's College, Belfast, and the Royal University. He became a clerk in the Dublin law courts, and in his spare time immersed himself in the study of early Irish history. His abiding interest in Irish then began, and he joined with DOUGLAS HYDE and others in the founding of the Gaelic League in 1893, editing its official organ, the *Gaelic Journal*. In 1908 his growing reputation as a scholar brought him appointment as professor of early Irish history at UCD. Through the Gaelic League he met leaders of Sinn Féin, and was elected chairman of the council that formed the Irish Volunteers in 1913, later becoming chief of staff. MacNeill set his face against an armed rising, seeing little hope of success, but without his knowledge the secret IRB proceeded with its plans with CONNOLLY and the Citizen Army, and with the support of PEARSE and other Volunteer officers. Easter Sunday 1916 was fixed as the day to take up arms; MacNeill learned of this the previous Thursday, agreed at first, but on hearing of the arrest of CASEMENT and the interception of German arms issued an order on Easter Sunday morning countermanding the mobilisation of the Volunteers. Despite the ensuing confusion Pearse, Connolly and the others decided that they must go forward, and the rising began on Easter Monday, 24 April 1916. After the surrender on 29 April MacNeill was arrested with hundreds of others and sentenced to penal servitude for life. Released in 1917 under a general amnesty, he was elected MP for NUI. He supported the Anglo-Irish Treaty of 1921 and became Minister for Education in the first Free State government. When the Boundary Commission was set up in 1924 he was nominated to represent the Free State, but resigned after a 'special forecast' of the findings was published in the *Morning Post* on 7 November 1925. In December 1925 the Free State government made a supplemental agreement with the British government, which, among other matters, confirmed the boundary as comprising the entire Six Counties, contrary to the hopes of nationalists. MacNeill became the object of intense criticism, was forced to resign his ministry, and lost his seat in the general election of 1927. He became chairman of the Irish Manuscripts Commission that year, retiring from politics, to which he was temperamentally unsuited, to devote himself to scholarship. His major works were *Phases of Irish History* (1919), and *Celtic Ireland* (1921), based on his critical investigations of native records of ancient Irish history. His publications covered a wide range, dealing with law tracts, annals, glossaries, and ogham writing, and included a study of ST PATRICK (1934). He died in Dublin, 15 October 1945.

MacNEILL, JAMES (1869–1938), administrator. Born at Glenarm, Co. Antrim, 27 or 29 March 1869. Educated at Belvedere College, Dublin, and Emmanuel College, Cambridge. He joined the Indian civil service and, after a successful career, retired at forty-five and came back to Ireland, where he joined the Sinn Féin movement. Appointed high commissioner for the Irish Free State in London, 1923, a post to which his administrative abilities were well suited. Succeeded T. M. HEALY as Governor-General, 1928. When Fianna Fáil came into power in February 1932 under DE VALERA it was made clear that MacNeill's post was regarded as an objectionable symbol of British monarchy, and the king finally agreed to his removal from office from 1 November 1932. MacNeill died in London on 12 December 1938.

MacNEILL, SIR JOHN BENJAMIN (*c.* 1793–1880), civil engineer. Born

Mount Pleasant, Co. Louth. Lieutenant in the Louth Militia, 1811-1815. He then obtained employment under the engineer Thomas Telford, who was engaged in road and bridge making in Scotland and England, and became one of Telford's principal assistants. About 1834 he set up as a consulting engineer, with offices in London and Glasgow. He constructed some small railway lines in Scotland, and carried out experiments on canal-boat traction, studying the 'swift' boats that carried passengers at eight miles an hour on the Firth and Clyde canal. His system of sectioplanography was adopted for railway plans by standing orders of the House of Commons. He was commissioned to undertake a survey of the north of Ireland for the railway commission, and came to live at the family house at Mount Pleasant. First professor of civil engineering at TCD, 1842-1852. He completed the Drogheda and Dublin line, and was knighted in 1844 on his completion of the Kildare section of the Great Southern and Western railway. During his later years he went blind, and retired. Died on 2 March 1880 in Cromwell Road, South Kensington, London. Fellow, Royal Society and other learned bodies.

MacNEILL, JOHN GORDON SWIFT (1849-1926), politician and jurist. Born in Dublin, 11 March 1849. Educated at TCD and Christ Church, Oxford. Called to the bar 1875. Professor of constitutional and criminal law, King's Inns, 1882-1888. Joined the Nationalist party; MP for South Donegal 1887-1918. His knowledge of constitutional history and parliamentary procedure proved most valuable to PARNELL and the party in their policy of obstruction in the House of Commons. He campaigned successfully for the principle that government ministers should not be directors of public companies, and for the abolition of flogging of boys in the Royal Navy. Professor of constitutional law at UCD 1909. Left politics in 1918 with the rise of

Sinn Féin. His books include *The Irish Parliament* (1885), *How the Union was Carried* (1887), *Titled Corruption* (1894), *Constitutional and Parliamentary History of Ireland* (1917), *Studies in the Constitution of the Irish Free State* (1925), and *What I Have Seen and Heard* (1925), memoirs written in a light vein. Died in Dublin, unmarried, 24 August 1926.

MacNEVIN, WILLIAM (1763-1841), United Irishman. Born 21 March 1763 at Ballymahowma, Aughrim, Co. Galway. Educated at Prague under the care of his uncle, Baron MacNevin, physician to the Empress Maria Theresa. Having graduated in medicine at Vienna in 1783 he returned to Ireland and began to practise in Dublin. He became an active worker for Catholic emancipation, joined the Catholic Committee, and was then inducted into the Society of United Irishmen by LORD EDWARD FITZGERALD. In 1798 he was arrested with other leaders and imprisoned at Kilmainham jail and later at Fort George in Scotland. After the Treaty of Amiens in 1802 he was released and joined the French army as a captain in the Irish Brigade. When his expectations of an invasion of Ireland were disappointed, he resigned his commission and sailed for New York. From 1805 until his death he held several important medical posts there and worked to promote the welfare of the Irish immigrants. He published books on chemistry, Irish history, and travel. Died at New York on 12 July 1841.

McQUAID, JOHN CHARLES (1895-1973), Archbishop of Dublin. Born at Cootehill, Co. Cavan, 28 July 1895. Educated at St Patrick's College, Cavan, Blackrock College, Dublin, and Clongowes Wood College. Entered the novitiate of the Holy Ghost Fathers at Kimmage Manor, Dublin, and continued his studies at UCD, where he distinguished himself in ancient classics, and at Rome. Ordained at St Mary's College, Rathmines, in 1924. Dean of studies, Blackrock College, 1925, and president 1931. Became a leading figure in Catholic secondary education. In November 1940 he was appointed Archbishop of Dublin, and was at the time, and throughout his episcopate, the only Irish bishop to come from a religious order. During the Second World War and the immediate post-war years he devoted himself particularly to social problems. In 1941 he established the Catholic Social Service Conference, to co-ordinate the work of Catholic charitable organisations, and in 1942 set up the Catholic Social Welfare Bureau to look after the welfare of emigrants; the work of the bureau was later extended to family welfare. With the return of normal conditions about 1948, he initiated and carried through an extensive building programme, under which thirty-four churches and sixty-seven secondary schools were provided by 1965. He had always held that education must be denominational and, in accordance with this view, in his Lenten pastoral of 1944 reiterated the ban on the attendance of Catholics at TCD without permission of their bishop, on pain of mortal sin. This instruction was renewed annually in his Lenten regulations for twenty years. He fostered the study of Catholic social teaching, and in 1950 founded the Dublin Institute of Catholic Sociology (now the Dublin Institute of Adult Education). When Dr Noël Browne, Minister for Health in the first Coalition government, proposed the 'Mother and Child' health scheme in 1950, Dr McQuaid took a leading part in opposing it. In the face of this opposition the Government abandoned the scheme, and Dr Browne resigned early in April 1951. The 1960s introduced a period of ferment in the Catholic Church, and the archbishop seemed to find difficulty in coming to terms with the new ways. On returning from the final session of the Second Vatican Council, he told his people: 'No change will worry the tranquillity of your Christian lives.' Nevertheless, in obedience to the new teaching on ecumenism he endeavoured to moderate his life-long aloofness from other Christian denominations. He was widely recognised as an administrator of outstanding ability. Less well known was his quality of compassion, shown in his almost secret care for the poor and ill. He retired on 4 January 1972, and died in Loughlinstown Hospital, Co. Dublin, on 7 April 1973.

MacRORY, JOSEPH (1861–1945), cardinal. Born in Ballygawly, Co. Tyrone, and educated at St Patrick's Seminary, Armagh, and Maynooth. He was ordained in 1885 and immediately appointed professor in Dungannon Academy. Two years later he became professor of moral theology and sacred scripture at Oscott College, Birmingham. He returned to Maynooth at twenty-seven to take the chair of sacred scripture and Hebrew, and became vice-president of Maynooth 1909. With colleagues he founded the *Theological Quarterly*, and contributed to many clerical periodicals. Became Bishop of Down and Connor 1915, Archbishop of Armagh and Primate of All-Ireland 1928, and received the red hat as cardinal in Rome 1929. Papal Legate to Liverpool 1933 for laying the foundation stone of the new cathedral, and to Eucharistic Congress in Melbourne 1934. He was a strong nationalist and condemned Partition as a grave injustice. He died in Armagh on 13 October 1945.

MacSWINEY, TERENCE (1879–1920), revolutionary. Born in Cork. Educated at North Monastery CBS. At fifteen he joined Dwyer and Co., Cork, to train as an accountant. In 1907 he took a degree in philosophy from the RUI and published his first book, a long poem, *The Music of Freedom*. Helped to form Cork Celtic Literary Society in 1901, and in 1908, with DANIEL CORKERY, founded the Cork Dramatic Society, for which he wrote several plays: *The Revolutionist, The Holocaust, The Warriors of Coole* and *The Wooing of Emer*. In 1911 Cork County Council appointed him commercial teacher and organiser of classes in the towns of Co. Cork. One of the principals in the forming of the Cork Volunteers in December 1913. Two years later he resigned from the Cork County Committee of Technical Instruction to become a full-time organiser for the Volunteers. In 1914 he published a weekly paper, *Fianna Fáil*, written almost entirely by himself. It was suppressed after eleven issues. A series of articles he wrote for *Irish Freedom* between 1912 and 1916 was published posthumously under the title *Principles of Freedom* (1921). Arrested in January 1916 and charged with making a seditious speech at Ballymoe, Co. Cork, but released in February without being brought to trial. On Easter Sunday 1916 MacSwiney obeyed MACNEILL's countermanding order and travelled to Tralee on a British army permit to persuade the Kerry Volunteers to give up their arms on conditions agreed with the army. Imprisoned for short terms in 1916 and 1917. Elected to first Dáil Éireann as member for West Cork. Continued to recruit and organise the Volunteers. Was active in setting up Dáil Éireann's Arbitration Courts. Following the murder of his friend TOMÁS MAC CURTAIN in March 1920, MacSwiney was elected Lord Mayor of Cork. On 12 August 1920 the military raided Cork City Hall and arrested him and others. It was agreed by the prisoners that they should go on hunger strike. All but the Lord Mayor were released three days later. On 16 August he was court-martialled and sentenced to two years' imprisonment. He told the court that by taking no food he would put a limit to any term of imprisonment imposed. On 18 August he was given into the custody of Brixton Prison in such a state of collapse that the prison doctor decided that he would not be able to survive forcible feeding. However, on 21 October, when his condition had worsened considerably, attempts were made to force-feed him. His case attracted world-wide attention and many efforts were made to persuade the British government to release him. He died at Brixton on 24 October, the 74th day of his fast.

McVEAGH, TREVOR GEORGE (1908–1968), lawyer and sportsman. Born at Drewstown, Co. Meath; educated at St Columba's College, Rathfarnham, and TCD. He qualified as a solicitor and built up an extensive practice. He showed extraordinary versatility as a sportsman, and represented Ireland more than seventy times in four different sports. In one year, 1938, he gained international caps for tennis, hockey, squash rackets, and cricket. Under his captaincy the Irish hockey team won the Triple Crown three years in succession. An ankle injury in 1939 ended his sporting career. He died suddenly at home in Dublin on 5 June 1968.

MADDEN, RICHARD ROBERT (1798–1886), historian of the United Irishmen. Born at 9 Wormwood Gate, Dublin, 20 August 1798. Educated at private schools. After serving a five-year apprenticeship with a Dr Woods of Athboy he continued his medical studies in Paris, London, and Naples. He travelled and practised in the Near East between 1824 and 1827, spent a few years in London, and then went to Jamaica in 1833 as a special magistrate to superintend the abolition of slavery. Difficulties arose with planters who resented his reforming zeal, and he resigned in 1834. He held somewhat similar posts in Havana 1836–1840 and in Africa 1841–1843. He was special correspondent of the *Morning Chronicle* in Lisbon for three years and was then appointed colonial secretary for West Australia, where he sought to improve the position of the aborigines. Became secretary of the Loan Fund Board in Dublin 1850–1880. His principal work is *The United Irishmen, their Lives and Times* (seven volumes, 1843–1846). He also wrote a number of works based on his travels and his experiences as physician, pilgrim, and abolitionist. Died at his house, 3 Vernon Terrace, Booterstown, Co. Dublin, 5 February 1886. Buried in Donnybrook churchyard.

MADDEN, SAMUEL (1686–1765), writer and philanthropist. Born Dublin, 23 December 1686. Educated at TCD. Took holy orders in the established church and obtained a living at Newtownbutler, Co. Fermanagh, near the family estates that he had inherited in 1703. His tragedy *Themistocles* was produced with considerable success in London in 1729. He supported THOMAS PRIOR in founding the Dublin Society in 1731, and settled premiums of £300 a year on it for the encouragement of manufactures and the arts. He also contributed financially to a scheme for premiums to students at TCD, and these benefactions gained him the name 'Premium Madden'. Published *Reflections and Resolutions Proper for the Gentlemen of Ireland, as to their Conduct for the Service of their Country* (1738), which advocated various measures to improve the distressed state of the country. SWIFT and Johnson were among his friends; Johnson said, 'His was a name which Ireland ought to honour.' He died at Manor Waterhouse, Co. Fermanagh, 31 December 1765. The Madden premiums for disappointed candidates for fellowship at TCD were established by his second son.

MAGAN, FRANCIS (*c.* 1772–1843), informer. Born Dublin. Graduated at TCD 1794, called to the bar 1796, first Catholic to be admitted under the Relief Act of 1793. He joined the United Irishmen, but having little success at the bar and being short of money was induced by the 'Sham Squire', FRANCIS HIGGINS, to become an informer. Through information supplied by him, LORD EDWARD FITZGERALD was arrested in 1798. So well did he avoid suspicion that on the night of the arrest he was elected a member of the head committee of the United Irishmen. He continued to pose as a patriot, opposed the union with England, and subscribed liberally to funds to advance the cause of Catholic emancipation. In 1821 he was appointed a commissioner for enclosing waste lands and commons. Until 1834 he received a government pension of £200 a year. He died unmarried, and by his will required a perpetual yearly mass to be celebrated by all the priests of St Michael and John's for the repose of his soul.

MAGEE, JOHN (1750–1809), printer and journalist. Born Belfast; went to Dublin and became proprietor and printer of *Magee's Weekly Packet* 1777 and the *Dublin Evening Post* 1779. He attacked the 'Sham Squire', FRANCIS HIGGINS, and the chief justice, Lord Clonmell, in his papers. Fiats were issued requiring bail for £7,800, and in default he was imprisoned. He was found guilty of libel on Higgins in 1789. The verdict aroused popular outcry. In revenge he arranged a Grand Olympic Pig-Hunt close to Clonmell's house in Blackrock, Co. Dublin, which was attended by thousands. The pigs broke into Clonmell's grounds and did much damage. Magee was imprisoned on and off in Newgate and by 1790 was broken in spirit and fortune but had achieved his aim of exposing both Higgins and Clonmell. He died in Dublin, November 1809.

MAGEE, JOHN, THE YOUNGER (1780–1814), journalist. Born Dublin. Succeeded his father, JOHN MAGEE, as proprietor of the *Dublin Evening Post* and conducted it on the same reforming lines. Found guilty of libel on Dublin police 1812 and on Duke of Richmond 1813 despite brilliant defence by DANIEL O'CONNELL. Fined £500 and sentenced to two years' imprisonment for Richmond libel. Died in Dublin.

MAGEE, MARTHA MARIA, née STEWART (died 1846), philanthropist. Born at Lurgan, Co. Armagh, and married a Presbyterian minister, Reverend William Magee, who died in 1800. Her two sons died in early manhood. After inheriting a large fortune from her two brothers she moved to Dublin, where she died on 22 June 1846. With other charitable bequests totalling £40,000, she left £20,000 to endow a college for the education of the Irish Presbyterian ministry. After prolonged controversy with the General Assembly, led by HENRY COOKE, the trustees were enabled, following a law suit, to establish Magee College in Derry in 1865. It became an integral part of the New University of Ulster in 1970.

MAGEE, WILLIAM KIRKPATRICK (1868-1961), essayist, under the pseudonym of John Eglinton. Born in Dublin and educated at the High School and TCD, where he won the Chancellor's prize for verse four times. He worked in the National Library 1898-1921, and appears in JOYCE's *Ulysses*. Secretary to GEORGE MOORE and a member of the Dublin theosophical movement. With Frederick Ryan he founded *Dana*, a short-lived literary magazine which in 1904-1905 published the leading writers of the Irish literary revival but rejected Joyce's *Portrait of the Artist as a Young Man* as a serial. Of interest still are his *Anglo-Irish Essays* (1917), *Irish Literary Portraits* (1935), and *Memoir of AE* (1937). When the Irish Free State was set up he moved to England and died in Bournemouth on 9 May 1961.

MAGINN, WILLIAM (1793-1842), poet and journalist. Born at Marlboro's Fort, Cork, 10 July 1793. Educated by his father, who kept a private school, and at TCD. A precocious student, he graduated in classics in 1811, returned to Cork to assist his father, and began to contribute poems and parodies to *Blackwood's Magazine*. He is credited with having originated the 'Noctes Ambrosianae', and written some of those 'dialogues of the day', which appeared in *Blackwood's* from 1822 to 1835. In 1823 he went to London, wrote stories and verse for various periodicals, and in 1830 jointly founded *Fraser's Magazine*, which soon became the leading English monthly. His 'Gallery of Literary Characters', illustrated by MACLISE, proved highly popular. His other works included novels, essays, and literary criticism. His intemperate habits

brought bankruptcy and illness: he was the original for Captain Shandon in Thackeray's *Pendennis*. He died at Walton-on-Thames, 21 August 1842.

MAGRATH, MEILER (c. 1523-1622), archbishop of Cashel, famed for his rapacity. Born in Co. Fermanagh. Became a Franciscan friar and spent much of his early life in Rome, from where he was sent on special missionary duty to Ireland. Appointed bishop of Down and Connor by papal decree 1565. In 1567 he professed himself ready to conform to the reformed church. In 1570 he was appointed to Clogher, and in 1571 he was made archbishop of Cashel and bishop of Emly. In 1571 he imprisoned friars at Cashel for preaching against the queen. The friars were later forcibly, or possibly collusively, released by Edward Butler. During the following years Magrath continued to make himself useful to the government and at the same time intrigued with the rebels. He was not always successful in keeping in with both sides, and eventually, in March 1580, the Pope deprived him of the see of Down and Connor for 'heresy and many other crimes', after nine years as both a Papal bishop and an Anglican archbishop. In October 1582 he went to England with a reputation as an informer against the rebels. On his complaint of poverty, he was given the sees of Waterford and Lismore. He completely ignored the spiritual care of his four bishoprics—as a rule, no provision was made for religious services—and in 1607, as a result of his negligence, he was forced to resign Waterford and Lismore and was given instead Killala and Achonry, both of small value, but retained Cashel. Although he was mistrusted and his evil influence feared, his ability for intrigue earned him relative indemnity from the authorities. In 1613 he attended parliament in Dublin. Died in his hundredth year. Buried in his own cathedral at Cashel.

MAGUIRE, CONOR ALEXANDER (1889-1971), lawyer and judge. Born at

236

Cong, Co. Mayo, son of a native Irish-speaker. Educated at Clongowes Wood College and NUI. Qualified as a solicitor in 1914 and began to practise in Claremorris, Co. Mayo. He soon became involved in the Sinn Féin movement and acted as a judge in the Republican courts from 1920 and 1922, and as a Dáil Éireann land settlement commissioner. These activities led to a period of internment. Called to the bar 1922; took silk 1932. TD for NUI 1932–1936; attorney-general in the first Fianna Fáil government 1932; High Court judge 1936. In June 1946 he was appointed Chief Justice. Chairman of the Irish Red Cross Society from its foundation in 1939 until 1946. In recognition of his services was awarded Cross of Commander, Legion of Honour, by the French government, 1948. Also honoured by Spanish government with Grand Cross of San Raimund de Penafort. A strong supporter of Irish, he was elected president of the International Celtic Congress 1956 and president of Oireachtas na Gaeilge 1962. Died in Dublin, 26 September 1971.

MAGUIRE, JOHN FRANCIS (1815–1872), journalist and politican. Born in Cork. Called to the bar 1843. In 1841 he founded the *Cork Examiner* in support of DANIEL O'CONNELL, and conducted it for many years. MP for Dungarvan 1852–1865, and Cork 1865 until his death. In Parliament he supported nationalist policies on the land question, disestablishment, and reform of the Poor Law. He made three visits to Rome to see Pope Pius IX, and published a book on the Pontificate for which the Pope named him a knight commander of St Gregory. Elected Lord Mayor of Cork four times. He published some half-dozen books, including *The Irish in America*, following a six-month visit to the USA and Canada. Died at Dublin on 1 November 1872. Buried in Cork.

MAHAFFY, SIR JOHN PENTLAND (1839–1919), scholar and Provost of TCD. Born in Switzerland of Irish parents on 26 February 1839. Educated at home in Donegal from the age of nine. Entering TCD in 1855 he read classics with distinction, took fellowship in 1864, and served the college until his death fifty-five years later. Professor of ancient history 1869–1899; published a number of books on the social life and civilisation of the ancient Greeks. Flinders Petrie entrusted him with the deciphering of papyri discovered in Egypt, and subsequently he published *The Empire of the Ptolemies* (1895). President RIA 1911–1916; knighted 1918. It is often forgotten that he was a clergyman, on account of which his knighthood was, strictly speaking, illegal. Holy orders were then essential for fellowship. Mahaffy was a first-rate shot, an accomplished musician, and an inveterate diner-out, welcomed for his brilliant if sometimes wounding talk. His *Principles of the Art of Conversation* appeared in 1887, as a headline for others. He dismissed the idea that any worthwhile literature could exist in Irish, and regarded nationalism as little better than provincialism. Nevertheless, at the Irish Convention, held in the college in 1917, he proposed that Ireland should have a federal constitution on the model of Switzerland, with Ulster as an autonomous province. Unexpectedly passed over for the provostship in 1904, he had to wait until 1914, when he was seventy-five, to get this coveted post. Died in the provost's house in 1919. Buried in Mount Jerome.

MAHON, Rt Hon SIR BRYAN (1862–1930), general. Born Belleville, Co. Galway, 2 April 1862. Lieutenant, 8th (King's Royal Irish) Hussars, 1883. Received DSO in Dongola campaign 1896. Fought at battles of Atbara and Omdurman. Sent to South Africa as brigadier-general and cut through Boer lines to relieve Mafeking. The scenes of delirious rejoicing in London added a new word, 'mafficking', to the English language. Awarded CB. Saw further service in Egypt and India; appointed KCVO 1913. At outbreak of First World War appointed to command 10th (Irish)

Division and took part in Gallipoli campaign. Commander-in-chief Ireland 1916–1918; retired 1921 to live in Ireland. KCB 1922. Nominated to first Irish Free State Senate 1922. Died Dublin, 24 September 1930.

MAHON, CHARLES JAMES PATRICK (1800–1891), the O'Gorman Mahon, politician and soldier. Born Ennis, Co. Clare, 17 March 1800. Educated at TCD; joined the Catholic Association, and played a prominent part in helping DANIEL O'CONNELL to win the Clare election of 1828. Elected MP for Clare 1830, but unseated on petition regarding a charge of bribery. O'Connell supported his opponent in the general election of 1831, in which O'Gorman Mahon was defeated, and this led to a quarrel, never healed, between O'Connell and himself. Called to the bar 1834 but did not practise. He set out on foreign travel the following year, visiting most countries in Europe, including France, where he was an intimate of Louis-Philippe and Talleyrand, and then going to Africa, the East, and South America. He was back in Ireland in 1846; MP for Ennis 1847–1852. On being defeated by thirteen votes in 1852 he again set out abroad. The Russian emperor appointed him a lieutenant in his international bodyguard, a rank that placed him above many generals. He fought against the Tartars, travelled in China and India, and fought under the Turkish and Austrian flags. In the 1860s he went to South America, served as a general under the government during a civil war in Uruguay, had command of a Chilean fleet with the rank of admiral in the war with Spain, was a colonel under the emperor of Brazil, and took part in the American Civil War on the side of the north. Returning to France he was made a colonel in a regiment of Chasseurs by Napoleon III. In Germany he was on good terms with Bismarck and the Crown Prince. He came back to Ireland in 1871 and joined PARNELL's party. MP for Clare 1879–1885; MP for Carlow

1887 until his death. His fellow-candidate for Clare in the general election of 1880 was CAPTAIN WILLIAM O'SHEA, and it was he who introduced O'Shea to Parnell. He has been described as one of the last of the old race of daredevil Irish gentlemen. He fought thirteen duels, and it is thought that several resulted in the death of his opponent. He later told Gladstone that, in every case, he had been the aggressor. Despite his great age he retained all his faculties to the end, dying in Sidney St, London, on 15 June 1891, at ninety-one. Many of the adventures attributed to him are of doubtful origin. The details of his life are difficult to establish with certainty, due to a lack of reliable sources.

MAHONY, FRANCIS SYLVESTER (1804–1866), humorist, better known as 'Father Prout'. Born at Cork, 31 December 1804, son of a prosperous woollen-manufacturer of Blarney. Educated at Clongowes Wood College. He wished to become a Jesuit, and after studying at Paris and Rome was appointed to the staff at Clongowes in 1830. A late-night frolic led to his resignation and to termination of his membership of the order. He then entered the Irish College in Rome. Ordained priest at Lucca 1832; assigned to a parish in Cork, and showed courage and devotion as a hospital chaplain during a cholera epidemic. After a sharp disagreement with his bishop he removed to London in 1834, and ceased to exercise his priestly functions. He began to write for *Fraser's Magazine*, and took his pen-name from a real Father Prout, parish priest of Watergrasshill, Co. Cork, who had died in 1830. His *Reliques of Father Prout* appeared in Fraser's between 1834 and 1836 and established his reputation as a writer of light verse, and parodies in Latin, Greek, and French. He contributed poems to *Bentley's Miscellany*, founded by Dickens in 1837, and then, after an extended tour of Europe, settled in Rome in 1846 as correspondent for the *Daily News*. In 1848 he moved to Paris and was correspondent for the *Globe* from 1858 until his death. Died in Paris, 18 May 1866. Buried in the vaults of Shandon Church, Cork, which he made widely known by his verses 'The Bells of Shandon'.

MALACHY (MAEL MAEDOC), SAINT (1094/97–1148), archbishop of Armagh. Brought up at Armagh after the death of his parents, under the care of a hermit, Eimar. Ordained by St Cellach or Celsus, archbishop of Armagh, at twenty-five. Vicar to the archbishop, responsible for eradicating abuses and superstitions. Substituted Roman for Celtic liturgy, settled the regular celebration of the canonical hours in all churches, and renewed the use of the sacraments, especially penance, confirmation, and matrimony. Studied the canons of the church with St Malchus at Lismore before becoming abbot of Bangor in 1123. Bishop of Connor 1124. In 1128 a raiding party forced him to go with one hundred and twenty monks from Bangor to Munster, where they received a grant of land at Iveragh in Kerry from Cormac MacCarthy, king of Desmond. Succeeded Cellach in the See of Armagh 1132 but, owing to intrigue, unable to take possession until 1134. His appointment broke the tradition of hereditary succession. Once discipline and peace were restored in Armagh he resigned and returned to his former diocese, Connor, in 1137. He set about dividing the diocese in two, Down and Connor, and founded a priory of Augustinian canons at Downpatrick. Went to Rome 1139, visiting St Bernard at Clairvaux en route. Pope Innocent II appointed him apostolic legate for Ireland. He established the first Cistercian abbey in Ireland, at Mellifont, Co. Louth, in 1142. Convoked the synod of Inis Phádraig (off Skerries, Co. Dublin), 1148. Set out again for Rome, reached Clairvaux, where he died in the arms of Bernard on 2 November 1148. Buried at Clairvaux. Canonised by Pope Clement III in 1190—the first papal canonisation of an Irishman. The so-called Prophecies of St Malachy concerning the Popes are spurious: they were unknown before 1590.

MALLET, ROBERT (1810–1881), civil engineer. Born Dublin. Graduated in engineering, TCD; became partner in his father's foundry in 1831 and expanded the business considerably. His projects included raising the roof of St George's Church, Dublin, weighing 133 tons; boring an artesian well for Guinness's brewery; building a number of swivel bridges on the Shannon; building the Nore viaduct and Fastnet Rock lighthouse 1848–1849. He surveyed the Dodder at his own expense as a possible water supply. In 1852 he invented the buckled plate for flooring bridges. Elected FRS 1854; moved to London 1861 and set up as consulting engineer. Awarded Telford Medal, Institution of Civil Engineers, 1859; Cunningham Medal, RIA, 1862; Wollaston Gold Medal, Geological Society, 1877. Contributed many papers to engineering journals and societies. Published *Great Neapolitan Earthquake of 1857* (1862). Died Clapham Road, Surrey, 5 November 1881.

MALLIN, MICHAEL (1880–1916), one of the sixteen leaders executed after the 1916 Rising. Born in Dublin, joined the British army as a drummer-boy. Served abroad, and was promoted non-commissioned officer. After fourteen years he left the army and returned to Dublin, where he worked as a silk weaver and became secretary of the Silk Weavers' Union. He became friendly with JAMES CONNOLLY and joined the Irish Citizen Army on its formation in 1913. He wrote military lectures that were published in *The Workers' Republic*, and gave training in street fighting to the Citizen Army. In the 1916 Rising he was in command of the College of Surgeons. He was court-martialled, condemned to death, and executed in Kilmainham jail on 8 May 1916.

MALONE, EDMUND (1741–1812), Shakespearian scholar. Born in Dublin, 4

239

October 1741. Educated at TCD and the Inner Temple. Called to the bar in 1767 and practised on the Munster circuit, but when left a modest income on the death of his father removed to London in 1777 to become a man of letters. He became friendly with Dr Johnson, Sir Joshua Reynolds, EDMUND BURKE and other members of the famous 'Club', of which he himself became a member. Devoting himself to Shakespearian criticism, he published in 1778 his *Attempt to Ascertain the Order in which the Plays of Shakespeare were Written*. His edition of Shakespeare, the fruit of seven years' labour, appeared in eleven volumes in 1790. Though criticised for showing more industry than imagination, the edition sold out quickly, and Malone then projected a new edition to include a life of Shakespeare and a history of the Elizabethan stage. He died while still working on it, and it was completed by James Boswell the younger (twenty-one volumes, 1821). It remained for over a hundred years the standard complete edition. He gave much help to Boswell in writing his life of Johnson. In 1796 he published an *Exposure of the Ireland Forgeries*, an enquiry into the authenticity of certain papers attributed to Shakespeare. In the *Gentleman's Magazine* for 1782 he exposed Chatterton's 'Rowley' forgeries. He spent a good part of his income collecting books, and after his death the major part of his valuable library was presented to the Bodleian Library, Oxford.

MALONE, REV. SYLVESTER (1822–1906), historian. Born Kilmally, Co. Clare. Educated Maynooth; ordained 1854. Curate in several parishes until 1873, when he became parish priest of Sixmilebridge, Co. Clare. Vicar-general Kilrush 1892; remained there until his death. Published *Church History of Ireland* (1867), a standard work. Supported language revival and bequeathed £100 for essays in Irish to Society for Preservation of the Irish Language. The prizes were won by HYDE and Ó DUINNÍN. Malone died at Kilrush, 21 May 1906.

MALTON, JAMES (died 1803), architectural draughtsman. Probably born in London. Came to Ireland in 1785 with his father. Employed for nearly three years as draughtsman in office of GANDON during building of Custom House. Dismissed for breaches of confidence and other irregularities. In 1791 completed a series of drawings showing views of Dublin. Twenty-five were reproduced by him in etching and aquatint, and engraved sets published from 1792. He went back to London about this time. Began to exhibit in the RA in 1792 and showed seventeen Dublin views in Indian ink and watercolour. With the engravings they constitute an invaluable record of Dublin architecture, executed with care and accuracy, probably the finest views of Dublin ever made. He died of brain fever in Norton, St Marylebone, 28 July 1803.

MANCHESTER MARTYRS, THE (ALLEN, LARKIN, and O'BRIEN). On 18 September 1867 a police van conveying two Fenian prisoners, Colonel Kelly and Captain Deasy, to Manchester jail was attacked by armed men. The prisoners were released and made good their escape. In the scuffle, Sergeant Charles Brett was shot and killed. William Philip Allen, Michael Larkin and 'William Gould' (Michael O'Brien) were arrested, with others, and tried in October before a special commission in Manchester. All three pleaded not guilty. Allen said that he was born and reared in Bandon, Co. Cork. O'Brien said that he was born in Cork and was a citizen of the USA. All three were condemned to death, and executed by public hanging at Manchester jail on 23 November 1867. Bitter public feeling was aroused in Ireland by their conviction on what many regarded as flimsy evidence. The song 'God Save Ireland', written to commemorate them by T. D. SULLIVAN, became widely popular.

MANGAN, JAMES CLARENCE (1803–1849), poet. Born 1 May 1803 at 3

240

Fishamble St, Dublin, son of an impoverished grocer. Educated at a school in Saul's Court by a Father Graham, who taught him Latin, Spanish, French, and German. He went to work at fifteen in a scrivener's office at miserable wages. After ten years' drudgery he left and managed to live by writing occasional pieces for magazines. Friends found him employment for short periods in the library of TCD and in the Ordnance Survey. His prose and verse, including translations from the German, appeared in the *Dublin University Magazine*. Becoming acquainted with GAVAN DUFFY, he wrote pieces for the *Nation* under Duffy's editorship, sometimes using the nom-de-plume 'The Man in the Cloak'. He knew no Irish, but working from translations made for him by O'CURRY and O'Daly produced memorable versions of Irish poems, notably 'My Dark Rosaleen' and 'The Woman of Three Cows'. His published work included a *German Anthology* (1845) and *The Poets and Poetry of Munster* (1849). His natural tendency to melancholy, aggravated by poverty, loneliness, and an unhappy love affair, drove him to alcoholism, and his last years were wretched in the extreme. He died of malnutrition in the Meath Hospital, Dublin, on 20 June 1849, during a cholera epidemic.

MANING, FREDERICK EDWARD (1812–1883), the 'Pakeha Maori.' Born 5 July 1812 at Johnville, Co. Dublin. His father emigrated to Van Diemen's Land (Tasmania) in 1824. In 1833, seeking adventure, Frederick set off in a small trading schooner for New Zealand, which was not then a British colony, and hardly open even to traders. His great height and strength, and his good humour, made him welcome among the Maoris, who soon installed him as Pakeha Maori, that is, a naturalised stranger. He acquired a tract of land, settled at Onaki, married a Maori wife, and adopted the customs of the tribe. In 1865 he became a judge in the courts established under British rule to settle land titles, and his judgements contain colourful accounts of Maori customs. He published two books, *Old New Zealand*, a record of Maori life, and *The History of the War in the North with Heke in 1845*. He became ill in 1881 and travelled to England in search of a cure, but died in London, 25 July 1883. At his own request his body was taken back to New Zealand for burial.

MANNIX, DANIEL (1864–1963), archbishop of Melbourne. Born Charleville (Ráth Luirc), Co. Cork, 4 March 1864. After a brilliant career at Maynooth College, was ordained there in 1890. Professor of mental and moral theology 1891, professor of theology 1894, and president of the college 1903. In 1912 he went to Melbourne, Australia, as coadjutor, and became archbishop in 1917. During the First World War he was a controversial figure as Australian spokesman for Irish independence and leader of the successful opposition of Australians to conscription for overseas service. In 1920 when he went to Rome for his *ad limina* visit, he travelled by way of the USA, and was greeted by huge crowds across the country. He proposed to visit Ireland on the way, but British destroyers intercepted his vessel, the *Baltic*, and he was arrested, landed at Penzance, and forbidden to speak at the main centres of Irish population in England. During his forty-seven years as archbishop he established 108 parishes, more than 150 primary schools, seventeen high schools, and fourteen schools for technical, commercial and domestic training. He founded the Newman College for men and St Mary's Hall for women at the University of Melbourne, as well as the provincial seminary of Corpus Christi College. He promoted Catholic Action, the Catholic press, the liturgical movement, and the Catholic social movement. Died in Melbourne, 6 November 1963. Buried there in St Patrick's Cathedral.

MARKIEVICZ, COUNTESS CONSTANCE, née GORE-BOOTH (1868–1927), revolutionary. Born at

Buckingham Gate, London, 4 February 1868. Educated by a governess at Lissadell, Co. Sligo, where the family held extensive estates. In 1887 she was presented at a court of Queen Victoria, was called 'the new Irish beauty', and took her place in Irish society as a member of the Anglo-Irish landed gentry. Wishing to become a painter, she studied at the Slade School in London in 1893 and in Paris from 1898 to 1900. In Paris she met Count Casimir Dunin-Markievicz, a Catholic six years younger than herself, who came from a long line of Polish landowners settled in the Ukraine and had met with fair success as a painter. He was already married, with two sons, but was estranged from his wife, who died in 1899. Constance married him in London on 29 September 1900; their only child, Maeve Alys, was born at Lissadell in November 1901. After periods in Paris and the Ukraine they settled in Dublin in 1903. The countess soon became attracted to Gaelic League and Abbey Theatre circles, while continuing to move in Dublin society, which was centred on the Lord Lieutenant. With Casimir and ELLEN DUNCAN she helped to found the United Arts Club in 1907. In 1906 she rented a cottage at Ballally in the Dublin mountains and came across back numbers of *The Peasant* and *Sinn Féin*, left by a previous tenant, PÁDRAIC COLUM. Her interest in her country's struggle for freedom was thus first aroused. In 1908 she entered nationalist politics, joining Sinn Féin and Inghinidhe na hÉireann, founded by MAUD GONNE. In 1909 she founded Na Fianna, an organisation for boys, who were taught drill and the use of arms. During the lockout of workers in Dublin in 1913 she ran a soup kitchen in Liberty Hall. About this time Casimir left for the Ukraine, and never lived in Dublin again. In the 1916 Rising she served at the College of Surgeons under MICHAEL MALLIN, and was condemned to death. Her sentence was commuted to penal servitude for life and she was imprisoned in Aylesbury jail. Released in the general amnesty of June 1917, she

was received into the Catholic Church a fortnight later. In August 1917 she was made a freeman of Sligo. In the general election of December 1918 she was returned for St Patrick's division of Dublin, the first woman ever to be elected to the British Parliament: in accordance with Sinn Féin policy she refused to take her seat. Member of the first Dáil Éireann, which met on 21 January 1919, and Minister for Labour. On the run like other ministers, she served two jail sentences, in Mountjoy and Cork. She opposed the Anglo-Irish Treaty of 1921 and toured America in 1922 to enlist support for the Republican cause. Defeated in the general election of 1922, she won Dublin Borough South in August 1923 when the Civil War had ended. She continued to advocate republican views, was arrested in November 1923, and went on hunger strike. Joined Fianna Fáil when it was founded by DE VALERA in 1926. Re-elected to the Dáil 1927. For some years her health had been failing, and she died in Dublin on 15 July 1927. Casimir came from Warsaw to be at her bedside. She was buried in Glasnevin cemetery.

MARMION, JOSEPH (1858–1923), monk and spiritual writer. Born in Dublin. Educated Belvedere College, Holy Cross College, Clonliffe, and Rome. Curate at Dundrum, Dublin, then professor at Clonliffe and chaplain to Mountjoy prison. After five years in Dublin he entered the Benedictine novitiate at Maredsous Abbey in Belgium, and in 1891 he was professed as Dom Columba. Represented Maredsous at the centenary celebrations of Maynooth College 1895. Prior at Mont César, Louvain, and examiner at Louvain University. Abbot of Maredsous September 1909. At the outbreak of the First World War he left Belgium, disguised as a cattle jobber, to seek asylum for his community. His mission failed in England, and eventually they settled at Edermine, Co. Wexford. He became known as a preacher of retreats. Preached retreat to monks of Caldey prior to their conversion to the Catholic faith. Returned to Maredsous at the end of the war. From notes taken by students at his lectures and submitted to him for correction he published *Le Christ, Vie de l'Ame* (1918), *Le Christ Dans ses Mystères* (1919), and *Le Christ, Idéal du Moine* (1922). They had a wide readership and were translated into nine languages. Died in Belgium, 30 January 1923.

MARSDEN, WILLIAM (1754–1836), orientalist and numismatist. Born 16 November 1754 at Verval, Co. Wicklow, son of a wealthy shipowner and banker. Joined the East India Company at Bengkulu in Sumatra in 1771. After serving for eight years he went to England and in 1785, with his brother John, who had also served in Sumatra, he founded an East India agency business in Gower St, London. In 1795 he was persuaded to accept the post of second secretary to the Admiralty, and in 1804 was promoted to be first secretary at a salary of £4,000 a year. After giving able service, he resigned in 1807 and received a pension for life of £1,500 a year. In 1831 he voluntarily relinquished his pension. Published a *History of Sumatra* (1783) and *A Dictionary and Grammar of the Malayan Language* (1812). *Numismata Orientalia* (1823–1825) established his fame as a numismatist. It describes his collection of oriental coins, some 3,447 in all, which he presented to the British Museum in 1834. Elected FRS 1783, and an original member RIA. Died at his house at Aldenham, Hertfordshire, 6 October 1836.

MARSH, NARCISSUS (1638–1713), provost of TCD. Born 20 December 1638 near Cricklade, Wiltshire. Educated at Magdalen Hall, Oxford; ordained 1662. Principal of St Alban Hall 1673. By favour of JAMES BUTLER, Duke of Ormond, appointed provost of TCD, January 1678. Employed Paul Higgins, Catholic priest turned Protestant, to teach Irish in TCD. Founder-member of Philosophical Society, and bishop of Ferns

and Leighlin 1683. Driven from his see in 1689 and fled to England. Returned in July 1690 after Battle of the Boyne. Archbishop of Cashel 1691; translated to Dublin 1694. Built library in garden of St Sepulchre's, close to St Patrick's Cathedral, 1701–1704. Marsh's is the oldest public library in Ireland. Gave SWIFT his first seat in chapter of St Patrick's Cathedral. Translated to Armagh 1703. Founded an almshouse at Drogheda for widows of clergymen. Died, unmarried, in Dublin, 2 November 1713.

MARTIN, (HARRIET) MARY LETITIA (1815–1850), novelist, 'Princess of Connemara'. Born 28 August 1815 at Ballynahinch Castle, Co. Galway, only child of Thomas Barnewall Martin MP, and granddaughter of 'HUMANITY DICK' MARTIN. On her father's death in 1847 she inherited large estates that he had mortgaged to the Land Life Assurance Company for £200,000. During the famine years of 1846–1847 the family spent large sums on food and clothing to relieve their tenants, as well as giving work to some hundreds of labourers. In 1847 she married Arthur Gonne Bell of Brookside, Co. Mayo, who had no money of his own and who assumed the surname of Martin by royal licence. When she was unable to meet the instalments on the mortgage the property was brought into the Encumbered Estates Court. Out of 200,000 acres she was able to retain nothing and became almost penniless. She went to Fontaine L'Évêque in Belgium and turned to novel-writing to support herself and her family. She wrote *St Etienne, a Tale of the Vendean War* (1845) and *Julia Howard, a Romance* (1850). She then went to New York in 1850 to seek better fortune and died there in childbirth, on 7 November 1850.

MARTIN, JOHN (1812–1875), nationalist. Born at Loughorne, near Newry, Co. Down, on 8 September 1812, son of a Presbyterian clergyman.

Educated at TCD. Studied medicine for a few years, but then gave it up. The death of an uncle in 1835 left him independent financially and he travelled to America and the Continent. On his return he joined the Young Irelanders, and when his brother-in-law and lifelong friend JOHN MITCHEL was arrested in 1848 and his paper, the *United Irishman*, suppressed, Martin founded the *Irish Felon* to continue the struggle. He was imprisoned, found guilty of treason-felony, and sentenced to transportation for ten years. After five years in Van Diemen's Land (Tasmania) he was pardoned on condition of exile from Ireland. This condition was removed in 1856 and he returned to Co. Down. Elected Home Rule MP for Co. Meath 1871, and for a time accepted the post of secretary to the Home Rule League, first on half-pay and then in an honorary capacity. Known throughout Ireland as 'Honest John Martin'. Died at Dromolane House, near Newry, 29 March 1875, a few days after attending the funeral of John Mitchel.

MARTIN, MOTHER MARY (1892–1975), founder of the Medical Missionaries of Mary. Born in Glenageary, Co. Dublin, eldest of the twelve children of a leading Dublin timber merchant. Educated Sacred Heart Convent, Leeson Street, Dublin, and Holy Child College, Harrogate, Yorkshire. During the First World War she trained as a Voluntary Aid nurse in England, and served there and in France and Malta. It was at this time that she formed the idea of devoting her life to the service of the sick. In 1918 she returned to Dublin and trained as a midwife at the National Maternity Hospital, Holles St. In January 1921, at the request of the African missionary, BISHOP SHANAHAN, she went to Calabar, Nigeria, and began to work in the village of Nsukara. Appalled at the conditions she saw, she became convinced that they should be remedied by the establishment of a religious order of dedicated women who would set up clinics and hospitals in

Africa. After two years on the mission she returned to Ireland in 1923 on the advice of Bishop Shanahan, to enter a new congregation then being formed, but left two years later after consulting her spiritual director. Years of ill-health followed. Nevertheless she continued to advocate that women religious should undertake maternity and medical work, and she was encouraged to persevere by Dr Paschal Robinson, Papal Nuncio to Ireland. In 1934 she became matron of Glenstal, a new school founded by the Benedictines in Co. Limerick. Two years later Pope Pius XI gave permission to women religious to devote themselves to medical work in all its branches, and on 11 May 1936 she received permission to found her congregation, the Medical Missionaries of Mary, which she did the following year in the southern Nigerian town of Anua. In April 1938, although seriously ill in hospital in Port Harcourt, she was professed as a nun. On medical advice she sailed for home the same month. Her work continued and a house for students was opened at Booterstown, Co. Dublin, and a novitiate was founded at Collon, Co. Louth. In response to local requests, the Medical Missionaries opened a maternity hospital in Drogheda in December 1939. Her work culminated in 1957 with the opening of the International Missionary Training Hospital at Drogheda. Cardinal Cushing, archbishop of Boston, became a patron, and through his assistance a hostel for extern sisters and students was founded in 1959. Received Florence Nightingale Medal from International Red Cross 1963. Honorary fellowship RCSI 1966 'for her singular achievements in the field of medical missions,' the first woman to be so honoured. First woman to be made a freeman of Drogheda, 1966. The Medical Missionaries now run hospitals throughout Africa as well as in the USA, Italy and Spain. Mother Mary's great achievement lay in securing permission for women religious to undertake medical work. Died 27 January 1975 in the hospital she had founded in Drogheda.

MARTIN, RICHARD (1754–1834), 'Humanity Dick'. Born February 1754, probably in Dublin. Educated at Harrow and Trinity College, Cambridge. From his family seat at Ballynahinch Castle he virtually ruled over Connemara, where his estates comprised 200,000 acres, stretching thirty miles from his hall door, to give him the longest front avenue in Europe. He sat in the Irish parliament 1776–1800, supported the Union, and represented Co. Galway 1801–1826. Widely known for love of animals and his readiness in duelling. In 1822 he succeeded in having passed 'the first modern enactment in Great Britain for protecting the right of animals.' One of the founders of the Royal Society for the Prevention of Cruelty to Animals 1824. In Parliament he supported Catholic emancipation, and tried to abolish the death penalty for forgery. His generosity to his tenants was on a princely scale. King George IV, long a personal friend, first called him 'Humanity Martin'. In 1827 he lost his seat in Parliament and retired to Boulogne, where he died on 6 January 1834. MARY LETITIA MARTIN was his granddaughter.

MARTIN, VIOLET FLORENCE (1862–1915), novelist, under pen-name Martin Ross. Born at Ross House, Co. Galway, 11 June 1862, daughter of James Martin, head of the ancient family of Martin, one of the 'Tribes of Galway'. Educated at Alexandra College, Dublin, and spent most of her life at Ross and at Drishane, the home of her cousin EDITH SOMERVILLE. Their literary partnership began with their first meeting in January 1886. In 1898 she had a serious accident while hunting, from which she never completely recovered. In addition to the well-known books written jointly by herself and her cousin, she published two volumes of autobiographical èssays, *Some Irish Yesterdays* (1906) and *Strayaways*, published posthumously in 1920. Died at Cork, 21 December 1915.

MARTYN, EDWARD (1859–1924), playwright. Born Co. Galway. His family were wealthy Catholic landlords who were exempted from the penal laws in 1709 by a special Act of Queen Anne, because of their moderation and charity to Protestants in troubled times. Educated at Beaumont College and Christ Church, Oxford. On his return to the family home, Tulira Castle, he became interested in Irish, and in traditional and church music. Founded the Palestrina Choir in the Pro-Cathedral, Dublin, in order to reform liturgical music. Also a founder of the Feis Cheoil, now an annual musical festival. Associated with GEORGE MOORE and W. B. YEATS in founding the Irish Literary Theatre in 1899, and his play *The Heather Field* was the second to be produced by this new group. His next play, *Maeve* (1899), was, like his first, a study in Ibsen's symbolism with an Irish setting. He wrote several more plays, including *The Tale of a Town* (1902), *Glencolman* (1912), and *The Dream Physician* (1914). In 1914 he withdrew from the Abbey, which had succeeded the Literary Theatre, and with JOSEPH PLUNKETT and THOMAS MACDONAGH founded the Irish Theatre, a short-lived venture in Hardwicke St, Dublin. He was a central figure in *Hail and Farewell* (1911–1914), George Moore's mordant account of the Irish literary revival. In his later years he became virtually a recluse in Tulira Castle. He died unmarried.

MASON, WILLIAM SHAW (1774–1853), statistician. Born Dublin; educated TCD. Appointed remembrancer or receiver of first fruits 1805. Secretary, Commissioners of Public Records, 1810. Encouraged by Sir Robert Peel, then Chief Secretary, he undertook *A Statistical Account or Parochial Survey of Ireland, Drawn up from the Communications of the Clergy* (three volumes, 1814–1819), a valuable record of the time. His *Survey, Valuation and Census of the Barony of Portnahinch* (1821) was submitted to King George IV on his visit to Ireland, as a model for a statistical survey of the whole country. He made a collection of books on Ireland for Peel, and prepared a printed catalogue. Died Camden St, Dublin, 11 March 1853.

MASSEY, WILLIAM FERGUSON (1856–1925), Prime Minister of New Zealand. Born at Limavady, Co. Derry, 26 March 1856, son of a farmer. Educated at local national schools and a private school in Derry. His parents emigrated to New Zealand in 1862 and he joined them in 1870 and took up farming near Auckland. In 1894 he won a seat in the conservative interest in the House of Representatives. Chief opposition whip 1895–1903, then leader of the opposition, which, in 1904, styled itself the Reform Party. He became Prime Minister in July 1912 and retained that office until his death thirteen years later. In August 1915 he formed a national government of the two chief parties, Reform and Liberal, and led New Zealand through the First World War with ability and firmness. The only premier in the world to retain office before, during and after that war. Plenipotentiary to the Paris Peace Conference 1919, and signed the Treaty of Versailles on behalf of New Zealand. Ten cities made him a freeman, including Belfast and Derry. Privy councillor 1914. His attendance at Imperial Conferences in 1917, 1921 and 1923 enabled him to meet the leading statesmen of the British Empire, with resultant benefit to New Zealand. Died at Wellington on 10 May 1925.

MATHEW, FATHER THEOBALD (1790–1856), apostle of temperance. Born 10 October 1790 at Thomastown Castle, Cashel, Co. Tipperary, where his father was agent to Lord Llandaff. Entered Maynooth seminary in 1807 but left after a short stay to join the Capuchins in Dublin, where he was ordained in 1814. He was sent to Cork, opened a free school for poor children, and formed a society of steady young men to help relieve the widespread

wretchedness and poverty. After twenty-five years' labour among the poor he was asked by non-conformist friends to lead their temperance society. On 10 April 1838 he signed a pledge of total abstinence with the historic words, 'Here goes in the name of the Lord,' and began his campaign. His success was remarkable: within six years his disciples included nearly half the adult population, the revenue from duties on spirits fell from £1.4 million to £0.8 million, and there was an extraordinary reduction in crime. Father Mathew extended his crusade to centres of Irish population in Britain with equal success. His later years were clouded by ill-health and financial difficulties; a public subscription relieved the debts he had incurred in founding temperance clubs and libraries throughout the country. He received a civil list pension of £300 a year in 1847. On his return to Ireland in 1851 from an extended visit to America he was told that Rome had proposed to make him a bishop but the state of his health precluded his acceptance. Retired to live with his brother Charles near Cork. Died in Queenstown (Cóbh), 8 December 1856.

MATURIN, BASIL WILLIAM (1847–1915), preacher and writer. Born at All Saints' vicarage, Grangegorman, Dublin, 15 February 1847, son of Rev. William Maturin. Educated at TCD; took holy orders, and served as a curate in England, later going to America where he became rector of St Clements in Philadelphia in 1881. Doubts as to his position in the Anglican Church led to his recall to England in 1888. He spent the next nine years preaching and conducting missions. In 1897, after much mental questioning and travail, he was received into the Roman Catholic Church in Beaumont, near Windsor, and ordained in Rome after two years' theological study. He spent the next sixteen years mainly in London, combining parish work with preaching and writing. His eloquent sermons and his sympathetic insight as director of penitents made him widely known. Chaplain at Oxford University 1914, but the outbreak of war emptied the colleges. Went to America to preach during the Lent of 1915 and was drowned when returning on the *Lusitania*, torpedoed and sunk on 7 May. His principal works were *Practical Studies on the Parables of Our Lord* (1897) and *Laws of the Spiritual Life* (1905).

MATURIN, CHARLES ROBERT (1782–1824), novelist and playwright. Born in Dublin of Huguenot stock; educated at TCD. Entering the Church of Ireland, he served as a curate in Loughrea and Dublin. He wrote a number of tragedies, but his only success was *Bertram*, produced at Drury Lane by Kean in 1816. He fared better with his novels, publishing six in all; the best-known, *Melmoth the Wanderer* (1820), a story in the Gothic style on the theme of the wandering Jew, had great influence on contemporary European writing. Balzac wrote a sequel, *Melmoth Réconsilié*, and Oscar Wilde took the pen-name Sebastian Melmoth after his downfall. Died in Dublin, 30 October 1824.

MAXWELL, CONSTANTIA (1886–1962), historian. Born in Dublin; educated at TCD and at Bedford College, London. Became assistant in history and later lecturer at TCD. Published works on Chateaubriand, and edited Arthur Young's *Tour in Ireland*. Other works were *Irish History from Contemporary Sources* (1923), *The English Traveller in France* (1932), *Dublin Under the Georges* (1936), *Irish Town and Country Under the Georges* (1940), *History of Trinity College* (1946), and *The Stranger in Ireland: From the Reign of Elizabeth to the Great Famine* (1954). Professor of economic history 1939, the first woman to be appointed to a chair in TCD. Lecky Professor of History 1945. Retired in 1951. Died at Pembury, Kent, in February 1962.

MAXWELL, WILLIAM HAMILTON (1792–1850), novelist. Born at Newry,

Co. Down; educated at TCD. Joined the British army and served in the Peninsular Wars and at Waterloo. Returning to Ireland he entered the Protestant Church and became rector of Balla, Co. Mayo, in 1820. Here he wrote *Wild Sports of the West of Ireland* (1832), his best-known work, and still well worth reading. He contributed to *Bentley's Miscellany* and the *Dublin University Magazine*, and wrote a number of popular novels and historical works based on his military and sporting experiences, as well as a *Life of Wellington* (three volumes, 1839–1841). After some years of ill-health and financial difficulties he retired to Musselburgh near Edinburgh, where he died, 29 December 1850.

MAY, FREDERICK (1911–1985), composer and pianist. Born in Dublin and educated at the RIAM, TCD, and the Royal College of Music, London. He won a travelling studentship in 1935 to work under Alban Berg in Vienna, but the great composer and teacher died before he reached Vienna and he studied instead under Berg's pupil, Egon Wellesz. From 1933 to 1956 his output was large and favourably received abroad. It included his setting of Ernst Toller's 'Songs from Prison', his 'Scherzo for Orchestra', 'Symphonic Ballad', 'Spring Nocturne', and 'Lyric Movement for String Orchestra'. He was director of the Abbey Theatre orchestra for fifteen years, and a talented accompanist. In later years he suffered from a form of tinnitus, which made composition impossible. He died in a Dublin hospital on 8 September 1985, survived by his niece, Nicola, daughter of his sister Sheila, first wife of DAVID GREENE.

MAYNE, RUTHERFORD. See under WADDELL, SAMUEL J.

MEAGHER, THOMAS FRANCIS (1823–1867), nationalist. Born in Waterford, 3 August 1823. Educated at Clongowes Wood College. Intended for the bar, he soon took up politics. In a speech to the Repeal Association in 1846 he hailed the sword as a sacred weapon, which led Thackeray to call him 'Meagher of the Sword'. A founder-member of the Irish Confederation, he stood unsuccessfully for Waterford in 1848. He was the first to formally propose the Tricolour as the national flag, in 1848. Arrested after the abortive rising of 1848 and sentenced to death; the sentence being commuted to penal servitude for life, he was sent to Van Diemen's Land (Tasmania). Escaping in 1852 he went to America, where he became a journalist and lecturer. In the Civil War he organised the Irish Brigade to fight for the North, and became a brigadier-general. After the war he was appointed temporary governor of Montana territory. He was accidentally drowned in the Missouri on 1 July 1867.

MEEHAN, REV. CHARLES PATRICK (1812–1890), author and translator. Born 141 Great Britain St (Parnell St), Dublin, 12 July 1812. Educated Irish College, Rome; ordained 1834. Curate, parish of Saints Michael and John, Dublin, until his death. Contributed verse to the *Nation* and articles to Catholic periodicals, besides publishing translations and historical compilations and editing the poems of DAVIS and MANGAN. His most valuable work is *Fate and Fortunes of Hugh O'Neill, Earl of Tyrone and Rory O'Donnell, Earl of Tyrconnel* (1870). Died Dublin, 14 March 1890.

MEENAN, JAMES (1910–1987), professor of economics and author. Born in Dublin in October 1910 and educated at Clongowes Wood College and UCD. He was called to the bar in 1938. He spent two years in Italy studying law and Mussolini's corporate state, then became part-time lecturer in political economy at UCD while practising law. He succeeded GEORGE O'BRIEN as professor of economics in 1961. He served on a number of Government commissions and was appointed a director of the Central Bank in 1949. He was a member of the RDS from the age of seventeen and was president 1980–1983. His published works include *The Italian Corporative System* (1944), *A View of Ireland* (1957), *The Irish Economy since 1922* (1970), and a biography of George O'Brien (1980). He was a founder-governor of the Irish Times Trust and a director of the *Irish Times*. He died in Dublin on 25 May 1987, survived by his wife, Annette, and three daughters.

MERRIMAN, BRIAN (c. 1740–1805), poet. Born in Ennistymon, Co. Clare, son of an itinerant stonemason. The family moved to Feakle shortly afterwards, and Brian taught school there between 1765 and 1785. His own education is not known, but it is probable that he attended a hedge school, and he may have picked up scraps of learning from wandering poor scholars and poets. At Feakle he had a small farm and cultivated it well enough to win two prizes from the Dublin Society in 1797 for his crop of flax. He married a woman from the parish about 1787 and they had two daughters. About 1802 they moved to Limerick, where Merriman continued to teach and where he died suddenly on 27 July 1805. He was buried in Feakle churchyard. His reputation rests on a poem of 1,206 lines, *Cúirt an Mheán-Oíche* ('The Midnight Court') (c. 1780). The plight of young women who lack husbands, clerical celibacy, free love and the misery of a young woman married to a withered old man are the principal themes. Merriman's vigour, fluency and earthy humour made his poem widely popular, and while he was still alive numerous manuscript copies were made and circulated. One authority has described it as the greatest humorous poem ever written in Irish. It has been translated into English by ARLAND USSHER, FRANK O'CONNOR, LORD LONGFORD and DAVID MARCUS. Cumann Merriman, a society devoted to the history and literature of Thomond, was founded by Con Howard in 1967. Under its auspices a Merriman Summer School is held annually in Co. Clare.

MEYER, KUNO (1858–1919), Celtic scholar. Born in Hamburg; educated at

Edinburgh and Leipzig universities. Lecturer in German, University College, Liverpool, 1884. Devoted himself to 'the fascinating study of the vernacular literature of ancient Ireland, the earliest voice from the dawn of West European civilisation.' Founded the School of Irish Learning in Dublin 1903, and *Ériu*, the school's journal, 1904. Also founded a number of Celtic reviews and journals in Germany. Professor of Celtic, University of Berlin, 1911. His publications include *The Voyage of Bran* (1895), *Stories and Songs from Irish Manuscripts* (1899), *Four Old Irish Songs of Summer and Winter* (1903), *Triads of Ireland* (1906), *Fianaigecht* (1910), and *Selections From Ancient Irish Poetry* (1911). He was made a freeman of Dublin in 1911 and of Cork in 1912. Died in Leipzig 1919. His portrait by Augustus John hangs in the National Gallery, Dublin.

MIDDLETON, COLIN (1910-1983), painter. Born in Belfast, son of a damask designer, and served an apprenticeship in the linen trade. He worked as a textile designer and then became an art teacher. An Arts Council award when he was sixty enabled him to devote himself full-time to painting. His first one-man exhibition in 1943 consisted of over a hundred paintings of astonishing variety and he continued to experiment throughout his career. He exhibited in Dublin, Belfast, Edinburgh, and Glasgow, and his work is included in the Municipal Gallery, Dublin, and the Ulster Museum. In 1970 he was made an MBE, elected to the RHA, and received an honorary degree from QUB. His first wife died young. He died in Belfast on 23 December 1983, survived by his second wife, Katie, and a daughter.

MILLER, LIAM (1924-1987), publisher. Born in Mountrath, Co. Laois, and studied architecture at UCD. He worked in London on city reconstruction projects at the end of the Second World War. Returned to Dublin and founded the Dolmen Press 1951, at first working from his home and using only a hand press. The quality of Dolmen productions soon gained for him an international reputation as a typographer and book designer. He published poets AUSTIN CLARKE, Thomas Kinsella, John Montague, and Richard Murphy. He was a director of the Lantern Theatre, and designed sets for the Abbey Theatre. He was first president of CLÉ (the Irish Book Publishers' Association). He died in Dublin on 17 May 1987, survived by his wife, Josephine, a son and three daughters.

MILLIGAN, ALICE L. (1865-1953), writer. Born in Omagh, Co. Tyrone, in September 1865, daughter of Seaton F. Milligan MRIA, wealthy businessman and antiquary, and sister of CHARLOTTE MILLIGAN FOX. Educated at Methodist College, Belfast, Magee College, Derry, and King's College, London. Refused to go to Germany to learn the language and chose to go to Dublin to learn Irish. Her first contact with it had been through her great-uncle, Armour Alcorn, an extensive farmer, whose dealings with his labourers were conducted through Irish. Her studies intensified her enthusiasm for the political independence of Ireland. As organising secretary of the 1798 centenary celebrations in Ulster she invited her friend, the Fenian JOHN O'LEARY, to Belfast. Organiser for the Gaelic League for some years and toured the country producing historical tableaux to raise funds to finance Irish classes with the support of W. B. YEATS and GEORGE RUSSELL. Her writings did much to stimulate the early Sinn Féin movement. With Anna Johnston (ETHNA CARBERY), she founded a monthly paper, the *Northern Patriot*, in conjunction with a national working-men's club in Belfast. The paper advocated the separation of Ireland from England. Following disagreement with the club, a new paper, the *Shan Van Vocht*, was founded in 1896 under the same joint editorship. Wrote several plays for the Irish Literary Theatre, forerunner of the Abbey. Published a book of poetry, a novel, and a *Life of Wolfe Tone* (1898). A founder-member of the Ulster Anti-Partition Council. Received honorary D.Litt., NUI, in 1941. Died at Tyrcar, Omagh, 13 April 1953.

MILLIN, TERENCE (1903–1980), surgeon. Born in Helen's Bay, Co. Down, and educated at St Andrew's College, Dublin, and TCD, where he won scholarships in mathematics and medicine. He captained the rugby team that won the Leinster Senior Cup and the Bateman Cup and beat both Oxford and Cambridge. He was capped for Ireland against Wales 1925. In 1928 he won a fellowship of the RCSI and moved to London, working at All Saints' Hospital and Royal Masonic Hospital. In 1954 he published in the *Lancet* an account of a new technique he had devised for operating on the prostate gland, which made him internationally famous; 'Millin's prostatectomy' reduced mortality dramatically and was recognised as a striking advance in surgical technique. He also published a textbook on retropubic surgery. Having won fame and fortune in London he moved to Cork in the 1950s and commuted to Harley Street as a part-time consultant. Later he lived in Co. Wicklow. His many honours included presidency of the RCSI and honorary fellowship of the American College of Surgeons. He died on 3 July 1980, survived by his wife and two daughters.

MILNE, EWART (1903–1987), poet. Born in Dublin on 25 May 1903 and educated at Christ Church Cathedral Grammar School. He ran away to sea but returned to Ireland, met Kathleen Bradner and married her in London. He served on the Republican side with Spanish Medical Aid in the civil war, following his friend CHARLIE DONNELLY to Madrid. During the Second World War he worked on a farm in England, then was divorced and married Thelma Dobson in 1948. He returned to Dublin in the 1960s. His wife died in 1964 and he went back to England in 1966. He published fourteen volumes of poetry and contributed for over forty years to leading Irish, British and American literary magazines. He died in Bedford on 14 January 1987, survived by the two sons of his second marriage.

MITCHEL, JOHN (1815–1875), patriot. Born in Dungiven, Co. Derry, son of a Presbyterian minister. Educated at Newry and TCD. He became a lawyer, practising in Newry and Banbridge. On visits to Dublin he made the acquaintance of DUFFY and DAVIS and began to write for the *Nation*, the organ of the Young Ireland party. The frightful miseries brought about by the Great Famine of 1845–1847 convinced Mitchel that constitutional agitation was useless. He founded the *United Irishman* to advocate passive resistance by the small farmers to protect their lives and homesteads; should this fail they would have to resort to arms. In 1848 he was arrested, tried for treason-felony, convicted by a packed jury, and sentenced to fourteen years' transportation. He was sent to Bermuda and then to Van Diemen's Land (Tasmania), but escaped to America in 1853. Here he published in 1854 his *Jail Journal*, a classic in prison literature. He founded a series of short-lived newspapers in New York. His outspoken championship of the southern states in the Civil War lost him many friends and readers and he suffered a term of imprisonment. His eldest and his youngest sons were killed in the war. In 1874 he returned to Ireland and was elected MP for Tipperary. The British government declared him ineligible as an undischarged felon, but the people re-elected him in 1875. He died on 20 March 1875 in Newry, where he is buried.

MITCHELL, ALEXANDER (1780–1868), civil engineer. Born in Dublin, 13 April 1780. Although he virtually lost his sight in 1802 he carried on a brick-making and building business in Belfast until 1832. He invented machines for brick-making, and by 1842 had invented and patented the Mitchell screw-pile and mooring, a simple and effective method of constructing lighthouses in deep water, on mud banks and shifting sands, and of fixing beacons and mooring ships. In 1848 he was elected a member of the Institution of Civil Engineers, and received the Telford Silver Medal for a paper on his invention. His screw-pile was used for the construction of lighthouses at Maplin Sand on the Thames estuary, at Morecambe Bay, and at Belfast Lough. The success of these undertakings led to the use of his invention on the breakwater at Portland, the viaduct and bridges on the Bombay and Baroda railway, and the whole system of Indian telegraphs. Died at Glen Devis, near Belfast, on 25 June 1868.

MITCHELL, SUSAN LANGSTAFF (1866–1926), author and hostess. Born at Carrick-on-Shannon, Co. Leitrim. Her father, manager of the Provincial Bank there, died when she was six, and she was sent to live in Dublin with two of her aunts, who were comfortably off. She attended a private school for girls in Morehampton Road, and in addition had lessons in music, singing, drawing, and dancing. In 1900 she went to London for treatment for an illness that had impaired her hearing, and stayed with the family of JOHN B. YEATS. In 1901 she became assistant editor of the *Irish Homestead*, which was edited by GEORGE RUSSELL from 1905, and contributed essays, book reviews, and drama notes. Her first collection of verse, entitled *Aids to the Immortality of Certain Persons, Charitably Administered*, appeared in 1908. In it she satirised lightly a number of people notable in literature and public life. *The Living Chalice and Other Poems*, a collection of religious verse, also appeared in 1908. Her third and last published collection, *Frankincense and Myrrh*, appeared in 1912. In 1916 she contributed a study of GEORGE MOORE to a series entitled *Irishmen Today*. In 1926 she became sub-editor of the *Irish Statesman*, which was edited by Russell. She was a prominent member of the

United Arts Club, many of whose members were singled out in her light satiric verse, and she was also celebrated in those circles as a generous, kind and witty hostess.

MOLINES or MULLEN, ALLAN (died 1690), anatomist. Born Ballyculter, Co. Down. Educated TCD, graduating MB 1676 and MD 1684. Elected fellow RCPI 1684. Contributed valuable paper to Dublin Philosophical Society on human and comparative anatomy. Described vascularity of lens of the eye, which he discovered by dissecting an elephant accidentally burnt in Dublin 1681. Published an *Account* of this in London, 1682, notable for the accuracy of its anatomical observations. Elected FRS 1683. A discreditable love affair obliged him to move to London 1686. He accompanied Lord Inchiquin to the West Indies in 1690, hoping to improve his fortunes. Died soon after landing at Barbados, reportedly from the effects of heavy drinking.

MOLONY, HELENA (1884–1967), actress and trade unionist. Joined the movement for national independence while still a young woman. Became a member of Inghinidhe na hÉireann in 1903. In 1908 she became editor of *Bean na hÉireann*, a monthly magazine founded by MAUD GONNE MACBRIDE at her suggestion. It advocated 'militancy, separatism, and feminism'. Helped CONSTANCE MARKIEVICZ to found Na Fianna in 1909. That year she joined the Abbey Theatre and played there until 1920, with interruptions from her political activities. Arrested in 1911 during protests organised by Sinn Féin against the visit of King George V. At the request of JAMES CONNOLLY she became secretary of the Irish Women Workers' Union in 1915. She joined the Citizen Army and took part in the attack on Dublin Castle in the 1916 Rising. Imprisoned in Aylesbury jail until December 1916. After the Treaty she took the Republican side. Became an organiser with her old union, and was honoured with presidency of the Irish Trade Union Congress. Shortly after the end of the Second World War she retired owing to ill-health. Died in Dublin, 28 January 1967.

MOLYNEUX, SIR THOMAS (1661–1733), physician, brother of WILLIAM. Born Dublin; educated TCD and Leiden University. Graduated M.D. 1687 and elected FRS. Practised successfully in Dublin. Published notes on the Giant's Causeway and was the first to assert that it is a natural phenomenon and not an artefact. Published first account of anatomy of the sea-mouse, and first scientific account of the Irish elk. Elected president, RCPI, 1702, 1709, 1713, and 1720. Founded Asylum for the Blind 1711. State physician 1715, and professor of medicine, DU, from 1717. Published *A Discourse on Danish Forts* (1725). Made baronet 1730. His portrait by Kneller is in TCD.

MOLYNEUX, WILLIAM (1656–1698), philosopher and patriot. Born in New Row, Dublin, 17 April 1656. Educated at TCD and the Middle Temple, London. He was a semi-invalid, and his wife, Margaret Domville, whom he married on his return to Dublin in 1678, went blind three months later and died in 1691 after much suffering. Having private means he had no need to practise law, and applied himself to the study of philosophy, optics, and astronomy. First secretary, Dublin Philosophical Society, founded in 1684, precursor of the RIA. Engineer and Surveyor of the King's Buildings 1684; elected FRS 1685. During the war of 1689–1691 he went to live at Chester, where he became friendly with Locke and wrote *Dioptrica Nova*, which was for a long time the standard work on optics. On return to Dublin elected MP for Dublin University. In 1698 published *The Case of Ireland's being Bound by Acts of Parliament in England Stated*. His assertion of the right of Ireland to legislative independence in order to secure its commercial interests created a sensation. The pamphlet was condemned by the Westminster House of Commons as 'of dangerous consequence to the Crown and Parliament of England', and burned by the common hangman. On returning from a visit to Locke in England he was taken ill and died on 11 October 1698.

MONAGHAN, JOHN JOSEPH ('RINTY') (1920–1984), world flyweight boxing champion. Born in the docks area of Belfast and became a professional boxer. He won the world title when he knocked out Jackie Paterson from Glasgow in the King's Hall, Belfast, on 23 March 1948. He successfully defended his title a year later against Maurice Sanderson and in 1949 drew with Londoner Terry Allen. He retired undefeated six months later. After each fight he sang 'When Irish Eyes are Smiling' from the ring. Of fifty-four professional fights he won forty-three, drew three, and lost eight. He held the British, European, Commonwealth and world championships simultaneously. After retiring he took to the cabaret circuit with little success, then worked as a taxi and lorry driver and garage attendant. It was said he got his nickname 'Rinty' from Rin-Tin-Tin, the dog film-star, because of his speedy footwork. He died in his Belfast home on 3 March 1984, survived by his wife, Frances, and six children.

MONRO, MONROE, or MUNRO, HENRY (1768–1798), United Irishman. Born at Lisburn, Co. Antrim, and became a linen-draper. In 1795 he joined the United Irishmen in order to forward the causes of Catholic emancipation and parliamentary reform. On the outbreak of the 1798 Rising he was chosen to command the insurgents in Co. Down, and seized Ballynahinch. Government troops under General Nugent succeeded in re-taking it. Monro was captured on 15 June, tried by court-martial, and hanged opposite his own door and in sight, it was said, of his wife and sisters.

MONTEZ, LOLA, stage-name of MARIE DOLORES ELIZA ROS-ANNA GILBERT (1818–1861), dancer. Born at Limerick, daughter of a British army officer. Educated at Montrose in Scotland and in Paris. At nineteen, to escape an arranged marriage with a gouty old judge, she eloped to Ireland with a Captain Thomas James; their marriage ended in divorce five years later. After studying dancing for a few months she made a disastrous début in London in 1843 as 'Lola Montez, Spanish dancer'. However, she secured engagements at Dresden and Berlin, met with great success, and was equally well received at St Petersburg (Leningrad) and Paris. Here she had a liaison with a young Republican editor, Dujarrier, who was killed in a duel. In 1847 she danced in Munich, and her beauty captivated the old king, Ludwig, who made her Comtesse de Lansfield, gave her a pension of 20,000 florins, and built her a magnificent mansion. As the king's favourite she became virtual ruler of Bavaria, but her liberal policies led to an insurrection, and she was banished in 1848. From 1851 to 1853 she danced and acted in America. After a period in Australia, where she horsewhipped the editor of the *Ballarat Times* for casting doubts on her character, she lectured in America on gallantry, beautiful women, heroines of history, and similar subjects. Her second marriage, in 1849 to a Lieutenant Heald, ended with his death; her third marriage, in 1853 to P. P. Hull of San Francisco, ended in divorce. From 1859 she settled in New York and devoted herself to the care of the inmates of the Magdalen Asylum. Died at Asteria, New York, 17 January 1861.

MONTGOMERY, LESLIE A. (1873–1961), writer. Born in Downpatrick, Co. Down, 5 October 1873. Educated at Dundalk. Joined Northern Banking Co. in Belfast at sixteen. After seventeen years he was transferred to Skerries. Manager there until his retirement in 1934. Under the pseudonym Lynn C. Doyle ('linseed oil'), he wrote more than twenty books, including the humorous Ballygullion series. The first collection of these stories about a fictitious border village appeared in 1908, and the final collection, *The Ballygullion Bus*, in 1957. Published a comedy, *Love and Land* (1913), which was produced at the Little Theatre, London. His first novel was *Mr Wildridge at the Bank* (1916), followed by a long succession of short stories, articles, poems, and plays. Member of Censorship of Publications Board 1937, but resigned because it was 'so terribly easy to read only the marked passages, so hard to wade through the whole book afterwards.' After 1935 his work appeared in the *Strand*, the *Century*, and *Passing Show*. He developed a reputation as a lecturer, and regularly broadcast his stories for the BBC in Belfast. His most productive period as a writer was in his sixties. President of the Consultative Council of Irish PEN 1954. Died in Dublin in August 1961.

MONTGOMERY, NIALL (*c.* 1914–1987), architect. Born in Dublin and educated at Ring College, Belvedere College and UCD, graduating in architecture 1938. After a short spell in the Office of Public Works, where he was involved in the award-winning design of Dublin Airport buildings, he went into private practice. He won a medal for his work on the Kilkenny Design Centre. He was president of the Royal Institute of the Architects of Ireland in the mid-1970s. In 1975 he won a Carroll's prize for an audio-visual work at the Living Art Exhibition and later held a one-man exhibition of drawings, paintings, and sculptures in the Peacock Theatre, Dublin. His poetry appeared in periodicals and anthologies. He died in Dublin on 12 March 1987, survived by his wife, two daughters and a son.

MOODY, JOHN (1727–1812), actor. Born in Cork, son of a hairdresser named Cochran. Followed his father's occupation for some years. In 1745 he went to Jamaica, and was so successful there as an actor that he was able to return home as a man of considerable means. He went to London, and played at Drury Lane until 1804. He excelled in the part of a comic Irishman. On retiring from the stage he settled at Barnes Common and made a comfortable living growing vegetables for the London market. Died 26 December 1812.

MOODY, THEODORE WILLIAM (1907–1984), historian. Born in Belfast and educated at RBAI and QUB. Became a lecturer at QUB; professor of modern history, TCD, 1940–1977. With R. Dudley Edwards he founded the *Journal of Irish Historical Studies* in 1938 and was joint editor until 1977. Leading spirit in the launching of *A New History of Ireland*, an ambitious project under the aegis of the RIA, of which six volumes have appeared. *The Course of Irish History* (1967), edited by him and Professor F. X. Martin, became widely used as a textbook. His *Davitt and the Irish Revolution* (1981), the work of a lifetime, is regarded as his greatest achievement. Also published a biography of THOMAS DAVIS (1945), and a history of QUB (1959) with J. C. Beckett. He died in Dublin on 11 February 1984.

MOONEY, RIA (1904–1973), actress and producer. Born in Dublin. Began acting as a child of six. At sixteen she was singing with the Rathmines and Rathgar Musical Society. Studied at the Metropolitan College of Art for some years. In 1924 she joined the Abbey Theatre company by invitation, after giving a striking performance at the Dublin Arts Club in Chekhov's *Proposal*. The personal choice of SEÁN O'CASEY for the part of Rosie Redmond in the first production of *The Plough and the Stars* (1926). Later she toured England and the USA with MOLLY ALLGOOD and remained in New York for some years as assistant director with the Civic Repertory Theatre. Returning to Ireland in the 1930s, she played with the Gate Theatre company, and in 1944 became director of the Gaiety Theatre School of Acting. Returned to the Abbey

as first woman producer there, a post she held for fifteen years. Died in Dublin in January 1973.

MOOR, REV. MICHAEL (1640–1726), Provost of TCD. Born Bridge St, Dublin; educated Nantes and Paris. Ordained 1684 on his return to Ireland, vicar-general of Dublin 1685. Chaplain and confessor to RICHARD TALBOT, by whose influence he was appointed Provost of TCD in 1689 despite Jesuit opposition. The only Catholic to hold the position. Protected Protestants, and saved the library from being burnt. Forced to resign in 1690 when his sermon in Christ Church Cathedral, reflecting on the Jesuits, offended King James II. Fled to Paris; became successively censor of books in Rome, rector of University of Paris (1701), principal of Collège de Navarre, and professor at Collège de France. Blind in his last years. Died in Paris, 22 August 1726, and left his fine library to the Irish College there.

MOORE, GEORGE AUGUSTUS (1852–1933), novelist. Born 24 February 1852 at Moore Hall, Ballyglass, Co. Mayo, son of a wealthy landlord. Educated at Oscott College, Birmingham. In 1873 he went to Paris to become a painter, but finding his talent insufficient went to London and turned to writing. His first novel, *A Modern Lover* (1883), showed promise, but it was not until the publication of *Esther Waters* in 1894 that he emerged as a major writer of power and realism. In 1901 he settled in Dublin and was associated with YEATS, MARTYN and LADY GREGORY in the Irish literary revival and the founding of the Abbey Theatre. His short stories, *The Untilled Field* (1903), received their inspiration from this return to Ireland. Difficulties arose with his literary associates, and Moore went back to London in 1911 and lived for the rest of his life at 121 Ebury Street. His autobiography, *Hail and Farewell* (three volumes, 1911–1914), gives a mordant account of his ten years in Dublin with a candour and directness new to his time.

He continued to write novels, publishing more than a dozen in all. *The Brook Kerith* (1916) and *Heloïse and Abelard* (1921) are generally taken as representing the summit of his achievement in this field. Died, unmarried, in London, 21 January 1933.

MOORE, THOMAS (1779-1852), poet. Born 28 May 1779 at 12 Aungier Street, Dublin, son of a grocer and wine merchant. Entered TCD 1794 and became friendly with ROBERT EMMET, but shunned the activities of the United Irishmen. In 1799 he entered the Middle Temple in London to study law. From an early age he had shown a talent for singing, acting, and versifying, and he was an immediate social success in London. In 1800 he published his *Odes of Anacreon*, which received high praise. The pseudonymous *Poetical Works of the late Thomas Little* was less successful in 1801. In 1803 he was appointed registrar of the Admiralty Prize Court in Bermuda but the seclusion of the islands was little to his taste, and he soon appointed a deputy and returned to London, visiting the USA and Canada en route. Resuming his career as a poet and socialite, he published *Odes, Epistles and other Poems* in 1806, and the following year undertook his *Irish Melodies*, which were published in parts between 1807 and 1834, with music arranged by SIR JOHN STEVENSON from 'traditional' Irish tunes. The *Melodies* earned him a considerable income · and he was accepted as the national lyric poet of Ireland. In 1812 Longman offered him £3,000 to write an oriental romance. The result, *Lalla Rookh*, was received very favourably. In 1818 it was discovered that his deputy at Bermuda had absconded, leaving Moore responsible for some £6,000, and he was obliged to live abroad for three years to avoid the debtor's prison. In Italy he renewed a friendship with Byron, who left him his 'Memoirs'. Moore sold them to the publisher John Murray, but repurchased and then burnt then, writing a life of Byron himself instead. He returned to his country home, Sloperton Cottage, Wiltshire, in 1822 and spent the rest of his life there. His other writings include formal satires, lighter prose pieces like *The Fudge Family in Paris* (1818), and a poor *History of Ireland* (1827), but he is now remembered chiefly for his *Melodies* and for his burning of Byron's memoirs. He received a civil list pension of £300 a year in 1835. His last years were clouded by the loss of his two sons and by mental illness. Died at Sloperton Cottage, 25 February 1852. Buried in Bromham churchyard.

MORAN, DAVID PATRICK (1871-1936), journalist. Born Waterford; educated Castleknock College. Founder, editor and proprietor of the *Leader* from 1900. In its first decade this weekly had great influence in drawing people into the national movement and won wide circulation, but declined later. Moran published essays, *The Philosophy of Irish Ireland*, and a novel, *Tom O'Kelly* (both 1905). Died Sutton, Co. Dublin.

MORAN, MICHAEL (1794-1846), 'Zozimus', balladeer. Born in a thatched cottage in Faddle Alley, off Dowker's Lane, between Clanbrassil Street and Blackpitts in Dublin's Liberties. When he was two weeks old he was blinded by illness. More of a reciter than a singer, he had no ear for music and depended on his eccentricity to make his name. He became known as Zozimus from his recitation of the history of St Mary of Egypt. In this metrical tale written by Dr Coyle, bishop of Raphoe, Mary is found, after fifty years of penance in the desert, by the Blessed Zozimus. Many of Moran's ballads, such as 'Saint Patrick was a Gentleman' and 'The Finding of Moses', survive to this day. Died on 3 April 1846, and buried in Glasnevin cemetery, Dublin, where a monument was unveiled on 6 April 1988.

MORAN, PATRICK FRANCIS (1830-1911), cardinal. Born at Leighlinbridge, Co. Carlow, on 16 September

1830. Educated Irish College in Rome and ordained by special permission at twenty-two. Vice-rector of the Irish College 1856 to 1866. Returned to Ireland as private secretary to his mother's stepbrother, CARDINAL CULLEN, Archbishop of Dublin. Bishop of Ossory 1873. In 1884 went to Australia as archbishop of Sydney, and in 1885 became the first Australian cardinal. He showed immense energy in building new schools, churches, and hospitals. He advocated home rule for Ireland and supported Australian federation. He had published a dozen books on Church history before his sudden death at Manby Palace, Sydney, on 16 August 1911. His best-known works were his *History of the Catholic Archbishops of Dublin* (1864) and *Spicilegium Ossoriense* (1873–84), a collection of documents illustrating Irish church history from the Reformation until 1800. He also wrote a *History of the Catholic Church in Australia* (1896).

MORGAN, LADY SYDNEY (1783–1859), novelist. Born in Dublin, eldest child of ROBERT OWENSON. Educated at the Huguenot School, Clontarf. Her father's affairs failed to prosper, and Sydney became a governess. Her first publication, a slight volume of poems, appeared in 1801, followed by *St Clair* (1804), a novel of ill-starred love, clearly deriving from Goethe's *Sorrows of Werther*. She collected and published *Twelve Original Hibernian Melodies* (1805), wrote a second novel, and in 1806 made her name with *The Wild Irish Girl*, extolling the scenery and traditions of Ireland in rhapsodic prose. The Marchioness of Abercorn invited the young novelist to become her companion and in 1812 persuaded her to marry the family surgeon, Thomas Charles Morgan, for whom the marquess arranged a knighthood. Her salon in Kildare St became a centre of social and literary life in Dublin. She continued to write novels, and travelled extensively in France and Italy. Her books on the politics and society of these countries, like her novels, were criticised severely in the *Quarterly Review*, but without impairing their success. In 1837 Lord Melbourne granted her a pension of £300 a year, the first of its kind given to a woman for her services to letters. Lady Morgan then removed to London, where she became well known in society but ceased to write. Died there, 14 April 1859, leaving a considerable fortune.

MORIARTY, DAVID (1814–1877), bishop. Born 18 August 1814 at Derryvin, Kilcarah, Co. Kerry. Educated Boulogne-sur-Mer and Maynooth. Vice-rector, Irish College, Paris, 1839; rector, All Hallows, Drumcondra, Dublin, 1845. Coadjutor 1854 and bishop of Kerry 1856. He bitterly opposed all movements against the government, and denounced the Fenian leaders, saying in a well-remembered phrase that 'eternity is not long enough nor Hell hot enough for such miscreants.' He subsequently opposed the Home Rule party. Nevertheless, his nominee was defeated by a Protestant home-ruler, Blennerhasset, in Kerry by-election 1872. He died 1 October 1877.

MORSHIEL, GEORGE. See under SHIELS, GEORGE.

MOSSE, BARTHOLOMEW (1712–1759), founder of the Rotunda Hospital. Son of the rector of Maryborough (Portlaoise). Apprenticed to John Stone, a Dublin surgeon, and on 12 July 1733 received a licence to practise surgery. After making an extensive tour of Europe to study the practice of medicine, he settled in Dublin in 1742 and obtained a licence in midwifery. Struck by the miseries suffered by poor expectant mothers, he rented a large house in George's Lane, and opened it on 15 March 1745 as the 'Lying-in Hospital', the first of its kind in Ireland or Britain, and the beginning of a revolution in maternity services. Encouraged by its success, he leased a large plot of ground on the north side of Dublin, and with only £500 in hands, began the building of the Rotunda Hospital, with

Richard Cassels as architect. Mosse laid out the gardens as a fashionable resort, and organised concerts and illuminations to raise funds for the building work. Further finance was provided by lotteries, subscriptions, and parliamentary grants. The hospital was opened on 8 December 1757, with Mosse as the first master. He formed a scheme, only partly executed, for nursing, clothing and maintaining all children born in the Rotunda whose parents entrusted them to his care. His philanthropic schemes involved him in debt and misrepresentation. He died at the house of Alderman Peter Barré at Cullenswood, near Dublin, on 16 February 1759. After his death, parliament at various times granted £9,000 to the hospital, and £2,500 to his widow for the maintenance of herself and her children.

MOSSOP, HENRY (c. 1729-1774), actor. Born probably at Tuam, Co. Galway, where his father was a clergyman. Educated at a grammar-school in Digges Street, Dublin, and TCD. Made his first appearance on the stage at Smock Alley Theatre, Dublin, on 28 November 1749. Well received, especially in Shakespearian tragedy, and in 1751 Garrick engaged him for Drury Lane Theatre in London. He became jealous of Garrick, and returned to Dublin in 1759 to play at Crow Street Theatre. In November 1760 he took over Smock Alley, and entered into intense rivalry with Crow Street, run by SPRANGER BARRY and Woodward, which involved both houses in financial difficulties. Mossop's troubles were increased by his heavy gambling. When he went to London in 1771 to seek recruits he was imprisoned for debt and released a bankrupt. Toured the Continent for a year in an effort to restore his fortunes, but returned to London depressed and in broken health. Died in a Chelsea garret in extreme poverty on 18 November 1773. Another account, in the *Gentleman's Magazine*, gives the date of his death as 27 December 1774.

MOSSOP, WILLIAM (1751-1805), medallist, and founder of the art in Ireland. Born in Dublin; educated at the Blue Coat School. In 1765 he was apprenticed to a seal-cutter and then set up in business for himself at 4 Bull Lane. His first recorded medal, a portrait of the Right Honourable JOHN BERESFORD and his wife, was struck in 1782. Made the prize medal for the RIA, and medals for the Dublin Society and for the Orange Association, as well as a number of portrait medals and large seals for corporate bodies. Between 1792 and 1797 he executed the dies for coinage made from Wicklow copper. Died at his house, 68 Mecklenburgh St, 28 January 1805.

MOSSOP, WILLIAM STEPHEN (1788-1827), medallist, son of WILLIAM. Born Dublin; educated at Whyte's Academy, Grafton Street, and under Francis West in Dublin Society's school. When his father died, in 1805, he took up the business. In 1816 he made the first medallic portrait of O'CONNELL but it failed to sell. In 1820 he began a projected series of forty medals of distinguished Irishmen. He finished one of GRATTAN but lack of public interest forced him to abandon the project in despair. His medal for the visit of King George IV in 1821 had a good sale. His Derry medal with portrait of WALKER for the Prentice Boys Club was also successful. He was an original member of the RHA in 1823 and secretary. His mind became unbalanced from unremitting hard work and disappointments, and he was committed to Richmond Asylum and died there 11 August 1827. He wrote an account of his father's and his own work in *History of Dublin* by J. T. GILBERT.

MULCAHY, GENERAL RICHARD (1886-1971), soldier and politician. Born in Waterford; educated CBS, Mount Sion, Waterford, and later at Thurles, where his father was postmaster. Joined the postal service and worked in Thurles, Bantry, and Dublin.

Joined the Irish Volunteers soon after their formation in 1913. Second-in-command to THOMAS ASHE in encounter with armed constabulary at Ashbourne, Co. Dublin, in Easter Week 1916. Arrested after the rising and interned at Frongoch until the general amnesty of 1917. He immediately re-joined the movement and became chief of staff of the republican army. Elected MP for Clontarf division 1918. In 1919 he married Josephine Ryan, sister of DR JAMES RYAN and Phyllis Ryan, wife of SEÁN T. Ó CEALLAIGH. He supported the Treaty of 1921 and became GOC the military forces of the provisional government during the Civil War. Minister for Defence, 1923-1924; TD, Dublin North-West, 1922-1923 and Dublin City North, 1923-1937. Defeated in the 1937 general election, re-elected for Dublin North-East 1938, and defeated again in the general election of 1943. Senator 1943-1944. Returned to the Dáil for Tipperary in 1944. After the resignation of W. T. COSGRAVE in June 1944, he became leader of Fine Gael. Minister for Education 1948-1951 in the first Coalition government, and from 1954 to 1957 in the second Coalition. Resigned leadership of Fine Gael in October 1959, and in October 1960 told his Tipperary constituents that he did not intend to contest the next election. He spent the last five years of his life arranging and annotating his papers, and presented seventy-five boxes of documents to UCD, where the Richard Mulcahy Trust has been established. An enthusiastic supporter of the language revival and an Irish-speaker, he was chairman of the Gaeltacht Commission 1925-1926, which enquired into conditions in the Irish-speaking districts. Died in Dublin on 16 December 1971.

MULHALL, MICHAEL GEORGE (1836-1900), statistician. Born 100 St Stephen's Green, Dublin, 29 September 1836. Educated Irish College, Rome. Went to South America in 1858 and in 1861 founded the *Standard*, in Buenos Aires, the first English paper in South America. Maintained his connection with it until 1894. Published *Handbook of the River Plate* (1869), first English book printed in Argentina. Returned to Ireland 1878. Published *Progress of the World* (1880), *The Balance Sheet of the World 1870-1880* (1881), and his famous *Dictionary of Statistics* (1883), which became a standard reference-book and went into several editions. Also published *History of Prices since 1850* (1885), and similar works. At request of HORACE PLUNKETT he toured Europe in 1896, collecting material for report on projected Irish department of agriculture. Died Killiney Park, Co. Dublin, 13 December 1900.

MULHOLLAND, ROSA (1841-1921), novelist. Daughter of a Dr Mulholland. Born Belfast and educated at home. Published her first novel, *Dumara* (1864), under the name 'Ruth Murray'. Received encouragement from Charles Dickens, who printed many of her earlier stories in his *Household Words*. In 1891 she married Mr (later Sir) JOHN GILBERT, who died in 1898. She continued to write for over fifty years, producing a great number of novels, of which the best-known was probably *A Fair Emigrant* (1888). Her sister married RUSSELL OF KILLOWEN. Died Dublin, April 1921.

MULREADY, WILLIAM (1786-1863), painter. Born in Ennis, Co. Clare, son of a leather-breeches maker. When he was six the family moved to London and he was educated at a school for Roman Catholics at Castle Street, Long Acre. After working in the studio of a sculptor called Banks, he entered the RA school in 1800, and won the Silver Palette of the Society of Arts. He earned his living at this time as a book illustrator and teacher of drawing, and at eighteen married a daughter of John Varley, a watercolour painter. They separated after four years. He began to exhibit at the RA in 1804, became an associate in 1815, a full member in 1816, and continued to show work there almost every year until 1862. His first pictures were landscapes; later, he turned to subjects like 'Old Caspar' and 'The Carpenter's Shop'. Most of his best pictures are in the Victoria and Albert Museum. 'The Bathers' and 'The Toyseller', his last work, are in the National Gallery of Ireland. He was still painting within two days of his death, and said, 'I have, from the first moment I became a visitor to the Life School, drawn there as if I were drawing for the prize.' His life was solitary and secluded; he died at his house in Linden Grove, Bayswater, on 7 July 1863.

MULVANY, GEORGE FRANCIS (1809-1869), painter. Born in Dublin, son of Thomas James Mulvany RHA, keeper RHA from its foundation in 1823 until his death in 1845. George Francis studied in the Academy School and in Italy, and began to exhibit in 1827. RHA 1835; elected to succeed his father as keeper 1845. Played a prominent part in the moves to found the National Gallery of Ireland, and on 6 September 1862 was appointed first director. Exhibited regularly in the RHA to the year of his death, and also exhibited at the RA, London, in 1836 and 1839. The National Gallery has portraits by him of JOHN BANIM and SIR FREDERICK W. BURTON RHA. Died at his house in Herbert Place, Dublin, 6 February 1869.

MURPHY, ARTHUR (1727-1805), actor and author. Born 27 December 1727 at Clonyquin, Roscommon. Educated at the English College, St Omer. Between 1747 and 1751 he worked as a clerk, first in Cork and then in London. He then published *Gray's Inns Journal* for two years, before taking to the stage, making his first appearance as Othello at Covent Garden Theatre in October 1754. He was well received, but he retired from the stage in 1756 and was called to the bar. He wrote or adapted a great number of tragedies, farces, and comedies, translated Tacitus and Sallust, and wrote biographies of Garrick and Johnson. His comedies were very popular and were revived many times. He retired from the bar in 1788, and was made a commissioner of bankruptcy in 1798. Despite his earnings from the stage and a bequest of West Indian slaves, which he sold for £1,000, he continually in need of money. King George III granted him a pension of £200 a year from 8 January 1803. Died at his house, 14 Queen's Row, Knightsbridge, on 18 June 1805.

MURPHY, FATHER JOHN (c. 1753-1798), leader in the 1798 Rising. Born at Tincurry, Ferns, Co. Wexford. Educated at a hedge school and at Seville, where he was ordained. On his return to Ireland he became assistant priest at Boolavogue, Co. Wexford. He was at first active in promoting loyalty to the government, but in May 1798 the outrages perpetrated by the military drove him into rebellion. At Oulart he routed the North Cork Militia, and then proceeded to take Ferns, Enniscorthy, and Wexford. He was repulsed from Arklow with heavy losses. After the defeat of the insurgents at Vinegar Hill he escaped to Wexford. His fate is uncertain, but it appears that he was later captured by the yeomen and hanged.

MURPHY, SEUMAS (1907-1975), sculptor and stone-carver. Born at Greenhill, near Mallow, Co. Cork, on 15 July 1907. Educated at St Patrick's NS in Cork, where DANIEL CORKERY was one of his teachers. Left school at fourteen, joined the School of Art with Corkery's encouragement, and a year later became an apprentice stone-carver. He continued to study at the School of Art, and when he was twenty-four he won a Gibson Bequest scholarship, which took him to Paris for a year. He studied at the Académie Colo Rossi and with Andrew O'Connor, the Irish-American sculptor. On his return to Cork in 1933 he held an exhibition and opened a studio, helped and encouraged again by Corkery. As his reputation grew he was commissioned to execute portrait heads of many famous people.

In the entrance to Áras an Uachtaráin are bronze busts by him of all the Presidents from DOUGLAS HYDE to CEARBHALL Ó DÁLAIGH. His other commissions included heads of SEÁN LEMASS, 'POPE' O'MAHONY, ARCHBISHOP MCQUAID, MÁIRTÍN Ó CADHAIN, MICHAEL COLLINS, SEÁN Ó RIADA, and FRANK O'CONNOR. His headstones were noted for the austerity of his designs and the graceful precision of the lettering; a fine example is the commemorative stone to Ó Riada in St Gobnait's cemetery in Cúil Aodha. In 1950 he published *Stone Mad*, an autobiographical account of the lives and characters of the 'stonies' or stone-carvers with whom he had worked. Became professor of sculpture, RHA, and exhibited there up to the last year of his life. Received honorary LL.D. from NUI 1969. Died suddenly on 2 October 1975 at his home at Wellesley Terrace, Wellington Road, Cork.

MURPHY, WILLIAM MARTIN (1844–1919), founder of Independent Newspapers. Born Bantry, Co. Cork, 21 November 1844. Educated at Belvedere College. Took over the family business at nineteen when his father, a building contractor, died. His enterprise and business acumen expanded the business and he built churches, schools and bridges throughout Ireland, as well as railways and tramways in Britain and Africa. Elected Nationalist MP for St Patrick's, Dublin, 1885–1892. In 1904 he bought three Dublin daily newspapers and replaced them in 1905 with the *Irish Independent*. In 1906 he founded the *Sunday Independent*. Refused knighthood from King Edward VII that year. He led Dublin employers against the trade unions, an opposition that culminated in the lockout of 1913. The workers were led by JAMES LARKIN. After the 1916 Rising he bought ruined buildings in Abbey Street as sites for his newspaper offices. He owned Clery's department store, the Dublin United Tramways Company, and other large concerns. Wrote one book, *The Home Rule Act 1914*

Exposed (1917). Died in Dublin, 25 June 1919.

MURRAY, DANIEL (1768–1852), archbishop. Born 18 April 1768 at Sheepwalk, Arklow, Co. Wicklow. Educated at Dublin and Irish College, Salamanca. Ordained 1792 and served as curate in Dublin and Arklow. Apprehensive of violence after 1798 Rising, he moved to Dublin, where he won the friendship of ARCHBISHOP TROY. Consecrated coadjutor 1809. Acted as president, Maynooth College, 1812–1813. He went to Rome in 1814 and 1815 to oppose granting the British government a veto on Irish ecclesiastical appointments. The proposal was dropped. Archbishop of Dublin 1823. Encouraged MARY AIKENHEAD to found the Irish Sisters of Charity, and CATHERINE MCAULEY to found the Sisters of Mercy. He opposed O'CONNELL's Repeal movement and supported the Queen's Colleges (so-called 'godless' colleges) against O'Connell and MACHALE. He enjoyed the respect of British governments and was offered seat in Privy Council but refused. Died Dublin, 26 February 1852.

MURRAY, SIR JAMES (1788–1871), physician. Born in Derry and educated at Edinburgh and Dublin. Practised in Belfast. Published paper in 1817 on value of fluid magnesia. Appointed resident physician to lord lieutenant 1829 and knighted. Inspector of anatomy in Dublin for nearly forty years. Established factory for making fluid magnesia and patented his process. Probably the first to suggest use of electricity as curative agent. Published *Cholera* (1849), which was translated into Italian, and other medical papers. Died Upper Temple St, Dublin, 8 December 1871.

MURRAY, RUTH. See under MULHOLLAND, ROSA.

MURRAY, THOMAS CORNELIUS (1873–1959), playwright. Born at

Macroom, Co. Cork, 17 January 1873. Entered St Patrick's Teachers' Training College, Drumcondra, in 1891. Taught in schools in Cork before being appointed headmaster of the Inchicore Model Schools, Dublin. Founded Cork Little Theatre with TERENCE MAC-SWINEY, Con O'Leary, and DANIEL CORKERY. His first play, a comedy, *Wheel of Fortune*, was produced there in 1909. In 1910 he offered another play, *Birthright*, to the Abbey. This launched his career as one of the leading Abbey playwrights. His plays *Maurice Harte* (1912) and *Autumn Fire* (1924) were regarded as masterpieces of the realistic school and, like his ten other plays, were faithful to the manners and speech of West Cork. Murray, who retired from teaching in 1932, also wrote lyric poetry and one novel, and contributed essays to the *New Ireland Review, Dublin Magazine*, and *The Bell*. President, Irish Playwrights' Association and vice-president, Irish Academy of Letters. Received honorary D.Litt. from NUI 1949. Died 7 March 1959.

MYLES NA gCOPALEEN. See under O'NOLAN, BRIAN.

N

NAGLE, HONORIA (NANO) (1728–1784), founder of the Presentation Order. Born at Balgriffin, near Mallow, Co. Cork; educated in Paris. Distressed at the lack of education for the Catholic poor, she opened a school in Cove Lane, Cork, about 1754. Although Catholic schools were illegal at that time, within four years several hundred girls and boys were attending seven of her schools; a considerable inheritance in 1757 enabled her to finance this development. Her health began to trouble her, and to ensure the continuance of the work she introduced the Ursuline nuns in 1771. This order was mainly devoted to the education of the well-to-do, and after some years she founded a new order, 'which excluded every exercise of charity which was not in favour of the poor,' and to which she gave the name 'the Order of the Presentation of the Blessed Virgin Mary'. A convent and school built at her own expense were opened in Cork in 1777. She died there, 20 April 1784. The rules of the community received papal approval in 1791 and it has since spread to England, America, Australia, and India.

NAPIER, SIR WILLIAM FRANCIS PATRICK (1785–1860), general and historian of the Peninsular War. Born at Celbridge, Co. Kildare, 17 December 1785. Educated at a local grammar school. Joined the British army at fourteen, took part in the Peninsular War, fought at La Coruña under Sir John Moore and was wounded several times. By 1813 he had reached the rank of colonel, but ill-health, resulting from a bullet lodged in his spine, obliged him to return to England, and he retired on half pay in 1819. From 1842 to 1848 he was lieutenant-governor of Guernsey, and was then knighted and made a general. In 1823 he began his *History of the War in the Peninsula* for which he was specially supplied with documents by ARTHUR WELLESLEY (the Duke of Wellington), and Marshal Soult. His wife, with infinite patience, deciphered a mass of correspondence from Joseph Bonaparte, king of Spain. The book appeared in six volumes between 1828 and 1840 and remains a classic of its kind. He also wrote several books on the career of his brother, Sir Charles Napier, the conqueror of Sind. Died at Clapham Park, Surrey, 10 February 1860.

NEILSON, SAMUEL (1761–1803), United Irishman. Born in September 1761 at Ballyroney, Co. Down, son of a Presbyterian minister. Educated at a local school. At sixteen he was apprenticed to his elder brother, a woollen-draper, and at twenty-four he married and set up in business for himself. He had made a fortune of £8,000 by 1790, when he abandoned business for politics. In 1791 he suggested to HENRY JOY MCCRACKEN the idea of a society of Irishmen of every persuasion to work for Catholic emancipation and parliamentary reform. He was thus the originator of the United Irishmen. He became acquainted with WOLFE TONE about this time and together they founded the society in Belfast with Tone the chief organiser. In 1792 Neilson established the *Northern Star*, the organ of the United Irishmen in the north, and became its editor. He had now adopted Tone's republican outlook and in his paper advocated complete separation from England. Several prosecutions followed, and in September 1796 he was arrested and imprisoned in Dublin, first in Newgate and then in Kilmainham.

His health suffered, and in February 1798 he was released on condition that he would abstain from 'treasonable conspiracy'. However, he was soon active in assisting LORD EDWARD FITZGERALD to prepare for a rising. After the arrest of Fitzgerald in May 1798 Neilson went to Newgate jail to reconnoitre for a rescue and was captured after a desperate resistance in which he was badly wounded. He was indicted for high treason with other leaders. Some of the prisoners, seeing that the rising had failed, and in order to stay further executions, agreed to disclose their plans without implicating individuals, and to submit to banishment. Neilson was included, probably because the government was unsure of being able to secure his conviction. Despite the agreement he was detained at Fort George in Scotland from 1799 to 1802, and then deported to the Netherlands. After making a secret visit to Dublin and Belfast, he made his way to America in December 1802 and was about to launch an evening paper when he died suddenly at Poughkeepsie, New York, on 29 August 1803.

NEWELL, EDWARD JOHN (1771–1798), informer. Born 29 June 1771 at Downpatrick, Co. Down. After a period as a sailor, he became a painter and glazier, and finally settled in Belfast and worked as a portrait painter in miniature. He joined the United Irishmen in 1796, and in revenge for the mistrust of him by the leaders he became an informer. Edward Cooke, the undersecretary at Dublin, paid him £2,000 for information, most of it invented, and hundreds were arrested as a result. Early in 1798 Newell said to Cooke that he would spy no longer. He then published *The Life and Confessions of Newell, the Informer*, which was privately printed in Belfast, and had a large sale. The authorities arranged that he should leave Ireland, and in June 1798 he was about to embark for America with the wife of an acquaintance who had agreed to elope with him, when he was assassinated.

NEWMAN, W. A. (ALEC) (1905–1972), journalist. Born in Waterford. The family moved to Belfast in 1912, and he was educated at RBAI and TCD. After some years as a schoolmaster at the High School, Dublin, he joined the *Irish Times* in 1930 as a leader writer. Assistant editor 1934, and editor 1954–1961. He then joined the *Irish Press* as leader writer and commentator on current affairs. His encyclopaedic memory made him a notable participant in radio quiz programmes. Died in Dublin, 6 March 1972.

NÍ CHONAILL, ÉIBHLÍN DHUBH (*c.* 1743–1800), author of the lament for her husband, *Caoineadh Airt Uí Laoghaire*. Born at Derrynane, Co. Kerry, one of the twenty-two children of Domhnall Mór Ó Conaill, grandfather of DANIEL O'CONNELL. When she was about fifteen her mother married her to an elderly O'Connor of Iveragh who died six months later. Tradition says that she was childishly cracking nuts for herself while he lay dying. In 1767 she was on a visit to her sister Máire, who was married to a landlord called Baldwin of Macroom. She saw and fell in love with Art Ó Laoghaire, who had just returned from serving as a captain in the Hungarian Hussars under the Empress Maria Theresa. He was noted for his boldness and fiery temper, and her family forbade her to marry him. Nevertheless, on 19 December 1767 a newspaper carried the notice, 'Married, Mr Arthur O'Leary, Macroom, to the Widow Connor of Iveragh.' They had two sons and she was expecting a third child when he was killed. The O'Connells of Derrynane wished above all to remain in quiet enjoyment of their estates by shunning public notice or any conflict with the law. The trouble they feared from Ó Laoghaire came soon. On 7 October 1771 the high sheriff of Cork, Abraham Morris, who lived near Macroom, offered twenty pounds to anyone who would seize Ó Laoghaire, 'a fellow of character most notoriously infamous.' Shortly afterwards the Muskerry Constitutional Society offered twenty guineas for him. Ó Laoghaire replied vigorously that he would answer any charges in court, and it is reasonably certain that he stood his trial and was acquitted. Tradition says that a quarrel over a woman first caused bitterness between Morris and Ó Laoghaire, and there is evidence in the lament that he was not free from blame in his dealings with local women. In 1773 at Macroom races Ó Laoghaire's mare won all before her, beating among others a horse belonging to Morris. Under a statute of King William III no Catholic could own a horse worth more than five pounds, and Morris at once offered that sum for the mare. Ó Laoghaire refused, was proclaimed, and went 'on his keeping' (on the run). Months later, in May the same year, Ó Laoghaire determined to bring matters to a head and lay in wait for Morris near Millstreet. Morris was warned by a man called Seán Mac Uaithne, and he procured an escort of soldiers for his return to Macroom. Ó Laoghaire retreated before them until they reached Carraig an Ime, and in an encounter there he was shot dead by a soldier. His riderless, bloodstained mare galloped home to Éibhlín Dhubh at Ráth Laoich, near Macroom. She mounted instantly, and at Carraig an Ime found her husband lying dead. She then composed the first part of her famous lament, with additions during his wake. His tomb in Kilcrea Abbey bears the inscription:

Lo; Arthur Leary, generous, handsome, brave,
Slain in his bloom, lies in this humble grave.
Died May 4th 1773. Aged 26 years.

A coroner's court found Morris guilty of Ó Laoghaire's death. In July 1773 he narrowly escaped assassination by a brother of the dead man. It appears that he was wounded, and he died in 1775. The lament gives a vivid account of the life of a wealthy Gaelic household in Munster in the eighteenth century. It has been edited by Professor Seán Ó Tuama and translated by FRANK O'CONNOR.

NÍ SCOLAÍ, MÁIRE (1909–1985), traditional singer. Born in Dublin and educated at Central Model Schools and Ring College. She went to Galway with her sister Mona and soon acquired a reputation as teacher of Irish singing and dancing. Appeared as Gráinne with MÍCHEÁL MAC LIAMMÓIR in his *Diarmaid agus Gráinne* in the Taibhdhearc in 1928. Married LIAM Ó BUACHALLA, then a lecturer in UCG. She became widely known for her interpretations of traditional Irish songs, won many prizes at feiseanna, broadcast frequently from Radio Éireann and the BBC and in France and the USA, and gave recitals in Covent Garden and Queen's Hall, London. She collected many songs in the Galway and Donegal Gaeltachtaí. Died in Galway on 29 June 1985.

NORBURY, EARL OF. See TOLER, JOHN.

NORTHCLIFFE, VISCOUNT. See under HARMSWORTH, ALFRED.

NORTON, WILLIAM (1900–1963), labour leader. Born in Dublin. Joined the postal service in 1916. After his election to the national executive of the Post Office Workers' Union in 1920 he became prominent in the trade union movement; full-time secretary of the union 1924–1948. Labour TD for Co. Dublin 1926–1927, and represented Kildare from 1932 until his death. Leader of the Labour Party from 1932. Tánaiste and Minister for Social Welfare 1948–1951 in the first Coalition government, and Tánaiste and Minister for Industry and Commerce 1954–1957. Unanimously elected president of the Postal, Telegraph and Telephone International 1957. Died in Dublin in December 1963.

NUGENT, COUNT LAVALL (1777–1862) Austrian field-marshal. Born at Ballincor, Co. Wicklow, in

November 1777. Little is known about his early years save that on 1 November 1793 he was appointed a cadet in the Austrian engineer corps, and served as lieutenant and then captain to the end of February 1799. He later distinguished himself in the Napoleonic wars, in battles at Monte Croce (1800) and Caldiero (1805). After a period of unemployment he was again placed on the active list of the Austrian army in 1813, shortly before Austria declared war against France, and defeated the French in a series of engagements in Italy. He commanded the Austrian troops in Naples in 1816, in which year he was made a prince of the Holy Roman Empire. This was a papal title, granted by Pope Pius VII. In 1826 he was created a magnate of Hungary with a hereditary seat in the upper house of the Hungarian Diet. He saw further service in 1848 during the revolt in Lombardy, and became a field-marshal in November 1849. His last service was at the age of eighty-two when he was present as a volunteer at the battle of Solferino on 24 June 1859. Died at Bosiljero, near Karlstadt (Karlovac) on 21 August 1862.

NUGENT, ROBERT, EARL NUGENT (1702-1788), politician and poet. Born at Carlanstown, Co. Westmeath. Inherited an estate of £1,500 a year. This he augmented by his skill in marrying rich widows, which caused Horace Walpole to invent the description 'to Nugentize'. His first wife, a daughter of the Earl of Fingal, died within a year in childbirth, and in 1736 he married Anne Knight, already twice a widow, and became owner of the parish of Gosfield in Essex, of a seat in Parliament for St Mawes in Cornwall, and £100,000 besides. From 1754 to 1774 he represented Bristol in Parliament, leaving St Mawes to a relative, but in 1774 he failed to secure re-election and returned to St Mawes, sitting for it until he retired in 1784. He became friendly with the Prince of Wales and lent him large sums, which were repaid by King George III in the form of 'places and peerages'. In 1766 he became Viscount Clare and Baron Nugent, and Earl Nugent in 1776. His second wife died in 1756, aged fifty-nine, and he then married Elizabeth, widow of the fourth Earl of Berkeley, with whom he secured a large fortune. A number of his poems appeared in Dodsley's *Collection*. He became friendly with GOLDSMITH, who acknowledged a present of venison from Gosfield Park in the poem *The Haunch of Venison: a Poetical Epistle to Lord Clare*. He had been brought up a Catholic, turned Protestant and then Catholic again. A contemporary, Glover, described him as 'a jovial and voluptuous Irishman who had left Popery for the Protestant religion, money and widows.' He died at the house of General O'Donnell in Rutland (Parnell) Square, Dublin, on 13 October 1788.

O

Ó BRIAIN, LIAM (1888–1974), patriot and scholar. Born in Dublin; educated at O'Connell CBS and RUI. Won the first NUI travelling studentship 1911; studied Early Irish in Germany and also studied in Paris. Lecturer in French, UCD, 1914. Joined the Irish Volunteers, fought in St Stephen's Green in the 1916 Rising, and was interned in Frongoch in Wales until the general release of prisoners in December of that year. Professor of Romance languages, UCG, 1917. He continued his activities in the movement for independence, and stood as Sinn Féin candidate for South Armagh in the general election of 1918. Although a total stranger to his constituents, he polled 6,000 votes to 8,000 for his Unionist opponent. In 1920 he became a judge in the Republican courts. These courts were illegal under British rule, and he was imprisoned for a year. He took the Treaty side in 1922, and after standing unsuccessfully in 1925 for election to Seanad Éireann retired from active participation in politics. He translated many books and plays from French, Spanish and English into Irish, and was a frequent broadcaster on radio and television. *Cuimhní Cinn* (1951) gives a vivid and candid account of the 1916 Rising. He took a leading part in the founding of Taibhdhearc na Gaillimhe, the Galway Irish-language theatre, in 1928 and often acted there. Chairman, An Club Leabhar, for eighteen years, and member of executive committee, Gaelic League, for ten years. His services in the cause of good relations between Ireland and France were recognised in 1951, when the French government made him a *chevalier* of the Legion of Honour. His conversational powers and wide range of interests earned him the description of 'a one-man open university'. He retired from his chair in 1959 and came to live in Dublin, where he died on 11 August 1974.

O'BRIEN, DERMOD (1865–1945), painter, grandson of WILLIAM SMITH O'BRIEN. Born at Mount Trenchard, Foynes, Co. Limerick. Educated at Harrow and Trinity College, Cambridge. Studied painting at the Academy of Antwerp with WALTER OSBORNE as fellow-pupil, then at the Académie Julien in Paris and the Slade School, London. He returned to Ireland in 1901 and exhibited at the RHA from 1904. Elected RHA 1907; president, RHA, from 1910 to his death. President, United Arts Club, and took leading part in cultural life of Dublin. Became recognised as the 'official' portrait painter of Ireland. Besides judges and generals he painted writers, including GEORGE BIRMINGHAM and CONAL O'RIORDAN. In his last twenty years he spent the winter in the south of France, painting landscapes. He sold the family home, Cahirmoyle, Co. Limerick, in 1920, and thereafter settled permanently in Dublin. He greatly encouraged young artists by visiting first exhibitions and buying their works. Died in his house, Fitzwilliam Square, 3 October 1945.

O'BRIEN, EDWARD CONOR MARSHAL (1880–1952), yachtsman and author. Born in Co. Limerick in November 1880, a grandson of WILLIAM SMITH O'BRIEN. Educated at Winchester, TCD, and Oxford. He was an architect by profession and became a member of the Royal Society of Antiquaries of Ireland. He was an original member of Sinn Féin and an Irish-speaker. He delighted in sports that had an element of danger in them, and was an expert yachtsman and mountaineer, often climbing in his bare feet. In 1914 in his yacht *Kelpie* he landed a cargo of German arms for the Irish Volunteers at Kilcoole, Co. Wicklow, assisted by Sir Thomas Myles, his sister Kate, and two men from Foynes. Afterwards he joined the Royal Navy and served as an officer during the First World War. Some time after the war he returned to Ireland and had the ketch *Saoirse* built to his own design at Baltimore, Co. Cork. On 20 June 1923 at 4.30 p.m. he sailed from Dún Laoghaire bound for New Zealand to join a mountaineering party. He arrived too late and sailed on, circumnavigating the globe and returning by way of Cape Horn. He sailed into Dún Laoghaire harbour precisely at 4.30 p.m. on 20 June 1925, the first Irishman to sail round the world in his own yacht. The Royal Cruising Club awarded him their challenge cup three times in succession for three successive stages of his voyage. In 1927 another small yacht, the *Ilen*, was built to his design and he sailed it to the Falkland Islands. He was an inspector of fisheries for a time under the Second Dáil and made an unsuccessful bid for the Senate in 1925. *Saoirse* was his only home until he sold it in 1940. In 1928 he married an artist, Kathleen Frances Clausen, and went to Ibiza in the Balearic Islands, which was his base in the Mediterranean until 1931. His wife died that year and he moved to Cornwall. In 1926 he had published his first book, *Across Three Oceans*, a description of his voyage in *Saoirse*, followed by *From Three Yachts* (1928). He wrote a further dozen books, mostly on sailing, but including several for boys: *Two Boys Go Sailing* (1936), *The Runaways* (1941), *The Castaways* (1946), and *The Luck of the Golden Salmon* (1951). Early in the Second World War he volunteered to serve in the Small Vessels' Pool, a voluntary civilian service of small-boat owners. He sailed several small boats across the Atlantic from America to British ports at a time when they were badly needed by the Allies. Died on 18 April 1952 at his sister's house at Foynes, Co. Limerick. *Saoirse* is still in commission, sailing from Royal Cornwall Yacht Club in Falmouth.

O'BRIEN, EILEEN (1925–1986), journalist. Born in Galway, only child of Helen and PROFESSOR LIAM Ó BRIAIN, and educated at UCG. She worked as a reporter on provincial newspapers in Ireland and England and with the Irish News Agency in the 1950s, was Belfast editor for the *Irish Press*, and PRO for Gael-Linn for a short period. In 1965 she joined the *Irish Times*, where she wrote a weekly 'Irishwoman's Diary' and 'A Social Sort of Column', and became Irish-language editor. Her republican sympathies were strong but did not impair her professional integrity in reporting on troubled times in Belfast and giving a voice to any who thought no-one wanted to listen. She died, unmarried, in a Dublin hospital on 1 January 1986.

O'BRIEN, FLANN. See under O'NOLAN, BRIAN.

O'BRIEN, GEORGE (1892–1973), economist. Born in Dublin; educated at UCD and the King's Inns. Called to the bar in 1913 and practised for some years before becoming professor of national economics, UCD, in 1926. Professor of political economy 1930, and held the joint chairs until his retirement in 1961. Published an *Economic History of Ireland* (three volumes, 1918–21), which broke new ground and has not yet been superseded. Served for some years as Government nominee on the board of the Abbey Theatre, and represented NUI in Seanad Éireann 1948–1965. Served on many important Government commissions on economic affairs, and on the committees of the Statistical Society, RDS, and RIA. In addition to many contributions to learned journals, his published work included *An Essay on the Economic Effects of the Reformation* (1923), *Agricultural Economics* (1929), and *The Four Green Fields* (1936), a penetrating study of the problem of partition. His exceptionally full career included directorships of Guinness and other commercial concerns, and he was a member of every leading club in Dublin. The brilliance of his lecturing drew undergraduates from other courses, and many of his former students remained his friends for life. He died, unmarried, in a Dublin hospital on 31 December 1973.

O'BRIEN, JAMES (BRONTERRE) (1805–1864), Chartist. Born Co. Longford; educated at Edgeworthstown school, TCD, and Gray's Inn, London. Joined the Chartist movement, and wrote revolutionary articles for the periodical press, using the pen-name Bronterre. In April 1840 he was sentenced to eighteen months' imprisonment for seditious speeches. On his release in September 1841 he quarrelled bitterly with FEARGUS O'CONNOR, another Irish Chartist leader, and opposed his land scheme. The movement began to decline after 1848, and he then made a precarious living by lecturing at the John Street Institute and the Eclectic Institute in Soho, London. Died in London in great poverty on 23 December 1864.

O'BRIEN, KATE (1897–1974), novelist and dramatist. Born in Limerick. Educated at Laurel Hill Convent, Limerick, and UCD. Worked in London as a journalist and then as a teacher. After a period in Washington as secretary to James O'Mara, who was organising a Dáil Éireann loan for DE VALERA, she went to Spain as a governess. In 1924 she returned to London and married a young Dutchman, Gustav Renier, author of *Are the English Really Human?* The marriage was not a success. Her writing career began in 1926 with a play, *Distinguished Villas*, which ran in London for three months. Her first novel, *Without My Cloak*, set in Limerick among the prosperous merchant class, appeared in 1931, and received the James Tait Black Memorial Prize and the Hawthornden Prize. It was followed by *The Ante-Room* (1934) and *Mary Lavelle* (1936). In 1937 she published a travel book, *Farewell*

Spain. Her novel *The Land of Spices* (1941) was banned by the Censorship Board. During the Second World War she worked in the Ministry of Information in London. *The Last of Summer* appeared in 1943, and a historical novel set in Spain, *That Lady*, was published in 1946. She was refused entry to Spain for some years because of her treatment of Philip II in that novel. It was dramatised in 1949 and played on Broadway with Katherine Cornell in the lead. In 1946 she won the Irish Women Writers' Club prize for her novel *For One Sweet Grape*, and in 1947 she was elected a member of the Irish Academy of Letters. In 1950 she bought a house at Roundstone, Co. Galway, and lived there until 1961. She continued to write novels, publishing *The Flower of May* in 1953 and *As Music and Splendour*, her last, in 1958. *English Diaries and Journals* appeared in 1943, and *My Ireland* in 1962. She returned to England in 1961 and lived in the little village of Boughton, not far from Canterbury. She visited Ireland and Spain regularly, having been allowed into Spain again in 1957 through the intervention of the Irish ambassador in Madrid. Died in hospital in Canterbury on 13 August 1974.

O'BRIEN, MICHAEL. See under MANCHESTER MARTYRS.

O'BRIEN, MURROUGH, first EARL OF INCHIQUIN (1614–1674), 'Murchadh na dTóiteán' ('Murchadh of the Burnings'). Married daughter of Sir William St Leger, lord president of Munster. Studied the art of war in the Spanish service in Italy. Returned 1639 and made vice-president of Munster 1640. Fought against the Irish rebels in 1641. Became governor of Munster after death of St Leger, July 1642. Approved of cessation of hostilities with the Confederates arranged by ORMOND at the king's command, 15 September 1643. Went to Oxford in February 1644 to obtain king's commission as president of Munster, but this had already been promised to the Earl of Portland, and he was put off with fair words and a warrant for an earldom, and came away discontented. Later that year he expelled nearly all the Catholics from Cork, Youghal, and Kinsale. The English parliament made him president of Munster. He attacked the Rock of Cashel, piled turf against the wooden enclosure and set fire to it, then massacred the garrison, including priests. At Knockanoss near Kanturk he defeated Lord Taaffe's Catholic army in November 1647 and became master of the south. Subsequently he made a truce with the Confederates, and allied himself with Ormond. After the arrival of Cromwell in 1649 with a large and efficient army, the Munster garrisons fell away from Inchiquin as the Protector took town after town. Inchiquin left for Brittany in 1650 and joined the court of Charles II. In May 1654 he received the earldom he had spurned ten years before and he became a Roman Catholic. He was made Governor of Catalonia, still subject to France, and then high steward to Henrietta Maria, the queen mother. Commanded an unsuccessful expeditionary force sent to help the Portuguese by Charles in 1662. He returned to England in 1663. His military career was now over and the presidency of Munster denied to him on account of his religion and given to the Earl of Orrery, who made him vice-president in 1664. He was restored to all his honours and given an estate of 10,000 acres in Munster with £8,000 compensation for his losses and suffering. Lived quietly for the rest of his days at Rostellan, Cork harbour, where he died 9 September 1674.

O'BRIEN, PETER (1842–1914), lord chief justice. Born Carnelly House, Co. Clare, 29 June 1842. Educated Clongowes Wood College and TCD; called to the bar 1865. Attorney-general 1888. Largely responsible for administering A. J. Balfour's Crimes Act, 1887, a coercive measure designed to repress attempts at winning Irish freedom. Became known as 'Peter the Packer' as he was accused of packing juries. Made

lord chief justice 1889, baronet 1891, raised to peerage 1900. Died Stillorgan, Co. Dublin, 7 September 1914.

O'BRIEN, RICHARD BARRY (1847–1918), lawyer and author. Born Kilrush, Co. Clare, 7 March 1847. Educated Catholic University, Dublin. Called to the bar 1874, English bar 1875. Gave up his practice and took to literature and politics. Editor of *The Speaker* and contributor to leading reviews. One of the founders of Irish Literary Society, London, and president 1906–1911. LL.D. from NUI. Published many historical and biographical works, including lives of Thomas Drummond, PARNELL, RUSSELL OF KILLOWEN, and John Bright. Died at his home at Kensington, London, 17 March 1918.

O'BRIEN, TOMMY (1905–1988), journalist and broadcaster. Born in Clonmel, Co. Tipperary, and joined the staff of the *Clonmel Nationalist*. As a junior reporter he carried dispatches for the IRA and was a close friend of DAN BREEN. A visit by a travelling company awakened in him a love of opera, and music became his lifelong passion. He spent his annual holidays visiting Covent Garden, London, and later La Scala, Milan, and collected a library of thousands of records. For forty years until shortly before his death he broadcast a weekly radio programme under the title 'Your Choice and Mine', which became immensely popular. His relaxed style and infectious enthusiasm created a country-wide awareness and appreciation of classical music. He was editor of the *Clonmel Nationalist* for some years, and was twice amateur billiards champion of Ireland. He died in a Clonmel nursing-home on 24 February 1988.

O'BRIEN, WILLIAM (1852–1928), nationalist and author. Born at Mallow, Co. Cork, on 2 October 1852. Though of Catholic parents, educated at the Protestant Cloyne Diocesan College and Queen's College, Cork. He took up journalism, became editor of the Land League journal, *United Ireland*, in 1881, and conducted it with such militancy that it was suppressed and O'Brien was arrested. Released in 1883, he was elected MP for Mallow and renewed his campaign in *United Ireland*. With JOHN DILLON he started the 'plan of campaign' in 1886, to force landlords to reduce exorbitant rents, and was imprisoned for six months. He took the anti-PARNELL side in 1891, founded the United Irish League in 1898, and played a leading part in the reunification of the party in 1900. With the passing of the Wyndham Land Act of 1903, which began the end of landlordism, O'Brien became convinced that the future for Ireland lay in agreement between unionists and nationalists. In 1910 he led a party of seven Cork MPs who combined in the 'All for Ireland' League under the motto 'Conference, Conciliation, Consent'. By 1918 Sinn Féin was sweeping the country and O'Brien and his followers did not contest the general election of that year. He wrote two novels: *When We Were Boys* (1890), a story of the Fenians, and *A Queen of Men* (1898) with GRACE O'MALLEY as the heroine. His *Recollections* (1906), *The Irish Revolution* (1928) and other volumes of reminiscences are useful source books. Died in London on 25 February 1928. Buried in Mallow.

O'BRIEN, WILLIAM (1881–1968), trade union pioneer. Born near Clonakilty, Co. Cork. Came to Dublin at fifteen. Joined Irish Socialist Republican Party in 1898 and became close friend and colleague of JAMES CONNOLLY. Actively associated with JAMES LARKIN in organising Irish workers. Helped to establish Irish Transport and General Workers' Union, 1909. Secretary of lockout committee in Dublin labour upheaval 1913. Organised committee that arranged return of Connolly from the USA in 1910. Deported and interned in Frongoch and Reading jails after 1916 Rising. Took prominent part in fight against conscription of 1918. Deported to Wormwood Scrubs in 1920. Released after hunger strike. TD for Dublin South City 1922–1923; for Tipperary, June–August 1927 and 1937–1938. Full-time trade union official with ITGWU from 1909 and general secretary for twenty-two years until his retirement. President, Trade Union Congress, 1913, 1918, 1925, and 1941. Died 30 October 1968 in convalescent home in Bray, Co. Wicklow.

O'BRIEN, WILLIAM SMITH (1803–1864), nationalist. Born at Dromoland, Co. Clare, 17 October 1803, son of Sir Lucius O'Brien. Educated at Harrow and Cambridge University. Conservative MP for Ennis 1825 and for Co. Limerick in 1835, but his views changed with experience of Parliament, and by 1844 he was a convinced Repealer. He became a leading member of the Young Irelanders, and with the help of GAVAN DUFFY and others who had seceded from O'CONNELL founded the Irish Confederation in 1847. At a great meeting of the Confederation in Dublin on 15 March 1848 he urged the formation of a National Guard, with the example of Paris in mind. After the arrest of most of their leaders later that year and the suspension of habeas corpus, the Confederates still at liberty decided on an armed rising. They had made no real preparations, and the Famine had left the countryside spiritless. In the closing days of July a small party under O'Brien clashed with forty-six policemen in the widow McCormack's cabbage-garden at Ballingarry, Co. Tipperary. This skirmish brought the rising of 1848 to an inglorious end. O'Brien was arrested shortly after, tried, and sentenced to death. The sentence was commuted to penal servitude for life and he served five years in Tasmania. He was released in 1854 on condition that he stayed outside the United Kingdom. His pardon was made unconditional in 1856. He returned to Ireland but took little part in politics. Died at Bangor in Wales on 16 June 1864.

Ó BRUADAIR, DÁIBHÍ (*c.* 1625–1698), poet. Born probably in East Cork, in comfortable circumstances. Received good education in Irish, Latin, and English, and was trained in poetry and genealogy, probably in a bardic school. He lived for long periods from about 1660 in Co. Limerick. In early life he spent lavishly, caring little for the future, which seemed assured. He wrote elegies, religious poems, and many verses about the political and historical events he witnessed. These are almost the only contemporary documents in Irish that exist to show the sentiments of the people. His 'Summary of Ireland's Purgatory' reviews the events of the years 1641-1684. About 1674 his poverty obliged him to work as a farm labourer and he lamented the crushing of the great Gaelic families, which had esteemed poetry and learning. A well-known poem begins: 'Woe to those who are not gloomy boors.' Sustained by the charity of a few friends, he found consolation in his last years in historical research and in transcribing records and genealogies. He died in January 1698 at a place unknown. Accounted a master of Irish style, one of the last who had been trained in the as yet unbroken traditions of the classical poetic schools.

Ó BUACHALLA, LIAM (1899-1970), professor of economics. Born in Dublin. Educated at Drogheda CBS. Joined the Irish Volunteers and served in the War of Independence. Worked as a cooper in Guinness's brewery, obtained a degree in economics by evening study, and secured a post as lecturer in UCG, later becoming professor of economics there. Lectured in Irish, published a number of textbooks in the language, and was president of the Gaelic League for a term. First nominated to the Seanad by DE VALERA in 1939, and cathaoirleach (chairman) from 1951 until he retired in 1969. Died at Drogheda, 16 October 1970, survived by his wife, MÁIRE NÍ SCOLAÍ.

O'BYRNE, DERMOT. See under BAX, SIR ARNOLD.

O'BYRNE, FIACH MacHUGH (*c.* 1544-1597), chief of the O'Byrnes of Wicklow. From his stronghold at Ballinacor at the head of the remote valley of Glenmalure he made frequent raids on the Pale. In February 1573 he was pardoned, and remained aloof for some years. But in 1580 the seneschal of Wexford, Captain Masterson, killed his kinsmen, the Kavanaghs, and he invaded Wexford and laid it waste. In August of that year the new lord justice, Lord Grey de Wilton, led a force into Glenmalure in an attempt to capture him, but was defeated with great loss. Fiach MacHugh continued to evade capture and was again pardoned in 1581. For several years following he caused little anxiety to the government in Dublin, but he was regarded with suspicion, and his very presence so near to the capital and the Pale was looked upon as a standing menace to the public peace. In March 1594 his sons attacked and burned the house of the sheriff of Kildare. Although Fiach asserted that he had no part in that exploit, the new deputy, Sir William Russell, seized on it to justify the capture and garrisoning of Ballinacor. Fiach was proclaimed a traitor, and a reward of £150 was offered for his capture and £100 for his head. He allied himself with HUGH O'NEILL, Earl of Tyrone, and recaptured Ballinacor in September 1596. Russell continued to pursue him, and on Sunday 8 May 1597 succeeded in capturing him. He was instantly beheaded, by a Sergeant Milborne.

Ó CADHAIN, MÁIRTÍN (1906-1970), writer. Born near Spiddal, in the Cois Fharraige Gaeltacht of Co. Galway. He was educated locally and became a teacher. In the 1930s he joined the IRA and in consequence was dismissed from his post. He made a living for some years as a freelance teacher, with intervals as a building labourer and turf-worker, while continuing to work for the IRA. In 1939 he was arrested and interned for five years at the Curragh Camp, Co. Kildare. He was a teacher of genius, and many fellow-internees who attended his Irish classes in the camp formed a lifelong attachment to the language. After his release he worked in various employments until 1949, when he joined the translation staff of Dáil Éireann. In 1956 he was appointed a lecturer in Modern Irish in TCD, and in 1969 was appointed to the chair of Irish. He was made a fellow of the college the following year. His first collection of short stories, *Idir Shúgradh agus Dáiríre*, appeared in 1939 and was followed by further short stories and his major work, *Cré na Cille* (1949), a novel portraying the intrigues and petty jealousies of a rural community, as told in conversations and monologues by the dead in the local cemetery. In his early days as a teacher he collected folklore in his native district, and compiled a major vocabulary of its dialect. In addition to Irish, Gaelic, Welsh, and Breton, he spoke and read German, Russian, Italian, and French. His reading was omnivorous and wide-ranging. He sought to make Irish a flexible instrument of modern thought and feeling. In his short stories he treated of life in the Connemara Gaeltacht with realism and authenticity. *Cré na Cille* was chosen by UNESCO for translation into several major European languages in a series devoted to masterpieces in the world's lesser-known languages. He was the first to be awarded the £2,000 prize of the Irish-American Cultural Institute of St Paul, Minnesota; the prize was given for *An tSraith ar Lár* (1967), a collection of short stories. He was elected to the Irish Academy of Letters, the first writer to be so honoured for writing in Irish only. He died in Dublin, 18 October 1970, leaving unpublished manuscripts of a novel, many short stories, and a critical work on modern Irish literature, as well as reviews and essays, together probably equal in extent to his published work.

O'CALLAGHAN, JOHN COR-NELIUS (1805–1883), author. Born in Dublin; educated Clongowes Wood College. Called to the bar 1829 but did not practise. Contributed to a weekly newspaper, *The Comet*, and to the *Irish Monthly Magazine*. These and other articles were published as *The Green Book* (1840). Joined staff of the *Nation* 1842. Edited O'Kelly's *Macariae Excidium* (1846), a secret history of the revolution in Ireland 1688–1691. His greatest work was *History of the Irish Brigades in the Service of France* (1870), to which he devoted twenty-five years' research. A strong supporter of O'CONNELL; with the sculptor JOHN HOGAN crowned O'Connell at a monster meeting on Hill of Tara. Died Dublin, 24 April 1883.

Ó CAOIMH, PÁDRAIG (1897–1964), general secretary of the GAA. Born in Roscommon. Educated at CBS in Cork. Became a teacher in Cork, joined the Irish Volunteers in 1916 and held the rank of captain on active service with the First Cork Brigade. Arrested in December 1920 and sentenced to fifteen years' penal servitude. Imprisoned in England until 1922. Opposed the Anglo-Irish Treaty of 1921 and fought on the Republican side in the Civil War. After some years' teaching he became general secretary of the GAA in 1929 and held the post until his death in Dublin on 15 May 1964. During his long term of office the association grew to be the largest and most powerful sporting organisation in the country.

O'CASEY, SEÁN (1880–1964), playwright. Born at 85 Upper Dorset Street, Dublin, on 30 March 1880 and worked there as a manual labourer until 1926. He was largely self-educated and read omnivorously, despite an eye complaint that troubled him all his life. He joined the Gaelic League, learned Irish, and for a time was secretary of the Irish Citizen Army. Left-wing in political sympathy, he was much influenced by JIM LARKIN, the labour leader in the Dublin lock-out of 1913. Encouraged by LADY GREGORY he began to submit plays to the Abbey Theatre, and after some years, success came with the production of *The Shadow of a Gunman* in 1923. With *Juno and the Paycock* (1924) and *The Plough and the*

Stars (1926) O'Casey became established as a playwright of power and originality. He left for London in 1926 to become a full-time writer. His next play, *The Silver Tassie*, was rejected by the Abbey. This was a bitter blow to O'Casey and estranged him from the directors. A London production in 1928 ran for two months. He wrote a further seven full-length plays, but none of them had the success or the critical acclaim of his first three, which seemed to have been written at white heat from his own experience of working-class Dublin in poverty, revolution, and civil war. Nor did they create characters like Joxer Daly and Fluther Good, who have passed into the mythology of the Irish stage. In 1927 O'Casey married Eileen Carey, an actress who had started her career with the D'Oyly Carte opera company. In 1939 he published *I Knock at the Door*, the first volume of a six-volume autobiography, ending with *Sunset and Evening Star* in 1954. Like all his writings, they show the man who wanted 'to make gold embroidery out of dancin' words.' He died at St Marychurch, Torquay, on 18 September 1964.

Ó CEALLAIGH, SEÁN T. (1882–1966), second President of Ireland. Born in Dublin on 25 August 1882. Educated at O'Connell CBS. In 1898 he joined the Gaelic League and then became active in the Celtic Literary Society with WILLIE ROONEY, ARTHUR GRIFFITH, and MAUD GONNE, and recruited for the IRB, which he had also joined. He was a founder-member of Sinn Féin in 1905, and the following year was elected to Dublin City Council, remaining a member for twenty-six years, during which time he campaigned vigorously for social reform. He became manager of *An Claidheamh Soluis*, the organ of the Gaelic League, and in 1915 was elected general secretary of the league. In Easter week 1916 he was staff captain to PATRICK PEARSE in the GPO. Although he avoided court-martial he was arrested, and interned in England. In the general election of 1918 he was returned as Sinn Féin MP for the College Green division of Dublin and represented Dublin until 1945. The First Dáil met in January 1919, and he was elected Ceann Comhairle (chairman) after the opening session. In an endeavour to secure international recognition, Dáil Éireann accredited him as envoy of the Republican government to the Peace Conference at Paris, and to Rome and the USA. His mission was not formally successful, but nevertheless he attracted international attention to the Irish struggle for independence. He opposed the Treaty of 1921 and was one of the founders of Fianna Fáil in 1926. When the party came into power in 1932 he became vice-president of the Executive Council (government) and Minister for Local Government and Public Health. In 1941 he became Minister for Finance, and held that post until his election as President of Ireland in 1945. In 1952 he was re-elected without opposition for a second term. He made state visits to Italy and France, and on St Patrick's Day 1959 addressed a joint session of the United States Congress in Washington. Pope Pius XI honoured him in 1934 with the Grand Cross of St Gregory the Great, and as president he received honours from France and Spain, and an honorary degree from NUI. Died in Dublin on 23 November 1966.

O'CLERY, MICHAEL (1575–1643), chronicler. Was born at Kilbarron, Co. Donegal, the son of a chief. He was baptised Tadhg but took the name Michael when he entered the Franciscan order at Louvain. He had already become known as an antiquary, and in 1620 the guardian at Louvain, Aodh Mac an Bhaird, sent him back to Ireland to collect manuscript material for the lives of the Irish saints. Assisted by other scholars, he collected everything he could find of historical interest, not confining himself to hagiography. His labours resulted in the compilation of *Réim Ríoghraidhe* (1630), a list of kings and their pedigrees, with lives and

273

genealogies of the saints, followed by *Leabhar Gabhála*, an account of the successive invasions of Ireland, and the famous *Annála Ríoghachta Éireann*, a chronicle of Irish history from the earliest days to 1616. A plain record of dates, kings, tribal raids and petty wars, burnings of monasteries and their rebuilding, it takes on a narrative form in the later stages nearer to the writer's own time, and is interspersed with occasional contemporary quotations. This invaluable source-book was written between 1632 and 1636 in a cottage on the banks of the River Drowse, which flows from Lough Melvin to Donegal Bay. JOHN COLGAN first called it the *Annals of the Four Masters*, in tribute to O'Clery and his three principal assistants, Cúchoigríche O'Duigeanáin, Fearfeasa O'Maolconaire and Cúchoigríche O'Clery. It was dedicated to their patron, Fergal O'Gara, Prince of Coolavin. O'Clery also compiled a *Martyrologium* of Irish saints and a glossary of Irish words, which was printed at Louvain in 1643. He died there at the end of that year, poor and modest, as he had lived all his life.

Ó COILEÁIN, SEÁN (1754–1817), poet. Born at Kilmeen, near Clonakilty, Co. Cork, and sent to Spain to prepare for the priesthood, but returned without completing his studies. He opened a school at Myross, in a remote part of Co. Cork, near Skibbereen. It is said that his wife left him, and that her sister, who remained in the house, burned it down with his manuscripts. Tradition says that he wrote his well-known 'Soliloquy' or 'Lament for Timoleague' when a priest read him 'Gray's Elegy' and asked him to write such a poem in Irish. PROFESSOR DAVID GREENE said that it is merely a translation, in a deliberately archaic style, of an English poem written by his friend Father Matthew Horgan. He died in Skibbereen, and was buried in Kilmeen, near Timoleague.

Ó CONAIRE, PÁDRAIC (1882–1928), writer. Born at 5 High Street, Galway, on 20 February 1882. His parents died when he was young, and he was brought up in Connemara by his grandparents. He was educated at Turlough Beg national school near Rosmuc in the Connemara Gaeltacht, and at Rockwell and Blackrock Colleges. He joined the civil service in London, taught Irish there in the Gaelic League, and began to write. By 1914 he had won several prizes at the Oireachtas and had published a play, a novel, and a number of short stories. He left the civil service that year and began a wandering life in Ireland, with occasional forays on foot across Europe. He continued to write in Irish only, although English offered a wider and much more lucrative market, and published another novel, collections of essays, and further short stories. *M'Asal Beag Dubh* (undated), essays on the delights of open-air life, was inevitably compared to Stevenson's *Travels with a Donkey*, and was reprinted several times. He spent his last few years teaching Irish in Galway. When he died in the Richmond Hospital, Dublin, on 6 October 1928, his sole possessions were his pipe and tobacco and an apple. He published more than a dozen books, the best-known being *Seacht mBua an Éirí Amach* (1918), *An Crann Géagach* (1919), *Síol Éabha* (1922), *Beagnach Fíor* (1927), and *Fearfeasa Mac Feasa* (1930).

O'CONNELL, COUNT DANIEL (1745–1833), soldier, uncle of the 'Liberator'. Born Derrynane, Co. Kerry, 21 May 1745. Joined French army as cadet 1761. Became adjutant in Clare's Regiment of the Irish Brigade about 1763, and later, officer of an engineer corps. Wounded at siege of Gibraltar and made colonel of the regiment. Appointed inspector-general of infantry and requested to edit *L'Ordonnance pour l'Infanterie*. This earned him the Cross of St Louis. Made a count in 1788. He remained in Paris for two years after the outbreak of the Revolution in 1789. Declined to accept command of a revolutionary army, and joined French émigrés at Koblenz. Fought as a private in Berchini's Hussars against the troops of the revolution. After the failure of that campaign in 1792 he went to London and submitted a scheme to re-organise the Irish Brigade in the service of King George III. Pitt accepted the scheme, and O'Connell was made colonel of the Fourth Regiment. Due to government mismanagement the brigade ceased to exist two years later. He retained his full pay to the end of his life as 'last colonel' of the brigade. He returned to France when the Treaty of Amiens was signed in 1802, but when hostilities broke out again he was detained by Napoleon for a short period as a British subject. Promoted lieutenant-general on the restoration of the Bourbons. After the revolution of 1830 he refused to take the oath of allegiance to Louis-Phillipe, was struck off the military list, and retired to private life. Died at his château of Madon, near Blois, 9 July 1833.

O'CONNELL, DANIEL (1775–1847), the 'Liberator'. Born near Cahirciveen, Co. Kerry, on 6 August 1775. He was adopted at an early age by his wealthy childless uncle, Maurice 'Hunting Cap' O'Connell, the head of the old Catholic family of the O'Connells, and brought up by him at Derrynane. He spoke Irish and absorbed the traditional culture of song and story still strong in Kerry at the time, acquiring a knowledge of the rural mind that served him in later years at the bar. In 1791 he was sent to school at St Omer and Douai, and his glimpses of the French revolutionary army in action left him with a life-long abhorrence of violence for political ends. In 1794 he entered Lincoln's Inn, but did not confine his studies to law-books. His reading of Voltaire, Rousseau, Godwin, Smith and Bentham moulded his political and economic thinking and influenced him towards Catholic liberalism and economic *laissez-faire*. He was called to the bar in 1798 and went on the Munster circuit, soon building up an enormous practice. The 1798 Rising and the terrible butchery that followed it confirmed him in his horror of violence. O'Connell married his cousin, Mary O'Connell, in 1802; their marriage was happy and they had five sons and three daughters. In 1815 he ridiculed the 'beggarly corporation of Dublin' and was challenged to a duel by a member, one D'Esterre. In the exchange of shots D'Esterre was fatally wounded, and O'Connell, stricken by remorse, vowed never to fight again, and settled a pension on the widow. He was later to say that 'not for all the universe contains' would he 'consent to the effusion of a single drop of human blood, except my own.'

Hopes of Catholic emancipation had been raised by the pledges given during the passage of the Act of Union, and O'Connell was soon drawn into political action. Before long he became the leader of the radical group in the Catholic Committee, who were opposed to the 'securities' proposed by a British government anxious to water down any concessions. The 'securities' included a veto on the appointment of Catholic bishops. Dissensions in the committee, and divergence between GRATTAN, who favoured compromise, and O'Connell, weakened the movement, and by 1823 O'Connell saw that a new departure was needed. He founded the Catholic Association, with the object of using all constitutional means to secure emancipation, and turned it into a mass crusade with the support of the Catholic clergy. Association membership at a penny a month brought in a large fighting-fund, and this 'Catholic rent' showed that a closely knit countrywide organisation supported the association. A turning-point came with the Clare election in 1828, when O'Connell, with the support of the forty-shilling freeholders, had an overwhelming victory against the government candidate. The whole country was aflame. Wellington and Peel feared a rising, and conceded Catholic emancipation in April 1829, but in the process the franchise was raised to £10, thus excluding the forty-shilling freeholders.

O'Connell was now the undisputed leader in Ireland, and he gave up his practice at the bar to devote his time wholly to politics. A special collection, 'the O'Connell Tribute', was made annually to compensate him for his heavy financial sacrifice; he had been earning £7,000 a year in fees. He now addressed himself to the task of winning repeal of the Act of Union and securing a representative Irish parliament for the Irish people. He was not a separatist in the republican sense, and indeed had a strong personal loyalty to the monarchy. Emancipation had been wrung from the British government by a massive display of the will of the people, and he thought that Repeal could also be won without firing a shot. But British political leaders feared Repeal as they did not fear emancipation. Behind Repeal they saw the spectre of an independent Irish nation, anathema to their imperial outlook, and they closed ranks. O'Connell, however, pressed on as before with agitation on constitutional lines. In 1832 he had thirty-nine Irish MPs pledged to his support. But the country was becoming more and more unsettled, there was violent agitation against the payment of tithes, crime was rampant; and the British government brought in a strong Coercion Act, which effectively hamstrung his tactics. A change came in 1835 with the arrival of Drummond as under-secretary at Dublin Castle; his liberal administration calmed the country for a time. The Irish MPs held the balance of power in the House of Commons and supported the Whigs. The Whig ministry, however, fell from power in 1841, and the scene changed. The Repeal movement began to gather momentum while the Young Ireland writers of the *Nation* rekindled the separatist spirit. In 1841 O'Connell was elected Lord Mayor of Dublin, and in 1843 the subscriptions to his Repeal Association, the Repeal 'rent', came to £48,400. He now began to organise monster meetings throughout the country. Three-quarters of a million people, it was estimated, assembled on the hill of Tara to hear the 'Liberator'. The government became alarmed at the fast-growing strength of the movement, and decided to act. O'Connell had arranged a meeting for 8 October 1843 at Clontarf, Dublin, to be the biggest yet held, and vast crowds were already on the way on 7 October when Peel banned it. O'Connell, unwilling to risk bloodshed, called off the meeting. He was arrested, charged with conspiracy, and sentenced to a year's imprisonment and a fine of £2,000. The House of Lords set aside the verdict after O'Connell had been three months in prison. On his release he continued his Repeal activities, although it was clear that a turning-point had been reached. The tactics that had won emancipation had failed, and O'Connell, now almost seventy, his health failing, had no clear plan for future action. Dissension broke out in the Repeal Association; the Young Irelanders withdrew. There were partial failures in the potato crop in the 1840s, a sinister prelude to the Great Famine of 1845–1847, and rural misery had reached new depths. Conscious that he had failed to reach his great goal, O'Connell left Ireland for the last time in January 1847, and made a touching but hardly audible speech in the House of Commons, reminding his hearers of the sufferings of his country. He left for the Continent in February, wishing to die in Rome, but did not survive the journey, dying in Genoa on 15 May 1847. At his wish his heart was sent to Rome; his body rests in a vault in Glasnevin cemetery under a round tower.

Tall and burly, he had inexhaustible energy, overflowing animal spirits, and great powers of work. He habitually rose at four in the morning and worked for three hours before breakfast. His mighty voice could command great crowds, and he turned with ease from passion to buffoonery to pathos. Not a great lawyer, his knowledge of Irish rural character made him unrivalled in cross-examination. Balzac said that he 'incarnated a whole people'. To the Catholic masses he was a leader beyond compare; as Ó Faoláin says, he was 'a hero-personification of themselves'. His coarse humour, his violent vituperation of opponents and his devious methods must be seen against the background of the Ireland of his day, with corruption and place-hunting accepted as commonplace, and the mass of the people misgoverned paupers. MITCHEL wrote of him in 1849: 'Poor old Dan! Wonderful, mighty, jovial and mean old man!... What a royal yet vulgar soul!... Pray ... that the good God who knew how to create so wondrous a creature may have mercy on his soul.' All public men have their detractors, and O'Connell has had his full share. Tradition calls him a great womaniser: the evidence shows that he was happiest in his family circle and that his hours of work left him leisure for little else. But it is true that as a widower of seventy he was seized with a wild passion for a young Protestant girl, to the great embarrassment of his sons and colleagues. His great achievement, Catholic emancipation, is overshadowed by his failure to win Repeal. But he showed the people of Ireland, long used to defeat, that victory could be achieved, and that the power to achieve it was theirs, given the right leadership. It was a lesson that sank deep into the Irish consciousness.

O'CONNELL, JOHN (1810–1858), politician, favourite son of the 'Liberator'. Born Dublin, 24 December 1810. Called to the bar 1837. Elected MP for Youghal 1832 and became member of his father's 'household brigade'. Later represented successively Athlone, Kilkenny, Limerick, and Clonmel. During his father's absences from Ireland he became virtual head of the Repeal Association. Opposed the Young Ireland party and earned their bitter enmity. After the death of his father the association collapsed under his inept leadership. Became a captain of militia after the 1848 Rising. Resigned as MP 1857 on being appointed clerk of the Hanaper Office, Dublin. Published a poor *Life and Speeches* of his father in 1846

and his own *Recollections* (1846). Died at his house in Kingstown (Dún Laoghaire), 24 May 1858.

O'CONNELL, MORGAN (1804–1885), politician. Second son of the 'Liberator'. Born 30 Merrion Square, Dublin, on 31 October 1804. In 1819 he enlisted in the Irish South American Legion to aid Bolivia, and saw further military service in Austria. Returned to Ireland and became MP for Meath 1832–1840. Resigned in 1840 in disagreement with his father's Repeal policy, and was appointed to Registry of Deeds at £1,200 a year, holding the post until 1868. Fought duel with Lord Alvanley on behalf of his father in 1835. Neither was hurt. In same year declined challenge from Disraeli. Died at 12 St Stephen's Green, Dublin, 20 January 1885.

O'CONNELL, PETER (1746–1826), lexicographer. Born at Carne, Co. Clare, and became a schoolmaster. He was befriended by CHARLES O'CONOR of Belnagare and a Dr O'Reardon of Limerick during the years 1785–1819 while he was working on his Irish-English dictionary. After failing to get help from DANIEL O'CONNELL towards publication, he pledged the manuscript in Tralee, and it was eventually sold to the British Museum. He died at Carne.

O'CONNELL, THOMAS J. (1882–1969), teacher and politician. Born near Knock, Co. Mayo. Educated at local national school and St Patrick's Training College, Dublin. He taught for fifteen years until his election as general secretary of the Irish National Teachers' Organisation in 1916. TD for Co. Galway 1922–1927 and for South Mayo 1927–1932. Leader of the Labour Party 1927–1932, and served in the Seanad until 1944. Founder-member of the Educational Building Society, and a director for many years. Died in Dublin, 22 June 1969.

O'CONNELL, TIMOTHY (1882–1970), agriculturist. Born at Aghabulloge, Co. Cork. Educated at Royal College of Science. Joined the Department of Agriculture technical staff, and was Director of Agriculture during the Second World War. He broadcast frequently on the growing of wheat, on which he was recognised internationally as an expert. From 1947 he was Irish delegate to the World Wheat Council in Washington. Although he retired from his post as assistant secretary of the department in 1948, he continued to represent Ireland at many international meetings, including those concerned with the Marshall Plan for the economic revival of Europe after the war. Died in Dublin in July 1970.

O'CONNOR, FEARGUS EDWARD (1794–1855), Chartist leader. Born at Connorville, Co. Cork, 18 July 1794, the son of ROGER O'CONNOR; claimed descent from the ancient kings of Ireland. Educated at Portarlington grammar school and TCD. Called to the bar, but turned to politics and became Repeal MP for Co. Cork in 1832. He began as a follower of O'CONNELL but soon quarrelled bitterly with him about policy, and lost his seat in 1835. Turning to radical agitation in England he drew enthusiastic crowds, particularly in the north, and in 1837 founded a weekly paper, the *Northern Star*, which achieved immediate success. The 'People's Charter' of the Working Men's Association was adopted in 1838, and O'Connor became the best-known Chartist leader. His energy and rough humour made Chartism a mass movement of protest, but its force was blunted by his quarrels with other leaders. Although he took no part in the 'rising' at Newport in 1839 he was imprisoned for a year for seditious libel. On his release he acquired a position of undisputed leadership in Chartism, but he had no clear policy, and rebuffed middle-class radicals. His energies in the 1840s were devoted to his 'National Land Company', an impractical scheme to settle urban workers on smallholdings, which ended in near-

bankruptcy. He was elected MP for Nottingham in 1847 and, after the Paris revolution of 1848, presided at a great Chartist meeting in London that ended inconclusively with the presentation of an ill-prepared petition. This was the beginning of the end for Chartism and for O'Connor. His egocentricity developed into insanity and he was committed to a private asylum in 1852. He died in London, 30 August 1855.

O'CONNOR, FRANK (1903–1966), author. Born Michael O'Donovan in Cork on 17 September 1903. Educated at St Patrick's NS, Cork, where one of his teachers was DANIEL CORKERY, who encouraged his literary talent. While still in his teens he fought in the War of Independence. His first job was as a clerk in the Great Southern Railway office in Cork. He later worked as a librarian in Wicklow, Cork and Dublin for varying periods. His first book of short stories, *Guests of the Nation*, appeared in 1931, followed in 1932 by a novel, *The Saint and Mary Kate*. From 1935 to 1939 he was a director of the Abbey Theatre and worked in close contact with W. B. YEATS. Two plays by him were produced at the Abbey, *In the Train* (1937) and *Moses' Rock* (1938). His biography of MICHAEL COLLINS, *The Big Fellow*, appeared in 1937. He became best-known for his short stories, publishing a number of collections from 1936. In 1939 he went to the USA, where he lectured in a number of universities and became a regular contributor to the *New Yorker*. Returned to Ireland in 1960; lecturer in English in TCD, 1963. Elected to the Irish Academy of Letters 1941. As well as fiction he wrote books of travel and comment on Ireland, literary criticism, an autobiography in two volumes, *An Only Child* and *My Father's Son*, and made many translations from the Irish, including a racy rendering of MERRIMAN's *Midnight Court* (1945). With DAVID GREENE he edited and translated *A Golden Treasury of Irish Poetry: A.D. 600 to 1200*, to bring to the general reader 'the most important branch of medieval poetry . . . from the only period when Ireland was an independent country.' Died in Dublin on 10 March 1966.

O'CONNOR, JAMES ARTHUR (1792-1841), landscape painter. Born in Dublin, the son of an engraver and print-seller. Except for a few lessons from William Sadler he was self-taught as an artist. He began to exhibit at the Dublin Society in 1809. He spent the years 1818 and 1819 in the west of Ireland, painting local views of Westport and Portumna districts for Lords Sligo and Clanricarde. In 1822 he moved to London, and exhibited at the RA and the British Institute from then until 1840. In 1826 he went to the Continent and stayed there until 1833, visiting Paris, Brussels, and other cities. The visit was successful: he sold a number of pictures, and did some of his best work at this period. On his return to London he found little demand for his pictures; his health began to fail, and on 7 January 1841 he died in humble lodgings at 6 Marlborough Street, Brompton.

O'CONNOR, MICHAEL P. (1896-1967), broadcaster and writer of children's stories. Born in Loughrea, Co. Galway. Served in the British forces in the First World War, then went to UCD, and graduated in medicine in 1925. Became director of medical services in Malaya, and was interned in Sarawak by the Japanese from 1941 to 1945. He wrote a number of novels and short stories based on his experiences in the Far East, but is best remembered for his simple and well-observed stories for children, which he broadcast from Radio Éireann over a period of seventeen years and which were widely popular. Died in Dublin on 5 December 1967.

O'CONNOR, ROGER (1762-1834), United Irishman. Born Connorville, Co. Cork. Educated TCD, and called to the English bar in 1784. As a young man he joined the yeomanry and hunted 'Whiteboys', but soon changed his out-look and joined the United Irishmen. He was arrested in 1797 at the instance of his brother, Robert, but was acquitted. Re-arrested in 1798 and sent to Fort George, Scotland. Released some years later; rented Dangan Castle, Trim, which was burnt down after he had insured it for £5,000. He then ran away with a married woman. In 1817 he was arrested for robbing the Galway coach. His defence pleaded that he wanted not money but love letters incriminating his friend Sir Francis Burdett, and he was acquitted. He published *The Chronicles of Eri* (1822), an alleged translation from the Phoenician but mostly his own fiction. Died at Kilcrea, Co. Cork, 27 January 1834. FEARGUS O'CONNOR was his son.

O'CONNOR, SEÁN (1910-1987), reforming civil servant. Born in Dingle, Co. Kerry, and educated at Dingle CBS and St Brendan's College, Killarney. He entered the Department of Education in 1931. In 1964 he became assistant secretary in charge of the new Development Section which, under DONAGH O'MALLEY as minister, introduced free post-primary education. In 1968 he published in *Studies*, the Jesuit periodical, a controversial article advocating a community-comprehensive system. At that time there were no secondary schools except those run by religious orders. In 1969, on ministerial instructions, he toured the country, organising public meetings to promote the new idea. He became secretary of the department in 1973 and chairman of the Higher Education Authority 1975-1979. Published *A Troubled Sky: Reflections on the Irish Education Scene, 1957-1968* (1986). Died in Dublin on 17 March 1987, survived by his wife, Máirín, two sons and a daughter.

O'CONNOR, THOMAS POWER (1848-1929), journalist and politician. Born in Athlone, 5 October 1848. Educated at the College of the Immaculate Conception, Athlone, and Queen's College, Galway. He became a journalist, working first for *Saunders' News-*

letter, Dublin, and then joining the *Daily Telegraph* in London. Elected Parnellite MP for Galway 1880, and in 1885 won the Scotland division of Liverpool and held the seat until his death. Combining politics and journalism with steady success, he founded an evening paper, the *Star*, and edited it from 1887 to 1890. In 1902 he started *T.P.'s Weekly*, a popular literary paper that flourished for many years. His books include *The Parnell Movement* (1886) and *Memories of an Old Parliamentarian* (1929). In 1917 he became the first film censor, a salaried appointment that made his name familiar to millions; he discharged his duties with skill and tact. Privy Councillor 1924, and 'father' of the House of Commons for many years. Died in London 18 November 1929.

O'CONOR, CHARLES (1710–1791), antiquary. Born at Kilmactranny, Co. Sligo, on 1 January 1710. Received his early education from a Franciscan who knew no English. In 1720 his father regained possession of the confiscated family estate of Belanagare, Co. Roscommon, and his education was continued by his brother-in-law, Bishop O'Rourke of Killala, who instructed him in English and Latin literature and urged him to continue his study of Irish. He married in 1731, and his wife's fortune enabled them to buy a farm in Co. Roscommon. Here they lived until 1749 when he succeeded to the Belanagare estate. At Belanagare he devoted himself to study and writing. His publications include *Dissertations on the Ancient History of Ireland* (1753), *A Statistical Account of the Parish of Kilronan* (1773), and a series of letters and pamphlets urging the removal of political disabilities of Catholics. As a young man he had been obliged to attend Mass in a cave, as the laws against priests were then enforced with severity. His youngest brother became a Protestant and filed a suit to obtain possession of Belanagare. Charles was obliged to buy him off with a large sum, which left him in reduced means in his

later years. In 1760, when his eldest son married, he gave him the house and went to live in a cottage in the demesne. He died there on 1 July 1791.

O'CONOR, CHARLES (1764–1828), antiquary and librarian. Born at Belanagare, Co. Roscommon, on 15 March 1764, grandson of CHARLES O'CONOR. Educated at the Ludovisi College in Rome, where he took the degree of DD in 1791. The following year he was appointed parish priest of Kilkeevin, Co. Roscommon, and remained there until 1798, when he was made chaplain to the Marchioness of Buckingham and librarian at Stowe to Richard Grenville, afterwards Duke of Buckingham and Chandos. In 1796 he published a memoir on the life and writings of his grandfather. Between 1810 and 1813 he published seven letters on *The Present Mode of Appointing Catholic Bishops in Ireland*. These letters supported the government veto, and he was declared unorthodox and suspended by ARCHBISHOP TROY in 1812. In 1814 he began his major work, *Rerum Hibernicarum Scriptores Veteres* (four volumes, 1814–1828), of which two hundred copies were printed at a cost of £3,000, which was met by the Duke of Buckingham. He also published in 1818 a catalogue of the manuscripts in the Stowe library. These manuscripts, which included the Annals of Ulster, Annals of Tighearnach, and the Annals of the Four Masters, were the originals on which *Rerum Scriptores* was based. Later scholars, including JOHN O'DONOVAN, asserted that his scholarship was faulty. His mind began to fail before the last volume of *Rerum Scriptores* was published and he suffered from the hallucination that he was deliberately being starved. He left Stowe on 4 July 1827 and was temporarily confined in Dr Harty's asylum at Finglas, Dublin, where DR LANIGAN was also an inmate. Died at his ancestral home at Belanagare on 29 July 1828.

O'CONOR, CHARLES OWEN (1838–1906), the 'O'Conor Don'. Born in Dublin on 7 May 1838, eldest son of Denis O'Conor of Belanagare and Clonalis, Co. Roscommon. The family being Catholics, he was educated at Downside by the Benedictines. He then studied at London University but did not graduate. Elected Liberal MP for Roscommon 1860, and held the seat until 1880, when he was defeated by a Parnellite. In Parliament he became a leading exponent of Roman Catholic opinion, especially on education, and he was appointed in 1878 to the Intermediate Examination Board. He urged reform of the land tenure system and supported the Home Rule movement led by BUTT. Member of royal commissions on the law relating to penal servitude (1863) and to factories and workshops (1873). For many years president of the Antiquarian Society of Ireland and of the RIA. President of the Irish Language Society, and procured the introduction of Irish into the curriculum of the Intermediate Board. Died at Clonalis, Castlerea, Co. Roscommon, on 30 June 1906.

O'CONOR, RODERIC (1860–1940), painter. Born in Co. Roscommon of a landed family on 17 October 1860 and educated at Ampleforth College, York, the Metropolitan College of Art, Dublin, and the RHA school. He then studied in Antwerp for a year, returned to Dublin, then left for France for good about 1885. He inherited large estates on his father's death in 1893 and sold them through the Land Commission in 1910. Investment of the proceeds yielded an income that gave him financial independence, especially as living in France was very cheap before the Second World War. He exhibited in Paris at the Salon des Indépendants with Van Gogh, Toulouse-Lautrec and Seurat in 1887 and 1888. In 1891 he moved to Brittany where he was one of the Pont Aven circle, which included Gauguin. They became close friends; Gauguin urged him vainly to accompany him back to Tahiti. He returned to Paris in 1904. Somerset Maugham based the character

Clutton in his novel *Of Human Bondage* on O'Conor: an unflattering portrait. A strongly individual painter who belonged to no school, his reputation has grown steadily. He died on 18 March 1940 at Neuilly-sur-Layon (Maine et Loire), survived by his wife, Renée Honta, formerly his mistress and thirty-four years younger, and is buried in the local cemetery. The English critic John Russell praised his 'tender and unaffected view of the world'.

Ó CRIOMHTHAIN, TOMÁS (1856–1937), author. Born on the Great Blasket Island off the coast of Kerry and lived there all his life, working a smallholding and fishing and beachcombing. Of his ten children, two boys were drowned, one in a fall from a cliff and the other trying to rescue a visitor; two girls died of measles. In 1917 Brian Ó Ceallaigh from Killarney spent a year on the island and read to him the stories of Pierre Loti and Maxim Gorki to show that a fisherman could write as well as any learned man. At Ó Ceallaigh's urging he wrote a diary, *Allagar na hInise* ('Island Talk'), which was published in 1928. He then wrote his autobiography, *An tOileánach* ('The Islandman'), which was published in 1929 and went into four editions. Both books were edited by PÁDRAIG Ó SIOCHFHRADHA. *Allagar na hInise* describes incidents in the daily life of the islanders with humour and insight. *An tOileánach* was written, Ó Criomhthain said, 'as there will not be our likes again,' and it recounts the hardships and isolation of island life, varied only by an occasional trip to Dún Chaoin on the mainland. The English scholar Robin Flower spent many summers there; his English translation of *An tOileánach* was published in 1934 but did not have the success of the original, which is regarded as a classic in Irish writing. Ó Criomhthain died on the island, which is now uninhabited. In 1953, when the population had dwindled to a few families, the Government resettled them on the mainland.

O'CURRY, EUGENE (1796–1862), scholar. Born at Dunaha, near Carrigaholt, Co. Clare, and received no formal education. In 1834 he obtained a post in the Ordnance Survey. When the survey was wound up by the British government in 1837 he had by then become known to scholars such as O'DONOVAN and TODD, and secured employment in cataloguing and arranging manuscripts in the RIA, TCD, and the British Museum. From this work he graduated to editing and translating Irish texts. In 1854 he was appointed professor of Irish history and archaeology in the new Catholic University of Ireland. His lectures were published in 1861 and gave a comprehensive account of the principal Irish mediaeval manuscripts, containing historical romances, chronicles, tales, and poems. A further series of lectures, *Manners and Customs of the Ancient Irish*, appeared posthumously in 1873. His industry was exceptional; he made facsimile copies of many lengthy manuscripts and transcribed others in a distinct and beautiful hand. He died in Dublin in July 1862.

Ó DÁLAIGH, CEARBHALL (1911–1978), fifth President of Ireland. Born in Bray, Co. Wicklow, on 12 February 1911 and educated at Scoil na Leanbh, Ring, Co. Waterford, Synge Street CBS, Dublin, and UCD, graduating in Celtic studies. He read law at King's Inns, was Irish-language editor of the *Irish Press*, and was called to the bar in 1934. Senior counsel 1945, Attorney-General 1946–1948 and 1951–1953. Appointed judge of the Supreme Court 1953, Chief Justice 1961. In 1972 he became Irish member of the EEC Court of Justice. He served as chairman of a number of Government commissions and of the Cultural Relations Committee. After the sudden death of President ERSKINE CHILDERS, all the political parties in the Dáil agreed that Ó Dálaigh should succeed him, and he was inaugurated on 19 December 1974. In office he made state visits to France and Spain and to the European Community institutions in Luxembourg. He was made an honorary fellow RCSI, and both he and his wife received honorary doctorates in Celtic literature from NUI. In September 1976, when an Emergency Powers Bill was presented to him for signature and promulgation, he decided after consulting the Council of State to refer it to the Supreme Court to test its constitutionality. The court judged that it was not repugnant to the Constitution, and he signed it. On 18 October, at an army function in Columb Barracks, Mullingar, the Minister for Defence, Patrick Donegan, called the President 'a thundering disgrace'. A Dáil motion by the opposition calling for the resignation of the minister, who had meanwhile offered an apology, was defeated on 21 October. The following day the President resigned, 'as the only way open to assert publicly my personal integrity and independence as President of Ireland and to protect the dignity and independence of the Presidency as an institution.' In retirement, the Ó Dálaighs went to live near Sneem, Co. Kerry. They made a fortnight's visit to China in May 1977 as guests of the Chinese government. On 21 March 1978 he died suddenly at home following a heart attack, and was buried in Sneem cemetery after a state funeral.

Cearbhall Ó Dálaigh had two abiding interests, the Irish language and the law. As Chief Justice he played a decisive part in liberalising the law and developing the position of the Supreme Court as guardian of the rights of citizens enshrined in the Constitution. He was a lover of the arts and a linguist, a man of wide culture, unaffected by high office.

O'DEA, DENIS (1903–1978), actor. Born in Dublin, worked in an insurance office, then took up acting professionally after successful appearances on the amateur stage. He joined the Abbey Theatre in the 1930s and became one of their leading players. He then went into films and had a succession of parts in Elstree and Hollywood productions, playing alongside Clark Gable, Grace

Kelly, and Marilyn Monroe. He married SIOBHÁN MCKENNA in 1946; in 1956 they starred in separate Broadway shows simultaneously. Sport was his relaxation: he enjoyed fishing, racing, and poker. He died in Dublin on 5 November 1978, survived by his wife and son, Donncha.

O'DEA, JAMES AUGUSTINE (JIMMY) (1899–1965), comedian. Born in Dublin. Qualified as an optician in Edinburgh. Returning to Dublin, he took part, in his spare time, in amateur productions of Ibsen and Chekhov. In 1927 he took to the stage full-time and formed a partnership with HARRY O'DONOVAN, who created for him his most famous part, Biddy Mulligan, 'the Pride of the Coombe'. In a successful career in pantomime and 'on the halls', he toured Ireland and England many times. Died in Dublin, 7 January 1965. A portrait of him by James Le Jeune RHA hangs in the National Gallery of Ireland.

Ó DEIRG, TOMÁS (1897–1956), politician. Born at Westport, Co. Mayo, 26 November 1897. Educated at local CBS and UCG. He organised a University Corps of the Irish Volunteers, and was arrested and deported after the 1916 Rising. On release he graduated in commerce, and was headmaster of Ballina Technical College 1918–1925. During the War of Independence he was interned in the Curragh, and while there was elected Sinn Féin MP for Mayo. He took the anti-Treaty side in 1922, and was captured by Free State troops. While attempting to escape he was shot in the eye. Elected Fianna Fáil TD for Carlow-Kilkenny in 1927. Minister for Education 1932–1939 and 1940–1948; Minister for Lands 1939–1943 and 1951–1954. In the Dáil he represented Carlow-Kilkenny or Kilkenny without a break from 1927 until his death in Dublin on 19 November 1956.

Ó DIREÁIN, MÁIRTÍN (1910–1988), poet. Born in Inis Mór, Aran Islands, on 26 November 1910 and educated at the local national school. His father died when he was seven, and his mother reared a family of four on twenty rocky acres. Máirtín, the eldest, secured a job in Galway Post Office in 1929. He acted in the Taibhdhearc and became secretary of the Galway branch of the Gaelic League. He moved to Dublin in 1937 and served in the Department of Posts and Telegraphs and then in the Department of Education until he retired in 1978. From 1948 to 1955 he was registrar of the National College of Art. His first collection of verse, *Coinnle Geala*, appeared in 1942, followed by *Dánta Aniar* (1943). *Rogha Dánta* (1949) firmly established him as a major voice in Irish poetry. *Ó Mórna* (1957) confirmed his position as the father of modern poetry in Irish. Two collections, *Dánta 1939–1979* (1980) and *Tacar Dánta—Selected Poems* (1984) showed his sustained creativity, and the translations into English in the 1984 volume introduced his poetry to a wider audience. The nostalgia for Aran of his early verse gave place in later work to an islander's bleak sense of urban alienation. He published nine volumes of verse in all, the last, *Craobhóg Dán*, appearing in 1986. *Feamainn Bhealtaine* (1961), essays on life in Aran, was his only prose work. In 1977 he received an honorary D.Litt. from NUI and the same year was awarded the Ossian Preis of £5,000 by the Freiherr von Stein Foundation, Hamburg. Elected member of the Irish Academy of Letters in 1970 after the death of MÁIRTÍN Ó CADHAIN. He received prizes for poetry from the Oireachtas and the Arts Council. He died in a Dublin hospital on 19 March 1988.

O'DOHERTY, SIR CAHIR (1587–1608), Lord of Inishowen. Knighted by Lord Mountjoy for bravery on the field of Augher. Favourably received in London by Queen Elizabeth I, and confirmed in his lands. On return to Ireland he married a daughter of Lord Gormanston and was made justice of the peace and alderman of the new city of Derry. After the Flight of the Earls in

1607 he was foreman of the jury that found them guilty of treason. But Sir George Paulet, governor of Derry, charged him with treason also, and he was obliged to find sureties. The following year, 1608, Paulet struck him while they were discussing a sale of land. In revenge he sacked and burned Derry, killed Paulet, and slaughtered the garrison. A force was despatched from Dublin against him and he was shot dead at the Rock of Doon near Kilmacrenan on 5 July 1608.

O'DOHERTY, KEVIN IZOD (1823–1905), nationalist. Born in Gloucester Street, Dublin, 7 September 1823. Educated at Dr Walls' School in Hume Street. While still a medical student at the Cecilia Street School he joined the Young Ireland movement. In 1849 he was convicted of treason-felony and sentenced to ten years' transportation to Van Diemen's Land (Tasmania). Pardoned in 1854, he returned to Dublin and qualified as a medical doctor. In 1862 he emigrated to Brisbane, and practised medicine there until 1885. He entered politics and was a member of the Queensland legislative assembly from 1877 to 1885. Returning to Dublin that year he was made a freeman of the city and elected MP for North Meath. In 1888 he went back to Brisbane, failed to recover his practice, and died there in poverty on 15 July 1905, survived by his wife, 'EVA' OF THE 'NATION'.

Ó DOIRNÍN, PEADAR (1682–1769), poet. Born, according to some sources, in the mountains north-west of Cashel, Co. Tipperary, in 1682; other authorities give the date of his birth as 1684 or 1685; yet more say he was born in Co. Louth in 1704. The following account of his subsequent career is by no means well authenticated and is given for what it is worth. From his name, an Ulster birthplace is the more likely, and Seán de Rís favours a village near Kilaury just north of Dundalk, Co. Louth. Political trouble obliged him to leave home, and he settled at Drumcree, Co. Armagh. He wrote a poem on the ancient divisions of Ireland, which brought him a meeting with Arthur Brownlow of Lurgan, then the possessor of the Book of Armagh, who took him into his house as tutor for his children and to impart to himself a knowledge of Irish literature. After a good many years, political differences ended the friendship. Ó Doirnín left the Brownlow household, married a Rose Toner, and settled as a schoolmaster near Forkhill, Co. Armagh. He wrote nature poems, political verses, and humorous verses. He died on 3 April 1769 at Forkhill, and was buried near the north-west wall of the churchyard of Urney, three miles north of Dundalk.

O'DONNELL, FRANK HUGH (1848–1916), author and politician. Born in Co. Donegal. Educated at St Ignatius' College, Galway, and Queen's College, Galway. Joined staff of the *Morning Post* and was foreign editor for many years. Elected MP for Galway 1874 but unseated on petition. MP for Dungarvan 1877–1885. PARNELL refused to allow him to be nominated in the general election of 1885. He took an unsuccessful and ill-judged action for libel against *The Times* in 1888 and, wittingly or unwittingly, revived the public outrage against Parnell aroused by the *Times* series 'Parnellism and Crime' in 1887; this led to the setting up of the Parnell Commission. He retired from politics 1885 and later lived on the Continent for many years. Published many books, the best-known *A History of the Irish Parliamentary Party* (two volumes, 1910). Died in London, 2 November 1916.

O'DONNELL, RED HUGH (*c.* 1571–1602), son of Sir Hugh O'Donnell, lord of Tír Chonaill. Grew up in fosterage with Mac Suibhne na dTuath. In 1587 the deputy, Sir John Perrott, fearing the power of the O'Donnells, decided to seize a hostage, and sent a merchant vessel to Lough Swilly with a cargo of Spanish wine. The young Hugh was enticed on board and, with two companions, Daniel MacSweeney and Hugh

284

O'Gallagher, was kidnapped and imprisoned in Dublin Castle. After three years Red Hugh escaped but was recaptured in a few days in the Wicklow mountains. On Christmas night 1591 he escaped again with Henry and Art O'Neill, sons of SHANE O'NEILL. They made for Glenmalure in bitter winter weather to seek refuge with FIACH MACHUGH O'BYRNE, but Art O'Neill died from exposure on the way. Red Hugh survived and later made his way to his father's castle at Ballyshannon, Co. Donegal. Here, physicians amputated his two great toes. In May 1592 he was inaugurated as chief of the O'Donnells, and before long seized Sligo and overran Connacht. He joined forces with HUGH O'NEILL and others and shared in the victory of the Yellow Ford in August 1598 when the English under Bagenal suffered a heavy defeat. The Irish cause prospered for the following two years. After the recall of Essex towards the end of 1599 and the arrival of Mountjoy in February 1600, their fortunes waned. They had long expected aid from Spain, and in September 1601 a Spanish fleet entered Kinsale, Co. Cork, with 3,400 troops under Don Juan del Aguila. O'Neill and O'Donnell at once marched south, while Mountjoy proceeded to lay siege to the Spaniards in Kinsale. The Battle of Kinsale took place on 24 December 1601, and resulted in a victory for Mountjoy; shortly after, del Aguila surrendered the town. The Irish decided to send Red Hugh to Spain for further help, and he sailed from Castlehaven on 6 January 1602. He was received by King Philip III with great honour and promised another force, but he fell suddenly ill at Simancas, and died there on 10 September 1602. From a letter from Carew to Mountjoy, it seems clear that he was poisoned by one James Blake of Galway, with the cognisance of Carew if not at his instigation. The body of Red Hugh was buried by command of King Philip with royal honours in the church of the Franciscan monastery at Valladolid, but no trace of the church now remains.

O'DONNELL, JAMES LOUIS (1738–1811), the 'Apostle of Newfoundland'. Born at Knocklofty, Co. Tipperary. At eighteen he entered the Franciscan convent of St Isidore in Rome. Ordained at Prague 1770; returned to Ireland 1775 and settled at Waterford, where he became prior of the Franciscan house; subsequently he became provincial of the order in Ireland. In 1784, at the request of leading Newfoundland merchants and their agents at Waterford, he was sent to Newfoundland as prefect and vicar apostolic. On 21 September 1796 he was consecrated at Quebec as titular bishop of Thyatira, and returned to Newfoundland to make his first episcopal visitation. He published a body of diocesan statutes in 1801, and divided the dioceses in missions, acting as a missionary priest himself because of the scarcity of clergy. He used his influence with the Catholics to restrain anti-government feeling, and in 1800 discovered and reported to the commandant, Major-General Skerret, a projected mutiny among the soldiers of the Newfoundland Regiment stationed at St Johns. The government awarded him a life pension of £50 annually for his service to the colony, and from then on his position in Newfoundland was equal to that of the governor in everything except name. His health failed, and in 1807 he was obliged to resign his see and return to Ireland. He spent his last years at Waterford, and died there on 15 April 1811.

O'DONNELL, MANUS (died 1563), lord of Tír Chonaill. Inaugurated at Kilmacrenan in 1537. Married Lady Eleanor Fitzgerald, sister of 'SILKEN THOMAS', and in 1539 invaded the Pale with O'Neill. In 1541 he submitted to the lord deputy. In 1555 he was deposed and taken prisoner by his son, Calvagh. He was released after a short time but did not recover his authority. In his castle at Lifford a life of ST COLMCILLE was written under his direction. The manuscript, completed in 1536, is now in the Bodleian Library, Oxford. He died at Lifford at an advanced age.

O'DONNELL, SIR NIALL GARBH (1569–1626). Born in Co. Donegal. Objected to the election of his cousin, Red Hugh, as chief. Captured Lifford and Donegal Abbey from him and had himself inaugurated at Kilmacrenan. He was accused of conspiring with CAHIR O'DOHERTY when the latter rebelled in 1608, but a Dublin jury refused to convict. In 1609 he was committed to the Tower of London and died there, 'a most unfortunate and badly-used man.'

O'DONNELL, PATRICK (1856–1927), cardinal. Born at Kilraine, near Glenties, Co. Donegal, on 28 November 1856. Educated at the local national school and at Letterkenny. Ordained at Maynooth in 1880 and appointed professor of theology there the same year. Bishop of Raphoe 1888. He completed the building of Letterkenny cathedral in 1901 and built many other churches, an industrial school at Killybegs, and a seminary at Letterkenny. He presided over the Irish Race Convention of 1896. Appointed coadjutor to Armagh 1922, archbishop 1924, and cardinal 1925. In 1927 he held a plenary synod at Maynooth, which introduced many reforms. A native Irish-speaker, he was a strong supporter of the language revival and issued his pastorals in Irish and English for many years. He helped to promote reunion among nationalists after the death of PARNELL in 1891, and presided at the National Convention of 1900, which elected JOHN REDMOND as leader of the Irish Party. He supported Redmond's policy in the First World War, and was an active member of the Irish Convention of 1917–1918. He helped to found the NUI in 1908. Died at his summer residence at Carlingford, Co. Louth, 22 October 1927.

O'DONNELL, PEADAR (1893–1986), revolutionary and writer. Born on a small farm at Meenmore, Co. Donegal, on 22 February 1893 and educated at St Patrick's Training College, Dublin. He taught on Arranmore and Inisfree islands but after visiting Scotland and seeing the hardships endured by migrant Irish labourers, he became a full-time organiser for the Irish Transport and General Workers' Union in 1918. In 1920 he joined the IRA and was wounded on active service in the War of Independence. He opposed the Anglo-Irish Treaty of 1921 and was imprisoned for two years, escaping in 1924. Elected Sinn Féin TD for Donegal in 1923 but did not take his seat or seek re-election. On 25 June 1924 he married Lile O'Donel, daughter of a wealthy Mayo landlord. He became editor of *An Phoblacht*, the IRA newspaper. With FRANK RYAN and GEORGE GILMORE he broke away from the IRA to found the short-lived Republican Congress to establish a workers' republic. He helped recruit volunteers to fight in the International Brigade on the Republican side in the Spanish Civil War. His first novel, *Storm*, appeared in 1926, followed by *Islanders* (1927), *Adrigoole* (1929), *The Knife* (1930), *On the Edge of the Stream* (1934), *The Big Windows* (1955), and *Proud Island* (1975). He published three autobiographical works, *The Gates Flew Open* (1932), *Salud!: an Irishman in Spain* (1937), and *There Will Be Another Day* (1963). He edited the literary monthly *The Bell* from 1946 until its demise in 1954. He received an award of £10,000 from the Irish-American Cultural Institute in 1982. All his life O'Donnell was an untiring champion of social reform and unpopular causes. In later years he campaigned for peace and nuclear disarmament. His novels depict the harsh realities of rural life as he knew them. He died in a Dublin hospital on 13 May 1986. His wife predeceased him in 1969. They had no children; he was survived by a nephew, Peadar Joe, whom he reared and regarded as a son.

O'DONNELL, RUAIDHRÍ (1575–1608), first Earl of Tír Chonaill. Accompanied his elder brother, RED HUGH, to Kinsale in 1601, and took over leadership when Hugh went to Spain after defeat there. He made submission to

Mountjoy in 1602, went with him to London in 1603, and was well received by the new king. He was knighted that year in Christ Church, Dublin, and created Earl of Tír Chonaill. He was dissatisfied with the lands granted to him and feared that the government intended to isolate and depose the chiefs under pretence of enforcing the recusancy laws. He thought to persuade Tyrone, Maguire and others to join him in seizing Dublin Castle, but his plans were discovered, and in 1607 he sailed from Lough Swilly with Tyrone and others. Died in Rome on 29 July 1608.

O'DONOGHUE, DAVID JAMES (1866–1917), man of letters. Born at Chelsea, 22 July 1866. Educated at local elementary schools. Read omnivorously in British Museum. Contributed articles to *Dublin Evening Telegraph* and other periodicals. Published valuable *Poets of Ireland* (1892–1893, revised and enlarged edition 1912). Also published *Humour of Ireland* (1894) and *Life of Carleton* (1896). He moved to Dublin about 1896 and continued a bookselling and publishing business established by his late brother. Published *Life of Mangan* (1897), *Life of Emmet* (1903), and many other works, the fruit of patient research. Appointed librarian, UCD, 1909. Died Dublin, 27 June 1917.

O'DONOGHUE, JOHN (1900–1964), novelist. Born in Kerry, son of a small farmer. Served in the Garda Síochána 1924–1931, then entered a monastery. Left after a few years and emigrated to England where he worked as a labourer. Published three novels, *In a Quiet Land* (1957), *In a Strange Land* (1958), and *In Kerry Long Ago* (1960). All are autobiographical, simple and moving accounts of rural life. He died in London in 1964 while working on a fourth book about his experiences as a policeman.

O'DONOVAN, EDMUND (1844–1883), war correspondent. Born in Dublin, 13 September 1844. Educated at St Francis Xavier College, Royal College of Science, and TCD. Began to contribute to the *Irish Times* in 1866, and when the Franco-Prussian War of 1870 broke out he joined the French Foreign Legion. Wounded and captured, he sent dispatches to Dublin and London from an internment camp. Correspondent for *The Times* of London during the Carlist rising in Spain in 1873, and went to Asia Minor in 1876 as correspondent for the *Daily News*. In 1879 he made a celebrated journey to Merv (Mary) in Central Asia, and was detained there for several months by the Turks on suspicion of being an agent for the Russians. His adventures are related in his book, *The Merv Oasis* (1882). In 1883 he went to Sudan as representative of the *Daily News* and joined the army of Hicks Pasha, which marched on Al-Obeid. In November 1883 the army was ambushed and annihilated. O'Donovan was never heard of again.

O'DONOVAN, GERALD (1871–1942), priest and novelist. Born in Co. Down on 15 July 1871, son of a peripatetic builder, and attended schools in Cork, Galway, and Sligo. Entered Maynooth and ordained in 1895 for the diocese of Clonfert. A socially minded liberal, interested in the arts, he was active in the Gaelic League and the co-operative movement led by SIR HORACE PLUNKETT and GEORGE RUSSELL. By the 1890s he had become administrator of Loughrea and brought JACK YEATS and SARAH PURSER to work on the new cathedral there. In 1903 a new bishop, Dr Thomas O'Dea, was appointed to Clonfert. It seems that the diocesan clergy had wished O'Donovan to get the post. Strained relations soon developed and in 1904 O'Donovan left Loughrea and the priesthood. He went to London to pursue a literary career, married Beryl Verschoyle, daughter of an Irish colonel, in 1911, and in 1915 published *Father Ralph*, the autobiographical novel by which he is best remembered. He published five more novels and established a close friendship with the novelist Rose Macaulay. He died in Surrey on 26 July 1942.

O'DONOVAN, HARRY (1896–1973), comedy scriptwriter. Born in Dublin; apprenticed to a house painter. After acting in amateur shows he joined a 'fit-up' company and toured Ireland for several years. He returned to Dublin in 1921 at the height of the War of Independence and, though times were lean, started a new troupe. About 1924 he met JIMMY O'DEA and formed with him 'O'Dea-O'Donovan Productions'. The partnership continued for thirty years, producing a pantomime and variety shows each year. The scripts were written by O'Donovan, and he also supplied hundreds of scripts to Radio Éireann. As well as producing the shows he acted as business manager, stage manager, and wardrobe master, and played occasional parts. He created Jimmy O'Dea's most famous part, Biddy Mulligan, the 'Pride of the Coombe'. During the Second World War he wrote eighty 'Irish half-hours' for the BBC. He died in Dublin on 3 November 1973.

O'DONOVAN, JOHN (1809–1861), scholar. Born 9 July 1809 at Attateemore, Co. Kilkenny, and educated in Dublin. In 1826 he obtained a post in the Irish Record Office, and in 1829 joined the Ordnance Survey. His work for the survey took him to every parish in Ireland, and the results of his examination of manuscripts and his local investigations into place-names were embodied in his *Letters*, edited long afterwards in fifty volumes by FR MICHAEL O'FLANAGAN. This was the first of a long series of scholarly works undertaken by O'Donovan. Many were published by the Irish Archaeological Society, which he founded in 1840 with EUGENE O'CURRY. His subjects included genealogy, history, poetry, law, and topography, and he included valuable maps in some volumes as well as translations of the Irish text. His greatest work was his edition and translation of the *Annals of the Four Masters* (seven volumes, 1848–1851). In 1852 he joined the commission for the publication of the ancient laws of Ireland and worked on an edition of the Seanchus Mór, but although he transcribed and translated nine volumes of legal manuscripts he did not live to edit the material. He also published a *Grammar of the Irish Language* (1845), and a supplement to O'Reilly's *Irish Dictionary*. He married a sister of O'Curry, and died in Dublin, 9 December 1861. Students of Irish topography, history, genealogy and language owe him an immense debt; the extent and accuracy of his researches place him in the first rank of Irish scholars.

O'DONOVAN ROSSA, JEREMIAH (1831–1915), nationalist. Born at Rosscarbery, Co. Cork, in September 1831. When JAMES STEPHENS came to Ireland in 1858 to organise the Fenians, Rossa and his Phoenix Society of Skibbereen were among the first to join. He was imprisoned for a short term. He became business manager of the Fenian organ, the *Irish People*, between 1863 and 1865, and contributed to the paper's leading columns and to its poets' corner. With other leading Fenians he was arrested in 1865 and sentenced to penal servitude for twenty years. Cruelly treated in prison, he was freed in 1871, on condition that he leave Ireland. He went to the USA where, during his long residence, he edited the *United Irishman* for a time. He published *O'Donovan Rossa's Prison Life: Six Years in Six English Prisons* (1874), re-published in 1882 as *Irish Rebels in English Prisons*. His *Rossa's Recollections: 1838 to 1898* appeared in 1898. Died in New York on 30 June 1915. His body was brought home, and an immense crowd followed the funeral to Glasnevin cemetery, Dublin, on 1 August 1915. PATRICK PEARSE, dressed in the uniform of the Irish Volunteers, delivered a funeral oration, ending with the words that became famous: 'The fools, the fools, the fools!—they have left us our Fenian dead, and while Ireland holds these graves, Ireland unfree shall never be at peace.'

Ó DUBHDA, PEADAR (1881–1971), teacher of Irish. Born near Dundalk on 7

288

November 1881. Educated at the local national school. At twelve he got his first job, delivering groceries for Leverett and Frye in country districts. While driving around in a horse and car he taught himself Irish from *Simple Lessons in Irish* by FATHER O'GROWNEY. He joined the local brass band, learned the cornet, and from that progressed, largely self-taught, to the violin, flute, and piano. In 1899 he was one of a small band of enthusiasts who founded a branch of the Gaelic League in Dundalk. He spent his weekends visiting the Gaeltacht areas of Armagh and Omeath to improve his Irish, and collected songs and stories from the surviving native speakers. In 1910 he became a múinteoir taistil (travelling teacher) of the Gaelic League at £55 a year, and covered 8,000 miles (13,000 km) a year by bicycle, organising classes all over the country. He went to Connemara in 1914 and was examined by PATRICK PEARSE for a certificate to teach Irish. Pearse gave him only a temporary certificate, to be renewed in a year, and he said that this was the only certificate he ever got. In the summer of 1915 the Gaelic League recognised the work of himself and his colleagues by holding their annual ardfheis in Omeath. In the 1930s he tried without success to interest the Catholic hierarchy in an Irish translation of the Douai Bible. Undaunted, he took on the work alone, completing it in 1953. The result, an illuminated manuscript of over three thousand pages, was presented to the National Library. He died in Dundalk in May 1971.

O'DUFFY, EIMAR ULTAN (1893–1935), writer. Born in Dublin, 29 September 1893, son of the dentist-in-ordinary to the viceregal household, and qualified in dentistry at NUI. He took an active part in the volunteer movement; at Easter 1916 he was one of the couriers who attempted to have the MACNEILL countermanding order transmitted throughout the country. In 1920, he married the daughter of Cruise O'Brien. During the Civil War period he took a liberal pro-Treaty view and was afterwards employed for a time in the Department of External Affairs. In 1925 he spent a short period in Paris as a journalist, then moved to England where he became an advocate of the social credit system, acted as a publicity agent for the Lloyd George Liberals in London, and practised as a writer. He wrote plays, novels, verse, journalism, satire, detective stories and economics textbooks. A noted work was *The Wasted Island* (1919), a long, autobiographical novel, with a major target the 'schemers' who, in his view, foisted an unwanted rebellion on the Irish Volunteers. In 1922–1923, with BULMER HOBSON, Colm Ó Lochlainn and P. S. O'HEGARTY he brought out a seven-issue series of the *Irish Review*. The first of a trilogy of economic satires, *King Goshawk and the Birds* appeared in 1926. At his direction, the incomplete drafts of his autobiography, *The Portrait Gallery*, were destroyed after his death. He died at New Malden, Surrey, England, on 21 March 1935.

O'DUFFY, GENERAL EOIN (1892–1944), Blueshirt leader. Born on 30 October 1892 near Castleblayney, Co. Monaghan. Apprenticed as an engineer to the county surveyor in Wexford, and then worked as an engineer and architect in his native county until 1919, when he became an auctioneer. He joined the IRA in 1917, saw active service in the War of Independence, and served several terms of imprisonment. He became director of organisation in 1921 and was appointed chief of staff in 1922 in succession to RICHARD MULCAHY. He supported the Anglo-Irish Treaty of December 1921, and when, in 1922, the Irish Free State government established a police force, the Civic Guard, later An Garda Síochána, he was named commissioner, in succession to Michael Staines. ÉAMON DE VALERA, who had come to power in 1932, held a sudden general election in January 1933, and two weeks after his re-election dismissed O'Duffy. In the Dáil he said that he had been dismissed because 'he was likely to be biased in his attitude because of past political affiliations', and that O'Duffy did not have his full confidence. O'Duffy refused an offer of an alternative position in the public service at the same salary. In July 1933 he was elected leader of the Army Comrades Association, and immediately changed its name to the National Guard. It ceased to be an organisation to look after the interests of ex-soldiers of the National Army and became an active political force. Soon it adopted blue as the colour of its uniform shirts, used a fascist-style salute, and became known as the Blueshirts. Their new leader proposed to hold a parade in Dublin on 13 August 1933 to commemorate GRIFFITH, COLLINS, and O'HIGGINS, but the government banned the parade, and he called it off. Later that month the organisation was proclaimed by government order. In September 1933 Cumann na nGaedheal and the Centre Party merged to form the United Ireland Party or Fine Gael, and O'Duffy was elected president. The National Guard was re-formed as the Young Ireland Association, but it was also banned by the government. It was then disbanded and replaced by the League of Youth. Meetings held by the Blueshirts in the provinces were marked by outbreaks of violence. They supported an anti-rates campaign mounted by farmers feeling the strain of the economic sanctions imposed by the British government because of the withholding of the land annuities during the 'economic war'. Suddenly, on 21 September 1934, O'Duffy resigned as president of Fine Gael, and said that he was glad to be out of politics. Although COSGRAVE and MACDERMOT had been unhappy with his leadership, the move was completely unexpected. In a sequence of events clouded in secrecy and confusion, the Blueshirt movement became divided and fell into disarray. Within a couple of years it had petered out completely. O'Duffy became interested in European fascist movements, and in June 1935 launched a new

party, the National Corporate Party. When the Spanish Civil War broke out in July 1936 he organised an Irish Brigade to fight for the Nationalists under Franco. The government decided on a policy of neutrality and passed legislation that made participation in the war illegal. In the end, some 700 volunteers from Ireland succeeded in making their way to Spain in 1936 and 1937. They served in O'Duffy's brigade for six months under trying conditions, and only a handful volunteered for a second term. O'Duffy regarded the venture as a contribution to a crusade against communism. After that he took no further part in politics. His health failed; he died on 30 November 1944, and was given a state funeral.

Ó DUINNÍN, FATHER PÁDRAIG (PATRICK DINNEEN)

Ó DUINNÍN, FATHER PÁDRAIG (PATRICK DINNEEN) (1860–1934), lexicographer and editor. Born on Christmas Day 1860 at Carn, Rathmore, Co. Kerry. Irish was his native language, and he attended a national school at Meentogues that was built in 1868–1870 from stones taken from the ruined house of EOGHAN RUA Ó SÚILLEABHÁIN. In 1880, after three years spent learning Latin and Greek from a Father O'Sullivan in Rathmore, he entered the Jesuit novitiate at Milltown Park, Dublin. In 1883 he was one of the first students to enrol in UCD when it passed to the care of the Jesuits: Gerard Manley Hopkins was his lecturer in Latin. He was ordained on 29 July 1894 and spent some years teaching English and mathematics in Jesuit schools at Mungret and Clongowes Wood. About August 1900 he left the Jesuits with the consent of his superiors and without canonical stain. The story that he left because of a disagreement over the fees he received for his editorial work is unfounded: he had published little by then. The most likely cause was his own highly individualistic character and habits, which found the rules of the society more irksome as he grew older. He joined the Gaelic League about this time and began his long career as an editor, author, and compiler. He turned first to the poets of his own district of Kerry, editing the poems of Ó RATHAILLE and Ó SÚILLEABHÁIN. In 1904 he prepared for the Irish Texts Society his remarkable *Irish-English Dictionary*, which bears the stamp of his own idiosyncratic personality and which has been ever since an invaluable reference-book for students of all ages. It superseded previous works of the kind and was republished in greatly enlarged editions in 1927 and 1934. Other important works were his editions of the poems of Ó Donncha (1902), MAC DOMHNAILL (1902), and FEIRITÉIR (1903), and of CÉITINN's *Foras Feasa ar Éirinn* (1908–1914). He also wrote a number of plays, essays, school texts, and a novel. From the time he left the Jesuits he made his living solely by writing in Irish, and claimed that he was the only person in Ireland doing so. In the preface to the 1927 edition of his dictionary he wrote: 'I reckon that, led by the lure and prompted by the pathos of unfinished or undeveloped undertakings, I have expended twenty years of severe labour.' He died in Dublin on 29 September 1934 and was buried in Glasnevin cemetery.

Ó FARACHÁIN, ROIBEARD (1909–1984), poet. Born Robert Farren in Dublin in April 1909 and educated at St Patrick's Training College and UCC. He taught in Dublin until 1939 when he joined Radio Éireann as talks officer. He became general features officer in 1943, deputy director in 1947 and controller of radio programmes from 1953 until his retirement in 1974. He published four books of verse, *Thronging Feet* (1936), *Time's Wall Asunder* (1939), *The First Exile* (1944)—a long epic poem on the life of COLMCILLE—and *Rime, Gentlemen, Please* (1945); also two critical works, *The Course of Irish Verse* (1947) and *Towards an Appreciation of Poetry* (1947), all as Robert Farren, and a volume of short stories in Irish. Two verse plays by him, *Convention at Druim Ceat* and *Lost Light*, were produced at the Abbey Theatre in 1943. He was a director of the Abbey from 1940 to 1973 and with AUSTIN CLARKE in 1941

formed the Dublin Verse-Speaking Society, from which evolved the Lyric Theatre Company, which produced a number of verse plays in the Abbey and Peacock theatres and on Radio Éireann. He died in Dublin on 29 December 1984, survived by his wife, Maureen, two sons and three daughters.

O'FLAHERTY, LIAM (1896–1984), novelist and short-story writer. Born on 28 August 1896 on a small farm at Gort na gCapall, Inishmore, Aran Islands. A visiting Holy Ghost father arranged schooling for him at Rockwell College, Co. Tipperary, Blackrock College, Dublin, and then UCD as a diocesan seminarian. Finding that he had no vocation, O'Flaherty left and joined the British Army in 1915 to fight in the First World War. He was invalided out in 1917 with shell-shock. For a couple of years he wandered through the USA, Canada and Latin America, working as deck-hand, beachcomber and lumberjack. Back in Ireland after the Treaty he joined the Communist Party and in January 1922 with a group of unemployed dockers took over the Rotunda Rooms for four days. He then left for London and began to write, encouraged by the critic Edward Garnett. His first novel, *Thy Neighbour's Wife*, appeared in 1923, followed by *The Black Soul* (1924) and *The Informer* (1925), which was awarded the James Tait Black Prize and made into a successful film (1935). He continued to write vigorously, publishing a further dozen novels, including *Skerret* (1932) and *Famine* (1937), acclaimed as masterpieces, and three volumes of autobiography, *Two Years* (1930), an account of his wandering life in his early twenties, *I Went to Russia* (1931), and *Shame the Devil* (1934). *A Tourist's Guide to Ireland* (1929) is a satire on social and political values that he viewed as shams. He wrote over a hundred and fifty short stories, mostly dealing with peasants and fishermen, the sea, wild birds and animals, and containing much of his best work. A collection of stories in Irish, *Dúil* (1953), shows his masterly command of the language. In 1926 he married Margaret Barrington (1895–1982); they had one child, and separated in 1932. Despite much success and the filming of three of his novels, he had financial troubles and two nervous breakdowns, possibly legacies from his shell-shock. Nevertheless his creative output from 1923 to 1953 was very large. After 1953 he wrote little. He travelled a great deal in South America, returned to Europe after the Second World War, and finally settled in Dublin in the 1960s. He was a founder-member of the Irish Academy of Letters, received an honorary doctorate from NUI in 1974 and the Allied Irish Banks Award for Literature in 1979. He died in a Dublin hospital on 7 September 1984. The realism and power of his writing is echoed in his saying: 'I was born on a windswept rock and hate the soft growth of sun-baked lands where there is no frost in men's bones.'

O'FLAHERTY, RODERIC (1629–1718), historian. Born at Moycullen Castle, Co. Galway. Educated at Lynch's school, Galway, and studied Irish literature and history under DUBHALTACH MAC FIRBISIGH, then living at St Nicholas' College, Galway. He was deprived of his estates after the war of 1641 but recovered some part in 1677. In 1685 he published in London *Ogygia*, a history of Ireland in Latin, the first to give readers in England an accurate and scholarly account. He also wrote a *Chorographical Description of West or H-Iar Connaught*, which was edited by JAMES HARDIMAN in 1846 for the Irish Archaeological Society. It is an interesting description of the area, with much local history. Edward Lhuyd of Oxford visited him in 1700 and described him as affable and learned, but 'the late revolution in Ireland had reduced him to great poverty and destroyed his books and papers.' SIR THOMAS MOLYNEUX found him in 1709 living in a miserable condition at Park, West Galway. He died there on 8 April 1718.

O'FLANAGAN, JAMES RODERICK (1814–1900), author. Born 1 September 1814 in Fermoy, Co. Cork, son of the barrack-master. Educated at Fermoy, TCD, and King's Inns. Called to the bar 1838, practised on the Munster circuit, then secured a post in Insolvency Court, Dublin, 1847. Published *The Blackwater in Munster* (1844) and contributed to the *Dublin University Magazine*. Edited *Irish National Magazine*. Published *History of Dundalk* (1861) with John D'Alton, and books on life at the bar. Moved to London about 1870 and lived on his pension, supplemented by literary work. About 1872 he built a mansion on parental property on the Blackwater near Fermoy. In 1885 he founded the *Fermoy Journal* and edited it, but it lasted little over a year. His chief work was *Lives of the Lord Chancellors of Ireland* (two volumes, 1870). He also wrote several novels. Died at Fermoy.

O'FLANAGAN, FATHER MICHAEL (1876–1942), priest and republican. Born at Cloontower, near Castlerea, Co. Roscommon. Educated at Cloonbonive NS and the Diocesan College, Summerhill, Co. Sligo. Ordained at Maynooth in 1900, then returned to Summerhill College to teach. Sent by his bishop to the USA in 1904 to raise funds to defray the debt on Loughlinn convent. His preaching ability brought him invitations to be Advent preacher in St Sylvester's in Rome in 1912 and 1914. Appointed curate at Cliffoney, Co. Sligo, 1914. He disputed the Congested Districts Board's reservation of turf banks for their own tenants, and in June 1915 led his congregation in cutting turf every day until the board secured an injunction to stop him. The turf rights were restored to the people in 1916. Shortly afterwards he was transferred to the parish of Crossna. He began to address nationalist meetings, and he gave the oration at the lying-in-state of O'DONOVAN ROSSA. In 1917 he managed COUNT PLUNKETT's successful campaign in the Roscommon by-election, and became vice-chairman of Sinn Féin. He said the prayers with which the First Dáil was opened at the Mansion House in January 1919. He was at the time 'silenced' by his bishop. He became an executive member of the Irish Agricultural Organisation Society and a vice-president of the Gaelic League. In November 1921 he went to America, and from there to Australia where, 'for some compliments paid to St George on the occasion of his feast,' he was arrested, held for three weeks, and finally deported on a French ship. He then worked for the republican cause in the USA until DE VALERA invited him back to assist in forming a new electoral policy. He acted as chairman of a sub-committee appointed to draw up a social programme for Sinn Féin, but later refused to join Fianna Fáil. In 1937 he again toured the USA, this time in support of the Spanish Republicans. During his career he was suspended several times by his bishop. His final suspension was removed in 1927, and he spent his last years in Sandyford, Dublin, acting as chaplain to nearby convents. He also undertook historical research, editing the fifty-volume *John O'Donovan Archaeological Survey* between 1924 and 1932, and between 1932 and 1942 preparing his *County Histories*. He died in August 1942.

O'FLYNN, FATHER JAMES CHRISTOPHER (1881–1962), 'Father O'Flynn of the Loft'. Born on 12 December 1881 in Mallow Lane, Cork; educated at North Monastery CBS. After two years as a clerk in a warehouse he felt the call to be a priest. He studied at Farranferris seminary and Maynooth, where he was ordained on 20 June 1909. Appointed to Farranferris in 1909 to teach elocution, and continued that work for over fifty years. Chaplain to Cork mental asylum 1910–1920, curate at North Cathedral, Cork, 1920–1946, and parish priest, Passage West, from 1946 until his death. The Flynn family was musical, and James had a fine voice, natural acting ability, and a love of Shakespeare from his Maynooth days.

In 1910 his first visit to the West Cork Gaeltacht awakened an abiding love of Irish song, story, and dance. He travelled through Munster on a motorcycle collecting traditional Irish songs and teaching singing classes. He became president of Cork City Gaelic League and chairman of the Munster Feis. In 1926 he rented a room, at once named 'the Loft', over a sweet-factory off Mulgrave St, Cork, to accommodate the increasing numbers attending his classes in Shakespearian acting, begun five years before in the choir-room of North Cathedral. Irish singing and dancing were also taught there. In May 1927 the 'Loft' produced six Shakespeare plays in Cork Opera House with great success. At Passage West he trained a girls' choir from the Mercy convent in traditional singing. The choir made many records and broadcast frequently from Radio Éireann. In June 1961 the BBC broadcast *It Happened to Me*, a half-hour documentary on his life and work, which took second prize at the International Conference of Catholic Television at Monte Carlo in March 1962. Father O'Flynn died in a Cork hospital in January 1962.

O'GORMAN, THOMAS (1732–1809), 'the Chevalier'. Born 16 September 1732 at Castletown, Co. Clare. Educated at Irish College in Paris and qualified as a physician in that city. While a student he married a daughter of Count d'Éon, who owned extensive vineyards in Burgundy. He entered the Irish Brigade and won the friendship of Louis XV, who made him a *chevalier*. Maintained a costly establishment in Paris, and moved in Court circles. Inherited the d'Éon estates and carried on a lucrative trade in wine. He was a native Irish-speaker, collected manuscripts on frequent visits to Ireland, and compiled pedigrees for expatriate Irish in France and Spain. Through his initiative the Book of Lecan, for a hundred years in the Irish College at Paris, was presented to the RIA. Lost his estates when the French Revolution broke out. Returned penniless to Ireland in 1793 and lived on bounty of relatives. Died at Drumelihy, Co. Clare, 18 November 1809.

O'GRADY, STANDISH HAYES (1832–1915), scholar. Born at Erinagh House, Castleconnell, Co. Limerick, son of Admiral Hayes O'Grady. Brought up and fostered in the Irish-speaking barony of Cloonagh. Received his formal education at Rugby School and TCD. Appointed president of the Ossianic Society in 1856 and shortly afterwards went to the USA, and worked there for thirty years as an engineer. During his student days he had been a friend of O'DONOVAN and O'CURRY, and had copied Irish manuscripts in the library of TCD. On his return from the USA he compiled a *Catalogue of Irish Manuscripts in the British Museum*. Owing to some disagreement with his publishers, the work was unfinished at O'Grady's death and was left to Robin Flower to complete. O'Grady's other principal work was *Silva Gadelica* (1892), a valuable compilation of tales from old manuscripts with translations and notes. He died in Cheshire.

O'GRADY, STANDISH JAMES (1846–1928), historian and novelist, cousin of STANDISH HAYES O'GRADY. Born at Castletown Bearhaven, Co. Cork, son of Viscount Guillamore, Church of Ireland rector there. Educated at the local school, Tipperary Grammar School, and TCD. Called to the bar, but soon turned to writing. O'CURRY's *Manners and Customs of the Ancient Irish* aroused his interest in Irish history and legend, and in 1878–1880 he published *The History of Ireland: Heroic Period*. He then wrote a series of novels based on Irish history and early mythology. *Red Hugh's Captivity* (1889) was followed by *Finn and His Companions* (1892). To these he added boys' adventure stories, *Lost on Du Corrig* (1894) and *The Chain of Gold* (1895), and further novels, *In the Wake of King James* (1896), *The Flight of the Eagle* (1897), etc. From 1900 to 1906 he edited the *All-Ireland Review* and wrote most of it

himself. He also edited the *Kilkenny Moderator*, and contributed articles on political and social questions to the *Irish Peasant* and the *New Age*. Through his writings he awakened his contemporaries to a creative sense of Ireland's epic past, and he has been called 'father of the Irish literary revival' and the Herodotus and prose Homer of his country. In 1918 he retired to the Isle of Wight for health reasons, and died there on 18 May 1928.

Ó GRIANNA, SÉAMUS (1891–1969), novelist and short-story writer, under the pen-name 'Máire'. Born in the Donegal Gaeltacht; became a teacher in 1912, and worked in Tyrone, Dublin, and Donegal. About 1919 he entered the service of the first Dáil Éireann as an organiser for the Ministry of Education. He took the Republican side after the Anglo-Irish Treaty of 1921 and was imprisoned for two years. In 1932, after the first Fianna Fáil government had taken office, he was reinstated in the civil service. His writing career began with two romantic novels, *Mo Dhá Róisín* (1921) and *Caisleán Óir* (1924). He then turned to short stories, where he was more successful. His first collection, *Cioth is Dealán* (1926), was well received, and he published a number of further volumes, mostly depicting the life and character of the people of his native Donegal. His autobiography, *Saoghal Corrach*, appeared in 1945. A good part of his official time was spent in producing translations into Irish from English and French; these were published by the Department of Education in an ill-advised attempt to provide reading material in Irish for the general public.

O'GROWNEY, FATHER EUGENE (1863–1899), leading figure in the Irish language revival movement. Born at Ballyfallon, Co. Meath, on 25 August 1863. Educated at the local national school, St Finian's diocesan seminary, Navan, and Maynooth College. As a youth his interest in Irish was aroused when he read lessons in Irish in *Young*

Ireland, a weekly published from the *Nation* office. He sought out local native speakers, and spent his holidays from Maynooth in the Gaeltacht to perfect his knowledge of the spoken language, visiting Cork, Kerry, Donegal, and Ring, but spending most time on the Aran island of Inis Meáin. He was ordained in 1889 and became curate at Ballynacargy, Co. Westmeath. He contributed articles in Irish to the *Gaelic Journal* and became editor in September 1891. His growing reputation led to his appointment as professor of Irish in Maynooth on 15 October 1891. He was in Scotland on a visit to the Gaelic-speaking areas when the Gaelic League was founded by DOUGLAS HYDE and others on 31 July 1893, but his work in the revival movement was recognised by his appointment as vice-president. That year he began a series of lessons on Irish in the *Gaelic Journal* and *Weekly Freeman*, published in book form in 1894 under the title *Simple Lessons in Irish*. Thousands of copies were sold, and for many years the lessons were regarded as the best available for learners. The strain of his duties as professor, editor, writer, and active worker in the revival told on his health, never robust, and in October 1894 he was obliged to leave Ireland for Arizona, where he hoped the dry climate would restore him. His ill-health continued and he resigned his Maynooth post on 23 June 1896. The trustees of the college granted him a pension, and he continued to contribute articles to the *Weekly Freeman* and to American papers. He died on 18 October 1899 at Los Angeles, where he was buried. Irish-Americans raised a subscription to return his body, and it was re-interred in Maynooth in 1901 with every mark of honour.

O'HALLORAN, SYLVESTER (1728–1807), surgeon and author. Born in Limerick on 31 December 1728 and studied medicine in London, Leiden, and Paris. He returned to Limerick in 1749 and practised as an ophthalmic surgeon. A treatise on glaucoma he had written in Paris was published in Limerick. He was mainly responsible for founding Limerick Infirmary. In *Insula Sacra* (1770) and *Ierne Defended* (1774) he urged preservation of Ireland's language and antiquities. Published also *A General History of Ireland* (1774). There is a contemporary description of him as 'the tall, thin doctor in his quaint French dress with his goldheaded cane, beautiful Parisian wig and cocked hat.' He first suggested the establishment of the College of Surgeons (founded 1784), and was elected an honorary member in 1786. He died in Limerick on 11 August 1807.

O'HANLON, COUNT REDMOND (died 1681), outlawed chief. His family were dispossessed of extensive estates in Ulster after the Cromwellian wars. He became leader of a band of outlaws or 'tories' about 1670 and kept the counties of Tyrone and Armagh under tribute. After many fruitless attempts to capture him, Dublin Castle put a price of £200 on his head. While hiding in the hills at Eightmilebridge, Co. Down, he was shot dead by his foster-brother, Arthur O'Hanlon, and his head was spiked over Downpatrick jail.

O'HANRAHAN, MICHAEL (1877–1916), author and revolutionary. Born in New Ross, Co. Wexford, on 17 March 1877. The family moved to Carlow and he was educated at the CBS there and at Carlow College Academy. He went to Dublin and became a freelance journalist and Irish reader at the Cló Cumann printing works. His father, a Fenian, had taken part in the 1867 Rising, and he joined the Irish Volunteers on their formation in 1913, and was also active in the Gaelic League. Later he became national quartermaster of the Volunteers and a full-time member of the headquarters staff. In the 1916 Rising he fought in Jacob's factory, was court-martialled and sentenced to death, and executed on 4 May 1916. He wrote two novels, *A Swordsman of the Brigade* (1914) and *When the Normans Came*, published posthumously in 1919.

Ó hÉANAÍ, SEOSAMH (1920–1984), traditional singer. Born in Muirgheas, Co. Galway. From his father, Pádhraic, he learned a great store of songs of the west. In 1943 he won the Gold Medal for sean-nós singing at the Oireachtas. Gael-Linn recorded many of his songs and promoted his singing career. After 1943 he worked for years as a labourer in Southampton. After unsuccessful attempts to find work in Ireland he emigrated to the USA where he became a well-paid doorman in a block of flats near Central Park, New York, a post that allowed him free time to continue his singing career. He appeared at most important folk festivals in the USA, including those at Newport and Philadelphia, made many recordings, and became well known on television. Some years before his death he was appointed to the Department of Musicology in Washington University, Seattle. In August 1982 he became the first European and the first folk-singer to be awarded the prestigious National Heritage Fellowship of the US National Endowment of the Arts. Further efforts to find employment in Ireland failed. He died in Seattle on 3 May 1984 and was buried in his native parish of Muirgheas.

O'HEGARTY, PATRICK SARSFIELD (1879–1955), public servant and writer. Born at Carrignavar, Co. Cork. Educated at North Monastery CBS, Cork. Entered the postal service in Cork. From 1902 to 1913 he served in London, was active in many Irish organisations, and edited the monthly *An tÉireannach* for the Gaelic League for a year. Transferred to Cóbh as postmaster in 1913. When the First World War broke out he was compulsorily appointed to Shrewsbury and then to Welshpool. In 1918, when the oath of allegiance became obligatory, he resigned and returned to Ireland to set up the Irish Bookshop in Dawson Street, Dublin. From 1922 to 1944 he served as secretary of the Department of Posts and Telegraphs. He was a regular contributor to the *Irish Book Lover* and *Irish Freedom*, which he edited between 1911 and 1914. He also edited a short-lived journal, the *Separatist*, which sought to heal the split caused by the Treaty and the Civil War. Editor of the *Irish World* 1918–1919. Among his publications were *John Mitchel: an Appreciation* (1917), *The Indestructible Nation* (1918), *Sinn Féin: an Illumination* (1919), *Ulster: a Brief Statement of Fact* (1919), *The Victory of Sinn Féin* (1924), and *A History of Ireland under the Union* (1952). He died in December 1955.

Ó hÉIGHEARTAIGH, SEÁN SÁIRSÉAL (1917–1967), publisher and civil servant. Born in Welshpool, Wales, son of P. S. O'HEGARTY. Educated at Scoil Bhríde, St Andrew's College, Dublin, and TCD, where he became a foundation scholar and graduated with first-class honours in science. He was auditor of An Cumann Gaelach (the Irish Society), and in 1939 arranged ÉAMON DE VALERA's first visit to TCD as Taoiseach, to attend a large meeting of the cumann. He played a leading part in the foundation of An Comhchaidreamh (the Union of University Irish Societies), Craobh na hAiséirí, a dynamic new branch of the Gaelic League, and An Club Leabhar, a book society that did much to encourage writing in Irish. On leaving university he entered the civil service, and rose rapidly to the rank of principal officer in the Department of Finance. He continued to work for the language, and was the first director of *Comhar,* the monthly magazine founded by An Comhchaidreamh in 1941. In 1945, with his wife, Bríd Ní Mhaoileoin, he founded the publishing firm of Sáirséal agus Dill. They revolutionised the publication of books in Irish, which had up till then relied almost exclusively on An Gúm, an unimaginative and highly conservative Government agency. A whole generation of writers found new hope in the encouragement and understanding they received from Sáirséal agus Dill. He carried on this work in addition to his official duties in the Department of Finance. He died suddenly on 14 June 1967 at his house in Highfield Road, Dublin.

O'HEMPSEY, DENIS (*c.* 1695–1807), harper. He was born, according to local tradition, on his father's farm at Craigmore, near Garvagh, Co. Derry. At three he lost his sight from smallpox. At twelve he began to learn to play the harp. When he was eighteen a group of local gentlemen presented him with a harp, and he travelled in Ireland and Scotland for ten years. He paid a second visit to Scotland in 1745 and played before Prince Charles Edward at Holyrood Palace. After further travel all over Ireland he was presented with a house at Magilligan, Co. Derry, by FREDERICK HERVEY, and there ended his days. In 1792 he attended the assembly of harpers in Belfast, and BUNTING speaks of the intricacy and peculiarity of his playing. In 1781, at the reputed age of eighty-six, he married a woman from Inishowen, and had one daughter. He was temperate throughout his life, drank milk and water and ate potatoes, and, according to current belief in the north of Ireland, reached the age of one hundred and twelve.

O'HICKEY, DR MICHAEL (1860–1916), professor of Irish. Born at Carrickbeg, Co. Waterford, the son of a Fenian, on 12 March 1860. Educated at Carrick-on-Suir CBS, and St John's College, Waterford. Ordained in 1884, served on the Scottish mission until 1893, and after a year in Kill parish was appointed diocesan inspector of schools. In 1896 he succeeded FR EUGENE O'GROWNEY as professor of Irish in Maynooth College. He became very active in the language revival movement, and while in Scotland contributed prose and verse in Irish to Irish newspapers and periodicals. On his return to Ireland he wrote propagandist articles for the Gaelic League, and delivered rousing addresses both at home and in England and Scotland in support of the movement. Elected vice-president of the League in 1903. He took a prominent part in the agitation to have Irish made a compulsory subject for matriculation at the NUI, and made public attacks on certain ecclesiastics, including two bishops who, as senators of the university, opposed the proposal. He described them as 'a worthless faction' and their policy as 'a squalid and foolish apostasy' and 'an act of treachery towards Ireland'. He was first reprimanded and then, in 1909, dismissed from his chair in Maynooth. The bishops considered that his conduct made him 'unfit to train ecclesiastics in habits of obedience, humility, and respect for authority'. In his defence he pleaded that he had attacked the ecclesiastics as university senators and not as clergymen, and that no question of faith or morals was involved. He appealed to Rome and went there in February 1910 to plead his case. An unfavourable verdict was given in April 1916. He returned to Ireland in July 1916 and died in his brother's house in Portlaw, Co. Waterford, on 19 November 1916.

O'HIGGINS, AMBROSE (*c.* 1720–1801), viceroy of Peru. Born near Dangan Castle, Co. Meath. He was sent to an uncle in Cádiz, a Jesuit, to be educated for the church, but found that he had no vocation and went to South America to try his fortune. After various unsuccessful commercial ventures he joined the Chilean army and rose rapidly to the rank of brigadier-general. In 1786 he became intendant of Concepción, where he entertained the French voyager Jean de La Pérouse. Appointed viceroy of Peru in 1795, he was active in the defence of the coast when war broke out between Spain and Italy in 1797. He died suddenly at Lima on 18 March 1801, leaving a natural son, BERNARDO.

O'HIGGINS, BERNARDO (1778–1842), the father of Chilean independence. Born in Chile 20 August 1778 of an Irish father, AMBROSE O'HIGGINS, and a Chilean mother. Educated in England, where he met supporters of Latin American independence, and on

297

his return to Chile in 1802 after his father's death he became an active member of the movement. A rising in 1814 under his command was defeated and O'Higgins fled to Argentina. A second attempt in 1817–1818 proved successful, and Chile's independence from Spain was proclaimed on 12 February 1818. O'Higgins became supreme director and was virtually a dictator from 1817 to 1823. He inaugurated reforms in education and land tenure and attempted to restrict bullfighting and gambling. These moves evoked strong opposition from the conservative elements, especially the landed aristocracy, and he was forced to resign in January 1823. He lived the rest of his life in Peru, where he died on 24 October 1842.

O'HIGGINS, KEVIN CHRISTOPHER (1892-1927), politician. Born at Stradbally, Co. Laois, 7 June 1892. Educated at Clongowes Wood College, Maynooth, and UCD. While still a student he joined Sinn Féin, was imprisoned for six months in 1918 for an anti-conscription speech, and while in jail was elected MP for Queen's County (Laois). He was 'on the run' in 1920, and in 1922 was elected TD for South Dublin. When Dáil Éireann was established in 1919 O'Higgins was appointed assistant minister for local government. He was a strong advocate of acceptance of the Treaty of 1921, and after the establishment of the Irish Free State in 1922 he became Minister for Economic Affairs and then Minister for Justice and External Affairs and vice-president of the Executive Council. When the Civil War broke out he took vigorous measures to restore law and order, and defended the execution of seventy-seven Republicans in 1922-1923. His father was shot dead when Republicans raided his house in February 1923. O'Higgins set up an unarmed police force, the Garda Síochána, to replace the RIC. His external policy aimed at a free and undivided Ireland within the British Commonwealth, and at the Imperial Conference of 1926 he took a leading part in re-defining Commonwealth relations on the basis of equality between members. While on his way to Mass at Booterstown on 10 July 1927 he was shot dead by unknown gunmen.

Ó hUIGINN, TADHG DALL (1550–1591), poet. Born probably in Co. Sligo, and fostered in Co. Donegal. It seems clear that he received the customary professional training in a bardic school, but where and when is unknown. His poems, of which only about forty survive, are addressed to the neighbouring lords, Maguires, O'Neills, O'Rourkes, his patron O'Connor Sligo, and William Burke, to whom he was united by 'a bond of art' in music, history, and poetry. Judged by them and the land he held at his death, his career was fairly prosperous. His poems represent the finest flowering of the bardic craft and give a vivid picture of life in the houses of the Gaelic lords. According to tradition he was murdered by six of the O'Haras, enraged by his satire describing them as thieving vagrants and lazy loons who ate all his food, but the documentary evidence for this is slender.

O'HURLEY, DERMOT (1519-1584), archbishop of Cashel. Born at Lycadoon, Co. Limerick, and educated at Louvain, where he became professor of philosophy. Subsequently he held the chair of canon law at Reims for four years. Proceeding to Rome, he was appointed archbishop of Cashel in 1581, and sailed for Ireland the following year. He escaped capture at Waterford and lay concealed for some time in a secret room at Slane Castle, Co. Meath. In 1583 he was arrested in Carrick-on-Suir and imprisoned in Dublin Castle. Examination by Lords Justices Loftus and Wallop revealed nothing, and Walsingham, secretary to Queen Elizabeth, ordered that he be put to the torture by roasting his feet in metal boots filled with oil. He denied charges of treason but refused religious conformity. As there was no evidence for conviction by civil courts, he was condemned by martial law, and hanged on 21 June 1584.

O'KEEFFE, JOHN (1747–1833), actor and playwright. Born in Abbey St, Dublin, on 24 June 1747, studied drawing under ROBERT WEST, then turned to acting and played for twelve years at Smock Alley Theatre. He married a daughter of Tottenham Heaphy, manager of a Limerick theatre; they separated in 1780. He wrote a total of sixty-eight comedies, farces, operas, and pantomimes. Blindness forced him to leave the stage in 1790 but he continued to write. His best play, *Wild Oats*, was immensely popular from its first production in 1791; a revival in London in 1976 ran for almost two years, and it was performed at the Abbey Theatre in 1977. His comic opera *Merry Sherwood* includes the famous song 'I am a Friar of Orders Grey'. He published his *Recollections* in 1826. He settled in London about 1780 and died in Southampton on 4 February 1833.

O'KELLY, DENNIS (*c.* 1720–1787), racehorse owner. Born in Ireland in poor circumstances. Went to England as a young man, and worked as a chair-man and then as a billiard and tennis marker. He then bettered his fortunes by permanent alliance with a noted courtesan, Charlotte Hayes, who afterwards became his wife. His first coup as a racehorse owner was the purchase of a share in Eclipse, then an untried horse, for 650 guineas, a very large sum in those days. At Winchester, in the Queen's Plate, when the horse won his first race, he won his famous bet, 'Eclipse first and the rest nowhere.' Not long afterwards he became sole owner of Eclipse for a further 1,000 guineas. Other famous horses that made large sums for him were Scaramouch and Gunpowder. He improved his social position by obtaining a commission in the Middlesex Militia, subsequently becoming a colonel. He bought a country house, Clay Hill, at Epsom, and later bought the famous estate of Cannons, near Edgeware, previously owned by the Duke of Chandos. Although he made large sums as a professional gamester, his will provided that his heir should forfeit £400 for every wager he made. He died at his house in Piccadilly, London, 28 December 1787.

O'KELLY, JAMES (1845–1916), war correspondent and politician. Born in Dublin; educated at TCD and the Sorbonne. Joined French Foreign Legion at eighteen. His regiment was sent to Mexico by Napoleon III in 1866 to support the Emperor Maximilian. He was made prisoner by the Mexican General Canales but escaped, returned to France, and served in the French army as a captain until the fall of Paris in 1870. He then joined the *New York Herald* and was sent to Cuba to report the Cuban revolt. He penetrated the Cuban lines to interview General Céspedes, president of the republic, and learn at first hand the reasons for the rising. Arrested by the Spaniards and condemned to be shot as a spy. Sent to Spain and saved by intervention of Castelar and ISAAC BUTT. Went to Brazil and later accompanied the emperor on tour of USA. With US troops in war against Sioux chief, Sitting Bull. Elected nationalist MP for Roscommon 1880 and served term in Kilmainham jail with PARNELL. Lost his seat to anti-Parnellite 1892, re-elected 1895, and held seat until his death. In Sudan as correspondent for London *Daily News* during Mahdi revolt. Press representative, *Irish Independent*, in House of Commons 1892–1895. Died in London, 23 December 1916. *The Mambi-land, or Adventures of a Herald Correspondent in Cuba* was published in Philadelphia in 1874.

O'KELLY, SÉAMUS (*c.* 1875–1918), author. Born at Loughrea, Co. Galway, and educated locally. Became a journalist, working first for the *Connaught Leader* and then for the *Southern Star*. In 1906 he joined the *Leinster Leader* in Naas, Co. Kildare, and spent his weekends in Dublin, where he became friendly with COLUM and GRIFFITH. His first important work, a collection of short stories under the title *By the Stream at Kilmeen*, appeared in 1906. He had several plays produced in the Abbey Theatre before moving to the *Saturday Evening Post* in 1912. *The Manchester Guardian* commissioned a series of Irish sketches, the Padna stories. A play, *Driftwood*, written for Miss Horniman, was well received in Manchester in 1915 and in London in 1916. His first novel, *The Lady of Deerpark*, appeared in 1917. For reasons of health he returned in 1915 to Naas, where his brother Michael was editor of the *Leinster Leader,* and took over the editorship when Michael was arrested in 1916. In May 1918, when Griffith was deported, he took charge of his paper, *Nationality*. British forces raided the offices in Harcourt Street, Dublin, in November 1918, and he died suddenly of a heart attack. His short story 'The Weaver's Grave' is regarded as his masterpiece. A radio adaptation won the Italia Prize in 1961 for Radio Éireann.

O'KELLY, SEÁN T. See under Ó CEALLAIGH.

O'KELLY de GALLAGH, COUNT GERALD EDWARD (1890–1968), diplomat. Born at Gurtray, Portumna, Co. Galway, on 11 March 1890. Educated at Clongowes Wood College and RUI. He travelled extensively in the Far East and in America, compiling commercial directories, served in the First World War, and was wounded. In 1919 he was sent to Switzerland by ARTHUR GRIFFITH to promote the cause of Irish independence at the League of Nations. He became Irish representative at Brussels in 1921, and first Irish minister to France in 1929. In 1935 he retired from the diplomatic service and started a wine business in France. During the Second World War he acted as special counsellor to the Irish mission in France, and negotiated the release of many Irish citizens interned during the German occupation. He returned to the diplomatic service in 1948 as chargé d'affaires in Lisbon, with the personal rank of minister. He retired again in 1955, was named as honorary counsellor to the Lisbon legation, and in 1962 was again invited by the Government to accept the post of chargé d'affaires there. He died in Lisbon, 3 January 1968, while still serving. He was a count of the Holy Roman Empire of the 1767 creation, a knight of Malta, grand officer of the Legion of Honour, and grand officer of the Order of Christ.

Ó LAOGHAIRE, FATHER PEADAR (1839–1920), priest and author. Born at Liscarrigane, near Macroom, Co. Cork. Educated at local schools and St Colman's College, Fermoy. He won a scholarship to St Patrick's seminary, Maynooth, and was ordained on 11 June 1867. He was first assigned to a parish near Mallow, and after further service at Rathcormack, Doneraile, and Rath, became parish priest at Castlelyons on 10 February 1891. He was a strong supporter of DAVITT and the Land League from its inception, and also worked hard to raise the local standard of education by founding small libraries and administering schools. His parents were native speakers of Irish, but also spoke English well, and he was bilingual from the cradle. At a prizegiving in Maynooth, ARCHBISHOP MACHALE reproached him for neglecting even to mention, in an essay on literature, that Ireland had its own Irish writers, but it was not until the foundation of the Gaelic League in 1893 that he became active on behalf of the language. He saw the need for reading-matter in Irish, especially for young people, and began in 1894 by writing *Ar nDóithín Araon*, a collection of short stories, and *Séadna*, a folk novel. He chose deliberately to use, in all his books, the speech of the people he had grown up with in west Cork, 'caint na ndaoine'. *Séadna* was followed by more short stories, religious essays, translations, and re-telling of classical mediaeval tales. Irrespective of subject-matter his style and language were the same, and the mediaeval tales were carefully edited by him for young readers. His autobiography, *Mo Sgéal Féin*, appeared in 1915. *Séadna* was the best-known and most widely read book in Irish for many years. An tAthair Peadar, as he was popularly called, was made a freeman of Dublin and Cork in 1912 in recognition of his services to the language. He was made a canon in 1906. Died at Castlelyons on 21 March 1920.

O'LEARY, JOHN (1830-1907), Fenian. Born 27 July 1830 in Tipperary, where he inherited some house property. Educated at local Erasmus Smith school and TCD. Abandoned his law studies when he found that barristers were required to take an oath of allegiance to the British crown, and, turning to medicine, attended the Queen's Colleges in Cork and Galway, but did not qualify. His strong nationalist sympathies involved him in skirmishes with the police near Clonmel, and in 1848 he spent several weeks in Clonmel jail. Later he became prominently identified with the Fenian movement, although never a sworn member, and in 1863 was appointed editor of the *Irish People*, a new Dublin weekly journal of Fenianism, with THOMAS CLARKE LUBY and CHARLES KICKHAM as his co-editors and chief contributors. An informer, Pierce Nagle, betrayed them, and O'Leary was arrested in 1865 and sentenced to twenty years' imprisonment. Released after nine years on condition of banishment from Ireland, he settled in Paris, but returned to Dublin in 1885 when the condition was removed. He occupied himself writing his reminiscences, published in 1896 under the title *Recollections of Fenians and Fenianism*. He died in Dublin, unmarried, on 16 March 1907. His portrait by JOHN B. YEATS in the National Gallery shows his fine presence and 'noble head' (W. B. YEATS), and his influence helped to turn W. B. Yeats towards historic Ireland for his themes.

O'MAHONY, EOIN (1904-1970), barrister, genealogist, lecturer, and raconteur. Born in Cork; educated at Presentation College, Cork, Clongowes Wood College, UCC, TCD, and the King's Inns. At university he distinguished himself as an orator. He was auditor and gold medallist of the Philosophical Society in Cork, and in Trinity was auditor and triple medallist of the College Historical Society and *reachtaire* of the Cumann Gaelach. As a law student he became centenary auditor and gold medallist of the Law Students' Debating Society. He practised on the Munster circuit for a while and then became interested in politics and joined Fianna Fáil in 1931. His efforts to secure election to the Dáil and Seanad were unsuccessful, as was his his attempt in 1966 to secure nomination as a presidential candidate. He was a Knight of Malta, and actively interested in the Military History Society and the Irish Georgian Society. He toured the USA and Canada to raise funds in an unsuccessful bid to save Georgian houses in Lower Fitzwilliam Street, Dublin. He was resident genealogist on the 'Meet the Clans' programme on Radio Éireann for seven years. He was founder and chief organiser of the annual gathering of the O'Mahony clan. Visiting professor at the University of South Illinois, 1966-1968, and annotated the university's large collection of Irish writings. His publications included *Catholic Organisation in Holland*, *The Pathology of Democracy*, and many contributions in prose and verse to various periodicals. He was well known in Europe, especially in Rome, and travelled extensively, calling on celebrities-in-residence in the style of the eighteenth century. He was widely and affectionately known as 'the Pope': of the various accounts of how he acquired the nickname, probably the most reliable ascribes it to a remark he made while a schoolboy at Clongowes, which was taken (mistakenly) to show an ambition to be Pope. Died in Dublin, unmarried, on 15 February 1970.

O'MAHONY, JOHN (1816-1877), Fenian. Born at Kilbenehy, Co.

Limerick. Educated at TCD. He joined the Young Irelanders and took part with SMITH O'BRIEN in the attempted rising of 1848. After the skirmish at Ballingarry, O'Mahony fled to France, and after several years of poverty joined MITCHEL in New York. He was active in associations formed by exiles to promote the cause of Irish freedom, and in 1858 he founded the Fenian Brotherhood, later known as the IRB, in association with MICHAEL DOHENY and JAMES STEPHENS. O'Mahony was the leading fugure, after Stephens, in the Fenians, and raised considerable sums of money to further their aims and became 'head centre' in the USA. After the failure of the rising in Ireland in 1867, O'Mahony dragged on a precarious existence in New York, and died there on 7 February 1877. He was buried in Glasnevin cemetery, Dublin, after a funeral followed by an immense crowd. A good classical and Irish scholar, O'Mahony published an English translation of CÉITINN's *Foras Feasa ar Éirinn* in New York in 1857.

O'MALLEY, DONOGH BRENDAN (1921–1968), engineer and politician. Born in Limerick; qualified as an engineer at UCG in 1943. Practised as a construction engineer in Limerick before being elected in 1954 to represent Limerick East in Dáil Éireann. Parliamentary secretary to the Minister for Finance 1961; Minister for Health, April 1965; Minister for Education, July 1966. He introduced free post-primary education and free school transport throughout the country. He also proposed a scheme to merge TCD and UCD into a new University of Dublin. This proposed merger aroused great controversy. O'Malley died suddenly in Limerick on 10 March 1968, before any steps could be taken towards implementing his proposal.

O'MALLEY, EARNÁN (1898–1957), writer and republican. Born at Castlebar, Co. Mayo. His family moved to Dublin when he was a boy. He was a medical student in 1916 and fought in the Easter Rising. He was wounded several times in the War of Independence. In March 1921 he was given command of the newly formed Second Southern Division of the IRA. During the Civil War he took the anti-Treaty side and became director of organisation. He took part in the fighting in the Four Courts and was captured, but escaped soon after. For a short period he was acting assistant chief of staff. He was re-arrested in Dublin, at a house in Ailesbury Road: after an hour's fighting he had been hit by twenty-one bullets, sixteen of which were later removed. He nevertheless took part in a 41-day hunger strike in 1923. His death sentence was reprieved when doctors said he would never walk again. While in prison he was elected to Dáil Éireann, but on his release he left Ireland for almost ten years. He recovered the use of his limbs, and travelled extensively. In 1927 he went to the USA to raise funds to launch the *Irish Press*, and then travelled all over North America, taking a variety of jobs, including school-teaching. He wrote articles and features for Irish and foreign journals, and broadcast on Radio Éireann and the BBC. His book *On Another Man's Wound* was published in 1936; a sequel, *The Singing Flame*, was published posthumously in 1978. In 1947 he was elected to the Irish Academy of Letters. He died at Howth, Co. Dublin, in March 1957.

O'MALLEY, GRACE (*c*. 1530–*c*. 1600). Born probably in Co. Mayo. Called Gráinne Umhaill or 'Granuaile' from her family's territories. (The popular form 'Gráinne Mhaol', with its meaning of 'bald' or 'cropped', is erroneous.) The O'Malleys were noted sea rovers, and she spent her childhood on the islands off the western coast. She was married twice, first to an O'Flaherty and then in 1582 to Richard Burke, chief of the Burkes of Mayo. She was a bold and independent leader; Sidney described her as 'a most famous feminine sea captain', and it is said that she visited

Queen Elizabeth in London and spoke to her as one queen to another. In 1586, after the death of her second husband, she was seized by Sir Richard Bingham, who accused her of plundering the Aran islands, and he prepared a gallows to execute her. She was released on a pledge from her son-in-law, Richard Burke; and when he rose against the English she fled to Ulster and stayed with O'Neill, being unable to return owing to the loss of her ships. Queen Elizabeth pardoned her and she returned to Connacht, dying there in great poverty a few years later. According to tradition, the source of most of her history, she is buried on Clare Island, in Clew Bay, Co. Mayo.

Ó MAOLCHONAIRE, FLAITHRÍ, or FLORENCE CONRY (1560–1629),

archbishop of Tuam. Born in Co. Roscommon of a family of hereditary poets and historians. Educated in Spain and the Netherlands, and became a Franciscan friar of the Strict Observance at Salamanca. In 1601, on the instructions of Pope Clement VIII, he accompanied Don Juan del Aguila on his expedition to Ireland. After the defeat of the Irish and Spanish at Kinsale in 1601 he returned to the Continent, and spent the rest of his life in exile. He was spiritual director to RED HUGH O'DONNELL, who died at Simancas in September 1602. In 1616, through his influence, Philip III founded a college at Louvain in the Spanish Netherlands, where Irish students could be trained for the church and Irish learning pursued. Pope Paul V nominated him to the archbishopric of Tuam in 1609, but he was never able to visit his see. During his long banishment he devoted himself to the study of the works of St Augustine, on which he became an international authority. He published treatises of great erudition on St Augustine and on grace, free will, original sin, and unbaptised children. His works in Irish included Sgáthán an Chrábhaidh ('Mirror of Faith') (1616), a devotional treatise translated from the Spanish, and a catechism, both published at Louvain. He died in a Franciscan convent in Madrid on 18 November 1629, and his body was transferred to the Irish College at Louvain in 1654.

O'MEARA, BARRY EDWARD

(1786–1836), surgeon to Napoleon. Born in Ireland, and joined the British army as an assistant surgeon in 1804. After serving in Sicily and Egypt he was obliged to leave the army in 1808 for having assisted at a duel, but he soon secured an appointment in the navy. He was serving in HMS *Bellerophon* when Napoleon surrendered himself on board on 14 July 1815. His personality and knowledge of Italian commended him to the ex-emperor, who asked that he accompany him to St Helena as his personal physician. Disagreements arose between SIR HUDSON LOWE, the governor, and O'Meara, who resented being asked to report Napoleon's private conversations, and culminated in the dismissal of O'Meara in 1818. On his return to England, O'Meara attached himself to the opposition and in 1822 published *Napoleon in Exile, or A Voice from St Helena*, in which he denounced Lowe's treatment of Bonaparte. The book created a sensation and quickly went into five editions. O'Meara died in London on 3 June 1836 of erysipelas, said to have been caused by catching cold at one of O'CONNELL's meetings. He was a founder-member of the Reform Club in London.

O'MEARA, ROBERT ALLEN QUAIN (1903–1974), professor of

medicine. Born at Bruff, Co. Limerick. Educated at Clongowes Wood College and TCD, where he graduated in natural science, became a research scholar in bacteriology, and qualified in medicine in 1927. Became fellow, RCPI, and Rockefeller Fellow in Bacteriology and Preventive Medicine, 1928–1931. In 1932 he joined the Wellcome research laboratories in England as a senior assistant bacteriologist. In 1938, at the request of the Medical Research Council of Ireland, he resigned from the Wellcome Foundation and returned to Dublin to study hypertoxic or virulent diphtheria, then the cause of heavy child mortality. Working at Cork Street Fever Hospital in collaboration with Dr C. J. McSweeney, he discovered a serum factor that he called the 'anti-B substance', which was extremely effective. This discovery brought about a dramatic drop in the expected mortality rate from the disease. In 1942 he became the first professor of experimental medicine at TCD, and was also professor of pathology, bacteriology, and preventive medicine 1945–1964. He became consultant pathologist to St Luke's Hospital and later director of research there. His studies of the role of fibrin in secondary cancer in humans brought him international recognition. Fellow, TCD, from 1941; senior fellow 1973. He retired from his chair in September 1974 but continued his research work in St Luke's. Died suddenly in Dublin, 5 December 1974.

O'MOORE, SIR RORY (died *c.* 1652), descended from chiefs of Laois. Inherited a castle and land at Ballina, Co. Kildare, from his father. Married into the Barnewells, a noted Catholic family of the Pale. Leading spirit in the rising of 1641, and enlisted help of OWEN ROE O'NEILL. 23 October 1641 was fixed for a general rising, including the seizure of Dublin Castle. The plot to seize the castle was betrayed, but Ulster rose as planned. When the supreme council of the Confederacy was formed, O'Moore was given command of troops in Laois and Offaly. The fortunes of war ebbed and flowed for the Confederacy for some years, but the arrival of Cromwell in August 1649 and the death of O'Neill in November signalled defeat. O'Moore was not a professional soldier, and played no great part in the campaign. His fate after the country had been subdued by Cromwell and Ireton is uncertain. He may have escaped to Scotland, but it is more likely that he died in Ireland.

O'MORPHI, MARIE-LOUISE (1736–1815), courtesan. Born in Rouen of Irish parents in 1736. In 1739 her father died and her mother, Margaret Murphy, moved to Paris, called herself Madame O'Morphi, and set up as a second-hand clothes dealer. She encouraged her five daughters in liaisons with rich Parisians. Marie-Louise was ravishingly beautiful and became the favourite model of the painter François Boucher and then his mistress. He called her Louison, and she posed for his voluptuous nudes. She attracted the notice of his patron, King Louis XV, and in 1753, aged seventeen, she became the king's mistress. After two years Madame de Pompadour, the king's favourite, arranged a marriage for Louison with an elderly army officer, but he was then posted to the Prussian frontier. A tactless remark about de Pompadour infuriated the king, who banished Louison to her husband's château in the Auvergne. Her husband was killed in battle in 1757 and in 1759 she was married to a court official. Louis XV died in 1774 and Louison's second husband died in 1790. During the Reign of Terror she was imprisoned for two years, then married a revolutionary called Dumont, twenty years her junior, who divorced her after a few years. She died in Paris on 17 January 1815 after the Bourbons were restored to the throne in the person of Louis XVIII; she had been his grandfather's mistress. She is the subject of paintings by the Irish artist Michael O'Farrell.

O'NEILL, CONN (*c.* 1484–1559), Conn Bacach (the lame). First of the O'Neills to emerge as leader of the Irish against the English in the sixteenth century. Inaugurated chief of the Tyrone O'Neills in 1519. After an invasion of his territory by the lord deputy, St Leger, in 1541, he went to England and made his submission in person to King Henry VIII, who created him Earl of Tyrone for life. This was resented by his son Shane and the majority of his clan. Their bitterness was increased by the nomination of Matthew, another son, whose legitimacy was disputed, as heir to Conn, with the title of Baron of Dungannon. Matthew was murdered by Shane's men in 1558. Conn fled for safety to the Pale, where he died.

O'NEILL, DANIEL (1920–1974), painter. Born Belfast. Served his time as an electrician, and took elementary lessons in art department of Belfast Technical School. First exhibition Mol's Gallery, Belfast, 1940. Took job on night shift so that he could paint by day. Victor Waddington, then in Dublin, guaranteed him an income so that he could paint full-time. His first one-man show in Dublin, 1946, was very successful. Later he spent several years abroad, returning in early 1960s to paint in Kerry. He showed occasionally at RHA, had a one-man show at Tooth's, London, and was represented in the Coronation exhibition of contemporary religious art and in the Boston Institute of Contemporary Art's travelling show. He was a natural expressionist, and considered by many to be the finest Irish romantic painter since JACK B. YEATS.

O'NEILL, ELIZA, LADY BECHER (1791–1872), actress. Born in Drogheda, Co. Louth. Her father was actor-manager of the local theatre, and she started her acting career there as a child. After playing for two years in Belfast she went to Dublin and soon made her name. She made a first appearance in Covent Garden, London, as Juliet on 6 October 1814. She had a great reception, and for the following five years had a career of unbroken success. A classical beauty, with a deep, clear and mellow voice, she was equally admired in comedy and tragedy. On 18 December 1819 she retired from the stage to marry William Becher, Irish MP for Mallow, Co. Cork, where he had considerable estates. He was created a baronet in 1831. She died at Mallow.

O'NEILL, FRANCIS (1849–1936), folklorist. Born at Tralibane, Co. Cork, 25 August 1849. Travelled the world as a seaman before emigrating to the USA in 1866. In 1873 he joined the Chicago police, and between 1901 and 1905 was general superintendent of the force. Throughout his tenure he sought out and employed Irish musicians, assuring them of stable jobs in the police and allowing them time to cultivate their music. He published several collections of traditional airs, among them *Music of Ireland* (1903), *Dance Music of Ireland: 1001 Gems of Irish Melody* (1907), *Irish Melodies*, and *Waifs and Strays of Gaelic Melody*, both of which appeared in the early 1920s. He told the story of his experiences collecting music in *Irish Folk Music, a Fascinating Hobby* (1910). *Irish Minstrels and Musicians* (1913) became a standard work but was a financial failure because of what he described as cultural apathy. He died in the USA.

O'NEILL, HUGH, third BARON DUNGANNON and second EARL OF TYRONE (1550-1616). Born at Dungannon. At nine he was taken by Sir Henry Sidney to his castle at Ludlow in Shropshire and brought up there, at Penshurst in Kent, and in London. Described by a contemporary, Sir John Dowdall, as 'a little rascal horse boy,' he was reared by his English patrons in 'the new religion'. His career after his return to Ireland in 1568 reflects the chaotic state of affairs. At first he remained loyal to his English connections and led a troop of horse in the queen's pay during the Desmond rebellion of 1569, but in 1588 he gave succour in Inishowen to survivors from the wreck of the Spanish Armada, and awakened in the English suspicions of his loyalty. In 1590 he was involved in the execution of Hugh Gavelock (Fettered Hugh), son of Shane O'Neill, but after a visit to London received the queen's pardon. He divorced his first wife in 1574; his second wife died in 1591, and in August of that year he eloped with Mabel Bagenal, daughter of Marshal Bagenal, who refused to give her her dowry and thus became O'Neill's implacable enemy. The marriage came under strain because, O'Neill said, 'I affected two other gentlewomen,' and Mabel left him and made public complaint against him to the Council. In the same year, 1591, he engineered the escape of RED HUGH O'DONNELL from Dublin Castle. In 1595, on the death of Turlough O'Neill, he was inaugurated as the O'Neill in traditional fashion. He was publicly proclaimed a traitor in Newry in June 1595, but in the autumn sued for peace and pardon. From subsequent events it would seem that he wanted temporary peace merely to gain time until Spanish aid should arrive. In December his wife died at Dungannon, and in the spring of 1596 he married his fourth wife, Catherine Magennis. The unrelenting enmity of Bagenal and his own ambition to regain all the hereditary powers of his family in Ulster gradually drew him to take arms against the English. In 1595 he defeated Sir John Norris in the Battle of Clontibret. As yet there was no open war, and O'Neill and other chiefs engaged the English in parleys and truces while opening secret communication with Spain. They demanded liberty of conscience, full pardon, and restoration of their titles and lands. Towards the end of 1596 an uneasy peace was arranged. In 1597, with the arrival of a new deputy, Lord Thomas Brough, hostilities broke out again and culminated in the battle of the Yellow Ford, near Armagh, in August 1598, in which the English suffered a heavy defeat, and their commander, Marshal Bagenal, was killed. O'Neill came to be spoken of as Prince of Ireland, and in great alarm the queen sent over Essex in 1599, providing him with an army of twenty thousand men and giving him almost as much power as if he had been made King of Ireland. O'Neill asked for a parley, and the two leaders met in the middle of a river near Dundalk in September 1599. They agreed on a truce until 1 May 1600, and Essex returned to England, where Elizabeth's displeasure resulted in his disgrace and execution. O'Neill, now at the summit of his power, asked in effect for autonomy, and Cecil,

the English Secretary, said, 'He means to be head and monarch of Ireland.' O'Neill made a royal progress through Ireland, taking submissions and preaching a holy war. Elizabeth then sent over Charles Blount, Lord Mountjoy, as Deputy, with Sir George Carew as president of Munster. Mountjoy proposed to ring Ulster with forts and use famine 'as the chief instrument of reducing this kingdom'. Sir Henry Dowcra persuaded Niall Garbh O'Donnell and Sir Art O'Neill to join him, and many Irish chiefs deserted O'Neill to side with Mountjoy. In September 1601 the long-awaited Spanish force arrived at Kinsale under Don Juan del Aguila. O'Neill decided to harass Leinster and the Pale in order to lure Mountjoy from the south, but the deputy would not be moved from his determination to attack the Spaniards, and he proceeded to besiege Kinsale. O'Neill arrived at Kinsale with Red Hugh O'Donnell in December 1601. The English supplies were precarious, their army had already been greatly reduced, and O'Neill's first plan was to avoid direct confrontation and wear down the enemy. The traditional view is that he was overruled by the impetuous O'Donnell and by del Aguila, who believed that the English would be no match for the combined Spanish and Irish forces. They decided to attack on 24 December 1601, but the battle ended in confusion and defeat, the Spaniards failing to sally out as arranged. Kinsale marked the end of the Gaelic order. O'Neill retreated to Ulster, and was harried there by Dowcra while he waited for further aid from Spain. In December 1602 he offered his submission, but this was rejected by Mountjoy. In March 1603 he again offered submission, which this time was accepted. Queen Elizabeth died the next day, 24 March, and O'Neill, unaware of her death, surrendered to Mountjoy at Mellifont, Co. Louth. When he learned in Dublin in April that the queen had died he wept for rage. In the years following his submission he was baited by the Dublin government, which took from him great tracts of his lands and forbade him to practise his religion. Abandoning hope, he sailed from Lough Foyle with other chiefs in September 1607 (the 'Flight of the Earls'), and settled in Rome. He was received with honour and given a Papal pension. The distinguished émigré, in Ó Faoláin's words, became 'habituated to melancholy and homelessness and the routine of idle days.' He died on 20 July 1616, and was buried with great pomp in San Pietro beside his son.

O'NEILL, JAMES (1849–1920), actor, father of Eugene O'Neill. Born in Kilkenny on 15 November 1849. Brought to America by his parents at five. After a sketchy education he went on the stage, making his first appearance in Cincinnati in 1867. After years in stock companies he obtained leading roles in New York in 1876 with the Union Square Theatre Co. In 1882 he appeared as Edmond Dantès in a stage version of *The Count of Monte Cristo*, and was so successful that it proved impossible for him to gain acceptance again in any other role; he played the part more than six thousand times. His health declined in his later years, following a motor-car accident. He died at New London, Connecticut, on 10 August 1920.

O'NEILL, JOSEPH (1878–1952), novelist and civil servant. Born in Tuam, Co. Galway, on 18 December 1878. He spent his early boyhood on the Aran Islands, where his father was stationed with the RIC. Educated from fifteen at St Jarlath's College, Tuam, and Queen's College, Galway. Studied Celtic languages under John Strachan in Manchester and comparative philology at Freiburg where OSBORN BERGIN, a fellow-student, became a close friend. Joined the Department of Education as an inspector in 1908 and rose to be secretary in 1923. With his wife, Mary Devenport O'Neill, he held a weekly salon in their Rathgar home, attended by distinguished literary figures. In 1917 he published *The Kingdom-Maker*, a verse

play. His first novel, *Wind from the North* (1934), received the Harmsworth Award of the Irish Academy of Letters and he was elected a member of the Academy in 1936. His second novel, *Land Under England* (1935), was a best-seller. He published three more novels, retired in 1944, and died in Stillorgan, Co. Dublin, on 6 May 1952.

O'NEILL, MÁIRE. See under ALLGOOD, MOLLY.

O'NEILL, OWEN ROE (*c.* 1590–1649), general, nephew of HUGH O'NEILL. Entered the Spanish military service about 1610. Served in the Netherlands with great distinction, and won particular renown for his defence of Arras against the French in 1640. In 1642 he decided to return to Ireland to help his fellow-Ulstermen in their rising against English domination. He arrived at Lough Swilly in July 1642 and was at once chosen as their general by the Ulstermen. He maintained that his position was that of a loyal follower of King Charles I, and in November 1642 he visited Kilkenny, where the General Assembly, styling itself 'the Confederate Catholics of Ireland', had established itself, and swore the oath of confederacy. In 1643 negotiations for peace were opened between the Confederates and Ormond, the king's deputy. Archbishop Giovanni Baptista Rinuccini arrived as papal legate in October 1645 and found in O'Neill a strong supporter of his policy of pushing the claims of the Catholic Church to the utmost. O'Neill inflicted a heavy defeat on the Scots parliamentarians under Monro in the battle of Benburb, Co. Tyrone, on 5 June 1646. Rinuccini left Ireland in February 1649, having lost control of the Supreme Council of the Confederacy. Cromwell landed at Ringsend, Dublin, in August of that year, and began the swift, terrible and decisive campaign that reduced Ireland to the status of a conquered colony. O'Neill died on 6 November 1649 at Cloughoughter Castle, Co. Cavan, on his way south to join Ormond and his royalist army. There is a tradition that he was poisoned by enemy agents, but there is no evidence to support it. He had shown exceptional military skill in keeping an army together in the chaotic conditions of the time, and Benburb was the only victory of consequence achieved by the Irish in the course of the war.

O'NEILL, SIR PHELIM (*c.* 1604–1653), military leader. Entered as a student at Lincoln's Inn. Appears to have embarked on an extravagant way of life, as he had mortgaged his estates heavily before 1641. Elected member for Dungannon in Irish parliament of 1641 and took leading part in rising of that year. Chosen as commander-in-chief of the Irish forces in the north, and issued forged commission from King Charles I. Superseded by OWEN ROE O'NEILL. After the death of Owen Roe, Sir Phelim expected to be restored to his former command. He was disappointed in this, but continued to fight against the parliamentarians until 1652. The following year his hiding-place in Co. Tyrone was betrayed by a kinsman. He was executed as a traitor on 10 March 1653.

Ó NÉILL, SÉAMUS (1910–1981), professor and writer. Born in Co. Down and educated at QUB. For over forty years he was professor of history at Carysfort College of Education, Dublin, and lectured widely in universities in the USA and Canada. His novel *Tonn Tuile* (1947) was a best-seller. He also wrote short stories, poetry and plays. *Iníon Rí Dhún Sobhairce* was produced at the Galway Taibhdhearc in 1953 with SIOBHÁN MCKENNA in a leading role. He died in a Dublin hospital on 2 June 1981.

O'NEILL, SHANE (1530–1567), 'Seán an Díomais' (Shane the Proud), chieftain. Born in Ulster, eldest son of CONN, first Earl of Tyrone. Became chief of the O'Neills in 1559. Queen Elizabeth withdrew her support and recognised Brian O'Neill, son of Conn's illegitimate son

Matthew. Shane was summoned to London in 1562 and persuaded the queen to recognise his rights and titles. Determined to remove all threats to his power he destroyed the Scottish settlements of the McDonnells in Antrim, although he supported Mary, Queen of Scots. He invaded the Pale and burned Armagh. He defeated the McDonnells at Ballycastle, taking SORLEY BOY MCDONNELL prisoner. Later he was defeated by Hugh Dubh O'Donnell at Lough Swilly in 1567. He sought refuge in Cushendun with the McDonnells, who murdered him on 2 June 1567.

O'NOLAN, BRIAN (1911–1966), author under the names Flann O'Brien and Myles na gCopaleen. Born in Strabane, Co. Tyrone, 5 October 1911. Graduated in Celtic languages from UCD in 1932. As a student he wrote comic verse in Old Irish for *Cothrom Féinne,* a college magazine. On graduation he joined the civil service, and laboured in the Department of Local Government until his retirement, in 1953, on the grounds of ill-health. His first book, *At Swim-Two-Birds,* was published in 1939; a comedy-fantasy, it has been described as 'a novel about a man who is writing a novel about a man who is writing a novel.' *An Béal Bocht,* a satire on aspects of 'Irishry', and his only book in Irish, appeared in 1941. About this time he began his column 'Cruiskeen Lawn' in the *Irish Times* under the nom-de-plume Myles na gCopaleen, and for over twenty years he captivated readers with his love and mastery of language and satiric humour. *The Hard Life* (1961), 'an exegesis of squalor', was dedicated to Graham Greene, 'whose own forms of gloom I admire.' His next book, *The Dalkey Archive* (1964), was dramatised by Hugh Leonard as *When the Saints Go Cycling In* for the 1965 Dublin Theatre Festival. *The Third Policeman,* written in 1940, was published posthumously in 1967 and confirmed his reputation as a master of comic invention. He also wrote two plays, *Faustus Kelly,* produced in the Abbey

Theatre in 1943, and *Thirst*. He died in Dublin on 1 April 1966.

Ó NUALLÁIN, CIARÁN (1910–1983), editor and writer. Born in Strabane, Co. Tyrone, on 2 February 1910, elder brother of BRIAN O'NOLAN, and educated at Synge St CBS, Blackrock College, and UCD. He worked as a sub-editor on the *Irish Independent* for some years, then on St Patrick's Day 1943, with Proinsias Mac an Bheatha, he founded the newspaper *Inniu*, published monthly for two years and then weekly until its demise in 1984, and edited it for twenty-five years. He published a memoir of his brother's early years, *Óige an Deartháir* (1973), a novel, *Oíche i nGleann na nGealt* (1939), and a collection of essays, *Amaidí* (1951). He died in Dublin on 23 February 1983.

O'RAHILLY, ALFRED (1884–1969), university professor and administrator. Born in October 1884 at Listowel, Co. Kerry. Educated at Blackrock College, Dublin, and RUI. Entered Stonyhurst College in 1908, intending to become a Jesuit, but found that the order did not suit his dynamic and highly individualist temperament, and left after taking his doctorate in philosophy. In 1914 he joined the staff of UCC as assistant in mathematics, and two years later was appointed to the chair of mathematical physics. In 1916 he joined Sinn Féin, and later was elected to Cork City Council, where he proposed TOMÁS MACCURTAIN and then TERENCE MACSWINEY as Lord Mayors. Imprisoned on Spike Island from January to June 1921 by the British authorities. Adviser to the Irish side on constitutional questions during the Treaty negotiations; supported the Treaty, and was elected TD for Cork City in 1923, but never spoke in the Dáil, and resigned his seat after a year, preferring to devote himself to his college duties. Registrar 1921. The new government made him their chief representative at an international conference at Geneva; he acted as arbitrator in many industrial disputes, and was a member of the banking commission. He visited Harvard to study social and political theory, and then persuaded UCC to found a lectureship in sociology, which he himself filled without salary. As director of the college library he reorganised and expanded it from 50,000 to 500,000 volumes. He established the Cork University Press, and launched a programme of adult education. He became president, UCC, in 1943, and retired in October 1954 to a house put at his disposal in the grounds of his old school, Blackrock. He was ordained priest on 18 December 1955 by ARCHBISHOP MCQUAID, and devoted the rest of his life to scriptural studies. After ordination he was made a knight of St Gregory and a monsignor. Besides devotional and scriptural works his main publications were a large book on *Money* and a study of *Electromagnetics* (1948). For the latter he was awarded a doctorate in science, and in 1939 the NUI conferred a doctorate in literature on him for his general published work. Died in Dublin on 2 August 1969.

O'RAHILLY, THOMAS FRANCIS (1883–1953), Celtic scholar. Born in Listowel, Co. Kerry. He began his career as a clerk in the Four Courts in Dublin, one of a group that included EOIN MACNEILL. One of the first students of the School of Irish Learning, established in 1903. Graduated from RUI, 1905. Soon became a leading authority on Irish dialects and on mediaeval and modern Irish. In 1912 he founded and edited the magazine *Gadelica*. Professor of Irish, TCD, 1919. In 1929 he went to UCC to take up a specially created post as research professor of Gaelic languages. Became research professor at UCD 1935. First director, School of Celtic Studies, DIAS, 1941. He resigned in 1947. In 1946 he published his monumental work on *Early Irish History and Mythology*. Among his other works are *Irish Dialects, Past and Present* (1932) and *The Two Saint Patricks* (1942). Between 1916 and 1927 he published a series of anthologies of Irish verse. Awarded honorary D.Litt by NUI

1928 and Litt.D. by DU 1948. In 1953 he became honorary professor of Irish language at Dublin University. Died in Dublin in November 1953.

Ó RAIFEARTAIGH, TARLACH (1905–1984), educationist. Born at Carrickmore, Co. Tyrone, and educated at St Patrick's College, Armagh, and UCD. He became professor of history at St Patrick's Training College, Dublin, then joined the Department of Education as inspector of secondary schools, rising to be secretary in 1956. On retiring he became chairman of the Higher Education Authority. Distinctions included honorary doctorates from NUI and DU, a papal knighthood, membership RIA and Legion of Honour. He died on 1 January 1984, survived by his wife, Nancy, three sons and three daughters.

Ó RATHAILLE, AODHAGÁN (1670–1726), poet. Born in the Sliabh Luachra district of Co. Kerry, near Killarney. Little is known about his life; he was probably educated at a bardic school, and was well versed in the genealogy of the great Gaelic families of Munster. He lived and died in great poverty, wandering through Munster among the houses of the last of the chiefs. He came to manhood as the Jacobite cause was defeated at the Boyne, Aughrim, and Limerick, and in stately elegies he lamented the decay of the old Gaelic order. He saw the new planters as upstarts and boors, and satirised their greed and ignorance. His lyrics speak of Ireland as a beautiful woman awaiting the return of her true lover from beyond the sea, and these 'aislingí' or visions are among the finest poems in the language. Pride of race speaks from many of his verses, as in his last poem, written on his death-bed: *Cabhair ní ghoirfead go gcuirtear mé i gcruinn-chomhrainn* ('I shall not cry for help until I am placed in a closed coffin'). He died near his birthplace, and is buried in Muckross Abbey.

O'REILLY, EDWARD (*c.* 1770–1829), lexicographer. Born in Co.

Cavan. Settled in Dublin around 1790. Used material gathered by WILLIAM HALIDAY, together with his own, to compile a dictionary of Irish. With little encouragement, he had the work printed by subscription in Dublin in 1817 as *Irish-English Dictionary*, prefixed with a 'concise introduction to Irish grammar'. In 1818 he was appointed assistant secretary to the Iberno-Celtic Society, established in Dublin that year. The society's principal aim was to preserve the remnants of Irish literature and to encourage its advancement. It published his *Dictionary of Irish Writers* in 1820. In 1824 he was awarded a medal by the RIA for an essay on the Brehon Laws, and a similar medal in 1829 for his discussion of the authenticity of the poems of 'Ossian' (Oisín) in Macpherson's 'translations'. He prepared catalogues of Irish-language manuscripts in Dublin libraries, and was employed in connection with Irish nomenclature for the maps of the Ordnance Survey of Ireland. Died in Dublin in August 1829.

O'REILLY, JOHN BOYLE (1844–1890), Fenian and writer. Born at Dowth Castle, near Drogheda, where his father was master of the national school that formed part of the Netterville Institute, founded by Viscount Netterville. Apprenticed as a printer to the *Drogheda Argus* at eleven at a wage of half-a-crown (12½ pence) a week; later he became a reporter on the *Guardian* in Preston, Lancashire. He joined the Fenians and came to Dublin in 1863 to enlist in the 10th Hussars, so that he could recruit Irishmen for the Fenians. He was betrayed by a fellow-soldier in 1866, tried, and sentenced to death. His sentence was commuted to life imprisonment the same day. He spent almost a year in solitary confinement in Millbank prison. He was then sent to Dartmoor, recaptured after escaping, and transported to Australia in 1867 on board the *Hougomont*. With the help of Father Patrick McCabe, a Catholic priest at the convict settlement near Fremantle, where O'Reilly was put working in a road gang, he succeeded in escaping on a New Bedford whaler, the *Gazelle,* in February 1869, and landed in Philadelphia in November. He settled in Boston, where he joined the *Boston Pilot,* an old-established weekly newspaper catering for the interests of Irish-American Catholics. In 1872 he married Mary Murphy, originally from Charlestown, Co. Mayo, in Boston. He made a name as a lecturer and writer. His *Songs, Legends and Ballads* (1878) went into eight editions. He became joint proprietor of the *Pilot* with Archbishop Williams of Boston in 1876, and was also editor from early in the 1870s until his death. His best-known work is a novel, *The Moondyne* (1880), based on his Australian experiences, which went into twelve editions. He also published a volume of poems, *Statues in the Block* (1881). Notre Dame University honoured him with an LL.D. that year. In 1880 he was selected to present an address of welcome to PARNELL in New York. Regular contributors to the *Pilot* under his editorship included T. W. ROLLESTON, DOUGLAS HYDE, LADY WILDE, KATHARINE TYNAN, and W. B. YEATS. He was noted for his liberal views, and in his paper and elsewhere he opposed anti-semitism and prejudice against blacks. He was invited to speak at Ottawa on St Patrick's Day 1885 but the British government refused him permission to visit Canada, although the Canadian government had raised no objection. He died at his summer cottage in Hull, Boston Harbour, in August 1890, from an accidental overdose of sleeping-tablets, and was buried in Holyhood cemetery, Brookline, Massachussets. He was survived by his wife and four daughters.

Ó RIADA, SEÁN (1931–1971), musician. Born in Cork on 1 August 1931. Educated at Adare CBS, Co. Limerick, and UCC, where he studied classics and music. Joined Radio Éireann as assistant director of music in 1952, but soon resigned to study in Paris and Italy. On returning to Ireland he became director of music for the Abbey Theatre, then in temporary exile in the Queen's Theatre.

His name became known all over Ireland when he wrote the music for the documentary film *Mise Éire,* covering Ireland's struggle for political freedom, which was made in 1959 for Gael-Linn by George Morrison. He revealed new depths in the air of 'Róisín Dubh', a song of lamentation and pride, and awakened a strong interest in Ireland's musical heritage. At the opening of the 1961 Dublin Theatre Festival his Ceoltóirí Chualann, a new type of band, won nationwide popularity for their restoration of life and nobility to traditional song and dance tunes. He became Cork Corporation Lecturer in music at UCC, and in 1964 went to live at Cúil Aodha in the West Cork Gaeltacht. Besides many broadcasts and recordings he wrote the music for the film version of *The Playboy of the Western World* (1962). He wrote a simple Mass in the idiom of traditional Irish music for Cúil Aodha parish church; a second setting was commissioned in 1970 by Glenstal Abbey. His other compositions include 'Hercules Dux Ferrariae', Hölderlin songs, the Olynthiac overture, piano concertos, and 'Vertical Man', art music recorded by Claddagh Records. He died in a London hospital on 3 October 1971.

Ó RÍORDÁIN, SEÁN (1916–1977), poet. Born in Ballyvourney, Co. Cork, 3 December 1916. Attended local national school, where he learned, he said, 'Caoineadh Airt Uí Laoghaire', the catechism, and 'Twinkle, twinkle, little star'. When he was fifteen the family moved near to Cork city, and he attended North Monastery CBS. Obtained post with Cork City Council; resigned owing to ill-health in late 1965. Published three books of poetry, *Eireaball Spideoige* (1952), *Brosna* (1964), and *Línte Liombó* (1971), which established him as one of the finest poets in modern Irish. With Rev. S. S. Ó Conghaile he published *Rí na nUile* (1967), translations of ninth to twelfth-century religious poetry. For some years he wrote a column in Irish in the *Irish Times,* a reflection of his Rabelaisian and impish conversation, in which he 'examined the conscience of the country'. In his later years he was a part-time staff member of UCG. Received honorary doctorate from NUI. Died at Cork, 21 February 1977.

Ó RÍORDÁIN, SEÁN P. (1905–1957), archaeologist. Born in Cork, started work as an apprentice in Cork dockyard, and qualified as a teacher by night study. While teaching he again studied at night to take his B.A. degree in 1928. He won a travelling studentship from NUI in 1931 and spent two years in Britain and the Continent studying excavation techniques and museum material in leading centres. Joined the National Museum antiquities division. Became professor of archaeology UCC in 1936. He spent eighteen years on research at Lough Gur, Co. Limerick, excavating Stone Age monuments and Early Christian sites, and introduced modern excavating techniques to Ireland. Published *Antiquities of the Irish Countryside* (1942), *Tara, the Monument on the Hill* (1954), and *Newgrange and the Bend of the Boyne* (1964), published after his death by co-author Glyn Daniel. He died in a Dublin hospital on 11 April 1957.

O'RIORDAN, CONAL HOLMES O'CONNELL (1874–1948), writer. Born in Dublin on 29 April 1874. Educated at Clongowes Wood College. A spinal injury suffered during a riding accident prevented him from obtaining a commission in the British army so he went on stage and began writing plays and novels. In 1909 he became managing director of the Abbey Theatre; he revived Synge's *Playboy of the Western World*, despite general opposition. In 1914 he led a YMCA Rest Hut group to the Front. After the war he wrote novels, many of them historical and with a strong theatrical quality. Among his works were his first novel, *In the Green Park* (1894), *The House of the Strange Woman* (1895), and a series, *Soldier Born* (1927), *Soldier of Waterloo* (1928), *Soldier's Wife* (1935), and *Soldier's*

End (1938). His plays include *The Piper* (1908), *An Imaginary Conversation* (1909), and *Time* (1909), all of which were performed at the Abbey. Made a fellow of the Royal Society of Literature, and served as a council member of PEN. He died on 18 June 1948. His earlier books were published under the nom-de-plume 'Norreys Connell'.

ORPEN, SIR WILLIAM (1878–1931), painter. Born at Stillorgan, Co. Dublin, 27 November 1878. Showing early talent for drawing, he entered the Metropolitan School of Art, Dublin, at eleven, and the Slade School in London at seventeen. When he began to exhibit, his success was immediate; he received many commissions for portraits, and was elected as associate of the RA in 1910. He exhibited annually at the RHA, and was elected RHA in 1908. He taught at the Metropolitan School of Art for five or six years before the First World War, and had considerable influence on contemporary Irish painters. He also ran a school in London with Augustus John for a time. From 1917 to 1919 he was in France as an official war artist, and executed a great number of paintings and drawings. He presented most of them to the British nation and they are now in the Imperial War Museum. He then attended the Peace Conference at Versailles and painted the signing of the treaty. He was made a KBE in 1918 and elected RA in 1921. He was in great demand as a fashionable portrait painter from then on, and was probably the most successful artist of his day. He wrote two autobiographical books, *An Onlooker in France 1917–1919* (1921) and *Stories of Old Ireland and Myself* (1924). He died in London, 29 September 1931.

ORR, WILLIAM (1766–1797), United Irishman. Born at Farranshane, Co. Antrim, of a respectable Presbyterian family, and owned a large farm and a bleach-green. Joined the United Irishmen, and advocated moderate views at meetings in Carrickfergus. In 1796 he was arrested on a charge of administering a treasonable oath to two soldiers. He was defended by CURRAN and denied the charge, but was found guilty and hanged at Carrickfergus on 14 October 1797. The execution aroused great public indignation as he was popularly thought to have been innocent, and 'Remember Orr' became a watchword for many years afterwards.

OSBORNE, WALTER FREDERICK (1859–1903), painter. Born 18 June 1859 at 5 Castlewood Avenue, Rathmines, Dublin, which was his home all his life. Educated at Rathmines School and the RHA. Won the Taylor Scholarship in 1881 and 1882, which enabled him to study under Verlat in Antwerp for two years; then devoted himself to painting, in oil and watercolour, the life of the Irish and English fields and towns, spending his summers in rural England. His reputation grew steadily, and in 1886 he was made RHA, receiving many commissions for portraits. He also exhibited at the RA. He died of pneumonia at his home in Dublin on 24 April 1903 and was buried in Mount Jerome cemetery. He was unmarried, and left substantial savings. The National Gallery of Ireland has some fine examples of his work. He taught at the RHA for three years before his death and had a great influence on young artists who studied under him.

O'SHANNON, CATHAL (1889-1969), trade unionist and journalist. Born in Randalstown, Co. Antrim. When he was six months old the family moved to Derry, and he was educated at St Columb's College. His first job was as a clerk in the Heysham Steamship Co. in Belfast. He joined the Gaelic League, met SEÁN MAC DIARMADA, and was sworn in as a member of the IRB. In 1913, at the request of JAMES CONNOLLY, he joined the staff of the Belfast office of the Transport and General Workers' Union. About this time he began to write for *The Peasant, Sinn Féin,* and other fugitive nationalist papers, and also for *An Claidheamh Soluis,* the Gaelic League organ. He mobilised at Coalisland, Co. Tyrone, on Easter Saturday 1916 with one hundred Volunteers but, without definite orders from Dublin, they dispersed. The following week he was arrested in Belfast, interned in Frongoch in Wales, and then transferred to Reading jail. On being released in the general amnesty of 1917 he became editor of the *Voice of Labour.* In 1920 he addressed meetings all over England, urging Irish independence, was arrested in London and imprisoned in Mountjoy jail, Dublin, but was released after a hunger strike of seventeen days. He then campaigned both as a Volunteer and as a trade union officer until the Treaty of 1921. In 1922 he was elected to the Dáil for Louth–Meath, and took a leading part in efforts by Labour members to mediate between the Republican and Free State sides in the Civil War. He continued to work as a trade union official, and in 1941 became secretary to the Irish Trade Union Congress, and then to the Congress of Irish Unions. On the establishment of the Labour Court in 1946 he was appointed as one of the workers' representatives, and served until his retirement in 1969. Died in Dublin on 4 October 1969.

O'SHEA, KATHARINE (KITTY) (1845–1921), mistress and later wife of CHARLES STEWART PARNELL. Born 30 January 1845 at Bradwell, Essex, daughter of Sir John Page Wood. Married CAPTAIN W. H. O'SHEA at Brighton, 24 January 1867. In 1875 she became companion to her wealthy widowed aunt, Mrs Benjamin Wood, then eighty-three. 'Aunt Ben' gave her a house at Eltham, Kent, close to her own, and a generous allowance. Captain O'Shea took rooms in London in 1878 and visited Eltham only occasionally. Hearing stories about Parnell from her husband and the O'GORMAN MAHON, she went to the House of Commons in July 1880 and asked to see him. Instant mutual attraction soon developed into passion, she became his mistress, and bore three children by him between 1882 and 1884. According to contemporary accounts she was not a beautiful woman, being at best striking or handsome, but had a vivacious personality, full of life and merriment. It is difficult to believe that O'Shea was as ignorant of the affair as he later testified in court. For whatever reasons—political ambition, or expectations from 'Aunt Ben'—he took no action until late in 1889, when he petitioned for divorce, naming Parnell as co-respondent. A decree nisi was given in November 1890. Parnell married Katharine at Steyning, near Brighton, on 25 June 1891. His health shattered, his career ruined, he died in Brighton on 6 October following. Katharine had recurring periods of mental breakdown, but survived until 5 February 1921, dying at 39 East Ham Road, Littlehampton, Sussex. There is no record that she ever visited Ireland.

O'SHEA, CAPTAIN WILLIAM HENRY (1840-1905), politician and adventurer. Born in Dublin, son of a wealthy solicitor. Educated at St Mary's College, Oscott, and TCD. His father bought him a commission in the 18th Hussars, a fashionable regiment. Married Katharine Wood, 24 January 1867. As his father had refused to pay his extravagant bills any longer, he sold his commission to buy a partnership in his uncle's bank in Madrid. Settled in Madrid after marriage, but soon quarrelled with his uncle and returned with his wife to England. Started a stud farm in Hertfordshire but went bankrupt. Financial support from his wife's Aunt 'Ben' kept them going. He became manager of a sulphur mine in Spain and stayed there for eighteen months, but this also failed. By this time he had ceased to live with his wife except for occasional visits. In 1880 he turned to politics, joined the Irish Party, and was elected MP for Clare 1880. Involved in the negotiations with Gladstone that led to the 'Kilmainham treaty'. Stood for Liverpool in the Liberal interest in general election 1885 but defeated.

Almost immediately PARNELL nominated him for a by-election in Galway. BIGGAR and T. M. HEALY opposed O'Shea strongly, and with reason, as he had neither voted nor sat with the Irish Party in the House of Commons. Parnell replied that rejection of O'Shea would be a blow to his own power and would imperil home rule. O'Shea was returned with a big majority. He resigned 1886 and in 1889 filed petition for divorce from his wife for adultery with Parnell. Decree nisi granted, November 1890. O'Shea then dropped out of public life. Died at Hove, 22 April 1905.

Ó SIOCHFHRADHA, PÁDRAIG (1883-1964), 'An Seabhach', author and teacher. Born in Dingle, Co. Kerry, on 10 March 1883. Became an active organiser for the Irish Volunteers in 1913. Imprisoned three times for his republican activities. Between 1904 and 1920 he was a teacher and organiser for the Gaelic League in Munster, and remained a life-long worker in the language movement. He held posts in the civil service from 1920 to 1932, including that of principal editor of An Gúm, the government publishing agency. In 1932 he became director of the Educational Company of Ireland and of the Talbot Press. Under the pen-name An Seabhach (the hawk) he published many volumes in Irish, including stories, plays, and new versions of old texts. Member of the Seanad 1946-1954. Two of his books, *Jimín Mháire Thaidhg* and *An Baile Seo 'Gainne*, were popular, even with schoolchildren, for their gentle humour. Died in Dublin on 11 November 1964.

Ó SÍOTHCHÁIN, FATHER MÍCHEÁL (1871-1948), assistant archbishop of Sydney. Born in Waterford. When he was ten his family moved to Dungarvan, where Irish was still spoken by the older people. Ordained at Maynooth in 1895; continued his studies at Oxford, where he took his MA in 1897, and at Bonn, where he received a Ph.D. in 1900. Appointed professor of classics at Maynooth, and became president in 1919. He founded Ring College in the Waterford Gaeltacht in 1906 with FATHER DE HINDEBERG and others. Their aim was to provide instruction entirely through Irish for a school year or a summer holiday term, so that the children would become fluent speakers. The college still continues successfully. In 1922 Father Ó Síothcháin was made assistant archbishop of Sydney, Australia. He published a number of books, the most important being *Seanchaint na nDéise* (1906), a study of the Irish of the Waterford Gaeltacht. He died in Sydney.

Ó SÚILLEABHÁIN, AMHLAOIBH

(1780-1838), diarist. Born 1 May 1780 in Killarney, Co. Kerry. When he was nine his father, a hedge schoolmaster, moved east in search of employment and settled near Callan, Co. Kilkenny. Amhlaoibh became a schoolmaster himself in Callan, which then had a population of about 5,600, the majority living in destitution in one-roomed mud hovels. He taught mathematics to a high standard, English, geography, and probably some Irish, as well as nature lore. Some time before 1824 he went into business as a linen-draper and also dealt in meal. The business thrived and he travelled to Clonmel, Waterford and Dublin to buy stock for the shop. He sowed crops, kept pigs, and was one of the solid men of the town. About 1831 he gave up his school. He collected the Catholic 'rent', spoke at one of O'CONNELL's monster meetings, and was a good friend to the poor and defenceless. His diary, for which he himself composed the name *Cín Lae,* runs from January 1827 to July 1835. It reveals a many-sided man: seanchaí, writer, collector of manuscripts, nature-lover. He was fond of company and games and well versed in Gaelic literature. In a simple direct prose he describes local customs and events, a thousand young men and women dancing on a low hill, 100,000 at a meeting, with 20,000 horsemen. He also wrote some romantic tales, sketches and poetry, of little value.

His large and good collection of ancient and modern Irish manuscripts and printed books was sold after his death. He died in Callan in November 1838. *Cinnlae Amhlaoibh Uí Shúilleabháin* was edited by Professor de Bhaldraithe and published 1970, also by Father Mícheál Mac Craith for the Irish Texts Society (four volumes, 1928-1931).

Ó SÚILLEABHÁIN, DIARMUID

(1932-1985), writer. Born in Béarra, Co. Cork, and trained as a national teacher in St Patrick's College, Dublin. Taught for over thirty years at Gorey CBS, Co. Wexford. He wrote novels, poetry, and a play. His novels, *Caoin Tú Féin* (1967) and *An Uain Bheo* (1968), won Oireachtas prizes. He also received awards from the Irish Academy of Letters and the Irish-American Cultural Institute. He was a member of the Ard-Chomhairle of Sinn Féin, contributed to *An Phoblacht,* and was jailed for three months in 1977 on conviction of inciting people to join the IRA at a public meeting in New Ross, Co. Wexford. Member, Irish Academy of Letters. Retired from teaching due to ill-health in 1982 and died in a Dublin hospital on 5 June 1985.

Ó SÚILLEABHÁIN, EOGHAN RUA

(1748-1784), poet. Born at Meentogues, seven miles east of Killarney, Co. Kerry. Educated at a bardic school at Faha, where poetry, music and the classics were taught. At eighteen he opened his own school at Gneeveguilla nearby, but after an 'incident nothing to his credit' (Ó Duinnín) he took to the road as *spailpín* or wandering farm-labourer. Returning to Faha the following Christmas he found a poetical contest in full swing between the married and the unmarried men, after a hurling match won by the married. Eoghan took the part of the younger men in a vigorous satire, buoyant with rhythm, that crushed the opposition. The next ten years were spent wandering over Munster, working as a hired labourer and sometimes as a schoolmaster. In his early thirties he became tutor to a Nagle family near Fermoy, but when discovered in misconduct with Mrs Nagle he had to fly for his life, pursued by her husband, who carried a gun. He took refuge in Fermoy barracks and joined the British navy (by his own account he was pressed into it). His ship joined the fleet under Vice-Admiral Rodney and sailed for the West Indies, where the English met and defeated the French off Dominica in April 1782. Eoghan wrote an ode in English, 'Rodney's Glory', to celebrate the victory. It was brought to the admiral, who sent for him and offered promotion, but the poet wanted only his freedom, which was refused. He returned to England where he served in the army. To secure his discharge he blistered his shins with spearwort; the army doctors could not cure the evil-smelling sores. Arrived home, he opened a school at Knocknagree Cross, but it lasted only a year. In June 1784 he was wounded in a drunken brawl with the servants of a Colonel Cronin, of Park, near Killarney, whom he had satirised. He died of fever a few days later in a mountain hut and was buried in Muckross Abbey. He was known as Eoghan an Bhéil Bhinn (Eoghan of the Sweet Mouth) from the richness and melody of his lyrics, which, though circulating only in manuscript, were known and recited throughout Munster or sung to well-known airs. His collected poems were not published in book form until 1901; the volume, edited by FATHER PÁDRAIG Ó DUINNÍN, includes nineteen 'aislingí' or visions as well as poems dealing with his own life as a wandering labourer or schoolmaster, satires, and poems in praise of women.

Ó SÚILLEABHÁIN, MUIRIS
(1904–1950), author. Born on 19 February 1904 on the Great Blasket Island, Co. Kerry. His mother died when he was six months old, and his father sent him to Dingle on the mainland. He stayed there until he was seven, attending the local school and speaking only English. His father then took him back to the island, where he continued his schooling and grew up speaking Irish with the other islanders. In 1927 he went to Dublin to join the Garda Síochána, and when his training was completed he was stationed at Indreabhán in the Connemara Gaeltacht. Here he wrote his autobiography, *Fiche Bliain ag Fás* (1933). An English translation was published in London the same year under the title *Twenty Years A-Growing*. 'I wrote it', he said, 'for the entertainment and laughter of the old women of the Blasket island... to send my voice into their ears again.' It had an instant success, and was translated into many languages. He then left the Guards, built himself a house and married and settled in Connemara. He was drowned while swimming on 25 June 1950.

O'SULLIVAN, DÓNAL JOSEPH
(1893–1973), scholar. Born in Liverpool of Irish parents. Joined the civil service in London as a first-division clerk, and was transferred to Dublin at his own request. Called to the bar in 1922, and appointed clerk to the Senate in 1925; when it was abolished by DE VALERA'S government in 1936 he retired and devoted himself to research. He had always been interested in traditional music, and between 1927 and 1939 he edited the *Bunting Collection of Irish Folk Music and Song* for the *Journal* of the Irish Folk Song Society. His chief work in this field, the monumental *Carolan: Life and Times of an Irish Harper*, appeared in 1958. *Songs of the Irish* (1960) included his own translations into English of many of the songs. *Irish Folk Music, Song and Dance* (1961) was commissioned by the Department of External Affairs for their series on Irish life and culture. In 1940 he published *The Irish Free State and Its Senate*, a useful source-book for students of Irish constitutional development. Lecturer on international affairs in TCD 1949–1965, and subsequently research lecturer in Irish folk music. Director of studies in Irish folk music at UCD 1951–1962. Died in Dublin on 15 April 1973.

O'SULLIVAN, SEÁN (1906–1964), painter. Born in Dublin. Educated at Synge Street CBS and Metropolitan School of Art, Dublin. He won a scholarship to England and France, and worked under Spencer Pryse and Zarraga at the Central School of Art in London and in the free schools. He then went to study at the Académie Julien in Paris. He returned to work in Ireland and at twenty-one was elected to the RHA, the youngest artist to be so honoured. He became a full member in 1931. He had a remarkable feeling for personality, and executed many portraits of distinguished Irish people, including DE VALERA, HYDE, YEATS, and JOYCE. Other notable works were a set of the Stations of the Cross in oils for a convent in Portarlington, and a mural for the hospital of the Medical Missionaries in Drogheda. He designed three commemorative postage stamps (the ROWAN HAMILTON, IGNATIUS RICE and DOUGLAS HYDE issues). He also painted a number of fine landscapes. Died in Nenagh district hospital, 4 April 1964.

O'SULLIVAN, SEAMUS, pen-name of James Sullivan Starkey (1879–1958), poet and bibliophile. Born 17 July 1879 in Dublin, son of a pharmacist at 80 Rathmines Road. Appeared as the Blind Man in W. B. YEATS's play *On Baile Strand*, on the opening night of the Abbey Theatre, 27 December 1904. The following year he published a volume of poetry, *The Twilight People*; this was succeeded by *Verses Sacred and Profane* (1908), *The Earth Lover* (1909), *Collected Poems* (1912), *Personal Talk* (1936), and *Collected Poems* (1940). A supporter of the Sinn Féin movement up to the time of the Anglo-Irish Treaty, he was a friend of ARTHUR GRIFFITH, OLIVER ST JOHN GOGARTY, JAMES JOYCE, and others, who frequented the old Martello Tower at Sandycove. In 1923 he founded the *Dublin Magazine*, which he edited until 1958. Almost every Irish writer of merit was a contributor. President of Dublin PEN for several years. In 1939 Dublin University conferred on him an honorary Litt.D. In 1957 the Irish Academy of Letters presented him with its Lady Gregory Medal. Among his prose works were *Mud and Purple* (1917), *Common Adventures* (1926), and *The Rose and Bottle* (1946). Died in Dublin on 24 March 1958.

O'SULLIVAN BEARE, DÓNALL (1560–1618), chief of the O'Sullivans of Beare, Co. Cork. Took a leading part in organising revolt against English rule. After the defeat of the Irish and Spanish forces at Kinsale in 1601, and the fall of his last stronghold, Dunboy Castle, in 1602, he hid in the glens of Cork and Kerry, hoping for further aid from Spain. When word came towards the end of the year that Phillip III had abandoned all thoughts of a further expedition, he resolved to seek refuge in Ulster. He set out from Glengariff on 31 December 1602 with four hundred fighting men and six hundred women, children, and servants. On their journey north in the depths of winter they were continually harassed by the English and by local chiefs. Only thirty-five survived to reach sanctuary with O'Rourke of Breffni in Leitrim Castle: the rest had either been killed or fallen behind from exhaustion, exposure, sickness, or wounds. He hoped to receive a pardon on the accession of King James I in 1603, but when this did not come he sailed for Spain with his wife and children. Phillip III conferred on him a knighthood of the Order of St Iago, a pension, and the title of Earl of Bearhaven. He was killed at Madrid by John Bathe, an Anglo-Irish refugee.

O'TOOLE, SAINT LAURENCE (c. 1130–1180), archbishop of Dublin. Born in Leinster of noble blood. While still young he was sent to be educated at the monastery of Glendalough, became a member of the community, and at twenty-five was made abbot. In 1162 the clergy and people of Dublin chose him as their first archbishop. The citizens of Dublin appointed him to treat with Strongbow when the Normans besieged the city in 1170, and after it had fallen to Strongbow he took a leading part in assembling an army to re-take it. The Irish, under Roderic O'Connor, were routed by Strongbow in 1171. Laurence perceived that the Normans were more than a match for the Irish, and when later that year King Henry II arrived with a large force and armed with papal authority, he submitted to the king. In 1175 he went to a council at Windsor, as ambassador from Roderic O'Connor to the king. In 1179 he was summoned by Pope Alexander III to the Third Lateran Council in Rome. In return for permission to travel through England, Henry exacted from him a promise to do nothing 'prejudicial to the King or his Kingdom'. Laurence was made papal legate, and given bulls guaranteeing papal protection for all the rights of his church. He went to England again in 1180 to make peace between O'Connor and the king, but Henry resented the tenor of the papal bulls and closed the ports to Laurence to prevent his return to Ireland. When Henry left for Normandy, Laurence followed him, hoping to obtain permission to return to Ireland. Before the king would agree to see him he died at the Augustinian canon's house at Eu on 14 November 1180. He was canonised in 1226, with 14 November as his feast-day.

Ó TUAIRISC, EOGHAN (1919–1982), soldier, schoolteacher, and writer. Born in Ballinasloe, Co. Galway, on 3 April 1919, son of a shoemaker, and educated at St Joseph's College. He joined the army in 1939 and after the Second World War trained as a teacher in St Patrick's College, Dublin. He travelled Ireland in a horse-drawn caravan with his artist wife, Una McDonnell, writing while she painted. In 1961 he left teaching to become a full-time writer. He won Oireachtas prizes in poetry, fiction, and drama, the Arts Council prize for a historical tragedy, and an Abbey Theatre prize for a Christmas pantomime in Irish. He published two novels in English and collections of verse in Irish and English. Died 24 August 1982, survived by his second wife, Rita Kelly, also a writer.

OTWAY, CAESAR (1780–1842), writer. Born in Co. Tipperary; educated at TCD. Took holy orders, and served as a curate in a country parish for seventeen years, then appointed assistant chaplain at Leeson Street Magdalen Chapel in Dublin. In 1826, with J. H. Singer, he founded the *Christian Examiner,* the first Irish religious magazine associated with the established church, and was the first to publish stories by WILLIAM CARLETON. He co-operated with GEORGE PETRIE in the first issue of the *Dublin Penny Journal.* His *Sketches in Ireland* (1827) and *A Tour in Connaught* (1839) give interesting contemporary accounts of Irish life. Ill-health curtailed his literary activities. Died in Dublin on 16 March 1842.

OWENSON, ROBERT (1744–1812), actor. Born in the barony of Tyrawley, Co. Mayo, the son of poor people called MacOwen, which he later changed to Owenson. Educated at a hedge school, and after working for a short time as steward to a neighbouring landowner he obtained an introduction to Garrick in 1771 through OLIVER GOLDSMITH, and went on the stage. He had a commanding figure and sang well and was already popular when he made his London début at Covent Garden in 1774. On Goldsmith's recommendation he was admitted a member of the 'Club'. In 1774 he married one Jane Mill; their first child was Sydney, later the celebrated LADY MORGAN. He appeared on the Dublin stage in 1776 and became part-proprietor of the Crow Street Theatre. In 1785, after a quarrel with his manager, he opened the Fishamble Street Theatre, but returned to Crow Street within the year. Attempts to conduct theatres in Kilkenny, Derry and Sligo were failures, and in 1798 he retired from the stage. He died in Dublin at the house of his son-in-law, Sir Arthur Clarke, at the end of May 1812, and was buried in Irishtown, then outside the city.

P

PAKENHAM, EDWARD ARTHUR HENRY, sixth EARL OF LONGFORD (1902-1961), theatrical producer and dramatist. Born 29 December 1902. When his father was killed at Gallipoli in 1915 he succeeded him as Earl of Longford and Baron Longford, peerage of Ireland, and Baron Silchester, peerage of the UK. Educated at Eton and Christ Church, Oxford. When the two-year-old Gate Theatre, founded by MÍCHEÁL MAC LIAMMÓIR and HILTON EDWARDS, ran into financial difficulties in 1931, Lord Longford offered to buy the outstanding shares. The arrangement lasted until 1936 when, following disagreements, the company was divided into two, Gate Company and Longford Players. Each company had six months in the theatre and six months touring. The Longford Players visited small towns as well as provincial cities and stimulated an extensive amateur drama movement in rural Ireland. Their repertoire included several original plays by Lord Longford and his translations from French and Greek drama. His most successful play was *Yahoo* (1933), based on the life of SWIFT. Other plays were *The Melians* (1931), *Carmilla* (1932), *Ascendancy* (1935), *Armlet of Jade* (1936), and *The Vineyard* (1943). From the beginning of his association, he contributed generously to the funds of the Gate and Longford companies from his private means. An Irish-speaker, he also translated a number of Irish poems, among them BRIAN MERRIMAN's *Midnight Court*. Member of Seanad Éireann on DE VALERA's nomination 1946-1948. MRIA 1952, and member of the Irish Academy of Letters. Received honorary D.Litt. from DU and NUI. In 1956 when Dublin City Council condemned the Gate Theatre building, he collected for a restoration fund in the streets of Dublin and at the theatre door each night; the building was restored largely at his own expense. Died in Dublin, 4 February 1961.

PALLES, CHRISTOPHER (1831-1920), lord chief baron of the exchequer in Ireland. Born in Dublin, 25 December 1831. Educated at Clongowes Wood College and TCD. Called to the bar in 1853, he quickly established himself as a leading junior, and on taking silk in 1865 was briefed in almost every important case. He became solicitor-general in 1872, attorney-general later that year, and also in 1872 made an unsuccessful bid for MP in the Liberal interest for Derry. Lord chief baron 1874, and held the office until 1916. The Exchequer, later merged in the High Court, became famous under Palles for the decisions handed down by him and for the lucidity and learning with which he expounded his judgements. He was also prominent in educational affairs as a commissioner for both national and intermediate education, and in his eightieth year virtually drafted the NUI constitution. He was a devout Catholic. Died at Dundrum, Co. Dublin, 14 February 1920.

PALMER, LADY ELEANOR (*c.* 1720-1818), beauty. Born in Co. Dublin, daughter of William Ambrose, a wealthy brewer. A leading beauty at the court of the viceroy, Lord Chesterfield, who called her 'the only dangerous papist in Ireland'. When she appeared at a court ball with an orange lily at her breast, Chesterfield improvised the lines:

'Say, lovely Tory, where's the jest
Of wearing Orange in the breast,

When that same breast uncovered shows

The whiteness of the rebel rose.'

In 1752 she married Roger Palmer of Castle Lacken, Co. Mayo, and Kenure Park, Co. Dublin. He was created baronet in 1777 and predeceased her. Though left a rich widow, she lived in a small lodging in Henry Street, Dublin. She died on 10 February 1818, aged ninety-eight, in full possession of her faculties.

PARKE, THOMAS HEAZLE (1857–1893), surgeon and traveller. Born 27 November 1857 at Clogher House, Drumsna, Co. Leitrim. Educated at RCSI. After a short time as dispensary doctor at Ballybay, Co. Monaghan, he joined the British army as a surgeon. He was posted to Egypt, accompanied the desert column sent to rescue Gordon, and saw active service in several engagements. In 1887 he volunteered for the expedition being organised by H. M. Stanley to relieve Emin Pasha, governor of the Equatorial Province of Africa. The expedition travelled more than 1,000 miles (1,600 km) up the Congo river, and then penetrated deep into the vast Congo forest, accomplishing its mission and reaching the eastern coast of Africa. Stanley said that without Parke the expedition would have been a failure. On his return to England in May 1890, Parke was honoured by the army and by many learned societies. He received the gold medals of the British Medical Association and of the Royal Geographical Societies of London and of Antwerp. He joined the staff of the Royal Victoria Hospital, Netley. His health had been undermined by the hardships he had suffered, and he died suddenly in Argyll. Buried in the family grave at Kilmessan, Co. Leitrim. Commemorated by a statue on Leinster Lawn, Dublin.

PARNELL, ANNA CATHERINE (1852–1911), political organiser, and sister of CHARLES STEWART PARNELL. Born at Avondale, Co. Wicklow. Active supporter of agitation led by her brother and founded Ladies' Land League in 1881, organised branches, and distributed £60,000 in relief. Charles Stewart distrusted his sister's understanding of the political situation. When the Ladies' Land League asked for funds to discharge heavy debts, he gave the money on condition that the league be disbanded. This was done in 1882, and Anna never forgave him. She wrote about him in *The Tale of a Great Sham*, which was not published until 1987. After his death in 1891 she seems to have become deranged. She moved from place to place, dressed strangely, and changed her name several times. She was drowned in Ilfracombe on 20 September 1911 after entering a rough sea despite warnings.

PARNELL, CHARLES STEWART (1846–1891), political leader. Born at Avondale, Co. Wicklow, on 27 June 1846. His father was a Protestant landowner of nationalist sympathies and his mother a daughter of Admiral Stewart of the US navy. He was educated at Yeovil and Chipping Norton, and later entered Magdalene College, Cambridge, but left without graduating. MP for Meath 1875, and joined the Home Rule party led by ISAAC BUTT. He soon gained a mastery of parliamentary procedure and made full use of the technique of obstruction in the House of Commons that had been pioneered by JOSEPH BIGGAR. His powers of leadership soon showed themselves, and after the death of Butt in 1879 he became the dominant figure in the Irish party. That year MICHAEL DAVITT founded the National Land League and invited Parnell to become the first president. In the land war of 1879–1882, which eventually led to the abolition of landlordism and the creation of a system of peasant proprietorship, the tenant farmers of Ireland defied their landlords for the first time. A new word was added to the English language when Captain Charles Boycott of Lough Mask House, Co. Mayo, was ostracised for opposition to the League. The agitation erupted at times into violence and outrage, the ordinary law ceased to function over large parts of the country and, like Sinn Féin in later years, the Land League set up its own land courts. The British government passed a new Coercion Act; Parnell and other leaders were arrested in October 1881, and the League was suppressed. Despite this show of strength, British political leaders had realised that the landlord system could no longer be defended. Gladstone came to terms with Parnell in March 1882 with the so-called 'Kilmainham treaty', under which the prisoners were released, the agitation was discontinued, and the policy of land reform initiated with the Land Act of 1881 was continued. On the release of Parnell, Lord Frederick Cavendish was immediately sent to Ireland as chief secretary to inaugurate the new era of peaceful progress, but on 6 May 1882, the day of his arrival, he and the under-secretary, Burke, were murdered in the Phoenix Park by members of a secret assassination society, the Invincibles. The British government reacted with a new Coercion Act. In the House of Commons, Parnell condemned the murders; despite this setback Gladstone's attitude towards him and the Irish question remained fundamentally unchanged.

Parnell saw the destruction of landlordism as merely a step towards the overthrow of English rule in Ireland. The Land League was replaced by the National League, and he set about strengthening the Irish party in preparation for the general election of 1885. This election was a triumph for him; his party, pledged to fight for legislative independence by constitutional means, won every seat outside eastern Ulster and Dublin University. Gladstone, who had won a victory for the Liberals in England, was convinced by Parnell's success of the justice of the home rule cause; he recognised it as 'the fixed desire of a nation', and gave it unwavering support for the rest of his career. But his

Home Rule Bill of 1886 aroused fierce antagonism from the Conservatives, who saw in it a betrayal of empire and of the loyalist and Protestant elements in Ireland. The extreme wings of the Liberal party—the aristocratic landowners and the radicals—defected on the issue, and the Bill was defeated. Gladstone lost office in the ensuing general election of 1886, the first to be fought in Britain on the home rule question, and in the next twenty years the Liberals held office for only one period of three years, 1892–1895. Nevertheless the year 1886 marked a turning-point in British relations with Ireland, as for the first time a major political party had committed itself to granting at least a measure of self-government to Ireland.

In 1887 the *Times* of London published a series of articles, 'Parnellism and Crime', in which the home rule leaders were accused of complicity in murder and outrage during the land war. The articles relied largely on letters supplied by RICHARD PIGOTT, a renegade nationalist, and in particular on an alleged facsimile of a letter from Parnell condoning the murder of undersecretary Burke. The articles caused a public furore, and a special commission of three High Court judges was appointed to enquire into the matter. Pigott broke down under the relentless cross-examination of SIR CHARLES RUSSELL and fled to Madrid, where he committed suicide. The commission found that the letters had been forged, and their verdict, delivered in February 1890, turned British public opinion, hitherto hostile, in favour of Parnell. He was now at the summit of his career, the uncrowned king of Ireland; but tragedy lay less than a year ahead. In November 1890, CAPTAIN WILLIAM O'SHEA, a former member of the Home Rule party, obtained a divorce from his wife, KATHARINE, naming Parnell as the co-respondent. The effect on Parnell's career was shattering. British nonconformists had rallied to Gladstone's crusade for home rule for Ireland as a great moral issue, and their continued support was vital to the Liberal party and thus to the cause of home rule. They took the view that Parnell was no longer a fit person to lead the Irish party, and Gladstone was forced to demand that he should retire, at least temporarily. In this the Liberal leader did not make any moral judgment on Parnell's conduct, but recognised the facts of the situation for his party. After this the standing committee of the Irish hierarchy adopted the nonconformist view. Parnell, a proud and passionate man beneath his aloof exterior, refused to step down, and this produced a bitter split in the party that he had welded into so powerful a political force. The majority went against him but he continued to fight for the leadership until his sudden death in Brighton on 6 October 1891, five months after he had married Kitty O'Shea. The great political party he had led fell apart, and the story of the ten years after his death is a record of futile divisions in an aftermath of corrosive bitterness. The tragic fall of Parnell was due to his insistence that his own personal conduct was in no way involved in the political struggle. In fact O'Shea was a man of inferior talents and doubtful character, who had been aware of Parnell's ten-year liaison with his wife almost since it began and had turned a blind eye in the hope of securing political advancement by his complaisance. He and his wife had virtually parted when she met Parnell. When at length O'Shea turned against Parnell and began the proceedings for divorce, Parnell refused to defend the action for fear that the evidence of O'Shea's collusion would influence the court to deny a decree. He wanted above all to make Kitty O'Shea his legal wife; and they had three children. These aspects of the affair meant a great deal to him and they clouded his political judgment, which until then had been marked by a cold and ruthless realism. Parnell was one of the greatest leaders Ireland ever had, and though his life seemed to end in failure his achievements remained. The reform of the land code, due to the combination of his leadership and the organising genius of DAVITT, brought about the greatest social revolution in modern Ireland. He made the British people conscious of his country's claim to self-government, and won to his side the large and influential liberal element that followed Gladstone.

PARNELL, SIR JOHN (1744–1801), chancellor of Irish exchequer, great-grandfather of C. S. PARNELL. Born 25 December 1744, probably at Rathleague, Queen's Co. (Laois). Studied at Lincoln's Inn, never called to Irish or English bar but elected bencher of King's Inns, Dublin, 11 February 1786. Appointed commissioner of customs and excise, December 1780. Succeeded his father as baronet April 1782. MP for Bangor 1761–1768, for Inistioge 1776–1783. Elected for Queen's Co. 1783–1800 and also for Maryborough (Portlaoise); chose to sit for Queen's Co. Represented Queen's Co. in UK parliament 1801. Chancellor of Irish exchequer 22 September 1785. Appointed member of British Privy Council, October 1786. Opposed concessions to Catholics 1793. Opposed the Union, and removed from office of chancellor, January 1799. Received £7,500 for loss of Maryborough representation on passing of Act of Union. Died suddenly in Clifford St, London, 5 December 1801. Buried in St George's Church, Hanover Square.

PARNELL, REV. THOMAS (1679–1718), poet. Born in Dublin; educated at TCD. Taking holy orders in 1700, he became archdeacon of Clogher in 1706. In 1716 he was presented with the vicarate of Finglas, Dublin, and resigned his archdeaconry. Friendship with SWIFT led to membership of the Scriblerus Club with Pope, Berkeley, and other leading writers. Visiting London frequently, Parnell contributed to Addison and STEELE's *Spectator*, helped Pope with his translation of the *Iliad*, and wrote an introductory essay. The death of his wife in 1711 aggravated his tendency to melancholia, and after living in retirement in Ireland from 1715 to 1718 he took ill after a visit to his old friends in London, and died at Chester in October 1718. His poems were published by Pope in 1721; 'The Hermit' and 'The Night-Piece on Death' still hold their place in anthologies.

PARSONS, SIR CHARLES ALGERNON (1854-1931), engineer and inventor. Born in London on 13 June 1854, youngest son of the third Earl of Rosse, and brought up at the family seat, Birr Castle, Co. Offaly. Educated at home by tutors then at TCD and Cambridge. Apprenticed to Sir William Armstrong at Elswick works, Newcastle upon Tyne. In 1884 he invented the high-speed turbine and in 1889 founded his own firm to develop his inventions, which included turbine generating plant for power stations and steam turbines for ships. He demonstrated his turbine on an experimental vessel, the *Turbinia*, at the naval review at Spithead in 1897 for Queen Victoria's diamond jubilee. The *Turbinia* steamed through the fleet at thirty-four knots, and no naval vessel could catch it. The Admiralty then ordered his turbine; the mercantile marine adopted it, and the Cunard Line's *Mauretania* held the Blue Riband of the Atlantic for nearly twenty-five years. He also produced glass for optical purposes, and many notable astronomical instruments. He received numerous honours and distinctions including FRS 1898, CB 1904, KCB 1911, Order of Merit 1927, the Faraday and Kelvin medals of the Institution of Electrical Engineers, and honorary degrees from eight universities, including TCD, Oxford, and Cambridge. He died at Kingston, Jamaica, on 11 February 1931.

PARSONS, WILLIAM, third EARL OF ROSSE (1800-1867), astronomer and constructor of the largest telescope then made. Born at York, England, 17 June 1800. Educated at TCD and Magdalen College, Oxford. MP for King's County (Offaly) 1831, resigning his seat in 1834 to devote all his time to scientific studies. He had begun experiments some years previously on his father's estate at Birr Castle towards improving the reflecting telescope. The pioneer in their construction, William Herschel, had not published his methods of casting and grinding specula or mirrors, and Parsons had to devise his own. The work was done by workmen from the district, and the tools, furnaces and ovens were constructed on the estate. His speculum metal was composed of four atoms (126.4 parts) of copper and one atom (30.9 parts) of tin, described as a brilliant alloy. He communicated the results of his experiments to Brewster's *Edinburgh Journal of Science* in 1828 and 1830. In 1839-1840 he successfully cast and mounted a solid three-foot (0.9 m) speculum. In 1842 he began a speculum of 6 feet (1.83 m) diameter, and in 1845 this great reflector was mounted and ready for work. The tube in which it was mounted was 58 feet (17.5 m) long and 7 feet (2 m) in diameter, slung in chains between two piers of masonry 50 feet (15 m) high. The cost of the entire machine was estimated at £20,000. Many visiting astronomers used this great telescope, the largest then made, from 1848 to 1878, and discovered many previously unknown features in nebulae, especially the similarity of annular and planetary nebulae. Rosse himself discovered the remarkable spiral configuration in many of the nebulae. He contributed papers to the Royal Society in 1850 and 1861 describing his methods of construction and giving some of the observations made by him with the telescope. He was honoured by many learned societies, was president of the Royal Society 1849-1854, and received a royal medal in 1851. The Imperial Academy of St Petersburg (Leningrad) admitted him to membership in 1853. He became chancellor of Dublin University in 1862. Succeeded his father as Earl of Rosse in 1841, elected to the House of Lords in 1845 as one of the representative peers for Ireland. A good landlord, he spent nearly all his Irish revenues on the relief of distress in the Great Famine of 1846–1847. Died at Monkstown, Co. Dublin, 31 October 1867. The remains of the great telescope are still in the grounds of Birr Castle; the mirror is in the Science Museum in London.

PATRICK, SAINT (died *c.* 490), apostle of Ireland. Fifth-century Ireland is a lost world, virtually closed both to historians and archaeologists, and what little is known about the life and work of Patrick comes from his own writings in Latin, now accepted as authentic, and from brief references in annals written about two centuries later. In his *Confessions*, an apologia written in his old age in rough Latin, Patrick says that he was a native of Roman Britain, the son of Calpurnius, a deacon who lived in the village of Bannaven Taberniae. (Scholars disagree about its location, ascribing it variously to Cumberland, the Severn valley, and the island of Anglesey.) He was captured by Irish raiders at the age of sixteen and sold into bondage to herd sheep and pigs on the slopes of Slemish, Co. Antrim, for a chief named Milchu. His thoughts turned to God, and he spent many hours in solitary prayer. After six years he escaped and made his way home. He relates how in a vision he saw a man who came from Ireland with letters, and how he heard the voices of the Irish imploring him to return. He does not say where he studied for the church, but tradition makes him a disciple of St Germanus of Auxerre, and he may also have spent some time at Tours and at the monastic island settlement on Lérins off the coast of Provence. According to the *Chronicle of Prosper of Aquitaine*, a contemporary source, Pope Celestine sent one Palladius in the year 431 to the Irish believing in Christ, to be their bishop. This fragment of evidence suggests that there were Christians in Ireland at that time in numbers sufficient to warrant the appointment of a bishop. According to tradition, Palladius' mission had little success, and he was forced to leave within a few

months, dying in Scotland about 431. The uncertainty surrounding the date of Patrick's arrival has occasioned the theory of two Patricks, whose careers were confused by later chroniclers, but this remains speculation. It seems reasonably certain that Patrick's mission spanned some thirty years, in the latter half of the fifth century; that it was very successful; and that Ireland, unlike any other country in western Europe, was converted to Christianity without the shedding of martyrs' blood. In his own words, the saint 'baptised thousands, ordained clerics everywhere, and rejoiced to see the flock of the Lord in Ireland growing splendidly.' It is probable that most of his missionary work was carried out in the northern half of the country. The date and place of his death are uncertain; tradition says that he died at Saul, near Downpatrick, Co. Down, on 17 March, the day now celebrated as the national festival.

The legends that accumulated around the saint's life go far beyond the meagre details related above, which include all that is known about him with any certainty. The story of his explaining the mystery of the Holy Trinity by showing a three-leaved shamrock (clover) to the king at Tara; the lighting of the Paschal fire on the hill of Slane; the destruction of the idol, *Crom Crúach*; the banishing of snakes from Ireland—these are all apocryphal accretions of later dates. So also is the identification of Saul as the site of his first church. Croagh Patrick, where he is said to have kept his Lenten fast and now a place of pilgrimage, has been claimed, with Slemish, as the scene of his captivity as a boy. His original Celtic name is said to have been Succat, Patricius being his Latin designation. Other writings attributed to Patrick are his *Epistle to Coroticus*, accepted as authentic, and a fine hymn in Irish, the *Breastplate of St Patrick*. The *Epistle*, written in Latin, beseeches Coroticus, a British chief, to free some Irish Christians whom he had taken captive. Whatever about the lack of knowledge of life in Ireland in the fifth century, the author of the *Confessions* and the *Epistle* emerges as a real personality; the vividness of his narrative and the undoubted success of his mission account for the central place he came to occupy in Irish tradition, and the hold he exercised over the imagination of the chroniclers and storytellers of later centuries.

PATTERSON, ROBERT (1802–1872), naturalist. Born Belfast, 18 April 1802. Educated RBAI. Apprenticed to his father, a merchant. Devoted his leisure to the study of natural history. With others founded Belfast Natural History Society in 1821, and was president for many years. Published *Zoology for Schools* (1846–1848), which had a wide circulation. Elected FRS and MRIA. Took active part in the public life of Belfast. Died there, 14 February 1872, at his home, College Square.

PEARCE, SIR EDWARD LOVETT (1699–1733), architect. Born probably in Co. Meath. Became cornet in Colonel Morris's dragoons at sixteen or seventeen. Visited Italy soon after and made drawings of buildings in Venice and other cities. Returned to Ireland and was elected MP for Ratoath 1727. Succeeded THOMAS BURGH as surveyor-general in 1730. Knighted 1732, and received freedom of Dublin 1733. His great work was the Houses of Parliament (now Bank of Ireland), College Green, Dublin. The first stone was laid in 1729; he did not live to see it finished. With its magnificent south colonnade to College Green it is one of the finest public buildings in Ireland. He also designed the obelisk at Stillorgan, and a theatre in Aungier Street. Died, of an abscess, at his house at Stillorgan, 7 December 1733.

PEARSE, MARGARET (1878–1968), teacher, sister of PATRICK PEARSE and WILLIAM PEARSE. Born in Great Brunswick (Pearse) Street, Dublin. Educated at the Holy Faith Convent, Glasnevin. Trained as a teacher. Helped her brothers in the establishment of St Enda's College, Rathfarnham, and was one of the group that carried it on for seventeen years after the execution of her brothers in 1916. In 1926 she made a lecture tour of the USA to raise funds for the school. TD for Co. Dublin 1933, and held the seat until 1937. In 1938 she was elected to Seanad Éireann and remained a member until her death. Died in Dublin, 7 November 1968, and was accorded a state funeral. She bequeathed St Enda's and the land with it to the nation to be maintained as a memorial to her brothers, and to their endeavours for the freedom of Ireland and for the Irish language.

PEARSE, PATRICK HENRY (1879–1916), educationist, writer, and revolutionary. Born 10 November 1879 at 27 Great Brunswick Street (Pearse Street). His father, a monumental sculptor, was an Englishman; his mother was a native of Co. Meath. Educated at a private school in Wentworth Place, Westland Row CBS, and RUI. Called to the bar. From his schooldays he was deeply interested in Irish language and culture. He joined the Gaelic League in 1895, became editor of its official organ, *An Claidheamh Soluis*, and lectured in Irish at University College. To advance his ideal of a free and Gaelic Ireland, he founded a bilingual school, Scoil Éanna (St Enda's), at Cullenswood House, Ranelagh, in September 1908. The school prospered and in 1910 moved to more extensive premises at the 'Hermitage', Rathfarnham. He built a cottage at Rosmuc in the Connemara Gaeltacht, and spent his summers there. In 1915 he joined the IRB, was co-opted to the Supreme Council, and elected to the Provisional Committee of the newly formed Irish Volunteers. When the remains of O'DONOVAN ROSSA were brought from America in 1915 for burial in the Fenian plot in Glasnevin cemetery, he delivered a historic oration at the graveside, ending with the words, 'Ireland unfree shall never be at peace.' In the 1916 Rising he was commander-in-chief of the forces of the Irish republic, president of the Provisional Government, and one of the signatories of the Proclamation of the Republic. After a week's fighting he agreed to an unconditional surrender 'to prevent further slaughter of Dublin citizens'. He was court-martialled, condemned to death, and executed in Kilmainham jail on 3 May 1916. He wrote stories, essays and poetry in Irish and English, a play, *The Singer*, and *The Story of a Success*, an account of Scoil Éanna.

PEARSE, WILLIAM (1881–1916), one of the sixteen leaders executed after the 1916 Rising. Born 15 November 1881 at 27 Great Brunswick Street (Pearse Street). Educated at Westland Row CBS; on leaving school he worked with his father, a monumental sculptor, and studied at the Dublin School of Art and in Paris. He became an Irish-speaker, and when his brother PATRICK founded Scoil Éanna in 1908 he taught art and drawing there; later, when Patrick became deeply involved with the Irish Volunteers, William was virtually headmaster. He joined the Volunteers on their formation in 1913, and in the 1916 Rising was a captain on the Headquarters Staff in the GPO. He was court-martialled, sentenced to death, and executed in Kilmainham jail on 4 May 1916.

PETRIE, GEORGE (1790–1866), antiquary, painter and musician. Born in Dublin, 1 January 1790. Educated at Samuel Whyte's School in Grafton Street and the art school of the Dublin Society. He contributed hundreds of illustrations to guide-books to Ireland, travelling all over the country and making a particular study of the ruins at Clonmacnoise, Cong, Killarney, and the Aran Islands. He exhibited many landscapes at the RHA. Elected academician 1828, and president 1857. Joining CAESAR OTWAY on the *Dublin Penny Journal* in 1832, he wrote numerous antiquarian articles, and was himself editor of the *Irish Penny Journal* during its single year's existence in 1842. He was attached to the Ordnance Survey from 1833 to 1839, when the government wound it up on grounds of expense, and did valuable work to preserve local history. His *Essay on the Antiquities of Tara* (1839) won him a gold medal from the RIA and he also received their gold medal for his famous *Essay on the Round Towers of Ireland*, published in 1845 with many additional studies under the title *Ecclesiastical Architecture of Ireland*. Many theories had previously been advanced about the purpose of the round towers, which were variously described as Phoenician fire-temples, minarets, phallic symbols, and tombs; in his closely argued and well-documented essay Petrie showed that they were Christian ecclesiastical buildings, erected for use as belfries, watch-towers, and keeps, and his findings have won general acceptance. Petrie was also a musician and on his travels collected a large number of airs, which he published in 1855 as *The Ancient Music of Ireland*. His sole interest lay in preserving as much as he could of Ireland's past culture, and he seemed devoid of any personal ambitions. His illustrations constitute a pictorial record of buildings of all periods, drawn with meticulous accuracy, and have never been surpassed. He received a civil list pension of £300 a year in 1849. His house in Great Charles Street was a social centre for the scholars and antiquaries of his day. He died there on 17 January 1866 and is buried in Mount Jerome cemetery.

PHILLIPS, MOLESWORTH (1755–1832), companion of Captain Cook. Born at Swords, Co. Dublin, on 15 August 1755. In 1776 he accepted a commission as second lieutenant in the Royal Marines, and was selected to accompany the explorer and navigator Captain James Cook on what proved to be his last voyage. He sailed with Cook from Plymouth for the Pacific in July 1776. When they landed at Hawaii with an escort of marines on 14 February 1779 to recover a stolen boat, they were attacked by the natives, who killed Cook and all but two of the marines. Phillips, though wounded, swam to a boat and escaped. On return to England he was promoted captain, and in January 1782 married a daughter of Dr Charles Burney. Through this association he met Samuel Johnson, Mrs Thrale, and others of the Burney circle. From 1796 to 1799 he lived on an estate he had inherited in Ireland at Ballycotton, Co. Cork. Promoted brevet lieutenant-colonel in 1798. Died of cholera at his home in Lambeth, London, 11 September 1832.

PIGOTT, RICHARD (c. 1828-1889), journalist and forger. Born in Co. Meath, probably at Ratoath. After working as an errand-boy in the *Nation* office, he found a post in Belfast as a clerk in the office of the *Ulsterman*, a nationalist newspaper. In 1858 the proprietor, Denis Holland, transferred it to Dublin and changed the name to the *Irishman*. In 1865 he presented the paper to Pigott. The following year Pigott started a weekly magazine, the *Shamrock*, and shortly afterwards another weekly, the *Flag of Ireland*. All three propagated extreme nationalist opinions and openly supported the Fenian movement. Pigott was imprisoned several times for publishing seditious matter. Although he made a large income from his papers, he was improvident and dissipated and continually in debt. About 1881 he sold his three papers to a publishing company owned by the Land League, and then began to write anonymous pamphlets libelling his political associates. In 1886 he sold information to the Irish Loyal and Patriotic Union, an anti-home-rule organisation, which accused PARNELL and his colleagues of complicity in murder and agrarian outrages. *The Times* of London secretly bought the papers from the union, and based on them a series of articles, 'Parnellism and Crime', which appeared in 1887. On 18 April 1887 *The Times* published a letter from Pigott's collection, purporting to have been signed by Parnell, condoning the Phoenix Park murders. In August 1888 a commission of three judges was appointed by Parliament to enquire into

the truth of the allegations made by *The Times*. Pigott was called as a witness, and on 21 February 1889 broke down under relentless cross-examination by SIR CHARLES RUSSELL. The next day he confessed his guilt to Henry Labouchere MP and fled the country. He was traced to Madrid, and as a police inspector entered his hotel room on 1 March 1889, he shot himself dead.

PILKINGTON, LAETITIA (1712-1750), adventurer. Born in Dublin. At seventeen she married Mathew Pilkington, a poor parson, who became chaplain to Lady Charlemont. Laetitia succeeded, by her wit and docility, in making friends with SWIFT, who secured a post in London for her husband in 1731. The marriage did not last. She was 'taken in the fact' (caught in the act) by her husband. Swift wrote: 'He is now suing for a divorce and will not get it: she is suing for a maintenance and he has none to give her.' In 1748 she published her *Memoirs* in Dublin; they included a valuable personal account of Swift's last days, for which they are the chief source. She opened a bookshop in St James's Street, London, but that venture failed, and she returned to Dublin, where she died on 29 August 1750.

PILKINGTON, REV. MATTHEW (c. 1700-1784), lexicographer. Born Ballyboy, Co. Offaly, and educated at TCD. Vicar of Donabate and Portrane, Dublin, from about 1724 until his death. Known as compiler of *Gentleman's and Connoisseur's Dictionary of Painters* (1770), the first of its kind published in England, with 1,400 entries, and a standard work until the publication of Bryan's *Dictionary of Painters and Engravers* (1813-1816), which was partly based on it. Pilkington's work went into ten editions, with further entries by later editors.

PLUNKETT, EDWARD JOHN MORETON DRAX, eighteenth BARON DUNSANY (1878-1957), author. Born in London, 24 July 1878.

327

Educated at Eton and Sandhurst. Succeeded to the title in 1899. Joined the Coldstream Guards and served in the Boer War. Then settled at Dunsany Castle, Co. Meath, and devoted himself to sport and to writing. His first play, *The Glittering Gate*, was produced at the Abbey Theatre in 1909. Joining the Royal Inniskilling Fusiliers on the outbreak of the First World War, he saw service in France, and was wounded and taken prisoner by the insurgents in the 1916 Rising. After the war Dunsany gained great popularity in the United States with his short plays, and became a successful lecturer and broadcaster. He poured out short stories, novels, and verse, as well as three autobiographical works, all beautifully written with a goose-quill without blotting a line. In his first book, *The Gods of Pegana* (1905), he invented his own idiosyncratic mythology. Other titles include *Time and the Gods* (1906), *The Sword of Wolfram* (1908), and *The Curse of the Wise Woman* (1933). He also published *Fifty Poems* (1929) and *Five Plays* (1914). His writings created a dream-world, suffused with the quality of fairy-tales, and at times bizarre and menacing. By contrast, the material for his Jorkens stories was furnished by his big-game hunting expeditions to Africa. Died in Dublin, 25 October 1957.

PLUNKETT, SIR HORACE CURZON (1854–1932), pioneer of agricultural co-operation. Son of Lord Dunsany. Born at Sherborne House, Gloucestershire, on 24 October 1854. Educated at Eton and University College, Oxford. Threatened by lung trouble in 1879, he sought health and fortune in ranching at Wyoming, on the foothills of the Rocky Mountains, and worked there for ten years, with annual visits to the family home at Dunsany, Co. Meath. He returned permanently to Ireland in 1889 and took a leading part in developing agricultural co-operation, particularly among dairy farmers in the south. In 1891 he was appointed a member of the newly constituted Congested Districts Board. Unionist MP for South Co. Dublin 1892, first president of the Irish Agricultural Organisation Society 1894. The report of the Recess Committee of 1895, convened largely through his initiative, led to the establishment in 1899 of the Department of Agriculture and Technical Instruction for Ireland. He was appointed vice-president, and guided the policy and administration of the department in its first seven critical years. The appointment was political, but although he lost his seat in Parliament in 1900 he was retained as vice-president until 1907. He believed that the industrial revolution needed to be redressed by an agricultural revolution through co-operation, and promulgated his ideas under the slogan, 'Better farming, better business, better living'. (President Theodore Roosevelt adopted the slogan for his conservation and country life policy.) He was re-elected president of the IAOS in 1907, and the following year public appreciation of his service was marked by the purchase and gift to him of 84 Merrion Square, Dublin, which became the headquarters of the agricultural co-operative movement under the name Plunkett House. He had at this time become an adherent of home rule, and in the years 1914–1922 worked to keep Ireland united and within the British Commonwealth, founding the Irish Dominion League to advance that aim. In 1922 he accepted membership of the new Irish Senate. His work on co-operation took him abroad frequently, and when he was in the USA during the Irish Civil War in 1923 his house, Kilteragh, Foxrock, Co. Dublin, was burned down. He moved to Weybridge, England, and continued to spread his gospel of co-operation. In 1924 he presided over a conference in Wembley on agricultural co-operation in the British Empire, and in 1925 visited South Africa to help the movement there. Elected FRS 1902, made a KCVO in 1903, and received honorary doctorates from the Universities of Oxford (1906) and Dublin (1908). He published two books, *Ireland in the New Century* (1904) and *The Rural Life Problem of the United States* (1910), as well as numerous pamphlets. Died at Weybridge, unmarried, 26 March 1932.

PLUNKETT, JOSEPH MARY (1887–1916), poet and revolutionary, son of George Noble, Count Plunkett. Born in Dublin. Educated at Belvedere College, Dublin, Stonyhurst, England, and UCD. His health was poor, and after graduation he spent some years in Italy, Egypt, and Algeria. On his return to Dublin in 1911 he renewed an earlier friendship with THOMAS MACDONAGH and with him launched the *Irish Review*, and helped EDWARD MARTYN to found the Irish Theatre in Hardwicke Street in 1914. Turning to politics, he joined the IRB and the Irish Volunteers, and in 1915 undertook a mission to Berlin to help ROGER CASEMENT in his efforts to secure German aid for a rising. He then went to New York to report to the Clan na Gael leaders on the progress of the preparations. On his return to Ireland he was made a member of the Military Council of the IRB. He fell seriously ill early in 1916 and had to undergo throat surgery. Nevertheless he took his place in the GPO during the 1916 Rising and was one of the signatories of the Proclamation of the Republic. He was court-martialled and sentenced to death. He married Grace Gifford in his cell in Kilmainham jail a few hours before his execution on 4 May 1916. His *Complete Poems* were published after his death.

PLUNKETT, SAINT OLIVER (1625–1681), archbishop of Armagh, and martyr. Born on 1 November 1625 at Loughcrew, near Oldcastle, Co. Meath, of a family closely related to the Earls of Fingall and Roscommon. In 1647 he went to Rome to study at the Irish College and was ordained in 1654. Remaining in Rome, he taught theology and became procurator, or representative, of the Irish bishops. When the see of Armagh became vacant in 1669 he was chosen to succeed, and having been consecrated archbishop in Ghent for prudence' sake, made his way to Dublin in 1670. In poverty and hardship he laboured to re-organise his diocese, holding a provincial synod and confirming ten thousand people within three months. He established the Jesuits at Drogheda, where they opened a school and a seminary, strove to maintain discipline in his diocese after years of neglect and to restore good relations between the secular and regular clergy, and worked to prevent the infiltration of Jansenism from priests who had been trained in France. After three years of comparative freedom from persecution he was forced to go into hiding in 1673, and from then until his arrest in 1679 his life was one of continual danger and grinding physical hardship. The 'Popish Plot' of Titus Oates caused panic in England in 1678, and the persecution in Ireland was intensified. An order of expulsion was made against all Catholic bishops and priests, and Plunkett was lodged in Dublin Castle in December 1679 on a charge of conspiring to bring about an armed rebellion. Only one witness, an apostate priest, could be found; the archbishop was then removed to Newgate prison in London. After months of delay a travesty of a trial took place, and he was found guilty of high treason for alleged complicity in the Titus Oates plot. He was hanged, drawn and quartered at Tyburn on 1 July 1681, the last Catholic to be martyred there. His relics are enshrined in Downside Abbey; the head is preserved in St Peter's Church, Drogheda He was beatified in 1920 and canonised on 12 October 1975, the first Irishman to be made a saint since ST LAURENCE O'TOOLE more than seven hundred years before.

POCKRICH, POCKERIDGE, OR PUCKERIDGE, RICHARD (1690–1759), inventor of the musical glasses. Born in Co. Monaghan. Left an income of £4,000 a year at the age of twenty-five. He spent it all on a succession of impractical schemes, such as planting vineyards in reclaimed bogs, providing men with wings, securing immortality by blood transfusion, and supplying men-of-war with unsinkable tin boats. He did succeed in inventing the musical glasses, or harmonically arranged goblets, and a new form of dulcimer. He gave many concerts in England, with practical exhibitions of his musical glasses. He was suffocated in a fire in his room at Hamlin's coffee-house in London.

POLLOCK, JOHN HACKET (1887–1964), physician and author. Born in Dublin. Educated at the Catholic University School and Cecilia Street Medical School. Became assistant pathologist at Richmond Hospital, Dublin. He resigned to enter a monastery, but after a short time resumed his medical career. Attached in turn to Cork Street Fever Hospital and Mercer's Hospital, and then re-appointed to his former post at the Richmond. He wrote poetry, plays, and novels, publishing some nineteen volumes in all under the pseudonym An Pilibín (the plover). *Peter and Paul* (1933) has interesting sidelights on Dublin's two universities, and *The Last Nightingale* (1951) was based on the life of JOHN DOWLAND, the seventeenth-century lutanist. Died in Dublin.

POOLE, JACOB (1774–1827), antiquary. Born 11 February 1774 at Growtown, Co. Wexford, to a Quaker family. Succeeded to family estate in 1800. Studied customs and language of baronies of Forth and Bargy. His collection of some 1,500 words of this old English dialect was edited by Rev. William Barnes and published in 1867. It is the sole authentic record of this speech. He died 20 November 1827. Buried in graveyard of Society of Friends, Forest, Co. Wexford.

POPE, ALEXANDER (1763–1835), actor and painter. Born in Cork. Studied painting under Francis West at the Dublin Art School. He practised for a time in Cork, executing portraits in crayon at a guinea each but, after success

in private theatricals, decided to go on the stage. He secured an engagement at Covent Garden theatre, London, in January 1785, and from then until his retirement in 1827 he was a principal actor either there or at Drury Lane or the Haymarket. He excelled in tragedy, and his Othello was unrivalled in his day. Throughout his life he continued to paint, and between 1787 and 1821 he exhibited fifty-nine miniatures at the RA. He delighted in good living, and, it was said, refused a benefit in Dublin arranged for him by Edmund Kean, saying: 'I must be at Plymouth at the time; it is exactly the season for mullet.' His first two wives predeceased him, and although they and his third wife brought him considerable property, he was seldom free of financial difficulties. In 1828 he obtained a pension of £100 a year from the Covent Garden Fund, to which he had contributed for forty-four years. Died at his house in Store Street, Bedford Square, London, 22 March 1835.

PORTER, JAMES (1753–1798), Presbyterian minister. Born at Tamna Wood, near Ballindrart, Co. Donegal, son of a farmer and scutch-miller. Became a schoolmaster at Dromore, Co. Down, in 1773. In 1780 he married and moved to Drogheda. Decided to enter the Presbyterian ministry, and studied divinity at Glasgow. Minister at Greyabbey, Co. Down, in 1787, and supplemented his income of £60 a year by farming. An open supporter of Catholic emancipation and parliamentary reform. He joined the Volunteers, though he did not take any active part with them, nor was he a United Irishman. In 1794 he became a contributor to the *Northern Star*, founded by SAMUEL NEILSON. A series of letters by 'a Presbyterian' reprinted under the title *Billy Bluff and Squire Firebrand* went into several editions. A satire on feudal tyranny and local espionage, it made his name throughout Ulster. Later, in 1796, he made a successful lecture tour of the province, his subject being natural philosophy. In 1797 he published a sermon, *Wind and Weather*, ridiculing the government's fast-day of thanksgiving for the dispersal of the French invasion fleet off Bantry Bay. On the outbreak of the rebellion of 1798 a large reward was offered for his capture, although he had never been a rebel and had always advocated peaceful means to achieve reform. He went into hiding, but was arrested in a cottage in the Mourne mountains in June 1798. After false testimony by an informer he was found guilty of treason by a court-martial, and, protesting his innocence to the last, was hanged on 2 July 1798 at Greyabbey, in full view of his home and meeting-house.

POTTER, ARCHIE J. (1918–1980), composer. Born on the Falls Road, Belfast, became a chorister at All Saints Church, Margaret St, London, and then an organ scholar at Clifton College, Bristol, 1932–1936. Later he studied composition under Vaughan Williams at the Royal College of Music, London. Finding it difficult to get employment in music, he worked in an optical factory. During the Second World War he spent six years in the British army, serving in Norway, Burma, and Indonesia. He then got a job with Unilever in West Africa. After three years he returned to Ireland and joined St Patrick's Cathedral Choir, Dublin. Was appointed professor of composition at RIAM 1956 and was also a governor; received D.Mus. (TCD) in 1953. Won Radio Éireann Carolan Prize for composition 1952 and 1953. Commissioned by RTE to write the television opera *Patrick* with script by DONAGH MACDONAGH. He wrote also three ballets and many choral and orchestral works, and received the Martin Toonders award from the Arts Council in 1978. He died suddenly on 5 July 1980.

POWER, ALBERT (1883–1945), sculptor. Born in Dublin. Studied at the Metropolitan School of Art under OLIVER SHEPPARD. He won many prizes there, including the Taylor awards for

statuettes, 1904–1907. Began to exhibit at the RHA in 1906, elected RHA in 1919. Lived all his life in Dublin, where he had a stone-yard in Berkeley Street. When the Tailteann Games were revived in 1924 he was commissioned to execute a statuette of Queen Maeve and to design gold, silver and bronze medals. He was represented at the exhibitions of Irish art in Paris in 1922 and in Brussels in 1930. His work to be seen in public places includes the figure of PÁDRAIC Ó CONAIRE in Eyre Square, Galway, a head of T. M. KETTLE in St Stephen's Green, head of W. B. YEATS in Sandymount Green, Dublin, and the tympanum in Mullingar Cathedral. He also executed portraits in marble or bronze of HUGH LANE, MICHAEL COLLINS, and ÉAMON DE VALERA. Died in Dublin, 10 July 1945.

POWER, ARTHUR (1891–1984), painter and writer. Born in Guernsey on 22 July 1891 and brought up in the family 'big house' in Waterford. He served in the British army in the First World War and then went to Paris, aspiring to be a writer, and became a close friend of JAMES JOYCE. He kept a record of their talks and in 1974 published *Conversations with James Joyce*. For several years he wrote a column for the *New York Herald* called 'Round the Studios'. He returned to Ireland, farmed for a while in Waterford, then sold the family property and moved to Dublin where he became art critic with the *Irish Times*. Although he had known Modigliani and Maillot and other artists in Paris, he did not begin to paint until his Dublin days. In 1940 he published the autobiographical *From the Old Waterford House*. He died in Leopardstown Park Hospital on 7 May 1984.

POWER, FRANK (1858–1884), war correspondent. Born Co. Laois. Became journalist in Dublin and then war correspondent in Bulgaria. In 1883 he accompanied EDMUND O'DONOVAN to Sudan as correspondent for *The Times* and *Pictorial World*. He fell ill at

Khartoum, was unable to join the army of Hicks Pasha, and so escaped the fate of O'Donovan. Appointed acting British consul, and welcomed General Gordon to Khartoum. During the siege of the city by the Mahdi he sent dispatches by telegram to *The Times*. In September 1884 Gordon sent him with Colonel Stewart by steamer down the Nile. They struck a rock near Berber, landed, and were killed by natives. His *Letters from Khartoum, Written During the Siege* was published in 1885.

POWER, RICHARD (1928-1970), novelist. Born in Kildare. Educated at the CBS and at TCD and Iowa University. Entered the civil service and began to write in Irish and English, contributing to many periodicals. His first book, *Úll i mBarr an Ghéagáin* (1959), which won a Club Leabhar prize of £200, described life on the Aran Islands and with Irish-speaking building labourers in England. In 1959 he obtained leave of absence from the civil service to take up a scholarship to a writers' workshop course in Iowa University. *Land of Youth* (1964) was named Book of the Month by the Booksellers' Guild of America. The last novel written before his untimely death, *The Hungry Grass* (1966), a study of the life of an Irish country priest, was acclaimed in Ireland, Britain, and America. He wrote scripts for films sponsored by the Department of Local Government, where he worked a full day as publications officer; two of the films won prizes at international film festivals in Cork and Milan. Died in Bray, 12 February 1970.

POWER, (WILLIAM GRATTAN) TYRONE (1797-1841), actor. Born near Kilmacthomas, Co. Waterford, on 2 November 1797. His father, a member of a prosperous Waterford family, died when he was a year old, and his mother then settled at Cardiff. He joined a company of strolling players at fourteen. After some years of indifferent success on the stage he made a hit at Covent Garden theatre in October 1826 in comic Irish parts, which he played with exuberance and rollicking humour. He then secured engagements at the leading London theatres at £100 a week, and made annual appearances at the Theatre Royal, Dublin, where he was received with enthusiasm. He made successful American tours in 1833, 1837, and 1838. In 1840 he visited America again to look after some property in Texas. For the return journey he embarked on 11 March 1841 on the *President*, the largest steamer afloat. During a gale on 17 March the steamer foundered, and all aboard were lost. The noted film actor Tyrone Power (1913-1958) was his great-grandson.

PRAEGER, ROBERT LLOYD (1865-1953), botanist. Born in August 1865 at Holywood, Co. Down, son of William Praeger of the Hague, a linen merchant, and Maria Patterson, daughter of ROBERT PATTERSON of Belfast. Educated at RBAI and Queen's College, Belfast. Began his career as a civil engineer with Belfast City and District Water Commissioners. Read his first geological paper in 1886, and subsequently made many contributions to Irish quaternary geology. Elected MRIA 1891. One of the founders and editor of the journal the *Irish Naturalist*. In 1893 he joined the staff of the National Library of Ireland and in 1920 became chief librarian. Retired at fifty-nine and granted full pension. On the last day of his service he set out for the Canary Islands to study the *Sempervivum* genus. His interest in botany had begun when he became a member of the Belfast Naturalists' Field Club at eleven. His *Flora of the County Armagh* (1893) was followed by many other publications, including surveys of Lambay and Clare Island, the flora of the west of Ireland, and books of essays and reminiscences. Twice president Dublin Field Club, received the Gold Medal of the Royal Horticultural Society of Ireland in 1940, and became its president in 1949-1950. Associate of the Linnean Society 1947. One of the founder-members of the Geographical Society of Ireland, its first president (1937), and also first secretary and president, Royal Zoological Society of Ireland. President, RIA, 1931; honorary life member of the Botanical Society of the British Isles 1951. The results of two major surveys, on the *Sedum* and *Sempervivum*, were published by the Royal Horticultural Society and rewarded with medals. *The Botanist in Ireland* (1934) was the last of Praeger's major scientific studies of Irish flora. *The Natural History of Ireland* was published in 1950. To the general reader, his best-known book is *The Way That I Went* (1939), a delightful account of his travels around Ireland. Died at Belfast, 5 May 1953.

PRIOR, THOMAS (1682–1751), founder of the Dublin Society, now the RDS. Born at Rathdowney, Co. Laois, and educated at Kilkenny School and TCD. A meeting of thirteen gentlemen in the college on 25 June 1731, with Prior the moving spirit, founded the Dublin Society for Improving Husbandry, Manufactures, and Other Useful Arts and Sciences. The society received a parliamentary grant of £500 a year in 1749. Prior wrote a number of tracts on *Absentees, The Virtues of Tar Water*, and questions of the day. Died 21 October 1751.

PROUT, FATHER. See under MAHONY, F. S.

PURCELL, NOEL (1900–1985), actor. Born in Dublin on 23 December 1900 and educated at Synge St CBS. He began his career at twelve as a call-boy in the Gaiety Theatre. In the 1930s he teamed up with JIMMY O'DEA and HARRY O'DONOVAN and toured Ireland and Britain. The revival of variety shows during the Second World War saw him playing to packed houses in Dublin, often as the dame in pantomime. He got his first film part in *Captain Boycott* (1947)

and continued in constant demand for character parts, playing in *The Blue Lagoon* (1949), *Moby Dick* (1956), and *Mutiny on the Bounty* (1962). He received the freedom of the city of Dublin in 1984 and was made a life member of Irish Actors' Equity. He died in a Dublin hospital on 3 March 1985, survived by his wife, Eileen, and four sons.

PURSER, SARAH HENRIETTA (1848–1943), artist. Born in Kingstown (Dún Laoghaire), 22 March 1848. Educated in Switzerland. Her father's business of flour-milling failed in 1873, and she decided to make her living as a portrait painter. Studied at the School of Art in Dublin and then in Paris. First exhibited at the RHA in 1880. Through the Gore-Booth family she obtained commissions for portraits in London, which were hung at the RA. Further commissions followed: 'I went through the British aristocracy like the measles.' Late in life she estimated that she had earned more than £30,000 from her painting. Shrewd investments in Guinness, when it became a public company in 1886, and on the Stock Exchange made her a wealthy woman. In 1903 she founded a stained-glass workshop, An Túr Gloine (the Tower of Glass), at 24 Upper Pembroke Street, Dublin. Distinguished artists who worked there included EVIE HONE and MICHAEL HEALY. In 1911, with her brother John, professor of medicine at TCD, she took a lease of Mespil House, an eighteenth-century mansion now demolished, on the Grand Canal, and held afternoon receptions there each month that were a feature of the literary and intellectual life of Dublin. In 1924 she founded the Friends of the National Collections, and some years later was mainly responsible for securing Charlemont House as the Municipal Gallery of Modern Art. She continued to paint until she was well over eighty. Died in Dublin, 7 August 1943.

Q

QUAIN, JONES (1796–1865), anatomist. Born Co. Cork; educated Adair's school, Fermoy, and TCD, graduating in medicine 1820. After further study on the Continent he became a teacher of anatomy in London 1825. Professor of anatomy, University College, London, 1831–1835; member of senate of the university 1835. Lived in retirement the last twenty years of his life, mostly in Paris, and devoted himself to literature and science. Published *Elements of Anatomy* (1828), which became a standard textbook. Died, unmarried, 31 January 1865.

QUAIN, RICHARD (1800–1887), surgeon, brother of JONES QUAIN. Born Fermoy, Co. Cork; educated Adair's school, Fermoy, and Aldergate School of Medicine, London, under his brother, and Paris. Became demonstrator to his brother. Surgeon, University College Hospital, 1834–1866, then consulting surgeon. FRCS 1843 and FRS 1844. President, RCS, 1868. Surgeon extraordinary to Queen Victoria. Published several books on medical subjects. Died 15 September 1887. Left bulk of his fortune of £75,000 to endow study of English language and literature and natural science at University College, London.

QUAIN, SIR RICHARD (1816–1898), physician. Born at Mallow, Co. Cork, 30 October 1816. Educated at Cloyne diocesan school and University College, London. Graduated in medicine with distinction in 1840, and embarked on a very successful career. Besides hospital appointments at Brompton, the Seamen's Hospital at Greenwich, and the Royal Hospital for Consumption at Ventnor, he acquired a large and fashionable practice in London, and became physician to Queen Victoria. Elected FRS 1871, honoured by the leading medical societies of England and Ireland, and created a baronet of the United Kingdom on New Year's Day 1891. He edited *A Dictionary of Medicine* (1882), which was the most successful medical publication of the time. Died in Harley Street, London, 13 March 1898.

QUIN, WINDHAM THOMAS WYNDHAM, fourth EARL OF DUNRAVEN AND MOUNT EARL (1841–1926). Born Adare, Co. Limerick, 12 February 1841. Educated privately at Rome and at Christ Church, Oxford. Joined Life Guards 1862. Became noted steeplechaser and yachtsman. War correspondent for *Daily Telegraph* in Abyssinia (Ethiopia) 1867 and Franco-Prussian War 1870. Succeeded to earldom 1871. Visited USA that year and hunted buffalo with Texas Jack and Buffalo Bill during the Indian wars. Unlike his forerunners, he made his home at Adare. Took deep interest in Irish affairs. Published *The Irish Question*, the first of many pamphlets, in 1880. Colonial under-secretary 1885–1887. Ran successful stud at Adare and was chairman of commission on Irish horse-breeding in 1896. He took his certificate as a master mariner and competed unsuccessfully for the America's Cup in 1893 and 1895 with *Valkyrie II* and *III*. His pamphlet protesting against the conduct of the 1895 races led to his being expelled from the New York Yacht Club. Published *Self-Instruction in the Practice and Theory of Navigation* (1900). In the First World War he commanded his steam yacht *Grianaig* as a hospital ship in the Mediterranean. He rendered his best service to Ireland as leader of the landlords who agreed to accept land purchase and so facilitated the Wyndham Land Act, 1903, which enabled tenants to become owners. He advocated devolution of legislation to an Irish parliament in 1905, and at the Irish Convention 1917 proposed a federal solution. Nominated by W. T. COSGRAVE to Free State Senate 1922. Published memoirs, *Past Times and Pastimes* (1922). Died London, 14 June 1926.

QUINN, EDEL MARY (1907–1944), Legion of Mary envoy to Africa. Born 14 September 1907 at Greenane, near Kanturk, Co. Cork. (Christened Edel by mistake; the priest was told the name Adèle but thought that Edel was intended, as a diminutive of Edelweiss.) Her father, a bank manager, was transferred frequently, and Edel was educated in Loreto convents in Clonmel and Enniscorthy and by the Faithful Companions of Jesus at their boarding-school in Upton, Cheshire. She had not finished her school career when a reversal in the family fortunes obliged her to return to Dublin, where they were now settled. She attended commercial school and obtained a post as secretary in the Chagny Tile Works, run by a young Frenchman. In 1927, when she had been about a year with the firm, he asked her to marry him. Her reply was that she had for some time past resolved to devote her life to the service of God, and intended to enter the Poor Clare convent in Belfast as soon as family circumstances allowed her to stop earning. Soon after this she joined the Legion of Mary, which had been founded by FRANK DUFF in Dublin in 1921. Early in 1932 she was making her final preparations to enter the Poor Clares when she contracted tuberculosis and had to spend eighteen months in Newcastle sanatorium, Co. Wicklow. On recovery, she took a secretarial post in Westland Row, Dublin, and continued her work with the legion. The organisation had spread rapidly to Britain and America, and a volunteer was required for Africa. Edel's offer was accepted, with some misgivings on account of her recent illness, and she left Ireland in October 1936. She worked as envoy first in Kenya, founding praesidia of the legion, and then in Mauritius and Nyasaland (Malawi). In 1941 her tuberculosis recurred and she spent six months in a sanatorium in Johannesburg. She then went to a Dominican mission hospital in the Cape Province. After a long convalescence she was back at her base in Kenya in 1943. She resumed her work, although much weakened in health. She died on 12 May 1944 in the convent of the Sisters of the Precious Blood at Nairobi, and is buried beside the grave of BISHOP SHANAHAN in the Missionaries' cemetery.

R

RAFTERY, ANTOINE (Antoine Ó Reachtabhra) (*c.* 1784–1835), poet. Born in Co. Mayo, probably near Kiltimagh. Smallpox blinded him in his youth and he became a travelling fiddler, and spent most of his life in the Gort-Loughrea district of Co. Galway. A folk-poet without formal education, he wrote poems and ballads on contemporary events, such as DANIEL O'CONNELL's victory in the Clare election, the drowning tragedy at 'Anach Cuain' (Eanach Dhúin), and hanging of a Whiteboy captain, Anthony O'Daly. His most ambitious work was a metrical history of Ireland, *Seanchas na Sceiche*, and he also wrote some pleasing love-poems. He was buried at Rahasane, near Craughwell, Co. Galway. His poems were preserved in oral tradition until collected and edited by DOUGLAS HYDE in 1903.

REA, JOHN (1822/23–1881), lawyer. Born in West Street, Belfast, and became a solicitor about 1847. Prominent in Young Ireland movement. Imprisoned in Kilmainham jail for nine months in 1848. Acted for Catholics in Dolly's Brae enquiry (see JOCELYN, Earl of Roden). His action against Belfast City Council for misappropriation of funds lasted for years; he won on appeal to the House of Lords. He was often imprisoned for contempt of court, and welcomed on release by torch-light processions. Contested Belfast unsuccessfully in 1874. Defended MICHAEL DAVITT 1879. Shot himself and was found dead in bed at 80 Donegall Street, Belfast, on 17 May 1881.

READ, CHARLES ANDERSON (1841–1878), author. Born Kilsella House, near Sligo. His father became a schoolmaster at Hilltown, near Newry,

on losing his inheritance. Charles failed in business as a merchant at Rathfriland, then obtained a post in Henderson's publishing house, London. Contributed stories to Henderson's journal *Young Folks*, including 'Aileen Aroon' and 'Savourneen Dheelish'. Major work: *Cabinet of Irish Literature* (1876–1878), selections from noted authors. The fourth and final volume was edited after his death by T. P. O'CONNOR. He died 23 January 1878 at Thornton Heath, Surrey.

REDDIN, KENNETH SHEILS (1895–1967), district justice and author. Born near Dublin; educated at Belvedere College, Dublin, Clongowes Wood College, and St Enda's, Rathfarnham, under PEARSE. Studied law at UCD; qualified as a solicitor in 1917. An active worker in Sinn Féin and the Gaelic League, took part in the 1916 Rising and was interned at Stafford, England. Appointed a district justice in 1922. Principal justice at Chancery St, Dublin, 1958–1964. He won a gold medal at the Tailteann Games in 1924 with his play *The Passing*, which was produced at the Abbey Theatre. *Old Mag* (1924) also had an Abbey production. He wrote several books for children, and three novels, sometimes using the pen-name 'Kenneth Sarr'. *Another Shore* (1945), his best-known novel, was made into a film by Ealing Studios in 1947. Died in Dublin, 17 August 1967.

REDMOND, JOHN EDWARD (1856–1918), political leader. Born at Ballytrent, Co. Wexford, on 1 September 1856, eldest son of William Redmond, MP for Wexford. Educated at Clongowes Wood College and TCD. He became a clerk in the House of

Commons and was called to the Irish bar in 1886. Elected MP for New Ross in 1881, he became a devoted follower of PARNELL. He made a successful political mission to Australia and the USA 1882–1884, raising £30,000 for the Irish Parliamentary Party funds. After the split in the party following the O'Shea divorce case in 1890, Redmond led the minority that supported Parnell. Elected Parnellite member for Waterford in 1891, and held the seat until his death. When the party was united again in 1900, Redmond became leader. He was an influential member of the Land Conference of 1902, from which came the Land Act of 1903, which gave a dramatic impetus to tenant land purchase. Involved in long-drawn-out negotiations that resulted in the foundation of the National University in 1908. After years of political manoeuvring against delaying tactics by the Liberals, he secured the introduction of the third Home Rule Bill in 1912. The opposition of the Ulster Unionists led by SIR EDWARD CARSON took him by surprise, and the Irish Volunteers were formed and led by men who had no sympathy with his policy of constitutional reform by parliamentary methods. When the First World War broke out in August 1914 Redmond proposed in the House of Commons that Ireland should be guarded by the Volunteers, North and South, and the British troops withdrawn. The British government ignored this, and thwarted his efforts to have a distinctive Irish division formed to correspond to that approved for Ulster. Despite these rebuffs he continued to encourage Irishmen to join the British forces. The 1916 Rising was a shattering and completely unexpected blow to his whole policy. Nevertheless he struggled on, and in 1917 suggested that a convention of Irishmen be held in Dublin to draft a constitution for Ireland within the empire. The convention met in July 1917 and had made little headway when Redmond died suddenly on 6 March 1918. He was buried in Wexford.

REDMOND, WILLIAM HOEY KEARNEY (1861–1917), nationalist, younger brother of JOHN REDMOND. Born at Ballytrent, Co. Wexford. Educated at Clongowes Wood College. He succeeded his father as MP for Wexford in 1883 and became a follower of PARNELL. He accompanied his brother John to Australia and America in 1882–1884 and revisited those countries several times on later missions. He wrote two books on Australia, *A Shooting Trip in the Australian Bush* (1898) and *Through the New Commonwealth* (1906). MP for North Fermanagh 1885. After a stormy election he was returned for East Clare in 1891 and held the seat unopposed until his death. When the First World War broke out, and John Redmond appealed for Irish volunteers, William responded by joining the British army. When on leave in March 1917 he appealed in the House of Commons on behalf of 'we who are about to die', for self-government within the empire for Ireland to place it on a par with Canada, New Zealand, and Australia. Killed in action on 7 June 1917. Buried in the garden of the hospice at Locre. *Trench Pictures from France* was published posthumously in 1917.

REEVES, WILLIAM (1815–1892), antiquary and bishop. Born at Charleville (Ráth Luirc), Co. Cork, 16 March 1815. Educated at private schools in Dublin and TCD, graduating in arts and medicine. Took holy orders in the Church of Ireland at Derry 1840. Served as curate in various Ulster parishes. Librarian at Armagh 1861–1886; made bishop of Down, Connor and Dromore in June 1886 and went to live at Conway House, Dunmurry, Co. Antrim. His best-known work, an edition of the *Life of St Columba* by ADAMNÁN, with extensive notes, appeared in 1857. His *Ecclesiastical Antiquities of Down, Conor and Dromore* (1847) and *Acts of Archbishop Colton* (1850) remain valuable source-books of church history. President, RIA, 1891 and contributed many original papers to its journal. Died of pneumonia in Dublin, 12 January 1892.

REHAN, ADA (1860–1916), actress. Born Limerick, real name Crehan. Taken to USA at five. Her older sisters were on the stage, and through her brother-in-law's help she made her début at thirteen. She was billed in Philadelphia as 'Rehan' by a printer's error, and retained the name. Became leading lady in Daly's Theatre on Broadway, scoring her greatest triumph as Katherina in *The Taming of the Shrew* in 1887. She made her first appearance in London in 1884, and laid the cornerstone of Daly's new theatre, Leicester Square, 30 October 1891. She was one of the best-loved actresses in New York and London, and much admired as Rosalind and Lady Teazle. Essentially a comedienne, her style of playing became somewhat outmoded in the early 1900s. She retired in 1905. Her life was devoted to the theatre, and she never married. Died New York.

REID, FORREST (1875–1947), novelist and critic. Born in Belfast, 24 June 1875. Educated RBAI and Christ's College, Cambridge, where he read mediaeval and modern languages. Returning to Belfast, he settled down there for the rest of his life. In 1904 he published *The Kingdom of Twilight*, the first of over a dozen novels. Boyhood and adolescence as seen through the sympathetic eyes of an older man are the themes of these books, which were strongly influenced by Henry James. His last novel, *Young Tom* (1944), was awarded the James Tait Black Memorial Prize. A little-known work is *Illustrators of the Sixties* (1928), an authoritative and original study of Victorian woodcut artists. Reid also published critical studies of W. B. YEATS and Walter de la Mare, and an autobiography, *Apostate* (1926). A founder-member of the Irish Academy of Letters. Died, unmarried, in Warrenpoint, Co. Down, 4 January 1947.

REID, REV. JAMES SEATON (1798–1851), church historian. Born Lurgan, Co. Armagh. Educated University of Glasgow. Ordained 1819 for Presbyterian church of Donegore, Co. Antrim. Ministered at Carrickfergus 1823; elected moderator of Synod of Ulster 1827. Founded *Orthodox Presbyterian* with others in 1829 and contributed frequently. Appointed professor of ecclesiastical history at Belfast College 1837. Professor of church history, Glasgow, 1841. His great work was his *History of the Presbyterian Church in Ireland* (three volumes, 1834–1851), based on original documents. Died 26 March 1851.

REID, NANO (1905–1981), painter. Born in Drogheda and educated at the local Siena Dominican convent. She won a scholarship to the Metropolitan School of Art, Dublin, and exhibited at the RHA when she was twenty. Between 1927 and 1932 she studied in Paris and London. Her reputation grew and she was selected with NORAH MCGUINNESS to represent Ireland at the Venice Biennale in 1950. In 1972 she won the Douglas Hyde gold medal and the Arts Council award at the Oireachtas exhibition. Her work is on permanent exhibition at the Municipal Gallery of Modern Art, Dublin, Santa Barbara Museum, California, and the Irish Institute, New York. She is remembered for her poetic evocation of the Irish countryside and especially the remote and hilly regions of her native Co. Louth. Despite critical acclaim she found it difficult to sell her paintings, and eventually retired to live with her sister in Drogheda where she died in hospital in November 1981.

REID, THOMAS MAYNE (1818–1883), novelist. Born at Ballyroney, Co. Down, 4 April 1818. Educated for the Presbyterian ministry, but emigrated to America in 1840. After a varied career as store-keeper, slave overseer, schoolmaster, and actor, with intervals spent hunting and at the Indian wars, he settled in Philadelphia in 1843 as a journalist. He took part in the Mexican War in 1847, and was severely wounded, being left for dead on the field. In June 1849 he sailed for Europe to take part in the revolution in Hungary, but arrived too late. He published his first novel, *The Rifle Rangers*, in London in 1850, and subsequently published more than thirty adventure novels, based on his own experiences. In 1867 he returned to New York, after the failure of building and journalistic ventures in England, and founded and conducted the *Onward Magazine*. In 1870, after a serious illness caused by his old wound, he returned to England, and died near Ross, Herefordshire, on 22 October 1883.

REILLY, THOMAS DEVIN (1824–1854), journalist. Born in Monaghan on 30 March 1824, son of a solicitor. Educated there and at TCD. Joined the staff of the *Nation* in 1845 and became a close friend of JOHN MITCHEL. After the arrest of Mitchel in 1848 he escaped to New York, where he worked as a journalist. Became editor of the New York *Democratic Review*, and later of the *Washington Union*. Died suddenly in Washington on 6 March 1854. Buried in Mount Olivet cemetery.

REYNOLDS, JAMES EMERSON (1844–1920), chemist. Born at Boterstown, Co. Dublin, 8 January 1844. Qualified at Edinburgh College of Physicians and Surgeons in 1865. Abandoned medicine two years later and devoted himself to chemistry. As analyst to the RDS he discovered thiocarbamide (thiourea), and devised a test for acetone. Professor of chemistry at RCSI 1870–1875 and at TCD 1875–1903. His *Experimental Chemistry for Junior Students* (1882) first introduced quantitative method into the teaching of chemistry. Elected FRS 1880. Resigned from TCD 1903. Died in London, 18 February 1920.

REYNOLDS, THOMAS (1771–1836), informer. Born on 9 March 1771 at 9 Park Street, Dublin, son of a prosperous poplin manufacturer, and educated at a Jesuit seminary at Liège.

He was related by marriage to WOLFE TONE, as they were married to sisters. About 1788 he inherited considerable property on the death of his father, but the dishonesty of a business partner and his own profligate life reduced him to virtual bankruptcy. He joined the United Irishmen, but in 1798, when he heard their plans for a revolution, he became alarmed and consulted one Cope, a friend and large creditor, who asked him to turn informer. The undersecretary, Cooke, authorised Cope to offer up to £100,000 if necessary to secure information. The government, through Reynolds's information, were able to arrest the Leinster Committee at the house of OLIVER BOND and so killed the conspiracy. Reynolds received £5,000 and an annual grant of £1,000. He left Ireland for his safety's sake, and after holding some British appointments abroad, settled in Paris where he died on 18 August 1836.

RICE, EDMUND IGNATIUS (1762–1844), founder of the Irish Christian Brothers. Born 1 June 1762 at Westcourt, near Callan, Co. Kilkenny. Educated at Kilkenny. Went to Waterford in 1779 as apprentice to his uncle, a wealthy export merchant, who died in 1790 and left him the business. Edmund married in 1785; his wife's sudden death in 1789 proved a turning-point in his life. Always devout and charitable, he decided to retire from business and devote himself to the service of God. With encouragement from Pope Pius VI and the permission of the bishop, he started a school for poor boys in Waterford in 1803 and soon had schools in several other towns. On 5 September 1820 Pope Pius VII approved the new congregation as 'the Institute of the Brothers of the Christian Schools of Ireland', and Brother Ignatius was elected the first superior-general. When he retired in 1838 the Brothers had twenty-two houses in Ireland and England; they have since extended throughout the English-speaking world. He died at Waterford, 29 August 1844.

RICHARDS, SHELAH (1903–1985), actress and producer. Born in May 1903 and educated at Alexandra College, Dublin, and a convent in Paris. She began her acting career with the Dublin Drama League and in 1924 joined the Abbey Theatre company and played many leading roles. She went to New York in 1938 to play with Gladys Cooper, returning to Ireland to run her own successful company at the Olympia Theatre, Dublin, during the Second World War with Nigel Heseltine. She joined RTE as a television producer soon after it was launched in 1962, specialising in drama. She retired in the 1970s and died in Ballybrack, Co. Dublin, on 19 January 1985. She was the first wife of playwright DENIS JOHNSTON and mother of novelist Jennifer Johnston.

RIDGEWAY, SIR WILLIAM (1853–1926), classical scholar. Born on 6 August 1853 at Ballydermot, Co. Offaly. Educated at Portarlington School, TCD, and Cambridge. Professor of Greek, Queen's College, Cork, 1883. Went back to Cambridge as Disney Professor of Archaeology 1892. In 1907 he was made Brereton Reader in Classics. His first book, *Origin of Metallic Currency and Weight Standards*, appeared in 1892. Other publications include *Origin and Influence of the Thoroughbred Horse* (1905), *Origin of Tragedy* (1910), and *The Oldest Irish Epic* (1907). He received many academic honours, was knighted in 1919, and died at his house at Fen Ditton, near Cambridge, on 12 August 1926.

ROBERTS, MICHAEL (1817–1882), mathematician. Born Peter St, Cork, on 18 April 1817. Educated Midleton School and TCD; fellow 1843 and professor of mathematics 1862; senior fellow 1879–1882. Won a high reputation by his contributions to learned journals, particularly his papers on the theory of invariants and covariants, and on hyperelliptic functions. Died Dublin, 4 October 1882.

ROBINSON, (ESMÉ STUART) LENNOX (1886–1958), playwright. Born 4 October 1886 in Douglas, Co. Cork. Educated at Bandon Grammar School. Became interested in the stage on seeing the Abbey Theatre Company perform in Cork. His first play, *The Clancy Name*, was produced in the Abbey in 1908 and ran for three months. Appointed manager of the Abbey in 1910 but resigned to devote himself to full-time writing. In 1915 he accepted a post as organising librarian for the Carnegie Trust, and travelled all over Ireland. He continued to write plays for the Abbey, and *The Whiteheaded Boy* (1916) was even more successful than his first. Returned to the Abbey as manager 1919; appointed a director in 1923. These were very difficult years financially for the theatre, as Annie Horniman had withdrawn her support in 1910. These straits were eased when the new Irish government decided to give the Abbey an annual grant, making it the first state-subsidised theatre in any English-speaking country. Robinson added to his reputation as a sound craftsman with *Crabbed Youth and Age* (1922), *The Far-Off Hills* (1928), *Drama at Inish* (1933), and *Church Street* (1934), and in these and other plays was one of the few Irish dramatists to deal with small-town middle-class life. For many years director of the Abbey School of Acting. He made a number of successful lecture tours of the USA, and also wrote a novel, a number of essays, short stories, and two volumes of autobiography, *In Three Homes* (1938) and *Curtain Up* (1941). In 1951 he published *Ireland's Abbey Theatre*, a valuable contribution to the history he had helped to make. Died at Monkstown, Co. Dublin, 14 October 1958. Buried in St Patrick's Cathedral.

ROBINSON, THOMAS ROMNEY (1792–1882), astronomer and mathematical physicist. Born in Dublin on 23 April 1792 and educated at Dr Bruce's academy in Belfast, and TCD. Became a fellow of the college in 1814 and lectured on natural philosophy for some years. In 1821 he obtained a college living at

Enniskillen, and in 1823 was appointed astronomer in charge of Armagh Observatory. Shortly afterwards he became rector of Carrickmacross, and held this post and the astronomership until his death fifty-nine years later. In 1859 he published his chief work, *Places of 5,345 Stars Observed at Armagh from 1828 to 1854*. The Royal Society awarded him a gold medal in 1862 for his astronomical work. He invented the cup-anemometer, and made many researches in physics. The numerous papers he published are to be found in the *Transactions* of the RIA, the Royal Society, and the Royal Astronomical Society. A friend of WILLIAM PARSONS, third Earl of Rosse, and helped in the erection of the great telescope at Parsonstown (Birr). Many learned societies and universities bestowed honours on him. Elected FRS 1856. Died suddenly at Armagh Observatory on 28 February 1882.

ROBINSON, SIR WILLIAM (died 1712), architect. Received his first patent as surveyor-general in 1670 at a salary of £300 a year. This was a military appointment; he is also described as owning land and as an importer of goods. He was first keeper of Parliament House in 1677. His masterpiece is the Royal Hospital, Kilmainham, built 1680-1684 for old soldiers, and sometimes erroneously attributed to Wren. About the same time he supervised the building of the two great forts at Kinsale Harbour, James's or Rincurran Fort and Charles's Fort, which still survive in massive ruins. He surrendered his patent in 1700 and was succeeded by BURGH. Knighted 1701. He was a foundation governor of the Royal Hospital until 1707. The only other surviving building that can with confidence be attributed to him is Marsh's Library (begun 1702). Died 13 November 1712.

ROBINSON, WILLIAM (1838-1935), gardener and author. Began as garden-boy at Ballykilcavan, Co. Laois. In 1861 went as under-gardener to Royal Botanic Society's gardens at Regent's Park, London. While there he was elected fellow, Linnean Society, one of his sponsors being Charles Darwin. He left after six years. Represented *The Times* in horticultural section of Paris Exhibition, 1867. Founded and conducted the *Garden*, a weekly, in 1872. Founded *Gardening Illustrated* in 1879 and ran it for forty years. Edited gardening column of the *Field* 1873-1903. With the earnings from writing he went to the USA about 1880 and studied the flora of the Rocky Mountains and California. His *English Flower Garden* (1883) went into sixteen editions. He published eighteen books in all, including *Parks and Gardens of Paris* (1878) and *Wood Fires for the Country House* (1924), his last. Also edited the weekly *Cottage Garden* (1892-1898) and *Flora and Sylva* (a 'monthly review for lovers of garden, woodland, tree or flower') (1903-1905). His income from journals enabled him to buy Gravetye Manor in Sussex with 200 acres about 1890, and in 1911 he published *Gravetye, an Account of 20 Years' Work*. He strove for simplicity in garden design and led the horticultural revolution against Victorian carpet-bedding. Died 12 May 1935.

ROCHE, SIR BOYLE (1743-1807), politician. Joined the British army at an early age and served in the war in America. Returning to Ireland, he entered parliament about 1776 and remained MP until the Act of Union of 1800, representing successively Tralee, Gowran, Portarlington, and Old Leighlin. For his constant support of the government he was granted a pension, appointed chamberlain to the vice-regal court, and in 1782 created a baronet. He opposed Catholic emancipation and fought hard for the Union, saying that his love for England and Ireland was so great that he 'would have the two sisters embrace like one brother.' Another 'bull' attributed to him was: 'Why should we put ourselves out of our way to do anything for posterity; for what has posterity done for us?' (He explained himself on this occasion by stating that by posterity he did not mean our ancestors but those who came immediately after them.) Died at his house, 63 Eccles St, Dublin, 5 June 1807.

ROCHE, 'TIGER' (born 1729), Dublin 'buck'. As a young man he attracted the favourable notice of the viceroy. Killed a watchman in a drunken riot, fled to North America, and fought with the French against the Indians. Accused of stealing a fowling-piece from a brother-officer, convicted at court-martial and dismissed the service in disgrace. Attacked his guard with such ferocity he was called 'Tiger'. Went to England in 1758; shortly afterwards, the real thief confessed on his death-bed. Roche was made lieutenant in a regiment, returned to Dublin, and was lionised at parties. He formed a body to patrol the streets and protect citizens from marauding 'pinkindindies'. He retired from the army after the Treaty of Paris 1763 and went to London, where he married a Miss Pitt, an heiress. He soon spent her fortune of £4,000, and treated his wife so cruelly that she abandoned him. Imprisoned for debt, he then received a small legacy, was released, and became more arrogant than ever. He so charmed a young woman that she allowed him to manage her fortune: he reduced her to destitution. He embarked for India in May 1773 as a captain of foot. On the voyage he quarrelled with a Captain Ferguson, who was murdered at night outside his lodgings at the Cape. Suspicion fell on Roche, who fled, taking refuge among the natives. He was arrested by the Dutch authorities, tried, and acquitted. He then took ship for Bombay, was arrested there by the British. He was tried again at the Old Bailey, December 1775, and again acquitted. He then sank into obscurity and was never heard of again.

RODGERS, WILLIAM ROBERT (1910-1969), poet. Born in Belfast; educated at QUB. Became a Presbyterian minister, and served in Loughgall, Co. Armagh, 1934-1946. His first volume of verse, *Awake, and Other Poems*, appeared in 1941. In 1946 he joined the BBC as a producer and script-writer, and was especially associated with Third Programme features of Irish literary interest. Elected to the Irish Academy of Letters 1951, and the following year published his second collection of verse, *Europa and the Bull*. He resigned from the BBC in 1952 but continued to contribute to their programmes. Poet-in-residence at Pitzer College, Clairmont, California, 1967-1969. Died in hospital in California on 1 February 1969. Renowned as a conversationalist, and remembered by one reviewer as 'a gentle genius'.

ROLLESTON, THOMAS WILLIAM HAZEN (1857-1920), writer. Born at Glasshouse, Shinrone, Co. Offaly, son of a County Court judge. Educated at St Columba's and TCD. Lived in Germany 1879-1883, studying German language and literature. On his return to Ireland founded the *Dublin University Review*, which he edited from May 1885 to December 1886. The *Review* published the earlier work of W. B. YEATS, KATHARINE TYNAN, and JANE BARLOW, and provided a forum for people of widely diverging views such as MICHAEL DAVITT, DOUGLAS HYDE, T. W. Russell and Sir Frederick Falkiner. It also introduced Turgenev to English readers. Rolleston went to London and was first honorary secretary of the Irish Literary Society 1892-1893. Delivered the Taylorian Lectures on 'Lessing and the Origins of Modern German Literature' at Oxford in 1892; was joint editor of the New Irish Library, and also contributed to various journals. Returned to Dublin as secretary to the Irish Industries' Association in 1894. Leader writer on the Dublin *Daily Express*, and correspondent of the London *Daily Chronicle*, 1898-1900. For the next five years he acted as organiser to the Department of Agriculture. In 1908 he settled in London, where he gave lectures and reviewed for *The Times*. One of the founders of the Rhymers' Club, and during the First World War acted as librarian to the Information Bureau. Publications include *Life of Lessing* (1889), *Imagination and Art in Gaelic Literature* (1900), *Parallel Paths: a Study in Biology, Ethics and Art* (1908), *Poems and Ballads of Young Ireland* (1888), and translations of German poetry. Died at Hampstead, London, 5 December 1920.

RONAYNE, JOSEPH PHILIP (1822–1876), civil engineer. Born in Cork and trained as a surveyor. Worked on design and construction of main-line railways in Ireland. In California from 1854 to 1859, superintending hydraulic works to supply water to the goldfields. On his return to Ireland he laid out the Cork-Macroom railway, being engineer, contractor, and largest shareholder. MP for Cork 1872–1876 and leading member of Home Rule party. Died at Queenstown (Cóbh), 7 May 1876.

ROONEY, WILLIAM (1872–1901), poet. Born in Dublin; classmate of ARTHUR GRIFFITH at Great Strand Street CBS. Became clerk in solicitor's office. Collaborated with Griffith in Leinster Literary Society and Celtic Literary Society. Contributed poems and articles to *United Ireland*, the *Shamrock, Northern Patriot, Shan Van Vocht*, and *Weekly Freeman*. On 4 March 1890 he founded the *United Irishman*, with Griffith as editor. Worked unsparingly for revival of Irish, travelling long distances to address small meetings, and wore himself out by his exertions. Died in Dublin, 6 May 1901. His *Poems and Ballads*, edited by Griffith, were published in 1902 and *Prose Writings* in 1909.

ROS, AMANDA McKITTRICK (1860–1939), novelist. Born near Drumaness, Co. Down, trained in Dublin as a teacher, and married Andy Ross, stationmaster at Larne. An admirer of Marie Corelli, she published *Irene Iddesleigh* (1897) at her own expense in Belfast. It was a novel written in high-flown alliterative prose. She followed this with two more novels in the same style, *Delina Delany* and *Donald Dudley*. These novels became the subject of a cult at Oxford and were re-published at the instance of Aldous Huxley. A club of her admirers met regularly in London; members included Desmond MacCarthy, E. V. Lucas, and F. Anstey. The titles of her collections of verse, *Poems of Puncture* and *Poems of Fomentation*, show that they were as eccentric as her novels. It appears that she did not realise the nature of the response to her writings, which varied from kindly laughter to derision.

ROSS, MARTIN. See under MARTIN, VIOLET FLORENCE.

ROSSE, EARL OF. See under PARSONS, WILLIAM.

ROTHWELL, RICHARD (1800–1868), painter. Born in Athlone, 20 November 1800. Began to study painting at fourteen in the school of the Dublin Society. Became a member RHA in 1824, and exhibited portraits there 1826–1829. Left for London, but after two years of fair success, decided that he needed to study the Old Masters, and went to Italy. Returned to London in 1834, but although he had several pictures accepted by the RA he received few commissions. Returned to Ireland in 1841, and settled at Rose Cottage, Rathfarnham, Dublin, contributing occasionally to the RA and the RHA. In London again in 1852, then made two visits to America, and a second visit to Italy. In 1858 he settled at Leamington, and in 1862 exhibited three pictures at the International Exhibition. He thought that they were badly hung and lighted, made a public protest, and took himself to the Continent again. Died in Rome on 13 September 1868. Buried beside the grave of the poet Keats by Joseph Severn, a mutual friend.

ROWAN, (ARCHIBALD) HAMILTON (1751–1834), United Irishman. Born 12 May 1751 in Rathbone Place, London, in the house of his grandfather, who bequeathed him considerable wealth. Educated at Westminster School and Queen's College, Cambridge. He married in Paris 1781, and settled at Rathcoffey, Co. Kildare, in 1784. He joined the Volunteers and attended the Dublin Convention of 1784. He was a founder-member of the Northern Whig Club, Belfast, in 1790 and, influenced by WOLFE TONE, joined the United Irishmen the following year. Tried for sedition 1794, and defended by CURRAN in a famous speech. Sentenced to two years' imprisonment in Dublin Newgate, but escaped to France where he became friendly with Mary Wollstonecraft. He went to America in 1795 and was joined by Tone and NAPPER TANDY at Wilmington on the Delaware. His vivid memory of the atrocities he saw in Paris during the Reign of Terror made it impossible for him to join their enterprise. Pardoned in 1803, he settled on his estate at Killyleagh Castle, Co. Down. Strong supporter of Catholic emancipation, and subscribed to the Catholic Association. He died in Dublin on 1 November 1834.

ROWSOME, LEO (1900–1970), 'King of the Irish Pipers'. Born in Co. Wexford. Well known in Ireland, the Continent and the USA as a gifted player of the Dublin Pipers' Club which, with the Meath Pipers' Club, founded Comhaltas Ceoltóirí Éireann at Mullingar in 1951. He made many recordings, and taught in Dublin for some years. Died suddenly in Riverstown parochial hall, Co. Sligo, on 20 September 1970 while adjudicating in the 'Fiddler of Dooney' traditional fiddle-playing championship.

RUSSELL, CHARLES, BARON RUSSELL OF KILLOWEN (1832–1900), lord chief justice of England. Born at Newry, Co. Down, 10 November 1832. Educated at Belfast diocesan seminary, a private school in Newry, and the Vincentian College, Castleknock, Dublin. Qualified as a solicitor in 1854 and, after practising successfully in Ulster for two years, entered Lincoln's Inn, London, and was called to the English bar in 1859. He soon made a name for himself on the northern circuit, and was able to take silk in 1872. Independent Liberal MP for Dundalk 1880; sat for South Hackney 1885–1894. While remaining independent of the Irish party, he gave strong and consistent support in Parliament to their home rule policy, and as attorney-general in Gladstone's administrations of 1886 and 1892 continued his work for the Irish cause. In 1880 he published *New Views of Ireland or Irish Land; Grievances; Remedies*, reprinted from the *Daily Telegraph*. Russell's powers as a cross-examiner were displayed during the Parnell Commission of 1888–1890, when as leading counsel for PARNELL he tore to shreds the evidence of PIGOTT, the author of forged letters that were the basis of the charges made in *The Times*. His advocacy for Britain in the Bering Sea arbitration of 1893 won him the Grand Order of St Michael and St George. His income at the bar was very great: as a junior he earned £3,000 a year, and in his last year as a QC he earned £20,000. Lord of appeal 1894, and created Baron Russell of Killowen; a month later appointed lord chief justice, the first Catholic to be appointed to the position since the Reformation. In his comparatively short tenure of office he won the confidence and good will of the public to a remarkable degree. Died in Kensington, 10 August 1900, after a short illness. Survived by his wife and nine children.

RUSSELL, GEORGE WILLIAM (1867–1935), poet and painter, also known by the pen-name AE (originally Æ, for 'Æon'). Born at Lurgan, Co. Armagh, 10 April 1867 and, the family removing to Dublin, was educated at Rathmines School and the Metropolitan School of Art, where he began his lifelong friendship with W. B. YEATS. After working as a clerk he joined the Irish Agricultural Organisation Society under SIR HORACE PLUNKETT in 1897 and became editor of its organ, the *Irish*

Homestead. His gifts as a writer and publicist gained it a wide influence in the cause of agricultural co-operation. His first book of poems, *Homeward: Songs by the Way* (1894) established him in the literary movement. His interests were wide: he became a theosophist, and wrote extensively on economics and politics, besides continuing to paint and write poetry. His *Collected Poems* appeared in 1913, with a second edition in 1926. From 1923 to 1930 he was editor of the *Irish Statesman*, and his house in Rathgar Avenue was a meeting-place for everyone interested in the artistic and economic future of Ireland. After his wife's death in 1932 he moved to England, and died in Bournemouth, 17 July 1935. The keynote of his work may be found in a motto from the Bhagavadgita, prefixed to one of his early poems: 'I am Beauty itself among beautiful things.'

RUSSELL, REV. MATTHEW (1834–1912), editor and writer. Born at Newry, Co. Down, brother of LORD RUSSELL OF KILLOWEN. Educated at Castleknock College and Maynooth. Ordained Jesuit 1864; taught at Crescent College, Limerick, 1864–1873. Founded *Irish Monthly* (first called *Catholic Ireland*) 1873, and edited it until his death. Encouraged many young writers, and wrote a number of devotional works, many in verse. From 1877 to 1886 and from 1903 until shortly before his death he also carried out priestly duties at St Francis Xavier's, Gardiner Street, Dublin. Died in Dublin, 12 September 1912.

RUSSELL, THOMAS (1767–1803), United Irishman, the 'Man from Godknows-where'. Born at Betsborough, Kilshanick, Co. Cork, on 21 November 1767. Although intended for the Church, joined the British army in 1782. His regiment was stationed at Belfast in 1791, and he became friendly with SAMUEL NEILSON, HENRY JOY MCCRACKEN, and other liberal politicians. About this time he was obliged to sell his commission, having gone bail for a swindler, and he became librarian of the Linen Hall Library. He then took an active part in the organising of the United Irish Society, and in 1796 he was arrested with Neilson and others. In July 1798 he was sent to Fort George in Scotland. Released in 1802 and went to Paris, where he met ROBERT EMMET, and became his follower. Returned to Ireland in April 1803 and was given the task of organising Ulster for Emmet's projected rising. After the failure of the rising he was arrested in Dublin in September by MAJOR HENRY SIRR, tried at Downpatrick for high treason, and hanged there on 21 October 1803. His story is told in a well-known poem 'The Man from God Knows Where' by Florence Wilson.

RUSSELL, THOMAS O'NEILL (1828–1908), author. Born at Lissonode, Moate, Co. Westmeath, son of a Quaker gentleman-farmer, and educated at the local national school. He worked as a commercial traveller for Jacob's, the biscuit manufacturers, learned Irish, and made its revival his life-long aim. Fearing arrest because of his association with the *Irishman*, an advanced nationalist paper, he emigrated to America, where he worked for thirty years as a commercial traveller while lecturing and writing on Irish. He returned to Dublin in 1895 and continued his work for the language revival, publishing volumes of essays, poems, translations from the Irish, and songs. He also wrote plays and a popular novel, *Dick Massey* (1860). Died in Synge Street, Dublin, 15 June 1908.

RUSSELL, SIR WILLIAM HOWARD (1820–1907), war correspondent. Born at Lily Vale, Tallaght, Co. Dublin, 28 March 1820. Educated at Dr Geoghegan's school in Hume St, TCD, and the Middle Temple. Called to the English bar 1850. Left college without a degree and joined *The Times*, reporting the Repeal agitation led by DANIEL O'CONNELL, and the general election of 1841. In 1854 he went to Gallipoli to report the Crimean War, and his letters describing the mismanagement of food supplies, the lack of medical care and the sufferings of the troops made him famous and popular in England, and an object of hatred to the army commanders. The phrase he applied to the infantry at Balaklava, the 'thin red streak', became part of the English language as the 'thin red line'. TCD honoured him with an LL.D. on his return. His next assignment brought him to India to report the campaign of 1858 to put down the 'Indian mutiny'. In 1860 he founded the *Army and Navy Gazette*, of which he was editor and principal owner to the end of his life, while still accepting important commissions from *The Times*. Went to the USA in 1861 and saw the first battle of Bull Run in the Civil War. His opposition to slavery had made him unpopular in the south; his faithful description of the disorderly retreat of the Federal troops at Bull Run brought down extreme northern anger, and he returned to England. He accompanied the Prussians in the 1870 Franco-German War; his last campaign was in South Africa during the Zulu War of 1879. He was knighted in 1895 and received orders from many European countries. He has been called 'the first modern war correspondent'. Died in Kensington. Buried at Brompton cemetery.

RYAN, CORNELIUS (1920–1974), war correspondent and author. Born in Dublin, 5 June 1920. Educated at Synge St CBS and RIAM. At twenty he went to London as secretary to Garfield Weston, an MP. He wanted to write, and joined the Reuters news agency a year later. In 1943 he became a war correspondent with the *Daily Telegraph*, and covered the D-Day invasion of Normandy on 6 June 1944 and the progress of General Patton's Third Army. Later, in 1945, he opened the *Daily Telegraph* bureau in Tokyo and reported the atomic bomb tests in the Pacific and the war in Palestine. In 1947 he went to New York as a staff writer for *Time*. He then worked for *Newsweek* and *Collier's Magazine* until 1956, when he became a roving correspondent for *Reader's Digest*, but devoted most of his time to his books. During these years as a working journalist he published six books on a variety of subjects, including two on General MacArthur and two on space, written in collaboration with Werner von Braun. After a visit to Normandy in 1949 on the fifth anniversary of D-Day he determined to write a history of the invasion. Having spent ten years on research, interviewed more than 1,000 participants and left himself 20,000 dollars in debt, he published *The Longest Day* in 1959. It was an instant best-seller, ending years of struggle for him and his family and making him a millionaire. It was made into a film that set box-office records. His wife was the main family support during those difficult years, when she worked as editor of *House and Home* and *Architectural Forum*. He had become an American citizen in 1950 and, after his success, settled in Ridgefield, Connecticut, and began research on his next book, on the fall of Berlin. Interviews and collection of data took five years and cost 60,000 dollars. *The Last Battle* was another best-seller. More than ten million hardcover copies of these two books were sold, and they appeared in twenty languages. His combination of tireless research and narrative skill earned him praise from Malcolm Muggeridge as 'the most brilliant reporter in the world'. His last work, *A Bridge Too Far*, which occupied him for seven years, was an account of the disastrous Allied 'Operation Market Garden' and battle of Arnhem in 1944. He died of cancer in New York in November 1974.

RYAN, DESMOND (1893–1964), journalist. Born in London. Educated at Scoil Éanna in Dublin. Acted as secretary to PEARSE; during the 1916 Rising he fought at the GPO, and after his release from internment became a journalist, like his father, W. P. RYAN. He wrote *The Man Called Pearse* (1919), *James*

Connolly (1924), *Remembering Sion* (1934), *Unique Dictator* (1936), *The Phoenix Flame* (1937), and *The Rising* (1949). Died in Dublin.

RYAN, FRANK (1902–1944), republican and socialist. Born near Elton, Co. Limerick. Educated at the local national school, St Colman's College, Fermoy, and UCD. His university career was interrupted in 1922 by service on the Republican side during the Civil War, and a year's internment. On graduating in Celtic studies in 1925 he worked first as a teacher of Irish and then with the Irish Tourist Association. By that time he was a member of the executive of the IRA and editor of its paper, *An Phoblacht*, and these activities led to his arrest and dismissal. In 1931 he helped to organise the socially radical Saor Éire movement, and in 1934, coming to believe that republicanism without democracy meant fascism, he broke with the IRA in an effort to build up a united front in Ireland against fascism. In 1936 he led a contingent of two hundred Irishmen to Spain to fight in the 15th or International Brigade for the Republic against General Franco. He reached the rank of major, was wounded early in 1937 at the battle of Jarama, and then ordered home to recuperate. He stood as a Republican candidate for the Dáil in the general election of that year but received only 875 votes. On his return to Spain he was appointed brigade adjutant to General Miaja, commander of the Spanish Republican army, and was editor of the *History of the 15th Brigade*, published in 1938 by the Spanish War Commissariat. He was captured by Italian forces in April 1938 and sentenced to death. ÉAMON DE VALERA, then Taoiseach, appealed at once to Franco for clemency, and a nation-wide campaign supported this appeal. Ryan spent thirteen months under sentence of death in a prison near Burgos, and then the sentence was commuted to thirty years' imprisonment. A year later he was set free by arrangement between the Irish, Spanish and German governments, and he was taken to Berlin in August 1940. The Germans proposed to send him to America to urge that the USA should stay neutral in the Second World War, but in Berlin he met Seán Russell, chief of staff of the IRA, and left with him for Ireland in a German submarine. Russell died suddenly on board, from peritonitis, and Ryan returned to Berlin, where German military intelligence treated him as a non-party neutral. In 1943 his health began to fail. Died in a sanatorium in Dresden, 10 June 1944.

RYAN, DR JAMES (1891–1970), politician. Born near Taghmon, Co. Wexford, 6 December 1891; went to school at St Peter's College, Wexford, and Ring College, and qualified in medicine at UCD. He had joined the Irish Volunteers as a student, and served as medical officer in the GPO in the 1916 Rising. Arrested, and interned at Frongoch until the general amnesty of December 1916; Sinn Féin MP for Wexford 1918. After the Treaty he took the Republican side, was elected TD for Wexford in 1923 and with DE VALERA and others founded Fianna Fáil in 1926. Minister for Agriculture 1932–1947; first Minister for Health and Social Welfare 1947. He held the same posts from 1954 until 1957, when he became Minister for Finance. With Dr T. K. Whitaker, then secretary of the department, he transformed it from its traditional role to a Department of Economic Affairs, by securing government backing for Whitaker's programme, aimed at finding and releasing a dynamic in Irish economic development. Whitaker's 'grey book', *Economic Development*, supplied the groundwork for the first Programme for Economic Expansion (1959), which marked a turning-point in the economy. He retired from politics in 1965. He was one of the founders of the New Ireland Assurance Company, and served as a director and as medical adviser. He farmed extensively at Delgany, Co. Wicklow. Died 25 September 1970.

RYAN, PATRICK J. (1883–1964), Olympic hammer-throwing champion. Born in Co. Limerick. Won his first Irish championship at Limerick in 1901 when he beat the world record holder, Tom Kiely. Emigrated to America and won the hammer-throwing championship of the USA every year from 1913 to 1921, except 1918, serving with the US forces in France in between these exploits. At Celtic Park in New York in August 1913 he set a world record at 189 feet 6½ inches (57.77 m), which stood until 1937 and was not beaten as an American record until 1952. He won his Olympic gold medal for the USA at Antwerp in 1920 and a silver medal for the 56 lb (25.5 kg) throw. A close friend of fellow-athletes John Kelly (father of Princess Grace of Monaco) and Gene Tunney, world heavyweight boxing champion. Returned to Ireland in 1919 and won the Irish championship at Croke Park. He took up farming in Limerick and died at Old Pallas, Pallasgreen, Co. Limerick, 13 February 1964.

RYAN, WILLIAM PATRICK (1867–1942), journalist. Born at Templemore, Co. Tipperary. He became a journalist in London but returned to Ireland in 1906 to edit John McCann's *Irish Peasant* at Navan. When the paper was suppressed by CARDINAL LOGUE, Ryan took it over and restarted it in Dublin as the *Peasant* (1907–1908). In 1909 it became the *Irish Nation*. In December 1910 Ryan returned to London, where he was involved in labour journalism for the rest of his life. Between 1911 and 1913 he edited *An tÉireannach* for the Gaelic League. He published fiction, drama, essays, poetry, and philosophy, in English and Irish, including *The Heart of Tipperary* (1893), *The Irish Literary Revival* (1894), *Plays for People* (1904), *The Pope's Green Island* (1912), *The Labour Revolt and Larkinism* (1913), and *The Irish Labour Movement* (1919). Died in London.

RYNNE, MICHAEL (1899–1981), revolutionary and ambassador. Born in 1899 and educated at Crescent College, Limerick, Our Lady's Bower, Athlone, Clongowes Wood College, UCD, and King's Inns. He joined the Irish Volunteers in 1917, became a captain in the Dublin Brigade, and saw active service in the War of Independence. After the Civil War he was called to the bar, studied law on the Continent, and received a doctorate from Munich University for a thesis on Ireland's constitutional and international position. In 1930 he returned to Ireland to work in O'Mara's, the family bacon company in Limerick. In 1932 he joined the Department of External Affairs as assistant legal adviser, soon became legal adviser, and was promoted assistant secretary in the 1950s. He served on many delegations to international conferences in Europe and America. Ambassador to Spain from 1954 until his retirement in 1961. He wrote many poems, short stories and radio plays under the pseudonym Andrew Lysaght (his middle names). He died in a Dublin hospital on 8 February 1981.

RYNNE, STEPHEN (1901–1980), writer, farmer and broadcaster. Born of wealthy Irish parents in Hampshire and educated at Clongowes Wood College and Reading University. He settled at Prosperous, Co. Kildare, where he farmed for the rest of his life. Wrote an autobiography, *Green Fields* (1938), a travel book, *All Ireland* (1956), and in 1960 a biography of CANON JOHN HAYES. Wrote many articles, and broadcast frequently on nature and farming subjects. Died on 12 December 1980 in a Dublin hospital.

S

SABINE, SIR EDWARD (1788–1883), soldier and scientist. Born 14 October 1788 in Great Britain Street (Parnell Street), Dublin. Educated at Marlow and Royal Military Academy, Woolwich. Commissioned in the artillery, and after serving in Gibraltar, on home stations, and in Canada, returned to England in 1816 and devoted himself to his favourite studies in astronomy, terrestrial magnetism, and ornithology. He was appointed astronomer to the Arctic expeditions of Ross (1818) and Parry (1819–1820), in search of a north-west passage. From 1821 to 1823 he conducted pendulum and magnetic experiments of great value on the coasts of Africa, America and the Arctic. In 1827 he was given general leave of absence from the army so that he could engage in scientific work. Most of his long life was devoted to research on terrestrial magnetism, and he superintended the establishment of magnetic observatories on British territory throughout the world. The results of his work were embodied in papers contributed to the British Association. Elected FRS 1818, president 1861–1871; KCB 1869, and honoured by learned institutions at home and abroad. Promoted general 1870, and in 1877, at eighty-nine, retired from the army on full pay. Died at Richmond, 16 June 1883.

SADLEIR, JOHN (1814–1856), politician and swindler. Born at Shronell, near Tipperary. Educated at Clongowes Wood College. He succeeded his uncle in a prosperous solicitor's practice in Dublin but left the legal profession in 1846 to devote himself to his business interests. He became a director of the Tipperary Joint-Stock Bank, which had been established about 1827 by his brother, and of a number of railway companies in England, France, and Switzerland. Elected MP for Carlow 1847; later sat for Sligo, and became one of the leaders of the group known as 'the Pope's Brass Band'. A junior lord of the Treasury 1843–1853. In 1856 he had overdrawn his account at the Tipperary bank by £200,000, and when a London bank refused to honour drafts on Tipperary, he committed suicide, his body being found on Hampstead Heath on 17 February 1856. It was discovered that the Tipperary bank was hopelessly insolvent, and depositors and others, mainly small farmers and clerks in the south of Ireland, lost about £400,000. To raise funds he had also forged land conveyances and railway share certificates. These revelations created a sensation. Dickens based the character of Mr Merdle in *Little Dorrit* on Sadleir.

SADLIER, MARY ANNE (1820–1903), novelist. Born Mary Madden, 31 December 1820 at Cootehill, Co. Cavan. Emigrated to Canada in 1844 and married well-known American publisher James Sadlier in 1846. She moved to New York in 1860, returning to Canada in 1869 after her husband's death. She wrote some sixty popular novels with Irish backgrounds, including *The Red Hand of Ulster* and *The Old House by the Boyne*. Died in Montreal, 5 April 1903.

SALMON, GEORGE (1819–1904), mathematician and theologian. Born at Cork, 25 September 1819. Educated there at Mr Porter's School and at TCD. After a brilliant academic career, became a fellow of the college 1841; professor of divinity 1866–1888. His *Conic Sections* (1847) was the leading textbook on the subject for fifty years and, with subsequent works on algebra and geometry, he established his reputation as a mathematician. His strong Protestant views found trenchant expression in *The Infallibility of the Church* (1889); he also published many studies of the New Testament. Appointed provost, TCD, 1888. Died in the Provost's House, 22 January 1904. Buried in Mount Jerome cemetery.

SANDS, BOBBY (1954–1981), revolutionary. Born in Belfast, left school at fifteen to become an apprentice to a coachbuilder. Complaining of intimidation by loyalists, the family moved from north Belfast to Twinbrook, west Belfast, in 1972, and shortly afterwards he joined the IRA. In 1973 he was charged with possession of four guns and sentenced to five years' imprisonment. He served his term as a 'special category' prisoner at the Maze prison, Long Kesh. Six months after release he was arrested following the bombing of a furniture factory and sentenced in September 1977 to fourteen years. While he was in prison his marriage broke up. 'Special category' or political status had been phased out from 1976, and he was imprisoned in the newly built 'H' blocks at Long Kesh. The IRA decided on a hunger strike in support of demands for civilian clothes and other marks of political status. On 1 March 1981 Bobby Sands began his fast. He was joined by three other IRA prisoners within three weeks. At a by-election on 9 April 1981 he was elected Westminster MP for Fermanagh-Tyrone in a straight fight against 'Official' Unionist Harry West. As the strikes went on and attempts at a settlement failed, tension mounted throughout the Six Counties, with rioting in Derry and Belfast. The British government remained inflexibly opposed to granting political status. Bobby Sands died on 5 May 1981, the sixty-sixth day of his hunger strike. Another prisoner took his place and the strike continued until the tenth prisoner died on 20 August. In 1981 Sinn Féin published Sands's prison diary and poems; an anthology of his writings, *Skylark, Sing Your Lonely Song*, appeared in 1982.

SANKEY, SIR RICHARD HIERAM (1829–1908), soldier and engineer. Born 22 March 1829 at Rockwell Castle, Co. Tipperary. Educated at Rev. D. Flynn's school, Harcourt Street, Dublin, and East India Company's military academy, Addiscombe. Appointed second lieutenant, Madras Engineers, in 1846. Served in the campaign against the 'Indian Mutiny'. Chief engineer at Mysore 1864–1877 and established irrigation department to deal scientifically with old native works. Commanded Royal Engineers on famous march from Kandahar to Kabul 1878–1879. Appointed major-general and received CB, 1883. On retiring from the army he was appointed chairman of the Irish Board of Works in 1884. Received KCB in 1892 and retired from board 1896. Died at his home, 32 Grosvenor Place, London, 11 November 1908.

SARGENT, FAY (1890–1967), actress and journalist. Born in Waterford. In 1907 married Philip Sargent, a timber merchant who was later prominent in the War of Independence. She raised funds for the cause by organising and singing at concerts, appeared in the Abbey Theatre under the name Dympna Daly, and with JIMMY O'DEA and RIA MOONEY in several silent films. She was best known for her regular column in the *Evening Herald*, featuring the conversations of Mrs Casey and Mrs Win-the-War, two typical Dublin 'characters'. Died in Dublin in December 1967.

SARR, KENNETH. See under REDDIN, KENNETH.

SARSFIELD, PATRICK, EARL OF LUCAN (died 1693), soldier. Born at Lucan, Co. Dublin, and educated at a French military school. On the death of his elder brother in 1675 he inherited an estate of £2,000 a year. He joined the

English Life Guards and fought for King James II against Monmouth at Sedgemoor in 1685. He accompanied the king to Ireland in 1689, was made brigadier-general, and expelled the Williamites from Connacht. He played only a minor role in command of cavalry at the Battle of the Boyne in 1690 but became second-in-command in the defence of Limerick under Boisileau. Guided by the rapparee 'Galloping' Hogan, he ambushed and blew up a Williamite convoy of guns and supplies at Ballyneety, near Limerick, in August 1690. The siege was abandoned the following month, and in February 1691 he was created Earl of Lucan. St Ruth then arrived from France to take command in Ireland, but was killed at the Battle of Aughrim in July 1691. The Jacobite forces were routed, as St Ruth had not communicated his plans to Sarsfield or any other of his officers. After 'Aughrim's dread disaster', Sarsfield defended Limerick for the second time, until September 1691, when a treaty was signed. The military articles allowed any of the Irish who so wished to depart from Ireland; about 12,000 troops left for France with Sarsfield and joined the Irish Brigade. He was mortally wounded two years later at the Battle of Landen and died 23 July 1693. He is credited with saying to the English after Limerick: 'Change kings and we will fight it over again with you,' and 'Oh, that this were for Ireland!' on seeing the blood from his wounds at Landen.

SAUL, CAPTAIN PATRICK J. (1894–1968), pioneer aviator. Born in Dublin; educated at St Patrick's Cathedral Grammar School. Went to sea in sail, and made several voyages around Cape Horn. Transferred to steam vessels, and took his master's certificate before the outbreak of the First World War. During the war he served with gunboats on the river Tigris, and was then posted to the Royal Engineers at Basra with the rank of captain. After the war he returned to the sea. His first wife was drowned when the ship he commanded sank off the French coast in 1922; he swam ashore with his baby daughter wrapped in a blanket. He then returned to the family coal business in Dublin and interested himself in the development of private flying in Ireland. In June 1930 he was navigator for Sir Charles Kingsford-Smith aboard the *Southern Cross* when it made a historic east-to-west trans-Atlantic flight from Portmarnock, Co. Dublin, to Harbour Grace, Newfoundland. In 1937 he became a civilian navigation instructor with the RAF. During the Second World War he was commissioned in the RAF and became a wing-commander. In 1941, at the request of the Irish government, he was transferred by the Air Ministry to take the post of chief of air traffic control at Foynes, Co. Limerick, then a flying-boat base. From 1950 to his retirement in 1959 he was chief of air traffic services in the Department of Industry and Commerce. He then took an active part in organising the Irish Federation of Sea Anglers. Died suddenly, 22 June 1968, while fishing on Lough Swilly.

SAURIN, WILLIAM (*c.* 1757–1839), attorney-general. Born in Belfast; educated at Dubourdieu's school at Lisburn, TCD, and Lincoln's Inn, London. Called to the Irish bar 1780, built up a large practice, and entered parliament in 1799 as member for Blessington. He prosecuted the 1798 leaders OLIVER BOND and the SHEARES BROTHERS. He opposed the Union of 1800 as weakening the Protestant ascendancy. Attorney-general for Ireland 1807, and showed uncompromising hostility to Catholic claims for emancipation. His intolerance became so virulent that Lord Wellesley felt obliged to remove him from office in 1822. He was offered a peerage and a judgeship as compensation but refused both and returned to practise at the bar. He retired in 1831. Died 11 January 1839.

SAYERS, PEIG (1873–1958), storyteller. Born at Vicarstown, Dún Chaoin, Co. Kerry. Nine of her brothers and sisters died young, only four of a family of thirteen surviving. At fourteen she went as servant-girl in the house of a large shopkeeper in Dingle, where she was treated with kindness and affection. After some years her health failed and she returned home. Recovering, she went to service in another house in Dingle, where she found a harsh mistress and poor living conditions. A few years later a match was arranged for her with Pádraig Ó Guíthín, 'Pats Flint', from the Great Blasket Island. She lived for over forty years on the island, and bore ten children, of whom six survived. One of her sons, Tomás, was killed when he fell down a cliff. Her husband died in his middle years, her children emigrated, and she was left alone. Her sole companion in her later years on the island was her blind brother-in-law. She had a great store of folklore, and had been noted among the islanders for her story-telling. Seosamh Ó Dálaigh of the Irish Folklore Commission took down from her 375 of the wonder tales of Gaelic Ireland, and forty folk-songs. Her autobiography, *Peig*, was taken down from her dictation by her son Mícheál, edited by Máire Ní Chinnéide, and published in 1936. An English translation by Bryan MacMahon appeared in 1973. *Machnamh Sheanmhná* (1939) was translated by Séamus Ennis in 1962 as *An Old Woman's Reflections*. A further instalment of her autobiography, *Beatha Pheig Sayers*, also dictated to her son, appeared in 1970. By 1953 the population of the island had dwindled to the point where community life could not continue, and the Government re-settled the remaining families on the mainland. Peig spent her last years in hospital in Dingle. Her sight failed, and she died there shortly before Christmas 1958. She was the last of the three famous writers from the Great Blasket. Her autobiography ranks with those of Ó CRIOMHTHAIN and MUIRIS Ó SÚILLEABHÁIN among the classics of their kind in modern Irish literature.

SCOTT, JOHN, EARL OF CLONMELL (1739–1798), chief justice. Born 8 June 1739 in Co. Tipperary. Educated at TCD and the Middle Temple. Called to the bar in 1765 and built up a large practice. His unblushing effrontery and bronzed appearance gained him the nickname 'copper-faced Jack'. Elected MP for Mullingar 1769; KC 1770. Turned from the patriotic side when promised office, saying, 'My Lord, you have spoiled a good patriot.' Appointed solicitor-general 1774, attorney-general 1777. He spoke strongly in favour of legislative independence in 1782 and was peremptorily dismissed from office, but with a change in the ministry he was soon restored to favour. Appointed chief justice 1784. Made Viscount Clonmell 1789. In the same year he ruined what judicial reputation he had by issuing a fiat for £4,000 against JOHN MAGEE. Following severe criticism in press and parliament, a law was specially passed to regulate the issue of fiats. He was made earl in 1793. His court was boycotted because of his gross rudeness to a barrister, and he had to apologise publicly. Died 23 May 1798. His *Diary*, printed privately by his family after his death, confirmed that he was 'unscrupulous, passionate and greedy'.

SEXTON, THOMAS (1848–1932), nationalist MP. Born at Ballygannon, Co. Waterford. Educated at local CBS. Starting his working life as a railway clerk, he became a leader-writer on the *Nation*, joined the Parnellite party, and was elected MP for Sligo in 1880. Lord Mayor of Dublin 1888–1889. Left politics soon after the Parnellite split. He was in charge of the *Freeman's Journal* from 1892 to 1912; thereafter, apart from business interests in insurance and a bakery, he lived a very retired life, dying in Dublin on 1 November 1932.

SHACKLETON, SIR ERNEST HENRY (1874–1922), explorer. Born at Kilkea, Co. Kildare, 15 February 1874. Educated at Dulwich College, London. He went to sea in the merchant service and qualified as a master mariner. His part in Captain Scott's Antarctic expedition of 1901–1903 strengthened his desire for adventure and fame, and in 1907 he led his own expedition in the whaler *Nimrod* and came within ninety-seven miles (156 km) of the South Pole. On his return he was knighted and granted £20,000 by Parliament towards the cost of the expedition. In 1914 he set out again for the Antarctic. His ship, the *Endurance*, was beset in pack-ice for nine months, and finally crushed. Shackleton led his men for five months across ice floes until they reached Elephant Island, and then made an 800-mile (1,300 km) journey with five companions in a 22-foot (6.7 m) boat through some of the stormiest seas in the world to reach a Norwegian whaling station in South Georgia Island. Relief expeditions under his command rescued the rest of his party from Elephant Island after three attempts. In 1921 he set out on a further Antarctic journey, but died suddenly in South Georgia, 5 January 1922. His explorations, which yielded considerable discoveries and valuable scientific results, are described by him in his two books, *The Heart of the Antarctic* (1909) and *South* (1919).

SHANAHAN, JOSEPH (1871–1943), missionary bishop. Born 6 June 1871 at Glenkeen, near Templederry, Co. Tipperary. After studying in France and at Rockwell College, ordained Holy Ghost father 1900; dean of discipline at Rockwell 1900–1902. Volunteered for the mission field and sent to southern Nigeria 1902. Prefect apostolic 1905; first vicar apostolic of southern Nigeria and titular bishop of Abila 1920. In his thirty years in southern Nigeria he directed the building up of a network of schools, hospitals, mission stations, and teachers' colleges, and the extensive Christianising of the area. His particular achievement was in the field of education. Member for twelve years of the Education Advisory Council set up by the British colonial authorities in 1906. Also instrumental in the forming of the Congregation of the Holy Rosary, an

order of missionary sisters, at Killeshandra, Co. Cavan, in 1924. In 1932 he returned to Ireland because of ill-health, but six years later he went to Zanzibar (Tanzania) as an assistant to the missionary in charge there. Died in December 1943. Buried in the missionaries' cemetery in Nairobi.

SHAW, SIR EYRE MASSEY (1830–1908), head of London Fire Brigade. Born Ballymore, Co. Cork, 17 January 1830. Educated TCD; served in British army 1854–1859. Chief constable of Belfast 1859, re-organised the fire brigade, and suppressed party disturbances with acknowledged impartiality. When the head of London Fire Brigade died in the great fire in Tooley Street in 1861 he was appointed in his place. Brought the brigade to a high degree of efficiency by unremitting attention. Twice severely injured while directing operations. Wrote many treatises on fire protection, which became standard works. CB 1879, KCB 1891. Received freedom of city of London 1892 after retirement. Managing director, Palatine Insurance and chairman, Metropolitan Electric Supply Co. Died at Folkestone, 25 August 1908.

SHAW, GEORGE BERNARD (1856–1950), playwright. Born 26 July 1856 at 3 Upper Synge Street (now 33 Synge Street), Dublin, the only son of an unsuccessful wholesale merchant, and educated at Wesley College. His mother was a good singer and formed a friendship with her teacher, George Vandeleur Lee, with whom the Shaws shared a house for some years. Lee also owned Torca Cottage, Dalkey, Co. Dublin, where they spent summers remembered with pleasure by Shaw many years later. Growing up shy, poor, and lonely, Shaw haunted the National Gallery in Merrion Square, and at home listened absorbedly to the music that filled the house. It was thus, he said later, that he got his real education. At sixteen he went into an estate office as a junior clerk.

Then Lee suddenly decided to remove to London in 1872, and Mrs Shaw, tired of genteel poverty with her tippling husband, followed him with her two daughters, leaving her husband and son to fend for themselves. Four years later young Shaw joined her, having made up his mind to be a writer. Her earnings as a music teacher, supplemented in 1877 by his share of a legacy, kept their ramshackle establishment going. From 1876 to 1885 Shaw laboured at the writing of five novels, none of which had any success. His perseverance in the face of these nine years of discouragement showed his resolution and courage; his industry earned him scarcely fifty pence a year. He joined the Fabian Society in 1884, and with a further display of will-power and persistence overcame his shyness to become one of the most effective speakers in the country. He also served as a local government councillor in the borough of St Pancras from 1897 to 1903. The drama critic Archer, who met Shaw in the reading-room of the British Museum, found him employment in 1885 as a book reviewer for the *Pall Mall Gazette* and as art critic for the *World*. In 1888 he became music critic on the *Star*, and under the pen-name Corno di Bassetto wrote a new kind of musical criticism, direct, clear and lively, which can be read to this day with pleasure. The tide had begun to turn, he was beginning to be known in literary circles, and the hard apprenticeship was nearly, but not quite, finished.

His first play, *Widowers' Houses*, was produced in London in 1892, and had for theme the evil of slum landlordism. He next wrote *The Philanderer, Mrs Warren's Profession, Arms and the Man, Candida,* and *You Never Can Tell*. Astonishing though it may seem today, none of these plays was a success, and it seemed that Shaw would fail as a dramatist just as he had failed as a novelist. He accepted a post as dramatic critic on the *Saturday Review* in 1895 under the editorship of FRANK HARRIS. Then recognition came from the USA,

where his next play, *The Devil's Disciple*, was acclaimed in New York and earned more than £2,000 in royalties in 1897. The following year he collapsed from overwork, and was nursed by Charlotte Payne-Townshend, a wealthy Anglo-Irishwoman whom he had met while staying with his Fabian friends Sidney and Beatrice Webb. They were married in 1898, and their happy union brought a settled way of life to Shaw. They settled at Ayot St Laurence in Hertfordshire in 1906. From 1898, almost every year saw a new play from his pen. But it was not until Harley Granville-Barker, a gifted producer, took over at the Royal Court Theatre in 1904 that Shaw's genius as a playwright was recognised in London. Here were seen for the first time *John Bull's Other Island, Man and Superman* and *The Doctor's Dilemma. John Bull's Other Island* was written at the request of W. B. YEATS for the Irish Literary Theatre, but Shaw was quite out of tune with the Celtic movement, and in addition, the play called for stagecraft beyond the compass of the comparatively inexperienced Irish players. In London it was well received, possibly because it showed Englishmen as sentimental but successful and the typical Irishman as clever but unsuccessful. By the outbreak of the First World War in 1914 Shaw was established as the leading dramatist and wit of his day. He quickly lost his popularity when he published *Common Sense About the War* in November 1914; his courageous stand for his native country after the 1916 Rising and his defence of ROGER CASEMENT increased public resentment against him. His idea of justice and his clear thinking on the real nature of war were anathema to a people caught up in the fever of the times. Those of the fighting men who survived the trenches showed that they had different views when they crowded the theatre at a revival of *Arms and the Man* in 1919.

Shaw himself considered *Heartbreak House*, produced in New York in 1920, to be his best play; most critics give the palm to *Saint Joan*, which, with Sybil Thorndike in the title role, was an immense success in London in 1924 and made him the world's most famous living dramatist. He was awarded the Nobel Prize in 1925. In 1928 he returned to political writing with *The Intelligent Woman's Guide to Socialism and Capitalism*, an example of English prose at its best: lucid, vigorous, and compelling. The Shaws travelled a great deal, for his wife delighted to visit foreign countries. He had become a vegetarian in 1881 after much reading of Shelley, whose works included the little-known *A Vindication of Natural Diet* (1813). He attributed his health and energy to this diet and to the fact that he neither smoked nor drank alcohol, but he became seriously ill with pernicious anaemia in 1938. His wife died in 1943 after a long illness; they had no children, and the remaining seven years of his life were quiet and solitary. He was made an honorary freeman of Dublin in his ninetieth year. In September 1950 he fell and fractured his thigh, dying at home on 2 November. His body was cremated and the ashes were scattered in the garden of the house, which he left to the National Trust. His will benefited the National Gallery of Ireland, where as a poor boy he had found the intellectual stimulus for which his heart and mind had craved. The enormous royalties from *My Fair Lady*, a film version of *Pygmalion*, multiplied the value of this bequest many times over.

Shaw was the first disciple of Ibsen to write for the English stage, and he aimed to stimulate the minds of playgoers rather than to titillate their emotions. His plays treated of themes previously aired only in parliament or pulpit: prostitution, war, religion, and economics. But the wit and eloquence with which he presented his ideas, the sparkling conversation he put into the mouths of his characters and the freshness of his approach brought a new intellectual life to the stage. He took to writing long prefaces to his plays, and these display to the full his mastery of English prose. His famous correspondence with the actress Ellen Terry has more of her in it than of

Shaw and is a singularly fascinating contribution to that branch of literature. His socialism could fairly be described as based on his view that human happiness is best served by the creation of an orderly community.

SHEARES, HENRY (1753–1798), elder brother of JOHN. Born at Cork; educated at TCD. Joined the British army, but resigned his commission after three years. Called to the bar 1789. His first wife died in 1791, and their four children were reared by her parents in France. While visiting them in 1792 with his brother he formed the revolutionary principles that brought him into the United Irishmen, and to his death.

SHEARES, JOHN (1766–1798), United Irishman. Born at Cork, son of a wealthy banker and MP. Educated at TCD; called to the bar 1788. Visited France in 1792 with his brother HENRY and became imbued with the political principles of the revolution. On his return to Dublin he joined the United Irishmen and became a frequent contributor to a nationalist paper, the *Press*. He was arrested with his brother on 21 May 1798, having been betrayed by a Captain Armstrong of the militia, to whom he had revealed his plans. The brothers were found guilty of high treason and publicly executed before Newgate prison on 14 July 1798. They were buried in the crypt of St Michan's Church.

SHEE, SIR MARTIN ARCHER (1769–1850), portrait painter. Born in Dublin, 20 December 1769. Studied painting in the school of the Dublin Society under Francis West. By the age of seventeen he was able to make a good living as a portrait painter in crayons. In June 1788 he left for London. After initial set-backs, on the advice of Sir Joshua Reynolds he entered the schools of the RA, and soon began to make steady progress. He had a number of portraits accepted by the academy in 1791 and 1792. Became an associate in

1798; elected full member 1800. He now had an assured position and a large practice as a portrait painter. Elected president of the RA 25 January 1830; knighted that year. He worked with skill and diplomacy to advance the interests of the academy and of the profession, and, in his own words, 'was always ready to break a lance with the vandalism of the day.' In 1826 the RHA made him an honorary member in recognition of his services in securing its charter. He published a number of poems, two novels, and a tragedy. His health began to decline about 1843, and he stopped painting and proposed to resign his presidency. The whole body of members and associates requested that he remain and voted him a salary of £300 a year for his life. Died at Brighton, 19 August 1850.

SHEEHAN, CANON PATRICK AUGUSTINE (1852–1913), priest and novelist. Born in Mallow, Co. Cork, 17 March 1852. Educated at St Colman's College, Fermoy, and Maynooth seminary. Ordained in Cork, 18 April 1875. Served as curate on the English mission at Plymouth and Exeter. After curacies in Co. Cork he was appointed parish priest of Doneraile in 1895, and made a canon in 1903. His first novel, *Geoffrey Austin, Student* (1895) and its sequel, *The Triumph of Failure* (1898), dealt with problems of Catholic adolescence. *My New Curate*, episodes of Irish clerical life, appeared in the *American Ecclesiastical Review* (1898). This and later books had wide popularity in Ireland and abroad; the best-known are *Glenanaar* (1905), *Luke Delmege* (1905), *Lisheen* (1907), and *The Graves at Kilmorna* (1916). Died at Doneraile, 5 October 1913.

SHEEHY, REV. NICHOLAS (1728–1766), patriot priest. Born in Clonmel. Educated at Santiago and Salamanca; ordained 1750. Served in Waterford and then became parish priest in Shanraghen and Templetenny. Took the part of his flock, forced to pay rack-rents and heavy tithes and without security of tenure. Accused in 1765 of complicity in Whiteboy offences. Fearing a packed jury in Clonmel, he succeeded in having his trial transferred to the King's Bench, Dublin, and was acquitted. Re-arrested for murder of an informer, one Bridge, and convicted in Clonmel on perjured evidence. Hanged in Clonmel on 15 March 1766.

SHEIL, RICHARD LALOR (1791–1851), dramatist and politician. Born at Drumdowney, Co. Kilkenny, 17 August 1791. Educated at Stonyhurst College and TCD. Called to the bar 1814; lacking briefs, he turned to writing, and was successful with his first play, *Adelaide*, produced in Dublin in 1814. Further successes followed in London with *The Apostate* (1817), *Bellamira* (1818), and *Evadne* (1819). His next two plays were poorly received; by this time he was active in politics, and his practice at the bar had improved. He opposed O'CONNELL's policies on Repeal but later joined him in the struggle for Catholic emancipation and was a prominent member of the Catholic Association. After the grant of emancipation in 1829 he became MP for Milborne Port, Somerset, and later sat for Co. Louth, Co. Tipperary, and Dungarvan successively. He supported the Whigs, and was appointed Master of the Mint in 1846 and British minister at the court of Tuscany in 1851. Died at Florence, 25 May 1851, shortly after he had taken up his post there.

SHEPPARD, OLIVER (1865–1941), sculptor. Born 10 April 1865 in Cookstown, Co. Tyrone, son of Simpson Sheppard, a sculptor. The family moved to Dublin soon after he was born, and he began to study at an early age in the Metropolitan School of Art. The school records of 1884 list him as an 'artisan'. In 1888 he won a scholarship to the South Kensington Art School and studied there from 1889 to 1891. About this time, he went to Paris for a year. He began to teach in Leicester and in 1895 moved to Nottingham, where he taught modelling.

He worked for two summers as assistant to Édouard Lantéri at South Kensington. He returned to Dublin in 1902 and took up a post as instructor in modelling at the Metropolitan School of Art, and later was professor of sculpture to the RHA. He first exhibited at the RHA in 1887 and continued to show there until his death. Exhibited eleven times at the RA between 1891 and 1928. Elected RHA, 1901. He exhibited with the Arts and Crafts Society of Ireland and was represented at the Irish Exhibition in Paris in 1922 and in Brussels in 1930. In 1905 he was a founder-member of the Royal Society of British Sculptors. His best-known piece, 'The Death of Cúchulain', was executed about 1911–1912, with JAMES SLEATOR as a model for the head. It was later chosen as a memorial to the 1916 Rising and is now in the GPO, Dublin. His work was mainly Celtic in inspiration, in contrast to the classical, Italianate style of his exact contemporary, JOHN HUGHES. Died in Dublin, 14 September 1941.

SHERIDAN, FRANCES, née CHAMBERLAINE (1724–1766), novelist and dramatist. Born in Dublin; her mother died soon after her birth, and her clergyman-father disapproved of his daughter's being taught to read or write. Her eldest brother, Walter, also a clergyman, taught her privately. At fifteen she wrote a romance, *Eugenia and Adelaide*, which was published after her death. When THOMAS SHERIDAN, manager of the Theatre Royal, was involved in a riot in 1745 after he had reprimanded a drunken patron, Miss Chamberlaine praised him in verses and in a pamphlet. They met, and were married in 1747. RICHARD BRINSLEY SHERIDAN was their second son. They moved to London in 1754, and Samuel Richardson encouraged Mrs Sheridan to write another novel. The result, *The Memoirs of Miss Biddulph*, appeared in 1761 and was warmly received. It was translated into German, and the Abbé Prévost made an adaptation in French. She wrote several comedies, *The Discovery* (1763) being the most successful. In 1764 the family moved to Blois in France to escape their creditors. She died there, 26 September 1766.

SHERIDAN, JOHN DESMOND (1903–1980), novelist and humorist. Born in Glasgow of Donegal parents and educated at O'Connell CBS, Dublin, St Patrick's Training College, and UCD. After teaching at East Wall NS he was for twenty-five years editor of the *Irish School Weekly*, and later became director of publications with the Educational Company of Ireland. He wrote a weekly humorous column for the *Irish Independent*, afterwards published in book form; novels, poetry, and humorous essays. His work was very popular and was translated into several languages. He died in a nursing home in Dalkey, Co. Dublin, on 1 May 1980.

SHERIDAN, MARTIN J. (1881–1918), athlete and Olympic gold-medallist. Born in Bohola, Co. Mayo, and at nineteen emigrated to New York and joined the police force. Won a gold medal in the discus at the Olympic Games in St Louis in 1904. At the special or intercalated games in Athens in 1906 he won two gold medals (discus and shot-put), three silver medals (standing high jump, standing long jump, and stone-cast), and scored more points than the team total of any other country. King George of Greece had a statue of a discus thrower erected in his honour in the Athens Stadium. He was selected to represent the USA in every field event at the London Olympics in 1908 and won two gold medals (free discus and Greek discus), and a bronze medal (standing long jump). During his career he set six-teen world records and won three world all-round ten-event athletic championships. He died of pneumonia in 1918. A memorial was erected to him in Bohola in 1966.

SHERIDAN, PHILIP HENRY (1831–1888), general. Born 6 March 1831 at

Killinkere, Co. Cavan. Taken to USA at an early age and educated at West Point Military Academy 1848–1853. He showed administrative talent, and then distinguished himself as a cavalry commander in 1862. Later in the Civil War he rose to be major-general in command of cavalry corps, Army of the Potomac, 1864. After successful engagements against Lee's forces he was appointed commander in Shenandoah Valley, and conducted a brilliant and decisive campaign. He won the last great battle of the war at Five Forks on 1 April 1865. When hostilities ended, he was appointed military governor of Texas and Louisiana, and then saw active service in Indian campaigns in the west. Succeeded Sherman as commander-in-chief in 1883. Published *Personal Memoirs* (1888). A leader of great natural magnetism and a strict disciplinarian. Died at Nonquitt, Massachusetts, 5 August 1888.

SHERIDAN, RICHARD BRINSLEY (1751–1816), playwright and orator. Born at 12 Upper Dorset Street, Dublin, 30 October 1751, son of THOMAS SHERIDAN and FRANCES CHAMBERLAINE SHERIDAN, and educated at Harrow. His first attempt at literature, a three-act farce, was written in collaboration with a school-friend. In 1771 the family settled in Bath, and the young Sheridan fell in love with Elizabeth Linley, the 'Maid of Bath', a girl of great beauty and musical talent, and eloped with her to France. After marriage they settled in London, and although Elizabeth's voice would have made their fortune, Sheridan would not allow her to sing professionally. To support their extravagant way of life he turned to writing for the stage in real earnest. *The Rivals*, produced at Covent Garden in 1775, shows the hand of the born dramatist, and quickly became popular. This was followed by two equally popular but poorly written farces. In 1776 Sheridan, now an established playwright, bought half the patent of Drury Lane Theatre from Garrick for £35,000 with the aid of his father-in-law and a friend, and in 1778 he bought the remaining half for £45,000. His masterpiece, *The School for Scandal*, was produced in 1777; equally brilliant in dialogue and in invention, it was an immediate and lasting success. The last of his three great comedies, *The Critic* (1779), showed no falling-off in his sparkling wit. Sheridan turned to politics in 1780, and sat in Parliament for thirty-two years. He was the friend of BURKE and Fox, but despite his brilliance as an orator, which held the house enthralled, he secured only minor appointments in government. In 1787 he made a famous speech supporting the impeachment of Warren Hastings. His parliamentary career came to an end when he lost his seat in 1812. During it, he opposed the Union and supported the liberty of the press. In 1792 his first wife died, and his second, whom he married in 1795, was as extravagant as Sheridan himself. Drury Lane Theatre did not prosper under his indifferent management, and the destruction of the new building by fire in 1809 put the finishing touches to his calamitous money troubles. His later days were full of trouble and privation and he died on 7 July 1816 in great poverty, with the bailiffs actually in possession of his house. His varied and tumultuous life had a fittingly ironic conclusion; his friends gave him a magnificent funeral in Westminster Abbey.

SHERIDAN, THOMAS (1646–1712), Jacobite. Born near Trim, Co. Meath. Educated TCD; elected fellow 1667. Entered Middle Temple 1670 but abandoned study of law to become collector of customs and excise at Cork, a lucrative post. Appointed commissioner of revenue 1675. Received DCL at Oxford, 1677. Published *A Discourse on the Rise and Power of Parliaments* (1677), dealing more with economics and religion than with government. Elected FRS, 1679. Came under suspicion in 1680 of complicity in the 'popish plot' and was imprisoned for some months. Won the favour of the king, and was released.

Declared himself a Catholic in 1686 and so eligible for public office under a legal decision delivered only days before. Appointed secretary to RICHARD TALBOT, Duke of Tyrconnell, in 1686, apparently against Tyrconnell's wishes. Received additional post as first commissioner of revenue in 1687. Strained relations soon developed, as the revenue commissioners deplored the adverse effects on trade and revenue of Tyrconnell's policy and would not co-operate with him by removing Protestants in their service to make room for Catholics. Tyrconnell accused Sheridan of corruption, and after a court hearing in 1688, King James replaced Sheridan as secretary and commissioner. Nevertheless he remained loyal to the king, followed him into exile after the revolution, and after the death of his enemy Tyrconnell in 1691 became James's personal secretary. In 1702 he wrote *A Narrative*, mainly devoted to a defence of himself, and, although partial, a valuable source for the history of his times. Died at Saint Germain.

SHERIDAN, THOMAS (1719–1788), actor, father of RICHARD BRINSLEY SHERIDAN. Born Quilca, Co. Cavan. SWIFT was his godfather. Educated at Westminster School and TCD. He chose the stage as his profession, appeared at Theatre Royal, Smock Alley, in 1743 and Drury Lane 1744. Appeared at Covent Garden, and was ranked by many as equal to Garrick. Became manager of Smock Alley, but when SPRANGER BARRY opened in opposition, Sheridan went to England, where he taught elocution with great success. Secured a pension of £300 a year for Dr Johnson but lost Johnson's friendship when he obtained a pension of £200 for himself to prepare a pronouncing dictionary. He published a number of works on education and elocution, *A General Dictionary of the English Language* (two volumes, 1780), and edited *The Works of Swift, with Life* (eighteen volumes, 1784). He died at Margate, 14 August 1788.

SHIELDS, ARTHUR (1896–1970), actor. Born in Dublin. Began to act at the Abbey Theatre as a young man. Influenced by the national spirit of the literary revival, he joined the Irish Volunteers, and served in the GPO in the 1916 Rising. Interned at Frongoch in Wales, but was released after a short time. Resumed his acting career at the Abbey, where his more famous brother, William, was playing under the name BARRY FITZGERALD. In 1936 John Ford brought him to America to play in a film version of *The Plough and the Stars*. In 1937 the Abbey gave him a year's leave of absence to try his luck again in America. Believing that he had tuberculosis, and that the dry climate of California would suit him better, he spent the rest of his life there, acting in films and television. Died at his home in Santa Barbara, 27 April 1970.

SHIELDS, JAMES (1806–1879), soldier and politician. Born Altmore, Co. Tyrone, on 12 May 1806. Emigrated to USA in 1826 and settled in Illinois. Studied law and became Supreme Court judge 1843–1845. Distinguished himself as brigadier-general in Mexican War 1846–1848. US Senator for Illinois 1849–1855 and for Minnesota 1858–1859. Fought on Unionist side in the Civil War against Stonewall Jackson in the Shenandoah Valley. Subsequently held various political offices until his death in Iowa on 1 June 1879.

SHIELDS, WILLIAM. See under FITZGERALD, BARRY.

SHIELS, GEORGE (1886–1949), playwright. Born at Ballymoney, Co. Antrim, and educated locally. Emigrated to Canada, where he was crippled for life after a railway accident. Returning to Ireland, he began writing, at first under the pseudonym George Morshiel. His first plays, *Bedmates* and *Insurance Money*, were performed at the Abbey in 1921. The following year *Paul Twyning* was particularly successful, and Shiels continued to write for the Abbey for the next twenty years. His other plays included *Passing Day, Professor Tim, The Fort Field,* and *The Summit. The Rugged Path* (1940) created a record for the Abbey when it ran for eight weeks and was seen by 25,000 people.

SIGERSON, GEORGE (1836–1925), physician, scientist, and man of letters. Born at Holy Hill near Strabane, Co. Tyrone, 11 January 1836. He attended Letterkenny Academy, and then, because of local pogroms, his father sent him to France to finish his schooling at St Joseph's College, Montrouge. Studied medicine at the Queen's Colleges in Galway and Cork, and attended surgery lectures at the Catholic University school of medicine in Cecilia St, Dublin. He taught himself Irish, and took honours and a prize at a special *ad hoc* Celtic examination in his final year in medical school. He took his degree at Queen's College in 1859, and spent some time in Paris studying medicine under Charcot and Duchenne. He then married and settled in Dublin to practise medicine, specialising as a neurologist. He did not secure any hospital appointment, but was professor of botany and later of zoology at the Catholic University medical school, and subsequently at NUI. His first book, *The Poets and Poetry of Munster,* appeared in 1860. He was actively engaged in political journalism for many years, contributing articles to the *Freeman's Journal,* the *Irishman*—then being edited by RICHARD PIGOTT—the *North British Review,* and other periodicals. His *History of the Land Tenures and Land Classes of Ireland* (1871) attracted the interest of Gladstone. He also wrote a number of scientific papers, and translated Charcot's *Diseases of the Nervous System* into English. His best-known work, *Bards of the Gael and Gall,* a collection of his translations from the Irish, appeared in 1897. He published his last book, *The Easter Song of Sedulius,* when he was eighty-six. His house at 3 Clare Street, Dublin, was a gathering-place for all interested in Irish literature and music. He was one of the founders of the Feis

Cheoil, president of the National Literary Society from 1893 until his death, and one of the first members of the Free State Senate. A commanding Viking-like figure, he enjoyed perfect health until his eighty-ninth year. Died at home, 17 February 1925, after a short illness.

SILKEN THOMAS. See under FITZGERALD, LORD THOMAS.

SIMPSON, ALAN (1920–1980), theatre director and army officer. Born in Dublin in 1920 and educated at Campbell College, Belfast, and TCD, graduating in engineering in 1946. He served with the Irish army during the Second World War, then transferred to the reserve and worked with EDWARDS and MAC LIAMMÓIR. In 1950 he joined the Corps of Engineers in the regular army and was commissioned as captain. His interest in the theatre continued and in 1953 with his wife, Carolyn Swift, he founded the Pike Theatre in a Dublin mews. Here was staged the first Irish production of Beckett's *Waiting for Godot* and of Behan's *The Quare Fellow.* In 1957 charges against him of staging an 'obscene production'—Tennessee Williams's *The Rose Tattoo*—were dismissed in Dublin District Court. The Pike closed in 1960 and he moved to England to work in theatre in London and Edinburgh. He told the story of the Pike in *Beckett and Behan and a Theatre in Dublin* (1962). From December 1968 to September 1969 he was artistic adviser to the Abbey Theatre. He then directed a number of successful musicals in Dublin. In 1978 he lectured at the State University of New York and directed productions in Illinois and off-Broadway. He died suddenly in Dublin on 15 May 1980.

SIRR, HENRY CHARLES (1764–1841), town-major of Dublin. Born in Dublin Castle, 25 November 1764, son of the town-major. Joined the British army in 1778 as an ensign, but left the service in 1791 to become a wine merchant in

Dublin. In 1796 he became acting town-major or head of police, and in 1798 his position was confirmed and he was given a residence in Dublin Castle. On 19 May 1798 he took part in the capture of LORD EDWARD FITZGERALD, and in 1803 he organised the arrest of ROBERT EMMET and other leaders. He retired on full pay in 1826 and was allowed to retain his residence in Dublin Castle. Died 7 January 1841. Buried in St Werburgh's, Dublin, near to Lord Edward. His valuable collection of antiques was bought by the RIA.

SKEFFINGTON, CLOTWORTHY, second EARL OF MASSEREENE (1742–1805). Born 28 January 1742, probably in Antrim. Succeeded to his father's titles in 1757. Educated at Corpus Christi College, Cambridge. On a visit to France about 1765 he was either cheated at cards or, according to another version, tricked into signing bonds for large amounts. Refusing to pay, he was imprisoned for nearly twenty years, first in a debtors' prison at Fort l'Évêque and then in La Force, Paris. He was allowed to entertain, and lived well for most of the time. Liberated by the mob on the eve of the fall of the Bastille on 14 July 1789, he escaped to England, accompanied by the daughter of the jail governor, whom he married in London soon after. His wife, celebrated for her beauty, died at thirty-eight. He died at Antrim Castle, 28 February 1805.

SKEFFINGTON, FRANCIS SHEEHY (1878–1916), writer. Born in Bailieborough, Co. Cavan. Educated at home by his father, Dr Joseph Skeffington, an inspector of schools, and at University College. Became known as a socialist, pacifist, and feminist, and in 1902 began a two-year term as the first lay registrar of the college. Married Hanna Sheehy, founder of the Women Graduates' Association, in 1903, and on principle adopted his wife's surname. Assisted TOM KETTLE to edit a small newspaper, the *Nationalist*, in 1905, and about the same time became a member of the Young Ireland branch of the United Irish League. Became active in the developing Irish labour movement. Wrote a *Life of Michael Davitt* (1908). Became editor of the *Irish Citizen* 1912. Also a regular contributor to the *Manchester Guardian*, the American *Call*, and the French *L'Humanité*. During the 1913 lock-out he was a member of the 'Peace Committee', which tried vainly to reconcile the workers and employers. When the Irish Citizen Army was formed in 1913 he was elected one of its vice-chairmen; he had joined on the understanding that its purpose was to defend workers against the police, and after it became a military organisation he left. On the outbreak of war he began to campaign against recruitment, was arrested in 1915 and sentenced to six months' imprisonment with hard labour, but after six days on hunger strike he was released. He then went to the USA to campaign for the cause of Irish freedom. A friend of some of the 1916 revolutionary leaders, Sheehy-Skeffington had tried to persuade them to organise instead of a military force a body 'armed and equipped with the weapons of the intellect and will'. His only part in the rising was an effort to organise citizens to stop looting. On 25 April 1916, however, he was arrested and taken to Portobello (Cathal Brugha) Barracks, Dublin. Later, as a hostage on a raiding expedition, he witnessed the shooting of an unarmed boy by his arresting officer, Captain Bowen-Colthurst. The following morning the captain had Sheehy-Skeffington, with two other prisoners, taken to the yard and shot. The senior officer discovered what had occurred and, after failing to induce Dublin Castle to act, reported it to the Prime Minister. As a result of a court-martial Bowen-Colthurst was declared of unsound mind at the time of his crime; he emigrated to Canada after a year in prison. An enquiry by royal commission was instituted on 23 August 1916 and it resulted in an offer of monetary compensation to Mrs Sheehy-Skeffington, which was refused. A novel by Sheehy-Skeffington, *In Dark and Evil Days*, was published after his death.

SKELTON, REV. PHILIP (1707–1787), philanthropist and writer. Born Derriaghy, Co. Antrim, and educated at TCD. Became curate to DR SAMUEL MADDEN and tutor to his sons. Curate at Monaghan 1732–1750, and then held the livings of Templecairn, near Lough Derg, Devenish, Co. Fermanagh, and Fintona. At Templecairn he often assembled his flock to see him die, until one parishioner said: 'Make a day, sir, and keep it, and don't be always disappointing us thus.' This remark cured his hypochondria. He sold his library to feed the poor of his parish during a famine in 1757, and again in 1778, after renewing it. He published a number of theological works and a *Description of Lough Derg* (1759). He retired to Dublin in 1780. Died there, 4 May 1787.

SLEATOR, JAMES (1889–1950), painter. Born in Co. Armagh. Studied at the Belfast School of Art. In 1910 he won a scholarship to the Metropolitan School of Art in Dublin, where he worked under ORPEN. He then went to the Slade in London and also studied for a time in Paris. In 1915 he returned to Dublin and took up a teaching post in the Metropolitan School of Art. That year he first exhibited at the RHA. Elected RHA in 1917. In 1922 he went to Florence and spent five years there painting portraits and landscapes. Then, on the advice of Orpen, he opened a studio in London and had Sir Winston Churchill as a pupil. He received many commissions for portraits. When Orpen died in 1931 Sleator was selected to finish a number of his uncompleted commissions. He exhibited at the RA and at the Royal Society of Portrait Painters. In 1941 he returned to Dublin, and remained there until his death. President, RHA, 1945. Among the distinguished people whose portraits he executed were RUTHERFORD MAYNE, THOMAS BODKIN, ALFRED O'RAHILLY and KATE O'BRIEN.

SLOANE, SIR HANS (1660–1753), physician and naturalist. Born at Killyleagh, Co. Down, 16 April 1660. An illness at sixteen led him to adopt temperate habits for the rest of his long life. He studied medicine at Paris and Montpellier, and graduated at the University of Orange in 1683. Between 1687 and 1689 he was physician to the governor of Jamaica, and collected about eight hundred new specimens of plants, publishing a catalogue of them in Latin in 1696. He settled in London and practised medicine with great success. Made a baronet in 1716, and appointed physician to King George II. His monumental work, *A Voyage to the Islands of Madeira, Jamaica, etc., with the Natural History of Jamaica,* appeared in two volumes in 1707 and 1725. President, Royal Society, 1727, and honoured by many foreign academies of science. He amassed a library of 50,000 books, 3,500 manuscripts, and numerous cabinets of specimens and curiosities, the whole forming a collection of immense value. He bequeathed this collection to the British nation on condition that his family should receive £20,000. The bequest was accepted and formed the nucleus of the British Museum, which was opened to the public 1759. Died in London, 11 January 1753.

SMITH, HENRY JOHN STEPHEN (1826–1883), mathematician. Born in Dublin, 2 November 1826. Educated at Rugby and Balliol College, Oxford. Took a double first-class degree. Elected a fellow of Balliol in 1849. He lectured in mathematics at Balliol until 1873, when he received a sinecure fellowship at Corpus Christi College. FRS 1861, and fellow of the Royal Astronomical Society. He was made keeper of the University Museum in 1874. He was a member of innumerable boards and committees, and his sense of public duty obliged him to devote much time to these activities to the exclusion of mathematical studies. Nevertheless he was the greatest authority of his day on the theory of numbers, and also wrote on elliptic functions and modern geometry. Died 9 February 1883. Buried at St Sepulchre's, Oxford. His *Collected Mathematical Papers* were published in 1894.

SMITH, JAMES (*c.* 1720–1806), signatory of the American Declaration of Independence. Born in Ireland. Emigrated to USA with his father in 1729. Educated at College of Philadelphia; practised law at York, Pennsylvania. Raised the first volunteer company in the state to resist British authority. Member of the Continental Congress 1775–1778, and signed the Declaration of Independence. High Court judge 1780. Friend and supporter of Washington, and sacrificed his personal fortune in the revolutionary cause. Died at York on 11 July 1806.

SMITH, VINCENT ARTHUR (1848–1920), historian of India. Born in Dublin, 3 June 1848; educated at TCD. Joined the Indian civil service in 1871, and after a successful career in the North-West Province retired at fifty-two to devote himself to research on the history and antiquities of India. His *Early History of India* (1904) became the authoritative work on the subject. He also published *A History of Fine Art in India and Ceylon* (1911) and the *Oxford History of India* (1918). Awarded the gold medal of the Royal Asiatic Society in 1918 and the Cross of the Indian Empire in 1919. Died at Oxford, 6 February 1920.

SMITHSON, ANNIE (1873–1948), nurse and writer. Born in Sandymount, Dublin, educated in Dublin and Liverpool. Trained as a nurse and midwife and practised as a district nurse in many parts of Ireland. Secretary and organiser of the Irish Nurses' Organisation 1929–1942. During the Civil War she took the Republican side, and was nursing the wounded in Moran's Hotel when it was under siege. In 1917 she published her first novel, *Her Irish Heritage*. It became a best-seller, and other novels, all romantic, followed with equal success. They include *By Strange Paths* and *The Walk of a Queen*. In 1944 she published her autobiography, *Myself—and Others*. One of the earliest members of the Old Dublin Society. Died in Dublin. Buried in Whitechurch, Co. Dublin.

SMITHSON, HARRIET CONSTANCE, afterwards **MADAME BERLIOZ** (1800–1854), actress. Born at Ennis, Co. Clare, 18 March 1800, daughter of a theatre manager. Made her first appearance at Crow Street Theatre, Dublin, about 1815. After playing in Belfast, Cork, and Limerick, she received an engagement in 1818 at Drury Lane Theatre, London, then at a low ebb in its fortunes. Her performances attracted little attention, and she remained comparatively unknown until 1828, when she went with Macready to Paris, and was received with acclamation. Her playing of Desdemona and Juliet aroused particular enthusiasm. Berlioz, the French composer, who was then unknown and poor, made advances to her, but without success. His *Symphonie Fantastique* (1830) was composed in her honour. When he returned to Paris from Italy in the summer of 1833 she was ill and in debt. He renewed his suit, and they were married in October 1833 at the British embassy in Paris. A special performance at the Théâtre Italien to pay her debts raised the inadequate sum of 7,000 francs, and she received no curtain calls. It was her last appearance on the stage. Sharing her husband's privations, she became, according to his account, sharp-tongued, jealous, and exacting. In 1840 they separated by mutual consent, and Berlioz chose another partner. He saw his wife occasionally, and contributed to her support. During the last four years of her life, paralysis left her without speech or movement. Died at Montmartre, 3 March 1854.

SMYLLIE, ROBERT MAIRE (1894–1954), journalist. Born in Glasgow, eldest son of Robert Smyllie, a Scottish journalist, and Elizabeth Follis of Cork.

While he was still a boy the family moved to Sligo, where his father edited the *Sligo Times*. He was educated at Sligo Grammar School and TCD. During the 1914 long vacation he was on the Continent as tutor to the son of a well-to-do American. At the outbreak of war he was interned by the Germans at Ruhleben civilian camp on the outskirts of Berlin, and he remained there until 1918. His fellow-internees included many distinguished men, and he was introduced to journalism through the pages of the camp's fortnightly magazine. On his return to Ireland he found the Sligo paper defunct, and was unable to resume his Trinity studies. He called at the *Irish Times* office looking for a job and the editor, JOHN EDWARD HEALY, asked him to cover the Versailles Peace Conference. His successful coverage, which included a scoop interview with Lloyd George, guaranteed him a place on the newspaper's staff, and he very shortly became Healy's trusted lieutenant. He succeeded to the editorship on Healy's death in 1934, and became an important and influential figure in Irish life, especially in his discerning encouragement of new writers. He held court each evening in the Palace Bar, Fleet Street, and here many writers later to become famous were first enrolled as contributors to the *Irish Times*. Among them were BRENDAN BEHAN and BRIAN O'NOLAN. Whilst he believed in the Commonwealth and Ireland's future as a member, he approached the problem from an Irish angle, unlike his predecessor. Articles he wrote led to his being decorated by the Czechoslovak government before it succumbed to Hitler's army. Smyllie, who for thirty years used the pen-name 'Nichevo', died at Dalkey, Co. Dublin, 11 September 1954.

SMYTH (OR SMITH), EDWARD (1749–1812), sculptor. Born in Co. Meath. Apprenticed to Simon Vierpyl, a sculptor, of Bachelor's Walk, Dublin. His design for a statue of CHARLES LUCAS MP, now in the City Hall, was accepted in 1772, and subsequently he was employed by GANDON to execute ornamental sculpture for the Custom House, including sixteen heads symbolising the principal rivers of Ireland, and a huge statue of 'Commerce'. Gandon then employed him for similar work for the House of Lords (now part of the Bank of Ireland) in Westmoreland Street, and for the Four Courts and the King's Inns. FRANCIS JOHNSTON commissioned him to execute various sculptured embellishments for Dublin Castle Chapel, including ninety heads over the doors and windows. In 1811 the Dublin Society established a school of modelling and sculpture and appointed him master at fifty guineas a year. He died suddenly, 2 August 1812, at his home at 36 Montgomery Street.

SMYTH, PATRICK JAMES (1826–1885), Young Irelander. Born in Dublin. Educated at Clongowes Wood College, where he became a close friend of THOMAS F. MEAGHER. Became an active member of the Young Ireland movement. After the abortive rising of 1848 he escaped to America, where he supported himself by journalism for some years. In 1854 he went to Tasmania, and planned and carried out the escape of JOHN MITCHEL. In 1856 he returned to Ireland. Called to the bar in 1858 but did not practise. He joined the Home Rule party of ISAAC BUTT and in 1871 was elected MP for Westmeath. From 1880 until 1882 he sat for Tipperary. He disapproved of the policy of PARNELL and made bitter attacks on the Land League. In December 1884 he was appointed secretary of the Irish Loan Reproductive Fund, and his acceptance of this semi-government post exposed him to strong criticism. He held it for only a few weeks, dying on 12 January 1885 at his house in Belgrave Square, Dublin.

SOMERVILLE, EDITH ANNA OENONE (1858–1949), novelist. Born 2 May 1858 in Corfu, where her father, Lt.-Col. Somerville, was stationed. The following year he retired to his home at Drishane, Skibbereen, Co. Cork, and she spent most of her long life there. She was educated at Alexandra College, Dublin, and studied painting in London, Düsseldorf, and Paris. Riding and painting were her absorbing interests; she became master of the West Carbery foxhounds, and held exhibitions of her paintings in London and New York. On 17 January 1886 she met her cousin VIOLET MARTIN, and thus began their literary partnership under the names Somerville and Ross. Their first book, *An Irish Cousin*, appeared in 1889, and when Violet Martin died in 1915 they had published fourteen titles, including *The Real Charlotte* (1894), *Some Experiences of an Irish R.M.* (1899), and *In Mr Knox's Country* (1915). Edith Somerville believed that her partner's death caused no break in their collaboration, and she continued to write and to publish as Somerville and Ross. *Irish Memories* appeared in 1917, and *The Big House at Inver* in 1925. Their books depict many aspects of the Anglo-Irish way of life of the period with wit and insight, and the Ascendancy's view of their Irish tenants and neighbours. In 1922 Dublin University conferred on her an honorary D.Litt., and in 1941 the Irish Academy of Letters, of which she was a founder-member, awarded her the Gregory gold medal, their principal honour. In 1948 *The Real Charlotte* was published in the World's Classics series, a rare accolade for a living author. She died at her home in Drishane on 8 October 1949.

SOUTHERNE, THOMAS (1660–1746), dramatist. Born at Oxmantown, Dublin. Educated at TCD and the Middle Temple, London. His first play, *The Loyal Brother*, was produced in 1682. He then served with success in the English army, but the revolution of 1688 ending his military prospects, he returned to play-writing, helped by his friend, Dryden. He was also also friendly with SWIFT, Pope, and Gray. His first success was *The Fatal Marriage* (1694); his *Oronoko, or the Royal Slave* (1696) was even more popular. Based on Mrs Aphra Behn's novel of the same title, it began the long campaign in England against the slave trade. Southerne was an extremely shrewd man of business, and retired wealthy, though his other plays met with indifferent success. Died in London, 22 May 1746.

SOUTHOUSE-CHEYNEY, REGINALD. See under CHEYNEY, PETER.

STACK, AUSTIN (1879–1929), revolutionary. Born at Ballymullen, Tralee, Co. Kerry, on 7 December 1879. Educated at local CBS; at fourteen he became a clerk in a Tralee solicitor's office. Captained the Kerry team that won the All-Ireland football final in 1904. President, Kerry GAA County Board 1918–1929. He joined the IRB in 1908. In 1916 as commandant of the Kerry Brigade, IRA, he made preparations for landing of arms by ROGER CASEMENT. He was arrested and sentenced to death, commuted to penal servitude for life. Released June 1917 and elected Sinn Féin MP for Kerry in 1918 general election. Honorary secretary of Sinn Féin from 1917 to his death. Minister for Home Affairs, Finance and Defence at different times between 1919 and 1922. Opposed the Treaty of 1921, took part in the Civil War, was captured in 1923 and went on hunger strike for forty-one days before being released in July 1924. When ÉAMON DE VALERA founded Fianna Fáil in 1926, Stack remained with Sinn Féin and was re-elected to the Dáil in 1927. On 10 August 1925 he married Una Gordon, a widow of considerable means, a member of Cumann na mBan who kept a 'safe house' for republicans during the War of Independence. His health never recovered after his hunger strike and he died in a Dublin hospital on 27 April 1929.

STACPOOLE, HENRY DE VERE (1863–1951), novelist. Born in Kingstown (Dún Laoghaire), son of Rev. William Stacpoole. Educated at Malvern College and St George's and St Mary's Hospitals, London. After qualifying in 1891 he made many voyages as a ship's doctor, gathering experiences that he later used in his novels. Settling down to write, he published about a dozen novels before making his name with *The Blue Lagoon* (1908), a romantic story of two children shipwrecked on a Pacific island. It appealed particularly to the Edwardian love of childhood fantasy, in the manner of *Peter Pan* and *The Blue Bird*, and was successful both on the stage and when made into a film. He followed this success with a long series of books with romantic and tropical appeal, publishing some fifty novels in all, and also two volumes of autobiography. Died at Shanklin in the Isle of Wight in April 1951. He had a life-long interest in seabirds, and founded the Penguin Club for their study and protection.

STANFORD, SIR CHARLES VILLIERS (1852-1924), composer and music teacher. Born in 2 Herbert Street, Dublin, 30 September 1852. Educated at Bassett's School in Dublin and Queen's College, Cambridge, where he went as a choral scholar in 1870. After further study at Leipzig and Berlin he soon won distinction as a composer, his music to the *Eumenides* of Aeschylus taking Cambridge by storm. Exceptionally versatile and prolific, he wrote operas, large-scale choral works, symphonies, chamber music, church music, and solo songs. His six *Irish Rhapsodies* drew largely on native melodies and have retained their popularity as the best of his orchestral works. His settings for Irish poems were published in several collections with great success; *An Irish Idyll* (1901), *Cushendall* (1910) and *Songs from Leinster* (1914) contain some of his best work. He also edited the *Petrie Collection of Irish Music*. He was appointed professor of composition and orchestral playing at the Royal College of Music in 1883 and professor of music at Cambridge in 1887, and held both posts until his death. A gifted teacher, many of his pupils later became distinguished musicians themselves: Walford Davies, Vaughan Williams, Gustav Holst, Eugene Goossens and Arthur Bliss studied under him. He was knighted in 1901. In 1911 he published *Musical Composition*, an exposition of his methods, and in 1914 *Pages from an Unwritten Diary*. Died in London, 29 March 1924; his ashes are buried in Westminster Abbey.

STANFORD, WILLIAM BEDELL (1910-1984), classical scholar. Born in Belfast on 16 January 1910 and educated at Bishop Foy School, Waterford, and TCD, where he excelled in classics. He was elected fellow 1934 and appointed regius professor of Greek 1940. Represented Dublin University in Seanad Éireann 1948-1969 and held firmly that Protestants had an important part to play in the republic and an equal stake in the life of the state. He was a visiting professor at Berkeley, McGill University, Toronto, and Wayne Park University, and lectured extensively throughout the USA. He also lectured on Hellenic cruises for a number of years. Member RIA and other learned bodies and of the General Synod of the Church of Ireland. He wrote widely on Greek literature and won international recognition for his edition of Homer's *Odyssey* (1947-1948). With R. B. McDowell he published a life of MAHAFFY in 1971. He died on 30 December 1984.

STANYHURST, RICHARD (1547-1618), author, uncle of ARCHBISHOP USSHER. Born in Dublin; educated at University College, Oxford, and Lincoln's Inn. Returning to Ireland with his tutor, Edmund Campion, he devoted himself to Irish history and literature, and contributed a *Description* and a *History* of Ireland to Holinshed's *Chronicles* in 1577. After the death of his wife in 1579 he left for the Netherlands, where he became a Catholic, took holy orders, and was made chaplain to the Archduke Albert. In 1584 he published *De Re Rebus in Hibernia Gestis*, a treatise on the early history of Ireland, which was severely criticised by CÉITINN. His chief work, his translation of the first four books of Virgil's *Aeneid* into English heroic verse (1582), is a literary curiosity. Thomas Nash said, 'he trod a foule, lumbering, boysterous, wallowing measure.' He died at Brussels.

STARKEY, JAMES SULLIVAN. See under O'SULLIVAN, SEUMAS.

STARKIE, ENID MARY (*c.* 1899–1970), critic. Born in Killiney, Co. Dublin. Educated at Alexandra College, Dublin, the RIAM, Somerville College, Oxford, and the Sorbonne. After some years as assistant lecturer in modern languages at Exeter University, she returned to Somerville College in 1929 as lecturer in modern languages. Elected a fellow of the college 1935. Appointed reader in French literature 1946. Her critical reputation rests on her biographies of Baudelaire, Rimbaud, and Flaubert. France honoured her with a doctorate from the Sorbonne and a prize from the French Academy, and made her a *chevalier* of the Legion of Honour. In 1941 she published *A Lady's Child*, an account of her life in Dublin and Oxford, which, by its unusual candour, failed to please many of her relations. Died in Oxford in April 1970.

STARKIE, WALTER FITZWILLIAM (1894–1976), author, and authority on gypsies. Born 9 August 1894. Brother of ENID STARKIE. Educated at Shrewsbury School and TCD. Lecturer in Romance Languages, TCD, 1920; fellow 1924; professor of Spanish and lecturer in Italian literature 1926–1947. Served with Red Cross in Europe during First World War and developed special interest in gypsies. Later he travelled among them, playing his fiddle, troubadour-fashion, and studying their music and folklore. Published *Raggle-Taggle* (1933), an account of his adventures in the Balkans, *Spanish Raggle-Taggle* (1934), and *Gypsy Folklore and Music* (1935). Director, Abbey Theatre, 1927–1942. In Madrid 1940–1954 as head of the British Institute. Lectured widely throughout Europe and North and South America. Professor-in-residence, University of California, 1962–1970 and lived in Los Angeles. Other books include *The Road to Santiago* (1957) and *Scholars and Gypsies* (1963), an autobiography. Received many honours, including CMG, OBE, *chevalier* of Legion of Honour. Retired to Spain. Died in Madrid, 2 November 1976.

STEELE, RICHARD (1672–1729), essayist. Born in Dublin in March 1672. Educated at Charterhouse and Merton College, Oxford. Enlisted in the Life Guards in 1694, and published a poem on the funeral of Queen Mary, which brought him a commission in the Coldstream Guards. In a duel with an Irishman named Kelly in 1700 he wounded his opponent seriously, and in remorse wrote *The Christian Hero*, a devotional manual that pleased the public but not his brother-officers. Between 1701 and 1705 he produced three unsuccessful plays. Marriage to a rich widow followed in that year. She died in 1707, and Steele secured an appointment as 'gazetteer' at £300 a year, leaving the army the same year and marrying the beautiful Mary ('Prue') Scurlock. As an habitué of the coffee-houses, with their good talk, Steele conceived the idea of a periodical for this public, and on 12 April 1709 published the first number of the *Tatler*, with his school-friend Addison as a contributor. Appearing thrice weekly, the *Tatler* advocated ideals of gentlemanly conduct and a new respect for women. In 1711 it was succeeded by the *Spectator*, which was followed in 1713 by the *Guardian*. Steele generously acknowledged the value of Addison's contributions to all his periodicals. He entered Parliament in 1713, and was knighted in 1715. He crossed swords with SWIFT in a pamphleteering duel, but was no match for him. In 1720 he issued pamphlets condemning the South Sea Bubble. After 1715 his literary work was of little importance, his political fortunes were mixed, and his financial position, never very easy, grew worse. He left London for Wales in 1724 and died in Carmarthen on 1 September

1729. Steele's collaboration with Addison in the *Spectator* is one of the famous partnerships in literature. Steele supplied originality, sympathy, and enthusiasm. Addison complemented these qualities with his ease, correctness, and exquisite art. Together they fashioned a model of English prose with an influence that has persisted through all the vagaries of style since their time. Steele himself was warm, impulsive, improvident, a devoted husband to his beloved 'Prue', and a loyal friend.

STEELE, THOMAS (1788–1848), landlord and repealer. Born at Derrymore, Co. Clare, 3 November 1788. Educated at TCD, and Magdalene College, Cambridge. Inherited a large estate in Co. Clare at an early age. Gave rein to his adventurous spirit by active service in the Spanish wars in 1823. On his return to Ireland he became a strong supporter of Catholic emancipation, though himself a Protestant, and was made 'head pacificator' by O'CONNELL, with the duty of quelling faction-fighting. Eccentric and wildly extravagant, his transparent sincerity made him known as 'Honest Tom Steele', and he dissipated his fortune in supporting the causes led by O'Connell. Overwhelmed by the death of his leader, he attempted suicide by throwing himself into the Thames from Waterloo Bridge, and, though rescued, died a few days later, on 15 June 1848. Buried in Glasnevin cemetery, Dublin, beside O'Connell.

STEEVENS, RICHARD (1653–1710), physician. Born probably in Athlone. Educated at the Latin School, Athlone, and TCD. His father, who was rector of Athlone, intended him for the Church, but after taking deacon's orders he turned to medicine, and took his MD at Trinity in 1687. He soon built up a lucrative practice in Dublin, and was elected president of the College of Physicians in 1710. He died shortly afterwards, and left his large fortune to his twin sister, Grizell, for life, and directed that it should then be applied towards

founding and maintaining a hospital in Dublin. His sister surrendered the estate, reserving only £100 a year and a right of residence for herself. The hospital, known as Dr Steevens', was completed in 1733, and was the first public hospital established in Dublin. Grizell died on 18 March 1746.

STEPHENS, JAMES (1825–1901), chief founder of the Fenians. Born in Kilkenny, and became a civil engineer on the Limerick and Waterford railway. Joined the Young Ireland movement and took part with SMITH O'BRIEN in the rising of 1848. Wounded in the skirmish at Ballingarry, he escaped to Paris, where he met T. C. LUBY, and returned with him to Ireland to sound out the possibilities of a new movement. Encouraged by the response of the people, Stephens, with Luby and others, founded the Irish Republican Brotherhood or the Fenian movement. It was organised by Stephens on military principles. A 'centre' or colonel was chosen, who in turn selected nine captains, each captain selecting nine sergeants, and each sergeant nine men. 'Circles' of 820 men formed in this way were soon organised throughout the country. Stephens went to America in 1858 and in 1864 on successful fund-raising missions, and in 1863 founded a newspaper, the *Irish People*, to forward the cause. It was edited by KICKHAM, LUBY, and O'LEARY, and proved a great success. Stephens had promised his American associates that he would lead a rising in 1865, but when dissensions in America delayed the sending of arms he postponed action. He was arrested in November that year but, escaping in a fortnight, he made his way to Paris and then to New York. The American Fenians denounced him as 'a rogue, impostor and traitor' and he fled for his life back to Paris. He earned a precarious living by journalism and teaching until a public subscription raised by friends in Ireland enabled him to return in 1886 and to live in comparative comfort at Blackrock, Co. Dublin, where he died on 29 April 1901.

STEPHENS, JAMES (1880-1950), poet and storyteller. Born in Dublin, date uncertain, but probably 9 February 1880. His father died when he was two, and on his mother's remarriage he was sent to an orphanage. He ran away, and after many vicissitudes found employment as a solicitor's clerk in Dublin. His first volume of poems, *Insurrections*, was published in 1909, and was followed by his first novel, *The Charwoman's Daughter* (1912), an appealing idyll of the Dublin slums. In his next book, *The Crock of Gold* (1912), he created a world of rich fantasy, and won recognition as a prose writer of originality, close to genius. He went to Paris in 1912, returning to Dublin in 1915 as registrar of the National Gallery, a post he held until 1924, when he removed to London. He was a founder-member of the Irish Academy of Letters, and received a civil list pension in 1942. His work after 1914 was confined to short stories and lyrics. In the last years of his life the BBC discovered his talent as a broadcaster, and he enthralled listeners with his verse and stories. He died at his home in London on 26 December 1950. Lord Grey said of him: 'He is a born bohemian, small in stature but quite big inside, large and roomy.' His eye-witness account of the 1916 Rising, *The Insurrection in Dublin,* was reprinted in 1965.

STERNE or STEARNE, JOHN (1624-1669), founder of the College of Physicians, Dublin. Born Ardbraccan, Co. Meath, on 26 November 1624. Educated at TCD. Fled to England on the outbreak of rebellion of 1641 and studied medicine at Sidney Sussex College, Cambridge. Returned to Dublin in 1651 to practise medicine. Appointed in 1656 first lecturer in Hebrew at TCD, and professor of law in 1660. He founded the College of Physicians in 1660 and became first president. Professor of medicine, TCD, 1662, and published a number of works on medicine and theology. Died in Dublin, 18 November 1669.

STERNE, LAURENCE (1713-1768), novelist. Born at Clonmel, Co. Tipperary, 24 November 1713, son of an impoverished army ensign. Spent his early years in Irish garrison towns. At ten he was sent to school in Halifax, Yorkshire, and through the generosity of a cousin went to Jesus College, Cambridge. After graduating he took holy orders, and through family influence secured a living near York in 1738. He wrote miscellaneous journalism for York periodicals. In 1759 he wrote *The History of a Good Warm Watchcoat*, an account of a local chapter quarrel, which was not published until after his death. He was an unfaithful husband, his marriage proved a failure, and in 1758 his wife was committed to a private asylum. Sterne then turned to literary work in earnest, and wrote the opening two volumes of *The Life and Opinions of Tristram Shandy, Gentleman*. Published in London in 1760, this work made him famous almost overnight, and he added a further seven volumes, although never completing it. He suffered from tuberculosis, and *A Sentimental Journey* (1768) describes his travels in France and Italy in search of health; the opening sentence—'They order, said I, this matter better in France'—is often quoted. He published *The Sermons of Mr Yorick* in seven volumes between 1760 and 1769. *Letters from Yorick to Eliza* (1773) contained his correspondence with a young married woman for whom he cultivated a platonic passion. He died in London, 18 March 1768. *Tristram Shandy* was an innovation; its insinuating humour and extravagances, reflecting his idiosyncratic personality, made it the first expressionistic novel in English literature.

STEVENSON, SIR JOHN ANDREW (*c.* 1760-1833), composer. Born in Dublin; became a chorister in Christ Church Cathedral and later in St Patrick's. A prolific composer, he wrote symphonies, operas, songs, services, and anthems, but is best-known for his arrangement of Irish airs for the *Melodies* written by THOMAS MOORE. Received the degree of doctor of music from Dublin University in 1791, was knighted in 1803, and died 14 September 1833 at Headfort House, Kells, Co. Meath, the seat of his son-in-law, the Marquess of Headfort.

STEWART, ROBERT, VISCOUNT CASTLEREAGH, second MARQUIS OF LONDONDERRY (1769–1822). Born in Dublin, 18 June 1769. Educated at the Royal School, Armagh, and St John's College, Cambridge. Elected to the Irish parliament in 1790. Became chief secretary in 1798. The rising that year convinced him that union with Britain was essential to preserve the empire, and he did not flinch from the huge outlay for 'compensation for disturbance' that secured the passage of the Act of Union in 1800. Descriptions of his tactics as wholesale bribery and corruption take little account of the facts of political life in the eighteenth century, when patronage was an accepted instrument of government policy. The Catholics had been led to believe that their emancipation would follow the Union, and when King George III refused his consent, Castlereagh resigned with Pitt. He was soon back in office as secretary for war in 1805, and from then until his suicide in 1822 played a dominant role in British policy. He became foreign secretary in 1812, and was the chief architect of the coalition against Napoleon. In the negotiations at the Congress of Vienna in 1815 his statesmanship secured the acceptance of terms that brought peace to Europe for forty years. After 1815 his popularity ebbed rapidly in England (he had none to lose in Ireland), as he was identified with the repressive policies of the post-Napoleon years. His attempts to have Queen Caroline divorced brought public odium and threats on his life. His duties had imposed severe and continuous strain on him for years, his mind gave way, and he cut his throat on 12 August 1822 at Footscray, his house in Kent. He left a widow but no children. Buried in Westminster Abbey.

STOCK, JOSEPH (1740–1813), bishop. Born at 1 Dame St, Dublin, on 22 December 1740, and educated at Mr Gast's school and TCD. In 1776 he published a life of GEORGE BERKELEY, the only one based on contemporary information. Took holy orders and after serving in Raphoe and Lismore became headmaster of Portora Royal School, Enniskillen, 1795–1798. Bishop of Killala 1798, and in 1800 published *Narrative of What Passed at Killala During the French Invasion of 1798*, a vivid account of the French landings written with unusual impartiality. He was translated to the diocese of Waterford and Lismore in 1810. An accomplished biblical scholar and theologian. TCD library contains letters written by him from Killala and Waterford to his son Henry in Dublin, which give interesting glimpses of life in an episcopal palace in a remote part of Ireland at the beginning of the nineteenth century. He died at Waterford on 18 August 1813.

STOKER, ABRAHAM (BRAM) (1847–1912), novelist. Born at 15 Marino Crescent, Fairview, Dublin. Educated at TCD. He entered the civil service, became interested in the theatre, and contributed unpaid reviews of plays to the *Evening Mail*. When Sir Henry Irving gave a season in Dublin in 1876, Stoker became his devoted admirer. Two years later Irving invited him to become his manager. Stoker held this post until Irving's death in 1905, and although his master made inordinate demands on him he found time to write a dozen novels. *Dracula* (1897) was influenced by *Carmilla*, a tale of vampirism by SHERIDAN LE FANU, and has won worldwide fame. Films, reprints, translations, even comic strips, have made Count Dracula familiar to millions. His other novels, though not without merit, are now forgotten. After the death of Irving in 1905, Stoker's health and fortunes declined. In 1906 he published *Personal Reminiscences of Henry Irving*. He was survived by his wife and only son.

STOKES, ADRIAN (1887–1927), pathologist. Born at Lausanne, 9 February 1887. Educated at St Stephen's

Green school and TCD. Graduated in medicine in 1910, and after service in English hospitals became assistant to the professor of pathology at TCD. In 1914, on the outbreak of the First World War, he joined the Royal Army Medical Corps, and did valuable work on gas gangrene, trench nephritis, dysentery, and jaundice. He invented the method of giving oxygen continuously through a nasal catheter to victims of gassing. For his war services he received the DSO and OBE. In 1919 he returned to Dublin as professor of bacteriology and preventive medicine at TCD. Appointed Dunn Professor of Pathology at London University 1922. In 1927 the Rockefeller Yellow Fever Commission asked him to visit Nigeria to investigate the causes of the fever. He carried out experiments at Lagos, which showed that it could be transmitted by monkeys and mosquitoes. On 15 September 1927 he developed yellow fever himself and died four days later.

STOKES, SIR GEORGE GABRIEL (1819–1903), mathematician and physicist. Born at Skreen, Co. Sligo, 13 August 1819. Educated at Bristol College and Pembroke College, Cambridge. Fellow of the college 1841. As Lucasian Professor of Mathematics (1849–1903), secretary (1854–1885), and president (1885–1890) of the Royal Society, he held three offices that had only once before been held by one person, Sir Isaac Newton. MP for Cambridge University 1887–1892; created a baronet in 1889. In 1902 he was elected master of Pembroke College. With James Clerk Maxwell and another Irishman, LORD KELVIN, he contributed significantly to the fame of the Cambridge school of mathematical physics in the mid-nineteenth century. The greater part of his work was concerned with waves and the transformations imposed on them during their passage through various media, and his researches placed the science of hydrodynamics on a new footing. His other well-known investigations are those he made on the wave theory of light. His

mathematical and physical papers were published in five volumes (1880–1905), three of which he edited himself, the other two being edited by SIR JOSEPH LARMOR. He also published *Light* (1884–1887), and *Natural Theology* (1891). In his later years he received nearly all the honours open to scientists, both at home and in Europe. Died at Cambridge, 1 February 1903.

STOKES, WHITLEY (1763–1845), physician, father of WILLIAM STOKES. Born in Dublin and educated at TCD. Took fellowship 1788 and graduated in medicine 1789. Joined the United Irishmen as a young man, and was suspended from his fellowship for three years by Lord Clare at his visitation of 1798. Regius professor of medicine 1830–1843. Published an English-Irish dictionary at his own expense. Described by WOLFE TONE as 'the very best man I have ever known.' Died at his house in Harcourt Street, Dublin, 13 April 1845.

STOKES, WHITLEY (1830–1909), Celtic scholar. Born in Dublin, 28 February 1830. Educated at St Columba's College, Rathfarnham, Co. Dublin, at TCD, and the Inner Temple, London. Called to the English bar in 1855 and practised law in England for six years. He then went to India and held several important legal posts in Madras and Calcutta. During his Indian service he published a number of works on Anglo-Indian law. He was made CSI in 1877, CIE in 1879, and returned to England in 1882. In his father's house in Dublin he had met PETRIE, O'DONOVAN, and O'CURRY, and from his early twenties he devoted himself to the study of the words and forms of the Irish language. His first publication, 'Irish Glosses from a MS in TCD', appeared in 1859 as a paper in the *Transactions of the Philological Society of London*. For his first book, *A Medieval Tract on Latin Declensions*, he received the gold medal of the RIA. With John Strachan he published a *Thesaurus Palaeohibernicus* (1901–1903), more than 1,200 pages of Old Irish glosses from manuscripts earlier than the eleventh century. This work rendered easily accessible for the first time the mass of Old Irish glosses on the Continent and in Ireland. Other texts edited and translated by him include *Fis Adamnáin*, *Tógáil Traoi*, the *Tripartite Life of St Patrick*, and the *Féilire* of Aengus. Besides these and many other Irish texts and glosses, he published editions and translations of Cornish and Breton texts, many papers on grammatical subjects, and critical reviews of the work of other scholars in this field. His whole life was one of unflagging industry in Celtic studies. Died at 15 Grenville Place, Kensington, London, 13 April 1909.

STOKES, WILLIAM (1804–1878), physician. Born in Dublin. Educated privately and at Edinburgh, where he qualified as a physician. In Dublin he was attached to the Meath Hospital and built up a large practice. In 1837 he published a treatise on *Diseases of the Chest*, and in 1854 *Diseases of the Heart and Aorta*, both long regarded as models of medical exposition. He was a friend of the painter BURTON and of PETRIE, whose *Life* he wrote, and his wide interests included art, music, and antiquities. Elected FRS, 1861, and the same year appointed physician-in-ordinary to Queen Victoria. President, RIA, 1874. He died at Howth, Co. Dublin, 10 January 1878.

STONE, GEORGE (*c.* 1708–1764), archbishop of Armagh. Born in London. Educated at Westminster School and Christ Church, Oxford. Took holy orders and came to Dublin as chaplain to the lord lieutenant, the Duke of Dorset. Rose rapidly in the church. Dean of Ferns 1733, of Derry 1734. Bishop of Ferns and Leighlin 1740; bishop of Kildare and dean of Christ Church 1743. Bishop of Derry 1745; archbishop of Armagh, March 1747. Lord justice and member of Irish Privy Council, April 1747. Supported claim of crown to surplus Irish revenues against HENRY BOYLE. The crown claim succeeded in 1751 The struggle was renewed in 1753 and the Irish House of Commons

rejected a Bill asserting the crown right. Servants of the crown who had voted against the Bill were dismissed, and some of the surplus was appropriated to the national debt by royal authority. Stone emerged as virtual dictator of Ireland. His power waned after Boyle became Earl of Shannon, but he succeeded in securing appointment as lord justice in April 1758 with Shannon and Ponsonby. This triumvirate carried on the government of Ireland down to 1764. Stone was accounted more of a politician than a churchman, a master of finesse and tact, but of unbounded ambition. He died in London on 19 December 1764.

STUART, JAMES (1764–1842), historian of Armagh. Born at Armagh and educated at Armagh Royal School and TCD. Called to the bar but never practised. He became first editor of the *Newry Telegraph* in 1812 and from 1815 to 1819 also edited the *Newry Magazine*. Published *Historical Memoirs of the City of Armagh* (1819), one of the most valuable works of its kind. He went to live in Belfast in 1821 and edited the *News Letter*. He founded and edited the *Guardian and Constitutional Advocate* in 1827, but ill-health forced him to abandon it. He died in Belfast in poor circumstances in September 1842.

SULLIVAN, ALEXANDER MARTIN (1830–1884), journalist and politician. Born at Bantry, Co. Cork. Educated at the local national school. After working as a clerk and reporter he joined the staff of the *Nation* in 1855 and became editor and sole proprietor in 1858 when GAVAN DUFFY left for Australia. Sullivan favoured constitutional agitation and opposed the Fenian movement. A Fenian council decided on his assassination, but the respect held for him by the rank and file secured his safety. In 1867 he was sentenced to six months' imprisonment for an article on the execution of the Manchester Martyrs. Released after three months, he insisted that £400, collected as a national testimonial to him, should be used to erect a statue of HENRY

GRATTAN in College Green, Dublin. Home Rule MP for Co. Louth 1874-1880 and for Meath 1880-1881. Called to the bar in 1876 and to the English bar the following year, he handed the *Nation* over to his elder brother in 1877 and removed to London to practise there. In 1881 his health broke down under the double strain of legal and parliamentary duties and he resigned his seat. Died at Dartry Lodge, Rathgar, Dublin, 17 October 1884. Sullivan's *Story of Ireland* (1870) had a very large circulation for many years among Irish people at home and abroad.

SULLIVAN, ALEXANDER MARTIN (1871-1959), barrister. Born at Belfield, Drumcondra, Dublin, 14 January 1871, second son of A. M. SULLIVAN. Educated at Ushaw, Belvedere, and TCD. Called to the bar in 1892 and quickly rose to the first rank, becoming King's Serjeant in Ireland in 1912, the last to hold that title. By family tradition he was a constitutional nationalist, and his life was threatened after the 1916 Rising because of his opposition to Sinn Féin and the physical force movement; he undertook the defence of SIR ROGER CASEMENT only from a sense of professional duty. After the establishment of an Irish state in 1922 he removed to England, being already a member of the English bar, and practised successfully there until 1949. When the Republic of Ireland Act was passed that year, he considered himself an alien disqualified from practice in England, and retired to Dublin. He retained his house at Beckenham, Kent, and died there 9 January 1959. He published two books of reminiscences, *Old Ireland* (1927) and *The Last Serjeant* (1952).

SULLIVAN, TIMOTHY DANIEL (1827-1914), politician and poet. Born in Bantry, Co. Cork, in May 1827. Educated at Bantry schools. He became a journalist and assisted his brother A. M. SULLIVAN in the management of the *Nation*. In 1867 the paper published his song 'God Save Ireland' to com-memorate the Manchester Martyrs, which became the *de facto* national anthem until 1924. He also wrote 'The Song of the Canadian Backwoods' or 'Ireland, Boys, Hooray', which was sung by both northern and southern troops on the eve of the battle of Fredericksburg in the American Civil War. MP for Westmeath 1880-1885, and subsequently sat for Dublin and then for Co. Donegal. Lord Mayor of Dublin 1886-1887. In 1890 he made a tour of America to raise funds for the Irish party. He published a number of volumes of poems, including *Greenleaves* (1868), *Lays of the Land League* (1887), and *Poems* (1888). His *Recollections* appeared in 1905.

SWANZY, MARY (1882-1978), painter. Born at 23 Merrion Square, Dublin, on 15 February 1882, a daughter of the distinguished eye specialist Sir Henry Swanzy. She was educated at Alexandra College, Dublin, Versailles and Freiburg, then returned to Dublin to study art under JOHN BUTLER YEATS at Miss Manning's School and at the Metropolitan School of Art. In 1905 she moved to Paris and was soon showing in group exhibitions with the then-unknown artists Picasso, Braque, and Vlaminck. Back in Ireland she exhibited at the RHA, then visited her sister in the Balkans in 1921-1922. In 1924 she went to Honolulu and Samoa and painted lush tropical landscapes. She continued to exhibit in Dublin and Paris and in 1946 had three pictures in a show in London that included Henry Moore, William Scott, Braque, Dufy, and Chagall. She was elected honorary RHA in 1949. She died on 7 July 1978 at her house in London where she had lived with her sister.

SWEETMAN, GERARD (1908-1970), lawyer and politician. Born in Dublin 10 June 1908. Educated at Beaumont and TCD. Admitted a solicitor in 1930 and built up a large practice. Became a member of Fine Gael and sat for the Seanad from 1943 to 1948. TD for Co. Kildare 1948 until his death. In the second Coalition government of 1954–1957 he was Minister for Finance, and advised the government to appoint T. K. Whitaker as secretary of the department and head of the civil service in 1956. Died in a motor accident, 28 January 1970.

SWIFT, JONATHAN (1667–1745), writer and dean of St Patrick's Cathedral, Dublin. Born 30 November 1667 at 7 Hoey's Court, Dublin. Educated at Kilkenny School and TCD. His university career was undistinguished and he obtained his degree only by special exemption. In 1689 he received an appointment as secretary to the statesman Sir William Temple at Moor Park, Surrey. In 1694, having taken holy orders, he became prebend of Kilroot, Co. Antrim, but soon tired of that isolated life and returned to Moor Park in 1696. He remained there until Temple's death in 1699, his duties including acting as tutor to the young and beautiful Hester Johnson ('Stella'), daughter of a companion of Temple's sister. Thus began the great enduring affection of his life. At Moor Park he wrote *A Tale of a Tub*, of which he said many years later, 'What a genius I had when I wrote that Book,' and *The Battle of the Books*. Both were published in 1704, anonymously, like most of his writings. In 1700 he was given the vicarage of Laracor near Trim, Co. Meath, and took his doctor's degree in TCD in February 1701. Between 1701 and 1710 he divided his time between Dublin and London, where he had some church business for the archbishop of Dublin. In London he soon made a reputation as a wit and conversationalist. Addison, Congreve and the famous men of the day were his constant companions in the clubs and coffee-houses. The following three years he spent almost entirely in London, where he had become closely involved in politics. The Tories sought the support of his powerful pen, and finding the lord treasurer, Harley, a man much to his liking, he espoused their cause. In pamphlets and lampoons he lacerated the Whigs for their war policy and contributed to the overthrow of Marlborough. His activities in these years are described in his delightful *Journal to Stella*, letters written to Hester Johnson, who at his advice had settled in Dublin after the death of Temple. The Tories rewarded him poorly. He hoped for a bishopric, but Queen Anne would not hear of such preferment for the author of the *Tale of a Tub* with its free-spoken attacks on religious cant, and he was given the deanery of St Patrick's, Dublin, in April 1713. He regarded this as banishment; within a year the Whigs were back in power, and his prospects in London were gone forever. He was followed to Ireland by 'Vanessa', Esther Vanhomrigh, twenty-year-old daughter of a rich widow with property at Celbridge, near Dublin, whom he had met in London. His poem 'Cadénus and Vanessa' indicated that his feelings for her were no more than those of a friend, but she had fallen passionately in love with him. Her presence in Dublin was a great embarrassment to him and almost estranged him from Stella, to whom he was tenderly devoted. Vanessa died of tuberculosis in 1723, and it is said that she and Swift had a violent quarrel shortly before. Very little is known for certain about the relations between Swift and these two women, although many explanations and interpretations have been offered. There is no conclusive proof that he was married to Stella, although this was the belief of many of his contemporaries.

His best-known book, popularly called *Gulliver's Travels*, was published in 1726 and became famous almost overnight. The work of his mature and disillusioned years, it reflects in its later parts his savage rage at the spectacle of human misery and depravity. It is one of the great ironies of literature that it has become a children's classic. Swift became increasingly incensed at the ill-treatment of Ireland, brought home to him by the wretched condition of the people he saw when he walked out from his deanery or travelled through the countryside. His first pamphlet on Irish affairs, published in 1720, advocated boycotting English fabrics. He won immense popularity in 1724 when his *Drapier's Letters* foiled a plan to foist on the Irish a new copper currency, 'Wood's Halfpence', the patent for which had been obtained by bribery. His *Modest Proposal* suggested that the people should be relieved by the sale of their numerous children as food for the rich. No more biting satire has been written in English. Stella died in 1728 when Swift was sixty, and his remaining years were clouded by infirmity and loneliness. This misanthrope, who was dearly loved by two beautiful women, had a genius for friendship, and still kept up a voluminous correspondence with Pope, Gay, Arbuthnot, and others of his English circle. But he was increasingly afflicted by giddiness and deafness, and lived in constant terror of mental decline. In 1742 he sank into a speechless lethargy and was committed to the care of guardians. He died 19 October 1745 and is buried in St Patrick's Cathedral, where, in the words written by him for his own epitaph, 'fierce indignation can no longer tear his heart.' He left £8,000 to build a home for the insane. While he lived, his private charity was extensive and well-judged. Swift was one of the most commanding intellects and the greatest writer of his day. His prose is unmatched for simple strength and clarity. His satire was savage in its mockery, overpowering in its sheer force of intellect. His letters are among the best in English literature, and show an ease and lightness that carry the reader along in sheer delight.

SWIFT, PATRICK (1928-1983), artist. Born in Dublin, and in his twenties left a job in the Dublin Gas Company to take up full-time painting. In 1953 he received an Arts Council grant to study in Italy and then spent some time in Paris and London, where he edited the literary magazine *X*. He settled in the Algarve in Portugal in the 1960s, revived an old pottery, painted landscapes, and

with David Wright wrote three well-received books on Portuguese regions, including the Algarve. In 1971 his portrait of his friend PATRICK KAVANAGH was exhibited in Dublin and excited much interest. He died in his home in the Algarve on 19 July 1983 after a long illness.

SYNGE, JOHN MILLINGTON (1871-1909), playwright. Born at Newtown Little, Rathfarnham, Co. Dublin, 16 April 1871. Educated privately and at TCD, where he won prizes in Irish and Hebrew. As a boy he showed an absorbing interest in nature, and roamed the Dublin mountains and the Wicklow glens. He studied at the RIAM while still an undergraduate, and became proficient on the piano, flute, and violin. Deciding to become a musician, he went to Germany in 1893 for further study, but after two years turned to literature and settled in Paris, making occasional trips to Ireland, including a visit to the Aran Islands. In Paris he met W. B. YEATS, who advised him to return to the Aran Islands and write about the way of life there. Synge spent the late summers of 1899-1902 on the islands, sharing the isolated life, playing his fiddle, and listening to the talk and stories around the firesides at night. He began a book, *The Aran Islands*, which found a publisher in 1907, and was illustrated by JACK B. YEATS. Meanwhile he wrote two plays for the newly founded Irish National Theatre, both based on stories he had heard on Aran. *The Shadow of the Glen* was produced in 1903 and *Riders to the Sea* the following year. At home they were received with hostility; English critics welcomed them and perceived a new and vitalising force in Synge's use of the speech of fishermen and country people. When the Abbey Theatre opened on 27 December 1904 Synge became literary adviser and later a director with Yeats and LADY GREGORY. *The Well of the Saints* was produced there in 1905. His great comedy, *The Playboy of the Western World*, now a classic of the Irish theatre, caused a riot on its first Abbey production in 1907; its ironic laughter and underlying note of tragedy seemed equally abhorrent to the Dublin audiences. Undeterred, Yeats put on *The Tinker's Wedding* the same year. Synge's last and unfinished play, *Deirdre of the Sorrows*, was said to have been inspired by his love for the actress MOLLY ALLGOOD, who played Pegeen Mike in *The Playboy*. His health was never robust; he died in Dublin on 24 March 1909, and was buried in the family tomb at Mount Jerome, Dublin. Besides his plays and his book on the Aran Islands, Synge wrote a number of occasional papers describing his travels through the wilder parts of Ireland; these have considerable charm, compounded of the personality of the writer, the remote beauty of the scenes, and the strange primitive way of life that he sets down.

T

TAAFFE, NICHOLAS (1677–1769), **sixth VISCOUNT TAAFFE**. Born at O'Crean's Castle, Sligo. Educated in Lorraine, and joined the Austrian service. Promoted lieutenant-general in 1752. Succeeded to his Irish title in 1738. His estates were sold and he received only one-third of the price, the rest going to a Protestant relative. At the battle of Kolin (1757) he rallied the Austrian cavalry. He introduced the potato on his large estate in Silesia. Published *Observations on Affairs in Ireland* (1766), a plea against the penal laws. Died at castle of Ellischau, Bohemia, 30 December 1769.

TALBOT, MATTHEW (1856–1925), 'servant of God'. Born 2 May 1856 at 13 Aldborough Court, Dublin, the second of twelve children of Charles Talbot, a labourer with Dublin Port and Docks Board. Educated at O'Connell CBS. At twelve he went to work as a messenger-boy with E. & J. Burke, wine merchants, and four years later obtained a job as a messenger with the Port and Docks Board. Heavy drinking was customary in working-class life of the period, and he began to drink in his early teens. He left the board after three years so as not to disgrace his father, although he also drank heavily. He then worked for many years as a builder's labourer, carrying a hod for the bricklayer. He spent all his wages on drink, sometimes holding horses for hours for a few pence when his money had gone. About 1884 he took a pledge of total abstinence, and his whole life changed. He began to attend again to his religious duties and gradually became more and more devout, and imposed severe mortifications on himself. He slept on a plank with a wooden block for a pillow, restricted his food most days to dry bread and cocoa without milk or sugar, and began to attend Mass daily, rising before 4 a.m. for this purpose. He gave up his pipe, although he had smoked an ounce of tobacco a day. It took him a considerable time to repay money he had borrowed to buy drink. About 1900 he left home and took a room in Gloucester Street. For spiritual guidance he went to Dr Hickey of Holy Cross College, Clonliffe Road, and to Fr O'Reilly of the Pro-Cathedral. He often went to Mass in the Jesuit Church in Gardiner St, and was well known to several members of that order. Early in the 1900s he began to work in the timber-yard of T. & C. Martin's. He joined his fellow-workers on strike in the famous labour troubles of 1913 but took no active part in it. He did not picket, but gave money to married men on strike. In 1923 he spent two periods in the Mater Hospital, receiving treatment for a kidney and heart condition. He was not able to work for some time after, and subsisted on disability benefit of 7s 6d (37½p) a week after his unemployment benefit had run out. He went back to work with Martins in the spring of 1925 and continued to work to the day before he died. On 7 June 1925 he collapsed and died in Granby Lane on the way from his room at 18 Rutland St to early Mass in St Saviour's, Dominick St. It was then discovered that he wore a chain on his waist and a lighter chain on one arm, on the other arm a cord, and a chain below one knee, immediately below the kneecap. He was described as a small, wiry man, inclined to be pugnacious, like his father. He was a good worker even in his hard-drinking days, and was put first by foremen to set the pace. In later days he was said to be cheerful and good-humoured, and laughed and talked pleasantly with visitors. He gave most of his wages to charity, and sought to conceal his prayers and fasts. In October 1976 the Catholic Church, which had already declared him to be a 'servant of God', gave him the title of Venerable. His remains are interred in a vault in Glasnevin cemetery, and a bronze head has been mounted on the wall of a block of flats near to the site of 18 Rutland St, where he lived in his last years.

TALBOT, PETER (1620–1680), archbishop, brother of RICHARD. Born in Dublin. Ordained Jesuit in Portugal and taught theology at Antwerp. Served on diplomatic missions for the exiled King Charles II, who had set up a court in Antwerp. On the Restoration, Talbot resigned from the Jesuits and joined the Court as queen's almoner. He was forced to flee to Europe when accused of a plot to assassinate Ormond. He was appointed archbishop of Dublin 1669. Banished in 1673, and lived in Paris until 1675, when he was allowed to return to England and in 1677 to Ireland. Arrested in 1678 on charge of complicity in the 'Popish Plot', imprisoned in Dublin Castle, and died there.

TALBOT, RICHARD (1630–1691), Earl and titular Duke of Tyrconnell. Born at Malahide, Co. Dublin, entered the English army, and fought in the defence of Drogheda against Cromwell in 1649. On the defeat of the Royalist cause in Ireland he fled to the Continent, but returned at the Restoration in 1660. He was given grants of land in Ireland and was well paid for securing the restoration of some estates to their former owners. By 1670 he had become chief spokesman for Irish Catholics who had suffered under the various Acts of Settlement. In 1678 he was arrested for supposed complicity in the 'Popish Plot', but was soon released. On the accession of King James II in 1685 he was given command of the army in Ireland and in June 1686 he was made lord-in-general at a salary of £1,410 and given independence from Clarendon, the lord lieutenant. His policy was to make the king independent in England by means of an Irish army, and to restore to Catholics the property and power they had formerly enjoyed in Ireland. He replaced Protestants with Catholic soldiers and officers, and appointed Catholic judges, sheriffs, and magistrates, making room for them, if necessary, by the removal of Protestants. He became viceroy of Ireland in January 1687, and in July 1688 the king made him a duke. During the Williamite wars the Anglo-Irish of the Pale, led by Tyrconnell, were regarded with distrust and jealousy by the native Irish, who numbered SARSFIELD among their leaders. Tyrconnell commanded a regiment of horse at the Battle of the Boyne in 1690 and after this defeat went to France, where James had already fled. He returned to Ireland in January 1691 as lord lieutenant with funds and a promise of French help. After the loss of Athlone and the heavy defeat at Aughrim, he was proceeding to prepare Limerick for a siege when on 14 August 1691 he died suddenly of apoplexy.

TANDY, (JAMES) NAPPER (1740–1803), United Irishman. Born in Dublin and started life as an ironmonger, later becoming a land agent and rent collector. Entered politics as a representative of the guild of merchants on the common council. Joined the Volunteers on their formation and commanded the approaches to the Houses of Parliament when their independence was announced on 27 May 1782. His influence declined as the Volunteer movement weakened. In 1791 he helped WOLFE TONE and THOMAS RUSSELL to found the Society of United Irishmen, and became the first secretary of the Dublin group. In 1793 he fled to America to avoid arrest for having taken the oath of the Defenders' Society. Hearing of developments at home, he went to Paris in 1798, was appointed a general by the French government, and sent to Ireland with a small force. He landed at Rutland Island off the Donegal coast but, learning of Humbert's defeat in Connacht, re-embarked and sailed for Norway. Eventually he was captured in Hamburg, handed over to the British, and sentenced to death after trial at Lifford, Co. Donegal. Napoleon demanded his extradition, and he was released unconditionally in 1802. Died at Bordeaux on 24 August 1803. His memory is kept alive in the ballad 'The Wearing of the Green': 'I met with Napper Tandy and he shook me by the hand.' SIR JONAH BARRINGTON said: 'He acquired celebrity without being able to account for it, and possessed an influence without rank or capacity.'

TATE, NAHUM (1652–1715), English poet laureate. Born in Dublin; educated at TCD. Moving to London, he wrote a number of plays and adapted others. His version of *Lear*, to which he gave a happy ending, with Cordelia marrying Edgar, superseded the original on the English stage until the 1850s. His poems, remarkable for quantity rather than merit, were mainly written for public occasions and to secure patronage from the wealthy. Dryden commissioned him to write the second part of 'Absalom and Architophel', and he had a hand in many other works, as translator, adaptor, or editor. His own best poem is 'Panacea, a Poem on Tea' (1700). In collaboration with Nicholas Brady, he published a metrical version of the Psalms, which included 'While Shepherds Watched' and 'Through All the Changing Scenes of Life', which found a lasting place in Protestant worship. Tate succeeded Shadwell as poet laureate in 1692, and died in London, deeply in debt, on 12 August 1715.

TAYLOR, GEORGE (1716–1781), signatory of the American Declaration of Independence. Born in Ireland; emigrated to North America in 1736. Worked as a clerk and then forge-manager in Chester Co. before moving to Durham, Pennsylvania, where he became an iron manufacturer in 1754. Served from 1764 to 1770 in provincial assembly and as colonel of militia, but did not see active service. Re-elected October 1775 and active in promotion of revolutionary measures. Member of Continental Congress 1776, and signed Declaration of Independence on 2 August. Helped to negotiate a treaty with several Indian tribes. Retired from Congress in March 1777. Died at Easton, 23 February 1781.

TEELING, BARTHOLOMEW (1774–1798), United Irishman. Born at Lisburn, Co. Antrim, son of a linen-draper. Educated in Dublin at a school conducted by the Rev. W. Dubordieu, a French Protestant clergyman. He joined the United Irishmen before he was twenty, and in 1796 went to France to assist WOLFE TONE in securing a French invasion of Ireland. He served a campaign under Hoche, and then in 1798 landed at Killala as aide-de-camp to General Humbert and was captured after the surrender of the French at Ballinamuck. He was tried by court-martial in Dublin, sentenced to death, and executed at Arbour Hill barracks on 24 September 1798.

TEELING, CHARLES HAMILTON (1778–1850), journalist. Born at Lisburn, brother of BARTHOLOMEW. Arrested in 1796 as a United Irishman. Settled in Dundalk in 1802 as a linen-bleacher. Became proprietor of Belfast *Northern Herald*. Moved to Newry and established the *Newry Examiner*, which was edited from 1836 to 1840 by Thomas, afterwards Lord O'Hagan, who married his daughter. He owned and edited the monthly *Ulster Magazine* 1832–1835. Published *Personal Narrative of the Rebellion of 1798* (1828), of considerable historical value, and a *Sequel* (1832). Also *The History and Consequences of the Battle of the Diamond* (1835), a Catholic version of the events in which the Orange Society originated. Died in Dublin.

TEMPLETON, JOHN (1766–1825), naturalist. Born in Belfast and educated privately. His private means enabled him to devote himself to study of local botany and zoology. He laid out an experimental garden on the family estate at Cranmore, near Belfast. He corresponded with leading British naturalists and contributed to their works but published very little himself. He left in manuscript a *Journal* (1806–1825), and *Hibernian Flora*, illustrated with his own watercolours (both in Belfast Museum) and *Catalogue of Native Plants*, in RIA. He was offered a post in New Holland (Australia) and a grant of land, but declined. Discovered *Rosa hibernica* in 1795 near Holywood. Associate of Linnean Society. Died at Cranmore, 15 December 1825.

TENNANT, MARGARET MARY EDITH, née ABRAHAM (1869–1946), pioneer in public social work. Born at Rathgar, Dublin, 5 April 1869. Educated privately, mainly by her father, a lawyer in the public service. On his death in 1887 she went to London to become secretary to Lady Dilke, scholar and promoter of trade unions among women. She became treasurer of the Women's Trade Union League, and in 1893 was appointed by Asquith to be the first woman factory inspector. She concerned herself chiefly with the three evils of illegal overtime, bad sanitation, and dangerous trades. In 1895 she was appointed to a departmental committee on dangerous trades, of which the chairman was Harold John Tennant, a Liberal MP who subsequently became secretary of state for Scotland. They were married in 1896, and she resigned her post. She kept in touch with her old activities, was chairman of the Industrial Law Committee, and in 1909 was appointed a member of the Royal Commission on Divorce. During the First World War she was chief adviser on women's welfare in the Ministry of Munitions, and was made a Companion of Honour in 1917. Her eldest son was killed on active service that year. Died at Cornhill, Rolvenden, Kent, 11 July 1946.

THOMAS, GEORGE (1756–1802), the 'Rajah from Tipperary'. Born on a small farm at Roscrea, Co. Tipperary. He joined the British navy as a sailor, and in 1781 deserted from a man-of-war at Madras and became a mercenary soldier in the army of the Nizam of Hyderabad. In 1787 he made his way to Delhi and entered the service of the Begum Sumru of Sirdhana. The begum appointed him commander of her army, and his career was successful until 1792, when he lost favour with her. He then transferred to the service of Appa Rao, the Muhratta governor of Meerut. Shortly after the death of Appa Rao in 1797 he seized power and made himself rajah of a wide territory, with revenues estimated at £200,000. He founded a mint and a gun factory, extended his territories by frequent raids, and proposed to the British government that he should conquer the Punjab for them. He was a military commander of genius, but the Sikhs, whom he had despoiled, at length obtained French aid, and he was deposed in 1802. He was escorted to the British frontier and intended to return to Ireland, but died of fever at Bahrampur, Bengal, 22 August 1802.

THOMPSON, WILLIAM (*c.* 1785–1833), political economist. Born in Rosscarbery, Co. Cork. A wealthy landlord, the contrast between his own affluence and the wretched condition of his tenants led him to study economic problems. He became friendly with Bentham, supported Robert Owen's ideas on co-operation, and in 1824 published *An Enquiry into the Principles of the Distribution of Wealth Most Conducive to Human Happiness*. He regarded unearned income and private property as leading to social injustice, and was the first writer to treat the just distribution of wealth as a cardinal principle in political economy. He was also a pioneer in his views on sexual equality, which he expounded in his book *Appeal of One Half* the Human Race, Women, against the Pretentions of the Other Half, Men, to Retain them in Political, and thence in Civil and Domestic Slavery (1825). He died at Cloonkeen, Rosscarbery, on 28 March 1833,and left most of his estate to aid the poor, with schemes based on the principles of Robert Owen. This provision was set aside by the courts after twenty-five years' litigation. Thompson was quoted by Marx, whom the Webbs described as 'Thompson's disciple'. A bust of Thompson is displayed in Prague's International Communist Museum.

THOMPSON, WILLIAM (1805–1852), naturalist. Born in Belfast, 2 December 1805, son of a linen-merchant. After local schooling, was apprenticed to the linen business in 1820. He soon abandoned business for science, and devoted himself to the study of natural history. After a tour of the Continent in 1826 he published his first paper, *On the Birds of the Copeland Islands*. At a meeting of the British Association in Glasgow in 1840 his *Report on the Fauna of Ireland—Division Vertebrata* attracted favourable notice. His chief work was his *Natural History of Ireland* (1849–1856), which became the standard book on the subject. He was the first observer to describe the wonderful breeding-places of many rare species of birds to be found along the coast of Co. Donegal. Died 17 February 1852 while on a visit to London. Buried in Belfast.

THOMPSON, WILLIAM MARCUS (1857–1907), journalist. Born at Derry, 24 April 1857, of a strongly Orange family, and educated privately. Started work on the *Belfast Morning News*, and joined the staff of the conservative *Standard* in London in 1877. Called to the bar in 1880, he developed radical sympathies and specialised in defending trade unionists. He defended John Burns twice in 1886 and again in 1888 on a charge of incitement to riot. A regular contributor to *Reynolds' Newspaper*, he became editor in 1894 and continued its policy of attack on privilege and rank. Died in London, 28 December 1907.

THOMSON, HUGH (1860–1920), illustrator. Born 1 June 1860 at Coleraine, Co. Derry. Educated at the Model School there. Went to London in 1883 and began to work for the *English Illustrated Magazine*. The publishers, the Macmillan family, became his friends, and commissioned him to illustrate a long series of English classics, including Jane Austen's novels, and works by Thackeray, George Eliot, Dickens, and J. M. Barrie. He also made many drawings for the leading magazines of the day, notably the *Graphic*. Imagination, charm and humour mark his work. Towards the end of his life he received a civil list pension. Died at Wandsworth Common, 7 May 1920.

THOMSON, JAMES (1822–1892), engineer. Born Belfast, 16 February 1822. Brother of LORD KELVIN. Educated by his father, a professor of mathematics. Entered Glasgow University at ten, graduated in 1839. Served apprenticeship in engineering works in England. Became civil engineer in Belfast in 1851 and waterworks engineer 1853. Professor of engineering, Queen's College, 1853–1873 and Glasgow University 1873–1889. Invented or improved centrifugal and jet pumps, paddle-boats, and water-wheels. Contributed papers to many learned journals on subjects including plasticity of ice, crystallisation, liquefaction, and air and water currents. Elected FRS 1877. Received honorary doctorates from Glasgow, QUB, and DU. Resigned in 1889 due to failing eyesight. Died 8 May 1892.

THORNTON, MATTHEW (1714–1803), signatory of the American Declaration of Independence. Born at Derry, and emigrated to USA with his parents in 1718. Educated at Worcester, Massachusetts, and became a medical doctor. Practised at Londonderry, New Hampshire. Presided over the Provincial Convention of 1775, delegate to the Continental Congress 1776, and signed the Declaration. Judge 1782. Died at Newburyport, 24 June 1803.

THURSTON, KATHERINE CECIL (1875–1911), novelist. Born at Wood's Gift, Cork, 18 April 1875. Educated privately by her wealthy parents. After her marriage in 1901 to E. Temple Thurston, the novelist, she began to write and won quick popularity, especially with her second novel, *John Chilcote MP* (1904). Her books were more successful than her marriage, which foundered in divorce in 1910. She died from asphyxia in Moore's Hotel, Cork, 5 September 1911.

TIERNEY, MICHAEL (1894–1975), president of UCD. Born 30 September 1894 at Ballymacward, Co. Galway. Educated at Esker National School, St Joseph's College, Ballinasloe, and UCD. Won a travelling studentship and studied classics at the Sorbonne, Athens, and Berlin. Joined the Department of Classics, UCD, in 1915; appointed to the chair of Greek 1923. Elected TD for North Mayo in 1925 for Cumann na nGaedheal. TD for NUI 1927–1932. When Seanad Éireann was reconstituted following the enactment of the new Constitution, he won a seat in 1938, became vice-chairman the following year, and held the post until the dissolution of the Seanad after the general election of 1944. In 1947, rather unexpectedly, he ran successfully for office as president of UCD and held the post until his retirement in 1964. For the greater part of his presidency his main object was to secure the support of the Government for the moving of the college from the confines of Earlsfort Terrace to a more spacious site on Stillorgan Road. Some circles thought that the college should be expanded by the acquisition of adjoining property so as to retain it in the city centre. Dr Tierney's view prevailed, and the college was enabled to acquire very extensive grounds at Belfield. He contributed many articles to learned journals, served on Government commissions, and was awarded the knighthood of the Order of St Gregory the Great. Author of *Daniel O'Connell* (1949), *Struggle with Fortune* (1954), and

Newman's University Sketches. Died at his home in Dublin, 10 May 1975.

TODD, JAMES HENTHORN (1805–1869), scholar. Born in Dublin, 23 April 1805. Educated at TCD; fellow of the college 1831. Took holy orders in the Church of Ireland 1832. Edited the *Christian Examiner*, a church periodical, and became a popular tutor in the college. In 1840 he founded the Irish Archaeological Society, and in 1843 he joined with Lord Adare, Dr Sewell and others in founding St Columba's College at Rathfarnham, Co. Dublin. Regius Professor of Hebrew 1849, and librarian 1852. With the help of JOHN O'DONOVAN and EUGENE O'CURRY he classified and arranged the valuable collection of Irish manuscripts in the library. President RIA 1856–1862, and contributed learned papers to its proceedings, as well as publishing a life of Saint Patrick (1864) and editing an important Irish manuscript, *Cogadh Gaedhil re Gallaibh* (1867), recounting the Norse invasions of Ireland. With WILLIAM REEVES he edited the Martyrology of Donegal (1864). Died at his house in Rathfarnham, 28 June 1869. His friends founded the Todd Lectureship in Celtic languages at the RIA in his memory.

TODHUNTER, JOHN (1839–1916), poet, playwright, and physician. Born Dublin, the son of a merchant, at 19 Sir John Rogerson's Quay, on 30 December 1839. Educated at the Quaker Schools at Mountmellick and York, and TCD. Practised medicine in Dublin at Cork Street Hospital 1870–1874, and lectured on English literature. Retiring from practice to devote himself to literature, he travelled much abroad, finally settling in London, where he was involved in the founding of the Irish Literary Society. His first play, *Helena in Troas* (1886), had Beerbohm-Tree and his wife in the leading parts. Further successful productions included *A Sicilian Idyll* (1890) and *The Black Cat* (1893). His published verse includes *Alcestis* (1879), *Forest Songs* (1881), and *How Dreams Come*

True (1890). He translated Heine's *Book of Songs* (1907) and wrote *A Study of Shelley* (1880) and *The Life of Patrick Sarsfield* (1895). Died at Chiswick, England, 25 October 1916.

TOLAND, JOHN (1670–1722), deist. Born 30 November 1670 in Inishowen, Co. Donegal. Brought up a Catholic, but turned Protestant at sixteen. Educated at Glasgow, Leiden and Oxford universities, he abandoned his intention of becoming a dissenting minister. In 1696 he published *Christianity Not Mysterious*, which caused great controversy and began the conflict between deists and orthodox believers. By order of the House of Commons the book was burned in Dublin by the common hangman, as atheistical and subversive. He paid a brief visit to Ireland in 1697 but had to run out of the country. His subsequent career is obscure; it seems that he made a difficult living as a half-recognised political agent and hack author for people in power, notably Harley and Lord Shaftesbury. He visited Hannover and Berlin in 1701, and was again in Berlin in 1707. He published a number of political and theological pamphlets. *Nazaremus* (1718) and *Tetradymus* (1720) discussed various points of ecclesiastical history. *Pantheisticon* (1720) outlined the principles of a supposed philosophical society of pantheists. He also wrote a life of Milton. He was a native Irish-speaker, and used his knowledge in a *History of the Druids* included in a 'collection of several pieces by Mr Toland' (1726). Died at Putney near London, 11 March 1722.

TOLER, JOHN, first EARL OF NORBURY (1745–1831), chief justice. Born at Beechwood, Co. Tipperary, 3 December 1745. Educated at TCD; called to the bar 1770. MP for Tralee 1776. His support of the government brought him appointment as solicitor-general in 1789 and as attorney-general in 1798. For his vote for the Union in 1800 he was created Baron Norbury, and appointed chief justice of the Court of Common Pleas. Notorious on the bench for his scanty knowledge of the law and his callousness, while his buffoonery often had the court in an uproar. O'CONNELL petitioned parliament to have him removed from office, but without avail. Eventually he was induced to resign in 1827, and was compensated by a pension of £3,046 a year and an earldom. O'Connell said that 'he was bought off the bench by a most shameful traffic.' He died in Dublin, 27 July 1831.

TONE, THEOBALD WOLFE (1763–1798), United Irishman. Born at 44 Stafford Street (now Wolfe Tone St), Dublin, 20 June 1763, son of a coach-maker. Educated at TCD and the Middle Temple, London. Called to the bar 1789 but had little inclination for the practice of law, and soon turned to politics. In 1791 he published a pamphlet, *An Argument on Behalf of the Catholics of Ireland*, and the same year founded the Society of United Irishmen with THOMAS RUSSELL and NAPPER TANDY. Tone defined his objects as 'to break the connection with England, the never-failing source of all our political evils...' and his means as 'to substitute the common name of Irishman in place of the denominations of Protestant, Catholic and Dissenter.' In July 1792 he became paid secretary of the Catholic Committee, and in December 1792 he organised a Catholic Convention of elected delegates in the Tailors' Hall in Dublin. The Catholic Relief Act of 1793 followed, but Tone was bitterly disappointed by the limited concessions it gave. The political thinking of Tone and his associates was strongly influenced by the democratic principles of the French revolutionary leaders and it was natural that they should turn to France for help. Early in 1794 a clergyman, WILLIAM JACKSON, came to Dublin on a mission from France to open talks with the United Irishmen. Tone prepared for him a memorandum to show that Ireland was ripe for a French invasion. The following April, Jackson was arrested for treason. Tone's association with him was known to the authorities, but they agreed not to proceed against him if he left the country. Tone accepted this condition but insisted that he should not be required to give evidence against Jackson, and in fact remained openly in Dublin until after Jackson's trial. Before sailing from Belfast to America with his wife and family in May 1795, he met his friends Russell, NEILSON, and MCCRACKEN on Cave Hill, and they solemnly undertook never to cease their struggles for the independence of Ireland. In Philadelphia he obtained letters of introduction from the French minister to the Committee of Public Safety in Paris. Arriving there in February 1796 he soon impressed the minister for foreign affairs, Delacroix, with his energy and ability. The Directory appointed General Hoche to command an expedition, and Tone was made an adjutant-general in the French army. He sailed with the expedition from Brest on 15 December 1796, with 43 ships and 15,000 men, but it proved abortive; the fleet was scattered by storms and returned to France. Tone then joined Hoche in Holland where he was organising another expedition with the help of the Dutch, but this also failed. The sudden death of Hoche in September 1797 was a blow to Tone's hopes, as the two men had a high regard for each other.

When news of the rising in Ireland came, in May 1798, Tone renewed his efforts, but owing to the disorganised state of the French forces the best that could be arranged was a number of small raids on different parts of the Irish coast. On 16 September, Tone sailed with General Hardy and 3,000 men, and reached Lough Swilly. A powerful English squadron hove in sight, and after a sharp engagement captured the small French fleet on 12 October. Tone was taken prisoner to Dublin and tried by court-martial on 10 November. He appeared in his French uniform, was found guilty, and sentenced to be hanged, though he pleaded for a soldier's death by firing-squad. Early on the morning fixed for his execution he opened an artery in his neck with a penknife, and died on 19 November 1798. He was buried with his ancestors in Bodenstown churchyard, Co. Kildare, and is commemorated in an annual pilgrimage to his grave.

While a student at TCD Tone had eloped with a girl of sixteen to make what proved, despite later sorrow and privation, a very happy marriage. His widow, Matilda, received a small grant from the French government. His *Journals* and a biography were published in America in 1826 by his son WILLIAM.

TONE, WILLIAM THEOBALD WOLFE (1791-1828), soldier and author, son of THEOBALD WOLFE TONE. Born Dublin, 20 April 1791. After his father's death, he was declared an adopted child of the French Republic and educated at public expense in the Prytaneum and Lyceum. He was appointed to the French army and fought under Napoleon, being severely wounded at Leipzig. After Waterloo he went to New York, where he studied law. He was appointed to the artillery in 1820 but resigned in December 1826. Married Catherine, daughter of his father's friend William Sampson, in 1825. Wrote a *System of Cavalry Instruction* (1824). Published his father's journals and political writings, adding a *Life of Theobald Wolfe Tone* (two volumes, 1826). Died of tuberculosis, 10 October 1828. Buried in Long Island.

TORRENS, ROBERT (1780-1864), political economist. Born Harveyhill, Derry. Served in the Royal Marines at Walcheren and as colonel of a Spanish legion in the Peninsular Wars. Retired as colonel in 1835. MP for Ashburton and Bolton successively 1831-1835. He advocated the colonisation of South Australia, and in 1835 was appointed chairman of the Crown Commissioners to establish provinces there. Lake Torrens and the River Torrens, on which Adelaide was built, were named after him. His economic writings include

An Essay on the External Corn Trade (1815), which went through several editions and influenced Peel's legislation, and *An Essay on the Production of Wealth* (1821), in which he was one of the first to emphasise the role of land, labour and capital as the three instruments of production, and to state the law of diminishing returns. He anticipated Mills's theory of international trade, and was highly praised by Ricardo, who made an addition to his own work to meet Torrens's objection to his theory of value. He was one of the proprietors of the *Traveller*, editor for a time of the *Globe*, and wrote two novels. Elected FRS 1818. Died at Craven Hill, London, 27 May 1864.

TOTTENHAM, CHARLES (1685–1758), politician. Born in Co. Wexford. MP for New Ross 1727. In 1731 the administration proposed that £60,000 surplus in the National Debt Fund should be handed over to the English government. The motion came forward in the first session held in the new Parliament House in College Green. Tottenham heard of it, rode 60 miles (97 km) through the night, and rushed into the chamber in his mud-splashed boots. An attempt was made to exclude him but the Speaker ruled in his favour, and his vote defeated the motion. For years afterwards 'Tottenham in his boots' was a standing toast in patriotic circles. Sheriff of Co. Wexford 1737, and had great influence locally. He held his seat in parliament until shortly before his death on 20 September 1758.

TRAILL, ANTHONY (1838–1914), provost of TCD. Born at Ballylough, Co. Antrim, 1 November 1838. Educated at TCD; fellow 1865. Having graduated in engineering, he proceeded to take degrees in law and medicine. His restless energy found further outlet in sport: he was captain of cricket, racquets champion, and golfer. In politics an Ulster Unionist and owner of a small estate in Antrim, he took the side of the landlords in the struggle for reform of land tenure in Ireland. High sheriff of Antrim 1884, and chairman of Portrush electric tramway, the first in the world, which ran from Portrush to Bushmills, a distance of 6 miles (10 km), from 1883 until 1947. Appointed provost, TCD, 1904. While resisting any changes in the constitutional position of the college, he carried out many internal reforms. Died at the Provost's House, 15 October 1914.

TRAYNOR, OSCAR (1886–1963), soldier and politician. Born in Dublin, 21 March 1886, of a strongly nationalist family. Educated at St Mary's Place CBS. When his father died in 1899 he was apprenticed to John Long, a noted Dublin wood-carver. Later he became a compositor. He joined the Irish Volunteers, took part in the 1916 Rising, and was interned at Knutsford and Frongoch. During the War of Independence he became brigadier of the Dublin Brigade and led the attack on the Custom House in 1921. Elected TD for Dublin North in 1925. Minister for Posts and Telegraphs 1936; Minister for Defence in several Fianna Fáil governments until his resignation because of ill-health in 1961. As a young man he was a noted footballer, and toured Europe as goalkeeper for Belfast Celtic. President, Football Association of Ireland, from 1948 until his death. Died in Dublin, 15 December 1963.

TRENCH, FREDERIC HERBERT (1865–1923), poet and playwright. Born at Avonmore, Co. Cork, 23 November 1865. Educated at Haileybury and Keble College, Oxford. Joined the Board of Education in 1891 but the work was uncongenial and he resigned in 1909 and became artistic director of the Haymarket Theatre until 1911, when he went to live near Florence. His four-act play *Napoleon* was produced by the Stage Society in 1919. He died at Boulogne-sur-Mer, 11 June 1923. His *Collected Works* were published in 1924.

TRENCH, MELASINA (1768–1827), author. Born in Dublin, 22 March 1768. Brought up by her grandfather, Richard

Chenevix Trench, bishop of Waterford. In 1786 she married Colonel Richard St George, who died two years later in Portugal. She began to travel through Europe in 1798, meeting, among others, Nelson, Lady Hamilton, and President John Quincy Adams. In 1803 she married Richard Trench of Moate, Co. Galway, in Paris. Her husband was detained in France until 1807 by Napoleon, although Melasina delivered a petition to him in person in 1805. She died at Malvern on 27 May 1827. Her letters and journals were edited by her son, RICHARD CHENEVIX TRENCH, as *Remains* (1862). Her poems were issued anonymously. She was noted for her beauty and simplicity, and was much sought after in society.

TRENCH, RT. REV. RICHARD CHENEVIX (1807–1886), archbishop.

Born in Dublin on 5 September 1807, son of MELASINA TRENCH. Educated at Harrow, and Trinity College, Cambridge. After travels on the Continent he was ordained deacon in 1833. Served as curate and rector. Professor of divinity at King's College 1846–1858; dean of Westminster 1856. Consecrated archbishop of Dublin on 1 January 1864. Fought against disestablishment of Church of Ireland, and after the Act of 1869 kept the church united through a difficult period. An accident in 1875 incapacitated him for some time. He resigned 1884 and died at 23 Eaton Square on 28 March 1886. Buried in Westminster Abbey. Some of his books of poetry went into many editions. Also published history, sermons, and other devotional works. Distinguished as a philologist, his *Study of Words* (1851) went into twenty editions.

TRENCH, WILLIAM STEUART

(1808–1872), land agent and author. Born 16 September 1808 at Bellegrove, near Portarlington, Co. Laois. Cousin of RICHARD CHENEVIX TRENCH. Educated at Armagh Royal School and TCD. Won gold medal of Royal Agricultural Society for essay on reclamation. Became agent for Shirley estate, Co. Monaghan, 1843, and afterwards for Lords Lansdowne, Bath, and Digby. In *Realities of Irish Life* (1868) he recorded his experiences of Irish rural life over twenty years, including the Famine times. It went into five editions in a year. The *Edinburgh Review* said that it had the force, humour and pathos of Dickens at his best. *Ierne, a Tale* (1871) was less successful. His *Sketches of Life and Character in Ireland* appeared in the monthly *Evening Hours*, 1871–1872. Died at Lord Bath's seat, Carrickmacross, Co. Monaghan, 10 August 1872.

TROY, DERMOT (1927–1962), tenor.

Born in Wicklow and joined the RAF at eighteen for a short period. He studied at the RIAM, won the *Irish Independent* Caruso competition in 1952, and was invited to join the Glyndebourne chorus. He then spent three years at Covent Garden and was invited to sing in Mannheim. This led to a successful tour in West Germany and a prestigious engagement in Hamburg, where he was offered a three-year contract. Early in 1961 he suffered a heart attack and was obliged to stop work for a year. Hamburg kept his place open and in April 1962 he returned to sing as Lensky in Tchaikovsky's *Eugene Onegin*. It was his last performance: he died in September 1962. His acting ability, gift for languages and fine natural tenor had won him an international reputation and opened a brilliant career before him when he died at the age of thirty-five.

TROY, JOHN THOMAS (1739–1823), archbishop of Dublin.

Born at Porterstown, Co. Dublin, 10 May 1739. Went to Rome at fifteen to enter the Dominican order. Ordained in 1762; prior of St Clement's in Rome 1772. In 1776 he was recalled to Ireland to become bishop of Ossory. He denounced the Whiteboys, and preached the duty of obedience to established government. Administrator of Armagh archdiocese 1781–1782; archbishop of Dublin 1786. He condemned the 1798 Rising and gave strong support to the legislative union with Britain in 1801. He opposed the principles and philosophy originating in revolutionary France, and helped to found Maynooth College with the aim of removing the necessity for clerical students to study on the continent. His views on the loyalty due to constitutional government led him to accept the principle of a government veto on clerical appointments, and he agreed that only those loyal to the government should be promoted to Irish bishoprics. He laid the foundation stone of the Pro-Cathedral in Marlborough Street, Dublin, in April 1815. Died 11 May 1823. Left barely enough money to pay his funeral expenses.

TUCKEY, JAMES KINGSTON (1776–1816), explorer. Born at Mallow, Co. Cork, in August 1776. Entered British navy in 1793. Served in the East Indies and wounded in both arms; appointed lieutenant 1800. Sent to Port Philip, New South Wales, in 1802 to establish a colony, and published an *Account* of his voyage in 1805. He was captured at sea about 1806 by the French and kept prisoner at Verdun until 1814. While there he married a fellow prisoner and wrote *Maritime Geography and Statistics*, published in 1815 on his return to London. Appointed in 1816 to command an expedition to the Congo in a specially built ship. His health, impaired in the tropics, broke down, and he died there 4 October 1816. His *Narrative of an Expedition to Explore the River Zaire* was published in 1818.

TUOHY, PATRICK (1894–1930), painter. Born at 15 North Frederick Street, Dublin. Educated by the Christian Brothers and at St Enda's, Rathfarnham, where he was one of the first pupils. WILLIAM PEARSE, teacher of art at the school, encouraged him to join the Metropolitan School of Art for evening classes, where he was taught by WILLIAM ORPEN. He won the Taylor Scholarship in 1912 and again in 1915. His first commission came from the Jesuit community in Rathfarnham

Castle, for whom he executed ten ceiling paintings. He also did ceiling paintings for the La Scala Theatre (later the Capitol Cinema, now demolished) in Dublin. He joined the Irish Citizen Army and served in the GPO in the 1916 Rising. After the surrender he escaped to Spain and taught in Madrid for eighteen months. On his return to Dublin in 1918 he took up a teaching post at the Metropolitan School of Art. That year he exhibited for the first time at the RHA, showing 'A Mayo Peasant Boy', now in the Municipal Gallery of Modern Art. This painting was sent to the exhibition of Irish art in Paris in 1922. In addition he contributed illustrations to books by STANDISH JAMES O'GRADY, painted a number of landscapes, and made some remarkable portraits of contemporaries, including the poet JAMES STEPHENS and Lord Fingall. He made lengthy visits to Paris, became friendly with JAMES JOYCE, and painted him and his family. In 1927 he went to Columbia, South Carolina, and later settled in New York. He returned to Ireland only once, for a brief visit. He died suddenly in New York.

TURNER, SAMUEL (1765–1810), informer. Born Turner's Glen, near Newry, Co. Down. Educated at TCD; called to the bar 1788. Joined the United Irishmen and became member of executive committee. Escaped to the Continent early in 1797. Lived in Hamburg and kept in contact with the Irish patriots. Included in the 1798 Act of Attainder as one concerned in the rebellion. Returned to Ireland in 1803 on death of his father and had attainder reversed on proof of his absence from Ireland a year prior to the rebellion. Settled in Dublin, enjoyed the esteem due to a patriot and the friendship of O'CONNELL until his death. W. J. FITZPATRICK established later that, in 1797, he betrayed his associates to the government through Lord Downshire and that he received a secret pension of £300 a year, afterwards increased to £500. Fitzpatrick states that he was killed in a duel with one Boyce in the Isle of Man.

TURNERELLI, PETER (1774–1839), sculptor. Born in Belfast, grandson of an Italian political refugee. The family moved to London when he was seventeen, and he became a pupil of Chenu, the sculptor, and a student at the RA. In 1797 he was appointed as instructor in modelling to the royal princesses, and lived at court for three years. In 1801 he was appointed sculptor-in-ordinary to the royal family, but declined a knighthood. He acquired a fashionable and lucrative practice, chiefly as a modeller of busts. The most distinguished people sat for him, including Wellington, Erskine, Pitt, and GRATTAN, and he was also asked to execute the 'jubilee' bust of King George III. It was modelled in 1809 and exhibited at the RA in the Jubilee Year, 1810. His bust of DANIEL O'CONNELL was extremely popular and it was said that 10,000 plaster copies were sold in Ireland. In 1814 his design for a monument to Robert Burns, showing the poet at the plough, was selected and erected at Dumfries. Exhibited regularly at the RA from 1802 until his death, which occurred after a few hours' illness at his house in Newman Street, London, 20 March 1839.

TYNAN, KATHARINE (1861–1931), novelist and poet. Born in Dublin, 23 January 1861. Educated at the Siena Convent, Drogheda. Her husband, H. A. Hinkson, whom she married in 1883, was a resident magistrate in Co. Mayo from 1914 until his death in 1919. She wrote over a hundred novels, many poems, and an autobiography in five volumes. Her novels included *Oh! What a Plague is Love* (1896), *She Walks in Beauty* (1899), *John-a-Dreams* (1916), and *They Loved Greatly* (1923). Her daughter was the novelist PAMELA HINKSON. Died at Wimbledon, 2 April 1931.

TYNDALL, JOHN (1820–1893), natural philosopher. Born at Leighlinbridge, Co. Carlow, 2 August 1820. Edu-cated at the local national school. Joined the Ordnance Survey of Ireland 1839; selected for the English survey in 1842. Worked as a railway engineer 1844–1847. Joined the staff of Queenswood College, Hampshire, but left after a year to study at the University of Marburg in Germany where he gained his doctorate in 1850. Returned to Queenswood in 1851, elected FRS 1852, and in 1853 became professor of natural philosophy at the Royal Institution. He became a close friend of Faraday, a colleague at the institution, and wrote his life under the title *Faraday as a Discoverer* (1868). His investigations into the properties of radiant heat probably constitute his major scientific contribution. An excellent lecturer and a pioneer in popular scientific writing, his books were translated into many European languages. In 1867 he succeeded Faraday as superintendent of the Royal Institution and as scientific adviser to Trinity House. A skilful mountaineer, he visited Switzerland regularly, published *Glaciers of the Alps* in 1860, and made the first ascent of the Weisshorn in 1861. In 1887 he resigned his posts because of continued ill-health, and retired to his country house at Hindhead, Surrey. Died there, 4 December 1893, from accidental poisoning with chloral.

TYRCONNELL, DUKE OF. See under TALBOT, RICHARD.

TYRRELL, ROBERT YELVERTON (1844–1914), classical scholar. Born 21 January 1844 at Ballingarry, Co. Tipperary, son of the vicar. Educated at home and TCD. Fellow 1868; professor of Latin 1871, of Greek 1880, and of ancient history 1900. Senior fellow and registrar 1904. In 1901 he was chosen one of 'the first fifty members of the British Academy. Published editions of Euripedes, Terence, and Sophocles, and of Cicero's *Correspondence*. Edited the TCD miscellany *Kottabos*, and one of the founders of *Hermathena* in 1874. Recognised as one of the greatest scholars of his day, with a keen wit and felicitous style. Died Dublin, 19 September 1914.

U

UA BUACHALLA, DOMHNALL (1865–1963), Seanascal (Governor-General) of Ireland. Son of a native Irish-speaker from Cork and active all his life in the language movement. He marched at the head of a small group of Irish Volunteers from Maynooth to take part in the fighting at the GPO in the 1916 Rising. He was imprisoned after the rising but released in 1917. Elected MP for Kildare 1918, and sat in the First Dáil. Voted against Treaty and fought in Four Courts in Civil War. Captured and imprisoned in Dundalk jail. Released by Republican troops August 1922. Elected Fianna Fáil TD for Kildare 1927 but lost his seat in general election of 1932. After the removal of JAMES MACNEILL from the office of Governor-General on 1 November 1932, Ua Buachalla was appointed in his place with the title of Seanascal until the post was abolished on the abdication of King Edward VIII. He did not live in the Viceregal Lodge but in a small suburban house, did not appear in public, and took no part in social affairs. He was the oldest surviving member of the 1916 Rising when he died in a Dublin nursing home on 30 October 1963.

USSHER, REV. HENRY (died 1790), astronomer. Born in Co. Wicklow. Educated at TCD; elected fellow 1764. Doctor of divinity 1779; professor of astronomy 1783. He chose the site of Dunsink, Co. Dublin, for the college observatory, planned the building, supervised construction and procured the equipment. Elected FRS 1785 and contributed papers including *An Account of an Aurora Borealis Seen in Full Sunshine*. Original member RIA. Died at his house in Harcourt Street, Dublin, 8 May 1790.

USSHER, JAMES (1581–1656), scholar and archbishop of Armagh. Born in Nicholas Street, Dublin, 4 January 1581. At thirteen entered TCD, where he was one of the first undergraduates. Ordained 1601; professor of theological controversies 1607–1621. In 1615 he helped to prepare strongly Calvinistic articles of belief for the Church of Ireland. Bishop of Meath 1621; archbishop of Armagh 1625. His toleration of pluralism and his obstruction of BEDELL in his plan to translate the Bible into Irish evoked strong contemporary criticism. While he was on a visit to England in 1640, dissensions between the Parliament and King Charles I came to a head, and he never returned to Ireland. He was respected by both sides, and in 1641 proposed a scheme for the combination of episcopacy and presbyterianism. Though he was a royalist, he advised Charles I against the execution of Strafford. He was granted the bishopric of Carlisle in 1642, but held it for only a short time. Moved to Oxford in 1642, and having declined an invitation to the Westminster Assembly of Divines took refuge in Wales in 1645. Became the guest of the dowager Countess of Peterborough at Reigate, Surrey, 1646. Died there 21 March 1656. A man of extensive learning, and a voluminous writer on ecclesiastical history, theology, and early Irish history; his *Works* were published in seventeen volumes in Dublin (1847–1864). His system of chronology, which placed the date of the Creation at 4004 B.C., was the source of the dates in many English editions of the Bible. His library, consisting of 10,000 volumes and many early Irish and Oriental manuscripts of great value, was bought for £2,200 after his death by contributions from the English army in Ireland, and after some vicissitudes placed in TCD on the order of King Charles II.

USSHER, (PERCY) ARLAND (1899–1980), writer. Born in Battersea, London, on 9 September 1899 and educated at Abbotsholme School, Derbyshire, at TCD, and St John's College, Cambridge, but took no degree. He returned to the family estate at Cappoquin, Co. Waterford, learned Irish, and published two books on the language and way of life of the Déise Gaeltacht. He was the first to publish (1926) a translation of *The Midnight Court* by BRIAN MERRIMAN. Bored with farming, he moved to Dublin in 1943. Wrote extensively on philosophy. Publications included *Journey Through Dread* (1955), a study of Kierkegaard, Heidegger and Sartre, *Three Great Irishmen* (1952) (SHAW, YEATS and JOYCE), and *The Face and Mind of Ireland* (1949). MIAL, president for twelve years, and received the academy's Gregory Medal. A forebear was ARCHBISHOP JAMES USSHER. He died in Dublin on 24 December 1980.

V

VIGNOLES, CHARLES BLACKER (1793–1875), engineer. Born at Wood-brook, Co. Wexford, son of an army ensign. As an infant he was taken prisoner by the French in the West Indies, and to secure his release was gazetted as an ensign when eighteen months old, and placed on half-pay. Brought back to England, and entered Sandhurst Military Academy in 1810. After service in Europe and Canada he returned to England in 1816, and secured employment on the construction of railways and canals. Engineer-in-chief in 1832 of the first Irish railway, from Dublin to Kingstown (Dún Laoghaire), opened on 17 December 1834. Acquired an international reputation as a civil engineer, and was employed as railway consultant in France, Switzerland, Germany, Spain, Russia and Brazil. Elected first professor of civil engineering at University College, London, 1841. Honoured by many learned societies; FRS 1855. Died at his house, the Villa Amalthea, Hythe, Hampshire, 17 November 1875.

W

WADDELL, HELEN (1889–1965), writer and scholar, sister of SAMUEL WADDELL. Born in Tokyo, daughter of a Presbyterian minister who returned to Ulster with his family when Helen was a young child. Educated in Belfast at Victoria College for Girls and QUB. Unable to pursue her academic career until 1920, as she had an invalid stepmother in her care. Meantime she published her first book, *Lyrics from the Chinese* (1915). Her first play, *The Spoilt Buddha*, was performed at the Opera House by the Ulster Literary Society. Also contributed articles to the *Standard, Manchester Guardian, Nation,* etc. In 1920 she began working towards a Ph.D. at Somerville College, Oxford. Her study of the secular origins of the stage led to her first major book, *The Wandering Scholars* (1927), followed by *Medieval Latin Lyrics* (1929), *Peter Abelard* (1933), *Beasts and Saints*, and *The Desert Fathers* (1936). *Peter Abelard,* the story of Abélard and Héloïse, went into thirty editions. She continued to contribute articles to journals, to lecture, and to broadcast, and became assistant editor to F. N. Voight on the magazine *The Nineteenth Century.* Her play *The Abbé Prévost* was staged in 1935. She settled in London and included among her friends the Shaws, GEORGE RUSSELL, Max Beerbohm, Stanley Baldwin, and Siegfried Sassoon. Received honorary degrees from Belfast, Columbia, Durham, and St Andrew's, and is the only woman to have gained the A. C. Benson Medal of the Royal Society of Literature. During the latter part of her life she suffered progressive loss of memory, and for the last ten years was completely incapacitated. Died in March 1965.

WADDELL, SAMUEL JOHN (1878–1967), playwright and actor under the name Rutherford Mayne. Born in Japan, son of the Rev. Hugh Waddell, a Presbyterian minister and lecturer at the Imperial University of Tokyo. Brought home to Ireland and educated at RBAI and Queen's College, Belfast, graduating in engineering at RUI. Helped to found the Ulster Literary Theatre 1904, and began to act and write for it. His first play, *The Turn of the Road*, was produced by the theatre in Belfast in 1906. His best-known work, *The Drone*, had its first performance in 1908 in the Abbey Theatre. He took his nom-de-plume from CAPTAIN MAYNE REID, his mother's maternal granduncle. As an actor he scored a great success in the title role in Eugene O'Neill's *Emperor Jones*. He toured Scotland and England for a season with the Mollison Repertory Company. He wrote a dozen plays in all, including *Red Turf, Peter,* and *Bridgehead*, which was based on his experiences as an inspector with the Land Commission, which he joined as a young engineer. He rose to be chief inspector and lay commissioner, retiring in 1950. Died in Dalkey, Co. Dublin, 25 February 1967.

WADDING, LUKE (1588–1657), Franciscan scholar. Born in Waterford, 16 October 1588. After studying in Lisbon and Coimbra, he entered the Franciscan order. Ordained at Vizeu in Portugal in 1613. President, Irish College, Salamanca, in 1617. In 1618 he went to Rome as theologian to the Spanish mission sent to promote the dogma of the Immaculate Conception. He remained there for the rest of his life. He founded the Irish Franciscan College of Saint

Isidore in 1625 and the Ludovisian College for Irish secular clergy in 1627. He kept in close contact with home, corresponding regularly with the Irish bishops, and after the insurrection of 1641 his influence at the Vatican secured valuable support for the Irish Catholic Confederation; as well as money, ships, and arms, the Pope sent Rinuccini as nuncio to Ireland in response to Wadding's advocacy of the Catholic cause. A scholarly and prolific writer, Wadding published thirty-six volumes in all. *Annales Minorum* (1625-1654), a monumental history of the Franciscan order in eight volumes, won him an international reputation. His other great achievement was the first critical edition of the entire works of DUNS SCOTUS, like himself a Franciscan (twelve volumes, 1639). The Confederation petitioned the Pope to make Wadding a cardinal. He found means to avoid this and other honours, and remained a simple priest until his death in Rome on 18 November 1657.

WADE, WALTER (died 1825), botanist. Practised in Dublin as a physician. He is credited with having secured a grant of £300 to establish a botanic garden at Dublin. Became professor and lecturer on botany to the Dublin Society (later the RDS). Elected associate, Linnean Society, 1792. Visited Kerry and Connemara and discovered new varieties of plants. He was the first scientific Irish botanist, and published a number of works on Irish flora. He died in Dublin.

WALKER, REV. GEORGE (1618-1690), governor of Derry. Born in Co. Tyrone, educated at Glasgow University. Little is known of him until his appointment as rector of Lissan, Co. Derry, in 1669. He also received the living of Donaghmore, near Dungannon, in 1674. He raised a regiment at Dungannon in 1688. Took refuge in Derry city, April 1689, and became joint governor, with the rank of colonel and 900 men under his command. After the

105-day siege was raised on 28 July 1689 he was selected to go to London with a royal address. He was received with rapture as a hero by the public, and warmly welcomed by King William III. Published *A True Account of the Siege of Londonderry* (1689), which was challenged by MACKENZIE. Appointed bishop of Derry. He was killed at the Battle of the Boyne, 12 July 1690.

WALKER, JOHN (1768-1833), founder of the Church of God. Born in Roscommon. Educated at TCD; elected fellow 1791 and ordained priest in Church of Ireland. About 1803, after a study of apostolic practices among the earliest Christians, he became convinced he could not continue in the church, and offered to resign his fellowship. He was expelled at once. He supported himself by lectures, and had a congregation of followers at Stafford Street, Dublin, who called themselves the Church of God, though more usually known as Separatists or Walkerites. He moved to London in 1819. Published a number of educational and religious works. TCD granted him a pension of £600 a year in 1833, as amends for their treatment of him. He returned to Dublin that year. Died 25 October 1833.

WALL, JOSEPH (1737-1802), governor of Goree. Born at Derryknavin, Co. Laois. Educated at TCD. Joined the British army in 1760 and served abroad until about 1773, when he returned to Ireland, 'to hunt for an heiress'. This failed, and after spending some time in England at gambling and amorous intrigues he secured by influence the governorship of Goree (Sénégal) in West Africa, in 1779. In 1782, in a drunken fit, he arrested an army sergeant called Armstrong on a charge of mutiny, and had him flogged by slaves. Armstrong received eight hundred lashes and died shortly afterwards. Wall, in poor health from the trying climate, was back in England later that year. Charges were laid against him by one of his officers, but during delay awaiting the arrival of witnesses from Sénégal he escaped to the Continent. In 1797 he returned to live in England, and in 1801 offered to stand trial. He was found guilty of the murder of Armstrong, and executed outside Newgate on 28 January 1802.

WALLACE, WILLIAM VINCENT (1812–1865), composer. Born in Waterford, 11 March 1812, son of a Scottish regimental bandmaster. He showed musical talent at an early age, and at sixteen was organist in Thurles Cathedral. After some years as a violinist in Dublin he married a Miss Kelly from Blackrock, gave up music, and emigrated to Australia to try sheep-farming in the bush. He soon separated from his wife, whom he never saw again. He then took to travel, wandered over Tasmania and New Zealand, and nearly lost his life on a whaling expedition. He visited India, Nepal, and Kashmir, and then went to South America and Mexico, making considerable sums from concerts in these countries. He invested his savings in piano and tobacco factories in America and sustained heavy losses when they went bankrupt. In 1844 he married a Miss Stoepel, a pianist, in New York, and they went to London the following year. After moderate success with a series of concerts, he wrote the opera *Maritana*, which was received with great enthusiasm at a production in Drury Lane Theatre on 15 November 1845. Visits to Germany and America followed, and he then wrote *Lurline*. When produced at Covent Garden in February 1860 this had an even greater success than *Maritana*. Wallace wrote several more operas and a great deal of pianoforte music. When he became seriously ill in 1864 he removed to France. Died at the Château de Bagen in the Pyrenees, 12 October 1865.

WALLER, JOHN FRANCIS (1810–1894), author. Born at Limerick. Educated at TCD, called to the bar 1833. Joined staff of *Dublin University Magazine*, and succeeded CHARLES LEVER as editor. His most notable contributions,

the *Slingsby Papers*, were published in book form in 1852. He published several volumes of poems and wrote popular songs, including 'Cushla Ma Chree' and 'The Song of the Glass'. Edited *Imperial Dictionary of Universal Biography* (three volumes, 1857–1863), *Gulliver's Travels* (1864), *Goldsmith's Works* (1864–1865), and MOORE's *Irish Melodies* (1867). Vice-president RIA. Appointed registrar of the Rolls court 1867. On retirement moved to London and engaged in literary work for Cassell and Co. Died at Bishop's Stortford, 19 January 1894.

WALSH, EDWARD (1805–1850), poet. Born in Derry. Educated at hedge school and became a hedge school-master. Imprisoned for taking part in tithe war. After release he became a national school teacher near Mallow but was dismissed for article 'What is Repeal, Papa?' in the *Nation*. Became national teacher again in Co. Waterford in 1837. Contributed poems and translations to the *Dublin Penny Journal* and *Nation*. Moved to Dublin, and for a brief period was sub-editor on the *Monitor*, a weekly newspaper. In 1847 adverse circumstances forced him to take a post as teacher to the convict establishment at Spike Island, Cork harbour. Dismissed for clandestine interview with JOHN MITCHEL. Became schoolmaster, Cork Union workhouse in August 1848. Published *Reliques of Irish Jacobite Poetry, with Metrical Translations* (1844), and *Irish Popular Songs, Translated with Notes* (1847). Died 6 August 1850.

WALSH, MAURICE (1879–1964), writer. Born near Listowel, Co. Kerry, and educated locally. Joined the civil service in Limerick 1901 and served as an excise officer for twenty years in the highlands of Scotland, Derbyshire, Staffordshire, the Yorkshire dales, and the west of Ireland. In 1923 he volunteered to return to Ireland to serve under the new Irish government. His first novel, *The Key above the Door* (1926), failed in a £500 first novel competition. Chambers, the Edinburgh publishers, bought it for £100, and sold 150,000 copies. Further novels include *While Rivers Run* (1928), *The Small Dark Man* (1929), *Blackcock's Feather* (1932), *The Road to Nowhere* (1934), *Green Rushes* (1935), and *And No Quarter* (1937). He also wrote a series of short stories, *Thomasheen James*, and *The Quiet Man*, later made into a film of the same name. Retired from the civil service in 1933. In 1939, with Seán Ó Faoláin, he wrote a special article for the *Saturday Evening Post* to present the case for Ireland's neutrality during the war. Died in Dublin.

WALSH, WILLIAM J. (1841–1921), archbishop. Born in Dublin, 30 January 1841. Educated at Catholic University under Newman, and at Maynooth. Professor of theology, Maynooth, 1867–1878; vice-president 1878, and president 1881. Appointed archbishop of Dublin 1885. Took active part in public affairs and was a strong supporter of the Republican leaders from 1918 until his death. First chancellor, NUI. Published works on Catholic education, Gregorian music, and bimetallism. Died in Dublin, 9 April 1921.

WARBURTON, BARTHOLOMEW ELLIOTT GEORGE, usually known as Eliot Warburton (1810–1852), author. Born near Tullamore, Co. Offaly. Educated at Cambridge University. Called to the bar 1837, but soon abandoned the law to manage his estates, travel abroad, and write. When he contributed articles on his travels in the Near East to the *Dublin University Magazine*, the editor, CHARLES LEVER, persuaded him to make them into a book. Under the title *The Crescent and the Cross, or the Romance and Realities of Eastern Travel* (1844), it went into seventeen editions. He continued to travel and to produce miscellaneous works, including historical novels and an edition of the *Memoirs of Horace Walpole and his Contemporaries* (1852). His last visit to Ireland was made to study the poverty in Dublin for a projected *History of the Poor*. His last book, *Darien, or The Merchant Prince* (1852), includes a description of the horrors of a ship on fire. On 4 January 1852 he perished off Land's End in a fire on board the mail steamer *Amazon* on its maiden voyage to Darien in the West Indies.

WARD, JOHN (1781–1837), mystic. Born Queenstown (Cóbh), Co. Cork, on 25 December 1781. Taken by his parents to Bristol in 1790, and apprenticed to a shipwright. Joined the navy and was present at battle of Copenhagen 1801. In 1803 he was paid off, got married, and supported himself as a shoemaker. He had been brought up a Calvinist, but now tried in succession Methodists, Baptists, Independents, Sandemanians, and Southcottians, but quarrelled with all of them. In 1826 he received, as he thought, 'an illumination', and gave up shoemaking to proclaim his divine mission. He called himself 'Zion', and his followers reckoned their calendar from 1826. He toured England making converts. In 1832 he was sentenced to eighteen months' imprisonment at Derby for blasphemy. On release he assembled a congregation at Bristol. He removed to Leeds in 1836 and died there, at 91 Park Lane, on 12 March 1837. Gentle in manner and a persuasive speaker, he published some thirty works on religion, based mainly on his reading of the Bible.

WARE, SIR JAMES (1594–1666), antiquary and historian. Born at his father's house, Castle Street, Dublin, on 26 November 1594. Educated at TCD. Collected and studied manuscripts and charters. Employed DUBHALTACH MAC FIRBISIGH to prepare transcripts and translations from the Irish for him. Knighted 1629, succeeded his father as auditor-general for Ireland 1632, and became MP for Dublin University and a member of the Privy Council. During the Civil War he was imprisoned by the Parliamentarians as a Royalist and then expelled from Dublin in 1649. After a year and a half in France, he settled in London and pursued his studies there until the restoration of 1660, when he returned to Dublin and was re-appointed auditor-general. From his emoluments of office he made generous contributions to widows and to fellow-Royalists who had been ruined by the war, while continuing to collect and preserve valuable historical material on Gaelic Ireland. He published a number of treatises in Latin on Irish literary and ecclesiastical antiquities, as well as editions of Campion's *History of Ireland* and Spenser's *View of the State of Ireland.* His son, Robert Ware, translated and republished his works, which gained wide circulation. *The Whole Works of Sir James Ware* were published in three volumes in Dublin (1739–1764) by Walter Harris, husband of his granddaughter. Ware died at his family house in Castle Street, Dublin, on 1 December 1666. Buried in St Werburgh's Church, Dublin. His manuscripts are in the Bodleian Library and British Library.

WARREN, SIR PETER (*c.* 1703–1752), admiral. Born at Warrenstown, Co. Meath, joined the British navy and served on the North American station. In 1745 he took part in an attack on the French-held port of Louisburg, Cape Breton Island, and captured prizes of immense value. Promoted rear-admiral that year and knighted in 1747 for successful action against a French squadron off Finistère. Married a Dutch heiress from New York and increased his fortune by shrewd investment in American real estate. Left the navy in declining health and settled in London. MP for Westminster 1747–1752. He died in July 1752 while on a visit to family estates in Ireland. Commemorated by an ornate monument in Westminster Abbey. He was said to have captured prizes to a value of two million dollars, and was known as the richest commoner in England.

WEBB, ALFRED JOHN (1834–1908), biographer. Born in Dublin on 10 June 1834. Educated at a Quaker day school and later at Dr Hodgson's High School, Manchester. On leaving school he was apprenticed to his father's printing business. In 1854 he was sent to Australia, partly for health reasons and partly to look for business opportunities. These were not forthcoming, and he was back in Dublin in a year. Although he had ample funds, he worked his passage home as deck-hand on a sailing vessel. He became manager and then owner of the printing business. Published a *Compendium of Irish Biography* (1878), which held the field for fifty years. He supported the home rule movement. Anti-Parnellite MP for West Waterford, 1890–1895. He travelled extensively, became interested in Indian politics, and on his last of many visits to India was elected president of the Indian National Congress of 1898. He contributed travel and general articles to the *Freeman's Journal, Irish Monthly,* and *New York Nation.* Other publications were *Opinions of Some Protestants Regarding their Irish Catholic Fellow-Countrymen* (1886), and *The Alleged Massacre of 1641* (1887). Died on 30 July 1908 while on holiday in the Shetland Islands. Buried in the Quaker burial ground at Blackrock, Co. Dublin.

WEBB, CAPTAIN JOHN HENRY (1870–1968), sailor. Born in Kinsale, Co. Cork. Went to sea at seventeen. He was a blue-water sailor for twenty-five years, and gained his extra master mariner's certificate before joining Dublin Port and Docks Board in 1912. Harbourmaster of Dublin 1914–1941, and became a Commissioner of Irish Lights. Died in Dublin, 30 November 1968.

WELD, ISAAC (1774–1856), author. Born in Fleet Street, Dublin, 15 March 1774. Educated at Whyte's school, Grafton Street, and in Norfolk and Norwich. In 1795 he sailed to Philadelphia from Dublin and spent two years travelling in America and Canada. Visited Mount Vernon and met George Washington. Returned in 1797 'without entertaining the slightest wish to revisit the American continent.' Published

Travels (1799), which quickly went into three editions and was translated into French, German, and Dutch. Visited Killarney, navigated the lakes in a boat he made from compressed brown paper, and published *Scenery of Killarney* (1807), illustrated by his own drawings. In May 1815 he sailed from Dunleary (Dún Laoghaire) to London in the fourteen horse-power steamboat *Thomas*, the first such vessel to make the passage. Compiled *Statistical Survey of the County of Roscommon* (1838) for the RDS, of which he was honorary secretary. Died at his home, Ravenswell, near Bray, Co. Wicklow, 4 August 1856.

WELDON, JOHN. See under MACNAMARA, BRINSLEY.

WELLESLEY, ARTHUR, first DUKE OF WELLINGTON (1769–1852), field-marshal. Born at Mornington House, 24 Upper Merrion Street, Dublin, 29 April 1769, fourth son of GARRETT WELLESLEY, first Earl of Mornington. His father died when he was twelve. He was sent to Eton, but his mother, now in reduced circumstances, removed him when he was fifteen, as she thought that he had little mental ability and was 'fit food for powder'. He was sent to Pignerol's military academy at Angers, where he learnt to ride and to speak French. He entered the army, and received his first commission as an ensign in 1787. He received rapid promotion, due to the growing political influence of his eldest brother, now Lord Mornington, and was aide-de-camp to the lord lieutenant in Ireland 1787–1793. Member for Trim in the Irish parliament 1790–1795, and according to SIR JONAH BARRINGTON, 'evinced no promise of that unparalleled celebrity and splendour which he has since reached, and whereunto intrepidity, decision, good luck and great military science have justly combined to elevate him.' He favoured a warlike policy towards France, and supported a government bill to grant the franchise to Catholics but opposed their admission to parliament. He saw active service in Flanders in 1794–1795, enduring a winter campaign of extreme hardship, and was critical of the disorganised state of the British army. Ordered to India, and landed in Calcutta in 1797, with rank of colonel. In the following eight years he gained a high military reputation. His brother, Lord Mornington, came to India as governor-general in May 1798, and Arthur Wellesley carried out in the field plans on which he was part-adviser in the cabinet. His despatches, begun at this time, show his ability, industry, and statesmanship. Knighted 1804; MP for Rye 1806, and Secretary for Ireland 1807–1809, with intervals on active service in Denmark and Portugal.

In 1809 he was made commander-in-chief in the Peninsula, and showing great generalship, foresight, and tenacity, finally drove the French from Spain and occupied Toulouse in April 1814. Made Duke of Wellington, created field-marshal, and given a parliamentary grant of £400,000. He also received all the most distinguished foreign orders. Appointed ambassador at Paris, and then went to the Congress of Vienna early in 1815. When news came of the escape of Napoleon from Elba in March 1815, Wellington took command of the British forces, and defeated Napoleon on 18 June at Waterloo. This victory gained him enormous prestige all over Europe, and the nation presented him with an estate in Hampshire at a cost of £263,000. On his return to England in 1819 he became a member of the cabinet and then commander-in-chief. Prime Minister in 1828 and, with Peel, saw that Catholic emancipation could no longer be denied and put it through in 1829. His opposition to parliamentary reform brought great unpopularity and the fall of his government in 1830. He held cabinet office again in 1834 and 1841–1846 and then retired from public life. Died at Walmer, Kent, 14 September 1852. Buried in St Paul's Cathedral.

WELLESLEY OR WESLEY, GARRETT, first EARL OF MORNINGTON (1735-1781). Born 19 July 1735 in Dublin. Educated at TCD. MP for Trim 1757, created Viscount Wellesley and Earl of Mornington 1760. Musically talented, played catches on the violin at nine, composed the glees 'Here in Cool Grot' and 'Come, Fairest Nymph'. Doctor of music, TCD, 1764. His five sons all became famous: one a duke, one a marquis, two barons, and one prebendary of Durham. Died at Kensington on 22 May 1781.

WELLESLEY OR WESLEY, RICHARD COLLEY, first BARON MORNINGTON (1690-1758), youngest son and eventual heir of Henry Colley of Carbury, Co. Kildare, whose family had come from England early in the sixteenth century. Educated at TCD, and became registrar and auditor of the Royal Hospital. In 1725 he published an account of this institution. Two years earlier he had succeeded to the Kildare estates, and in 1728 he inherited the estates of his cousin Garrett Wesley or Wellesley, of Dangan and Mornington, Co. Meath. He then assumed the name of Wesley, usually spelt Wellesley. Represented Trim 1729-1746; high sheriff of Co. Meath 1734. In 1746 he was created a peer of Ireland with the title of Baron Mornington of Meath. He built and endowed a charter school for fifty children near Trim. He died on 31 January 1758 at his house on the north-west side of Grafton Street in Dublin. Grandfather of ARTHUR WELLESLEY, first Duke of Wellington.

WEST, ROBERT (died 1770), draughtsman. Born in Waterford, son of an alderman. Studied art in Paris under Boucher and Vanloo. On his return to Ireland he established a drawing-school in George's Lane, Dublin. When the Dublin Society (later RDS) set up a drawing-school in 1757 in Shaw's Court, he was appointed master and taught there with great success. He became mentally deranged in 1763 and was replaced by Jacob Ennis, but was restored on death of Ennis in 1770. His son, Francis Robert, succeeded him as master and was succeeded in turn by his grandson, Robert Lucius.

WHALEY or WHALLEY, THOMAS (1766-1800), politician and eccentric, sometimes called 'Buck' or 'Jerusalem' Whaley. Born at 86 St Stephen's Green, Dublin. He inherited an income of £7,000 a year, together with £60,000 in cash, at thirteen. When placed under a tutor in Paris, he ran up enormous gambling debts and had to return to Ireland. In Dublin he accepted a wager, said to be for £20,000, that he would travel to Jerusalem and return within two years. He started in September 1788 and was back in Dublin in June 1789, having travelled 7,000 miles (11,250 km); his winning of the wager made him famous. MP for Newcastle, Co. Down, in 1785 while still under age, later sat for Enniscorthy and, according to SIR JONAH BARRINGTON, accepted bribes, first to vote for the Union and then to vote against it. While on his way to London he died at Knutsford in Cheshire on 2 November 1800. His memoirs, written in repentance as a warning to others, were published in 1906. His palatial house, 86 St Stephen's Green, now belongs to UCD.

WHALLY, JOHN (1653-1724), quack. Born 29 April 1653, son of a Cromwellian adventurer. A shoemaker by trade. Established himself in Dublin as vendor of unusual medicines, necromancer, and compiler of prophetic almanacs. Published translation of Ptolemy's *Quadripartite* (1701) and *A Treatise of Eclipses* (1702). Started *Whally's News Letter* in 1714, which satirised leading citizens. These were advertised in advance, and often earned him either hush-money or a horse-whipping. Died in Dublin, 17 January 1724.

WHARTON, ANTHONY. See under MCALLISTER, ALEXANDER.

WHEELER, SIR WILLIAM IRELAND DE COURCY (1879-1943), surgeon. Born in Dublin on 8 May 1879; educated at TCD. In 1904 he joined the staff of Mercer's Hospital and was also attached to the Rotunda and the National Children's Hospital. He lost an eye in an accident in his twenties, but did not let this handicap him in his career. In the First World War he served in France with the rank of lieutenant-colonel. Knighted in 1919. Became known as a leading surgeon throughout Great Britain and America. President RCSI 1923-1925. In 1932 he was invited to join the staff of the Southend General Hospital, and also worked at All Saints' Hospital and the Metropolitan Hospital. On the outbreak of the Second World War he was appointed consulting surgeon to the Royal Navy in Scotland with the rank of surgeon-rear-admiral. Author of *A Handbook of Operatic Surgery* (1918), *Injuries and Diseases of Bone* (1928), *Pillars of Surgery* (1933), and a large number of papers on almost every branch of surgery. Died suddenly in Aberdeen, 11 September 1943.

WHITE, SIR GEORGE STUART (1835-1912), field-marshal. Born at Whitehall, Co. Antrim. Educated at Sandhurst Military College. Posted to India, where his progress was slow until he distinguished himself in the Afghan War of 1870-1880, both by military skill and personal bravery. He received the VC, and became military secretary to the viceroy of India. Thereafter his advancement was rapid. After service in Burma and on the North-West Frontier, he was appointed commander-in-chief in India in 1893, passing over many senior officers. In September 1899, on the outbreak of the Boer War, he was sent to take command in Natal, and was besieged in Ladysmith with all his forces in November 1899. The defenders held out doggedly until relieved after 118 days. When Sir Redvers Buller suggested

to him that he should make terms, he replied 'The loss of 10,000 men would be a heavy blow to England. We must not think of it.' He returned to England in poor health and was appointed governor of Gibraltar, later being made field-marshal. Received the Order of Merit 1905, and was made governor of Chelsea Hospital, where he died, 24 June 1912.

WHITE, WILLIAM JOHN (JACK) (1920-1980), novelist, playwright and journalist. Born in Cork on 30 March 1920 and educated at Midleton College and TCD, where he twice won the Vice-Chancellor's prizes for English prose and verse. He joined the *Irish Times* on graduation in 1942, was London editor 1946-1952 and features and literary editor 1952-1961. He became head of public affairs in RTE in 1961, controller of television programmes in 1974, and then head of resources until his death. Wrote radio scripts, three novels, two plays, and *Minority Report* (1975), a study of the place of Protestants in the south of Ireland. His novels, *One for the Road* (1956), *The Hard Man* (1958), and *The Devil You Know* (1962), are closely observed and sharply written studies of the Dublin middle classes. His play *The Last Eleven* won the Irish Life Drama Award of 1967 and was produced at the Abbey Theatre in 1968. He was Irish correspondent of the *Observer* and *Manchester Guardian* for some years. He died suddenly on 13 April 1980 in Stuttgart, where he was attending a meeting of the European Broadcasting Union.

WHITELAW, REV. JAMES (1749-1813), statistician and philanthropist. Born in Co. Leitrim. Educated at TCD; ordained in Church of Ireland and obtained living of St Catherine's, in the Liberties of Dublin. Formed several charitable institutions to help the poor, and secured Erasmus Smith Free School for the Coombe. Made census of Dublin, published in 1805 as *Essay on the Population of Dublin in 1798*. Collaborated with Warburton in compiling history of Dublin, completed by Robert Walsh in

1818. Died 4 February 1813 from fever contracted while visiting poor parishioners.

WHITESIDE, JAMES (1804–1876), lord chief justice in Ireland. Born 12 August 1804 at Delgany, Co. Wicklow, son of local curate. Educated at TCD and Inner Temple; called to the bar 1830. While a student he wrote magazine articles, collected and re-published in 1870 as *Early Sketches of Eminent Persons*. He made rapid progress in his career and became QC in 1842. His speech in defence of DANIEL O'CONNELL at the state trials of 1844 placed him at the forefront of the bar. Shortly afterwards his health began to trouble him and he spent some time in Italy. Published *Italy in the Nineteenth Century* (1848). Returned to Ireland and defended SMITH O'BRIEN and others at state trials in Clonmel in 1848. Elected Conservative MP for Enniskillen 1851, and for Dublin University from 1859 until he became a judge. Appointed solicitor-general for Ireland 1852 and later attorney-general. After his celebrated speech in the Yelverton case he was greeted with cheers on entering the House of Commons. Regarded as one of the great orators of the century. Appointed chief justice, Queen's Bench, Ireland, 1866. Suffered much ill-health in his later years. Died at Brighton, 25 November 1876. Buried Mount Jerome cemetery, Dublin.

WHITLA, SIR WILLIAM (1851–1933), physician. Born at Monaghan, 15 September 1851. Educated at Model School, Monaghan. Apprenticed to a leading firm of dispensing chemists in Belfast. In 1872 he entered Queen's College, Belfast, to study medicine, and took his MD in 1877. He became physician to the Royal Victoria Hospital, the Belfast Ophthalmic Hospital, and the Belfast Hospital for Women and Children, and then set up in private practice, with great success. Elected professor of materia medica and jurisprudence at Queen's College, Belfast,

1890. Very many medical honours came his way, and in 1902 he was knighted and appointed physician to the king in Ireland. First MP for QUB 1918–1923. Author of three principal works, *Elements of Pharmacy, Materia Medica and Therapeutics* (1882, thirteenth edition 1939), *Dictionary of Treatment* (1891, seventh edition 1923), and *Manual of the Theory and Practice of Medicine* (1908). These have been translated into many languages. Died in Belfast, 11 December 1933.

WHITNEY, HARRY. See under KENNEDY, PATRICK.

WHITTY, MICHAEL JAMES (1795–1873), journalist. Born in Enniscorthy, Co. Wexford, son of a maltster. Began his literary career in London in 1821. Editor, *London and Dublin Magazine*, 1823. In 1824 he published anonymously two volumes of *Tales of Irish Life*, with illustrations by his friend Cruikshank, which met with great success. From 1823 to 1829 he contributed regularly to Irish periodicals, and strongly advocated Catholic emancipation. First editor of the *Liverpool Journal*, 1829–1836, when he was appointed chief constable of the borough. During his twelve years in this office he re-organised the police force and formed an efficient fire brigade. On his retirement in 1848 the town council presented him with £1,000 in recognition of his services. While chief constable he had not completely severed his connection with the *Liverpool Journal*, and in 1848 he bought it and resumed his journalistic career. For many years he was Liverpool correspondent and agent for the *Daily News*. In 1851 he gave evidence before a parliamentary commission on the Stamp Act, and recommended the abolition of the stamp duty, the advertisement duty, and the duty on paper. When these imposts were removed he founded, in 1855, the *Liverpool Daily Post*, the first penny daily published in the United Kingdom. In 1861–1864 he wrote in strong support of the northern states in the American Civil War. The last few years of his life were spent in retirement at Prince's Park, Liverpool, where he died, 10 June 1873.

WILDE, LADY JANE FRANCESCA

(1826–1896), 'Speranza' of the *Nation*. Born in Dublin, daughter of a solicitor and granddaughter of archdeacon Elgee of Wexford. On seeing the funeral of THOMAS DAVIS in 1845 and reading his poems she became an ardent nationalist, and contributed verse and prose to the *Nation* under the pen-name 'Speranza'. When DUFFY was prosecuted in 1849 for publishing seditious articles, she at once avowed her authorship of 'Jacta Alea Est', cited by the prosecution. In 1851 she married Dr (afterwards Sir) WILLIAM WILDE, and after his death in 1876 she removed to London. She had published a volume of poems in 1864 under her pen-name 'Speranza', and as Lady Wilde she published a number of works on folklore, *Driftwood from Scandinavia* (1884), *Ancient Legends of Ireland* (1887), and *Ancient Cures* (1891). She also published *Men, Women and Books* (1891) and *Social Studies* (1893). Although in straitened circumstances, she conducted a salon in London with great spirit for many years. In 1890 she received a civil list pension of £300 a year. Died in London, 3 February 1896, the year after her son OSCAR was sent to prison.

WILDE, OSCAR FINGAL O'FLAHERTIE WILLS (1854–1900),

wit and dramatist. Born at 21 Westland Row, Dublin, 16 October 1854, younger son of SIR WILLIAM WILDE and Jane Francesca Elgee, 'Speranza' of the *Nation*. Educated at Portora Royal School, Enniskillen, TCD, and Magdalen College, Oxford. At Oxford he won the Newdigate Prize for poetry in 1878, acquired a reputation for witty conversation, and graduated with first-class honours in classics and the humanities. In London he became known as the founder of the aesthetic cult, with its symbols of peacocks' feathers and blue china, and propounded the philosophy of 'art for art's sake'. His first publication was a volume of *Poems* (1881). In 1882 he made a successful tour of the USA and Canada, lecturing on 'aesthetic philosophy'. He spent the next six years in London working as a book reviewer. In 1884 he married Constance Lloyd. Edited the *Woman's World* from 1887 to 1889. Wilde's real literary career began in 1888 when he published *The Happy Prince and Other Tales*, a collection of charming fairy stories. His only novel, *The Picture of Dorian Gray* (1891), was badly received; the same year he published another book of fairy stories, *A House of Pomegranates*, which, he said, 'was intended neither for the British child nor the British public.' Two early plays, *Vera* (1883) and a blank verse tragedy, *The Duchess of Padua* (1891), had been unsuccessful, but his first comedy, *Lady Windermere's Fan*, produced in London in 1892, made an instant hit. He followed this success with three more comedies, *A Woman of No Importance*, produced in 1893, and *An Ideal Husband* and *The Importance of Being Earnest*, both produced in 1895. In them Wilde's characteristic witty and epigrammatic dialogue mirrored his conversation. His play *Salomé*, written in French and translated into English by Lord Alfred Douglas, was banned in England because it portrayed biblical characters. The English translation was published in 1894 with illustrations by Aubrey Beardsley. *The Importance of Being Earnest* is Wilde's masterpiece: the essence of pure comedy, it has become a classic and is frequently revived.

In 1891 Wilde had become friendly with Lord Alfred Douglas and appeared everywhere in his company. The Marquess of Queensberry, father of Lord Alfred, objected to his liaison, and in 1895 Wilde took an action against Queensberry for criminal libel, which was unsuccessful following a devastating cross-examination by EDWARD CARSON. He was then himself arrested, charged with homosexual offences, and on 25 May 1895, after trial by jury, sentenced to two years' imprisonment with hard labour. He served the greater part of his sentence in Reading jail, where the hardships and humiliations of prison caused him much suffering. In November 1895 he was declared a bankrupt. On his release in May 1897 he left England, and spent the rest of his life in Italy and France, depending on a small annuity bought for him by friends. In 1898 he published *The Ballad of Reading Gaol*, based on his prison experiences. In Paris he lived at the Hôtel d'Alsace, and on 30 November 1900 he died there of cerebral meningitis, after receiving the last rites of the Catholic Church. He is buried in the cemetery of Père Lachaise. His wife had died in 1896, and he was survived by their two sons. His prose apologia, *De Profundis*, was published in 1905.

WILDE, SIR WILLIAM ROBERT WILLS (1815–1876), surgeon and antiquary. Born in Castlerea, Co. Roscommon. Educated at Elphin Diocesan School. Qualified as a surgeon from Dr Steevens' Hospital, Dublin, 1837. A voyage with a patient led to his first book, *The Narrative of a Voyage to Madeira, Teneriffe, and Along the Shores of the Mediterranean* (1840). After further studies in London, Berlin, and Vienna, he settled in Dublin in 1841, and soon built up a large and rewarding practice as an oculist and ear specialist. He established his own hospital in Molesworth St in 1844, and later that year moved it to Mark St, off Great Brunswick St (Pearse St). He wrote several books on medical subjects, became editor of the *Dublin Journal of Medical Science* in 1845, and contributed many articles to it and other medical journals. He is now remembered as the father of OSCAR WILDE and the author of works on Irish antiquities and topography. *The Beauties of the Boyne and the Blackwater* (1849) and *Lough Corrib and Lough Mask* (1867) describe districts of scenic beauty, rich in antiquarian remains and historical associations. He also compiled a learned descriptive *Catalogue of the Contents of the Museum of the*

Royal Irish Academy (three volumes, 1858–1862). In 1849 he published a booklet, *The Closing Years of the Life of Dean Swift*, to show that SWIFT was not insane but ill in his last years.

Appointed medical commissioner for the Irish census in 1841, and in 1851 published a Blue Book on *The Epidemics of Ireland*. Knighted for his services to the census 1864; received the Cunningham Medal from the RIA, their highest award, 1873. In 1864 he was the central figure in a trial by jury that became a *cause célèbre* in Dublin. A Mary Josephine Travers had become a patient of his in 1854, when she was nineteen. Towards the end of 1864 she took an action for libel because of a letter written about her by LADY WILDE. ISAAC BUTT appeared for Miss Travers, who, in the course of the trial, accused Sir William of having raped her. The judge, having pointed out than an action for rape was not before the court, observed that such an action would not have succeeded. The jury found that the letter was libellous, and awarded damages of one farthing ($\frac{1}{10}$p), but gave costs against Sir William. Although it became clear in the course of the trial that Miss Travers was neurotic to the verge of derangement, Wilde's career was clouded for some years. He died in Dublin, 19 April 1876. Buried in Mount Jerome Cemetery. Survived by Lady Wilde and two sons, William and Oscar.

WILKS, ROBERT (*c.* 1665–1732), actor. Born at Rathfarnham, Co. Dublin, in 1665 or perhaps 1670. He made his first appearance on the stage at Smock Alley, in Dublin, in December 1691, and scored a great success in the part of Othello. His popularity in Dublin was so great that he had difficulty in making a visit to London with FARQUHAR in 1698. He stayed on, and played for many years at Drury Lane Theatre. He was also associated with the Haymarket Theatre. He excelled in comedy, and his most famous part was that of Sir Harry Wildair in Farquhar's *The Constant Couple*. Died at his house in

Bow St, Covent Garden, London, 27 February 1732.

WILLIAMS, CHARLES (1838–1904), war correspondent. Born at Coleraine, Co. Derry, 4 May 1838. Educated at Belfast Academy and at a private school in Greenwich. For health reasons he spent some years in the southern states of America. On his return he joined the staff of the *Evening Standard* in 1859. His first assignment as a war correspondent brought him to the French headquarters in the Franco-German War of 1870. In 1877 he reported the Armenian war from the headquarters of the Turkish commander. He accompanied the Nile expedition for the relief of General Gordon in 1884. Shortly afterwards he left the *Standard* to become correspondent for the *Daily Chronicle*, and reported the Bulgar-Serbian war of 1885 and the Greco-Turkish war of 1887. His last service in the field was in Kitchener's Sudanese campaign of 1898, and his despatches include an account of the battle of Omdurman and of the recapture of Khartoum in 1898. He founded the Press Club, and was president 1896-1897. Died in lodgings in Brixton, 9 February 1904.

WILLIAMS, RICHARD D'ALTON (1822–1862), poet, 'Shamrock' of the *Nation*. Born in Dublin, 8 October 1822, a natural son of Count D'Alton, landed proprietor, and Mary Williams, a farmer's daughter. Educated at the Jesuit College, Tullabeg, and St Partick's College, Carlow. Came to Dublin in 1843 to study medicine, and took out his diploma in 1849. Before this, he had begun to contribute verses to the *Nation* under the name 'Shamrock', and in 1848 he brought out a paper, the *Irish Tribune*, to take the place of the suppressed *United Irishman*, founded by JOHN MITCHEL. He was arrested that year, defended by SAMUEL FERGUSON, and found not guilty of treason-felony. In June 1851 he emigrated to America. Professor of belles-lettres in the Jesuit College, Springhill, Mobile, Alabama,

until 1856. He then married and moved to New Orleans, where he practised medicine until his health failed. He died of tuberculosis at Thibodeaux, Louisiana, 5 July 1862.

WILLIAMS, T. DESMOND (1921–1987), historian. Born in Dublin and educated privately, at UCD, and at Peterhouse, Cambridge, on a travelling studentship from NUI. He won the John Brooke Memorial Scholarship to King's Inns and was called to the bar. Worked at Cambridge University on historical research from 1944 and then invited by the British Foreign Office to assist in editing the archives of the German Foreign Office. He was appointed professor of modern history, UCD, in 1949, the youngest in that post, and introduced the tutorial system. He served on the Governing Body and Academic Council and on the Senate of NUI. Publications include *The Great Famine* (1956) with R. Dudley Edwards, *The Irish Struggle, 1916–26* (1966), *Ireland in the War Years and After* (1969) with Kevin Nowlan, and *Secret Societies in Ireland* (1973). Edited *Irish Historical Studies* and *The Leader* for some years. He retired in 1985 and died in a Dublin hospital on 18 January 1987 after many years of ill-health, which failed to diminish his delight in company and conversation.

WILLS, REV. JAMES (1790–1868), author. Born at Willsgrove, Co. Roscommon, on 1 January 1790. Educated at TCD. A large joint inheritance was squandered by his elder brother. He took holy orders in 1822, failed to get appointment to a living, and began to contribute to leading periodicals. He gave the manuscript of his poem 'The Universe' to C. R. MATURIN, who published it as his own for £500. Secured sinecure curacy at Suirville in 1835, became vicar 1846, and obtained additional livings at Kilmacow and Attanagh. Published poems and religious and philosophical works. His most important work was *Lives of Illustrious and Distinguished Irishmen* (six volumes, 1840–1847), for which he received £1,000. It was reissued as *The Irish Nation* (1875). Died at Attanagh in November 1868.

WILMOT, CATHERINE (1773–1824), traveller and diarist. Born in Drogheda, where her father was port surveyor. He transferred to a similar post in Cork in 1775. He was wealthy, and she led a full social life. She accompanied Lord Mountcashel's party on a grand tour of the Continent after the Peace of Amiens (1802). Her diary was published in 1920 by Thomas Sadleir as *An Irish Peer on the Continent, 1801–1803.* On her tour she dined with Napoleon in the Tuileries, met the licentious bishop LORD BRISTOL with his mistresses, made friends with Angelica Kauffmann, and had an hour's audience with Pope Pius VII. She then went to Russia on her parents' instructions, to bring home her sister MARTHA, who was staying with Princess Daschkaw on her extensive estates east of Moscow. The princess became very attached to the sisters. Martha refused to leave her, and Catherine returned alone in 1807. She had a private income, and settled in France. Died of tuberculosis in Paris, 28 March 1824.

WILMOT, MARTHA (1775–1873), diarist. Born in Cork. Went to Russia in 1803 to stay with wealthy family friend, Princess Daschkaw. The princess was director of the Academy of Arts and Sciences in St Petersburg (Leningrad), edited a monthly magazine, and wrote plays. When war broke out between Russia and England in 1808, Martha, regarded with suspicion by the authorities, was obliged to leave the elderly princess, who gave her gifts of jewels and money. She was shipwrecked off the coast of Finland, but reached Harwich in December 1808. The princess died soon after, feeling she had nothing to live for, having quarrelled with her surviving daughter. Martha published *Memoirs of Princess Daschkaw* (1840). She married Rev. William Bradford, rector of Storrington, Sussex, later chaplain to the British embassy, Vienna. When he died in 1857 she came to Dublin to live with her married daughter at Taney Hill House, where she died on 18 December 1873. The *Russian Journals of Martha and Catherine Wilmot, 1803–1808* (1834) and *More Letters from Martha Wilmot: Vienna, 1819–1829* (1935) were edited and published by Marchioness of Londonderry and Montgomery Hyde.

WILSON, SIR HENRY (1864–1922), field-marshal. Born 5 May 1864 at Currygrane, Edgeworthstown (Mostrim), Co. Longford. Educated at Marlborough College. Joined the British army in 1884 and saw service in the Boer War and in Burma. Commandant of the Camberley Staff College with the rank of brigadier-general 1907–1910; director of military operations 1910–1914. He was active behind the scenes in support of the Ulster Unionists in their opposition to home rule in 1914. Promoted lieutenant-general January 1915; corps commander 1916. During the First World War he formed a close association with Lloyd George, who made him chief of the Imperial General Staff in February 1918. Military representative at the Congress of Versailles, appointed field-marshal in July 1919, made a baronet and given a grant of £10,000. After the war he urged a policy of coercion in Ireland. In 1922, when his term as chief of staff expired, Lloyd George did not renew it, and he left the army. Elected Conservative MP for North Down and continued to urge repressive measures against the Sinn Féin movement. On 22 June 1922 he was shot dead on the doorstep of his London house by Reginald Dunne and Joseph O'Sullivan, two Irishmen and ex-British army soldiers (O'Sullivan had lost a leg at Ypres). The IRA disclaimed responsibility. The men were tried, found guilty, and executed.

WILSON, WALTER GORDON (1874–1957), engineer. Born at Blackrock, Co. Dublin, 21 April 1874. Started his career as a naval cadet in the *Britannia*. In 1894 he entered King's College, Cambridge, and graduated in mechanical engineering. With Percy Pilcher, a lecturer in naval architecture, he formed an engineering firm to design an internal combustion aero-engine. Pilcher was killed in a gliding accident in 1899 and the project was abandoned. Wilson then designed the Wilson-Pilcher motor-car, embodying epicyclic gears among other new features. In 1904 he joined the Armstrong-Whitworth Co. and designed the Armstrong-Whitworth car. From 1903 to 1914 he worked with Halls of Deptford, and designed for them the Hallford lorry, which was used extensively by the British army in the First World War. He re-joined the navy in 1914 and was assigned to the Armoured Car Division. Here, with Sir William Tritton, he was responsible for the successful development of a design for a tank. About 1917 he became chief of design in the Mechanical Warfare Department of the War Office, and was awarded the CMG. After the war he invented the Wilson self-changing gearbox, and founded the firm of Self-Changing Gears Ltd of Coventry. He was a great lover of the countryside, a fine shot and expert fly-fisherman. Died at his house in Itchen Abbas, near Winchester, 30 June 1957.

WILSON, WILLIAM EDWARD (1851–1908), astronomer and physicist. Born in Belfast 19 July 1851. Educated privately. Set up a private observatory on his father's estate at Daramona, Streete, Co. Westmeath, equipped with a 12-inch (305 mm) refractor by GRUBB. In 1881 he built a new observatory with 24-inch (610 mm) refractor, also by Grubb, and a physical laboratory. Made pioneering investigations into the temperature of the sun and radiation from sun-spots. Contributed papers to Royal Astronomical Society, collected and printed privately 1900. Elected FRS in 1896. High sheriff of Westmeath 1901. Died at Daramona, 6 March 1908.

WINGFIELD, LEWIS STRANGE (1842–1891). Born at Powerscourt, Co. Wicklow, son of the sixth Viscount Powerscourt. Educated at Eton and Bonn. Travelled widely in Europe, the Far East, and North Africa. He was in Paris during the siege of 1870 and in Sudan during Gordon's campaign. Acted in London theatres, designed theatre costumes for the Lyceum, was an attendant in a mental asylum, a journalist, and a painter. His pictures were exhibited at the RA and he was elected RHA. He wrote travel books based on his experiences, and many novels, including *My Lords of Strogue* (1879) and *The Maid of Honour* (1891). Died in London.

WOFFINGTON, MARGARET (PEG) (*c*. 1714–1760), actress. Born in Dublin on 18 October, year uncertain. Her father was a bricklayer and her mother a laundress. She made her stage début in a children's company at an amusement booth conducted by the famous rope-dancer Madame Violante in George's Lane. She was then engaged at the Smock Alley Theatre and played a wide variety of parts, including Ophelia, old ladies, and her famous 'breeches' part as Sir Harry Wildair in *The Constant Couple*. When Rich of Covent Garden Theatre saw her he engaged her immediately, and she took London by storm on her first appearance in November 1740. With her fine figure and flashing dark eyes she was described as the handsomest woman who ever appeared on the stage. Her love affairs were many. In 1741 she played in Drury Lane Theatre opposite David Garrick and became his mistress for some years. Her vivacity, intelligence and good humour made her a welcome guest, especially with men, and on her return to Dublin in 1751 she was made president of the 'Beefsteak Club', the only woman ever admitted to their weekly dinners. After three very successful seasons in Dublin she returned to Covent Garden in 1754. Her one defect was a rather harsh voice, which detracted from her acting in tragedy. She pensioned her mother and took good care of her younger sister, but her good nature did not extend to her rivals, and in 1756 in a fit of temper she stabbed another leading actress, GEORGE ANNE BELLAMY. On 3 May 1757, while playing Rosalind in *As You Like It*, she was taken ill on the stage. It was her last appearance; she lingered on for three years, devoting herself to charitable works and repentance and generously endowing alms houses at Teddington. Died in London, 28 March 1760. She is the subject of Charles Reade's first novel, *Peg Woffington* (1853).

WOGAN, SIR CHARLES (*c.* 1698–1754), Jacobite soldier of fortune, known as the Chevalier Wogan. Born at Rathcoffey, Co. Kildare. Little is known about his early years. In 1715 he fought in the Stuart rising at the battle of Preston and was taken prisoner. He escaped from Newgate jail and made his way to France where he served in Dillon's regiment until 1718. Selected by the exiled 'James III', the Old Pretender, to win him the hand of a Russian princess. When that attempt failed the choice fell on Maria Clementina Sobieski, granddaughter of Jan Sobieski, the deliverer of Europe from the Turks. On her way to meet Wogan at Bologna she was arrested at Innsbruck by order of the emperor, who wished to retain the good will of the British government. The Chevalier succeeded in rescuing her in April 1719 and escorting her to her future husband. James rewarded him with a baronetcy, and the Pope conferred on him the title of Roman senator. A number of novels were based on the episode. He then took service as a colonel in the Spanish army, distinguished himself at the relief of Santa Cruz, and was promoted brigadier-general and made governor of La Mancha. From there he sent to SWIFT several casks of wine and a parcel of writings, for which Swift was unable to find a publisher. Died at Barcelona, 21 July 1754.

WOLFE, ARTHUR, first VISCOUNT KILWARDEN (1739–1803), lord chief justice. Born 19 January 1739 at Forenaughts, Co. Kildare. Educated at TCD. Called to the bar 1766, built up a large practice, and took silk in 1778. MP for Coleraine 1783; solicitor-general 1787; and attorney-general 1789. Chief justice of the King's Bench 1798, and created Baron Kilwarden. He supported the Union with Britain in 1800 and received a viscountcy and a peerage. On 23 July 1803, the night of the rising led by ROBERT EMMET, his carriage was stopped by a mob in Thomas St and he and his nephew were murdered.

WOLFE, CHARLES (1791–1823), poet. Born at Blackhall, Co. Kildare, 14 December 1791. Educated at the Abbey High School, Winchester, and TCD. In November 1817 he took holy orders, and became a curate at Ballyclog, Co. Tyrone, and later at Donoughmore, Co. Down. His health began to fail; his courtship of a beautiful young woman proved unsuccessful; and in 1821 he resigned his curacy. He died of tuberculosis at Cóbh, Co. Cork, on 21 February 1823, and is buried there. He is remembered for one poem, his ode 'On the Burial of Sir John Moore', which was first published in the *Newry Telegraph* on 19 April 1817. Byron praised it extravagantly in 1822, and so rescued it from obscurity. After that, many sought to claim it for their own, but Wolfe's authorship is now undisputed.

WOOD, CHARLES (1866–1926), composer. Born at Armagh, 14 June 1866. Educated at the Cathedral School there. In 1883 he won a scholarship to the Royal College of Music in London where he studied under STANFORD. His scholarship was made tenable at Cambridge where he took his Mus.Bac. degree in 1890. He taught at the Royal College and became organist at Caius College. In 1924 he succeeded Stanford as professor of music at Cambridge. He wrote a number of songs, string quartets, and organ preludes. His church music is still performed regularly and may be said to have reached classical status. Died at Cambridge, 12 July 1926.

WOODWARD, BENJAMIN (1816–1860), architect. Born in Tullamore, Co. Offaly, on 16 November 1816, son of Captain Charles Woodward of the Royal Meath Militia, and educated at Carrickmacross Grammar School. He joined the architectural firm of SIR THOMAS DEANE in Cork. They built the Museum Building in TCD, with carvings by the O'Shea brothers. Ruskin came from England to see it, declared that Woodward was the only architect in Europe, and brought him to Oxford with Deane and the O'Sheas to build the Museum there. His sumptuous style, using coloured stone and brick, appealed to the Pre-Raphaelites. His other buildings include the Kildare St Club, with its diverting exterior carvings by the O'Sheas, now deprived of its fine interior; St Anne's School, Molesworth St, now demolished; UCC; and Kilkenny Castle. He died in 1860 in a hotel in Lyon while on his way back to England.

WOULFE, PETER (*c.* 1727–1803), chemist. Born in Co. Limerick. Moved to London and lived at Clerkenwell, spending most summers in Paris. Elected FRS in 1767. Noted for his eccentricities. Searched for the elixir of life, and attributed failure to his lack of pious and charitable acts. Contributed papers to *Transactions of the Royal Society* and delivered first Bakerian lecture 1776. Invented 'Woulfe's bottle', two-necked apparatus now standard in chemical laboratories.

WYATT, THOMAS HENRY (1807–1880), architect. Born at Loughlin House, Co. Roscommon, 9 May 1807. He was placed as a pupil with Hardwick in London and superintended several public works. Began his own practice in 1832, and was also district surveyor of Hackney until 1861. His practice prospered, and he designed assize courts and asylums, Liverpool Exchange, and Knightsbridge Barracks. With his brother, Sir Mathew Digby, he designed the garrison chapel at Woolwich. Also designed Stockwell Fever Hospital, two hospitals in Malta, the Adelphi Theatre, and Brook House, Park Lane, long known as the most beautiful private house in London. Connected as designer or restorer with more than 150 churches. President, Royal Institute of British Architects, 1870–1873, gold medallist 1873. Died at his house, 77 Great Russell Street, London, 5 August 1880.

WYSE, SIR THOMAS (1791–1862), politician and diplomat. Born at St John, Co. Waterford, 9 December 1791. Educated at Stonyhurst, TCD, and Lincoln's Inn. In 1814 he went on the Grand Tour, spending two years in Italy, mainly in Rome and Florence, and a further two years visiting Athens, Constantinople, Egypt, and the Middle East. In March 1821 he married Laetitia, eldest daughter of Lucien Bonaparte, and went to live in Viterbo. There were two sons of the marriage but it was not a success, and Laetitia left him in 1828. A deed of separation was executed and they never met again; she died at Viterbo in 1872. Wyse returned to Ireland in 1825 and entered politics, taking a leading part in the struggle for Catholic emancipation. MP for Tipperary 1830 and for Waterford 1835–1847. In his parliamentary career he was an enlightened liberal and was particularly interested in education. Many reforms were introduced as a result of his advocacy. Simultaneously he engaged in literary work and published *Walks in Rome, Oriental Sketches*, and other volumes. Appointed British minister in Athens 1849; KCB 1857. Died in Athens, 16 April 1862.

Y

YEATS, JACK BUTLER (1871–1957), artist. Born 29 August 1871 at 23 Fitzroy Road, London, youngest of five children of JOHN BUTLER YEATS and his wife, Susan Pollexfen. At eight he went to live in Sligo with his Pollexfen grandparents, and his boyhood there awakened his lifelong delight in country scenes, travelling people, circuses, and seafarers. His exiguous formal education was received at a private school run by the Misses Blythe. He returned to London at seventeen, and studied at the Westminster, South Kensington and Chiswick schools of art. Between 1890 and 1910 he worked as a professional illustrator, contributing to the *Vegetarian, Judy, Paddock Life, Boy's Own Paper* and other periodicals, as well as schoolbooks and racing papers. In 1894 he married Mary Cottenham White, a fellow art student, and in 1897 they settled in Devon. They visited Ireland frequently, staying with LADY GREGORY at Coole, and Yeats went on a walking-tour in the west of Ireland with J. M. SYNGE. At this period he held a number of one-man shows of drawings and watercolours at the Clausen Galleries, New York. Despite his long residence there, he felt England to be an alien country and in 1910 returned to live in Ireland for the rest of his life, settling first at Greystones, Co. Wicklow, and then in Dublin. He illustrated a large number of broadsheets, and in 1912 published a book of paintings and drawings, *Life in the West of Ireland.* About this time he turned to painting in oils, and had five works shown in the Armory International Exhibition of Modern Art in New York in 1913. Elected RHA 1915. The 1916 Rising and the subsequent struggle for independence inspired some of his best-known paintings, the elegiac

'Bachelor's Walk, In Memory', 'Communicating With Prisoners', and 'Funeral of Harry Boland'. His reputation grew steadily in the 1930s. In 1942 he had a retrospective exhibition at the National Gallery, London, and in 1945 a loan exhibition of almost a hundred pictures was held in the National College of Art, Dublin. A loan exhibition was held in the Tate Gallery, London, in 1948, and a first retrospective American exhibition was held in the principal cities of the USA in 1951. His use of vivid and vital colour, which he began in the late 1920s, shows its full development in his later work. Sir Kenneth Clark said: 'Colour is Yeats's element, in which he dives and splashes with the shameless abandon of a porpoise.' He wrote a number of prose works. Some, like *Sligo* (1930) and *Sailing, Sailing Swiftly* (1933), were reminiscences, with little consecutive narrative thread; others were leisurely novels, like *The Amaranthers* (1936). His plays *La La Noo* (1942) and *In Sand* (Abbey Experimental Theatre, 1949) reflect, like the other books, his own view of his inspiration, for both painting and writing, as 'affection, wide, devious, and sometimes handsome.' He received many honours, principally honorary degrees from TCD and NUI and the Legion of Honour. Died Dublin 28 March 1957.

YEATS, JOHN BUTLER (1839–1922), painter. Born 16 March 1839 at Tullylish, Co. Down, where his father was rector. Educated at Atholl Academy, Isle of Man, and TCD. On his father's sudden death in 1862 he inherited a small estate in Kildare, which brought him an income of a few hundred pounds a year. He married Susan Pollexfen the following year, and was called to the bar in 1866 but did not practise. In 1867 he went to London to become a painter, and studied at Heatherley's Art School. He returned to Ireland in the early 1880s and began to exhibit at the RHA, meeting with fair success as a portrait painter but making little money. Elected RHA 1892. He returned to London in 1887, but was back in Dublin in 1901, the year after his wife died, and in October of that year had a joint exhibition with NATHANIEL HONE. SIR HUGH LANE secured commissions for him, and many of his portraits of the leading personages in Irish literary and political life are in the National Gallery of Ireland. The writers and talkers of Dublin were all his friends, and THOMAS BODKIN said that 'his portraits have an air of mingled intimacy and dignity.' He went to New York in 1908, intending to stay only a short while, but spent the rest of his life there, becoming known as the best conversationalist in New York. John Quinn, a wealthy lawyer, gave him help and encouragement, but he never became fashionable, as he charged too little for his portraits. His friends said that he received greater consideration as a critic, philosopher and conversationalist than as a painter. He lectured, and wrote essays for *Harper's Weekly* and other magazines, collected in a book called *Essays Irish and American* (1918). *Early Memories, a Chapter of Autobiography* was published posthumously. He died in New York on 2 February 1922, and was buried in the village of Chestertown in the Adirondacks. His *Letters to His Son, W. B. Yeats, and Others* (1944), with a memoir by JOSEPH HONE, show the discerning encouragement he gave both to W. B. and his other son, JACK B.

YEATS, WILLIAM BUTLER (1865–1939), poet and dramatist. Born in Sandymount Avenue, Dublin, 13 June 1865, eldest son of JOHN BUTLER YEATS. Shortly after his birth the family moved to London, and remained there until 1880. He attended the Godolphin School, Hammersmith, but spent his holidays in Sligo with his grandparents, the Pollexfens, millers and small shipowners. He was a gentle and delicate child and he was unhappy at school in London. When the family returned to Dublin in 1880 he went to the High School, then in Harcourt Street. His father wished him to enter TCD in the family tradition, but he refused, fearing that he would be unable to meet the entrance requirements. Instead he studied at the Metropolitan School of Art from 1884 to 1885, and then in 1886 at the RHA School. At the Metropolitan he became friendly with GEORGE RUSSELL and a group of mystics. From seventeen he had been writing poetry and plays in imitation of Shelley and Spenser, and about 1886 he decided to abandon art and devote himself to writing. His first publication, *Mosada, a Dramatic Poem* (1886), had nothing Irish about it, but shortly afterwards he met two men, JOHN O'LEARY and STANDISH JAMES O'GRADY, and under their influence 'I turned my back on foreign themes, decided that the race was more important than the individual, and began *The Wanderings of Oisín.*' The family went back to London in 1887. He maintained his interest in the occult, joining Madame Blavatsky's Theosophists in 1887 and the Order of the Golden Dawn in 1890. He met most of the poets of his generation at the Rhymers' Club, which he helped to found, and in 1891 founded the Irish Literary Society of London. The following year in Dublin he joined with John O'Leary in founding the National Literary Society, whose immediate object was to publicise the literature, folklore and legends of Ireland. In 1889 he published *The Wanderings of Oisín*, a long poem based on Irish mythology, and in 1892 *The Countess Cathleen*, his first poetic play. His first volume of folkstories, *The Celtic Twilight*, appeared in 1893. In 1895 he edited *A Book of Irish Verse*, and published *Poems*. Three books of prose appeared in 1897, *The Secret Rose, The Tables of the Law,* and *The Adoration of the Magi.*

In 1889 he met Maud Gonne (see under MACBRIDE) and then 'all the trouble of my life began.' His long, frustrated obsession with her was one of the great traumatic experiences of his life. He proposed marriage to her in 1891 but was refused. Under her influence he joined the IRB and played a prominent part in the celebrations of the centenary of the 1798 Rising. She was the subject of many of his love poems. Through EDWARD MARTYN he met LADY AUGUSTA GREGORY, and in 1897 he spent the first of many summers at her house, Coole Park, Co. Galway. His health was then poor, and he was suffering from nervous strain, but the peace of Coole and Lady Gregory's solicitude greatly helped him. With her he planned an Irish Literary Theatre, which had its beginning in 1899 with the first performance of his poetic play *The Countess Cathleen*. He collaborated with GEORGE MOORE in *Diarmuid and Grainne*, produced in 1901, and with Lady Gregory in a series of one-act plays. In 1902 he wrote *Cathleen Ni Houlihan* for Maud Gonne to act. Collaboration with Frank and WILLIAM FAY led to the founding of the Irish National Theatre, with Yeats and Lady Gregory as co-directors. Annie Horniman, a wealthy Englishwoman from Manchester, bought the Mechanics' Institute in Abbey Street, Dublin, for them in 1904 and provided a subsidy for some years. On the first night, 27 December 1904, the Abbey Players presented a double bill, *On Baile's Strand* by Yeats and *Spreading the News* by Lady Gregory. In 1906, under a new constitution, Yeats, Lady Gregory and J. M. SYNGE were appointed directors, and Yeats remained a director until his death. The founding of the Abbey, in his own later words 'a small, dingy and impecunious theatre,' marked the launching of a dramatic movement that made Dublin an important literary capital in the first quarter of the century. He took a firm and uncompromising stand against any attempt to curb the freedom of expression of the theatre.

After the turn of the century he abandoned active politics and devoted himself to writing and to the affairs of the Abbey. He published *The Green Helmet and Other Poems* in 1910 and *Responsibilities* in 1914. In this productive period he wrote some of his best plays, including *On Baile's Strand* (1904) and *The King's Threshold* (1904). Ezra Pound, who acted as his secretary during the winters of 1913 and 1915, introduced him to the Japanese *noh* drama, and his imagination was kindled by the discovery that it contained many elements of his own philosophy of art, as in the wearing by the actors of masks, and in the ritual dances. Under the influence of *noh* he wrote *Four Plays for Dancers* (1921): *At the Hawk's Well, The Only Jealousy of Emer, The Dreaming of the Bones,* and *Calvary*. He published literary and critical essays in *Ideas of Good and Evil* (1903), *The Cutting of an Agate* (1912), and *Per Amica Silentiae Lunae* (1918).

He still felt deeply about Maud Gonne, and he again proposed to her in 1916, after the execution of JOHN MACBRIDE, her husband. She refused him again, and he then became infatuated with her daughter, Iseult, and proposed to her—but with equal lack of success. His major achievement in poetry came with the publication of four volumes between 1919 and 1933. *The Wild Swans at Coole* (1919), *Michael Robartes and the Dancer* (1921), *The Tower* (1928) and *The Winding Stair* (1933) contain his finest work, poetry of sustained strength and vision. His themes are his recollections of his friends, political turmoil in Ireland, his examination of his own emotions, and his questioning of the values of life. Since 1911 he had known an English girl, George Hyde-Lees, a friend of Ezra Pound, who shared his interest in theosophy. They were married on 21 October 1917, and his life changed and became 'serene and full of order'. Later, in a letter to Tagore, he said that as a husband and a father he felt 'more knitted into life'. The Rising of 1916 made a deep impression on him and he wrote several poems in homage to the executed leaders, some of whom had been his fellow-workers in the literary movement. After 1916 he resolved to return to live in Ireland. In 1915 he had bought Thoor Ballylee, a small derelict Norman castle in east Galway, close to Lady Gregory's Coole Park, and now he refurnished it and went to live there in 1922.

In the twenties he received many honours; in 1922 both QUB and TCD gave him honorary degrees, and President Cosgrave appointed him to the Senate of the newly established Irish Free State, in recognition of his services to Ireland. In 1923 he was awarded the Nobel Prize for literature, and in 1932, with GEORGE BERNARD SHAW, he founded the Irish Academy of Letters, for the promotion of creative writing in Ireland. He made a number of successful lecture tours in America, the first in 1903, and each time carried out an exacting programme with unfailing punctuality. These tours were undertaken to augment his slender income from writing; in 1919 he set out, he said, 'to earn a roof for Ballylee'; and his last tour, in 1932, was made to earn money for improvements to the house at Riversdale, Rathfarnham, outside Dublin, which he had just bought. On his tour he also raised funds for the Irish Academy of Letters by a series of drawing-room lectures.

His creative vitality continued into his sixties and seventies, although he raged against old age, and his later poems are full of violence and excitement. His *Collected Poems* appeared in 1933 and his *Collected Plays* in 1934. The *Plays* were reissued in 1952 with later additional works. His autobiography is contained in three volumes, *Reveries over Childhood and Youth* (1915), *The Trembling of the Veil* (1922), and *Dramatis Personae* (1936). On medical advice he had spent many winters in Italy and France from 1927 onwards. Late in the winter of 1938 he left Ireland for the Riviera in failing health. He died at Roquebrune, overlooking Monaco, on 28 January 1939, and was buried there. In September 1948 his remains were brought to Ireland on board the LÉ *Macha*, and he was re-interred in the churchyard of his grandfather's parish at Drumcliffe, Co. Sligo, 'under bare Ben Bulben's head'. A stone, inscribed as he had directed, marks the grave:

No marble, no conventional phrase;
On limestone quarried near the spot
By his command these words are cut:
> Cast a cold eye
> On life, on death.
> Horseman, pass by!

He was undoubtedly the greatest poetical figure of his age, and since his death his works have been the subject of intensive analysis by legions of critics and scholars, particularly in America. T. S. Eliot said that 'he was one of those few poets whose history is the history of our own time, who are a part of the consciousness of their age, which cannot be understood without them.'

Z

ZOZIMUS. See under MORAN,
MICHAEL.

SELECT BIBLIOGRAPHY

GENERAL HISTORIES
Arnold, Bruce, *A Concise History of Irish Art*, London 1969.
Dudley Edwards, R., *A New History of Ireland*, Dublin 1972.
Joyce, P. W., *An Illustrated History of Ireland*, Dublin 1923.
————*A Short History of Gaelic Ireland*, Dublin 1924.
Lecky, W. E. H., *A History of Ireland in the Eighteenth Century* (5 vols.), London 1892–1896.
Lydon, J., and MacCurtain, M. (eds.), *Gill History of Ireland* (11 vols.), Dublin 1972–1973.
Lyons, F. S. L., *Ireland Since the Famine*, London 1971.
Macardle, Dorothy, *The Irish Republic*, Dublin 1951.
MacLysaght, Edward, *Irish Life in the Seventeenth Century*, Dublin 1939.
Moody, T. W., and Martin, F. X., *The Course of Irish History*, Cork 1967.

NEWSPAPERS, PERIODICALS AND OFFICIAL PUBLICATIONS
Annual Register (London)
The Bell (Dublin)
Bulletin, Department of Foreign Affairs (Dublin)
Capuchin Annual (Dublin)
Dublin Magazine (Dublin)
Eason's Bulletin, new series, vols. 1–10 (Dublin)
Evening Telegraph (Dublin)
Freeman's Journal (Dublin)
Irish Book Lover (London)
Irish Historical Studies (Dublin)
Irish Independent (Dublin)
Irish Monthly (Dublin)
Irish Press (Dublin)
Irish Times (Dublin)
Keesing's Contemporary Archives (London)
Sinn Féin (Dublin)
Studies (Dublin)

REFERENCE WORKS AND MANUSCRIPT MATERIAL

Australian Encyclopaedia, Sydney 1958

Ballard, George, *British Ladies*, Oxford 1752.

Blackburne, E. Owens, *Illustrious Irishwomen*, London 1877.

Boase, Frederick, *Modern English Biography*, Truro 1892–1901.

Brady, Anne M., and Cleeve, Brian, *A Biographical Dictionary of Irish Writers*, Mullingar 1985.

Brown, Stephen J., *An Index of Catholic Biographies*, Dublin 1890.

Burke's Irish Family Records, London 1976.

Butler, Alban, *Lives of the Saints*, London 1956.

Chambers Biographical Dictionary, Edinburgh 1974.

Cleeve, Brian, *Dictionary of Irish Writers*, Cork 1966–1971.

Concise Cambridge History of English Literature, Cambridge 1941.

Crone, J. S., *A Concise Dictionary of Irish Biography*, Dublin 1937.

Dictionary of American Biography, New York 1928–1974.

Dictionary of American History, New York 1940.

Dictionary of Catholic Biography, London 1961.

Dictionary of National Biography, London 1890–1960.

Dictionary of Scientific Biography, New York 1976.

Encyclopaedia Americana, New York 1966.

Encyclopaedia Britannica, Chicago 1973.

Encyclopaedia of Canada, Toronto 1935.

Encyclopaedia of Ireland, Dublin 1968.

Grehan, Ida, *Irish Family Names*, London 1973.

Groves's Dictionary of Music and Musicians, London 1954.

Hayes, Richard, *Biographical Dictionary of Irishmen in France*, Dublin 1949.

Hickey, D. J., and Doherty, J. E., *A Dictionary of Irish History since 1800*, Dublin 1980.

Hogan, Robert, *Dictionary of Irish Literature*, Dublin 1980.

Joly Papers, 'Battle of Magheramayo: Report', National Library of Ireland.

Joly Papers, 'Orange Institution of Ireland: Report of Special Committee', National Library of Ireland.

Nealon, Ted, *Ireland: a Parliamentary Directory*, Dublin 1974.

Neeson, Eoin, *The Book of Irish Saints*, Cork 1967.

New Catholic Encyclopaedia, New York 1967.

Oxford Companion to English Literature, London 1932.

Oxford Companion to the Theatre, London 1957.

Oxford Literary Guide to the British Isles, Oxford 1977.

Penguin Companion to Literature, Volume 1: Britain and the Commonwealth, Harmondsworth 1971.

Royal Dublin Society, *Proceedings*, 1911–1913, 1931.

Royal Irish Academy, *Proceedings*, 1836–.
Royal Society of London, *Biographical Memoirs*.
———— *Obituary Notices.*
———— *Year Book*, London 1897–.
Strickland, W. G., *Dictionary of Irish Artists*, Dublin 1913.
Taibhdhearc na Gaillimhe, Cláracha, Galway.
Thom's Irish Who's Who, Dublin 1923.
Webb, A. J., *A Compendium of Irish Biography*, Dublin 1878.
Who Was Who, London 1916–1970.

BIOGRAPHIES, AUTOBIOGRAPHIES AND GENERAL WORKS
Adamnán (ed. Reeves), *Life of St Columba*, Edinburgh 1874.
Anonymous, *The Life and Times of G. R. Fitzgerald*, Dublin 1787.
Armour, W. D., *Armour of Ballymoney*, London 1934.
Barrington, Sir Jonah, *Personal Sketches of His Own Times*, London 1827–1832.
Berry, H. F., *A History of the Royal Dublin Society*, London 1915.
Bew, Paul, *C. S. Parnell*, Dublin 1980.
Bodkin, Thomas, *Hugh Lane and His Pictures*, Dublin 1934.
Bowen, Zack, *Pádraic Colum*, Carbondale 1970.
Bowman, J., and O'Donoghue, R., *Portraits: Belvedere College, 1832–1982*, Dublin 1982.
Brown, Stephen J., *Ireland in Fiction*, Dublin 1919.
Buckland, P., *James Craig*, Dublin 1980.
Butler, Hubert, *Ten Thousand Saints*, Kilkenny 1973.
Cameron, Sir Charles, *History of the Royal College of Surgeons of Ireland*, Dublin 1886.
Carroll, Mary Teresa Airtin, *Life of Catherine McAuley*, New York 1887.
Carroll, M. G., *The Story of Matt Talbot*, Cork 1948.
Collis, W. Robert, *The Silver Fleece*, London 1936.
Colum, Mary, *Life and the Dream*, Dublin 1966.
Colum, Pádraic, *Arthur Griffith*, Dublin 1959.
Corkery, Daniel, *The Hidden Ireland*, Dublin 1925.
Costello, Peter, *James Joyce*, Dublin 1980.
Costello, P., and van de Kemp, P., *Flann O'Brien: an Illustrated Biography*, London 1987.
Coxhead, Elizabeth, *Daughters of Erin*, London 1965.
Craig, Maurice James, *Dublin, 1660–1860*, London 1952.
Cullen, L. M., *Life in Ireland*, London 1968.
Cummins, N. Marshall, *Some Chapters of Cork Medical History*, Cork 1957.
Cusack, Mary F., *The Nun of Kenmare*, London 1889.
Daly, Dominic, *The Young Douglas Hyde*, New Jersey 1974.

De Blaghd, Earnán, *Trasna na Bóinne*, Dublin 1957.

De Breffny, B., and ffolliott, R., *The Houses of Ireland*, London 1975.

Denson, Alan, *James H. Cousins and Margaret E. Cousins*, Kendal 1967.

——— *John Hughes, Sculptor*, Kendal 1969.

——— *Thomas Bodkin*, Dublin 1966.

De Rís, Seán, *Peadar Ó Doirnín*, Dublin 1969.

De Vere White, Terence, *Parents of Oscar Wilde*, London 1967.

——— *The Story of the Royal Dublin Society*, Tralee 1955.

Devoy, John, *Recollections of an Irish Rebel*, New York 1929.

——— *Rescue of the Military Fenians*, Dublin 1929.

Digby, M., *Horace Plunkett*, Oxford 1949.

Donnelly, J., *Charles Donnelly: Life and Poems*, Dublin 1988.

Doyle, Paul A., *Paul Vincent Carroll*, Lewisburg 1971.

Dudley Edwards, Ruth, *James Connolly*, Dublin 1981.

Duffy, Joseph, *Patrick in His Own Words*, Dublin 1972.

Dwyer, T. Ryle, *Éamon de Valera*, Dublin 1980.

Edgeworth, R. L., *Memoirs*, London 1820.

Elles-Fermor, Una, *The Irish Dramatic Movement*, London 1939.

Ellman, Richard, *James Joyce*, New York 1982.

——— *Oscar Wilde*, London 1987.

Falkiner, C. L., *Studies in Irish History and Biography*, London 1902.

Farrell, Brian, *Seán Lemass*, Dublin 1983.

Fay, Gerard, *The Abbey Theatre*, Dublin 1958.

Fenton, Seumas, *The Honourable Emily Lawless*, n.p. 1944.

Fisher, M., and Fisher, J., *Shackleton*, London 1957.

FitzGerald, Desmond, *Memoirs*, London 1968.

Fleetwood, John, *History of Medicine in Ireland*, Dublin 1951.

Flynn, W. J., *Free State Parliamentary Companion 1932*, Dublin 1932.

——— *Irish Parliamentary Handbook 1939*, Dublin 1939.

——— *Irish Parliamentary Handbook 1945*, Dublin 1945.

——— *Oireachtas Companion for 1930*, Dublin 1930.

Fox, R. M., *Rebel Irishwoman*, Dublin n.d.

Gilbert, J. T., *A History of Dublin*, Dublin 1854–1859.

Greene, David, *Writing in Irish Today*, Cork 1972.

Gregory, Isabella Augusta, *Our Irish Theatre*, New York 1914.

Gwynn, Denis, *Life of John Redmond*, London 1932.

——— *The O'Gorman Mahon*, London 1934.

Hayes, Richard, *Some Notable Limerick Doctors*, Limerick 1938.

Hazard, T. G., *Life of Daniel Donnelly*, Dublin 1820.

Hennessy, Maurice, *The Wild Geese: the Irish Soldier in Exile*, London 1973.

Hogan, Robert, *Eimar O'Duffy*, Lewisburg 1972.

Hone, Joseph, *Life of George Moore*, London 1936.

———*W. B. Yeats, 1865-1939*, London 1962.

Hull, Eleanor, *A Text Book of Irish Literature*, Dublin 1906.

Hunt, Hugh, *The Abbey: Ireland's National Theatre, 1904-1979*, Dublin 1979.

———*Seán O'Casey*, Dublin 1980.

Hyde, Montgomery, *The Life of Oscar Wilde*, London 1976.

Johnson, R., *Parnell and the Parnells*, Dublin 1888.

Kain, Richard M., *Susan Mitchell*, Lewsiburg 1972.

Keaney, Marion, *Westmeath Authors*, Mullingar 1969.

Kiely, Benedict, *Poor Scholar: a Study of the Works and Days of William Carleton*, New York 1947.

Lambert, Eric, *Mad with Much Heart*, London 1967.

Larkin, Emmet, *James Larkin*, London 1968.

Lenihan, Maurice, *Limerick, Its History and Antiquities*, Dublin 1866.

Levenson, Samuel, *Maud Gonne*, London 1977.

Longford, Earl of, and O'Neill, Thomas P., *Éamon de Valera*, Dublin 1970.

Luce, A. A., *The Life of George Berkeley*, London 1949.

Lynam, Shevaun, *Humanity Dick*, London 1975.

Lynch, Patrick, and Vaizey, John, *Guinness's Brewery in the Irish Economy*, Cambridge 1960.

Lyons, F. S. L., *Parnell*, London 1977.

Lyons, J. B., *Brief Lives of Irish Doctors*, Dublin 1978.

———*The Enigma of Tom Kettle*, Dublin 1983.

———*Oliver St John Gogarty*, Dublin 1980.

MacBride, Maud Gonne, *A Servant of the Queen*, Dublin 1950.

McCann, Seán, *The Story of the Abbey Theatre*, London 1967.

MacColl, René, *Roger Casement*, London 1960.

McCready, C. T., *Dublin Street Names, Dated and Explained*, Dublin 1892.

McDowell, R. B., and Stanford, W. B., *Mahaffy*, London 1971.

McDowell, R. B., and Webb, D. A., *Trinity College, Dublin, 1592-1952*, Cambridge 1982.

Mac Fhinn, Pádraig, *An tAthair Mícheál P. Ó hÍceadha*, Dublin 1974.

MacLysaght, Edward, *Changing Times*, Gerrards Cross 1978.

Madden, R. R., *Ireland in '98: Sketches of the Principal Men of the Time*, n.p. 1888.

———*The United Irishmen, Their Lives and Times*, London 1858-1860.

Maddox, Brenda, *Nora: a Biography of Nora Joyce*, London 1988.

Mangan, James Clarence (ed.), *The Poets and Poetry of Munster*, n.p. 1850.

Manning, Maurice, *The Blueshirts*, Dublin 1970.

Mapother, *Lessons from the Lives of Irish Surgeons*, Dublin 1873.

Marlow, Joyce, *The Uncrowned Queen of Ireland*, London 1975.

Marreco, Anne, *The Rebel Countess*, London 1967.

Martin, Augustine, *James Stephens*, Dublin 1977.

Maxwell, Constantia, *Dublin Under the Georges*, London 1956.

————*A History of Trinity College, Dublin, 1592–1892*, Dublin 1946.

Mitchel, John, *Jail Journal*, New York 1854, Dublin 1913.

Moody, T. W., *Davitt and the Irish Revolution*, New York 1981.

Morgan, Lady, *Memoirs, etc.*, London 1862.

Murphy, Seumas, *Stone Mad*, Dublin 1966.

Murphy, William, *Prodigal Father: the Life of John Butler Yeats*, Ithaca 1978.

Ó Briain, Liam, *Cuimhní Cinn*, Dublin 1971.

Ó Broin, Leon, *Frank Duff: a Biography*, Dublin 1980.

————*An Maidíneach*, Dublin 1971.

————*Michael Collins*, Dublin 1980.

————*Parnell*, Dublin 1937.

Ó'Bruadair, David (ed. McErlean), *Poems*, London 1908–1916.

O'Casey, Eileen, *Seán*, London 1971.

O'Casey, Seán, *I Knock at the Door*, London 1939.

Ó Ceallaigh, Seán T., *Seán T.*, Dublin 1972.

Ó Conluain, Proinsias, and Ó Céileachair, Donncha, *An Duinníneach*, Dublin 1958.

O'Connor, Ulick, *Brendan Behan*, London 1970.

————*The Campbell Companion*, London 1987.

————*Celtic Dawn*, London 1984.

————*Oliver St John Gogarty*, London 1964.

Ó Criomhthain, Tomás, *An tOileánach*, Dublin 1929.

Ó Cuív, Brian, *Irish Men of Learning*, Dublin 1961.

O'Donnell, Manus, *Life of Colmcille*, Illinois 1918.

O'Donoghue, D. J., *Geographical Distribution of Irish Ability*, Dublin 1906.

————*The Poets of Ireland*, Dublin 1912.

O'Donoghue, R., *Like a Tree Planted*, Dublin 1967.

O'Donovan, John, *George Bernard Shaw*, Dublin 1983.

Ó Faoláin, Seán, *Constance Markievicz*, London 1954.

————*The Great O'Neill*, London 1942.

O'Ferrall, Fergus, *Daniel O'Connell*, Dublin 1981.

Ó Fiaich, Tomás, *Columbanus in His Own Words*, Dublin 1974.

————*Oliver Plunkett*, Dublin 1975.

O'Flanagan, James R., *An Octogenarian Literary Life*, Cork 1896.

Ó hUiginn, Tadhg Dall (ed. Knott), *Bardic Poems*, London 1920.

Ó Lúing, Seán, *Art Ó Gríofa*, Dublin 1953.

O'Neill, Francis, *Irish Minstrels and Musicians*, Chicago 1913.

O'Neill, J. J., *Irish Theatrical History*, Dublin 1907.

Ó Néill, Tomás, and Ó Fiannachta, Pádraig, *De Valera* (2 vols.), Dublin 1968–1970.

Ó Súileabháin, Muiris, *Fiche Bliain ag Fás*, Dublin 1933.

Ó Súilleabháin, Amhlaoibh (ed. de Bhaldraithe), *Cinn-Lae,* Dublin 1970.

O'Sullivan, Thomas F., *The Story of the GAA*, Dublin 1916.

Ó Tuama, Seán, *Caoineadh Airt Uí Laoghaire*, Dublin 1961.

Pakenham, Thomas, *The Year of Liberty*, London 1969.

Partington and Wheeler, *Life and Work of William Higgins*, London 1960.

Pearson, Hesketh, *Bernard Shaw*, London 1951.

————*The Life of Oscar*, London 1954.

Pine, Richard, *Oscar Wilde*, Dublin 1983.

Plummer, Charles, *Lives of Irish Saints*, Oxford 1922.

Power, Frank, *Letters from Khartoum*, London 1885.

Praeger, Robert Lloyd, *Some Irish Naturalists*, Dundalk 1949.

Purcell, Mary, *Matt Talbot and His Times*, Dublin 1954.

Pyle, Hilary, *Jack B. Yeats*, London 1970.

Robinson, Hilary, *Somerville and Ross*, Dublin 1980.

Robinson, Lennox, *Palette and Plough*, Dublin 1948.

Roche, J. Jeffrey, *Life of John Boyle O'Reilly*, New York 1891.

Russell, W. Howard, *Dispatches from the Crimea, 1854–1856*, London 1966.

Ryan, R., *Worthies of Ireland*, London 1821.

Saul, G. Brandon, *Daniel Corkery*, Lewisburg 1973.

————*Séamus O'Kelly*, Lewisburg 1971.

Sayers, Peig, *Peig*, Dublin 1973.

Shannon, Martin, *Sixteen Roads to Golgotha*, Dublin n.d.

Share, Bernard, *Irish Lives*, Dublin 1971.

Sixty Glorious Years of the GAA, Dublin 1947.

Skinner, Liam C., *Politicians by Accident*, Dublin 1948.

Somerville-Large, Peter, *Irish Eccentrics*, London 1975.

Stewart, A. T. Q., *Edward Carson*, Dublin 1981.

Suenens, Léon-Joseph, *Edel Quinn*, Dublin 1954.

Taylor, W. D., *Jonathan Swift*, London 1933.

Teeling, C. H., *History of the Irish Rebellion of 1798*, Glasgow 1876.

Tucker, Bernard, *Jonathan Swift*, Dublin 1983.

Ua Laoghaire, Peadar, *Mo Sgéal Féin*, Dublin 1915.

Ua Muireadhaigh, Lorcán, *Amhráin Sheumais Mhic Chuarta*, Dundalk 1925.

Van Voris, J., *Constance Markievicz*, Amherst 1967.

Walsh, John Edward, *Ireland Sixty Years Ago*, Dublin 1847; reprinted in 1877 as *Ireland Ninety Years Ago*; reprinted in 1911 (ed. Dillon Cosgrave) as *Ireland One Hundred and Twenty Years Ago.*

Whaley, Thomas, *Buck Whaley's Memoirs*, London 1906.

Wills, James, *Lives of Illustrious and Distinguished Irishmen*, Dublin 1840–1847.

Wilmot, Martha, *Russian Journals*, London 1934.

Wilson, T. G., *Victorian Doctor*, London 1942.

Woodgate, M. V., *The Abbé Edgeworth,* Dublin n.d.
Yeats, William Butler, *Autobiographies*, London 1955.
Younger, Calton, *Arthur Griffith*, Dublin 1981.